Paul McFedries

Microsoft® Windows® Vista™

UNLEASHED

SAMS | 800 East 96th Street, Indianapolis, Indiana 46240 USA

Microsoft® Windows® Vista™ Unleashed

International Standard Book Number: 0-672-328941

Library of Congress Cataloging-in-Publication Data

McFedries, Paul.
Microsoft Windows Vista unleashed / Paul McFedries.
p. cm.
ISBN 0-672-32894-1
1. Microsoft Windows (Computer file) 2. Operating systems (Computers) I. Title.

QA76.76.063M398175 2006
005.4'46—dc22

2006038141

Printed in the United States of America

First Printing: December 2006

09 08 07 06 4 3 2 1

Trademarks

All terms mentioned in this book that are known to be trademarks or service marks have been appropriately capitalized. Sams Publishing cannot attest to the accuracy of this information. Use of a term in this book should not be regarded as affecting the validity of any trademark or service mark.

Warning and Disclaimer

Every effort has been made to make this book as complete and as accurate as possible, but no warranty or fitness is implied. The information provided is on an "as is" basis. The author and the publisher shall have neither liability nor responsibility to any person or entity with respect to any loss or damages arising from the information contained in this book.

Bulk Sales

Sams Publishing offers excellent discounts on this book when ordered in quantity for bulk purchases or special sales. For more information, please contact

U.S. Corporate and Government Sales
1-800-382-3419
corpsales@pearsontechgroup.com

For sales outside of the U.S., please contact

International Sales
international@pearsoned.com

The Safari® Enabled icon on the cover of your favorite technology book means the book is available through Safari Bookshelf. When you buy this book, you get free access to the online edition for 45 days.

Safari Bookshelf is an electronic reference library that lets you easily search thousands of technical books, find code samples, download chapters, and access technical information whenever and wherever you need it.

To gain 45-day Safari Enabled access to this book:

- Go to http://www.samspublishing.com/safarienabled
- Complete the brief registration form
- Enter the coupon code **BKHN-YTWI-TD5W-F1I8-M9RV**

If you have difficulty registering on Safari Bookshelf or accessing the online edition, please e-mail customer-service@safaribooksonline.com.

Acquisitions Editor
Loretta Yates

Development Editor
Todd Brakke

Managing Editor
Gina Kanouse

Project Editor
Andy Beaster

Copy Editor
Mike Henry

Indexer
Cheryl Lenser

Proofreader
Linda Seifert

Technical Editor
Terri Stratton

Team Coordinator
Cindy Teeters

Book Designer
Gary Adair

Page Layout
Bronkella Publishing

Contents at a Glance

Table of Contents

Part VI Appendixes

About the Author

Paul McFedries is the president of Logophilia Limited, a technical writing company. He has worked with computers in one form or another since 1975 and has used Windows since version 1 was foisted upon an unsuspecting (and underwhelmed) world in the mid-1980s. He is the author of more than 50 computer books that have sold over three million copies worldwide. His recent titles include the Sams Publishing book *Windows Vista Unveiled* and the Que Publishing books *Formulas and Functions with Microsoft Excel 2003, Tricks of the Microsoft Office Gurus*, and *Microsoft Access 2003 Forms, Reports, and Queries*. Paul is also the proprietor of Word Spy (www.wordspy.com) a website devoted to tracking new words and phrases as they enter the English language.

Dedication

To my wife (yes!), Karen

Acknowledgments Kudos, Plaudits, and Assorted Pats on the Back

The English essayist Joseph Addison once described an editor as someone who "rides in the whirlwind and directs the storm." I don't know if that's true for editors in some of the more sedate publishing nooks (novels and cookbooks and such), but I think it applies perfectly to the rigors of computer book editing. Why? Well, the computer industry is so fast-paced that any kind of editorial (or authorial) dawdling could mean a book will be obsolete before it even hits the shelves.

The good folks at Sams avoid premature book obsolescence by subjecting each manuscript to a barrage of simultaneous edits from a number of specialists (I call it "gang editing"). So a process that normally might take months is knocked down to a few short weeks. This means you get a book that contains timely and relevant information, and a book that has passed muster with some of the sharpest eyes and inner ears in the business. My name may be the only one that appears on the cover, but tons of people had a big hand in creating what you now hold in your hands. You'll find a list of all the people who worked on this book near the front, but there are a few I'd like to thank personally:

Loretta Yates: Loretta is the Acquisitions Editor for this book, which means that she "acquired" me to write it. I'm honored that she would choose me for such an important project, and I thank her for the confidence she has shown in my abilities over the years.

Todd Brakke: As Development Editor, it was Todd's job to work with me in determining the overall structure of the book and to make sure that all the relevant topics were covered in an order that made sense. If we succeeded in this (and I think we did), it's due in no small part to Todd's excellent instincts, his keen sense of how a book should flow together, and his own considerable Windows knowledge and skills.

Andy Beaster: Andy is the book's Project Editor, which means he works long hours making sure the manuscript is ready for the page layout and proofreading process. We've worked together before, and I never cease to be amazed at Andy's professionalism, competence, and good humor. Thanks, Andy, for yet another outstanding effort.

Mike Henry: As Copy Editor, Mike has the often thankless task of cleaning up authors' slapdash punctuation, rearranging their slipshod sentence structure, and just generally dotting their i's and crossing their t's. This requires an unerring eye for detail and the patience of a saint, so I extend a big thank you to Mike: Once again, you've made me look good.

Terri Stratton: Terri was the book's Technical Editor. This means that she verified all my facts and tried out all my techniques to make sure I didn't steer you in the wrong direction. This requires patience and perseverance in equal amounts, and Terri was more than up to the task.

We Want to Hear from You!

As the reader of this book, *you* are our most important critic and commentator. We value your opinion and want to know what we're doing right, what we could do better, what areas you'd like to see us publish in, and any other words of wisdom you're willing to pass our way.

As an associate publisher for Sams Publishing, I welcome your comments. You can email or write me directly to let me know what you did or didn't like about this book—as well as what we can do to make our books better.

Please note that I cannot help you with technical problems related to the topic of this book. We do have a User Services group, however, where I will forward specific technical questions related to the book.

When you write, please be sure to include this book's title and author as well as your name, email address, and phone number. I will carefully review your comments and share them with the author and editors who worked on the book.

Email: feedback@samspublishing.com

Mail: Greg Wiegand
Associate Publisher
Sams Publishing
800 East 96th Street
Indianapolis, IN 46240 USA

Reader Services

Visit our website and register this book at www.samspublishing.com/register for convenient access to any updates, downloads, or errata that might be available for this book.

Introduction

We shall not cease from exploration

And the end of all our exploring

Will be to arrive where we started

And know the place for the first time.

—*T. S. Eliot*

My goal in writing *Microsoft Windows Vista Unleashed* is to cover the good, the bad, and, yes, even the ugly of Windows Vista. In particular, I give you complete coverage of the intermediate-to-advanced features of Windows Vista. This means that I bypass basic topics, such as wielding the mouse, in favor of more complex operations, such as working with the Registry, maintaining and troubleshooting your system, networking, and getting around the Internet.

I've tried to keep the chapters focused on the topic at hand and unburdened with long-winded theoretical discussions. However, there are plenty of situations in which you won't be able to unleash the full power of Windows Vista and truly understand what's going on unless you have a solid base on which to stand. In these cases, I'll give you whatever theory and background you need to get up to speed. From there, I'll get right down to brass tacks without any further fuss and bother.

Who Should Read This Book

All writers write with an audience in mind. Actually, I'm not sure whether that's true for novelists and poets and the like, but it *should* be true for any technical writer who wants to create a useful and comprehensible book. Here are the members of my own imagined audience:

- **IT professionals**—These brave souls must decide whether to move to Vista, work out deployment issues, and support the new Vista desktops. The whole book has information related to your job and Vista.

- **Power users**—These elite users get their power via knowledge. With that in mind, this book extends the Windows power user's know-how by presenting an exhaustive account of everything that's new and improved in Windows Vista.
- **Business users**—If your company is thinking of or has already committed to moving to Vista, you need to know what you, your colleagues, and your staff are getting into. You also want to know what Vista will do to improve your productivity and make your life at the office easier. You learn all of this and more in this book.
- **Road warriors**—If you travel for a living, you probably want to know what Vista brings to the remote computing table. Will you be able to synchronize data, connect to the network, and manage power better than before? What other new notebook features can be found in Vista? You'll find out in this book.
- **Small business owners**—If you run a small or home business, you probably want to know whether Vista will give you a good return on investment. Will it make it easier to set up and maintain a network? Will Vista computers be more stable? Will your employees be able to collaborate easier? The answer turns out to be "Yes" for all of these questions, and I'll show you why.
- **Multimedia users**—If you use your computer to listen to music or radio stations, watch TV, work with digital photographs, edit digital movies, or burn CDs and DVDs, you'll be interested to know that Vista has a handful of new features that affect all of these activities.

Also, to keep the chapters uncluttered, I've made a few assumptions about what you know and what you don't know:

- I assume that you have knowledge of rudimentary computer concepts such as files and folders.
- I assume that you're familiar with the basic Windows skills: mouse maneuvering, dialog box negotiation, pull-down menu jockeying, and so on.
- I assume that you can operate peripherals attached to your computer, such as the keyboard and printer.
- I assume that you've used Windows for a while and are comfortable with concepts such as toolbars, scrollbars, and, of course, windows.
- I assume that you have a brain that you're willing to use and a good supply of innate curiosity.

How This Book Is Organized

To help you find the information you need, this book is divided into six parts that group related tasks. The next few sections offer a summary of each part.

Part I: Unleashing Day-to-Day Windows Vista

Part I takes your basic, workaday Windows chores and reveals their inner mysteries, allowing you to become more productive. After an initial chapter on what's new in Vista, topics include the myriad ways to get Windows Vista off the ground (Chapter 2), how to use Windows Vista to work with files and folders (Chapter 3), getting the most out of file types (Chapter 4), installing and running applications (Chapter 5), working with user accounts (Chapter 6), dealing with digital media (Chapter 7), using Contacts, Calendar, and faxing (Chapter 8), and Vista's mobile computing tools (Chapter 9).

Part II: Unleashing Essential Windows Vista Power Tools

The chapters in Part II get your advanced Windows Vista education off to a flying start by covering the ins and outs of four important Vista power tools: Control Panel and group policies (Chapter 10), the Registry (Chapter 11), and the Windows Script Host (Chapter 12).

Part III: Unleashing Windows Vista Customization and Optimization

In Part III, you dive into the deep end of advanced Windows work: customizing the interface (Chapter 13), performance tuning (Chapter 14), maintaining Windows Vista (Chapter 15), troubleshooting problems (Chapter 16), and working with devices (Chapter 17).

Part IV: Unleashing Windows Vista for the Internet

Part IV shows you how to work with Windows Vista's Internet features. You learn how to get the most out of a number of Internet services, including the Web (Chapter 18), email (Chapter 19), and newsgroups (Chapter 20). I close this part with an extensive look at the Internet security and privacy features that come with Windows Vista (Chapter 21).

Part V: Unleashing Windows Vista Networking

To close out the main part of this book, Part V takes an in-depth look at Windows Vista's networking features. You learn how to set up a small network (Chapter 22), how to access and use that network (Chapter 23), and how to access your network from remote locations (Chapter 24).

Part VI: Appendixes

To further your Windows Vista education, Part VI presents a few appendixes that contain extra goodies. You'll find a complete list of Windows Vista shortcut keys (Appendix A), a detailed look at using the Windows Vista command prompt (Appendix B), and a batch file primer (Appendix C).

Conventions Used in This Book

To make your life easier, this book includes various features and conventions that help you get the most out of this book and Windows Vista itself:

Steps	Throughout the book, I've broken many Windows Vista tasks into easy-to-follow step-by-step procedures.
Things you type	Whenever I suggest that you type something, what you type appears in a **`bold monospace`** font.
Filenames, folder names, and code	These things appear in a `monospace` font.
Commands	Commands and their syntax use the `monospace` font as well. Command placeholders (which stand for what you actually type) appear in an *`italic monospace`* font.
Pull-down menu commands	I use the following style for all application menu commands: *Menu, Command*, where *Menu* is the name of the menu that you pull down and *Command* is the name of the command you select. Here's an example: File, Open. This means that you pull down the File menu and select the Open command.
Code continuation character	When a line of code is too long to fit on only one line of this book, it is broken at a convenient place and continued to the next line. The continuation of the line is preceded by a code continuation character (➥). You should type a line of code that has this character as one long line without breaking it.

This book also uses the following boxes to draw your attention to important (or merely interesting) information:

NOTE

The Note box presents asides that give you more information about the current topic. These tidbits provide extra insights that give you a better understanding of the task. In many cases, they refer you to other sections of the book for more information.

TIP

The Tip box tells you about Windows Vista methods that are easier, faster, or more efficient than the standard methods.

CAUTION

The all-important Caution box tells you about potential accidents waiting to happen. There are always ways to mess things up when you're working with computers. These boxes help you avoid at least some of the pitfalls.

PART I

Unleashing Day-to-Day Windows Vista

CHAPTER 1

An Overview of Windows Vista

IN THIS CHAPTER

- The Development of Windows Vista
- Windows Vista System Requirements
- Windows Vista Editions
- Windows Anytime Upgrade
- New Interface Features
- What's New Under the Hood
- New and Improved Programs and Tools

It's hard to believe, but when Windows Vista shipped in 2007, it will be a full quarter of a century after Microsoft released its first version of MS-DOS, and an astonishing 23 years since the company announced the original version of Windows (which eventually shipped—to almost no acclaim—in 1985). Windows 2.0, released in 1987, was marginally more promising, but it resolutely failed to light any fires on the PC landscape. It wasn't until Windows 3.0 was released in 1990 that Windows finally came into its own and its utter dominance of the desktop began. With the release of Windows 95 on August 24, 1995, Windows became the rock star of the computing world, beloved by many, hated by some, but known to all.

It's also hard to believe that people were actually lining up outside computer stores on the night of August 23, 1995, to be among the first to purchase Windows 95 at midnight. Why on earth would anyone *do* that? Were they insane? Perhaps some were, but most were just caught up in the hype and hope generated by both Microsoft's marketing muscle and the simple fact that Windows 95 *was* light-years ahead of any previous version of the operating system.

By comparison, the Windows world since that hot summer night in 1995 has been decidedly—some would say *depressingly*—quiet. There have been plenty of new versions—Windows 98 and Windows Me on the consumer side, Windows NT 4 and Windows 2000 on the corporate side, and then Windows XP in all its flavors—but there has been a distinct lack of *buzz* associated with each release. True, nothing will ever live up to the hype (and hokum) that surrounded Windows 95, but the versions since have had a ho-hum quality to them. Sure, Windows 98 (particularly the Second Edition release) was solid (and is still used by many people to this day), Windows 2000 was a favorite business operating system (OS) for many years, and XP has been the best Windows yet, but nobody lined up at midnight to buy any of these products.

Will any of this change with the release of Windows Vista? True, nobody's all that excited about the name, but the name is meaningless in the long run. (In 2001, most folks thought XP—based, head-scratchingly, on the word *eXPerience*—was the dumbest name since Microsoft BOB, but everyone got used to it within a month or two and the "controversy," such as it was, faded quickly.) What might get people talking about Vista isn't the name, but the simple fact that we're *finally* seeing some interesting OS technology from Microsoft. Vista is beautiful to look at, promises to make our day-to-day computing lives a bit easier, and contains some compelling architectural improvements. I doubt few people outside of Microsoft will trumpet Vista as the greatest OS ever, but many months of delving into Vista's innards has convinced me that it has at least a few things to get excited about.

This chapter gets your Windows Vista introduction off the ground by giving you an overview of the operating system. I'll start with a brief history of Longhorn/Vista, and then give you a quick tour of what's new and interesting.

The Development of Windows Vista

In 2000, Bill Gates, chairman and chief software architect of Microsoft, announced that the successor to the forthcoming Whistler operating system—later renamed as Windows XP—would be a new OS codenamed Blackcomb. A year later, however, just a few months before the release of XP, Microsoft announced a change of plans: Blackcomb would come much later than expected, and between XP and Blackcomb, probably around 2003, we'd see a minor update codenamed Longhorn.

NOTE

Microsoft has long applied codenames to prerelease versions of its products. For Windows, the practice began with Windows 3.1, which used the codename Janus. The first of these temporary monikers that was in any way "famous" (that is, known reasonably widely outside of Microsoft) was Chicago, the codename for Windows 95. Since then, we've seen, among many others, Memphis for Windows 98, Cairo for Windows NT 4.0, Millennium for Windows Me, and Whistler for Windows XP.

Why the codename *Longhorn*? Legend has it that Bill Gates has fond feelings for British Columbia's Whistler-Blackcomb ski resort (the name of which has given us two previous codenames for Windows, so it's clear that *someone* at Microsoft loves the place). At the base of Whistler Mountain, in the Carleton Lodge, there is an après-ski bar called the Longhorn Saloon. The burgers, I hear, are quite good.

There is an impressively exhaustive list of Microsoft codenames on the Bink.nu site: http://bink.nu/Codenames.bink.

However, Microsoft's approach to Longhorn soon began to change. By the time the Windows Hardware Engineering Conference (WinHEC) rolled around in mid-2003, Microsoft was describing Longhorn as a "huge, big, bet-the-company move." Windows XP was being kept current with new updates, including Windows XP Service Pack 2, and new versions of Windows XP Tablet PC Edition and Windows XP Media Center Edition. Meanwhile, Longhorn gradually began to accumulate new features originally intended for Blackcomb. By the summer of 2004, Microsoft realized that Longhorn had become the next major Windows OS, so the company revamped the entire Longhorn development process and more or less started the whole thing from scratch. This delayed the release of Longhorn, of course, and the dates kept getting pushed out: first to 2005, then to early 2006, and finally to later in 2006 and early 2007.

But it wasn't just a revamped development process that was delaying Longhorn. In conferences, demos, and meetings with hardware vendors, developers, and customers, Microsoft had described the new OS and features in the most glowing terms imaginable. This had become a seriously ambitious project that was going to require an equally serious commitment of resources and, crucially, *time* to make the promises a reality. Unfortunately, time was the one thing that Microsoft didn't have a lot of. Yes, XP was a fine OS and was being kept fresh with updates, but the gap between XP and Vista was unprecedented.

By the time 2006 rolled around, Microsoft knew that it had to complete Longhorn as soon as humanly possible. Microsoft briefly considered an interim version of Windows that would ship between Windows XP Service Pack 2 and Longhorn. (This stopgap release was codenamed Oasis, but some wags dubbed it Shorthorn.)

"Vista" Unveiled

The codename Longhorn was finally retired when Microsoft announced on July 22, 2005, that the new OS would be called Windows Vista. Why *Vista*? Because, according to one Microsoft spokesperson, the new OS is "about providing clarity to your world and giving focus to the things that are important to you," and it "provides your view of the world." That sounds like a lot of marketing hoo-ha to my ears, but it's true that Vista does offer some new features that enable you to view your documents in radically new ways (radical for Windows, that is).

To give just one example, you can run a local search from the Start menu. The resulting window displays a list of all the files—documents, email messages, favorites, music files, images, and more—that contain the search term. You can then save the results as a search folder. The next time you open the search folder, Vista shows not only the files from the original search, but also any new files you've created that include the search term.

NOTE

Windows version numbers haven't mattered very much since the days of Windows 3.*x* and NT 4.0. However, all Windows releases do carry a version number. For example, Windows XP is version 5.1. Just for the record, Windows Vista is version 6.0. If you have Vista, you can see this for yourself: press Windows Logo+R (or select Start, All Programs, Accessories, Run); type **winver**; and click OK.

What's *Not* in Windows Vista

However, what of all those fancy new technologies that promised to rock the Windows world? Well, there was simply no way to include all of those features *and* ship Vista by early 2007. Reluctantly, Microsoft had to start dropping features from Vista.

The first major piece to land in the Recycle Bin was Windows Future Storage (WinFS), a SQL Server–based file system designed to run on top of NTFS and to make it easier to navigate and find documents. WinFS is expected to ship separately after Windows Vista, although as you'll see in this book, some features of WinFS *did* make it into Vista (see Chapter 4, "Mastering File Types").

Microsoft also removed the Windows PowerShell (codenamed Monad and also called the Windows Command Shell or Microsoft Command Shell), a .NET-based command-line scripting language. (However, PowerShell is undergoing a separate beta cycle as I write this, and it's expected to be released around the same time as Vista.)

Microsoft also "decoupled" some important technologies from Vista, which meant that these technologies were developed separately and released for Vista and "backported" to run on Windows XP and Windows Server 2003. Two major technologies are being backported:

- A new graphics architecture and application programming interface that was codenamed Avalon and is now called Windows Presentation Foundation (WPF)
- A new programming platform for building, configuring, and deploying network-distributed services, codenamed Indigo and now called Windows Communications Foundation (WCF)

In both cases, it doesn't mean that Windows XP and Windows Server 2003 will suddenly look and feel like Windows Vista after you install WPF and WCF. Instead, it means that the older operating systems will be capable of running any applications that use WPF and WCF code. This gives developers more incentive to build applications around these technologies because it ensures a much larger user base than they would otherwise have if WPF and WCF ran only on Vista installations.

Finally, there are also several Vista tools that will also be XP "down-level" tools (as this book went to press, it wasn't clear when these tools would ship; they may be available as you read this). This means that they will be made available as XP downloads, although without certain features that you get in the Vista versions:

- **Internet Explorer 7**—The XP version doesn't come with Protected Mode or Parental Controls (see "Security Enhancements" and "Internet Explorer 7," later in this chapter).
- **Windows Defender**—On XP, scan times will be slower because XP doesn't track file changes the way Vista does (see "Transactional NTFS," later in this chapter).
- **Media Player 11**—The XP version won't play content from another PC or device; it won't view content from a Vista Media Library; it won't integrate with the Windows shell; and it won't have Vista's advanced DVD playback features.

The upshot of these deletions, backports, and down-level tools is that Vista is not quite as compelling a release as it was once touted to be, but there are still plenty of new improvements to make it worth your time.

Windows Vista System Requirements

Personal computing is governed by two inexorable, and not unrelated, "laws":

> **Moore's Law**—Processing power doubles every 18 months (from Gordon Moore, cofounder of Intel).
>
> **Parkinson's Law of Data**—Data expands to fill the space available for storage (from the original Parkinson's Law: Work expands to fill the time available).

These two observations help explain why, when the computers we use are becoming increasingly powerful, our day-to-day tasks never really seem all that much faster. The leaps in processing power and memory are being matched by the increasing complexity and resource requirements of the latest programs. Therefore, the computer you're using today might be twice as muscular as the one you were using a year and a half ago, but the applications you're using are twice the size and require twice as many resources.

Windows fits neatly into this scenario. With each new release of Microsoft's flagship operating system, the hardware requirements become more stringent, and our computers' processing power is taxed a little more. Windows Vista is no exception. Even though Microsoft spent an enormous amount of time and effort trying to shoehorn Vista into a minimal system configuration, you need a reasonably powerful computer if you don't want to spend most of your day cursing the dreaded hourglass icon. The good news is that Windows Vista's hardware requirements are nowhere near as onerous as many people believed they would be. In fact, most midrange or better systems purchased in the past year or two should run Vista without a problem.

The next few sections present a rundown of the system requirements you need to meet in order to install and work with Windows Vista. Note that I give both the minimum requirements as stipulated by Microsoft, and a set of "reasonable" requirements that I believe you need to make working with Vista more or less pleasurable.

Processor Requirements

Vista desktop minimum: 800MHz modern processor

For adequate Vista performance, you need at least a midrange processor, which means an Intel Pentium 4 or Celeron, or an AMD Athlon XP, Athlon 64, or Sempron running at 2.0–3.0GHz. Faster is better, of course, but only if money is no object. Moving up to 3.2GHz or 3.6GHz might set you back a few hundred dollars, but the performance improvement won't be all that noticeable. You'd be better off investing those funds either in extra memory (discussed later) or in a dual-core processor.

NOTE

What does *dual-core* mean? It describes a CPU that combines two separate processors, each with its own cache memory, on a single chip. (The cache memory is an onboard storage area that the processor uses to store commonly used bits of data. The bigger the cache, the greater the performance.) This enables the operating system to perform two tasks at once without a performance hit. For example, you could work in your word processor or spreadsheet program in the foreground using one processor, while the other processor takes care of a background spyware or virus check. Current examples of dual-core processors are the Intel Core 2 and Pentium D series and Pentium Extreme Edition, and the AMD Athlon 64 X2.

The 64-bit processors are becoming more affordable, and they run the 64-bit version of Vista like a dream (one of my Vista test machines was 64-bit, and it was a pleasure to use). Look for a 64-bit Pentium 4 or any of the several x64 chips available from AMD. Note, however, that although these 64-bit machines can run 32-bit applications without a performance hit, those programs will *not* run any faster with the wider bus. To see a speed boost with your applications, you have to wait for 64-bit versions of the applications you intend to run on it.

Memory Requirements

Vista minimum: 512MB

You can run Vista on a system with 512MB of RAM, but the performance will be quite slow. Admittedly, I've been running beta versions of Vista, which are always slower than release versions because they contain debugging code and are works-in-progress as far as optimization goes. However, I believe that, for most people, 1GB is a more realistic minimum for day-to-day work, and that's how much RAM Microsoft recommends for "Windows Vista Premium Ready" systems. If you regularly have many programs running at the same time, or if you use programs that manipulate digital photos or play music, consider moving up to 1.5GB. If you do extensive work with large files such as databases, or if you use programs that manipulate digital videos, 2GB should be your RAM goal.

Note, however, that if you select a 64-bit processor, you should seriously consider upgrading your system RAM. The conventional wisdom is that because 64-bit machines deal with data in chunks that are twice the size of those in 32-bit machines, you need twice the memory to take full advantage of the 64-bit advantage. Therefore, if you'd normally have 1GB of RAM in a 32-bit machine, opt for 2GB in your 64-bit computer.

Finally, consider the speed of the memory. Older DDR (double data rate) memory chips typically operate at between 100MHz (PC-1600) and 200MHz (PC-3200), whereas newer DDR2 chips run between 200MHz (PC2-3200) and 533MHz (PC2-8500). The up-and-coming DDR3 chips will operate at between 400 and 800MHz, which is a substantial speed boost and should improve Vista performance noticeably.

NOTE

Memory module numbers such as PC-3200 and PC2-8500 tell you the theoretical bandwidth of the memory. For example, PC-3200 implies a theoretical bandwidth of 3200MBps. To calculate theoretical bandwidth, you first multiply the base chip speed by 2 to get the effective clock speed. (Modern memory is **double-pumped**, which means data transfers at the beginning and the end of each clock cycle.) You then multiply the effective clock speed by 8 (because the memory path is 64 bytes wide and there are 8 bits in each byte). A 100MHz chip has an effective clock speed of 200MHz and, therefore, a theoretical bandwidth of 1600MBps, so it is called PC-1600 memory.

Storage Requirements

Vista hard disk free space minimum: 15GB

The disk space requirements depend on which version of Vista you're installing, but count on the new OS requiring at least 15GB free space to install. The OS will use perhaps another few gigabytes for the storage of things such as the paging file, System Restore checkpoints, Internet Explorer temporary file, and the Recycle Bin, so Vista will require at least 20GB of storage. These days, of course, it's not the operating system that usurps the most space on our hard drives; it's the massive multimedia files that now seem to be routine for most of us. Multimegabyte digital photos and spreadsheets, and even *multigigabyte* database files and digital video files are not unusual. Fortunately, hard disk storage is dirt cheap these days, with most disks costing less—often *much* less—than a dollar a gigabyte.

Note, too, that the type of hard drive can affect performance. For desktop systems, an older IDE drive that spins at 5,400RPM will be a significant performance bottleneck. Moving up to a 7,200RPM drive will help immeasurably, and a 10,000RPM drive is even better if you don't mind the extra expense. You should also consider moving from the older, parallel IDE technology to the new Serial Advanced Technology Attachment (SATA) drives, which are at least theoretically faster (with data-transfer rates starting at 150MBps). Look for a SATA drive with an 8MB cache and Native Command Queuing (NCQ).

NOTE

Native Command Queuing (NCQ) is a relatively new hard-disk technology aimed at solving a long-standing hard-disk performance problem. Requests for hard-drive data are stored in the memory controller and are handled in sequence by the disk's onboard controller. Unfortunately, whenever the controller processes requests for data that is stored in areas that are far away from each other, it causes a significant performance hit. For example, suppose that request 1 is for data stored near the start of the disk, request 2 is for data near the end of the disk, and request 3 is again for data near the start of the disk. In a typical hard disk, the read/write heads must travel from the start of the disk to the end, and then back again, processing each request in the order it was received. With NCQ, the controller reorders the requests so that the 1 and 3, which are close to each other, are carried out first, and only then is the distant request 2 carried out.

Unfortunately for laptop users, most portable hard drives fall into the 5,400RPM range, and some are even slower than that. You can pay more to get a 7,200RPM drive, but in most instances, the performance improvement you'll see from such an upgrade isn't necessarily worth the additional cost.

Finally, you should also bear in mind that one of Windows Vista's new features is the ability to burn data to recordable DVDs. To take advantage of this, your system requires a DVD burner, preferably one that supports both the DVD-RW and DVD+RW disc formats (that is, a DVD±RW drive) .

NOTE

To learn more about Vista's new DVD features, see the section "DVD Burning and Ripping," in Chapter 7, "Working with Digital Media."

Graphics Requirements

Vista graphics memory minimum: 32MB

You'll be learning a lot more about Vista's graphical underpinnings in Chapter 13, "Customizing the Windows Vista Interface." For now, however, it's important to note that Microsoft is taking a sensibly cautious route to graphics requirements. Vista's interface is graphics intensive, but it will be smart enough to adopt a less intensive interface based on what your PC can handle. Whether Vista holds back on the visual bells and whistles depends on whether you have a separate AGP or PCI Express graphics adapter (as opposed to an integrated motherboard graphics chip), the capability of the card's graphics processing unit (GPU), and how much graphics memory the card has on board:

- If Vista detects a low-end card, it defaults to the Windows Classic theme, which offers a Windows 2000–like interface.
- If Vista detects a card with medium-range capabilities, it uses the new Aero theme, but without the Glass effects (such as transparency).
- If Vista detects a high-end card, it defaults to the full Aero Glass interface.

To get the beautiful Aero Glass look as well as the new 3D and animated effects, your system should have a graphics processor that supports DirectX 9, Pixel Shader 2.0 (in hardware, not as a software emulation), and 32 bits per pixel, and comes with a device driver that supports the new Windows Vista Display Driver Model (WDDM). (If you purchase a new video card, look for the Windows Vista Capable or Windows Vista Premium Ready logo on the box. If you just need to upgrade the driver for an existing graphics card, look for "WDDM" in the drive name or description.)

The amount of onboard memory you need depends on the resolution you plan to use (assuming that you're using a single monitor; for dual monitors, double the memory):

- If you'll be using a basic 800×600 or 1024×768 resolution, 32MB is enough.
- If you want to run up to 1280×1024, you need at least 64MB.
- If you want to run up to 1920×1200, you need at least 128MB.

TIP

Graphics memory is like system memory: You can never have too much, and it's always a good investment to buy a card that has much as you can get. One of Microsoft's Vista FAQs said it best: "The most [graphics] memory your bank account can afford is the ticket."

Before the final release of Vista, it wasn't clear whether *any* integrated graphics chips would support the full Aero Glass interface, although I've seen reports that some integrated graphics hardware—such as the Intel 945 and the ATI Radeon XPress X200—can handle Aero Glass.

Hardware Requirements for Various Vista Features

Windows Vista is a big, sprawling program that can do many things, so it's not surprising that there is a long list of miscellaneous equipment you might need, depending on what you plan to do with your system. Table 1.1 provides a rundown.

TABLE 1.1 Equipment Required for Various Windows Vista Tasks

Task	Required Equipment
Using the Internet	For a dial-up connection: A modem, preferably one that supports 56Kbps connections.
	For a broadband connection: A cable or DSL modem and a router for security.
Networking	For a wired connection: A network adapter, preferably one that supports Fast Ethernet (100Mbps) connections, a network switch or hub, and network cables.
	For a wireless connection: A wireless adapter that supports IEEE 802.11a, b, or g, and a wireless access point.
Handwriting	A Tablet PC with a digital pen, or a graphics tablet.
Photo editing	A USB slot for connecting the digital camera. If you want to transfer the images from a memory card, you need the appropriate memory card reader.
Document scanning	A document scanner or an all-in-one printer that includes scanning capabilities.
Faxing	A modem that includes fax capabilities.

TABLE 1.1 Continued

Task	Required Equipment
Ripping and burning CDs	For ripping: A CD or DVD drive. For burning: A recordable CD drive.
Burning DVDs	A recordable DVD drive.
Video editing	An internal or external video-capture device, or an IEEE 1394 (FireWire) port.
Videoconferencing	A webcam or a digital camera that has a webcam mode.
Listening to digital audio files	A sound card or integrated audio, as well as speakers or headphones. For the best sound, use a subwoofer with the speakers.
Listening to radio	A radio tuner card.
Watching TV	A TV tuner card (preferably one that supports video capture). A remote control is useful if you are watching the screen from a distance.

Windows Vista Editions

For many years, the Windows world was divided into two camps: the so-called "consumer" editions—Windows 95, 98, and Me—aimed at individuals and home office users, and the "business" editions—Windows NT and 2000—aimed at the corporate market. With the release of Windows XP, Microsoft merged these two streams into a single code base. However, that didn't mean the end to having multiple editions of the operating system. In fact, XP ended up with six major editions: Starter (for users with low-cost PCs in emerging markets outside North America), Home (individuals), Professional (corporate users and the SOHO crowd), Professional x64 (the 64-bit version for power users), Media Center (multimedia users), and Tablet PC (with digital pen support for Tablet PC users). Many people found the existence of so many versions of XP confusing, and it certainly was a head-scratching situation for anyone not versed in the relatively subtle differences among the editions.

Given this widespread confusion, you would think that Microsoft would simplify things with Windows Vista. After all, a case could be made that the reason so many people did not upgrade to XP was that they simply were not sure which edition they should purchase. Therefore, no one would blame you for thinking that the road to Vista is going to be straighter than the twisting XP path.

In the end, Vista has shipped with the same number of versions as XP—six in all—although Vista's versions are configured completely differently than XP's. First, the home market has two editions:

Vista Home Basic

- **Windows Vista Home Basic**—This edition is available in North America and other developed nations, and it represents the simplest Vista option. The Home Basic Edition is aimed at individuals using their computer at home who want security without complexity. Home Basic includes Windows Defender, Windows Mail with its antispam features, Internet Explorer 7 with its antiphishing features and protected mode, the improved Windows Firewall, the revamped Security Center, and Vista's enhanced parental controls. It also features Windows Media Player 11, Windows Movie Maker, Windows Photo Gallery, Windows Calendar, Windows Sidebar, Windows Search, the Games Explorer, partial support for the Mobility Center for notebook users, and basic networking (wired and wireless). However, Home Basic does not support the new Aero shell.

Vista Home Premium

- **Windows Vista Home Premium**—This edition includes everything in Home Basic, plus the Aero shell, Media Center, support for Tablet PCs, Windows Collaboration, Windows DVD Maker, scheduled backups, and advanced networking capabilities (such as ad hoc peer-to-peer networks and multiple-machine parental controls). This edition is aimed at networked household, multimedia enthusiasts, and notebook users.

The business market also has two editions:

Vista Business

- **Windows Vista Business**—This edition is analogous to Windows XP Professional and includes the same corporate features as XP Pro: support for domains, multiple network protocols, offline files, Remote Desktop, file and folder encryption, roaming user profiles, and group. Vista Business also comes with the Aero shell, Internet Information Server, Windows Fax and Scan, support for Tablet PCs, and the full Mobility Center. This edition does *not* come with Media Center, Movie Maker, and DVD Maker. In short, it's a no-nonsense OS for the business professional.

Vista Enterprise

- **Windows Vista Enterprise**—This edition is optimized for corporate desktops. It includes everything that's in the Vista Business edition, plus features such as Windows BitLocker (drive encryption for sensitive data), Virtual PC Express, Multilanguage User Interface (MUI), and Subsystem for UNIX-Based Applications (SUA). It also allows IT personnel to deploy the OS in different languages using a single disk image. Note, however, that Enterprise Edition will be made available only to Enterprise Agreement (EA) and Software Assurance (SA) volume-licensing customers. (Or, of course, you can just buy the Ultimate Edition, which I discuss next.)

Bestriding the canyon that exists between the home and business editions is an everything-but-the kitchen sink version:

Vista Ultimate Edition

- **Windows Vista Ultimate**—This edition comes with all the features of the Home Premium and Enterprise editions. It also offers enhanced game performance, access to online subscription services, custom themes, and enhanced support.

Here's the sixth Vista version:

- **Windows Vista Starter**—This is a stripped-down edition of Vista that is available only in emerging markets. It's designed for low-cost PCs and is optimized to run on machines with relatively slow CPUs and small memory footprints. This means that the Starter Edition won't support features such as the Aero shell, networking, image editing, and DVD burning. As with XP Starter Edition, Vista Starter Edition is limited to an 800×600 display and won't allow users to open more than three programs or three windows at once.

In addition to these editions, there are original equipment manufacturer (OEM) equivalents for all versions, as well as 64-bit versions for everything except the Starter Edition. Finally, Microsoft also released special versions of Vista—a Home Edition and a Professional Edition—that are customized for Europe to satisfy antitrust legal obligations in that region, which means these editions come without Microsoft's media features, including Media Player and Media Center.

Windows Anytime Upgrade

Microsoft is building Windows Vista as a *modularized* OS. This means that *every* edition of Vista rests on a subset—sometimes called MinWin—that contains the core functionality of the OS. Microsoft says that base contains about 95% of the Vista functionality. To create any of the Vista editions that you learned about earlier in this chapter, Microsoft simply adds the appropriate module (or *SKU*) on top of the base. This also works for language packs. The base OS has no language-specific code (it's *language-agnostic*, in the vernacular). Not even English is in the base OS. Therefore, you can apply only the languages you need on top of the base.

NOTE

SKU—short for *stock keeping unit* and pronounced *skew*—is a retailing term that refers to a unique code assigned to a product, which makes it easy for retailers to receive, identify, and inventory their stock. It also has the broader meaning of "a separate product," which is the meaning that Microsoft is using with the Vista components.

One of the big advantages of shipping multiple Vista SKUs in a single disc image is that all the modules I listed in the previous section are present on the disc. Therefore, it should be easy to "upgrade" to a higher version of Vista by simply adding the appropriate modules. That's exactly what Microsoft is doing with its new Windows Anytime Upgrade feature in the Home Basic, Home Premium, and Business editions. For example, if you are currently running the Home Basic edition of Windows Vista, you can use Windows Anytime Upgrade to jump up to Home Premium or even Ultimate. Similarly, Vista Business users can move to Vista Ultimate.

Figure 1.1 shows the Windows Anytime Upgrade window for Home Basic users (select Start, Control Panel, System and Maintenance, Windows Anytime Upgrade).

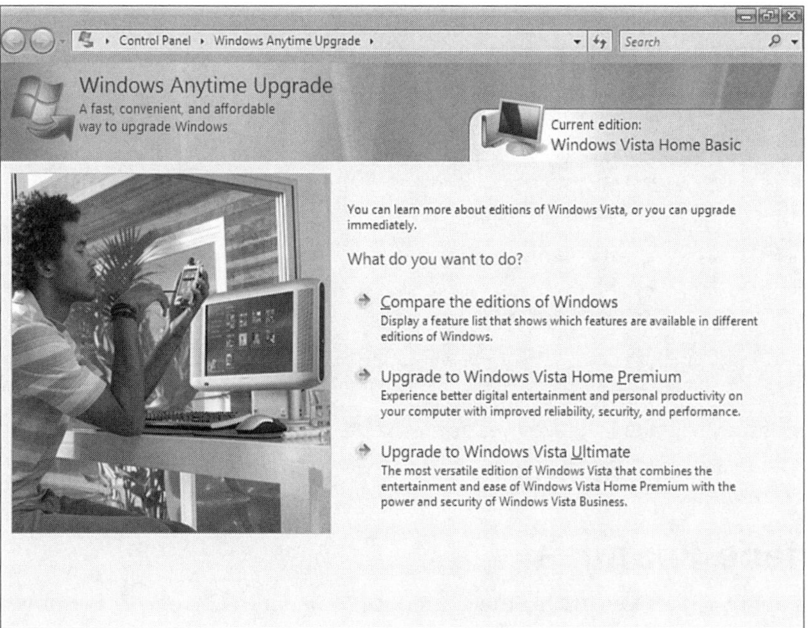

FIGURE 1.1 Windows Vista Home Basic users can upgrade to Home Premium or Ultimate.

Clicking one of the upgrade links takes you to another window that explains the upgrade process (see Figure 1.2):

1. Purchase a license from a Microsoft partner.
2. Download and install the license.
3. Insert your original Vista disc and follow the instructions to add the modules for the new version to your system.

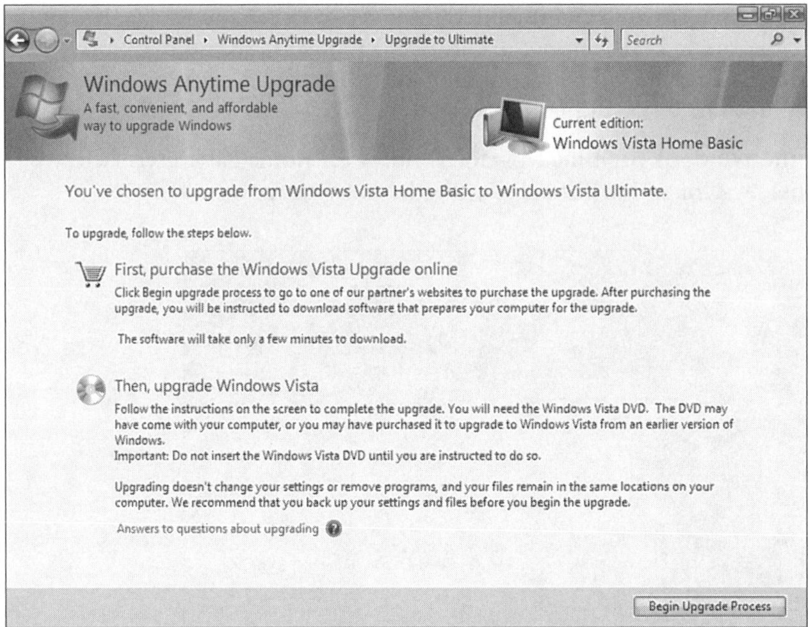

FIGURE 1.2 Clicking an upgrade link takes you to this page, where you can begin the upgrade process.

New Interface Features

You'll be learning about what's new with Vista's interface in detail in Chapter 7. For now, here's a summary of what to expect:

- **The Start "Orb"**—The Start button—a fixture in the computing firmament since Windows 95—has been replaced by an "orb" with the Windows logo, as shown in Figure 1.3.

FIGURE 1.3 Windows Vista replaces the Start button with an orb.

- **The Start Menu**—The Windows Vista Start menu has a new look, as you can see in Figure 1.4. There are still Internet and Email icons pinned to the top of the left side of the menu (although the Email icon now points to Windows Mail, the Vista replacement for Outlook Express), and the collection of links to Windows features on the right has been reconfigured. In addition, the icon at the top of the menu changes depending on which link is highlighted. The new Start menu has an integrated Search box as well, which I discuss a bit later in this section.

NOTE

Note also that the names of many Windows features have changed. In particular, Windows Vista no longer tacks on the word *My* to your personal folders (for example, My Documents is now just Documents).

FIGURE 1.4 The Windows Vista reconfigured Start menu.

- **The Desktop**—The desktop itself hasn't changed much, although the new high-resolution icons are much prettier than in previous versions. The big change related to the desktop is the new customization interface—called Desktop Background—which is much nicer than the old dialog box of controls and also offers a much wider variety of wallpapers, some of which are quite stunning. Figure 1.5 shows the Control Panel's Desktop Background window.
- **Aero Glass**—This is the new look of Vista's window, controls, and other elements. The "Glass" part means that for systems with relatively high-end graphics capabilities, the Vista window title bars and border will have a transparency effect.
- **Window Thumbnails**—These are scaled-down versions of windows and documents. For supported file types, these thumbnails are "live," which means they reflect the current content of the window or document. For example, in folder windows, the icon for an Excel workbook shows the first worksheet, and an icon for a Word document shows the first page. Similarly, a Windows Media Player thumbnail shows live content, such as a running video.

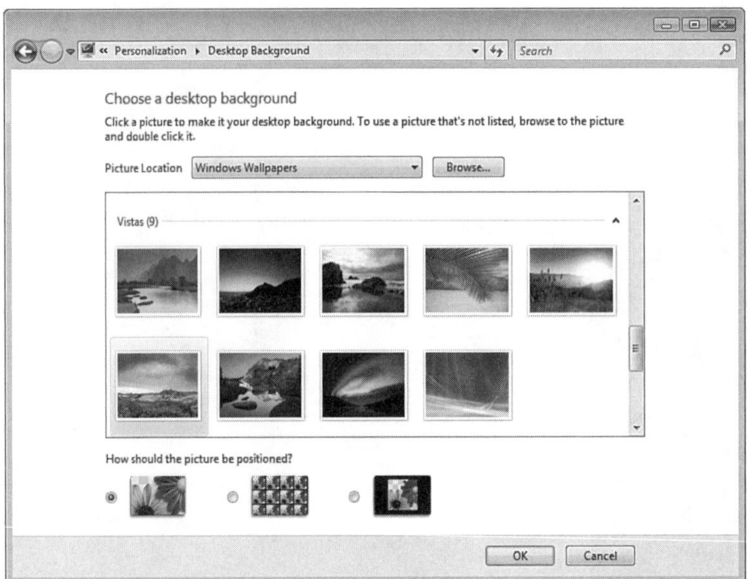

FIGURE 1.5 The Control Panel's Desktop Background window makes it easy to customize the desktop wallpaper, color, and more.

- **Flip and Flip 3D**—When you hold down Alt and press Tab, Vista displays not an icon for each open window, but a thumbnail for each window. Each time you press the Tab key, Vista "flips" to the next window (hence the name of this new feature: Flip). You can also press Windows Logo+Tab to organize the open windows in a 3D stack. Pressing the arrow keys or scrolling the mouse wheel flips you from one window to another (this feature is called Flip 3D). In Chapter 7, see the section titled "Better Cool Switches: Flip and Flip 3D" for screenshots that show you these features in action.
- **Taskbar Thumbnails**—The live thumbnails idea also extends to the taskbar. If you mouse over a taskbar button, Vista displays a live thumbnail for the window associated with the button, as shown in Figure 1.6.

FIGURE 1.6 When you hover the mouse pointer over a taskbar button, Vista displays a live thumbnail image of the associate window.

- **Folder Windows**—Windows Vista has given folder windows a considerable makeover, as shown in Figure 1.7. The "address" of the folder is hidden in favor of a hierarchical "breadcrumb" folder path, the Task pane is now a strip below the address bar, and the Classic (as they're now called) menus are hidden (you can display them by pressing Alt). Each window can be divided into as many as five sections: Besides the folder content, you can display the Navigation pane on the left, the Preview pane on the right, the Search pane above, and the Details pane below.

FIGURE 1.7 Folder windows in Windows Vista have been given a serious makeover.

- **Instant Search**—Vista's new Windows Search Engine (WSE) promises to be a more powerful alternative to the search capabilities of previous Windows versions. This is partially because WSE supports searching via tags, comments, and other document metadata (see "Support for Document Metadata," later in this chapter). Nevertheless, perhaps the biggest and potentially most useful search innovation in Vista is the Instant Search box that appears at the bottom of the Start menu (refer to Figure 1.4) and within every folder window (refer to Figure 1.7). The Instant Search box enables you to perform as-you-type searches, which means that when you type even a single character in the Instant Search box, Vista automatically begins searching all your programs, documents, Internet Explorer favorites, email messages, and contacts (in the case of the Start menu's Instant Search box) or all the files in the current folder (in the case of a folder window's Instant Search box). There are also on-the-fly Instant Search boxes within Windows Media Player, Windows Mail, Windows Photo Gallery, and many other locations.

NOTE

Folder windows come with a new Search pane that you can use to perform much more sophisticated searches, including searching by file date and size, and also metadata searches on file tags and authors.

- **Windows Sidebar**—The Windows Sidebar is a pane that appears on the right side of the Vista desktop. You can populate the Sidebar with a new technology called *gadgets*, which are mini-applications that can display the local weather, stock quotes, the current time, RSS newsfeeds, and much more.

What's New Under the Hood

The Windows Vista interface has been garnering most of the attention in the beta program, but Vista also offers plenty of new and improved features under the hood, as the next few sections show.

Support for Document Metadata

Metadata is data that describes data. For example, if you have some digital photos on your computer, you could use metadata to describe each image: the person who took the picture, the camera used, tags that describe the image itself, and so on. Windows Vista comes with built-in support for document metadata, enabling you to add and edit properties such as the `Title`, `Comments`, `Tags`, `Author`, and `Rating` (1 to 5 stars).

Windows not only gives you easier ways to edit metadata (for example, you can click the Edit link in the folder window's Preview pane), but it also makes good use of metadata to make your life easier:

- **Searching**—The Windows Search service indexes metadata so that you can search for documents using any metadata property as a query operand.
- **Grouping**—This refers to organizing a folder's contents according to the values in a particular property. This was also possible in Windows XP, but Windows Vista improves on XP by adding techniques that enable you to quickly select all the files in a group and to collapse a group to show only its header.
- **Stacking**—This is similar to grouping because it organizes the folder's contents based on the values of a property. The difference is that a stack of files appears in the folder as a kind of subfolder.

- **Filtering**—This refers to changing the folder view so that only files that have one or more specified property values are displayed. For example, you could filter the folder's files to show only those in which the `Type` property was, say, `Email` or `Music`.

NOTE

For the complete details on metadata, see the "Metadata and the Windows Explorer Property System" section in Chapter 3.

Performance Improvements

When I tell people that a new version of Windows is available, the first question they inevitably ask is, "Is it faster than [insert their current Windows version here]?" Everybody wants Windows to run faster, but that's primarily because most of us are running systems that have had the same OS installed for several years. One of the bitter truths of computing is that even the most meticulously well maintained system will slow down over time. On such systems, the only surefire way to get a big performance boost is to wipe the hard drive and start with a fresh OS install.

The Windows Vista Setup program essentially does just that (preserving and restoring your files and settings along the way, of course). Therefore, the short answer to the previous question is, "Yes, Vista will be faster than your existing system." However, that performance gain comes not just from a fresh install, but also because Microsoft has tweaked the Windows code for more speed:

- **Faster startup**—Microsoft has optimized the Vista startup code and implemented asynchronous startup script and application launching. This means that Vista doesn't delay startup by waiting for initialization scripts to complete their chores. It simply completes its own startup tasks while the scripts run in their own good time in the background.
- **Sleep mode**—Actually, you can reduce Vista startup to just a few seconds by taking advantage of the new Sleep mode, which combines the best features of the XP Hibernate and Standby modes. Like Hibernate, Sleep mode preserves all your open documents, windows, and programs, and it completely shuts down your computer. However, like Standby, you enter Sleep mode within just a few seconds, and you resume from Sleep mode within just a few seconds.
- **SuperFetch**—This technology tracks the programs and data you use over time to create a kind of profile of your disk usage. Using the profile, SuperFetch can then make an educated guess about the data that you'll require; like XP's Prefetcher, it can then load that data into memory ahead of time for enhanced performance. SuperFetch can also work with Vista's new ReadyBoost technology, which uses a USB 2.0 flash RAM drive as storage for the SuperFetch cache, which should provide improved performance even further by freeing up the RAM that SuperFetch would otherwise use.

- **Restart Manager**—This feature enables patches and updates to install much more intelligently. Now you often have to reboot when you install a patch because Windows can't shut down all the processes associated with the application you're patching. Restart Manager keeps track of all running processes and, in most cases, can shut down all of an application's processes so that the patch can be installed without requiring a reboot.

Stability Improvements

The second thing that people always ask about a new version of Windows is, "Will it crash less often? Microsoft has had nearly a quarter of a century to get Windows right, so why can't it produce a glitch-free operating system?" I have to break the news to my frustrated interlocutors that what they seek is almost certainly impossible. Windows is just too big and complex, and the number of software permutations and hardware combinations is just too huge to ensure complete system stability in all setups.

That doesn't mean that Microsoft isn't at least *trying* to make Windows more stable. Here's what it did in Vista:

- **I/O cancellation**—Windows often fails because some program has crashed and brought the OS down with it. The usual cause of this is that a program has made an input/output (I/O) request to a service, resource, or another program, but that process is unavailable; this results in a stuck program that requires a reboot to recover. To prevent this, Vista implements an improved version of a technology called **I/O cancellation**, which can detect when a program is stuck waiting for an I/O request and then cancel that request to help the program recover from the problem.
- **Reliability monitor**—This new feature keeps track of the overall stability of your system, as well as **reliability events**, which are either changes to your system that could affect stability or occurrences that might indicate instability. Reliability events include Windows updates, software installs and uninstalls, device driver installs, updates, rollbacks and uninstalls, device driver problems, and Windows failures. Reliability monitors graphs these changes and a measure of system stability over time so that you can graphically see whether any changes affected system stability.
- **Service recovery**—Many Windows services are mission-critical, and if they fail, it almost always means that the only way to recover your system is to shut down and restart your computer. With Windows Vista, however, every service has a **recovery policy** that enables Vista not only to restart the service, but also to reset any other service or process that depends on the failed service.
- **Startup Repair Tool**—Troubleshooting startup problems is not for the faint-of-heart, but you might never have to perform this onerous core again, thanks to Vista's new Startup Repair Tool (SRT), which is designed to fix many common startup problems automatically. When a startup failure occurs, Vista starts the SRT immediately. The program then analyzes the startup logs and performs a series of diagnostic tests to determine the cause of the startup failure.

- **New diagnostic tools**—Windows Vista is loaded with new and improved diagnostic tools. These include Disk Diagnostics (which monitors the Self-Monitoring, Analysis, and Reporting Technology, or SMART, data generated by most modern hard disks); Windows Memory Diagnostics (which works with Microsoft Online Crash Analysis to determine whether program crashes are caused by defective physical memory); Memory Leak Diagnosis (which looks for and fixes programs using increasing amounts of memory); Windows Resource Exhaustion Detection and Resolution (RADAR, which monitors virtual memory and issues a warning when resources run low, and also identifies which programs or processes are using the most virtual memory and includes a list of these resource hogs as part of the warning); Network Diagnostics (which analyzes all aspects of the network connection and then either fixes the problem or gives the user simple instructions for resolving the situation); and the Windows Diagnostic Console (which enables you to monitor performance metrics).

Security Enhancements

With reports of new Windows XP vulnerabilities coming in with stomach-lurching regularity, we all hope that Vista has a much better security track record. It's still too early to tell—and nefarious hackers are exceptionally clever—but it certainly looks as though Microsoft is heading in the right direction with Vista:

- **User Account Control**—This new—and *very* controversial—feature ensures that every Vista user runs with only limited privileges, even those accounts that are part of the Administrators group (except the Administrator account itself). In other words, each user runs as a "least privileged user," which means users have only the minimum privileges they require for day-to-day work. This also means that any malicious users or programs that gain access to the system also run with only limited privileges, thus limiting the amount of damage they can do. The downside (and the source of the controversy) is that you are constantly pestered with security dialog boxes that ask for your approval or credentials to perform even trivial tasks, such as deleting certain files.
- **Windows Firewall**—This feature is now **bidirectional**, which means that it blocks not only unauthorized incoming traffic, but also unauthorized outgoing traffic. For example, if your computer has a Trojan horse installed, it might attempt to send data out to the Web, but the firewall's outgoing protection will prevent this.
- **Windows Defender**—This is the Windows Vista antispyware program. (**Spyware** is a program that surreptitiously monitors a user's computer activities or harvests sensitive data on the user's computer, and then sends that information to an individual or a company via the user's Internet connection.) Windows Defender prevents spyware from being installed on your system and monitors your system in real-time to look for signs of spyware activity.
- **Internet Explorer Protected mode**—This new operating mode for Internet Explorer builds on the User Account Control feature. Protected mode means that Internet

Explorer runs with a privilege level that's enough to surf the Web, but that's about it. Internet Explorer can't install software, modify the user's files or settings, add shortcuts to the Startup folder, or even change its own settings for the default home page and search engine. This is designed to thwart spyware and other malicious programs that attempt to gain access to your system through the web browser.

- **Phishing Filter**—**Phishing** refers to creating a replica of an existing web page to fool a user into submitting personal, financial, or password data. Internet Explorer's new Phishing Filter can alert you when you surf to a page that is a known phishing site, or it can warn you if the current page appears to be a phishing scam.
- **Junk Mail Filter**—Windows Mail (the Vista replacement for Outlook Express) comes with an antispam filter based on the one that's part of Microsoft Outlook. The Junk Mail Filter uses a sophisticated algorithm to scan incoming messages for signs of spam. If it finds any, it quarantines the spam in a separate Junk Mail folder.
- **Windows Service Hardening**—This new technology is designed to limit the damage that a compromised service can wreak on a system by (among other things) running all services in a lower privilege level, stripping services of permissions that they don't require, and applying restrictions to services that control exactly what they can do on a system.
- **Secure Startup**—This technology encrypts the entire system drive to prevent a malicious user from accessing your sensitive data. Secure Startup works by storing the keys that encrypt and decrypt the sectors on a system drive in a Trusted Platform Module (TPM) 1.2 chip, which is a hardware component available on many newer machines.
- **Network Access Protection (NAP)**—This service checks the health status of a computer, including its installed security patches, downloaded virus signatures, and security settings. If any health item is not completely up-to-date or within the network guidelines, the NAP enforcement service (running on a server that supports this feature) either doesn't let the computer log on to the network or shuttles the computer off to a restricted area of the network.
- **Parental Controls**—This feature enables you to place restrictions on the user accounts that you've assigned to your children. Using the new User Controls window in the Control Panel, you can allow or block specific websites, set up general site restrictions (such as Kids Websites Only), block content categories (such as Pornography, Mature Content, and Bomb Making), block file downloads, set time limits for computer use, allow or disallow games, restrict games based on ratings and contents, and allow or block specific programs.

Windows Presentation Foundation

The Windows Presentation Foundation (WPF) is Vista's new graphical subsystem, and it's responsible for all the interface changes in the Vista package. WPF implements a new graphics model that can take full advantage of today's powerful graphics processing units.

With WPF, all output goes through the powerful Direct3D layer (so that the CPU doesn't have to deal with any graphics); this output also is all vector based, so WPF produces extremely high-resolution images that are completely scalable.

Desktop Window Manager

The Desktop Window Manager (DWM) is a new technology that assumes control over the screen display. With Vista, applications draw their graphics to an offscreen buffer, and then the DWM composites the buffer contents on the screen.

Improved Graphics

The combination of the WPF and DWM means that Vista graphics are the best Windows graphics ever. Program and document windows no longer "tear" when you move them quickly across the screen, animations applied to actions such as minimizing a window are richer and more effective, icons scale up and down with no loss of quality, and transparency effects are applied to window title bars and borders.

Transactional NTFS

The Windows Vista file system implements a new technology called Transactional NTFS, or TxF, for short. TxF applies transactional database ideas to the file system. This means that if some mishap occurs to your data—it could be a system crash, a program crash, an overwrite to an important file, or even just imprudent edits to a file—Vista allows you to roll back the file to a previous version. It's a lot like the System Restore feature, except that it works not for the entire system, but for individual files, folders, and volumes.

XML Paper Specification

Windows Vista supports a new Microsoft document format called the XML Paper Specification, or XPS. This is an XML schema designed to create documents that are high-fidelity reproductions of existing documents. In other words, documents published as XPS and opened in an XPS viewer program should look the same as they do in the original application. Microsoft has incorporated an XPS viewer into Windows Vista, so any Vista user will automatically be able to view XPS documents. (The viewer runs within Internet Explorer.)

Microsoft is also licensing XPS royalty-free so that developers can incorporate XPS viewing and publishing features into their products without cost. This means it should be easy to publish XPS documents from a variety of applications.

New and Improved Programs and Tools

All new versions of Windows come with a few brand-new programs and tools, as well as a bunch of existing features that have been overhauled, tweaked, or merely prettified. Windows Vista is no exception, and I've talked about a few of these already (including Windows Sidebar, Windows Defender, and the Reliability Monitor). The next few sections take you through the main highlights of the rest of Vista's new and improved programs and tools.

Welcome Center

When you start Windows Vista, you automatically see the new Welcome Center window, shown in Figure 1.8. This window tells you your Vista version and activation status, and provides you with some basic details about your PC (processor, RAM, computer name, and so on). There are also several links for tasks such as setting up devices, working with user accounts, transferring files from your old computer, and viewing more details about your computer.

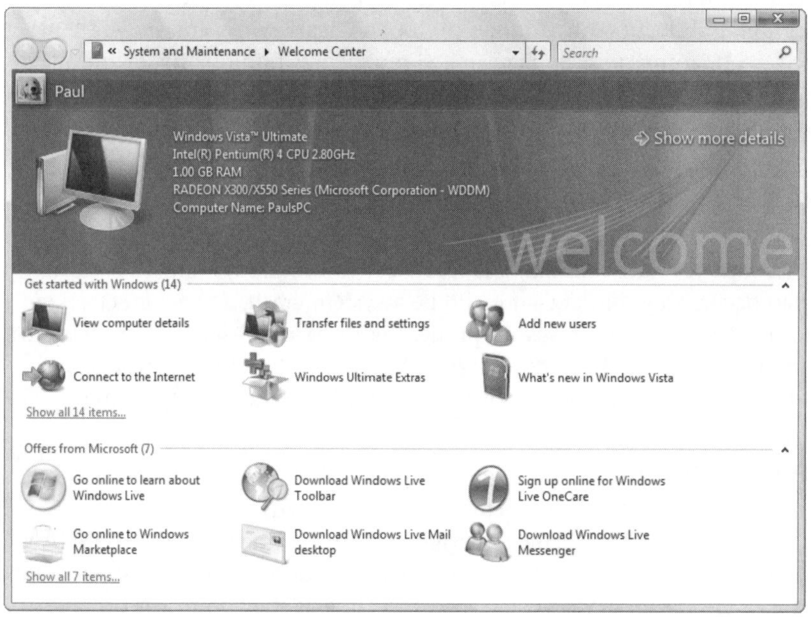

FIGURE 1.8 The new Welcome Center window appears automatically each time you start Vista.

Control Panel

The Control Panel received a major overhaul in Windows XP, which consisted of a new Category view that divided the icons into 10 categories, such as Appearance and Themes, Printers and Other Hardware, and Network and Internet Connections. This was a boon to novice users because it meant they no longer had to be intimidated by the 30-plus Control Panel icons that came with a default XP install. Power users, of course, *hated* the Category View because it required far too many extra clicks to get at the icon we wanted. Fortunately, Microsoft made it easy to switch between Category view and Classic view, the new name for the old all-icon arrangement of the Control Panel window.

Microsoft has tried again to reconfigure Control Panel in Windows Vista. Perhaps that's because the sheer number of Control Panel icons has exploded in Vista, with a default install foisting more than 50 icons onto your system. That's a lot of icons, even for power users to deal with, so clearly some kind of reorganization is required. Fortunately, Microsoft did *not* simply come up with a new set of Control Panel categories that everyone but beginners would ignore. Yes, there are categories, but with a number of twists:

- There are more categories than in XP. There are 11 sections in all (including the Mobile PC category that appears in notebook installations), so the categorization is a bit finer grained. This is particularly true because several XP "categories"—User Accounts, Add or Remove Programs, and Security Center—were actually icons that launched features.

- The categories are supplemented with links to specific features, as shown in Figure 1.9. For example, besides clicking the Hardware and Sound category to see all Control Panel's hardware- and audio-related icons, you can also click Printers or Mouse to go directly to those features.

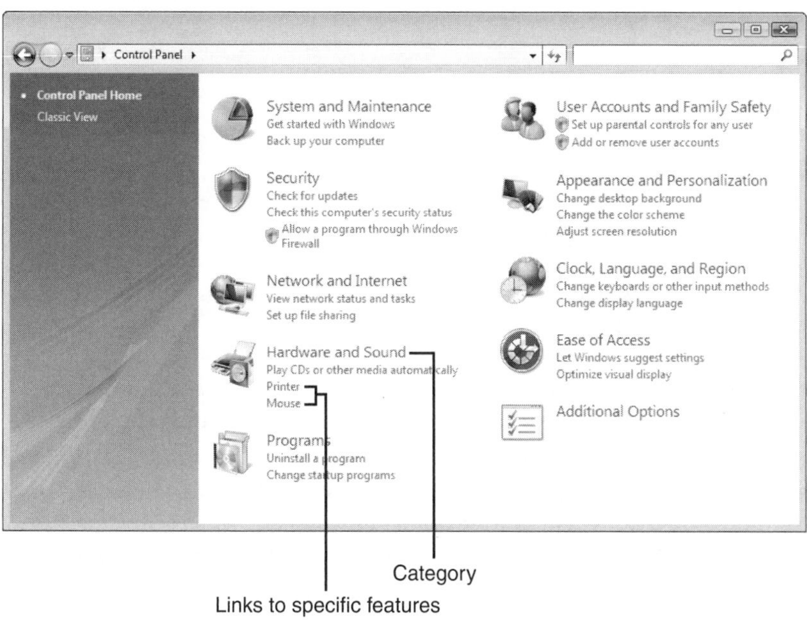

FIGURE 1.9 The Vista Control Panel supplements icon categories with links to specific features.

- Some icons are cross-referenced in multiple categories to make them easier to find. For example, you can find the Power Options icon in both the Hardware and Sound category and the Mobile PC category, and you can find the Windows Firewall icon in both the Security category and the Network and Internet category.

- When you open a category, Control Panel displays a list of all the categories on the left pane, as shown in Figure 1.10. That way, if you pick the wrong category or want to work with a different category, you don't need to navigate back to the Control Panel Home window.

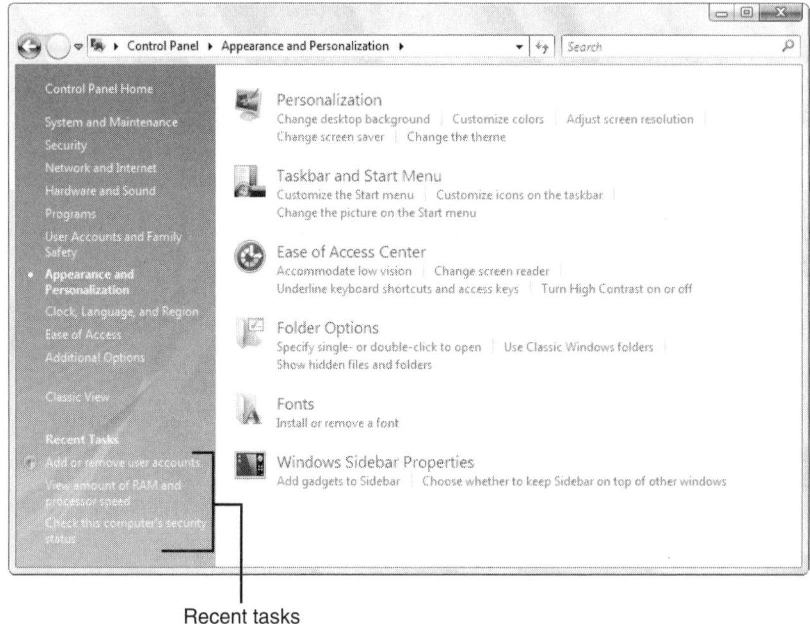

FIGURE 1.10 When you navigate into a category, Control Panel displays a list of all the categories in the left pane for easy access.

- Control Panel remembers your most recent tasks in each Windows session, as shown in Figure 1.10. This makes it easy to rerun a task that you use frequently.

The Vista Control Panel is clearly superior to its XP predecessor. It's easy to navigate for novices, but it also minimizes mouse clicks for experienced users. However, my guess is that most power users will still use the Classic view and, even faster, will set up the Control Panel as a submenu of the Start menu.

Internet Explorer 7

We haven't seen a new web browser from Microsoft for several years, so you'd expect that Internet Explorer 7 would be chock full of new features. Alas, it's not. The most important new features are the security enhancements that I mentioned earlier (the Phishing Filter and Protected mode). Other than those and a slightly revamped interface, the list of significant new features is disappointingly meager:

- **Tabbed browsing**—Like Firefox, Opera, Safari and quite a few other browsers, Internet Explorer finally has tabbed browsing, in which each open page appears in its own tab within a single Internet Explorer window. Internet Explorer ups the tab ante a bit with a new feature called Quick Tabs that displays a live thumbnail of each tabbed page, as shown in Figure 1.11.

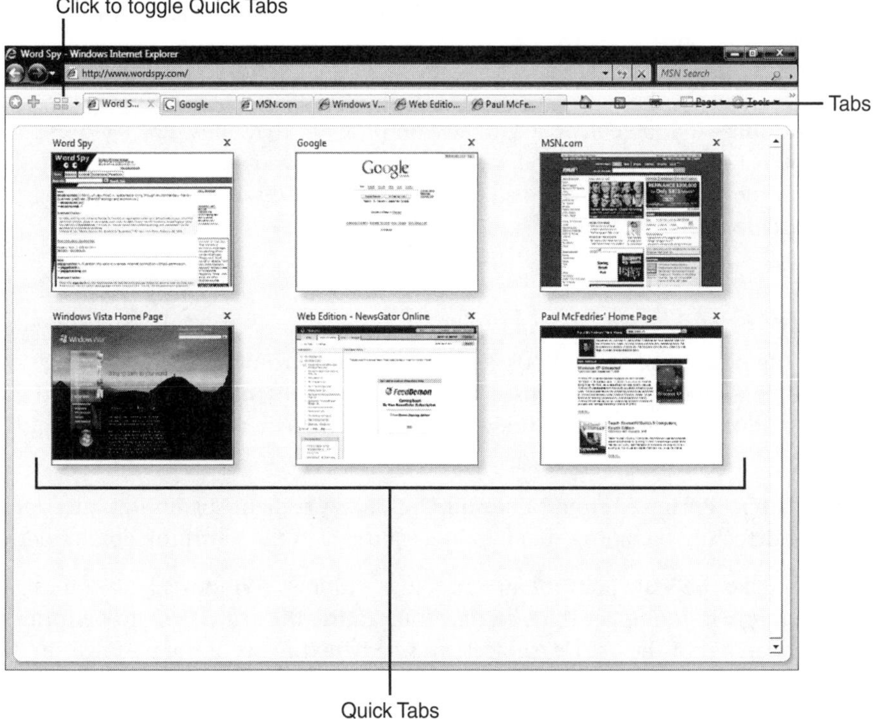

FIGURE 1.11 Internet Explorer 7 finally has tabbed browsing, but it improves on this feature with Quick Tabs, which provides live thumbnails of the tabbed pages.

- **Support for RSS feeds**—RSS (Real Simple Syndication) is becoming the preferred method for sites to enable readers to stay up-to-date with changing content. Internet Explorer 7 recognizes when a site has one or more RSS feeds available and enables you to view the feed. You can also subscribe to a feed to have Internet Explorer alert you when new content is available. Subscribed feeds appear in the new Feeds folder, which is part of the Favorites Center, a pane that also includes the Favorites and History folders.

- **Delete Browsing History**—This new feature gives you an easy way to delete the following data related to your past web browsing: temporary Internet files, cookies, history, saved form data, and remembered passwords. You can delete any one of these options, or you can delete all of them with a single click.

- **Multiple home pages**—Internet Explorer 7 enables you to specify up to eight home pages. When you launch Internet Explorer or click the Home button, Internet Explorer loads each home page in its own tab. This is a great new feature if you always open the same few sites at the start of each browsing session.

CAUTION

There's no such thing as a free browsing lunch, of course. The more home pages you have, the longer it takes Internet Explorer to launch.

- **Manage Add-ons**—If you've installed an add-on program that adds new features such as a toolbar to Internet Explorer, you can use the new Manage Add-ons dialog box to see all the add-ons. You can also use it to enable or disable an add-on and delete an installed ActiveX control.

Windows Mail

Windows Mail is the new name for Outlook Express, which Microsoft needed to change because some people were getting it confused with Microsoft Outlook. Unfortunately, the name is just about all that's new with Windows Mail. Only three new features are of any significance:

- **Junk Mail Filter**—Borrowed from Microsoft Outlook's excellent spam filter, this does a fine job of detecting incoming spam and relegating it to the new Junk Email folder.
- **Search box**—Like the Vista Start menu and folder windows, Windows Mail comes with a Search box in the upper-right corner. You can use the Search box to perform as-you-type searches of the To, Cc, subject, and body text fields of the messages in the current folder.
- **Microsoft Help Groups**—Windows Mail comes with a preconfigured account for Microsoft's msnews.microsoft.com news server, which hosts more than 2,000 `microsoft.public.*` newsgroups. If you have a Microsoft Passport ID (such as a Hotmail address), you can log in and rate newsgroup posts as either Useful or Not Useful.

Windows Calendar

Windows is slowly evolving into a complete computing system in the sense that it contains everything that a user with simple needs could want. It has long had a word processor, text editor, graphics editor, web browser, email client, media player, and backup program. What's missing? On the security side, it's essential to have a bidirectional firewall and antispyware tool, and Vista has both of those. In addition, all of us need some way to track appointments and to-do lists, so we need a calendar application; Vista now comes with one of those, too, called Windows Calendar, and it's actually not bad for an operating system freebie. It has a nice, clean interface (see Figure 1.12), and it does all the basic jobs that a calendar should:

- ▶ Create appointments, both one-time and recurring
- ▶ Create all-day events
- ▶ Schedule tasks, with the ability to set a priority flag and a completed flag
- ▶ Set appointment and task reminders
- ▶ View appointments by day, week, or month
- ▶ Publish and subscribe to calendars using the iCal standard
- ▶ Import Calendar (`.ics`) files
- ▶ Create multiple calendars

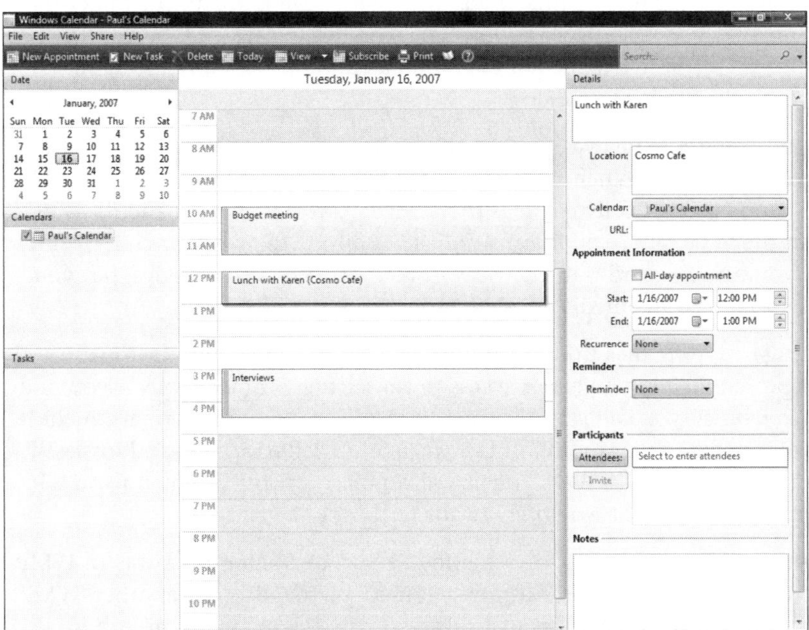

FIGURE 1.12 Windows Calendar is a reasonably competent calendar program.

Media Player

Vista ships with Windows Media Player 11 (WMP 11), a major update that includes quite a few new features:

- ▶ **Cleaner interface**—The overall interface is a bit simpler than in previous versions.
- ▶ **Album art**—If you've downloaded or scanned album art, it appears throughout the WMP 11 interface, which is much nicer than previous versions, in which album art appeared only rarely.

- **Grouping and stacking of media**—The grouping and stacking techniques that I mentioned earlier for folder windows also apply to the WMP library. For music, for example, WMP offers several views based on media metadata, including Songs view, which groups songs according the values in the `Album Artist` property and then by the values in the `Album` property, and `Genre`, which stacks the albums using the values in the `Genre` property. You get a different set of views for each category (Music, Pictures, Video, Recorded TV, or Other Media).
- **Advanced Tag Editor**—You can easily apply media metadata by downloading the relevant information from the Internet, but most WMP metadata is editable. An innovation in WMP 11 is the Advanced Tag Editor, which gives you a front-end for much of the metadata available for a particular media file.
- **Instant Search**—The WMP 11 window has an Instant Search box in the upper-right corner that enables you to perform as-you-type searches. After you type your text in the Search box, WMP searches filenames and metadata for matching media files; it shows the results in the WMP window.
- **Synching with media devices**—Synching items from the Library to a media device is a bit easier in WMP 11. When you insert a WMP-compatible media device, WMP recognizes it and automatically displays the device, its total capacity, and its available space in the Sync tab. In addition, WMP 11 supports two-way synching, which means that you can synch files not only from your PC to a media device, but you can also synch files from a media device to your PC.
- **Easier ripping**—Ripping files from an audio CD is more convenient in WMP 11 because the program gives you easier access to rip settings. For example, if you pull down the Rip tab list, you can select Format to display a list of file formats, including various Windows Media Audio formats (regular, variable bit rate, and lossless), MP3, and—new in WMP 11—WAV. You can also pull down the Rip menu and select Bit Rate to choose the rate at which you want to rip the media.
- **Burning options**—Burning music or other media to a disc is more flexible in WMP 11. For one thing, WMP supports burning media to a DVD disc. For another, WMP 11 comes with a new Burn tab in its Options dialog box, which you can use to select the burn speed, apply volume leveling to audio CDs, select the file list format for a data disc, and set the file quality.
- **URGE support**—WMP 11 automatically downloads and installs the URGE store, which is the online music store that Microsoft has created in collaboration with MTV.
- **Media Sharing**—This feature enables you to share your WMP Library with other network users, just like you'd share a folder or a printer.
- **DVD playback**—When you play a DVD in WMP 11, a DVD button is added to the playback controls. Clicking that button displays the DVD menu, which offers a much wider array of DVD-related commands than in previous versions. Welcome additions to the DVD arsenal are the capabilities to select audio and language tracks (if available), display subtitles (if any), and capture frames.

Media Center

You'll find no separate Media Center Edition of Windows Vista as there was with Windows XP. Instead, Vista comes with Media Center as part of its Home Premium and Ultimate editions. Here's a summary of the changes Microsoft has made to the Vista version of Media Center:

- **Interface improvements**—Microsoft has tweaked the Media Center interface to make it easier to use. The top-level tasks (TV, Music, and so on) appear more like a list than menu choices, as they do in XP Media Center. When you select a top-level task, Vista Media Center bolds the task text and displays the available second-level tasks below. When you select a second-level task, Media Center displays a graphic along with the task text to illustrate the task's function. As the displayed tasks move away from the center of the screen (whether up or down, left or right), they become progressively lighter. This focuses the user's attention on the task at hand in the center of the screen.
- **New menu structure**—The Vista Media Center comes with quite a few top-level tasks, including Pictures + Videos (work with your picture and video libraries), Movies (work with DVD movies), TV (work with your TV tuner), Music (work with music and radio), Spotlight (access media online and run other Media Center programs installed on your computer), Tools (access Media Center tools), and Tasks (run other Media Center features).
- **Show notifications for incoming phone calls**—You can set up Media Center to display these notifications for all incoming calls or just for calls with caller ID.
- **Wireless networking**—You can now use the Media Center to join your computer to an existing wireless network.
- **Parental controls**—You can set up parental controls to restrict the content viewed through Media Center.
- **Program optimization**—Vista Media Center comes with an optimization feature that ensures maximum performance from your system. Optimization occurs automatically every morning at 4 a.m., but you can set your own schedule.

Windows Photo Gallery

Windows Photo Gallery is a new program that can import images and videos from a camera, a scanner, removable media, the network, or the Web. You can then view the images, add metadata such as captions and tags, rate the images, search for images, and even apply common fixes to improve the look of photos. You can also burn selected images to a DVD disc.

DVD Burning and Authoring

Windows Vista offers DVD-burning capabilities in a number of places, including Windows Photo Gallery, Windows Media Player, Media Center, and Windows Movie Maker.

Vista also comes with Windows DVD Maker, a program that enables you to author actual DVD discs, complete with menus, chapters, and other elements of a typical DVD disc interface.

Per-Application Volume Control

Windows Vista implements a new technology called *per-application volume control*. This means that Vista gives you a volume-control slider for every running program and process that is currently producing audio output. Figure 1.13 shows the new Volume window that appears when you double-click the Volume icon in the notification area. The slider on the left controls the speaker volume, so you can use it as a systemwide volume control. The rest of the window contains the **application mixer**—sliders and mute buttons for individual programs.

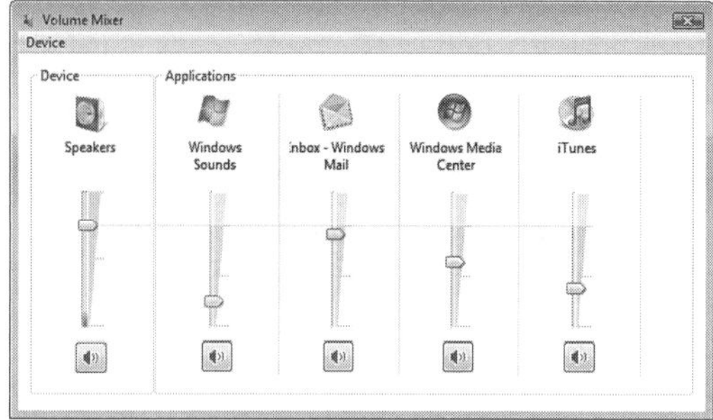

FIGURE 1.13 Windows Vista uses per-application volume control to enable you to set the volume level for each program that outputs audio.

Sound Recorder

Vista's Sound Recorder program is completely new and improves on its predecessors by offering unlimited recording time and the capability to record to the Windows Media Audio file format (previous versions were limited to one minute of WAV audio).

Windows Easy Transfer

Windows Transfer is the replacement for the XP Files and Settings Transfer Wizard. It works in much the same way as the XP wizard, but Windows Easy Transfer supports a broader range of transfer media, including Flash drives.

Windows Backup

The Windows Vista new backup program—now called Windows Backup—is quite an improvement on its predecessors:

- You can back up to a writeable disc, USB Flash drive, or other removable media.
- You can back up to a network share.

- When you set up the program, backing up is completely automated, particularly if you back up to a resource that has plenty of room to hold your files (such as a hard disk or roomy network share).
- You can create a system image backup—which Microsoft calls a *CompletePC backup*—that saves the exact state of your computer and thus enables you to completely restore your system if your computer dies or is stolen.

The Game Explorer

The Game Explorer is a special shell folder that offers several new features for gamers and game developers:

- A repository for all installed games.
- Game-related tasks such as launching a game, linking to the developer's website, and setting up parental controls.
- Support for games metadata, such as the game's publisher and version number and the last time you played the game. The Game Explorer also supports ratings from various organizations, including the Entertainment Software Rating Board (ESRB).
- Auto-update of games. With the new Game Update feature, Vista automatically lets you know if a patch or a newer version is available for an installed game.

The Game Explorer is initially populated with the eight games that come in the Vista box. These games include updates to venerable Windows favorites (FreeCell, Hearts, Minesweeper, Solitaire, Spider Solitaire, and InkBall) and a few new additions (Chess Titans, Mahjong Titans, and Purble Place).

Mobility Center

The new Windows Mobility Center offers a convenient overview of the state of various mobility features on your notebook computer. As you can see in Figure 1.14, the Mobility Center enables you to view and control the brightness, volume, battery status, wireless network connection, screen orientation for a Tablet PC, external display, and current synchronization status of your offline files.

Network Center

Network Center is the new Vista networking hub that shows you the current status of your connection and gives you quick access to all the most common networking tasks: connecting to a network, browsing a network, setting up a network (including new **ad hoc connections**, which are temporary hookups between two or more nearby PCs), and diagnosing network problems.

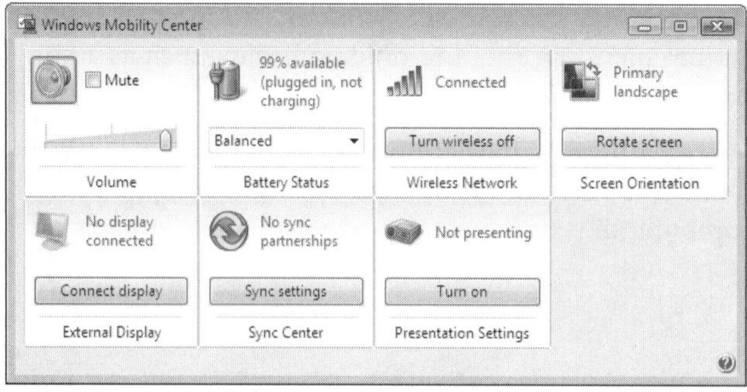

FIGURE 1.14 The new Mobility Center offers a selection of information and controls for notebook-related features.

Network Map

The Network Center displays a subset of the new Network Map feature, which gives you a visual display of everything your computer is connected to: network connections (wired and wireless), ad hoc connections, Internet connections, and more. Network Map also gives you a visual display of the connection status so that you can easily spot problems. Windows Vista comes with a more detailed version of Network Map, an example of which is shown in Figure 1.15.

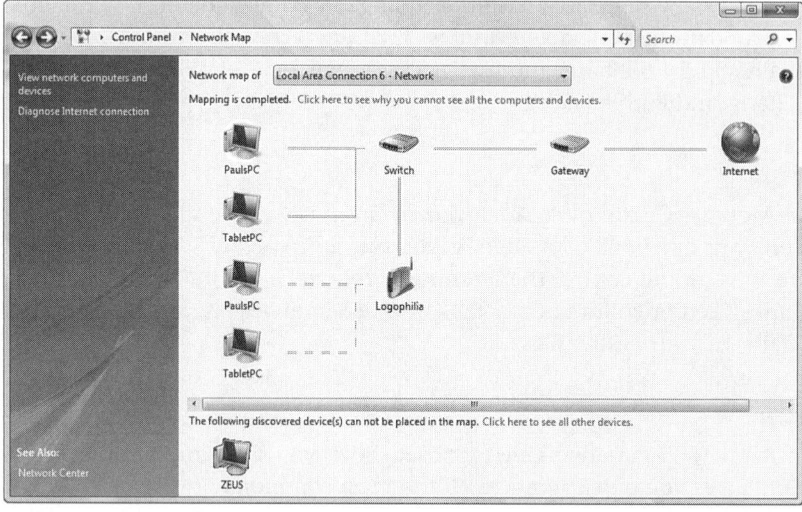

FIGURE 1.15 The full version of the Network Map.

Windows Collaboration

Vista's replacement for NetMeeting is an entirely new program called Windows Collaboration. As with NetMeeting, you can use Windows Collaboration to show a local program or document to any number of remote users, and you can collaborate on a document with remote users. Windows Collaboration uses several new Vista technologies, including Peer-to-Peer Networking, Distributed File System Replicator, and People Near Me. The latter is an opt-in list of people on the same network that you are. The idea is that you start a collaboration session and then invite one or more people from the People Near Me list to join the session. You can then start a presentation, which involves one of the participants performing some sort of action on his or her computer, and the other participants seeing the results of those actions within their session window. For example, you can demonstrate how a program works, collaborate on a document, or share your desktop, which enables remote users to view everything you do on your computer.

From Here

This chapter gave you an overview of what's new and noteworthy in Windows Vista, and you saw that there is quite a bit to sink your teeth into. That's just what we'll do in the rest of this book and I take you inside Windows Vista and show you how to take full advantage of its features, both new and old.

CHAPTER 2

Customizing and Troubleshooting the Windows Vista Startup

IN THIS CHAPTER

- The Boot Process, from Power Up to Startup
- Custom Startups Using the Boot Configuration Data
- Custom Startups with the Advanced Options Menu
- Useful Windows Vista Logon Strategies
- Troubleshooting Windows Vista Startup

Assuming that you have Windows Vista safely installed on your computer, you can begin your journey, appropriately enough, at the beginning: the startup process. At first blush, this might seem like a surprising topic for an entire chapter. After all, the Windows Vista startup procedure gives new meaning to the term no-brainer: You turn on your system, and a short while later, Windows Vista reports for duty. What's to write about?

You'd be surprised. The progress of a typical boot appears uneventful only because Windows Vista uses a whole host of default options for startup. By changing these defaults, you can take control of the startup process and make Windows Vista start your way. This chapter takes you through the entire startup process, from go to whoa, and shows you the options you can use to customize it and to troubleshoot it should things go awry.

The Boot Process, from Power Up to Startup

To better help you understand your Windows Vista startup options, let's take a closer look at what happens each time you fire up your machine. Although a computer performs dozens of actions during the boot process, most of them appeal only to wireheads and other hardware hackers. (A **wirehead** is, broadly speaking, an expert in the hardware aspects of PCs.) For our purposes, we can reduce the entire journey to the following 12-step program:

1. When you flip the switch on your computer (or press the Restart button, if the machine is already running), the system performs various hardware checks. The system's microprocessor executes the ROM BIOS code, which, among other things, performs the **Power-On Self Test** (POST). The POST detects and tests memory, ports, and basic devices such as the video adapter, keyboard, and disk drives. (You hear your floppy disk motors kick in briefly and the drive lights come on.) If the system has a Plug and Play BIOS, the BIOS also enumerates and tests the PnP-compliant devices in the system. If the POST goes well, you hear a single beep.

2. Now the BIOS code locates the **Master Boot Record** (MBR), which is the first 512-byte sector on your system's hard disk. The MBR consists of a small program (the **boot code**) that locates and runs the core operating system files, as well as a **partition table** that contains data about the various partitions on your system. At this point, the BIOS code gives way to the MBR's boot code.

3. On machines that come with a floppy drive (increasing rare nowadays) the boot code looks for a boot sector on drive A (the drive light illuminates once more). If a bootable disk is in the drive, the system will boot to the A:\ prompt; if a nonbootable disk is in the drive, the boot code displays the following message:

   ```
   Non-system disk or disk error
   Replace and press any key when ready
   ```

   If no disk is in the drive, most modern systems will then check for a bootable disc in the CD or DVD drive. If there's still no joy, the boot code turns its attention to the hard disk and uses the partition table to find the active (that is, bootable) partition and its boot sector (the first sector in the partition).

4. With the boot sector located, the MBR code runs the boot sector as a program. The Windows Vista boot sector runs a program called Windows Boot Manager (`BOOTMGR`).

5. Windows Boot Manager switches from **Real mode** (a single-tasking mode in which the processor can access only the first 640KB of memory) to **Protected mode** (a multitasking mode in which the processor can access all memory locations).

6. Windows Boot Manager reads the **Boot Configuration Data** (BCD) and displays the Windows Boot Manager menu (assuming that your system can boot to two or more operating systems; see "Custom Startups Using the Boot Configuration Data," next). Note, too, that at this point you can invoke the Advanced Options Menu for custom startups; see "Custom Startups with the Advanced Options Menu," later in this chapter.

7. Windows Boot Manager queries the BIOS for information about the system hardware, including the system buses, the disk drives, the ports, and more, and then stores the data in the Windows Vista Registry (in the `HKEY_LOCAL_MACHINE\HARDWARE` key).

NOTE

I mention the Windows Vista Registry in several places throughout this chapter. If you're not familiar with the Registry, please see Chapter 11, "Getting to Know the Windows Vista Registry."

8. The `Starting Windows` message and the progress bar appear. The progress bar tracks the loading of the device drivers that Vista needs at startup. The bar advances each time a driver is loaded.
9. Windows Boot Manager loads the Windows kernel—`NTOSKRNL.EXE`—which handles the loading of the rest of the operating system.
10. The kernel launches the Session Manager—`SMSS.EXE`—which initializes the system environment variables and starts the Windows logon process by running `WINLOGON.EXE`.
11. If your system has multiple user accounts or a single user account protected by a password, Windows Vista displays the Welcome screen to prompt you to pick a user or type your password.
12. New Plug and Play devices are detected and the contents of the `Run` Registry key and the Startup folder are processed.

Windows Vista also provides several routes for personalizing your startup:

- Invoke the Windows Vista Startup menu when the POST is complete
- Edit the BCD to change the default startup options
- Add programs or documents to the Windows Vista Run Registry key
- Add programs or documents to the Windows Vista Startup folder

The next few sections cover these techniques.

Custom Startups Using the Boot Configuration Data

If your system can boot to one or more operating systems other than Windows Vista, or to multiple installations of Windows Vista, you'll see a menu similar to the following during startup:

```
Choose the operating system or tool you want to start:
(Use the arrow keys to highlight your choice.)

    Earlier version of Windows
    Microsoft Windows Vista
```

```
To specify an advanced option for this choice, press F8.
Seconds until highlighted choice will be started automatically: 30

Tools:
    Windows Memory Diagnostic
```

If you do nothing at this point, Windows Vista will boot automatically after 30 seconds. Otherwise, you select the operating system you want and then press the Enter key to boot it. (To switch between the operating system menu and the Tools menu, press the Tab key.) The specifics of this menu are determined by the **Boot Configuration Data**, a new data store that replaces the `BOOT.INI` file used in previous versions of Windows. `BOOT.INI` still exists, but it's used only for loading the legacy operating systems in multiboot setups. Why the change? There are three main reasons:

- It didn't make sense to have two different types of boot information stores: one for BIOS-based systems and another for EFI-based systems. BCD creates a common store for both types of operating systems.
- The need to support **boot applications**, which refers to any process that runs in the boot environment that the Windows Boot Manager creates. The main types of boot applications are Windows Vista partitions, legacy installations of Windows, and startup tools, such as the Windows Memory Diagnostic that appears in the Windows Boot Manager menu. In this sense, Windows Boot Manager is a kind of miniature operating system that displays an interface (the Windows Boot Manager menu) that lets you select which application you want to run.
- The need to make boot options scriptable. The BCD exposes a scripting interface via a Windows Management Instrumentation (WMI) provider. This enables you to create scripts that modify all aspects of the BCD.

Windows Vista gives you four methods to modify some or all the data in the BCD store:

- The Startup and Recovery feature
- The System Configuration Utility
- The `BCDEDIT` command-line utility
- The BCD WMI provider

NOTE

I don't discuss the BCD WMI provider in this chapter. To get more information, see the following page:

msdn.microsoft.com/library/en-us/BCD/bcd/bcd_reference.asp

Using Startup and Recovery to Modify the BCD

You can modify a limited set of BCD options using the Startup and Recovery dialog box: the default operating system, the maximum time the Windows Boot Manager menu is displayed, and then maximum time the Windows Vista startup recovery options are displayed. Here are the steps to follow:

1. Select Start, right-click Computer, and then click Properties. Vista displays Control Panel's System window.
2. Click Advanced System Settings.
3. If you see the User Account Control dialog box, either click Continue or type an administrator password and click Submit. The System Properties dialog box appears.

TIP

A quicker way to get to the System Properties dialog box is to press Windows Logo+R (or select Start, All Programs, Accessories, Run), type **`systempropertiesadvanced`**, and click OK.

4. In the Advanced tab, click the Settings button in the Startup and Recovery group. Vista displays the Startup and Recovery dialog box, shown in Figure 2.1.

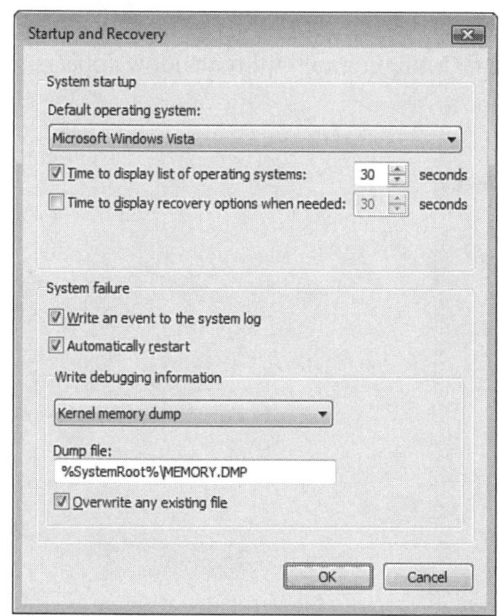

FIGURE 2.1 Use the Startup and Recovery dialog box to modify some aspects of the Boot Configuration Data.

5. Use the Default Operating System list to click the operating system that Windows Boot Manager highlights by default at startup. (In other words, this is the operating

system that runs automatically if you do not make a choice in the Windows Boot Manager menu.)

6. Use the Time to Display List of Operating Systems spin box to set the interval after which Windows Boot Manager launches the default operating system. If you don't want Windows Boot Manager to select an operating system automatically, deactivate the Time to Display List of Operating Systems check box.

7. If Windows Vista is not shut down properly, Windows Boot Manager displays a menu of recovery options at startup. If you want the default options selected automatically after a time interval, activate the Time to Display Recovery Options When Needed check box and use the associated spin box to set the interval.

8. Click OK in all open dialog boxes to put the new settings into effect.

Using the System Configuration Utility to Modify the BCD

For more detailed control over the BCD store, you can modify the data by using the System Configuration Utility. To start this program, follow these steps:

1. Press Windows Logo+R (or select Start, All Programs, Accessories, Run) to open the Run dialog box.

2. Type **`msconfig`** and then click OK.

3. If you see the User Account Control dialog box, either click Continue or type an administrator password and click Submit. The System Configuration Utility window appears.

4. Select the Boot tab, shown in Figure 2.2.

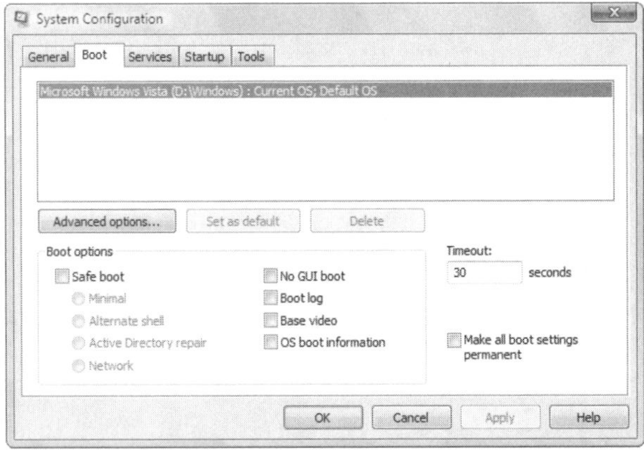

FIGURE 2.2 In the System Configuration Utility, use the Boot tab to modify the BCD store.

The large box near the top of the tab displays the Vista installations on the current computer. You see `Current OS` beside the Vista installation you are running now; you see `Default OS` beside the Vista installation that is set up as the default. There are four main tasks you can perform:

- Click the Set as Default button to set the highlighted Vista install as the default for the Windows Boot Manager menu.
- Use the Timeout text box to set the maximum time that Windows Boot Manager waits before selecting the default OS.
- Use the check boxes in the Boot Options group to set the following startup options for the currently highlighted Vista install:

Safe Boot: Minimal	Boots Windows Vista in **Safe mode**, which uses only a minimal set of device drivers. Use this switch if Windows Vista won't start, if a device or program is causing Windows Vista to crash, or if you can't uninstall a program while Windows Vista is running normally.
Safe Boot: Minimal (Alternate Shell)	Boots Windows Vista in Safe mode but also bypasses the Windows Vista GUI and boots to the command prompt instead. Use this switch if the programs in which you need to repair a problem can be run from the command prompt or if you can't load the Windows Vista GUI.

NOTE

The shell loaded by the `/safeboot:minimal(`*`alternateshell`*`)` switch is determined by the value in the following Registry key:

```
HKEY_LOCAL_MACHINE\SYSTEM\CurrentControlSet\SafeBoot\AlternateShell
```

The default value is `CMD.EXE` (the command prompt).

Safe Boot: Active Directory Repair	Boots Windows Vista in Safe mode and restores a backup of the Active Directory service (this option applies only to domain controllers).
Safe Boot: Network	Boots Windows Vista in Safe mode but also includes networking drivers. Use this switch if the drivers or programs you need to repair a problem in exist on a shared network resource, if you need access to email or other network-based communications for technical support, or if your computer is running a shared Windows Vista installation.
No GUI Boot	Tells Windows Vista not to load the VGA display driver that is normally used to display the progress bar during startup. Use this switch if Windows Vista hangs while switching video modes for the progress bar, or if the display of the progress bar is garbled.

Boot Log	Boots Vista and logs the boot process to a text file named `ntbtlog.txt` that resides in the `%SystemRoot%` folder. Move to the end of the file and you might see a message telling you which device driver failed. You probably need to reinstall or roll back the driver (see Chapter 17, "Getting the Most Out of Device Manager"). Use this switch if the Windows Vista startup hangs, if you need a detailed record of the startup process, or if you suspect (after using one of the other Startup menu options) that a driver is causing Windows Vista startup to fail.

NOTE

`%SystemRoot%` refers to the folder into which Windows Vista was installed. This is usually `C:\Windows`.

Base Video	Boots Vista using the standard VGA mode: 640×480 with 256 colors. This is useful for troubleshooting video display driver problems. Use this switch if Windows Vista fails to start using any of the Safe mode options, if you recently installed a new video card device driver and the screen is garbled, the driver is balking at a resolution or color depth setting that's too high, or if you can't load the Windows Vista GUI. After Windows Vista has loaded, you can reinstall or roll back the driver, or you can adjust the display settings to values that the driver can handle.
OS Boot Information	Displays the path and location of each device driver as it loads, as well as the operating system version and build number, the number of processors, the system memory, and the process type.

- Click the Advanced Options button to display the BOOT Advanced Options dialog box shown in Figure 2.3.

Number of Processors	In a multiprocessor system, specifies the maximum of processors that Windows Vista can use. Activate this check box if you suspect that using multiple processors is causing a program to hang.

Maximum Memory	Specifies the maximum amount of memory, in megabytes, that Windows Vista can use. Use this value when you suspect a faulty memory chip might be causing problems.
PCI Lock	Activate this check box to tell Vista not to dynamically assign hardware resources for PCI devices during startup. The resources assigned by the BIOS during the POST are locked in place. Use this switch if installing a PCI device causes the system to hang during startup.
Detect HAL	Activate this check box to force Vista to detect the computer's hardware abstraction layer (HAL) at startup. The HAL is a software layer that resides between the computer's hardware and the operating system kernel, and its job is to hide hardware differences so that the kernel can run on a variety of hardware. If you force Vista to detect the HAL, it can use the HAL to interact with the computer's hardware at startup. This is useful if dealing with the hardware directly is causing startup problems.
Debug	Enables remote debugging of the Windows Vista kernel. This sends debugging information to a remote computer via one of your computer's ports. If you use this switch, you can use the Debug Port list to specify a serial port, IEEE 1394 port, or USB port. If you use a serial port, you can specify the transmission speed of the debugging information using the Baud Rate list; if you use an IEEE 1394 connection, activate Channel and specify a channel value; if you use a USB port, type the device name in the USB Target Name text box.

Using BCDEDIT to Customize the Startup Options

The System Configuration Utility makes it easy to modify BCD store items, but it doesn't give you access to the entire BCD store. For example, the Boot tab doesn't list any legacy boot items on your system, and there are no options for renaming boot items, or changing the order in which the boot items are displayed in the Windows Boot Manager menu. For these tasks, and indeed for every possible BCD task, you need to use the BCDEDIT command-line tool.

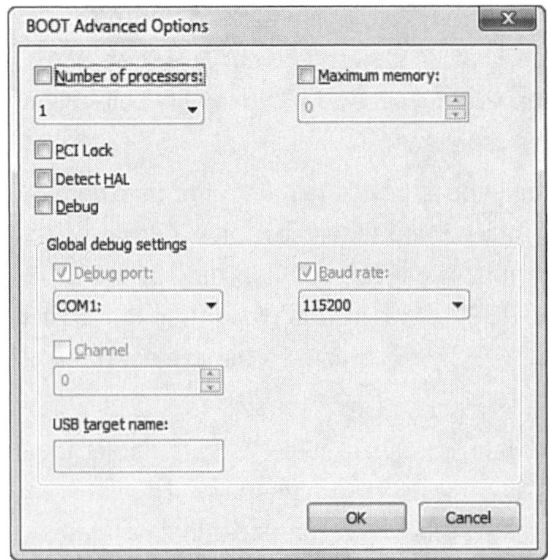

FIGURE 2.3 In the Boot tab, click Advanced Options to display the dialog box shown here.

Note that BCDEDIT is an Administrator-only tool, so you must run it under the Administrator account (not just any account in the Administrators group). The easiest way to do this is elevate your privileges when running the Command Prompt, as described in the following steps:

1. Select Start, All Programs, Accessories.
2. Right-click Command Prompt and then click Run as Administrator. The User Account Control dialog box appears.
3. Either click Continue or type an administrator password and click Submit. The Command Prompt window appears

See Chapter 6, "Getting the Most Out of User Accounts," to learn more about elevating privileges in Windows Vista.

Table 2.1 summarizes the switches you can use with BCDEDIT.

TABLE 2.1 Switches Available for the BCDEDIT Command-Line Tool

Switch	Description
/bootdebug	Toggles boot debugging for a boot application on and off
/bootems	Toggles Emergency Management Services for a boot application on and off
/bootsequence	Sets the one-time boot sequence for the boot manager
/copy	Makes a copy of an entry
/create	Creates a new entry
/createstore	Creates a new and empty BCD store
/dbgsettings	Sets the global debugger settings
/debug	Toggles kernel debugging for an operating system entry

Switch	Description
/default	Sets the default entry
/delete	Deletes an entry
/deletevalue	Deletes an entry value
/displayorder	Sets the order in which Boot Manager displays the operating system entries
/ems	Enables or disables Emergency Management Services for an operating system entry
/emssettings	Sets the global Emergency Management Services settings
/enum	Lists the entries in the BCD store
/export	Exports the contents of the BCD store to a file
/import	Restores the BCD store from a backup file created with the /export switch
/set	Sets an option value for an entry
/store	Specifies the BCD store to use
/timeout	Sets the Boot Manager timeout value
/toolsdisplayorder	Sets the order in which Boot Manager displays the Tools menu
/types	Displays the data types required by the /set and /deletevalue commands.
/v	Displays all entry identifiers in full, instead of using well-known identifiers

To help you understand how BCDEDIT works, let's examine the output that appears when you run BCDEDIT with the /enum switch:

```
Windows Boot Manager
--------------------
Identifier:              {bootmgr}
Type:                    10100002
Device:                  partition=C:
Description:             Windows Boot Manager
Inherit options:         {globalsettings}
Boot debugger:           No
Default:                 {current}
Display order:           {ntldr}
                         {current}
                         {a8ef3a39-a0a4-11da-bedf-97d9bf80e36c}
Tools display order:     {memdiag}
Timeout:                 30

Windows Legacy OS Loader
------------------------
Identifier:              {ntldr}
Type:                    10300006
```

```
Device:                 partition=C:
Path:                   \ntldr
Description:            Earlier version of Windows
Boot debugger:          No

Windows Boot Loader
-------------------
Identifier:             {current}
Type:                   10200003
Device:                 partition=C:
Path:                   \Windows\system32\winload.exe
Description:            Microsoft Windows Vista
Locale:                 en-US
Inherit options:        {bootloadersettings}
Boot debugger:          Yes
Windows device:         partition=D:
Windows root:           \Windows
Resume application:     {c105ff07-b93e-11da-82e5-ae629af91d6e}
No Execute policy:      OptIn
Kernel debugger:        No
EMS enabled in OS:      No

Windows Boot Loader
-------------------
Identifier:             {a8ef3a39-a0a4-11da-bedf-97d9bf80e36c}
Type:                   10200003
Device:                 partition=G:
Path:                   \Windows\system32\winload.exe
Description:            Microsoft Windows Vista
Locale:                 en-US
Inherit options:        {bootloadersettings}
Boot debugger:          No
Windows device:         partition=G:
Windows root:           \Windows
Resume application:     {a8ef3a3a-a0a4-11da-bedf-97d9bf80e36c}
No Execute policy:      OptIn
No integrity checks:    Yes
Kernel debugger:        No
EMS enabled in OS:      No
```

As you can see, this BCD store has four entries: one for Windows Boot Manager, one for a legacy Windows install (on partition C:), and two for Vista installs (on my text machine, partitions D: and G:). Notice that each entry has an `Identifier` setting, and these IDs are unique to each entry. All IDs are actually 32-digit **globally unique identifiers** (GUIDs) such as the one shown earlier for the second Windows Boot Loader item:

```
a8ef3a39-a0a4-11da-bedf-97d9bf80e36c
```

The other entries have GUIDs, as well, but by default BCDEDIT works with a collection of *well-known identifiers*, including the following (type **`bcdedit id /?`** to see the complete list):

`bootmgr`	The Windows Boot Manager entry
`ntldr`	An entry that uses a legacy operating system loader (NTLDR) to boot previous versions of Windows
`current`	The entry that corresponds to the operating system that is currently running
`default`	The entry that corresponds to the Windows Boot Manager default operating system
`memdiag`	The Windows Memory Diagnostics entry

If you want to see the full GUIDs for every entry, add the `/v` (verbose) switch:

```
bcdedit /enum /v
```

It would take dozens of pages to run through all the BCDEDIT switches, so I'll just give you a few examples so you can get a taste of how this powerful utility operates.

Making a Backup Copy of the BCD Store

Before you do any work on the BCD store, you should make a backup copy. That way, if you make an error when you change something in the BCD, you can always restore the backup copy to get your system back to its original state.

You create a backup copy using the `/export` switch. For example, the following command backs up the BCD store to a file named `bcd_backup` in the root folder of drive C:

```
bcdedit /export c:\bcd_backup
```

If you need to restore the backup, use the `/import` switch, as in this example:

```
bcdedit /import c:\bcd_backup
```

Renaming an Entry

The names that Windows Boot Manager assigns to the boot applications leave a lot to be desired. For a legacy operating system entry, for example, the default `Legacy (pre-Longhorn) Microsoft Windows Operating System` name is overly long and not particularly descriptive. A simpler name such as `Windows XP Pro` or `Windows 2000` would be much more useful. Similarly, all Vista installs get the same name: `Microsoft Windows`, which can be quite confusing. Names such as `Vista Home Premium` and `Vista Ultimate` would be much more understandable.

To rename an entry using BCDEDIT, use the following syntax:

```
bcdedit /set {id} description "name"
```

Here, replace *id* with the entry identifier (the GUID or the well-known identifier, if applicable) and replace *name* with the new name you want to use. For example, the following command replaces the current name of the legacy operating system entry (`ntldr`) with `Windows XP Pro`:

```
bcdedit /set {ntldr} description "Windows XP Pro"
```

TIP

GUIDs are 32-character values, so typing them by hand is both time-consuming and error-prone. To avoid this, first run the `bcdedit /enum` command to enumerate the BCD entries, and then scroll up until you see the GUID of the entry with which you want to work. Pull down the system menu (click the upper-left corner of the window or press Alt+Spacebar), select Edit, Mark, click-and-drag over the GUID to select it, and then press the Enter key to copy it. Begin typing your BCDEDIT command and when you get to the part where the identifier is required, pull down the system menu again and select Edit, Paste.

Changing the Order of the Entries

If you'd prefer that the Boot Manager menu entries appear in a different order, you can use BCDEDIT's `/displayorder` switch to change the order. In the simplest case, you might want to move an entry to either the beginning or the end of the menu. To send an entry to the beginning, include the `/addfirst` switch. Here's an example:

```
bcdedit /displayorder {a8ef3a39-a0a4-11da-bedf-97d9bf80e36c} /addfirst
```

To send an entry to the end of the menu, include the `/addlast` switch instead, as in this example:

```
bcdedit /displayorder {current} /addfirst
```

To set the overall order, include each identifier in the order you want, separated by spaces:

```
bcdedit /displayorder {current} {a8ef3a39-a0a4-11da-bedf-97d9bf80e36c} {ntldr}
```

Custom Startups with the Advanced Options Menu

When the Windows Boot Manager menu appears at startup, you see the following message when you highlight a Windows Vista install:

```
To specify an advanced option for this choice, press F8.
```

If you press F8, you get to the Advanced Boot Options menu, which looks like this:

TIP

If your system doesn't automatically display the Windows Boot Manager menu at startup, you can display it manually. After you start your computer, wait until the POST is complete, and then press F8 to display the Windows Boot Manager menu. If your computer is set up to "fast boot," it might not be obvious when the POST ends. In that case, just turn on your computer and press F8 repeatedly until you see the Windows Boot Manager menu. Note, however, that if your system picks up two separate F8 presses, you might end up directly in the Advanced Boot Options menu.


```
        Advanced Boot Options
Choose Advanced Options for: Microsoft Windows Vista
(use the arrow keys to highlight your choice.)

    Safe Mode
    Safe Mode with Networking
    Safe Mode with Command Prompt

    Enable Boot Logging
    Enable low-resolution video (640×480)
    Last Known Good Configuration (advanced)
    Directory Services Restore Mode
    Debugging Mode
    Disable automatic restart on system failure
    Disable Driver Signature Enforcement

    Start Windows Normally
```

The `Start Windows Normally` option loads Windows Vista in the usual fashion. You can use the other options to control the rest of the startup procedure:

Safe Mode — If you're having trouble with Windows Vista—for example, if a corrupt or incorrect video driver is mangling your display, or if Windows Vista won't start—you can use the Safe Mode option to run a stripped-down version of Windows Vista that includes only the minimal set of device drivers that Vista requires to load. You could reinstall or roll back the offending device driver and then load Vista normally. Starting in Safe mode displays the Administrator account in the Welcome screen, which is the account to use when troubleshooting problems. When Windows Vista finally loads, the desktop reminds you that you're in Safe mode by displaying `Safe Mode` in each corner. (Also, Windows Help and Support appears with Safe mode-related information and links.)

NOTE

If you're curious to know which drivers are loaded during a Safe mode boot, see the subkeys in the following Registry key:

`HKEY_LOCAL_MACHINE\SYSTEM\CurrentControlSet\Control\SafeBoot\Minimal\`

Safe Mode with Networking	This option is identical to plain Safe mode, except that Windows Vista's networking drivers are also loaded at startup. This enables you to log on to your network, which is handy if you need to access the network to load a device driver, run a troubleshooting utility, or send a tech support request. This option also gives you Internet access if you connect via a gateway on your network. This is useful if you need to download drivers or contact online tech support.
Safe Mode with Command Prompt	This option is the same as plain Safe mode, except that it doesn't load the Windows Vista GUI. Instead, it runs `CMD.EXE` to load a command prompt session.
Enable Boot Logging	This option is the same as the `Boot Normally` option, except that Windows Vista logs the boot process in a text file named `ntbtlog.txt` that resides in the system root.
Enable Low-Resolution Video (640×480)	This option loads Windows Vista with the video display set to 640×480 and 256 colors. This is useful if your video output is garbled when you start Vista. For example, if your display settings are configured at a resolution that your video card can't handle, boot in the low-resolution mode and then switch to a setting supported by your video card.
Last Known Good Configuration	This option boots Windows Vista using the last hardware configuration that produced a successful boot.

Directory Services Restore Mode	Boots Windows Vista in Safe mode and restores a backup of the Active Directory service (this option applies only to domain controllers).
Debugging Mode	Enables remote debugging of the Windows Vista kernel.
Disable Automatic Restart on System Failure	Prevents Windows Vista from restarting automatically when the system crashes. Choose this option if you want to prevent your system from restarting so that you can read an error message or deduce other information that can help you troubleshoot the problem.
Disable Driver Signature Enforcement	Prevents Windows Vista from checking whether devices drivers have digital signatures. Choose this option to ensure that Windows Vista loads an unsigned driver, if failing to load that driver is causing system problems.

For more information about these options, see the section titled "When to Use the Various Advanced Startup Options," later in this chapter.

Useful Windows Vista Logon Strategies

When you install Windows Vista, the setup program asks you to supply a username and optional password for one or more people who will be accessing the computer. How you initially log on to Windows Vista depends on what you did at that point of the install:

- If you didn't specify a password with the new username and your computer is not part of a network domain, Windows Vista logs on that username automatically.
- If you specified a password, if your computer is part of a domain, or if you have subsequently created multiple usernames, Windows Vista displays the Welcome screen, which lists the users (Figure 2.4 shows an example). Click the username you want to use, type the password (if the account has one), and press the Enter key to log on.

The default logon is fine for most users, but there are many ways to change Windows Vista's logon behavior. The rest of this section looks at a few tips and techniques for altering the way you log on to Windows Vista.

FIGURE 2.4 You see the Windows Vista Welcome screen if your workgroup or standalone computer is set up with a password or multiple users, or if you computer is part of a network domain.

Requiring Ctrl+Alt+Delete at Startup

Protecting your Windows Vista user account with a password (as described in Chapter 6), though an excellent idea, is not foolproof. Hackers are an endlessly resourceful bunch, and some of the smarter ones figured out a way to defeat the user account password system. The trick is that they install a virus or Trojan horse program — usually via an infected email message or malicious Web site — that loads itself when you start your computer. This program then displays a *fake* version of the Windows Vista Welcome screen. When you type your user name and password into this dialog box, the program records it and your system security is compromised.

To thwart this clever ruse, Windows Vista enables you to configure your system so that you must press Ctrl+Alt+Delete before you can log on. This key combination ensures that the authentic Welcome screen appears.

To require that users must press Ctrl+Alt+Delete before they can log on, follow these steps:

1. Press Windows Logo+R to display the Run dialog box.
2. Type **`control userpasswords2`** and then click OK.

3. If you see the User Account Control dialog box, either click Continue or type an administrator password and click Submit. The User Accounts dialog box appears.
4. Display the Advanced tab.
5. Activate the Require Users to Press Ctrl+Alt+Delete check box.
6. Click OK.

Logging On to a Domain

In previous versions of Windows, when you logged on to a domain you always used the Classic Windows logon, which consisted of pressing Ctrl+Alt+Delete and then typing your username and password in the Log On to Windows dialog box. (You also had the option of specifying a different domain.) However, the Classic Windows logon is gone from Windows Vista. You saw in the previous section how to require Ctrl+Alt+Delete before logging on. To log on to a domain in Windows Vista, you must specify the domain as part of the username. You have two choices:

- ***NetBIOSName\UserName***—Here, replace *NetBIOSName* with the NetBIOS name of the domain, and replace *UserName* with your network username (for example, logophilia\paulm).
- ***UserName@Domain***—Here, replace *Domain* with the domain name, and replace *UserName* with your network username (for example, paulm@logophilia.com).

See Chapter 6 to learn how to set up new user accounts in Windows Vista.

Accessing the Administrator Account

One of the confusing aspects about Windows Vista is that the Administrator account seems to disappear after the setup is complete. That's because, for security reasons, Windows Vista doesn't give you access to the all-powerful Administrator account, and I explain why in Chapter 6. I should say it doesn't give you *easy* access to this account. The Welcome screen doesn't include an option to choose the Administrator, and there is no option anywhere in the main Vista interface to enable this account to log on.

That's probably just as well because it keeps most users much safer, but it's annoying for those of us who might occasionally require the Administrator account. For example, tools such as the Windows Automated Installation Kit require the Administrator account. Fortunately, there are a couple of workarounds, both of which involve editing the Registry (see Chapter 11), so begin by opening the Registry Editor (click Start, type **regedit** in the Search box, and then click the `regedit` program that appears) and then navigating to the following key:

```
HKLM\SOFTWARE\Microsoft\Windows NT\CurrentVersion\Winlogon
```

You now have two choices:

- **Set Up an Automatic Logon for the Administrator**—See the next section for the details.
- **Include Administrator in the Welcome screen**—Create a new subkey under `Winlogon` named `SpecialAccounts`, and then create a new subkey under `SpecialAccounts` named `UserList`. In the `UserList` key, create a `DWORD` value named `Administrator` and set its value to `1`.

Setting Up an Automatic Logon

If you're using a standalone computer that no one else has access to (or that will be used by people you trust), you can save some time at startup by not having to type a username and password. In this scenario, the easiest way to do this is to set up Windows Vista with just a single user account without a password, which means Windows Vista logs on that user automatically at startup. If you have multiple user accounts (for testing purposes, for example) or if you want the Administrator account to be logged on automatically, you need to set up Windows Vista for automatic logons.

CAUTION

Setting up an automatic logon is generally not a good idea for notebook computers because they're easily lost or stolen. By leaving the logon prompt in place, the person who finds or steals your notebook will at least be unlikely to get past the logon, so your data won't be compromised.

Open the Registry Editor and head for the following Registry key:

```
HKLM\Software\Microsoft\Windows NT\CurrentVersion\Winlogon\
```

You need to do three things:

1. Double-click the `AutoAdminLogon` setting and change its value to `1`.
2. Double-click the `DefaultUseName` setting and change its value to the username you want to log on automatically.
3. Create a `String` setting named `DefaultPassword` and change its value to the password of the user you specified in step 2. Note that your password appears as plain text, so anyone can read it or even change it.

TIP

You can temporarily suspend the automatic logon by holding down the Shift key while Windows Vista starts up.

Disabling Automatic Logon Override

As you saw in the Tip sidebar in the previous section, you can hold down the Shift key to override an automatic logon. There are situations where this is not preferable. For example, you might have a computer set up for a particular user and you want only that user to log on. In that case, you don't want the user overriding the automatic logon.

To prevent the override of an automatic logon using the Shift key, open the Registry Editor once again and navigate to the following key:

```
HKLM\Software\Microsoft\Windows NT\CurrentVersion\Winlogon\
```

Create a new `String` value named `IgnoreShiftOverride` and set its value to `1`.

Troubleshooting Windows Vista Startup

Computers are often frustrating beasts, but few things in computerdom are as hair-pullingly, teeth-gnashingly frustrating as an operating system that won't operate. To help save some wear and tear on your hair and teeth, this section outlines a few common startup difficulties and their solutions.

When to Use the Various Advanced Startup Options

You saw earlier that Windows Vista has some useful options on its Advanced Options menu. But under what circumstances should you use each option? Because there is some overlap in what each option brings to the table, there are no hard and fast rules. It is possible, however, to lay down some general guidelines.

You should use the Safe Mode option if one of the following conditions occurs:

- Windows Vista doesn't start after the POST ends.
- Windows Vista seems to stall for an extended period.
- You can't print to a local printer.
- Your video display is distorted and possibly unreadable.
- Your computer stalls repeatedly.
- Your computer suddenly slows down and doesn't return to normal without a reboot.
- You need to test an intermittent error condition.

You should use the Safe Mode with Networking option if one of the following situations occurs:

- Windows Vista fails to start using any of the other safe mode options.
- The drivers or programs you need to repair a problem exist on a shared network resource.

- You need access to email or other network-based communications for technical support.
- You need to access the Internet via a network gateway device to download device drivers or visit an online tech support site.
- Your computer is running a shared Windows Vista installation.

You should use the Safe Mode with Command Prompt option if one of the following situations occurs:

- Windows Vista fails to start using any of the other Safe mode options.
- The programs you need to repair a problem must be run from the command prompt.
- You can't load the Windows Vista GUI.

You should use the Enable Boot Logging option in the following situations:

- The Windows Vista startup hangs after switching to Protected mode.
- You need a detailed record of the startup process.
- You suspect (after using one of the other Startup menu options) that a Protected-mode driver is causing Windows Vista startup to fail.

After starting (or attempting to start) Windows Vista with this option, you end up with a file named `ntbtlog.txt` in the `%SystemRoot%` folder. This is a text file, so you can examine it with any text editor. For example, you could boot to the command prompt (using the Safe Mode with Command Prompt option) and then use Notepad to examine the file. Move to the end of the file and you might see a message telling you which device driver failed. You probably need to reinstall or roll back the driver.

You should use the Enable VGA Mode option in the following situations:

- Windows Vista fails to start using any of the Safe mode options.
- You recently installed a new video card device driver and the screen is garbled or the driver is balking at a resolution or color depth setting that's too high.
- You can't load the Windows Vista GUI.

After Windows Vista has loaded, you can either reinstall or roll back the driver, or you can adjust the display settings to values that the driver can handle.

Use the Last Known Good Configuration option under the following circumstances:

- You suspect the problem is hardware related, but you can't figure out the driver that's causing the problem.
- You don't have time to try out the other more detailed inspections.

The Directory Services Restore Mode option is only for domain controllers, so you should never need to use it.

Use the Debugging Mode option if you receive a stop error during startup and a remote technical support professional has asked you to send debugging data.

What to Do If Windows Vista Won't Start in Safe Mode

If Windows Vista is so intractable that it won't even start in Safe mode, your system is likely afflicted with one of the following problems:

- Your system is infected with a virus. You need to run an antivirus program to cleanse your system.
- Your system has incorrect CMOS settings. Run the machine's CMOS setup program to see whether any of these settings needs to be changed or whether the CMOS battery needs to be replaced.
- Your system has a hardware conflict. See Chapter 17 for hardware troubleshooting procedures.
- There is a problem with a SCSI device. In this case, your system might hang during the SCSI BIOS initialization process. Try removing devices from the SCSI chain until your system starts normally.

Recovering Using the System Recovery Options

If your system still won't start, all is not yet lost. Windows Vista comes with a new feature called System Recovery Options, a collection to tools available on the Vista installation disc. The idea is that you boot your computer using the disc, and then select the recovery tool you want to use. To try this out, first follow these steps:

1. Insert your Windows Vista disc and reboot your computer.
2. When you're prompted to boot from the CD, press the required key (or, in most cases, any key). The Windows Vista setup program launches and after it loads a few files, you see the Install Windows screen.

NOTE

If your system won't boot from the Windows Vista disc, you need to adjust the system's BIOS settings to allow this. Restart the computer and look for a startup message that prompts you to press a key or key combination to enter the system's BIOS and modify the settings (which might be called Setup or something similar). Find the boot options and either enable a CD-based boot or make sure that the option to boot from the CD comes before the option to boot from the hard disk.

2. Click Next.
3. Click Repair Your Computer. The System Recovery Options dialog box appears and displays a list of your Windows Vista partitions.
4. Click your Windows Vista partition you want to repair and then click Next. The System Recovery Options dialog box displays a list of recovery tools.

System Recovery Options offers you the following five tools to help get your system back on it feet:

- **Startup Repair**—This tool checks your system for problems that might be preventing it from starting. If it finds any, it attempts to fix them automatically.
- **System Restore**—This tool runs System Restore so that you can revert your system to a protection point (see "Recovering Using System Restore" in Chapter 16, "Troubleshooting and Recovering from Problems").
- **Windows Complete PC Restore**—This tool restores your system using a CompletePC system image backup, which you learn how to create in Chapter 15, "Maintaining Your Windows Vista System."
- **Windows Memory Diagnostic Tool**—This tool checks your computer's memory chips for faults, which may be why your system isn't starting up. Click this option and then click Restart Now and Check for Problems. If it finds a problem in your chips, then you'll need to take your machine into the shop and get the chips replaced.
- **Command Prompt**—This tool takes you to the Windows Vista command prompt, where you can run command-line utilities such as CHKDSK. See Appendix B, "Using the Windows Vista Command Prompt," to learn the ins and outs of command prompt sessions.

Troubleshooting Startup Using the System Configuration Utility

If Windows Vista won't start, troubleshooting the problem usually involves trying various advanced startup options. It's almost always a time-consuming and tedious business.

However, what if Windows Vista *will* start, but you encounter problems along the way? Or what if you want to try a few different configurations to see whether you can eliminate startup items or improve Windows Vista's overall performance? For these scenarios, don't bother trying out different startup configurations by hand. Instead, take advantage of Windows Vista's System Configuration Utility which, as you saw earlier in this chapter, gives you a graphical front-end that offers precise control over how Windows Vista starts.

Launch the System Configuration Utility and display the General tab, which has three startup options (see Figure 2.5):

Normal Startup — This option loads Windows Vista normally.

Diagnostic Startup — This option loads only those device drivers and system services that are necessary for Vista to boot. This is equivalent to deactivating all the check boxes associated with the Selective Startup option, discussed next.

Selective Startup — When you activate this option, the following check boxes become available. Use these check boxes to select which portions of the startup should be processed.

For a selective startup, you control how Windows Vista processes items using the following two categories:

Load System Services — This category refers to the system services that Windows Vista loads at startup. The specific services loaded by Windows Vista are listed in the Services tab.

NOTE

A **service** is a program or process that performs a specific, low-level support function for the operating system or for an installed program. For example, Windows Vista's Automatic Updates feature is a service.

NOTE

The Services tab has an Essential column. Only those services that have Yes in this column are loaded when you choose the Selective Startup option.

Load Startup Items — This category refers to the items in your Windows Vista Startup group and to the startup items listed in the Registry. For the latter, the settings are stored in one of the following keys:

```
HKEY_CURRENT_USER\SOFTWARE\Microsoft\Windows\
➥CurrentVersion\Run
HKEY_LOCAL_MACHINE\SOFTWARE\Microsoft\Windows\
➥CurrentVersion\Run
```

The specific items loaded from the Startup group or the Registry are listed in the Startup tab.

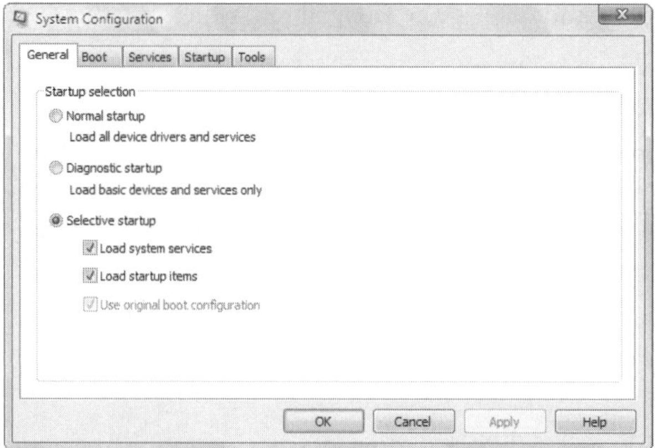

FIGURE 2.5 Use the System Configuration Utility's General tab to troubleshoot the Windows Vista startup.

To control these startup items, the System Configuration Utility gives you two choices:

- To prevent Windows Vista from loading every item in a particular category, activate Selective Startup in the General tab and then deactivate the check box for the category you want. For example, to disable all the items in the Startup tab, deactivate the Load Startup Items check box.
- To prevent Windows Vista from loading only specific items in a category, display the category's tab and then deactivate the check box beside the item or items you want to bypass at startup.

Here's a basic procedure you can follow to use the System Configuration Utility to troubleshoot a startup problem (assuming that you can start Windows Vista by using some kind of Safe mode boot, as described earlier):

1. In the System Configuration Utility, activate the Diagnostic Startup option and then reboot the computer. If the problem did not occur during the restart, you know the cause lies in the system services or the startup items.
2. In the System Configuration Utility, activate the Selective Startup option.
3. Activate Load System Services, deactivate Load Startup Items, and then reboot the computer.
4. Deactivate Load System Services, activate Load Startup Items, and then reboot the computer.
5. The problem will reoccur either during the step 3 reboot or the step 4 reboot. When this happens, you know that whatever item you activated before rebooting is the source of the problem. Display the tab of the item that is causing the problem. For example, if the problem reoccurred after you activated the Load Startup Items check box, display the Startup tab.

6. Click Disable All to clear all the check boxes.
7. Activate one of the check boxes to enable an item and then reboot the computer.
8. Repeat step 7 for each of the other check boxes until the problem reoccurs. When this happens, you know that whatever item you activated just before rebooting is the source of the problem.

Troubleshooting by Halves

If you have a large number of check boxes to test (such as in the Services tab), activating one check box at a time and rebooting can become very tedious very fast. A faster method is to begin by activating the first half of the check boxes and reboot. One of two things will happen:

- **The problem doesn't reoccur**—This means that one of the items represented by the deactivated check boxes is the culprit. Clear all the check boxes, activate half of the other check boxes, and then reboot.
- **The problem reoccurs**—This means that one of the activated check boxes is the problem. Activate only half of those check boxes and reboot.

Keep halving the number of activated check boxes until you isolate the offending item.

9. In the System Configuration Utility's General tab, activate the Normal Startup option.
10. Fix or work around the problem:
    - If the problem is a system service, you can disable the service. In Control Panel, click System and Maintenance, Administrative Tools, Services. Double-click the problematic service to open its property sheet. In the Startup Type list, select Disabled and then click OK.
    - If the problem is a Startup item, either delete the item from the Startup group or delete the item from the appropriate `Run` key in the Registry. If the item is a program, consider uninstalling or reinstalling the program.

What to Do If Windows Vista Still Won't Start

If Windows Vista won't start no matter what you try, you're not out of luck just yet. You still have another couple of things to try:

System Restore	This feature enables you to restore your system to a previous (and, presumably, operational) setup. To learn how to use System Restore, see the "Recovering Using System Restore" section in Chapter 16.
Complete PC Restore	This feature enables you to restore your entire system from a backup copy. For the details, see the "Recovering Using a System Image Backup" section in Chapter 16.

From Here

Here are some other places in the book where you'll find information related to startup:

- In Chapter 5, see the section titled "Launching Applications and Scripts at Startup."
- In Chapter 14, see the section titled "Optimizing Startup."
- In Chapter 16, see the section titled "Booting Using the Last Known Good Configuration."
- See Appendix B, "Using the Windows Vista Command Prompt," to learn more about command prompt sessions.

CHAPTER 3

Exploring Expert File and Folder Techniques

IN THIS CHAPTER

- Navigating Vista's New Folder Windows
- Basic File and Folder Chores: The Techniques Used by the Pros
- Metadata and the Windows Explorer Property System
- Desktop Searching with the Windows Search Engine
- Grouping, Stacking, and Filtering with Metadata
- Shadow Copies and Transactional NTFS
- Customizing Windows Explorer

Windows Vista was supposed to be the operating system that finally realized Microsoft's long-sought dream of a major file system breakthrough. Windows Vista was supposed to include WinFS (Windows Future Storage), a file-storage subsystem that runs on NTFS. WinFS not only uses SQL Server–related technology to create sophisticated indexes of a wide variety of data—documents, images, email messages, and so on—but it also leverages the power of XML to create metadata schemas for your data. **Metadata** is information that describes data. For example, you could implement a `Tags` property. If you then applied the tag `Budget2007` to all your data related to next year's budget—Excel workbooks, Word documents, PowerPoint presentations, Access databases, Outlook email messages, and so on—WinFS would not only index all this content, but it also would relate them together based on the common `Tag` metadata.

It's really the Holy Grail of file systems, but, alas, Microsoft had to drop support for WinFS in Vista so it could ship in a reasonable timeframe. Not that WinFS is dead: On the contrary, a group at Microsoft is still working on this technology, and Microsoft has promised that WinFS will be available for Windows Vista sometime after Vista hits the shelves.

In the meantime, you'll have to content yourself with the changes that Microsoft made to Vista's implementation of the NTFS file system. As you'll see in this chapter, Vista has cobbled quite a few WinFS-like features onto NTFS, including some support for metadata and advanced searching.

Overall, what we're seeing in Vista is a move away from the venerable drive-and-directory storage model that has been the only way of doing things in the PC world since MS-DOS 1.0. For the past quarter-century, we've been taught to think of a file as something that resides, say, on hard disk 0, in partition C:, in the directory/folder named `Data`. This location-based storage model worked more or less efficiently in the days of 100MB hard drives, but now 100GB drives are common, and mainstream terabyte (1000GB) drives are just around the corner. We fill these massive disks, of course (see my discussion of Parkinson's Law of Data in Chapter 14, "Tuning Windows Vista's Performance"), so these days we're dealing with anywhere from 1,000 to 10,000 times the amount of data that we were 10 years ago.

But it's not just the amount of data to deal with—it's also the number of places where that data is stored. If you have a floppy drive, a couple of hard disks, several partitions on each hard disk, a couple of optical drives, and a memory card reader, your system could easily use 15 drive letters. A well-used system might have more than 10,000 folders scattered across those drives. In addition, of course, plenty of data is stored in hundreds of email folders, RSS feeds, address books, and calendars. With numbers like these, it's clearly time to look for an alternative to location-based file storage. Vista is the first step toward that new storage mechanism, and this chapter gives you a preview of what's new.

Over and above the new Vista features, whether you're looking to master Windows Vista or just get your work done quickly and efficiently, a thorough knowledge of the techniques available for working with files and folders is essential. Or perhaps I should say that a thorough knowledge of *certain* techniques is essential. That's because, like the rest of Windows Vista, Windows Explorer (the file management accessory) offers a handful of methods for accomplishing most tasks. Not all of these techniques are particularly efficient, however. Therefore, my other goal in this chapter is to tell you not only *how* to do file management chores, but also to tell you the *best* ways to do those chores.

Navigating Vista's New Folder Windows

New Microsoft has spent a lot of time rethinking document storage and has incorporated into Vista some substantial changes in the way we view, navigate, and use folders. I discuss many of these innovations later in this chapter. For now, let's take a tour of the new interface features that you'll find in Vista's folder windows. Figure 3.1 shows a typical example of the species, the Documents window (formerly My Documents; click Start, Documents to open your version of this window).

Folder Navigation

One of the most fundamental and possibly far-reaching of Vista's innovations is doing away with—or, technically, hiding—the old drive-and-folder-path method of navigating the contents of your computer. You could go your entire Vista career and never have to view or type a backslash. Instead, Vista implements drives and folders as hierarchies that you navigate up, down, and even across. As you can see in Figure 3.1, the address bar doesn't show any drive letters or backslashes. Instead, you get a hierarchical path to the current folder. The path in Figure 3.1 has three items, separated by right-pointing arrows:

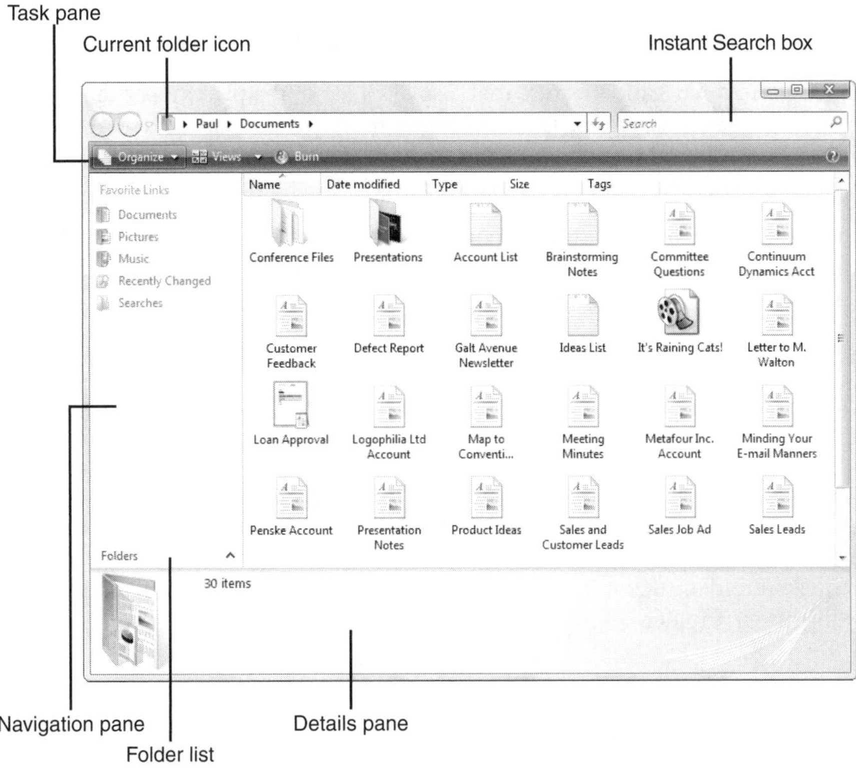

FIGURE 3.1 Vista's folder windows boast a significantly changed design.

- **Current folder icon**—This icon represents the current folder. You'll see a bit later that you can use this icon to navigate to your computer drives, your network, the Control Panel, your user folder, and more.
- **Paul**—This represents the second level of the sample hierarchy. In the example, this level represents all the folders and files associated with the account of a user named Paul.
- **Documents**—This represents the third level of the sample hierarchy. In the example, this level represents all the folders and files that reside in the user Paul's Documents folder.

TIP

If you miss the old pathname way of looking at folders, you can still see the drive letters and backslashes in Vista. Either right-click the path and click Edit Address, or press Alt+D. To return to the hierarchical path, press Esc.

This is a sensible and straightforward way to view the hierarchy, which is already a big improvement over previous versions of Windows. However, the real value here lies in the navigation features of the Address bar, and you can get a hint of these features from the nickname that many people have applied to the new Address bar: the *breadcrumb bar*.

Breadcrumbing refers to a navigation feature that displays a list of the places a person has visited or the route a person has taken. The term comes from the fairy tale of Hansel and Gretel, who threw down bits of bread to help find their way out of the forest. This feature is common on websites where the content is organized as a hierarchy or as a sequence of pages.

Vista introduces breadcrumb navigation to Windows not only by using the address bar to show you the hierarchical path you've taken to get to the current folder, but also by adding interactivity to the breadcrumb path:

- You can navigate back to any part of the hierarchy by clicking the folder name in the address bar. For example, in the path shown in Figure 3.1, you could jump immediately to the top-level hierarchy by clicking the Desktop icon on the far left of the path.
- You can navigate "sideways" to any part of any level by clicking the right-pointing arrow to the right of the level you want to work with. In Figure 3.2, for example, you see that clicking the Paul arrow displays a list of the other navigable items that are in the Paul folder, such as Downloads, Music, and Pictures. Clicking an item in this list opens that folder.

Click the arrow to see the items in that level

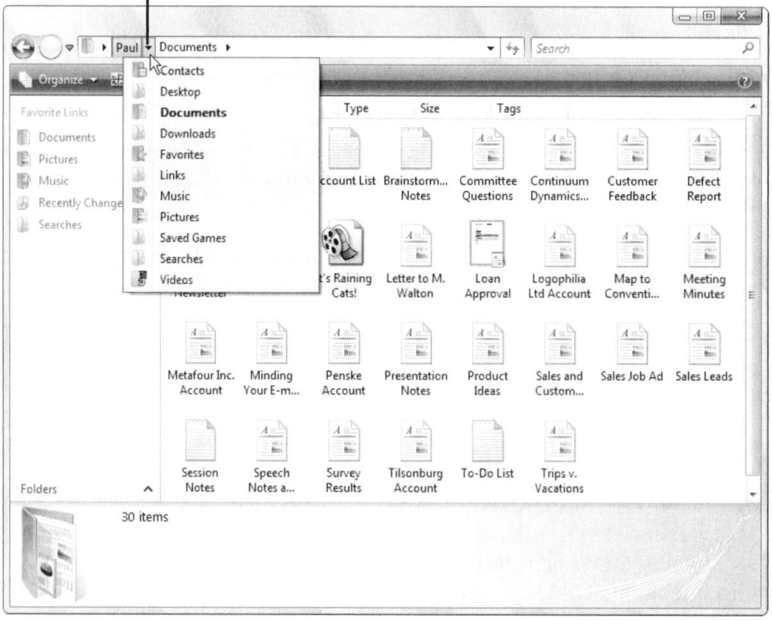

FIGURE 3.2 Breadcrumb navigation: In the Address bar, click a folder's arrow to see a list of the navigable items in that folder.

Instant Search

The next major change to the folder window interface in Windows Vista is the Instant Search box, which appears to the right of the address bar in all folder windows. Search is everywhere in Vista, and I go into it in much more detail later in this chapter (see "Desktop Searching with the Windows Search Engine"). For folder windows, however, the Instant Search box gives you a quick way to search for files within the current folder. Most of us nowadays have folders that contain hundreds or even thousands of documents. To knock such folders down to size in Vista, you need only type all or part of a filename, and Vista filters the folder contents to show just the matching files, as shown in Figure 3.3. Vista also matches those files that have metadata—such as the author or tags—that match your text.

Instant Search is a nice addition to the folder interface, but it's probably not going to be much of a productivity booster because it does *not* search within document text, and that's how most of us find the files we need. Of course, that might change when we all get into the habit of adding tags and other metadata to all our documents.

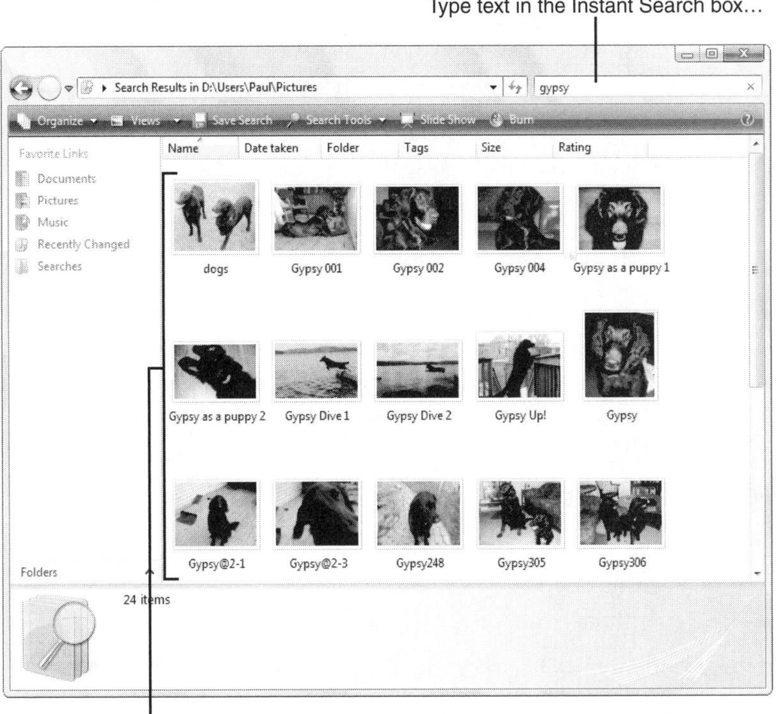

FIGURE 3.3 With Instant Search, Vista displays just those files with names or metadata that match your search text.

The Task Pane

The Task pane resides just below the Address bar. This pane contains task-related buttons, and its configuration depends on the type of folder you're viewing. For example, in the Pictures folder, there are buttons related to images, such as Burn and Slide Show (see Figure 3.4). However, all folder windows have the following two buttons:

- **Organize**—This button drops down a menu that enables you to perform basic file tasks (such as renaming, moving, copying, and deleting). It also includes a Layout command that displays a submenu of commands for configuring the folder window's layout by toggling the Details pane, Preview pane, and Navigation pane (discussed in the next three sections), and the menu bar (see the following Tip sidebar).
- **Views**—This button drops down a slider that enables you to change the folder view (see "Changing the View," later in this chapter).

TIP

Yes, the "classic" menus (as they're now called) are still available. If you want to use them only occasionally, press Alt to display the menu bar. (Press Alt again to hide the menu bar.) If you want the menus to remain onscreen in the active Windows Explorer window, click Organize, Layout, Menu Bar. (Repeat the command to hide the Classic menus.) If you want the menus to appear by default in all Windows Explorer windows, click Organize, Folder and Search Options, display the View tab, and activate the Always Show Menus check box.

The Details Pane

The Details pane resides at the bottom of the folder window, and it gives you information about the current folder (if no files are selected), the currently selected file or folder, or the current multiobject selection. If a document is selected (see Figure 3.4), the Details pane shows the following data:

- **A thumbnail of the document**—Vista's document thumbnails are much more informative than XP's. Here are some examples:
  - **Image**—The thumbnail shows a scaled-down version of the image.
  - **Video**—The thumbnail shows the first frame.
  - **Word 2007 document**—The thumbnail shows the first page.
  - **PowerPoint 2007 presentation**—The thumbnail shows the first slide.
  - **Excel 2007 workbook**—The thumbnail shows the first worksheet.
- **The document's metadata**—This includes the title, rating, and tags, as well as metadata specific to the document type, such as Genre for a music file and Camera Model for a digital photo. Some of this data is editable.

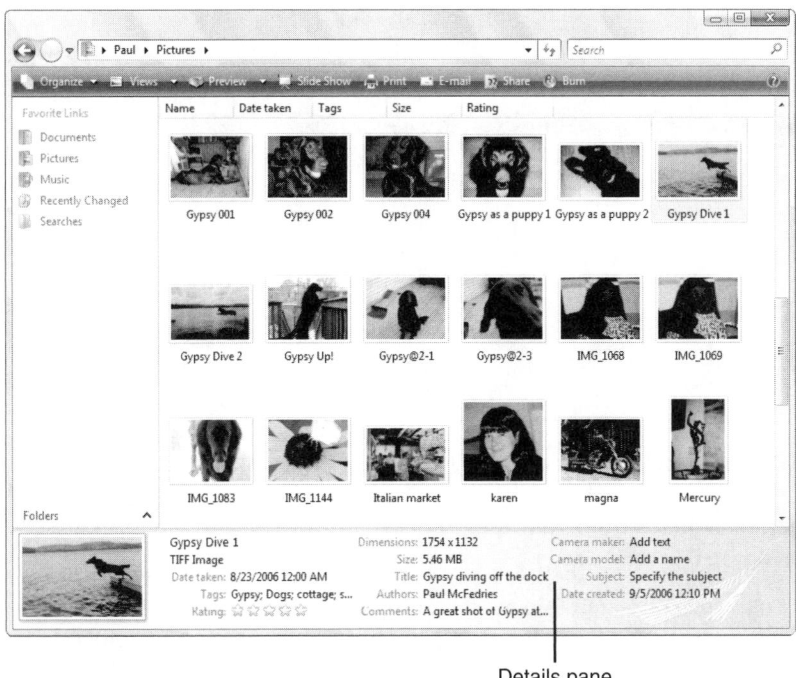

Details pane

FIGURE 3.4 The Details pane shows information about the selected file or folder.

The size of the Details pane is also configurable. You can use two methods:

- Click and drag the top edge of the Details pane up or down.
- Right-click an empty part of the Details pane, click Size, and then click Small, Medium, or Large.

The Preview Pane

The Preview pane offers yet another thumbnail view of the selected object. (It should be apparent to you by now that Vista is big on thumbnails.) As with the thumbnail in the Details pane, the Preview pane shows you the actual content from file types that support this feature, including images, videos, text files, and Office documents. Figure 3.5 shows the opening text from a text document previewed in the Preview pane. To display the Preview pane, select Organize, Layout, Preview Pane.

The Navigation Pane

The Navigation pane appears on the left side of each folder window and the Favorite Links section offers access to a few common folders. The top three icons—Documents, Pictures, and Music—are links to those folders. The other two links in the Navigation pane are special folders related to searching, which I discuss in detail later in this chapter (see "Saving Searches"). For now, here's a summary of what these two folders represent:

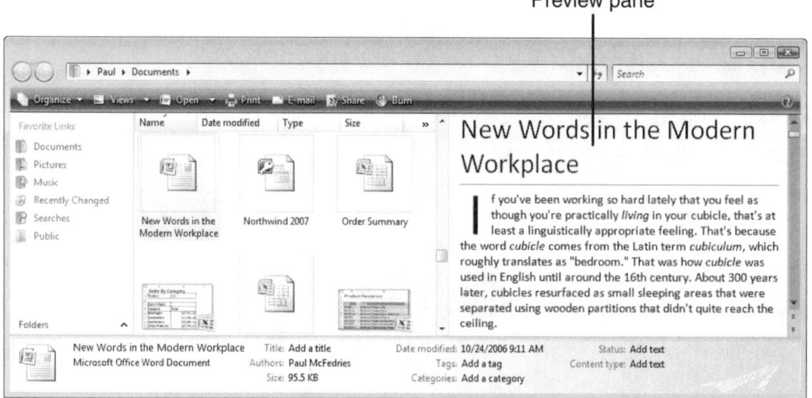

FIGURE 3.5 The Preview pane shows a thumbnail version of the selected file.

- **Recently Changed**—Items from your user folder that you have created or modified in the past 30 days.
- **Searches**—A collection of search folders, including Recently Changed, Important E-mail, and Favorite Music. Any searches that you save also appear in this folder.

TIP

The Favorite Links section is fully customizable. For example, you can add a link to one of your own favorite folders by clicking-and-dragging that folder and dropping it inside the Favorite Links section. You can also rename links (right-click a link and then click Rename) and remove links you don't use (right-click a link and click Remove Link).

TIP

What happened to the Folders list? It's still around, but it's hidden from view by default. However, it's easy enough to get at it: click Folders at the bottom of the Navigation pane.

Live Folder Icons

Do you ever wonder what's inside a folder? In previous versions of Windows, the only way to find out was to open the folder and look at the files. With Vista, however, that extra step isn't always necessary. That's because Vista introduces a new feature called Live Icons; each folder icon is an open folder filled not with generic "documents," but with actual folder content. For example, if you have a folder that you use to store PowerPoint presentations, that folder's icon will show the first slides from several of those presentation files. Figure 3.6 shows an example.

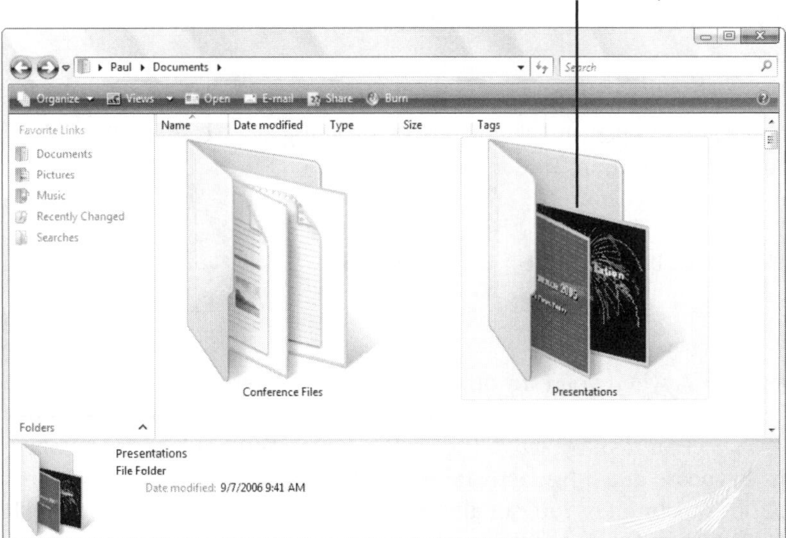

FIGURE 3.6 With Live Icons, the folder icon is filled with actual content from the folder.

Basic File and Folder Chores: The Techniques Used by the Pros

Now that you're familiar with what's new in Windows Vista's folders, it's time to put them through a workout. The next few sections take you through a few basic file and folder chores: selecting, moving and copying, and renaming.

Selecting Files with Check Boxes

New In this chapter, you learn about quite a few substantive changes to the Windows file system: metadata, the Windows Search engine, grouping, stacking, filtering, and search folders, previous versions, and transactional NTFS. All of these are fairly sophisticated and useful innovations. However, sometimes it's the small, incremental changes that make your life with a new operating system easier and more efficient. In this section, you learn about one of my favorites of Vista's many small but quite useful tweaks: a change that affects the way you select files.

When you need to select multiple, noncontiguous objects, the easiest method is to hold down the Ctrl key and click each item you want to select. However, when I use this technique to select more than a few files, I *always* end up accidentally selecting one or more files that I don't want. It's not a big deal to deselect these extra files, but it's one of those small drains on productivity that bugs me (and many other users).

Windows Vista introduces a new file-selection technique that promises to eliminate accidental selections. It's called Use Check Boxes to Select Items, and you activate it by following these steps:

1. Select Organize, Folder and Search Options to open the Folder and Search Options dialog box. (You can also open this dialog box by selecting Start, Control Panel, Appearance and Personalization, Folder Options.)
2. Click the View tab.
3. Activate the Use Check Boxes to Select Items check box.
4. Click OK.

As you can see in Figure 3.7, when you turn on this feature, Explorer creates a column to the left of the folder contents. When you point at a file or folder, a check box appears in this column, and you select an item by activating its check box. You don't need to hold down Ctrl or use the keyboard at all. Just activate the check boxes for the files and folders you want to select. Bonus technique: You can also select all the items in the folder quickly by clicking the check box that appears in the Name column.

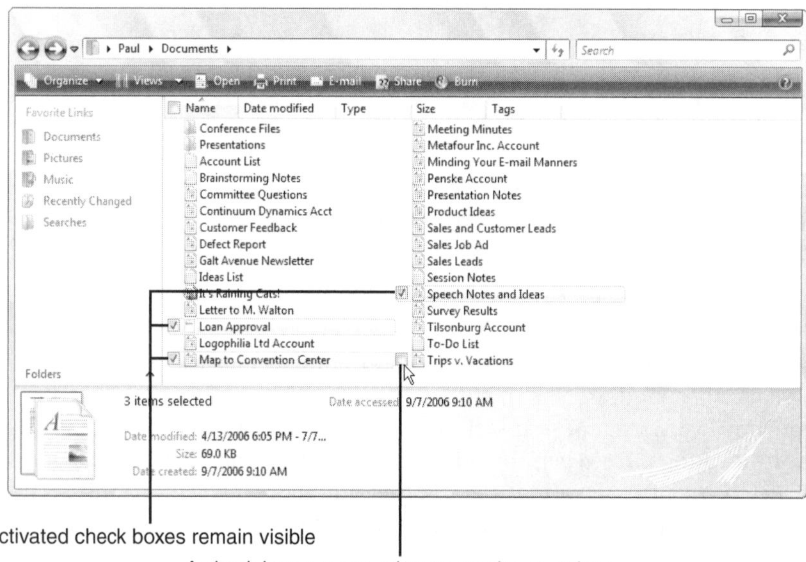

FIGURE 3.7 In Windows Vista, you can select files and folders using check boxes.

Understanding Size on Disk

The Windows Explorer Details pane shows you how many objects you've selected and the total size of the selected objects. However, it doesn't take into account any objects that might be inside a selected subfolder. To include subfolders, right-click the selection and then click Properties. Windows Vista counts all the files, calculates the total size as well as the total size on the disk, and then displays this data in the property sheet that appears.

What's the difference between the Size and Size on Disk values? Windows Vista stores files in discrete chunks of hard disk space called **clusters**, which have a fixed size. This size depends on the file system and the size of the partition, but 4KB is typical. The important thing to remember is that Windows Vista always uses full clusters to store all or part of a file. For example, suppose that you have two files, one that's 2KB and another that's 5KB. The 2KB file will be stored in an entire 4KB cluster. For the 5KB file, the first 4KB of the file will take up a whole cluster, and the remaining 1KB will be stored in its own 4KB cluster. Therefore, the total size of these files is 7KB, but they take up 12KB on the hard disk.

Resolving File Transfer Conflicts

New When you move or copy a file into the destination folder, it sometimes happens that a file with the same name already resides in that folder. In previous versions of Windows, you'd see a dialog box asking whether you want to replace the existing file, and you'd click Yes or No, as appropriate. Unfortunately, Windows didn't give you much information to go on to help you make the choice. Windows Vista takes a step in the right direction by displaying the Copy File (or Move File) dialog box, instead. Figure 3.8 shows an example of the Copy File dialog box.

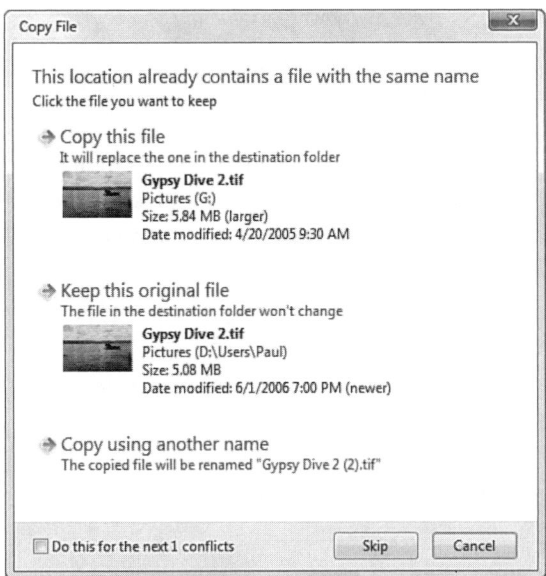

FIGURE 3.8 This dialog box appears if a file with the same name already exists inside the destination folder.

This dialog box gives you much more data: You see thumbnails for both versions, you get the dates and times when the files were last modified, the file extensions (so you can figure out the type), and file sizes. You also get three choices for resolving the conflict:

Copy (or Move) This File	The file you are copying (or moving) will replace the existing file.
Keep This Original File	The file will not be copied (or moved), so the original remains in the destination folder.
Copy (or Move) Using Another Name	The existing file remains as is, and the file being copied or moved is placed in the folder with (2) appended to the filename.

If Windows Vista detects multiple conflicts (as shown in Figure 3.8), you can also click Skip to avoid copying or moving a file. If you want to resolve the conflict in the same way with each file, be sure to activate the Do This for the Next *X* Conflicts check box to save time.

Expert Drag-and-Drop Techniques

You'll use the drag-and-drop technique throughout your Windows career. To make drag and drop even easier and more powerful, here are a few pointers to bear in mind:

"Lassoing" multiple files	If the objects you want to select are displayed in a block within the folder list, you can select them by dragging a box around the objects. This is known as **lassoing** the objects.
Drag-and-scroll	Most drag-and-drop operations involve dragging an object from the contents area and dropping it on a folder in the Folders list (be sure to display the Folders list first). If you can't see the destination in the Folders list, drag the pointer to the bottom of the Folders list. Windows Explorer will scroll the list up. To scroll the list down, drag the object to the top of the Folders list.
Drag-and-open	If the destination is a subfolder within an unopened folder branch, drag the object and hover the pointer over the unopened folder. After a second or two, Windows Explorer opens the folder branch.
Inter-window dragging	You can drag an object outside of the window and then drop it on a different location, such as the desktop.

TIP

You can't drop an object on a running program's taskbar icon, but you can do the next best thing. Drag the mouse over the appropriate taskbar button and wait a second or two. Windows will then bring that application's window to the foreground, and you can then drop the object within the window.

Drag between Explorers	Windows Vista lets you open two or more copies of Windows Explorer. If you have to use several drag-and-drop operations to get some objects to a particular destination, open a second copy of Windows Explorer and display the destination in this new window. You can then drag from the first window and drop into the second window.
Canceling drag-and-drop	To cancel a drag-and-drop operation, either press Esc or click the right mouse button. If you're right-dragging, click the left mouse button to cancel.

Taking Advantage of the Send To Command

For certain destinations, Windows Vista offers an easier method for copying or moving files or folders: the Send To command. To use this command, select the objects you want to work with and then run one of the following techniques:

- Display the Classic menus and select File, Send To
- Right-click the selection and then click Send To in the shortcut menu

Either way, you see a submenu of potential destinations, as shown in Figure 3.9. Note that the items in this menu (except the disk drives) are taken from the following folder that contains shortcut files for each item:

```
%UserProfile%\appdata\roaming\Microsoft\Windows\SendTo
```

This means that you can customize the Send To menu by adding, renaming, and deleting the shortcut files in your SendTo folder.

NOTE

The user profile folder for a user is the following:

`%SystemDrive%\Users\`*`User`*

Here, `%SystemDrive%` is the drive on which Vista is installed (such as C:), and *`User`* is the person's username. Windows Vista stores the user profile folder for the current user in the `%UserProfile%` environment variable.

FIGURE 3.9 The Send To command offers a menu of possible destinations.

Click the destination you want and Windows Vista sends the object there. What do I mean by *send*? I suppose that *drop* would be a better word because the Send To command acts like the drop part of drag-and-drop. Therefore, Send To follows the same rules as drag-and-drop:

- If the Send To destination is on a different disk drive, the object is copied.
- If the Send To destination is on the same disk drive, the object is moved.

TIP

As with a drag-and-drop operation, you can force the Send To command to copy or move an object. To force a move, hold down Shift when you select the Send To command. To force a copy, hold down Ctrl when you select the Send To command. To force a shortcut, hold down Shift and Ctrl when you select the Send To command.

The Recycle Bin: Deleting and Recovering Files and Folders

In my conversations with Windows users, I've noticed an interesting trend that has become more prominent in recent years: People don't delete files as often as they used to. I'm sure that the reason for this is the absolutely huge hard disks that are offered these days. Even entry-level systems come equipped with 40GB or 80GB disks, and hard disks with capacities of several hundred gigabytes are no longer a big deal. Unless someone's working with digital video files, even a power user isn't going to put a dent in these massive disks any time soon. So, why bother deleting anything?

Although it's always a good idea to remove files and folders you don't need (it makes your system easier to navigate, it speeds up defragmenting, and so on), avoiding deletions does have one advantage: You can never delete something important by accident.

Just in case you do, however, Windows Vista's Recycle Bin can bail you out. The Recycle Bin icon on the Windows Vista desktop is actually a front-end for a collection of hidden folders named Recycled that exist on each hard disk partition. The idea is that when you delete a file or folder, Windows Vista doesn't actually remove the object from your system. Instead, the object moves to the Recycled folder on the same drive. If you delete an object by accident, you can go to the Recycle Bin and return the object to its original spot. Note, however, that the Recycle Bin can hold only so much data. When it gets full, it permanently deletes its oldest objects to make room for newer ones.

TIP

If you're absolutely sure that you don't need an object, you can permanently delete it from your system (that is, bypass the Recycle Bin) by highlighting it and pressing Shift+Delete.

It's important to note that Windows Vista bypasses the Recycle Bin and permanently deletes an object under the following circumstances:

- You delete the object from a floppy disk or any removable drive.
- You delete the object from the DOS prompt.
- You delete the object from a network drive.

Setting Some Recycle Bin Options

The Recycle Bin has a few properties you can set to control how it works. To view these properties, right-click the desktop's Recycle Bin icon and then click Properties. Windows Vista displays the property sheet shown in Figure 3.10.

Here's a rundown of the various controls:

Recycle Bin Location	Choose the Recycle Bin you want to configure: the one for your user folder or you see an icon for each of the hard drive partitions on your computer.
Custom Size	Enter the size of the Recycle Bin. The larger the size, the more disk space the Recycle Bin takes up, but the more files it will save.
Do Not Move Files to the Recycle Bin	If you activate this option, all deletions are permanent.
Display Delete Confirmation Dialog	If you don't want Windows Vista to ask for confirmation when you delete an object, deactivate this check box.

FIGURE 3.10 Use this property sheet to configure the Recycle Bin to your liking.

TIP

You can clean out your Recycle Bin at any time by right-clicking the desktop's Recycle Bin icon and then clicking Empty Recycle Bin. The Recycle Bin contents can also be purged using Windows Vista's Disk Cleanup utility.

Click OK to put the new settings into effect.

Recovering a File or Folder

If you accidentally delete the wrong file or folder, you can return it to its rightful place by using the following method:

1. Open the desktop's Recycle Bin icon, or open any Recycled folder in Windows Explorer.
2. Select the object.
3. Click Restore This Item in the taskbar. (You can also right-click the file and then click Restore.)

NOTE

If deleting the file or folder was the last action you performed in Windows Explorer, you can recover the object by selecting the Edit, Undo Delete command (or by pressing Ctrl+Z). Note, too, that Windows Vista enables you to undo the 10 most recent actions.

File Maintenance Using the Open and Save As Dialog Boxes

One of the best-kept secrets of Windows Vista is the fact that you can perform many of these file maintenance operations within two of Windows Vista's standard dialog boxes:

Open — In most applications, you display this dialog box by selecting the File, Open command, or by pressing Ctrl+O.

Save As — You usually display this dialog box by selecting File, Save As. Or, if you're working with a new, unsaved file, by selecting File, Save, or by pressing Ctrl+S.

Here are three techniques you can use within these dialog boxes:

- To perform maintenance on a particular file or folder, right-click the object to display a shortcut menu like the one shown in Figure 3.11.
- To create a new object, right-click an empty section of the file list, and then click New to get the New menu.
- To create a new folder within the current folder, click the New Folder button.

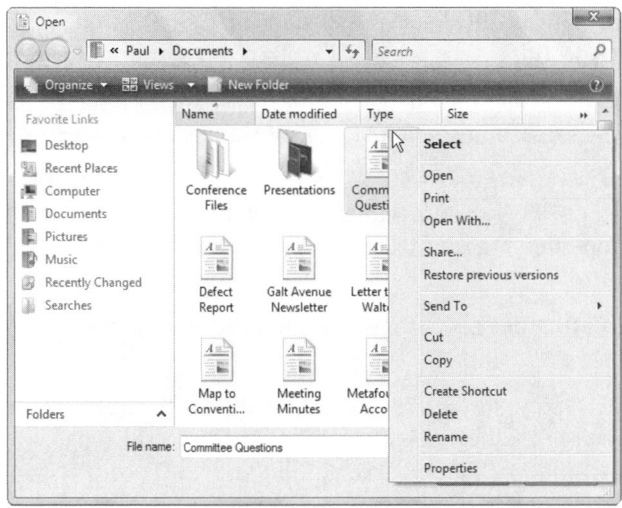

FIGURE 3.11 You can perform most basic file and folder maintenance right from the Open and Save As dialog boxes.

Metadata and the Windows Explorer Property System

If file location will become less important, what can you use to take its place as a basis for file organization? Content seems like a pretty good place to start. After all, it's what's inside the documents that really matters. For example, suppose that you're working on the Penske account. It's a pretty good bet that all the Penske-related documents on your system actually have the word *Penske* inside them somewhere. If you want to find a Penske document, a file system that indexes document content sure helps because then you need only do a content search on the word *Penske*.

However, what if a memo or other document comes your way with an idea that would be perfect for the Penske account, but that document doesn't use the word *Penske* anywhere? This is where purely content-based file management fails because you have no way of relating this new document with your Penske documents. Of course, you could edit the new document to add the word *Penske* somewhere, but that's a bit kludgy and, in any case, you might not have write permission on the file. It would be far better if you could somehow identify all of your documents that have "Penske-ness"—that is, that are directly or indirectly related to the Penske account.

This sounds like a job for metadata, and that's appropriate because metadata is all the rage these days, particularly on the Web. At sites such as Flickr.com and del.icio.us, surfers are categorizing the data they find online by applying descriptive keywords—called **tags**—to the objects they come across. **Social software**—software that enables users to share information and collaborate online—makes these tags available to other users, who can then take advantage of all this tagging to search for the information they need. At the del.icio.us site, for example, users bookmark interesting pages and assign tags to each site, and those tags can then be searched. This is called **social bookmarking**. Certainly, metadata is nothing new in the Windows world, either:

- Digital photo files often come with their own metadata for things such as the camera model and image dimensions, and some imaging software enables you to apply tags to pictures.
- In Windows Media Player, you can download album and track information that gets stored as various metadata properties: `Artist`, `Album Title`, `Track Title`, and `Genre`, to name just a few.
- The last few versions of Microsoft Office have supported metadata via the File, Properties command.
- For all file types, Windows XP displays in each file's property sheet a Summary tab that enables you to set metadata properties such as `Author`, `Comments`, and `Tags`.

New What's different in Vista is that metadata is a more integral part of the operating system. With the new Windows Search Engine, you can perform searches on some or all of these properties (see "Desktop Searching with the Windows Search Engine" later in this chapter). You can also use them to create virtual folders, file stacks, and file filters (see "Grouping, Stacking, and Filtering with Metadata," later in this chapter).

As you saw earlier, Windows Explorer displays some of a document's metadata in the Details pane (see Figure 3.4). To edit a document's metadata, Vista gives you two methods:

- In the Details pane, click the property you want to edit. Vista displays a text box in which you can type or edit the property value. Click Save when you're done.
- Right-click the document and click Properties to display the property sheet, and then click the Details tab. As you can see in Figure 3.12, this tab displays a list of properties and their values. To edit a property, click inside the Value column to the right of the property.

NOTE

By default, in most folder windows Vista displays the `Tags` and `Author` properties in Windows Explorer's Details view. (Specialized folders such as Music, Pictures, and Videos display other properties in Details view.) To toggle a property's column on and off, right-click any column header and then click the property. Click More to see a complete list of the available properties.

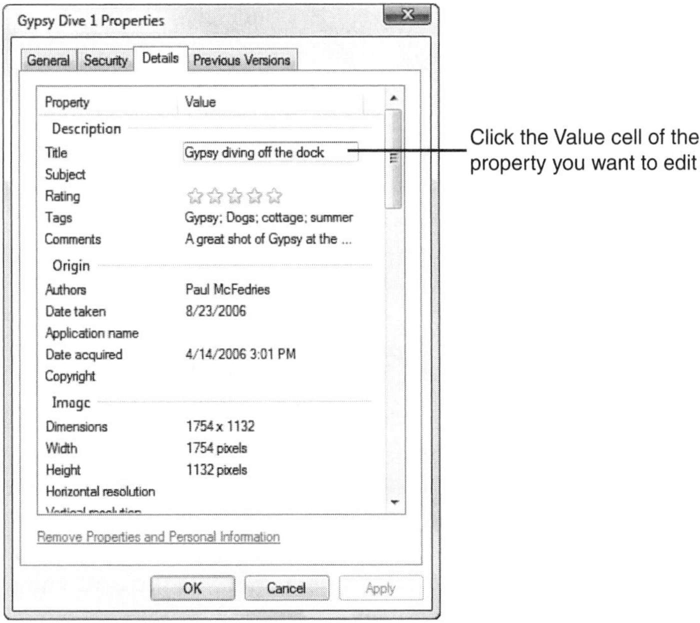

FIGURE 3.12 You can edit all of a document's configurable metadata in the document's property sheet.

Putting metadata at the heart of the operating system is a welcome innovation. Throw in the capability to sort, group, stack, filter, and create search folders based on such metadata, and few would dispute the value of this enhanced file system.

It's also a good thing that metadata is easy to implement for individual files, but will people get into the habit of adding metadata for each new document that they create? Time will tell, but it's certainly true that metadata has been underutilized so far. I think people will have to be convinced that taking a little time now to add metadata will save them more time in the future because the metadata makes documents easier to find and manage. It also helps if software vendors can make it easier for users to add metadata to documents. Having to switch over to Windows Explorer to add or edit metadata is not a big productivity booster. Instead, I hope Vista-aware programs will offer metadata-friendly interfaces and prompt for properties when users save new documents.

NOTE

The latest versions of Microsoft Word have a feature that, when enabled, prompts you to enter document metadata. In Word 2003 or earlier, select Tools, Options; display the Save tab; and activate the Prompt for Document Properties check box. Now, after you save a new document, Word displays the Properties dialog box automatically. Alas, this useful option appears to have been deleted from the Word 2007 interface, although it's still accessible via a macro:

```
Sub PromptForPropertiesInWord()
    Application.Options.SavePropertiesPrompt = True
End Sub
```

A much bigger problem is applying metadata to existing documents. I have thousands of them, and you probably do, too. Who has the time or motivation to set even just a few property values for thousands of old files? Nobody does, of course, and I suspect most of us will simply ignore the vast majority of our existing files (after all, we might never use 95% of them again) and move forward into the metadata future.

Desktop Searching with the Windows Search Engine

New Searching your computer in Windows XP wasn't a terrible experience, but no one raved about it, either. First, there was Microsoft's inexplicable decision to ship XP with the Indexing service turned off by default. Without the Indexing service, the search function was next-to-useless in XP, but turning it on required several relatively obscure clicks in the Search Companion. Even with the Indexing service running, searches that included entire partitions could take a frustratingly long time to complete.

Microsoft's goal in Vista is to make search a truly useful tool that provides complete results quickly. Did it succeed? For the most part, yes. The Windows Search Engine (WSE) service starts by default, which all by itself is a big improvement over XP. On the downside, it can still take Vista an absurdly long time to search, say, all of drive C:. However, that's because the Windows Search Engine does *not* index the entire drive. Instead, it just indexes your documents, your offline files (local copies of network files; see Chapter 22), and your email messages. If you're searching for one of these types of files, Vista searches are lightning quick.

Note that you can control what WSE indexes and force a rebuild of the index by selecting Start, Control Panel, System and Maintenance, Indexing Options. This displays the dialog box shown in Figure 3.13. To customize the search engine, you have two choices:

- **Modify**—Click this button to display the Indexed Locations dialog box, which enables you to change the locations included in the index. Activate the check box for each drive or folder you want to include.
- **Advanced**—Click this button to display the Advanced Options dialog box, which enables you to index encrypted files, change the index location, specify the file types (extensions) that you want include in or exclude from the index. You can also click Rebuild to re-create the index.

CAUTION

The Windows Search Engine takes a *long* time to index even a relatively small amount of data. If you're asking WSE to index dozens of gigabytes of data, wait until you're done working for the day and let the indexer run all night.

FIGURE 3.13 Use Control Panel's Indexing and Search Options to control the Windows Search Engine.

As-You-Type Searches with Instant Search

Vista's searching interface is also radically different from XP's simple but forgettable Search Companion. The most obvious—and, for simple searches, certainly the most useful—innovation is the Instant Search box on the Vista Start menu. As shown in Figure 3.14, as you type characters in the Instant Search box, the Start menu replaces the list of pinned and recently used programs with a new list that displays the following search links:

- A list of programs with names that include the typed characters
- A list of files (documents) with content or metadata that include the typed characters
- Other data—such as Contacts, email messages, and sites from Internet Explorer's Favorites and History lists—with content or metadata that include the typed characters
- A See All Results link
- A Search the Internet link

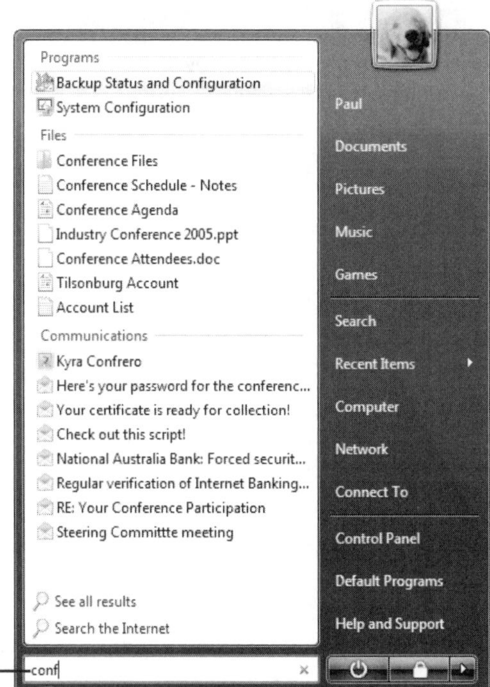

FIGURE 3.14 As-you-type searching using the Start menu's Instant Search box.

If you see the program or file you want, click it to open it. Otherwise, you can click Search the Computer to see the complete list of matches from the files in your user profile. If you prefer to search the Web for your text, click the Search the Internet link instead.

You can also perform these as-you-type searches in any folder by using the Instant Search box that appears in every Explorer window. As you type, Explorer displays those files in the current folder with names or metadata that matches your search text, as shown in Figure 3.15.

TIP

In a folder window, you can access the Instant Search box via the keyboard by pressing Ctrl+E.

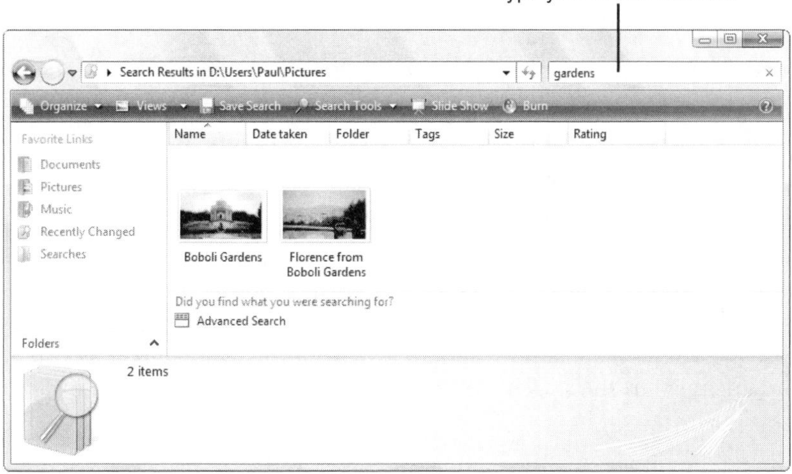

FIGURE 3.15 As-you-type searching using the Explorer window's Instant Search box.

Advanced Searches

As-you-type searches are handy and fast, but they tend to return too many results because they look for your search text in documents' metadata and contents. However, to find what you're looking for in a hard disk with dozens or even hundreds of gigabytes of data and many thousands of files, you need a more sophisticated approach. Windows Vista can help here, too.

Run an as-you-type search and then click the Advanced Search link. (Alternatively, select Search Tools, Search Pane to add the Search pane, and then click Advanced Search.) Vista displays the search controls shown in Figure 3.16.

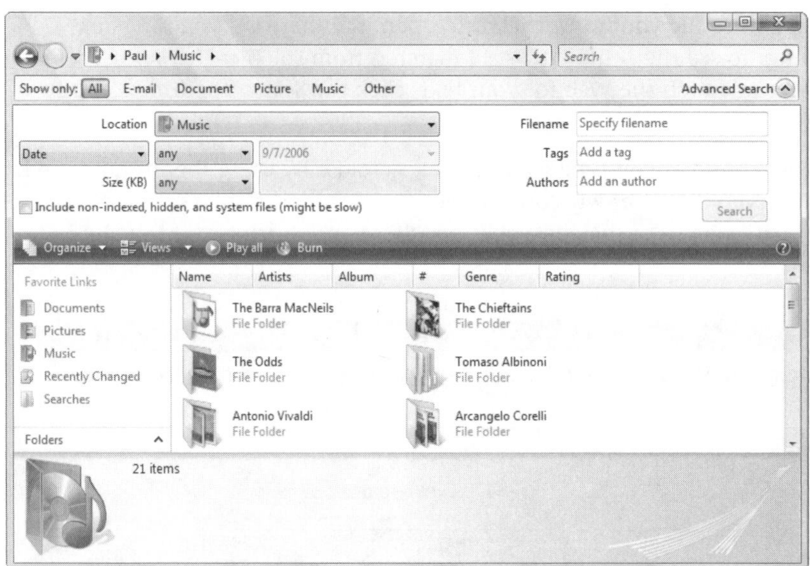

FIGURE 3.16 Use the Search pane to perform more advanced searches.

Vista assumes that you want to search by file type, so click one of the displayed types: All (matches any file type), E-mail, Document, Picture, Music, or Other.

To modify where Vista searches, pull down the Location list and click a location (for example, click Indexed Locations to search in all the folders included in the Search index). You can also click Choose Search Locations to display the Choose Search Locations dialog box, shown in Figure 3.17. The bottom part of the dialog box tells you the locations that are included in the search. You have three ways to modify these locations:

- To add a folder, activate the check box beside the folder in the Change Selected Locations list.
- To add any path, type it in the Or Type a Location Here text box, and then click Add.
- To remove a folder, either deactivate the check box beside the folder in the Change Selected Locations list, or click the folder in the Summary of Selected Locations and then click Remove.

Finally, you can add metadata filters that specify the properties in which you want Vista to look and how you want it to look there. In the Advanced Search pane, use some or all of the Date, Size, Filename, Tags, and Authors controls to enter your criteria.

With your search criteria set up, you can run the search by clicking the Search button or by pressing the Enter key. Figure 3.18 shows some example results.

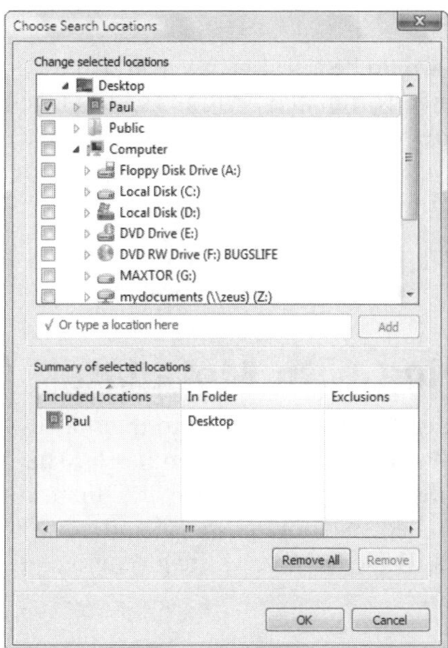

FIGURE 3.17 Use the Choose Search Locations dialog box to configure the folders included in your search.

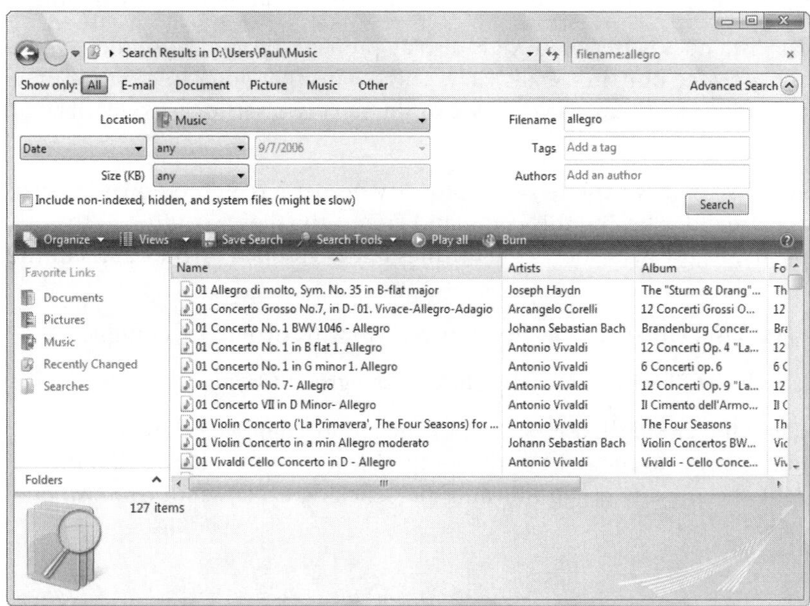

FIGURE 3.18 The results of a search.

Saving Searches

After taking all that time to get a search just right, it would be a real pain if you had to repeat the entire procedure to run the same search later. Fortunately, Windows Vista takes pity on searchers by enabling you to save your searches and rerun them anytime you like. After you run a search, you save it by clicking the Save Search button in the task pane. In the Save As dialog box that appears, type a name for the search and click Save.

Vista saves your searches in the Searches folder, appropriately enough. To rerun a search, click the Searches folder in the Navigation pane and then double-click the search.

Grouping, Stacking, and Filtering with Metadata

I mentioned earlier that people might not be motivated to apply metadata to their documents unless they could be convinced that metadata is worth the short-term hassle. The Windows programmers seem to understand this because they built three new file-management techniques into Windows Explorer, all of which become more powerful and more useful the more metadata you've applied to your files. These techniques are grouping, stacking, and filtering.

Grouping Files

New **Grouping** files means organizing a folder's contents according to the values in a particular property. You could do this in Windows XP, but you'll see that Windows Vista implements a couple of new techniques that make its grouping feature far more useful.

The first thing that Vista does better than XP is display property headers full time, whereas in XP they appeared only in Details view. This means that you can group your files (as well as stack and filter them, as you'll see in the next two sections) no matter which view you're using.

In the Vista version of Windows Explorer, each property header has a drop-down list that includes a Group command. Clicking this command groups the files according to the values in that property. Figure 3.19 shows the Pictures folder grouped by the values in the `Type` property.

As Figure 3.19 shows, Vista enhances the grouping feature with two new techniques:

- You can select all the files in a group by clicking the group title.
- You can collapse the group (that is, show just the group title) by clicking the upward-pointing arrow to the right of the group title. (You can collapse all the groups by right-clicking any group title and then clicking Collapse All Groups.)

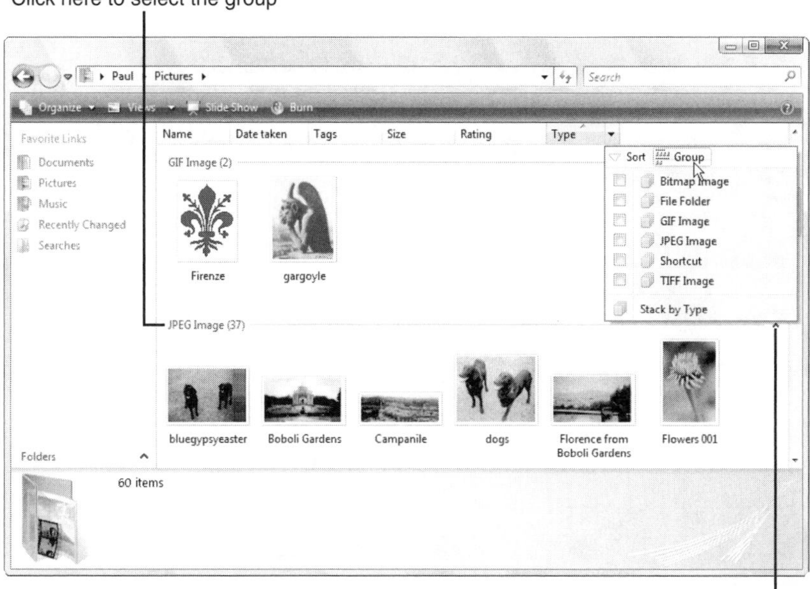

FIGURE 3.19 Windows Vista enables you to group and work with files based on the values in a property.

Stacking Files

New **Stacking** files is similar to grouping them because it organizes the folder's contents based on the values of a property. The difference is that a stack of files appears in the folder as a kind of subfolder. You stack files according to a property's values by pulling down the list associated with that property's header and clicking the Stack command. For example, Figure 3.20 shows the Pictures folder stacked according to the values in the `Size` property.

Filtering Files

New **Filtering** files means changing the folder view so that only files that have one or more specified property values are displayed. Returning to the `Type` property example, you could filter the folder's files to show only those where `Type` was, say, `JPEG Image` or `File Folder`.

When you pull down the list associated with a property's header, you see an item for each discrete property value, along with a check box for each value. To filter the files, activate the check boxes for the property values you want to view. For example, in Figure 3.21 I've activated the check boxes beside the `Bitmap Image` and `TIF Image` values in the `Type` property, and only those two types appear in the folder.

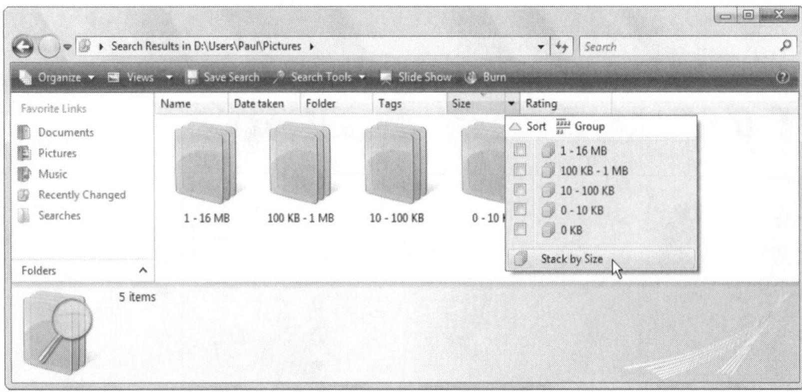

FIGURE 3.20 The Pictures folder stacked according to the values in the `Size` property.

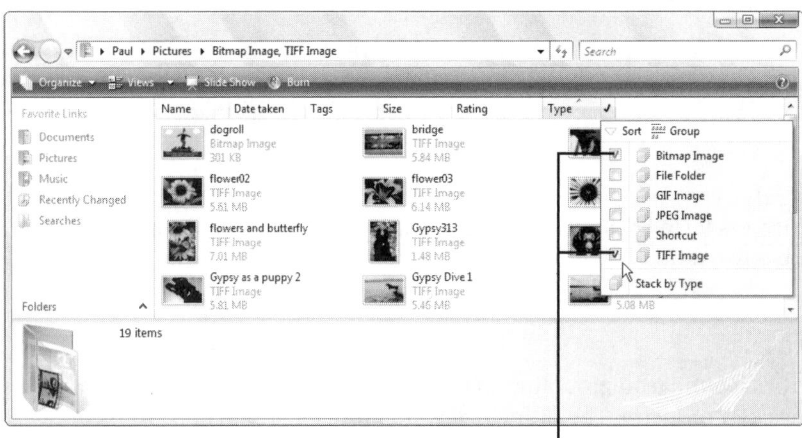

FIGURE 3.21 You can filter a folder to show only those files that have the property values you specify.

Shadow Copies and Transactional NTFS

New High-end databases have long supported the idea of the **transaction**, a collection of data modifications—inserts, deletions, updates, and so on—treated as a unit, meaning that either all the modifications occur or none of them does. For example, consider a finance database system that needs to perform a single chore: transfer a specified amount of money from one account to another. This involves two discrete steps (I'm simplifying here): debit one account by the specified amount and credit the other account for the same amount. If the database system did not treat these two steps as a single transaction, you could run into problems. For example, if the system successfully debited the first account but for some reason was unable to credit the second account, the system would be left in an unbalanced state. By treating the two steps as a single transaction, the system does not commit any changes unless both steps occur successfully. If the credit to the second account fails, the transaction is **rolled back** to the beginning, meaning that the debit to the first account is reversed and the system reverts to a stable state.

What does all this have to do with the Vista file system? It's actually directly related because Vista implements an interesting new technology called **Transactional NTFS**, or TxF, for short. TxF applies the same transactional database ideas to the file system. Put simply, with TxF, if some mishap occurs to your data—it could be a system crash, a program crash, an overwrite of an important file, or even just imprudent edits to a file—Vista enables you to roll back the file to a previous version. It's kind of like System Restore, except that it works not for the entire system, but for individual files, folders, and volumes.

Windows Vista's capability to restore previous versions of files and folders comes from two new processes:

- Each time you start your computer, Windows Vista creates a shadow copy of the volume in which Vista is stored. A **shadow copy** is essentially a snapshot of the volume's contents at a particular point in time.
- After creating the shadow copy, Vista uses transactional NTFS to intercept all calls to the file system. Vista maintains a meticulous log of those calls so that it knows exactly which files and folders in the volume have changed.

Together these processes enable Vista to store previous versions of files and folders, where a "previous" version is defined as a version of the object that changed after a shadow copy was created.

For example, suppose that you reboot your system three mornings in a row, and you make changes to a particular file each day. This means that you'll end up with three previous versions of the file: today's, yesterday's, and the day before yesterday's.

Reverting to a Previous Version of a Volume, Folder, or File

Windows Vista offers three different scenarios for using previous versions:

- If a system crash occurs, you might end up with extensive damage to large sections of the volume. Assuming that you can start Windows Vista, you might then be able to recover your data by reverting to a previous version of the volume (although this means that you'll probably lose any new documents you created since then). Note, however, that this means that *every* file that changed since creation of the associated shadow copy will be reverted to the previous version, so use this technique with some care.
- If a system crash or program crash damages a folder, you might be able to recover that folder by reverting to a previous version.

- If a system crash or program damages a file, or if you accidentally overwrite or miss-edit a file, you might be able to recover the file by reverting to a previous version.

To revert to a previous version, open the property sheet for the object you want to work with and then display the Previous Versions tab. Figure 3.22 shows the Previous Versions tab for a volume, whereas Figure 3.23 shows the Previous Versions tab for a file.

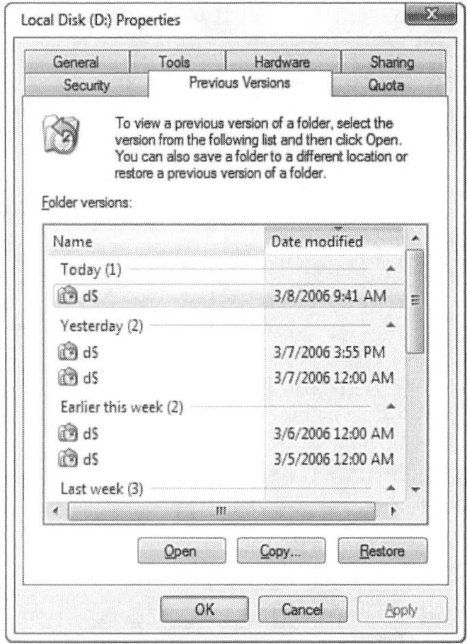

FIGURE 3.22 The Previous Versions tab for a volume.

Clicking a version activates the following three command buttons:

- **Open**—Click this button to view the contents of the previous version of the volume or folder, or to open the previous version of the file. This is useful if you're not sure which previous version you need.
- **Copy**—Click this button to make a copy of the previous version of the volume, folder, or file. This is useful if you're not sure that you want to restore *all* of the object. By making a copy, you can restore just part of the object (say, a few files from a volume or folder, or a section of a file).
- **Restore**—Click this button to roll back changes made to the volume, folder, or file to the previous version.

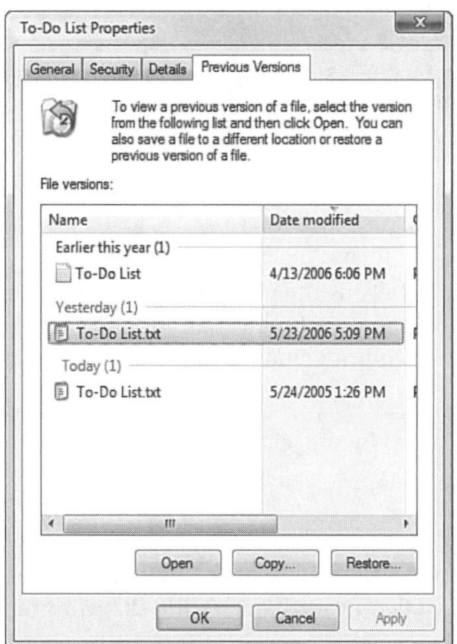

FIGURE 3.23 The Previous Versions tab for a file.

Customizing Windows Explorer

I close this chapter by examining various ways to customize the Windows Explorer interface. You'll likely be spending a lot of time with Windows Explorer over the years, so customizing it to your liking will make you more productive.

Changing the View

The icons in Windows Explorer's contents area can be viewed in five or six different ways, depending on the type of folder. To see a list of these views, either pull down the Views button in the Task pane or click View in the Classic menus. You get four choices for icon sizes: Extra Large Icons, Large Icons, Medium Icons, and Small Icons. You also get two other choices:

Tiles	Displays the icons in columns and for each one shows the filename, file type, and size.
Details	Displays a vertical list of icons, where each icon shows the data in all the displayed property columns (such as Name, Date Modified, Authors, Type, and Tags).

NOTE

To change the folder type, right-click the folder, click Properties, and then display the Customize tab. In the Use This Folder Type as a Template list, choose the type you want: Documents, Pictures and Videos, Music, or E-mail.

Viewing More Properties

Explorer's Details view (click Views and then select Details) is the preferred choice for power users because it displays the most information about each object and it gives you a great deal of flexibility. For example, here are some techniques you can use when working with the Details view:

- You can change the order of the property columns by dragging the column headings to the left or right.
- You can sort on a column by clicking the column heading.
- You can adjust the width of a column by pointing the mouse at the right edge of the column's heading (the pointer changes to a two-headed arrow) and dragging the pointer left or right.
- You can adjust the width of a column so that it's as wide as its widest data by double-clicking the right-edge of the column's heading.

TIP

To adjust all the columns so that they're exactly as wide as their widest data, right-click any column header and then click Size All Columns to Fit.

In addition, the Details view is informative because it shows you not only the name of each file, but also other properties, depending on the folder:

Documents—Name, Date Modified, Authors, Type, and Tags

Pictures and Videos—Name, Date Taken, Tags, and Rating

Music—Name, Artists, Album Title, Year, Genre, Length, and Rating

Contacts—Name, Full Name, Email, Business Phone, and Home Phone

These are all useful, to be sure, but Explorer can display many more file properties. In fact, there are nearly 300 properties in all, and they include useful information such as the dimensions of a picture file, the bit rate of a music file, and the frame rate of a video file. To see these and other properties, you have two choices:

- To see the most common properties for the current folder type, right-click any column header and then click the property you want to add.

- To see the complete property list, right-click any column header and then click More. The Choose Details dialog box that appears (see Figure 3.24) enables you to activate the check boxes for the properties you want to see, as well as rearrange the column order.

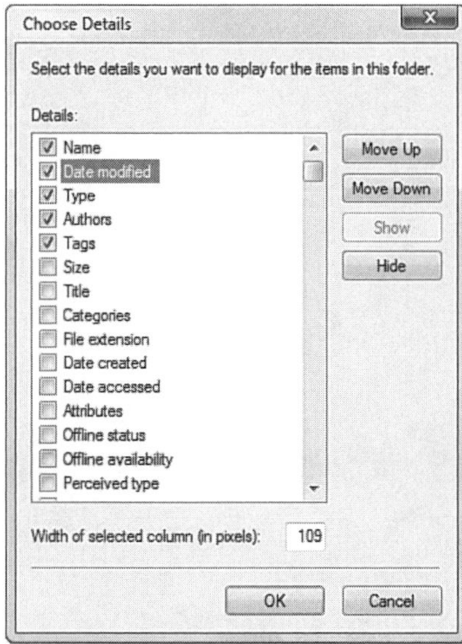

FIGURE 3.24 Use the Choose Details dialog box to add or remove property columns in Windows Explorer.

Running Explorer in Full-Screen Mode

If you want the largest possible screen area for the contents of each folder, you can place Windows Explorer in full-screen mode by pressing F11. (You can also hold down Ctrl and click the Maximize button; if Explorer is already maximized, you first have to click the Restore button.) This mode takes over the entire screen and hides the title bar, menu bar, status bar, address bar, and search bar. To work with the address bar or search bar, move your mouse pointer to the top of the screen. To restore the window, either press F11 again or display the address bar and search bar and then click the Full Screen button.

Exploring the View Options

Windows Explorer boasts a large number of customization options that you need to be familiar with. To see these options, you have two choices:

- In Windows Explorer, select Organize, Folder and Search Options
- Select Start, Settings, Control Panel, Appearance and Personalization, Folder Options

Either way, the view options can be found, appropriately enough, on the View tab of the Folder Options dialog box, as shown in Figure 3.25.

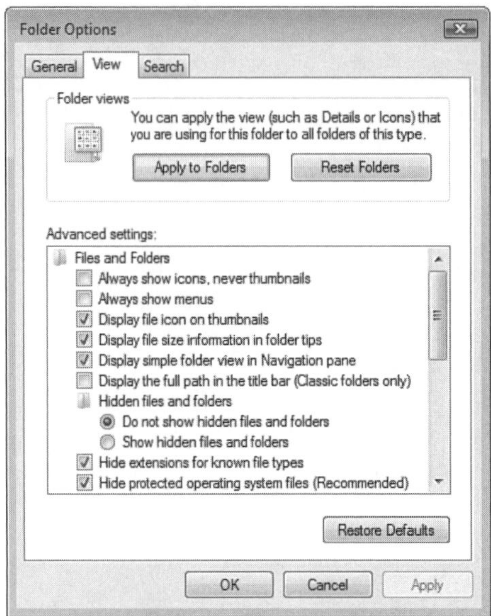

FIGURE 3.25 The View tab has quite a few options for customizing Windows Explorer.

The Folder Views group contains just the Reset All Folders button, which reverts all the Windows Vista folders back to their default configuration.

Here's a complete list of the various items in the Advanced Settings list:

Always Show Icons, Never Thumbnails	Activate this check box to prevent Windows Explorer from displaying file thumbnails.
Always Show Menus	Activate this check box to display the Classic menu bar full-time in Windows Explorer.

Display File Icon on Thumbnails	When this check box is activated, Windows Explorer superimposes the file type icon on the lower-right corner of each file's thumbnail. This is usually a good idea because the extra icon allows you to figure out the file type at a glance. However, if you find the icon getting in the way of the thumbnail image, deactivate this setting.
Display File Size Information in Folder Tips	When this setting is activated and you hover your mouse pointer over a folder icon, Windows Explorer calculates the size of the files and subfolders within the folder, and displays the size in a pop-up banner. This is useful information, but if you find that your system takes too long to calculate the file size, consider deactivating this setting.

NOTE

If you activate the Display File Size Information in Folder Tips setting, you must also activate the Show Pop-Up Description for Folder and Desktop Items setting, described later.

Display Simple Folder View in Navigation Pane	If you deactivate this setting, Explorer displays dotted lines connecting folders and subfolders in the Folders bar. If you prefer not to see these lines, leave this setting activated.
Display the Full Path in the Title Bar	Activate this setting to place the full pathname of the current folder in the Windows Explorer title bar. The full pathname includes the drive, the names of the parent folders, and the name of the current folder. Note that this only applies to Classic folders, which you activate by clicking the Use Windows Classic Folders option in the General pane.

Hidden Files and Folders	Windows Vista hides certain types of files by default. This makes sense for novice users because they could accidentally delete or rename an important file. However, it's a pain for more advanced users who might require access to these files. You can use these options to tell Windows Explorer which files to display: ▶ Do Not Show Hidden Files and Folders—Activate this option to avoid displaying objects that have the hidden attribute set. ▶ Show Hidden Files and Folders—Activate this option to display the hidden files.

NOTE

Files are hidden from view by having their Hidden attribute activated. You can work with this attribute directly by right-clicking a visible file, clicking Properties, and then toggling the Hidden setting on and off.

Hide Extensions for Known File Types	When you read Chapter 4, "Mastering File Types," you'll see that file extensions are one of the most crucial Windows Vista concepts. That's because file extensions define the file type and automatically associate files with certain applications. Microsoft figures that, crucial or not, the file extension concept is just too hard for new users to grasp. Therefore, right out of the box, Windows Explorer doesn't display file extensions. To overcome this limitation, deactivate this setting.

CAUTION

If you elect not to display file extensions, note that you won't be able to edit the extension when you rename a file. For example, if you have a text file named `Index.txt`, it will be displayed only as `Index` with the file extension hidden. If you edit the filename to `Index.htm`, Windows Vista actually renames the file to `Index.htm.txt`! To rename extensions, you must display them.

Hide Protected Operating System Files	This setting is activated by default, and it tells Windows Vista to hide files that have the System attribute activated. This is not usually a problem because you rarely have to do anything with the Windows system files. However, if you do need to see one of these files, deactivate this setting. When Windows Vista asks whether you're sure, click Yes.
Launch Folder Windows in a Separate Process	Activating this setting tells Windows Vista to create a new thread in memory for each folder you open. This makes Windows Explorer more stable because a problem with one thread won't crash the others. However, this also means that Windows Explorer requires far greater amounts of system resources and memory. Activate this option only if your system has plenty of resources and memory.
Remember Each Folder's View Settings	Activate this setting to have Windows Explorer View keep track of the view options you set for each folder. The next time you display a folder, Windows Explorer will remember the view options and use them to display the folder.
Restore Previous Folder Windows at Logon	If you activate this setting, Windows Vista makes note of which folders you have open when you log off. The next time you log on, Vista displays those folders again. This is a very useful option if you normally have one or two particular folder windows open all day long: It saves you having to reopen those folders each time you start Windows Vista.
Show Drive Letters	If you deactivate this check box, Windows Explorer hides the drive letters in the Computer folder and in the address bar when you open a drive.

NOTE

If you hide drive letters, Windows Explorer displays drive names such as `Local Disk - Unlabeled Volume 1`. This isn't particularly useful, so consider renaming your drives. Right-click the drive and then click Rename. Note that you must enter administrator credentials to perform this operation.

Show Encrypted or Compressed NTFS Files in Color	When this setting is activated, Windows Explorer shows the names of encrypted files in a green font and the names of compressed files in a blue font. This is a useful way to distinguish these from regular files, but you can deactivate it if you prefer to view all your files in a single color. Note that this only applies to files on NTFS partitions because only NTFS supports file encryption and compression.
Show Pop-Up Description for Folder and Desktop Items	Some icons display a pop-up banner when you point the mouse at them. For example, the default desktop icons display a pop-up banner that describes each icon. Use this setting to turn these pop-ups on and off.
Show Preview Handlers in Reading Pane	When this check box is activated, Windows Explorer includes controls for previewing certain types of files in the Reading pane. For example, when you display a video file in the Reading pane, Windows Explorer includes playback controls such as Play, Pause, and Stop.
Use Check Boxes to Select Items	I discussed this setting earlier in this chapter (refer to "Selecting Files with Check Boxes").
Use Sharing Wizard	When this check box is activated, you can share your files with other users on your computer. For the details, see the "Sharing Files with Other Users" section in Chapter 6, "Getting the Most Out of User Accounts." Deactivating this setting deactivates local file sharing.

When Typing Into List View	These options determine Windows Explorer's behavior when you open a folder and begin typing: ▶ Automatically Type Into the Search Box—Activate this option to have your typing appear in the Search box. ▶ Select the Typed Item in the View—Activate this option to jump to the first item in the folder with a name that begins with the letter you type.

Moving User Folders

By default, all your user folders are subfolders of the %USERPROFILE% folder, which is usually the following (where *User* is your username):

```
C:\Users\User
```

This is not a great location because it means that your documents and Windows Vista are on the same hard disk partition. If you have to wipe that partition to reinstall Windows Vista or some other operating system, you'll need to back up your documents first. Similarly, you might have another partition on your system that has lots of free disk space, so you might prefer to store your documents there. For these and other reasons, moving the location of your user folder is a good idea. Here's how:

TIP

An ideal setup is to have Windows Vista and your programs in one partition and your documents (that is, your user folders) in a separate partition. That way your documents remain safe if you have to wipe the system partition.

1. Create the folder in which you want your user folder to reside.
2. In Windows Explorer or the Vista Start menu, right-click the user folder you want to move, and then click Properties. The folder's property sheet appears.
3. In the Location tab, use the text box to enter the drive and folder where you want your documents stored. (Or click Move to select the folder using a dialog box.)
4. Click OK. If Explorer asks whether you want to create the new folder and then to move your documents to the new location, click Yes in both cases.

From Here

Here are some places in the book that contain information related to the material in this chapter:

- For an in-depth look at file types, see Chapter 4, "Mastering File Types."
- For file maintenance, see the sections titled "Deleting Unnecessary Files," "Defragmenting Your Hard Disk," and "Backing Up Your File." in Chapter 15, "Maintaining Your Windows Vista System."
- To learn how to access network folders and files, see Chapter 23, "Accessing and Administering the Network."
- To share your folders and files on a network, see the "Sharing Resources with the Network" section in Chapter 23.

CHAPTER 4

Mastering File Types

IN THIS CHAPTER

- Understanding File Types
- Working with Existing File Types
- Creating a New File Type
- Associating Two or More Extensions with a Single File Type
- Customizing the New Menu
- Customizing Windows Vista's Open with List

Amazingly, a long list of useful and powerful Windows Vista features are either ignored or given short shrift in the official Microsoft documentation. Whether it's the Windows Vista startup options, group policies, or the Registry (to name just three that I discuss in this book), Microsoft prefers that curious users figure these things out for themselves (with, of course, the help of their favorite computer book authors).

The subject of this chapter is a prime example. The idea of the **file type** can be described, without hyperbole, as the very foundation of the Windows Vista file system. Not only does Microsoft offer scant documentation and tools for working with file types, but also seems to have gone out of its way to hide the whole file type concept. As usual, the reason is to block out this aspect of Windows Vista's innards from the sensitive eyes of the novice user. Ironically, however, this just creates a completely new set of problems for beginners and more hassles for experienced users.

This chapter brings file types out into the open. You'll learn the basics of file types and then see a number of powerful techniques for using file types to take charge of the Windows Vista file system.

Understanding File Types

To get the most out of this chapter, you need to understand some background about what a file type is and how Windows Vista determines and works with file types. The next couple of sections tell you everything you need to know to get you through the rest of the chapter.

File Types and File Extensions

One of the fictions that Microsoft has tried to foist on the computer-using public is that we live in a "document-centric" world. That is, that people care only about the documents they create and not about the applications they use to create those documents. This is pure hokum. The reality is that applications are still too difficult to use and the capability to share documents between applications is still too problematic. In other words, you can't create documents unless you learn the ins and outs of an application, and you can't share documents with others unless you use compatible applications.

Unfortunately, we're stuck with Microsoft's worship of the document and all the problems that this worship creates. A good example is the hiding of file extensions. As you learned in Chapter 3, "Exploring Expert File and Folder Techniques," Windows Vista turns off file extensions by default. Here are just a few of the problems this allegedly document-centric decision creates:

Document confusion — If you have a folder with multiple documents that use the same primary name, it's often difficult to tell which file is which. For example, Figure 4.1 shows a folder with 18 different files named `Project`. Windows Vista unrealistically expects users to tell files apart just by examining their icons. To make matters worse, if the file is an image, Vista shows a thumbnail of the image instead of an icon. The result is that in Figure 4.1 it's impossible to tell at a glance which image is a GIF, which is a JPEG, and so on.

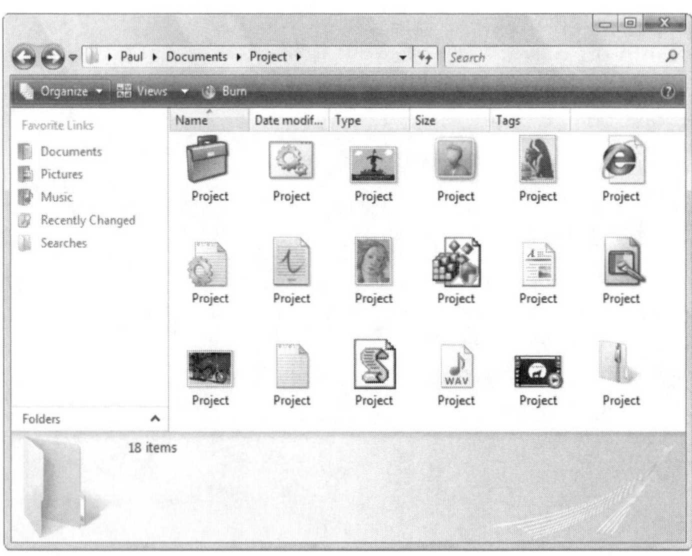

FIGURE 4.1 With file extensions turned off, it's often difficult to tell one file from another.

The inability to rename extensions	If you have a file named `index.txt` and you want to rename it to `index.html`, you can't do it with file extensions turned off. If you try, you just end up with a file named `index.html.txt`.
The inability to save a document under an extension of your choice	Similarly, with file extensions turned off, Windows Vista forces you to save a file using the default extension associated with an application. For example, if you're working in Notepad, every file you save must have a `txt` extension. If you create your own web pages, for example, you can't rename these text files with typical web page extensions such as `.htm`, `.html`, `.asp`, and so on.

TIP

There is a way to get around the inability to save a document under an extension of your choice. In the Save As dialog box, use the Save as Type list to select the All Files option, if it exists. You can then use the File Name text box to type the filename with the extension you prefer to use.

You can overcome all these problems by turning on file extensions. Why does the lack of file extensions cause such a fuss? Because file extensions *solely and completely* determine the file type of a document. In other words, if Windows Vista sees that a file has a `.txt` extension, it concludes the file uses the Text Document file type. Similarly, a file with the extension `.bmp` uses the Bitmap Image file type.

NOTE

As a reminder, you turn on file extensions by selecting Windows Explorer's Organize, Folder Options command, displaying the View tab, and deactivating the Hide File Extensions for Known File Types check box.

The file type, in turn, determines the application that's associated with the extension. If a file has a `.txt` extension, Windows Vista associates that extension with Notepad, so the file will always open in Notepad. Nothing else inherent in the file determines the file type so, at least from the point of view of the user, the entire Windows Vista file system rests on the shoulders of the humble file extension.

This method of determining file types is, no doubt, a poor design decision. For example, there is some danger that a novice user could render a file useless by imprudently renaming its extension. Interestingly, Microsoft seems to have recognized this danger and programmed a subtle behavior change into Vista: When file extensions are turned on and you activate the Rename command (click the file and then press F2), Vista displays the usual text box around the entire filename, but it selects *only* the file's primary name (the part to the left of the dot), as shown in Figure 4.2. Pressing any character obliterates the primary name, but leaves the extension intact.

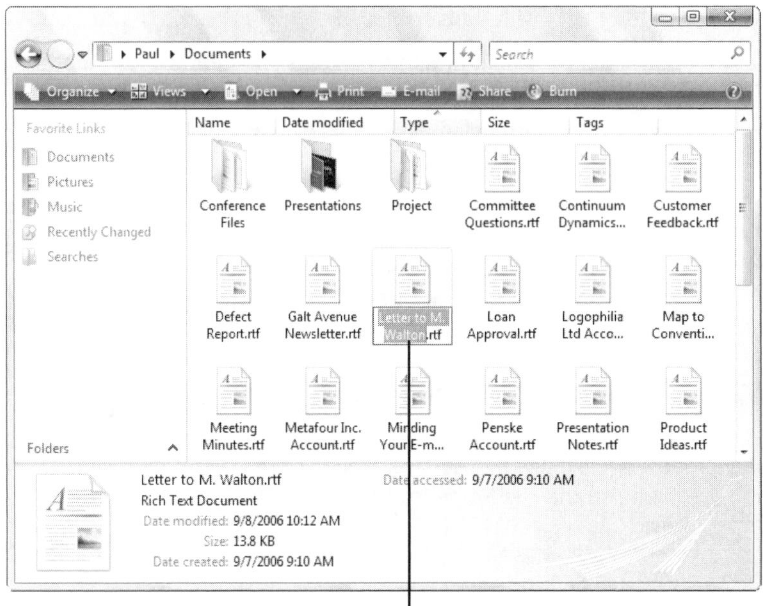

FIGURE 4.2 When you activate the Rename command with file extensions turned on, Windows Vista selects just the file's primary name.

Despite the drawbacks that come with file extensions, they lead to some powerful methods for manipulating and controlling the Windows Vista file system, as you'll see in this chapter.

File Types and the Registry

As you might expect, everything Windows Vista knows about file types is defined in the Registry. (See Chapter 11, "Getting to Know the Windows Vista Registry," for the details on understanding and using the Registry.) You use the Registry to work with file types throughout this chapter, so let's see how things work. Open the Registry Editor (press Windows Logo+R—or select Start, All Programs, Accessories, run—type **`regedit`**, click OK, and enter your credentials) and examine the `HKEY_CLASSES_ROOT` key. Notice that it's divided into two sections:

- The first part of `HKEY_CLASSES_ROOT` consists of dozens of file extension subkeys (such as `.bmp` and `.txt`). There are well over 400 such subkeys in a basic Windows Vista installation, and there could easily be two or three times that number on a system with many applications installed.

- The second part of HKEY_CLASSES_ROOT lists the various file types that are associated with the registered extensions. When an extension is associated with a particular file type, the extension is said to be **registered** with Windows Vista.

NOTE

HKEY_CLASSES_ROOT also stores information on ActiveX controls in its CLSID subkey. Many of these controls also have corresponding subkeys in the second half of HKEY_CLASSES_ROOT.

To see what this all means, take a look at Figure 4.3. Here, I've selected the `.txt` key, which has `txtfile` as its `Default` value.

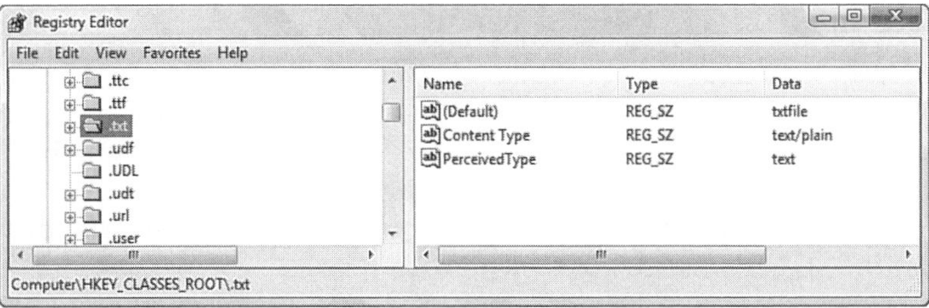

FIGURE 4.3 The first part of the HKEY_CLASSES_ROOT key contains subkeys for all the registered file extensions.

That `Default` value is a pointer to the extension's associated file type subkey in the second half of HKEY_CLASSES_ROOT. Figure 4.4 shows the `txtfile` subkey associated with the `.txt` extension. Here are some notes about this file type subkey:

- The `Default` value is a description of the file type (Text Document, in this case).
- The `DefaultIcon` subkey defines the icon that's displayed with any file that uses this type.
- The `shell` subkey determines the actions that can be performed with this file type. These actions vary depending on the file type, but `Open` and `Print` are common. The `Open` action determines the application that's associated with the file type. For example, the `Open` action for a Text Document file type is the following:

```
%SystemRoot%\system32\NOTEPAD.EXE %1
```

NOTE

The `%1` at the end of the command is a placeholder that refers to the document being opened (if any). If you double-click a file named `memo.txt`, for example, the `%1` placeholder is replaced by `memo.txt`, which tells Windows to run Notepad and open that file.

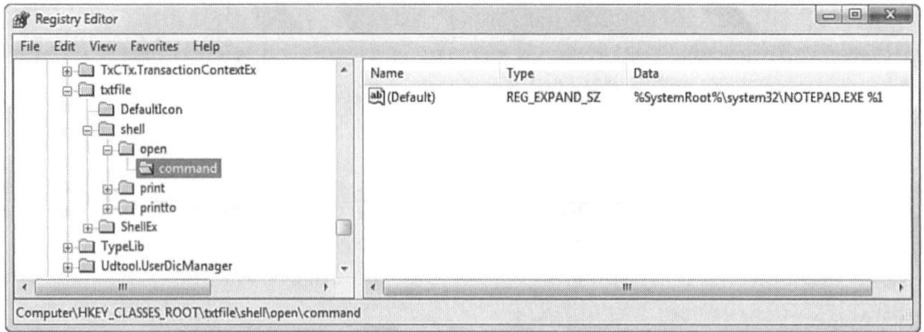

FIGURE 4.4 The second part of `HKEY_CLASSES_ROOT` contains the file type data associated with each extension.

Working with Existing File Types

In this section, you'll learn how to work with Windows Vista's existing file types. I'll show you how to change the file type description, modify the file type's actions, associate an extension with another file type, and disassociate a file type and an extension. Note that previous versions of Windows had a decent front-end for these types of hacks: the File Types tab in the Folder Options dialog box. Alas, that tab is nowhere in sight in Windows Vista, so you must use the Registry directly for some of what follows.

Setting the Default Action

Many file types have a default action that Windows Vista runs when you double-click a document of that file type. You can see the default action by right-clicking a document and examining the shortcut menu for the command that appears in bold type. You can edit the Registry to change the default action for a file type. Why would you want to do this? Here are some examples:

- For HTML documents (`.htm` or `.html` extension), the default action is `Open`, which opens the document in Internet Explorer. If you hand-code HTML pages, you might prefer the default action to be Edit so that you can quickly load the documents in your text editor.
- For images, the default action is `Preview`, which opens images in the Photo Gallery Viewer. Again, if you work with images frequently (creating them, cropping them, converting them, and so on), you might prefer that Edit be the default action.
- For Windows Scripting Host file types such as VBScript Script File (`.vbs` extension) and JScript Script File (`.js` extension), the default action is `Open`, which runs the script. However, these scripts can contain malicious code, so you can boost the security of your system by changing the default action for these file types to Edit.

To change the default action for a file type, follow these steps:

1. Open the Registry Editor.
2. Navigate to the key associated with the file type you want to work with.
3. Open the key and click the `Shell` branch.
4. Double-click the `Default` value to open the Edit String dialog box.
5. Type the name of the action that you want to be the default. For example, if you want the `Edit` action to be the default, type **`Edit`**.
6. Click OK.

Figure 4.5 shows the `VBSFile` file type (VBScript Script File) with the `Shell` branch's `Default` setting changed to `Edit`.

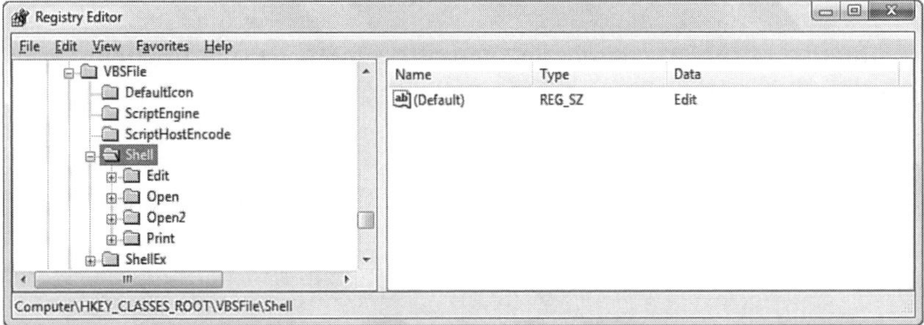

FIGURE 4.5 To change a file type's default action, change the value of the `Shell` branch's `Default` setting.

TIP

When you want to open a folder window in the two-paned Explorer view, you have to right-click the folder and then click Explore. To make the latter the default action for a folder, edit the Folder file type, select `explore` in the Actions list, and then click Set Default.

Creating a New File Type Action

You're not stuck with just the actions that Windows Vista has defined for a file type. You can add as many new actions that you can think of. For example, if you work with HTML documents, you could keep the default `Edit` action as it is (this opens the file for editing in Notepad) and create a new action—called, for example, `Open in HTML Editor`—that opens the file in an HTML editor that you have installed. When you right-click an HTML file, the menu that appears will show both commands: Edit (for Notepad) and Open in

HTML Editor (for the other editor; note that, for simplicity's sake, I'm assuming here that when you installed the HTML editor, it didn't modify the `Edit` action to point to itself).

To create a new action for an existing file type, follow these steps:

1. Open the Registry Editor.
2. Navigate to the key associated with the file type you want to work with.
3. Open the key and click the `Shell` branch.
4. Select Edit, New, Key, type the name of the new action, and press Enter.
5. Select Edit, New, Key, type **`command`**, and press Enter.
6. In the `command` branch, double-click the `Default` value to open the Edit String dialog box.
7. Type the full pathname of the application you want to use for the action. Here are some notes to bear in mind:

    - If the pathname of the executable file contains a space, be sure to enclose the path in quotation marks, like so:

    ```
    "C:\Program Files\My Program\program.exe"
    ```

    - If you'll be using documents that have spaces in their filenames, add the `%1` parameter after the pathname:

    ```
    "C:\Program Files\My Program\program.exe" "%1"
    ```

    The `%1` part tells the application to load the specified file (such as a filename you click), and the quotation marks ensure that no problems occur with multiple-word filenames.

    - If you're adding a `Print` action, be sure to include the `/p` switch after the application's pathname, like this:

    ```
    "C:\Program Files\My Program\program.exe" /p
    ```

TIP

You can define an accelerator key for the new action. Click the branch that holds the action name, and then double-click the `Default` value. In the Edit String dialog box, type the action name and precede a letter with an ampersand (&). That letter will be the menu accelerator key. For example, entering **`Open in &HTML Editor`** defines H as the accelerator key. When you right-click a file of this type, you can then press H to select the command in the shortcut menu.

8. Click OK.

Example: Opening the Command Prompt in the Current Folder

When you're working in Windows Explorer, you might find occasionally that you need to do some work at the command prompt. For example, the current folder might contain multiple files that need to be renamed—a task that's most easily done within a command-line session. Selecting Start, All Programs, Accessories, Command Prompt starts the session in the %USERPROFILE% folder, so you have to use one or more CD commands to get to the folder you want to work in.

An easier way would be to create a new action for the Folder file type that launches the command prompt and automatically displays the current Windows Explorer folder. To do this, follow these steps:

1. Open the Registry Editor.
2. Navigate to the `Folder` key.
3. Open the key and click the `shell` branch.
4. Select Edit, New, Key, type **`Open with Command Prompt`**, and press Enter.
5. Select Edit, New, Key, type **`command`**, and press Enter.
6. In the `command` branch, double-click the `Default` value to open the Edit String dialog box.
7. Type the following:

```
cmd.exe /k cd "%L"
```

NOTE

The `cmd.exe` file is the command prompt executable file. The `/k` switch tells Windows Vista to keep the command prompt window open after the `CD` (change directory) command completes. The `%L` placeholder represents the full pathname of the current folder.

8. Click OK.

Figure 4.6 shows two windows. The top window is the Registry Editor showing the new `Open with Command Prompt` action added to the `Folder\shell` key; in the bottom window, I right-clicked a folder. Notice how the new action appears in the shortcut menu.

Hiding a File Type's Extension

A **shortcut** is a file that points to another object: a document, folder, drive, printer, and so on. Shortcuts use the `.lnk` extension, which is associated with the `lnkfile` file type. Strangely, if you turn on file extensions, you still never see the `.lnk` extension when you view a shortcut file. Presumably, Windows Vista hides the extension because we're not supposed to think of the shortcut as an actual file, just a pointer to a file. That's fine with me, but how does Vista accomplish the trick of always hiding a shortcut's file extension?

4

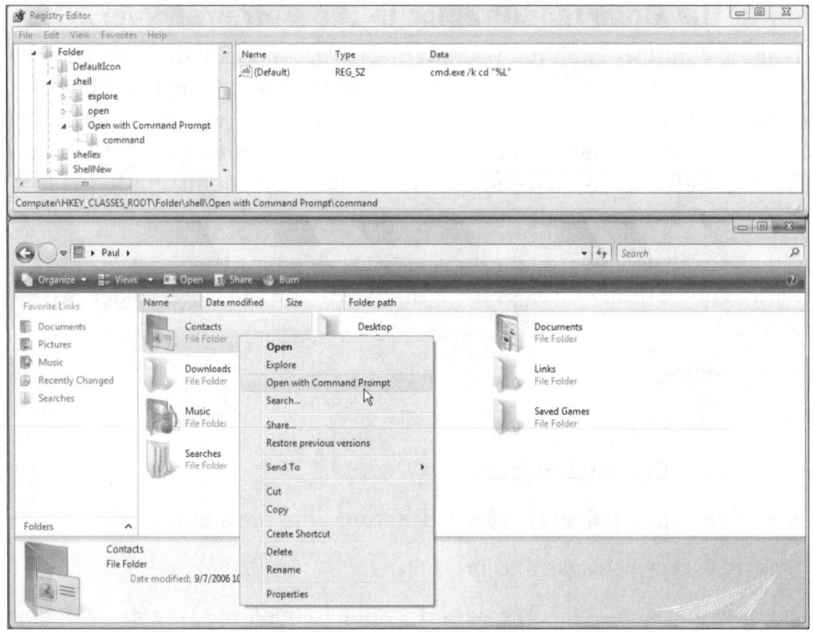

FIGURE 4.6 After you add the new action to the file type's `shell` key, the action appears in the file type's shortcut menu.

The secret is that the Registry's `lnkfile` (shortcut) key has an empty string setting named `NeverShowExt`. When Vista comes across this setting, it always hides the file type's extension.

You might want to duplicate this effect for another file type. If you have multiple users on your computer, for example, you might want to turn on file extensions, but hide the extensions of an important file type to ensure that users can't change it. Follow these steps to always hide a file type's extension:

1. Open the Registry Editor.
2. Navigate to the key of the file type you want to work with.
3. Select Edit, New, String Value.
4. Type **`NeverShowExt`** and press Enter.

Associating an Extension with a Different Application

There are many reasons you might want to override Windows Vista's default associations and use a different program to open an extension. For example, you might prefer to open text files in WordPad instead of Notepad. Similarly, you might want to open HTML files in Notepad or some other text editor rather than Internet Explorer.

In those cases, you need to associate the extension with the application you want to use instead of the Windows default association. In Windows Vista, you use the Open With dialog box to change the associated application, and Vista gives you many different ways to display this dialog box:

Right click With this method, right-click any file that uses the extension and then click Open With. If the file type already has multiple programs associated with it, you'll see a menu of those programs. In this case, click the Choose Default Program command from the menu that appears.

Task pane When you click a file, Windows Explorer's Task pane displays a button that represents the default action for the file type. For example, if you click an image, a Preview button appears in the Task pane; if you click an audio file, you see a Play button in the Task pane. In most cases, this default action button also doubles as a drop-down list. Display the list and click Choose Default Program.

Set Associations Select Start, Default Programs, Associate a File Type or Protocol With a Program. This displays the Set Associations window, shown in Figure 4.7, which displays a list of file extensions. Click the file type you want to work with and then click Change Program.

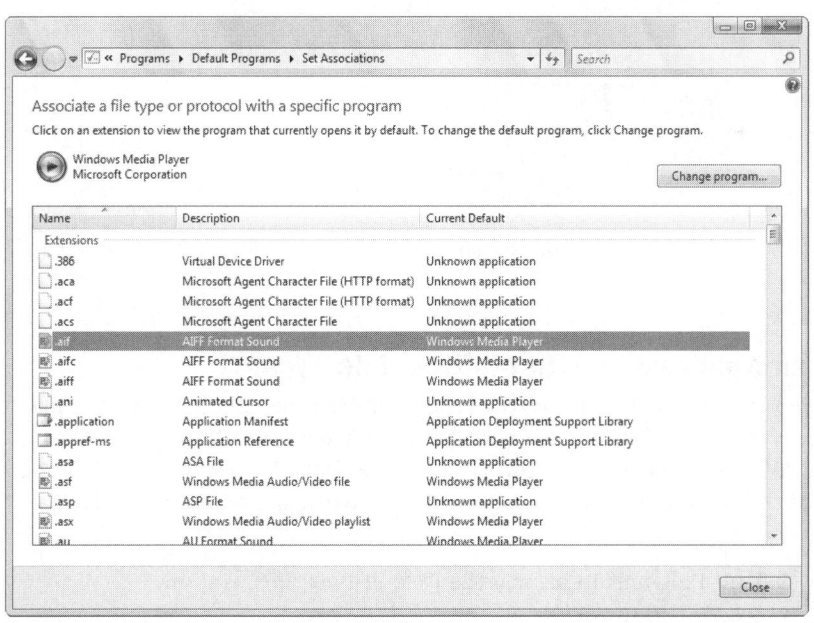

FIGURE 4.7 Use the Set Associations dialog box to change the application associated with any of the displayed file extensions.

No matter which method you use, you end up in the Open With dialog box, shown in Figure 4.8. From here, you follow these steps:

1. Select the program you want to associate with the file type. (If you don't see the program, click Browse, use the new Open With dialog box to select the program's executable file, and then click Open.)

2. Make sure that the Always Use the Selected Program to Open This Kind of File check box is activated. (If you arrived at the Open With dialog box via the Set Associations window, this check box is always activated and disabled.)

3. Click OK.

FIGURE 4.8 Use the Open With dialog box to associate a file type with a different application.

Associating an Application with Multiple File Types

Many applications can work with multiple file types. For example, Media Player can play more than 30 file types, including Windows Media Audio (`.wma`), MP3 (`.mp3`), CD Audio Track (`.cda`), and AVI (`.avi`). Windows Vista has a new Set Default Programs window that enables you specify which file types are associated with a particular application. Here's how to use it:

1. Select Start, Default Programs to display the Default Programs window.

2. Select Set Your Program Defaults to display the Set Default Programs window.

3. Use the Programs list to select the application you want to work with.

4. You now have two choices:

   - If you want to associate with the program all the file types that the program is capable of handling, click the Set As Default button.
   - If you want to associate with the program only some of the file types that it can handle, click Choose Defaults to display the Set Program Associations window. Activate the check box for each file type you want to associate with the program, and then click Save.

5. Click OK.

Creating a New File Type

Windows Vista comes with a long list of registered file types, but it can't account for every extension you'll face in your computing career. For rare extensions, it's best just to use the Open With dialog box. However, if you have an unregistered extension that you encounter frequently, you should register that extension by creating a new file type for it.

TIP

Text files, in particular, seem to come with all kinds of nonstandard (that is, unregistered) extensions. Rather than constantly setting up file types for these extensions or using the Open With dialog box, I created a shortcut for Notepad in my `%USERPROFILE\SendTo` folder. That way, I can open any text file by right-clicking it and then selecting Send To, Notepad.

Our old friend the Open With dialog box provides a quick-and-dirty method for creating a simple file type for an unregistered extension:

1. In Windows Explorer, select the file you want to work with.
2. Click Open. (For unregistered file types, Windows Vista doesn't display the Open With command.) Vista displays a dialog box telling you that it cannot open the file.
3. Activate the Select a Program from a List of Installed Programs option and then click OK. The Open With dialog box appears.
4. Select the application you want to use to open the file or click Browse to choose the program from a dialog box.
5. Use the Type a Description That You Want to Use for this Kind of File text box to enter a description for the new file type.
6. Make sure that the Always Use the Selected Program to Open This Kind of File check box is activated.
7. Click OK.

This method creates a new file type with the following properties:

- The number of actions Windows Vista creates for the file type depends on the application you selected. If you can use the application to both display and edit the file, Windows Vista creates `Open` and `Edit` actions; if you can use the application only to display the file, Windows Vista creates just the `Open` action.
- The icon associated with the file is the same as the one used by the associated application.
- In the Registry, you see the extension in `HKEY_CLASSES_ROOT` and the associated file type name is *`ext_auto_file`*, where *`ext`* is the file's extension.

Associating Two or More Extensions with a Single File Type

The problem with creating a new file type is that you often have to reinvent the wheel. For example, let's say you want to set up a new file type that uses the `.1st` extension. These are usually text files (such as `readme.1st`) that provide pre-installation instructions, so you probably want to associate them with Notepad. However, this means repeating some or all of the existing Text Document file types. To avoid this, it's possible to tell Windows Vista to associate a second extension with an existing file type. Here are the steps to follow:

1. Open the Registry Editor.
2. Select the `HKEY_CLASSES_ROOT` key.
3. Select Edit, New, Key.
4. Type the file extension used with the new file type (such as `.1st`), and press Enter.
5. In the new file extension key, double-click `Default`.
6. Type the name of the existing file type key that you want to associate with the new file type. For example, if you want the new file type to be associated with the Text Document (`.txt`) file type, enter **`txtfile`**.
7. Click OK.

Customizing the New Menu

One of Windows Vista's handiest features is the New menu, which enables you to create a new file without working within an application. In Windows Explorer (or on the desktop), right-click an empty part of the folder and then select New. In the submenu that appears, you'll see items that create new documents of various file types, including a folder, shortcut, bitmap image, WordPad document, text document, compressed folder, and possibly many others, depending on your system configuration and the applications you have installed.

What mechanism determines whether a file type appears on the New menu? The Registry, of course. To see how this works, start the Registry Editor and open the `HKEY_CLASSES_ROOT` key. As you've seen, most of the extension subkeys have only a `Default` setting that's either blank (if the extension isn't associated with a registered file type) or a string that points to the extension's associated file type.

However, many of these extension keys also have subkeys and a few of them have a subkey named `ShellNew`, in particular. For example, open the `.bmp` key and you see that it has a subkey named `ShellNew`. This subkey is what determines whether a file type appears on the New menu. Specifically, if the extension is registered with Windows Vista and it has a `ShellNew` subkey, the New menu sprouts a command for the associated file type.

The `ShellNew` subkey always contains a setting that determines how Windows Vista creates the new file. Four settings are possible:

`NullFile` This setting, the value of which is always set to a null string (""), tells Windows Vista to create an empty file of the associated type. Of the file types that appear on the default New menu, three use the `NullFile` setting: Text Document (`.txt`), Bitmap Image (`.bmp`), and Shortcut (`.lnk`).

`Directory` This setting tells Windows Vista to create a folder. The New menu's Briefcase (see the `Briefcase\ShellNew` key in the Registry) command uses this setting.

`Command` This setting tells Windows Vista to create the new file by executing a specific command. This command usually invokes an executable file with a few parameters. Two of the New menu's commands use this setting:

- **Contact**—The `.contact\ShellNew` key contains the following value for the `Command` setting:

  ```
  "%ProgramFiles%\Windows Mail\Wab.exe" /CreateContact "%1"
  ```

- **Journal Document**—In the `.jnt\jntfile\ShellNew` key, you'll see the following value for the `Command` setting:

  ```
  "%ProgramFiles%\Windows Journal\Journal.exe" /n 0
  ```

`Data` This setting contains a value, and when Windows Vista creates the new file, it copies this value into the file. The New menu's Rich Text Document (`.rtf`) and Compressed (Zipped) Folder (`.zip`) commands use this setting.

Adding File Types to the New Menu

To make the New menu even more convenient, you can add new file types for documents you work with regularly. For any file type that's registered with Windows Vista, you follow a simple three-step process:

1. Add a `ShellNew` subkey to the appropriate extension key in `HKEY_CLASSES_ROOT`.
2. Add one of the four settings discussed in the preceding section (`NullFile`, `Directory`, `Command`, or `Data`).
3. Type a value for the setting.

In most cases, the easiest way to go is to use `NullFile` to create an empty file.

Deleting File Types from the New Menu

Many Windows Vista applications (such as Microsoft Office) like to add their file types to the New menu. If you find that your New menu is getting overcrowded, you can delete some commands to keep things manageable. To do this, you need to find the appropriate extension in the Registry and delete its `ShellNew` subkey.

CAUTION

Instead of permanently deleting a `ShellNew` subkey, you can tread a more cautious path by simply renaming the key (to, for example, `ShellNewOld`). This still prevents Windows Vista from adding the item to the New menu, but it also means that you can restore the item just by restoring the original key name. Note, however, that some third-party Registry cleanup programs flag such renamed keys for deletion or restoration. The better programs—such as Registry Mechanic (www.pctools.com)—enable you to specify keys that the program should ignore.

Customizing Windows Vista's Open with List

You've used the Open With dialog box a couple of times so far in this chapter. This is a truly useful dialog box, but you can make it even more useful by customizing it. The rest of this chapter takes you through various Open With customizations.

Opening a Document with an Unassociated Application

From what you've learned in this chapter, you can see the process that Windows Vista goes through when you double-click a document:

1. Look up the document's extension in `HKEY_CLASSES_ROOT`.
2. Examine the `Default` value to get the name of the file type subkey.
3. Look up the file type subkey in `HKEY_CLASSES_ROOT`.
4. Get the `Default` value in the `shell\open\command` subkey to get the command line for the associated application.
5. Run the application and open the document.

What do you do if you want to bypass this process and have Windows Vista open a document in an **unassociated** application? (That is, an application other than the one with which the document is associated.) For example, what if you want to open a text file in WordPad?

One possibility would be to launch the unassociated application and open the document from there. To do so, you'd run the File, Open command (or whatever) and, in the Open dialog box, select All Files in the Files of Type list.

That will work, but it defeats the convenience of being able to launch a file directly from Windows Explorer. Here's how to work around this:

1. In Windows Explorer, select the document with which you want to work.
2. Select File, Open With. (Alternatively, right-click the document, and then click Open With in the shortcut menu.)
3. The next step depends on the file you're working with:
    - For most files, Windows Vista goes directly to the Open With dialog box. In this case, skip to step 4.
    - For a system file, Windows asks whether you're sure that you want to open the file. In this case, click Open With.
    - For some file types, Windows Vista displays a submenu of suggested programs. In this case, if you see the alternative program you want, select it. Otherwise, select Choose Default Program.
4. Select the unassociated application in which you want to open the document. (If the application you want to use isn't listed, click Browse and then select the program's executable file from the dialog box that appears.)
5. To prevent Windows Vista from changing the file type to the unassociated application, make sure that the Always Use the Selected Program to Open this Kind of File check box is deactivated.
6. Click OK to open the document in the selected application.

4

Note that Windows Vista remembers the unassociated applications that you choose in the Open With dialog box. When you next select the Open With command for the file type, Windows Vista displays a menu that includes both the associated program and the unassociated program you chose earlier.

How the Open with Feature Works

Before you learn about the more advanced Open With customizations, you need to know how Windows Vista compiles the list of applications that appear on the Open With list:

- Windows Vista checks `HKEY_CLASSES_ROOT\.ext` (where *.ext* is the extension that defines the file type). If it finds an `OpenWith` subkey, the applications listed under that subkey are added to the Open With menu and they appear in the Open With dialog box in the Recommended Programs section.

- Windows Vista checks `HKEY_CLASSES_ROOT\.ext` to see whether the file type has a `PerceivedType` setting. If so, it means the file type also has an associated **perceived type**. This is a broader type that groups related file types into a single category. For example, the Image perceived type includes files of type BMP, GIF, and JPEG, whereas the Text perceived type includes the files of type TXT, HTM, and XML. Windows Vista then checks the following:

  `HKEY_CLASSES_ROOT\SystemFileAssociations\PerceivedType\OpenWithList`

  Here, *`PerceivedType`* is value of the file type's `PerceivedType` setting. The application keys listed under the `OpenWithList` key are added to the file type's Open With menu and dialog box.

- Windows Vista checks `HKEY_CLASSES_ROOT\Applications`, which contains subkeys named after application executable files. If an application subkey has a `\shell\open\command` subkey, and if that subkey's `Default` value is set to the path name of the application's executable file, the application is added to the Open With dialog box.

- Windows Vista checks the following key:

  ```
  HKEY_CURRENT_USER\Software\Microsoft\Windows\CurrentVersion\Explorer\
  ➥FileExts\.ext\OpenWithList
  ```

  Here, *`ext`* is the file type's extension. This key contains settings for each application that the current user has used to open the file type via Open With. These settings are named `a`, `b`, `c`, and so on, and there's an `MRUList` setting that lists these letters in the order in which the applications have been used. These applications are added to the file type's Open With menu.

Removing an Application from a File Type's Open with Menu

When you use the Open With dialog box to choose an alternative application to open a particular file type, that application appears on the file type's Open With menu (that is, the menu that appears when you select the File, Open With command). To remove the application from this menu, open the following Registry key (where *`ext`* is the file type's extension):

```
HKEY_CURRENT_USER\Software\Microsoft\Windows\CurrentVersion\Explorer\
➥FileExts\.ext\OpenWithList
```

Delete the setting for the application you want removed from the menu. Also, edit the `MRUList` setting to remove the letter of the application you just deleted. For example, if the application setting you deleted was named `b`, delete the letter `b` from the `MRUList` setting.

Removing a Program from the Open with List

Rather than customizing only a single file type's Open With menu, you might need to customize the Open With dialog box for all file types. To prevent a program from appearing in the Open With list, open the Registry Editor and navigate to the following key:

```
HKEY_CLASSES_ROOT/Applications
```

Here you'll find a number of subkeys, each of which represents an application installed on your system. The names of these subkeys are the names of each application's executable file (such as `notepad.exe` for Notepad). To prevent Windows Vista from displaying an application in the Open With list, highlight the application's subkey, and create a new string value named `NoOpenWith`. (You don't have to supply a value for this setting.) To restore the application to the Open With list, delete the `NoOpenWith` setting.

NOTE

The `NoOpenWith` setting works only for applications that are not the default for opening a particular file type. For example, if you add `NoOpenWith` to the `notepad.exe` subkey, Notepad will still appear in the Open With list for text documents, but it won't appear for other file types, such as HTML files.

Adding a Program to the Open with List

You can also add an application to the Open With dialog box for all file types. Again, you head for the following Registry key:

```
HKEY_CLASSES_ROOT/Applications
```

Display the subkey named after the application's executable file. (If the subkey doesn't exist, create it.) Now add the `\shell\open\command` subkey and set the `Default` value to the pathname of the application's executable file.

Disabling the Open with Check Box

The Open With dialog box enables you to change the application associated with a file type's Open action by activating the Always Use the Selected Program to Open This Kind of File check box. If you share your computer with other people, you might not want them changing this association, either accidentally or purposefully. In that case, you can disable the check box by adjusting the following Registry key:

```
HKEY_CLASSES_ROOT\Unknown\shell\opendlg\command
```

The `Default` value of this key is the following:

```
%SystemRoot%\system32\rundll32.exe %SystemRoot%\system32\shell32.dll,
➥OpenAs_RunDLL %1
```

To disable the check box in the Open With dialog box, append `%2` to the end of the `Default` value:

```
%SystemRoot%\system32\rundll32.exe %SystemRoot%\system32\shell32.dll,
➥OpenAs_RunDLL %1 %2
```

From Here

Here are some other places in the book where you'll find related information:

- For a primer on Vista file techniques, see Chapter 3, "Exploring Expert File and Folder Techniques."
- For more information on application settings written to the Registry, see the section in Chapter 5 named "Applications and the Registry."
- For the details on understanding and working with the Registry, see Chapter 11, "Getting to Know the Windows Vista Registry."
- To learn how to create VBScript scripts, see Chapter 12, "Programming the Windows Scripting Host."

CHAPTER 5

Installing and Running Applications

IN THIS CHAPTER

- Practicing Safe Setups
- Applications and the Registry
- Launching Applications
- Understanding Application Compatibility

It's a rare (and no doubt unproductive) user who does nothing but run Windows on his or her computer. After all, when Windows starts, it doesn't do much of anything. No, to get full value for your computing dollar, you have to run an application or two. As an operating system, it's Windows' job to help make it easier for you to run your programs. Whether it's loading them into memory, managing their resources, or printing their documents, Windows has plenty to do behind the scenes. Windows Vista also comes with a few tools and techniques that you can use to make your applications run faster and more reliably. In this chapter, you'll learn how to install applications safely, how to launch applications, and how to solve program incompatibility issues.

Practicing Safe Setups

Outside of hardware woes and user errors (what IT personnel call a **PEBCAK—Problem Exists Between Chair And Keyboard**), most computer problems are caused by improperly installing a program or installing a program that doesn't mesh correctly with your system. It could be that the installation makes unfortunate changes to your configuration files, or that the program replaces a crucial system file with an older version, or that the program just wasn't meant to operate on (or wasn't tested with) a machine with your configuration. Whatever the reason, you can minimize these kinds of problems by understanding the installation process as it relates to user accounts and by following a few precautions before installing a new software package.

User Account Control and Installing Programs

In Windows Vista, something as apparently straightforward as installing a program isn't straightforward at all. The biggest hurdle you face is the Windows Vista security model—specifically, the User Account Control feature—which doesn't let just anyone install a program. More specifically, it doesn't let just anyone run unknown programs, and install programs for new applications are, by definition, unknown. Why the paranoia? Simply because Windows Vista wants to give you complete control over what gets installed on your system and what doesn't, particularly the latter. Lots of spyware programs and other malware run "stealth" installs and you never know they're on your system until things start to crash or other weirdness ensues. That won't happen under Windows Vista, at least not without your permission, because it prevents stealth installs by intercepting all installation attempts.

Therefore, unless you're running Windows Vista using the built-in Administrator account, when you launch an installation program, Windows Vista displays a User Account Control dialog box similar to the one shown in Figure 5.1. If you initiated the install, click Allow (if you're running Vista has a standard user, type an administrator password and click Submit, instead); otherwise, click Cancel.

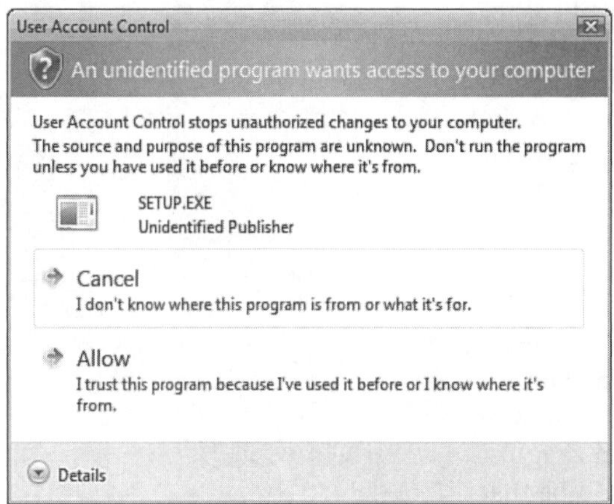

FIGURE 5.1 The User Account Control dialog box appears when you attempt to run an unknown program, such as an installation program.

Running Through a Pre-Installation Checklist

For those who enjoy working with computers, few things are as tempting as a new software package. The tendency is to just tear into the box, liberate the source disks, and let the installation program rip without further ado. This approach often loses its luster when, after a willy-nilly installation, your system starts to behave erratically. That's usually because the application's setup program has made adjustments to one or more important configuration files and given your system a case of indigestion in the process. That's the hard way to learn the hazards of a haphazard installation.

To avoid such a fate, you should always look before you leap. That is, you should follow a few simple safety measures before double-clicking that `setup.exe` file. The next few sections take you through a list of things to check before you install any program.

Check for Vista Compatibility

Check to see whether the program is compatible with Windows Vista. The easiest and safest setups occur with programs certified to work with Windows Vista. See "Understanding Application Compatibility," later in this chapter, to learn how to tell whether a program is Windows Vista–compatible.

Set a Restore Point

The quickest way to recover from a bad installation is to restore your system to the way it was before you ran the setup program. The only way to do that is to set a system restore point just before you run the program. In Chapter 15, "Maintaining Your Windows Vista System," see the section titled "Setting System Restore Points."

Read `Readme.txt` and Other Documentation

Although it's the easiest thing in the world to skip, you really should peruse whatever setup-related documentation the program provides. This includes the appropriate installation material in the manual, `Readme` text files found on the disk, and whatever else looks promising. By spending a few minutes looking over these resources, you can glean the following information:

- Any advance preparation you need to perform on your system
- What to expect during the installation
- Information you need to have on hand to complete the setup (such as a product's serial number)
- Changes the install program will make to your system or to your data files (if you're upgrading)
- Changes to the program and/or the documentation that were put into effect after the manual was printed

Virus-Check Downloaded Files

If you downloaded the application you're installing from the Internet, or if a friend or colleague sent you the installation file as an email attachment, you should scan the file using a good (and up-to-date) virus checker.

Although most viruses come to us via the Internet these days, not all of them do. Therefore, there are other situations in which it pays to be paranoid. You should check for viruses before installing if

- You ordered the program directly from an unknown developer.
- The package was already open when you purchased it from a dealer (buying opened software packages is never a good idea).
- A friend or colleague gave you the program on a floppy disk or recordable CD.

Understand the Effect on Your Data Files

Few software developers want to alienate their installed user base, so they usually emphasize upward compatibility in their upgrades. That is, the new version of the software will almost always be able to read and work with documents created with an older version. However, in the interest of progress, you often find that the data file format used by the latest incarnation of a program is different from its predecessors, and this new format is rarely *downward*-compatible. That is, an older version of the software will usually gag on a data file that was created by the new version. So, you're faced with two choices:

- Continue to work with your existing documents in the old format, thus possibly foregoing any benefits that come with the new format
- Update your files and thus risk making them incompatible with the old version of the program, should you decide to uninstall the upgrade

One possible solution to this dilemma is to make backup copies of all your data files before installing the upgrade. That way, you can always restore the good copies of your documents if the upgrade causes problems or destroys some of your data. If you've already used the upgrade to make changes to some documents, but you want to uninstall the upgrade, most programs have a Save As command that enables you to save the documents in their old format.

Use the Add or Remove Programs Feature

Click Start, Control Panel, Programs, Installed Programs to display the Installed Programs window shown in Figure 5.2. This is Windows Vista's replacement for the venerable Add or Remove Programs window, and it operates as a kind of one-stop shop for your installed applications. The items you see here come from the following Registry key:

```
HKLM\SOFTWARE\Microsoft\Windows\CurrentVersion\Uninstall
```

As shown in the bottom window of Figure 5.2, each installed application (as well as many installed Windows components) have a subkey in the `Uninstall` key. This subkey provides the data you see in the Installed Programs window, including the program Name (from the `DisplayName` setting), Publisher (the `Publisher` setting), Installed On (the `InstallDate` setting), Size (the `EstimatedSize` setting), Support link (the `HelpLink` setting), and File version (the `DisplayVersion` setting).

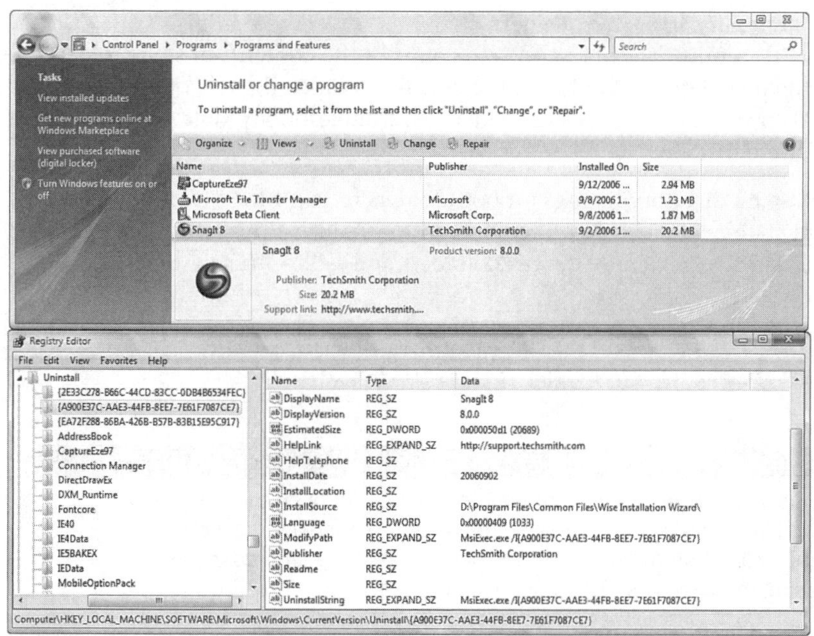

FIGURE 5.2 Items that can be uninstalled via Add or Remove Programs have corresponding Registry entries.

Click an installed program to activate the following three items on the Task pane:

Remove — Click this button (or Change/Remove) to uninstall the program. Note that each uninstallable item in the Installed Programs list has a corresponding `UninstallString` setting in the program's `Uninstall` subkey (see Figure 5.2).

Change — Click this button (or Change/Remove) to modify the program's installation. Depending on the program, modifying its installation might mean adding or removing program components or modifying settings.

Repair — Click this button to repair the program's installation, which usually means either reinstalling files or repairing damaged files.

TIP

After you've uninstalled a program, you might find that it still appears in the Installed Programs list. To fix this, open the Registry Editor, display the `Uninstall` key, and look for the subkey that represents the program. (If you're not sure, click a subkey and examine the `DisplayName` setting.) Delete that subkey and the uninstalled program will disappear from the list.

5

Save Directory Listings for Important Folders

Another safe setup technique I recommend is to compare the contents of some folders before and after the installation. Windows programs like to add all kinds of files to the `%SystemRoot%` and `%SystemRoot%\System32` folders. To troubleshoot problems, it helps to know which files were installed.

To figure this out, write directory listings for both folders to text files. The following two command prompt statements use the `DIR` command to produce alphabetical listings of the `%SystemRoot%` and `%SystemRoot%\System32` folders and redirect (using the > operator) these listings to text files:

```
dir %SystemRoot% /a-d /on /-p > c:\windir.txt
dir %SystemRoot%\system32 /a-d /on /-p > c:\sysdir.txt
```

NOTE

You need administrator privileges to write files to the root. To open the command prompt as an administrator, select Start, All Programs, Accessories, right-click Command Prompt, click Run As Administrator, and then enter your credentials. See Appendix B, "Using the Windows Vista Command Prompt."

When the installation is complete, run the following commands to save the new listings to a second set of text files:

```
dir %SystemRoot% /a-d /on /-p > c:\windir2.txt
dir %SystemRoot%\system32 /a-d /on /-p > c:\sysdir2.txt
```

The resulting text files are long, so comparing the before and after listings is time-consuming. To make this chore easier, use the `FC` (File Compare) command. Here's the simplified syntax to use with text files:

```
FC /L filename1 filename2
```

`/L`	Compares files as ASCII text
`filename1`	The first file you want to compare
`filename2`	The second file you want to compare

NOTE

The `FC` command can also compare binary files, display line numbers, perform case-insensitive comparisons, and much more. For the full syntax, enter the command `fc /?` at the command prompt.

For example, here's the command to run to compare the files `sysdir.txt` and `sysdir2.txt` that you created earlier:

```
fc /l c:\sysdir.txt c:\sysdir2.txt > fc-sys.txt
```

This statement redirects the `FC` command's output to a file named `fc-sys.txt`. Here's an example of the kind of data you'll see in this file when you open it in Notepad:

```
Comparing files C:\sysdir.txt and C:\sysdir2.txt
***** C:\sysdir.txt
09/04/2006  07:00 AM              657,920 WMVXENCD.DLL
09/04/2006  07:00 AM              272,384 WOW32.DLL
***** C:\SYSDIR2.TXT
09/04/2006  07:00 AM              657,920 WMVXENCD.DLL
11/22/2006  08:56 PM              913,560 wodFtpDLX.ocx
09/04/2006  07:00 AM              272,384 WOW32.DLL
*****
```

In this case, you can see that a file named `wodFtpDLX.ocx` has been added between `WMVXENCD.DLL` and `WOW32.DLL`.

5

TIP

The `FC` command is useful for more than just directory listings. You could also export Registry keys before and after and then use `FC` to compare the resulting registration (`.reg`) files. See Chapter 11, "Getting to Know the Windows Vista Registry."

TIP

Most high-end word processors have a feature that enables you to compare two documents (or any file type supported by the program). In Word 2003, for example, open the post-installation file, select Tools, Compare and Merge Documents, and then use the Compare and Merge Documents dialog box to open the pre-installation file. Word examines the documents and then inserts the changes using revision marks.

Take Control of the Installation

Some setup programs give new meaning to the term *brain-dead*. You slip in the source disk, run `Setup.exe` (or whatever), and the program proceeds to impose itself on your hard disk without so much as a how-do-you-do. Thankfully, most installation programs are a bit more thoughtful than that. They usually give you some advance warning about what's to come, and they prompt you for information as they go along. You can use this newfound thoughtfulness to assume a certain level of control over the installation. Here are a couple of things to watch for:

- **Choose your folder wisely**—Most installation programs offer to install their files in a default folder. Rather than just accepting this without question, think about where you want the program to reside. Personally, I prefer to use the Program Files folder to house all my applications. If you have multiple hard disks or partitions, you might prefer to use the one with the largest amount of free space. If the setup program lets you select data directories, you might want to use a separate folder that makes it easy to back up the data.

TIP

Most installation programs offer to copy the program's files to a subfolder of `%SystemDrive%\Program Files` (where `%SystemDrive%` is the partition on which Vista is installed). You can change this default installation folder by editing the Registry. First, display the following key:

```
HKLM\SOFTWARE\Microsoft\Windows\CurrentVersion\
```

The `ProgramFilesDir` setting holds the default install path. Change this setting to the path you prefer (for example, one that's on a drive with the most free disk space).

- **Use the Custom install option**—The best programs offer you a choice of installation options. Whenever possible, choose the Custom option, if one is available. This will give you maximum control over the components that are installed, including where and how they're installed.

Installing the Application

After you've run through this checklist, you're ready to install the program. Here's a summary of the various methods you can use to install a program in Windows Vista:

AutoPlay install—If the program comes on a CD or DVD that supports AutoPlay, it's likely that the installation program will launch automatically after you insert the disc into the drive. To prevent the install program from launching automatically, hold down the Shift key while you insert the disc.

TIP

Rather than holding down Shift each time you insert an install disc, you can configure Vista to never launch a disc's AutoPlay program. Follow the steps later in this chapter in the "Controlling AutoRun Behavior for Programs" section, and be sure to select the Take No Action option for the Software and Games setting.

Run `setup.exe`—For most applications, the installed program is named `setup.exe` (sometimes it's `install.exe`). Use Windows Explorer to find the install program and then double-click it. Alternatively, select Start, Run, enter the path to the `setup.exe` file (such as `e:\setup`), and click OK.

Decompress downloaded files—If you downloaded an application from the Internet, the file you receive will be either an `.exe` file or a `.zip` file. Either way, you should always store the file in an empty folder just in case it needs to extract files. You then do one of the following:

- If it's an `.exe` file, double-click it; in most cases, the install program will launch. In other cases, the program will extract its files and you then launch `setup.exe` (or whatever).
- If it's a `.zip` file, double-click it and Windows Vista will open a new compressed folder that shows the contents of the `.zip` file. If you see an installation program, double-click it. It's more likely, however, that you won't see an install program. Instead, the application is ready to go and all you have to do is extract the files to a folder and run the application from there.

Install from an `.inf` file—Some applications install via an information (`.inf`) file. To install these programs, right-click the file and then click Install in the shortcut menu that appears.

Applications and the Registry

As you'll see in Chapter 11, the Registry is perhaps Windows Vista's most important component because it stores thousands of settings that Windows needs. The Registry is important for your applications, as well, because most Windows applications use the Registry to store configuration data and other settings.

When you install an application, it typically makes a half-dozen different Registry modifications:

- Program settings
- User settings
- File types
- Application-specific paths
- Shared DLLs
- Uninstall settings

Program Settings

Program settings are related to the application as a whole: where it was installed, the serial number, and so on. The program settings are placed in a new subkey of `HKEY_LOCAL_MACHINE\Software`:

```
HKLM\Software\Company\Product\Version
```

Here, *`Company`* is the name of the program vendor, *`Product`* is the name of the software, and *`Version`* is the version number of the program. Here's an example for Office 2007:

```
HKLM\Software\Microsoft\Office\12.0
```

User Settings

User settings are user-specific entries, such as the user's name, preferences and options the user has selected, and so on. The user settings are stored in a subkey of `HKEY_CURRENT_USER\Software`:

```
HKCU\Software\Company\Product
```

File Types

File types refer to the file extensions used by the program's documents. These extensions are associated with the program's executable file so that double-clicking a document loads the program and displays the document. The extensions and file types are stored as subkeys within `HKEY_CLASSES_ROOT`. See Chapter 4, "Mastering File Types," for details.

If the application comes with **OLE** (object linking and embedding) support, it will have a unique class ID, which will be stored as a subkey within `HKEY_CLASSES_ROOT\CLSID`.

Application-Specific Paths

In computing, a **path** is a listing of the folders that the operating system must traverse to get to a particular file. Windows Vista uses a variation on this theme called **application-specific paths**. The idea is that if you enter only the primary name of a program's executable file in the Run dialog box (press Windows Logo+R), Windows Vista will find and run the program. For example, WordPad's executable file is `Wordpad.exe`, so you type **`wordpad`** in the Run dialog box, click OK, and WordPad opens.

NOTE

A file's **primary name** is the part of the filename to the left of the dot (.). For example, the primary name of the file `Excel.exe` is `excel`.

Windows finds the program because the application's executable file is associated with the particular path to the folder in which the file resides. These application-specific paths are set up in the following key:

```
HKLM\Software\Microsoft\Windows\CurrentVersion\App Paths
```

Each application that supports this feature adds a subkey that uses the name of the application's executable file (for example, `Wordpad.exe`). Within that subkey, the value of the `Default` setting is the full pathname (drive, folder, and filename) of the executable file. Note, too, that many applications also create a `Path` setting that specifies a default folder for the application.

TIP

It's possible to set up your own application-specific paths. See "Creating Application-Specific Paths," later in this chapter.

Launching Applications

Launching programs is one of the most fundamental operating system tasks, so it isn't surprising that Windows Vista offers an impressive number of ways to go about this:

- Use the Start menu—Click the Start button to open the Start menu. If you've used the program a lot, it should appear in the list of most frequently used (MFU) applications, so click its icon. Otherwise, click All Programs and then open the menus until you see the program icon, and then click the icon.
- Double-click the executable file—Use Windows Explorer to find the application's executable file, and then double-click that file.
- Double-click a shortcut—If a shortcut points to a program's executable file, double-clicking the shortcut will launch the program.
- Double-click a document—If you can use the application to create documents, double-clicking one of those documents should launch the program and load the document automatically. (If the document was one of the last 15 that you used, select Start, My Recent Documents, and then click the document in the submenu that appears.)
- Use the Open With command—If double-clicking a document opens the file in the wrong application, right-click the file and then click Open With. For the details on the Open With command, refer to the section in Chapter 4 titled "Customizing Windows Vista's Open With List."
- Insert a CD or DVD disc—Most CDs and DVDs support Windows Vista's AutoPlay feature that automatically starts a default program when the disc is inserted. The program that launches is determined by the contents of the `Autorun.inf` file in the disc's root folder. Open the file in Notepad and look for the `open` value in the `[AutoRun]` section. (See also "Controlling AutoRun Behavior for Programs," later in this chapter.)

Use the Run dialog box—Select Start, All Program, Accessories, Run (or press Windows Logo+R) to display the Run dialog box. Use the Open text box to specify the application (click OK when you're done):

TIP

One of the most annoying interface changes in Windows Vista is the burying of the Run command in the Accessories menu. If you use Run frequently, you might want to restore it to its rightful place on the main Start menu. Here's how: right-click the Start button, click Properties, and then click Customize. In the list of Start menu item, scroll down to the Run Command check box and activate it. Click OK to make it so.

- If the application resides within the `%SystemRoot%` or `%SystemRoot%\System32` folder, within a folder listed as part of the `PATH` environment variable, or if it has an application-specific path in the Registry (as described earlier in this chapter), just type the primary name of the executable file.
- For all other applications, enter the full pathname (drive, folder, and filename) for the executable file.
- You can also enter the full pathname of a document. If you want to open the document using a program other than the one associated with the document's file type, precede the document pathname with the application's pathname (separate the two paths with a space).

Use the Task Scheduler—You can use the Task Scheduler to run programs automatically at a given date and time, or on a regular schedule. Select Start, Control Panel, System and Maintenance, Scheduled Automated and Periodic Tasks. (See also "Using the Task Scheduler," later in this chapter.)

In addition to these methods, you can also control AutoRun behavior, set up the program to run automatically at startup, use the Run As Administrator command, and create your own application-specific paths. I discuss these methods in detail in the next three sections. To learn how to launch programs from the command prompt or a batch file, see the section in Appendix B titled "Starting Applications from the Command Prompt."

Controlling AutoRun Behavior for Programs

If you prefer to have some control over what happens when you insert a program's CD or DVD, you can modify the default AutoRun behavior for programs. Follow these steps:

1. Click Start, Default Programs to display the Default Programs window.
2. Click Change AutoPlay Settings. Windows Vista displays the AutoPlay window, shown in Figure 5.3.
3. Use the Software and Games list to click the AutoPlay behavior you prefer.
4. Click Save.

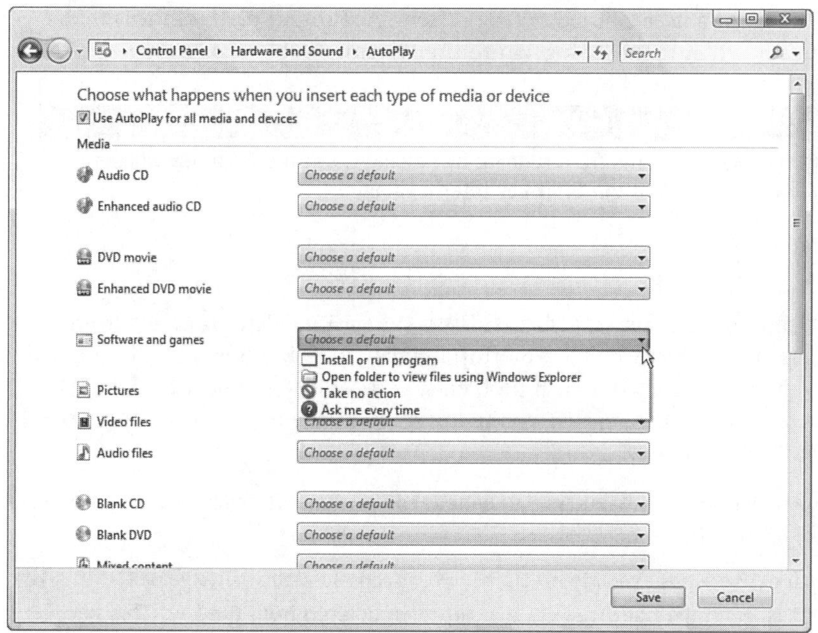

FIGURE 5.3 Use the AutoPlay window to set the default action Windows Vista will take when you insert a software CD or DVD.

Launching Applications and Scripts at Startup

If you have one or more programs that you use each day, or that you use as soon as Windows Vista starts, you can save yourself the hassle of launching these programs manually by getting Windows Vista to do it for you automatically at startup. Similarly, you can also get Windows Vista to automatically launch scripts or batch files at startup. You could set up a program or script for automatic startup launch using the Startup folder, the Registry, and the Group Policy snap-in.

Using the Startup Folder

The Startup folder is a regular file folder, but it has a special place in Windows Vista: You can get a program or script to run automatically at startup by adding a shortcut for that item to the Startup folder. (Adding shortcuts to the Startup folder is part of the Start menu customizations that I discuss in more detail in Chapter 13, "Customizing the Windows Vista Interface.") Note that the Startup folder appears twice in the Windows Vista interface:

- Via the Start menu (click Start, All Programs, Startup)
- Via Windows Explorer as the following subfolder:

```
\user\AppData\Roaming\Microsoft\Windows\Start Menu\Programs\Startup
```

Here, *user* is the name of a user defined on the system. A shortcut placed in this folder will run automatically when this user logs on to the system.

TIP

You can prevent the Startup items from running by holding down the Shift key while Windows Vista loads (hold down the Shift key after logging on).

Using the Registry

The Startup folder method has two drawbacks: Users can easily delete shortcuts from their own Startup folders, and users can bypass Startup items by holding down the Shift key while Windows Vista loads. To avoid both problems, you can use the Registry Editor to define your startup items. Assuming that you're logged in as the user you want to work with, the Registry offers two keys:

`HKCU\Software\Microsoft\Windows\CurrentVersion\Run`—The values in this key run automatically each time the user logs on.

`HKCU\Software\Microsoft\Windows\CurrentVersion\RunOnce`—The values in this key run only the next time the user logs on, and are then deleted from the key. (This key might not be present in your Registry. In that case, you need to add this key yourself.)

If you want an item to run at startup no matter who logs on, use the following keys:

`HKLM\Software\Microsoft\Windows\CurrentVersion\Run`—The values in this key run automatically each time any user logs on.

`HKLM\Software\Microsoft\Windows\CurrentVersion\RunOnce`—The values in this key run only the next time any user logs on, and are then deleted from the key. Don't confuse this key with the `RunOnceEx` key. `RunOnceEx` is an extended version of `RunOnce` that's used by developers to create more robust startup items that include features such as error handling and improved performance.

To create a startup item, add a string value to the appropriate key, give it whatever name you like, and then set its value to the full pathname of the executable file or script file that you want to launch at startup.

CAUTION

Placing the same startup item in both the `HKCU` and the `HKLM` hives will result in that item being started twice: once during the initial boot and again at logon.

TIP

If the program is in the `%SystemRoot%` folder, you can get away with entering only the name of the executable file. In addition, if the program you want to run at startup is capable of running in the background, you can load it in this mode by appending `/background` after the pathname.

Using Group Policies

If you prefer not to edit the Registry directly, or if you want to place a GUI between you and the Registry, Vista Pro's Group Policy snap-in can help. (See Chapter 10, "Using Control Panel and Group Policies," for details on using this snap-in.) Note, however, that Group Policy doesn't work directly with the Run keys in the `HKLM` and `HKCU` hives. Instead, these are considered to be **legacy keys**, meaning that they're mostly used by older programs. The new keys (new as of Windows 2000, that is) are the following:

```
HKLM\Software\Microsoft\Windows\CurrentVersion\policies\Explorer\Run

HKCU\Software\Microsoft\Windows\CurrentVersion\Policies\Explorer\Run
```

These keys do not appear in Windows Vista by default. You see them only after you specify startup programs in the Group Policy editor, as discussed in the next section. Alternatively, you can add these keys yourself using the Registry Editor.

NOTE

The startup items run in the following order:

```
HKLM\Software\Microsoft\Windows\CurrentVersion\RunOnce
HKLM\Software\Microsoft\Windows\CurrentVersion\policies\Explorer\Run
HKLM\Software\Microsoft\Windows\CurrentVersion\Run
HKCU\Software\Microsoft\Windows\CurrentVersion\Run
HKCU\Software\Microsoft\Windows\CurrentVersion\Policies\Explorer\Run
HKCU\Software\Microsoft\Windows\CurrentVersion\RunOnce
```

Startup folder (all users)

Startup folder (current user)

Adding Programs to the Run Keys As mentioned, you can either add values to these keys via the Registry Editor or you can use the Group Policy snap-in. To open the Group Policy window in Windows Vista Professional, select Start, Run, type **`gpedit.msc`**, and then click OK. In the Group Policy window, you have two choices:

- To work with startup programs for all users, select Computer Configuration, Administrative Templates, System, Logon. The items here will affect the Registry keys in the `HKLM` (all users) Registry hive.

- To work with startup programs for the current user, select User Configuration, Administrative Templates, System, Logon. The items here will affect the Registry keys in the `HKCU` (current user) hive.

Either way you'll see at least the following three items:

Run These Programs at User Logon—Use this item to add or remove startup programs using the `\Policies\Explorer\Run` keys in the Registry. To add a program, double-click the item, select the Enabled option, and then click Show. In the Show Contents dialog box, click Add, enter the full pathname of the program or script you want to run at startup, and then click OK.

Do Not Process the Run Once List—Use this item to toggle whether Windows Vista processes the `RunOnce` Registry keys (discussed in the previous section). Double-click this item and then activate the Enabled option to put this policy into effect; that is, programs listed in the `RunOnce` key are not launched at startup.

Do Not Process the Legacy Run List—Use this item to toggle whether Windows Vista processes the legacy `Run` keys. Double-click this item and then activate the Enabled option to put this policy into effect; that is, programs listed in the legacy Run key are not launched at startup.

Specifying Startup and Logon Scripts You also can use the Group Policy snap-in to specify script files to run at startup. You can specify script files at two places:

- Computer Configuration, Windows Settings, Scripts (Startup/Shutdown)—Use the Startup item to specify one or more script files to run each time the computer starts (and before the user logs on). Note that if you specify two or more scripts, Windows Vista runs them synchronously. That is, Windows Vista runs the first script, waits for it to finish, runs the second script, waits for it to finish, and so on.
- User Configuration, Windows Settings, Scripts (Logon/Logoff)—Use the Logon item to specify one or more script files to run each time any user logs on. Logon scripts are run asynchronously.

Finally, note that Windows Vista has policies dictating how these scripts run. For example, you can see the startup script policies by selecting Computer Configuration, Administrative Templates, System, Scripts. Three items affect startup scripts:

Run Logon Scripts Synchronously—If you enable this item, Windows Vista will run the logon scripts one at a time.

Run Startup Scripts Asynchronously—If you enable this item, Windows Vista will run the startup scripts at the same time.

Run Startup Scripts Visible—If you enable this item, Windows Vista will make the startup script commands visible to the user in a command window.

For logon scripts, a similar set of policies appears in the User Configuration, Administrative Templates, System, Scripts section.

CAUTION

Logon scripts are supposed to execute before the Windows Vista interface is displayed to the user. However, Windows Vista's improved logon can interfere with that by displaying the interface before all the scripts are done. Windows Vista runs both the computer logon scripts and the user logon scripts asynchronously, which greatly speeds up the logon time because no script has to wait for another to finish.

To prevent this, select Computer Configuration, Administrative Templates, System, Logon and enable the Always Wait for the Network at Computer Startup and Logon setting.

Using the Task Scheduler

Yet another way to set up a program or script to run at startup is to use the Task Scheduler. Here are the steps to follow:

1. Select Start, Control Panel, System and Maintenance, Scheduled Automated and Periodic Tasks.
2. Click Create Task.
3. In the General tab, use the Name text box to enter a name for the task.
4. In the Triggers tab, click New to display the New Trigger dialog box.
5. In the Begin the Task list, click one of the following and then click OK:

   At Log On—Choose this option to run the program only when you log on to Windows Vista.

   At Startup—Choose this option to run the program when your computer boots, no matter which user logs in.
6. In the Actions tab, click New to display the New Action dialog box.
7. In the Action list, select Start a Program.
8. Use the Program/Script text box to enter the path of the program or script.
9. Click OK.
10. Click OK.

Running a Program with the Administrator Account

As I explained earlier in this chapter, Windows Vista's User Account Control feature requires credentials from you when you attempt to run certain programs. This is not always the case, however. For example, if you start a command prompt session and attempt to redirect the output of a `DIR` command to a file in the root (as described earlier), the command will fail with an `Access is denied` error. Vista doesn't prompt you for credentials, it just aborts the operation.

To work around this problem, right-click the program you want to run and then click Run As Administrator. Enter your credentials and Windows Vista starts the program with the privileges of the Administrator account, which allows you to do anything you want.

TIP

In some cases, you might be able to set things up to always run a program under the Administrator account. Create a shortcut to the executable file, right-click the shortcut, and then click Properties. In the Compatibility tab, activate the Run This Program As an Administrator check box. Click OK.

It's worth noting here that if you need to run a program as a specific user, you can use the `RUNAS` command-line tool. You use `RUNAS` at the command prompt to specify the username, and Windows Vista then prompts you to enter the user's password. Here's the basic syntax (type **`RUNAS /?`** for the complete list of switches):

```
RUNAS /user:domain\user program
```

`/user:`*`domain\user`*	The *`user`* name under which you want the program to run. Replace *`domain`* with either the computer name (for a standalone or workgroup machine) or the domain name.
`program`	The full pathname and filename of the application. You need only use the file's primary name if the application resides within the current folder, the `%SystemRoot%` folder, the `%SystemRoot%\System32` folder, or a folder in the `PATH` variable.

Creating Application-Specific Paths

Earlier I told you about application-specific paths, which enable you to launch almost any 32-bit application simply by typing the name of its executable file, either in the Run dialog box or at the command prompt. You don't need to spell out the complete pathname. This pathless execution is handy, but it doesn't work in the following two situations:

- **16-bit applications**—These older programs don't store the paths to their executables in the Registry.
- **Documents**—You can't load a document just by typing its filename in the Run dialog box or at the command prompt unless the document is in the current folder.

To solve both these problems, and to handle the rare case when a 32-bit application doesn't create its own application-specific path, you can edit the Registry to add a path to an executable file (an application-specific path) or to a document (a document-specific path).

In the Registry Editor, open the following key:

```
HKLM\Software\Microsoft\Windows\CurrentVersion\App Paths
```

The `App Paths` key has subkeys for each installed 32-bit application. Each of these subkeys has one or both of the following settings:

`Default`—This setting spells out the path to the application's executable file. All the `App Paths` subkeys have this setting.

`Path`—This setting specifies one or more folders that contain files needed by the application. An application first looks for its files in the same folder as its executable file. If it can't find what it needs there, it checks the folder or folders listed in the `Path` setting. Not all `App Paths` subkeys use this setting.

5

To create an application-specific path, select the `App Paths` key, create a new subkey, and assign it the name of the application's executable file. For example, if the program's executable filename is `OLDAPP.EXE`, name the new subkey **`OLDAPP.EXE`**. For this new subkey, change the Default setting to the full pathname of the executable file.

TIP

You don't have to give the new `App Paths` subkey the name of the executable file. You can use any name you like as long as it ends with `.exe` and doesn't conflict with the name of an existing subkey.

Why does it have to end with `.exe`? Unless you specify otherwise, Windows Vista assumes that anything you enter in the Run dialog box or at the command prompt ends with `.exe`. Therefore, by ending the subkey with `.exe`, you need to type only the subkey's primary name. For example, if you name your new subkey `OLDAPP.EXE`, you can run the program by typing **`oldapp`** in the Run dialog box or at the command prompt.

You create document-specific paths the same way. (However, the document's file type must be registered with Windows Vista.) In that case, though, the Default setting takes on the full pathname of the document. Again, if you want to load the document just by typing its primary name, make sure that the new `App Paths` subkey uses the `.exe` extension.

Controlling Startup Programs with Windows Defender

Windows Defender is Vista's antispyware program, and you'll learn about its capabilities in detail in Chapter 21, "Implementing Windows Vista's Internet Security and Privacy

Features." For our purposes, Windows Defender comes with a feature called Software Explorer that enables you to view information about four types of programs: startup programs, currently running programs, network connected programs, and Winsock service providers. For the startup programs, you can use Software Explorer to either temporarily disable a program from running at startup, or you can remove it altogether from whatever startup nook it resides in (the Startup folder, a Registry key, and so on). Here are the steps to follow:

1. Select Start, All Programs, Windows Defender.
2. Click Tools.
3. Click Software Explorer and then enter your credentials when the User Account Control dialog box appears.
4. In the Software Explorer window, make sure that Startup Program is selected in the Category list. Windows Defender displays a list of programs that run at startup, as shown in Figure 5.4.

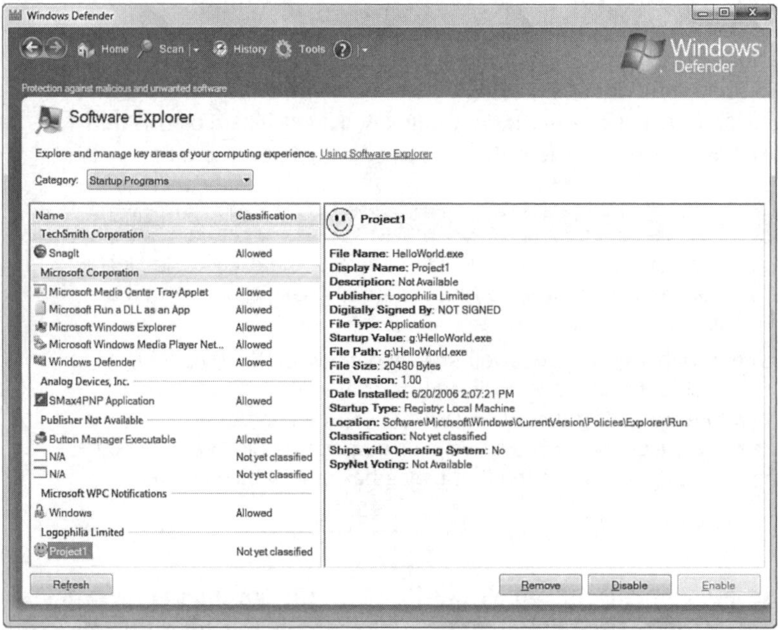

FIGURE 5.4 With Windows Defender's Software Explorer, you can display and control startup programs.

5. Click the program you want to work with. The Software Explorer displays the program's details on the right side of the window.

6. To temporarily prevent a program from running at startup, click Disable. If you never want to run the program at startup, click Remove instead.
7. When Windows Defender asks you to confirm, click Yes.

Understanding Application Compatibility

Most new software programs are certified as Windows Vista–compatible, meaning that they can be installed and run without mishap on any Windows Vista system. But what about older programs that were coded before Windows Vista was released? They can be a bit more problematic. Because Windows Vista is based on the code for Windows 2000—which was in turn based on Windows NT—programs that are compatible with those operating systems will probably (although not definitely) be compatible with Windows Vista. But the real problems lie with programs written for Windows 9x and Me. Windows Vista—even Windows Vista Home—uses a completely different code base than the old consumer versions of Windows, so it's inevitable that some of those legacy programs will either be unstable while running under Windows Vista or they won't run at all.

Why do such incompatibilities arise? One common reason is that the programmers of a legacy application hardwired certain data into the program's code. For example, installation programs often poll the operating system for its version number. If an application is designed for, say, Windows 95, the programmers might have set things up so that the application installs if and only if the operating system returns the Windows 95 version number. The program might run perfectly well under any later version of Windows, but this simplistic brain-dead version check prevents it from even installing on anything but Windows 95.

Another reason incompatibilities arise is that calls to **API** (application programming interface) functions return unexpected results. For example, the programmers of an old application might have assumed that the **FAT** (file allocation table) file system would always be the standard, so when checking for free disk space before installing the program, they'd expect to receive a number that is 2GB or less (the maximum size of a FAT partition). However, FAT32 and **NTFS** (NT file system) partitions can be considerably larger than 2GB, so a call to the API function that returns the amount of free space on a partition could return a number that blows out a memory buffer and crashes the installation program.

These types of problems might make it seem as though getting older programs to run under Windows Vista would be a nightmare. Fortunately, that's not usually true because the Windows Vista programmers did something very smart: Because many of these application incompatibilities are predictable, they gave Windows Vista the capability to make allowances for them and so enable many older programs to run under Windows Vista without modification. In Windows Vista, **application compatibility** refers to a set of concepts and technologies that enable the operating system to adjust its settings or behavior to compensate for the shortcomings of legacy programs. This section shows you how to work with Windows Vista's application compatibility tools.

CAUTION

Although application compatibility can work wonders to give aging programs new life under Vista, it doesn't mean that *every* legacy program will benefit. If history is any guide, some programs simply will not run under Vista, no matter which compatibility rabbits you pull out of Vista's hat. In some of these cases you may be able to get a program to run by installing a patch from the manufacturer, so check the program's website to see if updates are available that make the program Vista-friendly.

Determining Whether a Program Is Compatible with Windows Vista

One way to determine whether an application is compatible with Windows Vista is to go ahead and install it. If the program is not compatible with Windows Vista, you might see a dialog box similar to the one shown in Figure 5.5.

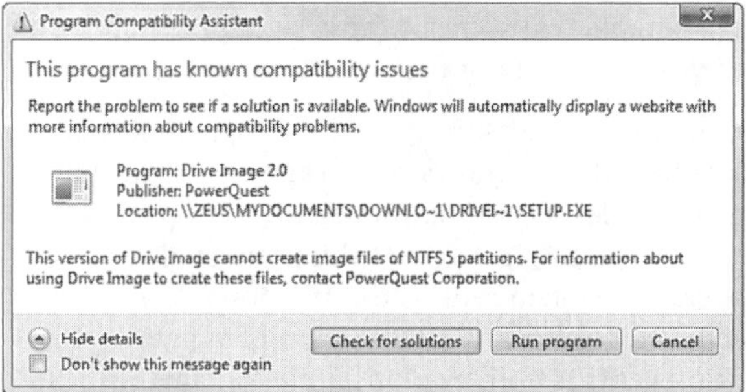

FIGURE 5.5 You might see a dialog box such as this if you try to install a program that isn't compatible with Windows Vista.

At this point you could click Run Program (in some dialog boxes, the button is named Continue), but this is a risky strategy because you can't be sure how the program will interact with Windows Vista. This approach is riskiest of all when dealing with disk utilities, backup software, antivirus programs, and other software that requires low-level control of the system. It's extremely unlikely that Windows Vista would ever allow such programs to run, but you should always upgrade such products to Windows Vista–compatible versions. A much safer route is to click Cancel to abort the installation and then visit the vendor's website or the Windows Update site to see whether a Windows Vista–friendly update is available. (You can often get the company's web address by clicking the Details button.)

NOTE

Where does the information in these dialog boxes come from? In the `%SystemRoot%\AppPatch` folder, Windows Vista has various system database (`.sdb`) files that contain messages such as the one shown in Figure 5.5 for all known applications that don't have compatibility fixes (discussed later in this section). The system database files aren't text files, so opening them with Notepad or WordPad will not allow you to read any of these stored messages.

A better approach is to find out in advance whether the program is compatible with Windows Vista. The most obvious way to do this is to look for the Designed for Windows Vista logo on the box. For older programs, check the manufacturer's website to see whether the company tells you that the program can be run under Windows Vista or if an upgrade is available. Alternatively, Microsoft has a web page that enables you to search on the name of a program or manufacturer to find out compatibility information: `http://www.microsoft.com/windows/catalog/`.

What if you're upgrading to Windows Vista and you want to know whether your installed software is compatible? The easiest way to find out is to use the Upgrade Advisor tool, which is available on the Windows Vista Professional CD. (The Windows Vista Home CD doesn't have the Upgrade Advisor.) Insert the Windows Vista Pro CD and, when the Welcome to Microsoft Windows Vista screen appears, click Check System Compatibility. Run through the Advisor's dialog boxes until you get to the report on system compatibility. This report will list software that doesn't support Windows Vista and possibly software that needs to be reinstalled after the Windows Vista setup has finished.

Understanding Compatibility Mode

To help you run programs under Windows Vista, especially those programs that worked properly in a previous version of Windows, Windows Vista offers a new way to run applications using **compatibility layers**. This means that Windows Vista runs the program by doing one or both of the following:

- **Running the program in a compatibility mode**—This involves emulating the behavior of previous version of Windows. Windows Vista can emulate the behavior of Windows 95, Windows 98, Windows Me, Windows NT 4.0 with Service Pack 5, and Windows 2000, as well as two more versions that are new to Windows Vista: Windows 2003 with Service Pack 1 and Windows XP with Service Pack 2.
- **Temporarily changing the system's visual display so that it's compatible with the program**—There are five possibilities here: setting the color depth to 256 colors, changing the screen resolution to 640×480, disabling Windows Vista's visual themes, disabling desktop composition, and disabling displaying scaling on high-DPI settings. Note that the last two settings are new to Windows Vista.

NOTE

Windows Vista and Microsoft often use the terms *compatibility layer* and *compatibility mode* interchangeably, depending on which compatibility tool you're using. In some cases, the emulations of previous Windows versions are called **operating system modes**.

These are the broad compatibility layers that Windows Vista supports. As you'll see a bit later, Windows Vista also offers fine-tuned control over these and other compatibility settings. For now, however, to set up a compatibility layer, you right-click the program's executable file or a shortcut to the file, click Properties, and then display the Compatibility tab in the property sheet that appears. To set the compatibility mode, activate the Run this Program in Compatibility Mode For check box (see Figure 5.6), and then use the list to choose the Windows version the program requires. You can also use the check boxes in the Display Settings group to adjust the video mode that Windows Vista will switch to when you use the program.

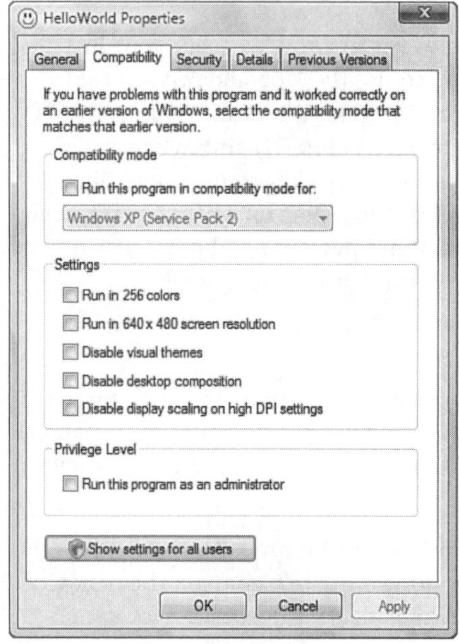

FIGURE 5.6 In the property sheet for an executable file, use the Compatibility tab to set the compatibility layer for the program.

Scripting Compatibility Layers

What do you do if you have a batch file that needs to run one or more programs within a temporary compatibility layer? You can handle this by using the following command within the batch file before you start the program:

```
SET __COMPAT_LAYER=[!]layer1 [layer2 ...]
```

Here, *layer1* and *layer2* are codes that represent the compatibility layers. Table 5.1 lists the 16 codes you can use.

TABLE 5.1 Codes to Use When Scripting Compatibility Layers

Code	Compatibility Layer
Win95	Windows 95
Win98	Windows 98 / Windows Me
Win2000	Windows 2000
NTSP5	Windows NT 4.0 SP 5
WinXPSp2	Windows XP (Service Pack 2)
WinSrv03Sp1	Windows Server 2003 (Service Pack 1)
256Color	256 color
640x480	640×480 screen resolution
DisableThemes	Disable visual themes
DisableDWM	Disable desktop composition
HighDpiAware	Disable display scaling on high DPI settings
RunAsAdmin	Run this program as an administrator
International	This layer handles incompatibilities caused by double-byte character sets
LUA	**Limited User Access**—This layer redirects some Registry and file operations to nonrestricted areas for users that don't have permission to access restricted areas (such as the HKLM key)
LUACleanup	**Limited User Access Cleanup**—This layer removes the Registry settings and files that were redirected using the LUA layer
ProfilesSetup	**Profile Setup Support**—This layer is used for older programs that install only for the current user; the layer ensures that the program is installed for all users

5

If you've already applied one or more layers to the program using the techniques from the previous section, you can tell Windows Vista not to use one of those layers by preceding its keyword with the ! symbol. Also, to turn off the compatibility layers, run the command without any parameters, like so:

```
SET __COMPAT_LAYER=
```

For example, the following commands set the compatibility layers to Windows 95 and 256 colors, run a program, and then remove the layers:

```
SET __COMPAT_LAYER=Win95 256Color
D:\Legacy\oldapp.exe
SET __COMPAT_LAYER=
```

NOTE

The compatibility layers created by SET __COMPAT_LAYER apply also to any processes that the affected application spawns. For example, if you set the Windows 95 layer for Setup.exe, the same layer will also apply to any other executable called by Setup.exe. You can find more information about the SET __COMPAT_LAYER command and its parameters at http://support.microsoft.com/default.aspx?scid=kb;en-us;286705.

NOTE

When you execute a program using a compatibility layer, Windows Vista creates an environment within which the program can function properly. For example, a program running under the `Win95` layer actually believes that Windows 95 is the operating system. Windows Vista accomplishes that not only by returning the Windows 95 version number when the program calls the `GetVersion` or `GetVersionEx` API functions, but also by "fixing" other incompatibilities between Windows 95 and Windows Vista. For example, Windows 95 programs expect components such as Calculator and Solitaire to be in the `%SystemRoot%` folder, but in Windows Vista these are in the `%SystemRoot%\System32\` folder. The `Win95` layer intercepts such file calls and reroutes them to the appropriate location.

The `Win95` layer consists of dozens of such fixes, which are part of a large database of incompatibilities maintained by Microsoft. As of this writing, hundreds of incompatibilities have been identified, and others might be found in the future. To get access to all these fixes and so get fine-tuned control over the compatibility issues relating to any legacy program, you need to use Application Compatibility Toolkit (ACT). Download and install the latest version of ACT (version 5.0 was in beta testing as of this writing) from the following Microsoft web page: go.microsoft.com/fwlink/?LinkID=36665

From Here

Here are a few other places in the book where you'll find information related to the material presented in this chapter:

- For more startup options, see Chapter 2, "Customizing and Troubleshooting the Windows Vista Startup."
- You can use the Open With list to open a document with a different program. For the details, see the section in Chapter 4 titled "Customizing Windows Vista's Open With List."
- For more information about group policies, see the section in Chapter 10 titled "Implementing Group Policies with Windows Vista."
- For a complete look at the inner workings of the Registry, see Chapter 11, "Getting to Know the Windows Vista Registry."
- To learn how to run programs using a script, see the section in Chapter 12 titled "Programming the WshShell Object."
- To maximize program performance, see the section in Chapter 14 titled "Optimizing Applications."
- For the details on Windows Defender, see the section in Chapter 21 titled "Thwarting Spyware with Windows Defender."
- To learn how to run programs from the command prompt, see the section in Appendix B titled "Starting Applications from the Command Prompt."

CHAPTER 6

Getting the Most Out of User Accounts

IN THIS CHAPTER

- Understanding Security Groups
- User Account Control: Smarter User Privileges
- Creating and Managing User Accounts
- Working With the User Accounts Dialog Box
- Working with the Local Users and Groups Snap-In
- Setting Account Policies
- Working with Users and Groups from the Command Line
- Creating and Enforcing Bulletproof Passwords
- Sharing Files with Other Users
- Using Parental Controls to Restrict Computer Usage
- Sharing Your Computer Securely

Do you share your computer with other people either at work or at home? Then you're no doubt all too aware of one undeniable fact of human psychology: People are individuals with minds of their own! One person prefers Windows in a black-and-purple color scheme; another person just loves that annoying Peace wallpaper; yet another person prefers to have a zillion shortcuts on the Windows desktop; and, of course, everybody uses a different mix of applications. How can you possibly satisfy all those diverse tastes and prevent people from coming to blows?

It's a lot easier than you might think. Windows Vista lets you set up a different user account for each person who uses the computer. A **user account** is a username (and an optional password) that uniquely identifies a person who uses the system. The user account enables Windows Vista to control the user's **privileges**; that is, the user's access to system resources (**permissions**) and the user's ability to run system tasks (**rights**). Standalone and workgroup machines use *local* user accounts that are maintained on the computer, whereas domain machines use *global* user accounts that are maintained on the domain controller. This chapter looks at local user accounts.

Understanding Security Groups

Security for Windows Vista user accounts is handled mostly (and most easily) by assigning each user to a particular security group. For example, the built-in Administrator account and the user account you created during the Windows Vista setup process are part of the Administrators group. Each security group is defined with a specific set of permissions and rights, and any user added to a group is automatically granted that group's permissions and rights. There are two main security groups:

Administrators—Members of this group have complete control over the computer, meaning they can access all folders and files, install and uninstall programs (including legacy programs) and devices, create, modify, and remove user accounts, install Windows updates, service packs, and fixes, use Safe mode, repair Windows, take ownership of objects, and more.

Users—Members of this group (also known as **Standard Users**) can access files only in their own folders and in the computer's shared folders, change their account's password, picture, and run programs and install programs that don't require administrative-level rights.

In addition to those groups, Windows Vista also defines up to 11 others that you'll use less often. Note that the permissions assigned to these groups are automatically assigned to members of the Administrators group. This means that if you have an administrator account, you don't also have to be a member of any other group in order to perform the task's specific to that group. Here's the list of groups:

Backup Operators—Members of this group can access the Backup program and use it to back up and restore folders and files, no matter what permissions are set on those objects.

Cryptographic Operators—Members of this group can perform cryptographic tasks.

Distributed COM Users—Members of this group can start, activate, and use Distributed COM (DCOM) objects.

Guests—Members of this group have the same privileges as those of the Users group. The exception is the default Guest account, which is not allowed to change its account password.

IIS_USRS—Members of this group can work with a remote Internet Information Server.

Network Configuration Operators—Members of this group have a subset of the Administrator-level rights that enables them to install and configure networking features.

Performance Log Users—Members of this group can use the Windows Performance Diagnostic Console snap-in to monitor performance counters, logs, and alerts, both locally and remotely.

Performance Monitor Users—Members of this group can use the Windows Performance Diagnostic Console snap-in to monitor performance counters only, both locally and remotely.

Power Users—Members of this group (also known as **Standard Users**) have a subset of the Administrator group privileges. Power Users can't back up or restore files, replace system files, take ownership of files, or install or remove device drivers. In addition, Power

Users can't install applications that explicitly require the user to be a member of the Administrators group.

Remote Desktop Users—Members of this group can log on to the computer from a remote location using the Remote Desktop feature.

Replicator—Members of this group can replicate files across a domain.

Each user is also assigned a **user profile** that contains all the user's folders and files, as well as the user's Windows settings. The folders and files are stored in `\%SystemDrive%\Users\user`, where *user* is the username; for the current user, this folder is designated by the `%UserProfile%` variable. This location contains a number of subfolders that hold the user's document folders (Documents, Pictures, Music, and so on), desktop icons and subfolders (Desktop), Internet Explorer favorites (Favorites), contacts (Contacts), saved searches (Searches), and more.

There are also a number of user folders within the hidden `%UserProfile%\AppData` folder that contain the user's application data. Some are in `%UserProfile%\AppData\Local`, whereas others are in `%UserProfile%\AppData\Roaming` (supposedly because they'll be used with a **roaming profile**—a network-based user profile that enables you to log on to any computer and see your profile data. Table 6.1 lists some of the more important of these application data subfolders.

TABLE 6.1 Some Hidden User Profile Folders

Content	Location
Internet Explorer Cache	`\Local\Microsoft\Windows\Temporary Internet Files`
Internet Explorer History	`\Local\Microsoft\Windows\History`
Internet Explorer Cookies	`\Roaming\Microsoft\Windows\Cookies`
All Programs	`\Roaming\Microsoft\Windows\Start Menu\Programs`
Recent Items	`\Roaming\Microsoft\Windows\Recent`
Send To	`\Roaming\Microsoft\Windows\SendTo`
Start Menu	`\Roaming\Microsoft\Windows\Start Menu`
Startup	`\Roaming\Microsoft\Windows\Start Menu\Programs\Startup`

User Account Control: Smarter User Privileges

New Most (I'm actually tempted to say the vast majority) of the security-related problems in recent versions of Windows boiled down to a single root cause: Most users were running Windows with administrator-level permissions. Administrators can do *anything* to a Windows machine, including installing programs, adding devices, updating drivers, installing updates and patches, changing Registry settings, running administrative tools, and creating and modifying user accounts. This is convenient, but it leads to a huge problem: Any malware that insinuates itself onto your system will also be capable of operating with administrative permissions, thus enabling the program to wreak havoc on the computer and just about anything connected to it.

Windows XP tried to solve the problem by creating a second-tier account level called the **limited user**, which had only very basic permissions. Unfortunately, there were three gaping holes in this "solution":

- XP prompted you to create one or more user accounts during setup, but it didn't force you to create one. If you skipped this part, XP started under the Administrator account.
- Even if you elected to create users, the setup program didn't give you an option for setting the account security level. Therefore, any account you created during XP's setup was automatically added to the Administrators group.
- If you created a limited user account, you probably didn't keep it for long because XP hobbled the account so badly that you couldn't use it to do anything but the most basic computer tasks. You couldn't even install most programs because they generally require write permission for the `%SystemRoot%` folder and the Registry, and limited users lacked that permission.

Windows Vista tries once again to solve this problem. The new solution is called User Account Control and it uses a principle called the **least-privileged user**. The idea behind this is to create an account level that has no more permissions than it requires. Again, such accounts are prevented from editing the Registry and performing other administrative tasks. However, these users can perform other day-to-day tasks:

- Install programs and updates
- Add printer drivers
- Change wireless security options (such as adding a WEP or WPA key)

In Windows Vista, the least-privileged user concept arrives in the form of a new account type called the standard user. This means that Vista has three basic account levels:

- **Administrator account**—This built-in account can do anything to the computer.
- **Administrators group**—Members of this group (except the Administrator account) run as standard users but are able to elevate their privileges when required just by clicking a button in a dialog box (see the next section).
- **Standard users group**—These are the least-privileged users, although they, too, can elevate their privileges when needed. However, they require access to an administrator password to do so.

Elevating Privileges

This idea of elevating privileges is at the heart of Vista's new security model. In Windows Vista, you could use the Run As command to run a task as a different user (that is, one with higher privileges). In Vista, you usually don't need to do this because Vista prompts you for the elevation automatically.

If you're a member of the Administrators group, you run with the privileges of a standard user for extra security. When you attempt a task that requires administrative privileges, Vista prompts for your consent by displaying a User Account Control dialog box similar to the one shown in Figure 6.1. Click Control to permit the task to proceed. If this dialog box appears unexpectedly, it's possible that a malware program is trying to perform some task that requires administrative privileges; you can thwart that task by clicking Cancel instead.

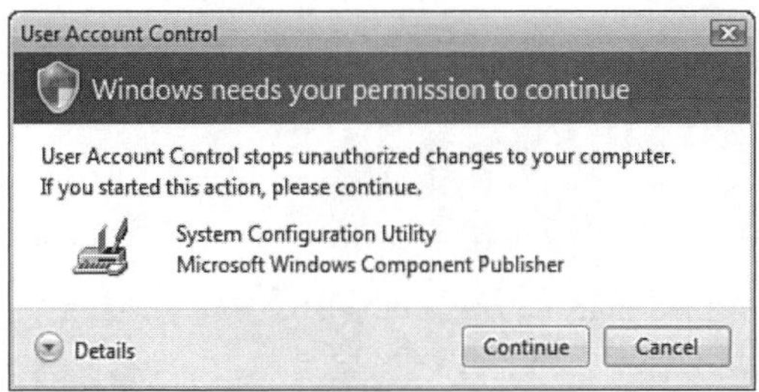

FIGURE 6.1 When an administrator launches a task that requires administrative privileges, Windows Vista displays this dialog box to ask for consent.

If you're running as a standard user and attempt a task that requires administrative privileges, Vista uses an extra level of protection. That is, instead of just prompting you for consent, it prompts you for the credentials of an administrator, as shown in Figure 6.2. If your system has multiple administrator accounts, each one is shown in this dialog box. Type the password for any administrator account shown, and then click Submit. Again, if this dialog box shows up unexpectedly, it might be malware, so you should click Cancel to prevent the task from going through.

Note, too, that in both cases Windows Vista switches to Secure Desktop mode, which means that you can't do anything else with Vista until you give your consent or credentials or cancel the operation. Vista indicates the secure desktop by darkening everything on the screen except the User Account Control dialog box.

NOTE

User Account Control seems eminently sensible on the surface, but Microsoft has not always implemented it in a sensible way. For example, sometimes you are prompted for elevation during simple tasks such as file deletions and renames, or when you change the system date or time. This has led to a backlash against User Account Control in some circles, and I'm sympathetic to a point. However, all the people who are complaining about User Account Control are Alpha Geeks who, by definition, are tweaking settings, installing drivers and programs, and generally pushing Vista to its limits. Of course, you're going to get hit with lots of UAC dialog boxes under those conditions. However, the average user—even the average power user—doesn't tweak the system all that often, so I think UAC will be much less of a problem than its critics suggest.

FIGURE 6.2 When a standard user launches a task that requires administrative privileges, Windows Vista displays this dialog box to ask for administrative credentials.

As you saw in the "Running a Program with the Administrator Account" section of Chapter 5, "Installing and Running Applications," it's also possible to elevate your privileges for any individual program. You do this by right-clicking the program file or shortcut and then clicking Run as Administrator.

File and Registry Virtualization

You might be wondering how secure Windows Vista really is if a standard user can install programs. Doesn't that mean that malware can install as well? No—Vista implements a new model for installation security. In Vista, you need administrative privileges to write anything to the `%SystemRoot%` folder (usually `C:\Windows`), the `%ProgramFiles%` folder (usually `C:\Program Files`), and the Registry. Vista handles this for standard users in two ways:

- During a program installation, Vista first prompts the user for credentials (that is, Vista displays one of the Windows Security dialog boxes shown earlier in Figures 6.1 and 6.2). If they are provided, Vista gives permission to the program installer to write to `%SystemRoot%`, `%ProgramFiles%`, and the Registry.
- If the user cannot provide credentials, Vista uses a technique called **file and Registry virtualization**, which creates virtual `%SystemRoot%` and `%ProgramFiles%` folders, and a virtual `HKEY_LOCAL_MACHINE` Registry key, all of which are stored with the user's files. This enables the installer to proceed without jeopardizing actual system files.

User Account Control Policies

You can customize User Account Control to a certain extent by using group policies. In the Local Security Settings snap-in (press Windows Logo+R, type **`secpol.msc`**, click OK, and then provide your credentials), open the Security Settings, Local Policies, Security Options branch. Here you'll find nine policies related to User Account Control (as shown in Figure 6.3):

- **User Account Control: Admin Approval Mode for the Built-In Administrator Account**—This policy controls whether the Administrator account falls under User Account Control. If you enable this policy, the Administrator account is treated like any other account in the Administrators group and you must click Continue in the consent dialog box when Windows Vista requires approval for an action.
- **User Account Control: Behavior of the Elevation Prompt for Administrators in Admin Approval Mode**—This policy controls the prompt that appears when an administrator requires elevated privileges. The default setting is Prompt for Consent, where the user clicks either Continue or Cancel. You can also choose Prompt for Credentials to force the user to type his or her password. If you choose No Prompt, administrators cannot elevate their privileges.
- **User Account Control: Behavior of the Elevation Prompt for Standard Users**—This policy controls the prompt that appears when a standard user requires elevated privileges. The default setting is Prompt for Credentials, to force the user to type an administrator password. You can also choose No Prompt to prevent standard users from elevating their privileges.
- **User Account Control: Detect Application Installs and Prompt for Elevation**—Use this policy to enable or disable automatic privilege elevation while installing programs.
- **User Account Control: Only Elevate Executables That Are Signed and Validated**—Use this policy to enable or disable whether Vista checks the security signature of any program that asks for elevated privileges.
- **User Account Control: Only Elevate UIAccess Applications That Are Installed in Secure Locations**—Use this policy to enable or disable whether Vista allows elevation for accessibility applications that require access to the user interface of another window only if they are installed in a secure location (such as the `%ProgramFiles%` folder).
- **User Account Control: Run All Administrators in Admin Approval Mode**—Use this policy to enable or disable running administrators (excluding the Administrator account) as standard users.
- **User Account Control: Switch to the Secure Desktop When Prompting for Elevation**—Use this policy to enable or disable whether Vista switches to the secure desktop when the elevation prompts appear.

- **User Account Control: Virtualize File and Registry Write Failures to Per-User Locations**—Use this policy to enable or disable file and Registry virtualization for standard users.

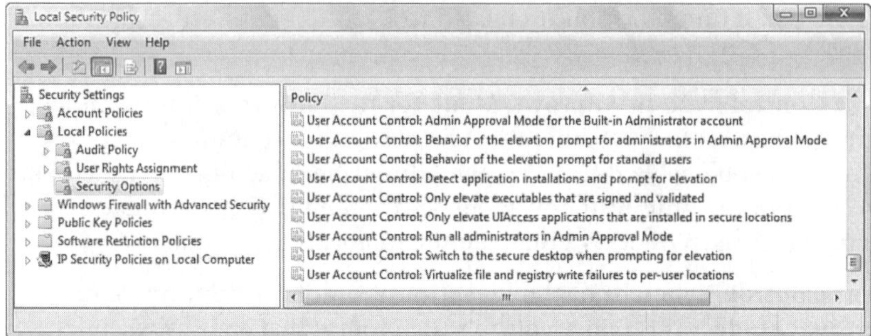

FIGURE 6.3 Vista policies related to User Account Control.

The rest of this chapter shows you the various methods Windows Vista offers to create, modify, and remove local user accounts.

Creating and Managing User Accounts

Windows Vista has a number of methods for working with user accounts. The most direct route is to use Control Panel's Manage Accounts window (select Start, Control Panel, Add or Remove User Accounts, and then enter your credentials). You create a new user account by following these steps:

1. Click Create a New Account. The Create New Account window appears.
2. Type the name for the account. The name can be up to 20 characters and must be unique on the system.
3. Activate either Administrator (to add the user to the Administrators group) or Standard User (to add the user to the Users group).
4. Click Create Account.

To modify an existing account, you have two choices:

- To modify your own account, click Go to the Main User Accounts Page to open the User Accounts window. Note that the links you see are slightly different from the ones listed next. For example, instead of Change Name, you see Change Your Name.
- To modify another user's account, click the account in the Manager Accounts window.

The latter technique opens the Change an Account window, shown in Figure 6.4, which includes some of or all the following tasks:

- **Change the Account Name**—Click this link to change the account's username. In the Rename Account window, type the new name and click Change Name.
- **Create a Password**—You see this task only if the user doesn't yet have an account password. Click the link to open the Create Password window, type the password twice, type a password hint, and then click Change Password.

NOTE

A strong password is the first line of defense when it comes to local computer security. Before setting up a password for an account, check out the section "Creating and Enforcing Bulletproof Passwords," later in this chapter.

CAUTION

The **password hint** is text that Vista displays in the Welcome screen if you type an incorrect password (see "Recovering from a Forgotten Password," later in this chapter). Because the hint is visible to anyone trying to log on to your machine, make the hint as vague as possible but still useful to you if you forget your password.

- **Change the Password**—If the user already has a password, click this link to change it. In the Change Password window, type the password twice, type a password hint, and then click Change Password.
- **Remove the Password**—If the user already has a password, click this link to delete it. In the Remove Password window, click Remove Password.
- **Change the Picture**—Click this link to change the random picture that Vista assigns to each account. In the Choose Picture window, either click one of the displayed images and then click Change Picture, or click Browse for More Pictures to use the Open dialog box to pick out an image from the `Pictures` folder (or wherever you like).
- **Set Up Parental Controls**—Click this link to apply Parental Controls to the user. See "Using Parental Controls to Restrict Computer Usage," later in this chapter.
- **Change the Account Type**—Click this link to open the Change Account Type window. Click either Standard User or Administrator and then click Change Account Type.
- **Delete the Account**—Click this link to delete the user account. In the Delete Account window, click either Delete Files or Keep Files (to delete or keep the user's documents), and then click Delete Account.

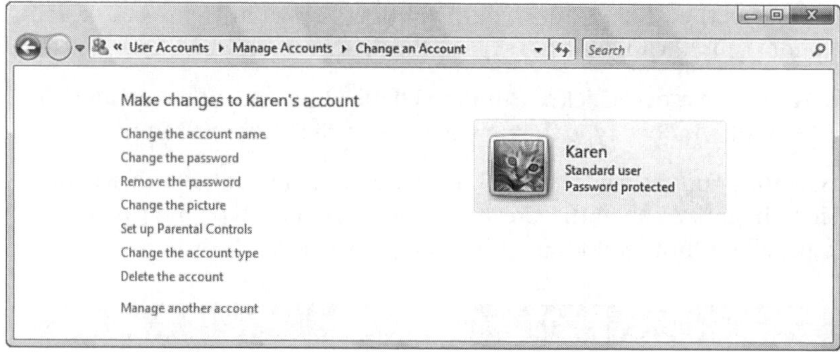

FIGURE 6.4 In the Manage Accounts window, click an account to see this list of tasks for changing the user's account.

Working with the User Accounts Dialog Box

Control Panel's User Accounts window has one major limitation: It offers only the Administrator and Limited (Users) account types. If you want to assign a user to one of the other groups, you have to use the User Accounts dialog box. You get there by following these steps:

1. Press Windows Logo+R (or select Start, All Programs, Accessories, Run) to display the Run dialog box.
2. In the Open text box, type **`control userpasswords2`**.
3. Click OK.
4. Enter your User Account Control credentials. Windows Vista displays the User Accounts dialog box, shown in Figure 6.5.

To enable the list of users, make sure that the Users Must Enter a User Name and Password to Use This Computer check box is activated.

Adding a New User

To add a new user via the User Accounts dialog box, follow these steps:

1. Click Add to launch the Add New User Wizard.
2. Type the new user's User Name (no more than 20 characters, and it must be unique). You can also type the user's Full Name and Description, but these are optional. Click Next.
3. Type the user's Password and type it again in the Confirm Password text box. Click Next.

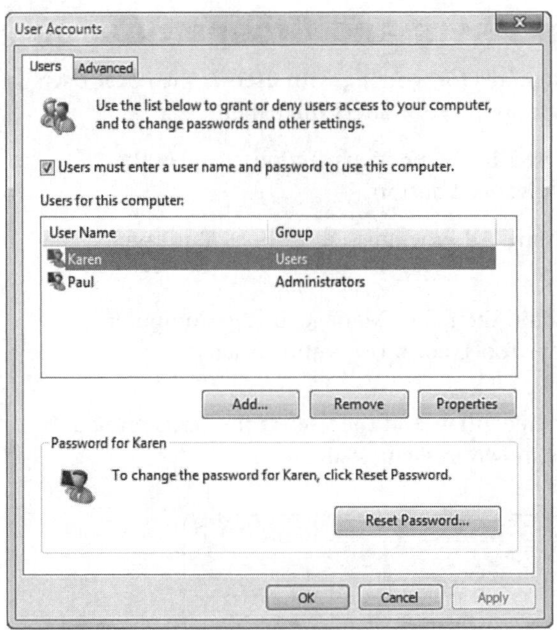

FIGURE 6.5 The User Accounts dialog box enables you to assign users to any Windows Vista security group.

4. Activate the option that specifies the user's security group: Standard User (Users group), Administrator (Administrator group), or Other. Activate the latter to assign the user to any of the 13 default Windows Vista groups.

5. Click Finish.

Performing Other User Tasks

Here's a list of the other tasks you can perform in the User Accounts dialog box:

- **Delete a user**—Select the user and click Remove. When Vista asks you to confirm, click Yes.
- **Change the user's name or group**—Select the user and click Properties to display the user's property sheet. Use the General tab to change the username; use the Group Membership tab to assign the user to a different group. Note that you can only assign the user to a single group using this method. If you need to assign a user to multiple groups, see "Working with the Local Users and Groups Snap-In," next.
- **Change the user's password**—Select the user and click Reset Password. Type the password in the New Password and Confirm New Password text boxes and click OK.

Working with the Local Users and Groups Snap-In

The most powerful of the Windows Vista tools for working with users is the Local Users and Groups MMC snap-in. To load this snap-in, Vista offers three methods:

- In the User Accounts dialog box (refer to the previous section), display the Advanced tab and then click the Advanced button.
- Press Windows Logo+R (or select Start, All Programs, Accessories, Run) type **`lusrmgr.msc`**, and click OK.
- Select Start, right-click Computer, and then click Manage. In the Computer Management window, select System Tools, Local Users and Groups.

Whichever method you use, enter your credentials and then select the Users branch to see a list of the users on your system, as shown in Figure 6.6.

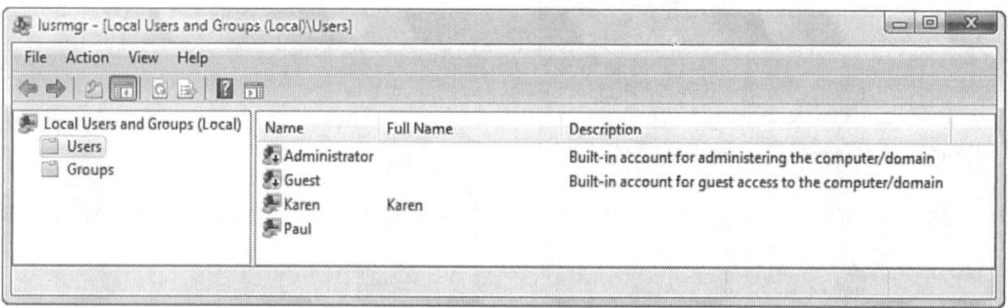

FIGURE 6.6 The Users branch lists all the system's users and enables you to add, modify, and delete users.

From here, you can perform the following tasks:

- **Add a new user**—Make sure that no user is selected and then select Action, New User. In the New User dialog box, type the User Name, Password, and Confirm Password. (I discuss the password-related check boxes in this dialog box later in this chapter; see "User Account Password Options.") Click Create.
- **Change a user's name**—Right-click the user and then click Rename.
- **Change a user's password**—Right-click the user and then click Set Password.
- **Add a user to a group**—Double-click the user to open the user's property sheet. In the Member Of tab, click Add and use the Enter the Object Names to Select box to enter the group name. If you're not sure of the name, click Advanced to open the Select Groups dialog box, click Find Now to list all the groups, select the group, and then click OK. Click OK to close the property sheet.

NOTE

Another way to add a user to a group is to select the Groups branch in the Local Users and Groups snap-in. Right-click the group you want to work with, and then click Add to Group. Now click Add, type the username in the Enter the Object Names to Select box, and then click OK.

- **Remove a user from a group**—Double-click the user to open the user's property sheet. In the Member Of tab, select the group from which you want the user removed, and then click Remove. Click OK to close the property sheet.
- **Change a user's profile**—Double-click the user to open the user's property sheet. Use the Profile tab to change the profile path, logon script, and home folder (activate the Local Path option to specify a local folder; or activate Connect to specify a shared network folder).
- **Disable an account**—Double-click the user to open the user's property sheet. In the General tab, activate the Account Is Disabled check box.
- **Delete a user**—Right-click the user and then click Delete. When Vista asks you to confirm, click Yes.

Setting Account Policies

Windows Vista Pro offers several sets of policies that affect user accounts. There are three kinds of account policies: security options, user rights, and account lockout policies. The next three sections take you through these policies.

Setting Account Security Policies

To see these policies, you have two choices:

- Open the Group Policy editor (press Windows Logo+R, type **`gpedit.msc`**, and click OK) and select Computer Configuration, Windows Settings, Security Settings, Local Policies, Security Options, as shown in Figure 6.7.
- Launch the Local Security Settings snap-in (press Windows Logo+R, type **`secpol.msc`**, and click OK) and select Security Settings, Local Policies, Security Options.

The Accounts grouping has five policies:

- **Administrator Account Status**—Use this policy to enable or disable the Administrator account. This is useful if you think someone else might be logging on as the Administrator. (A less drastic solution would be to change the Administrator password or rename the Administrator account.)

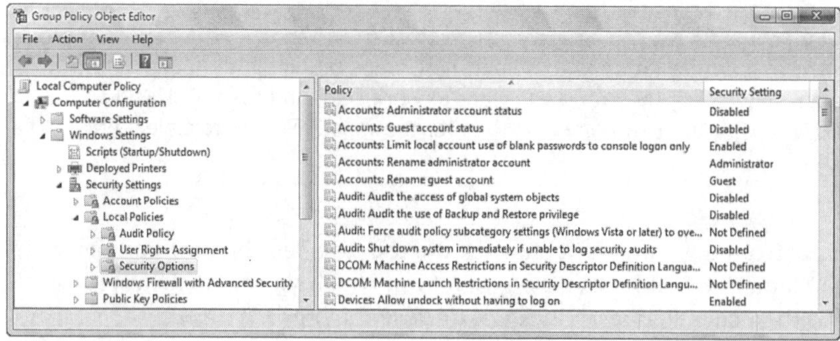

FIGURE 6.7 In the Security Options branch, use the five Accounts policies to configure security for your accounts.

NOTE

The Administrator account is always used during a Safe Mode boot, even if you disable the account.

- **Guest Account Status**—Use this option to enable or disable the Guest account.
- **Limit Local Account Use of Blank Passwords to Console Logon Only**—When this option is enabled, Windows Vista allows users with blank passwords to log on to the system directly only by using the Welcome screen. Such users can't log on via either the `RunAs` command or remotely over a network. This policy modifies the following Registry setting:

  ```
  HKLM\SYSTEM\CurrentControlSet\Control\Lsa\limitblankpassworduse
  ```

- **Rename Administrator Account**—Use this option to change the name of the Administrator account.
- **Rename Guest Account**—Use this option to change the name of the Guest account.

Setting User Rights Policies

Windows Vista has a long list of policies associated with user rights. To view these policies, you have two choices:

- In the Group Policy editor, select Computer Configuration, Windows Settings, Security Settings, Local Policies, User Rights Assignment, as shown in Figure 6.8.
- In the Local Security Policy snap-in, select Security Settings, Local Policies, User Rights Assignment.

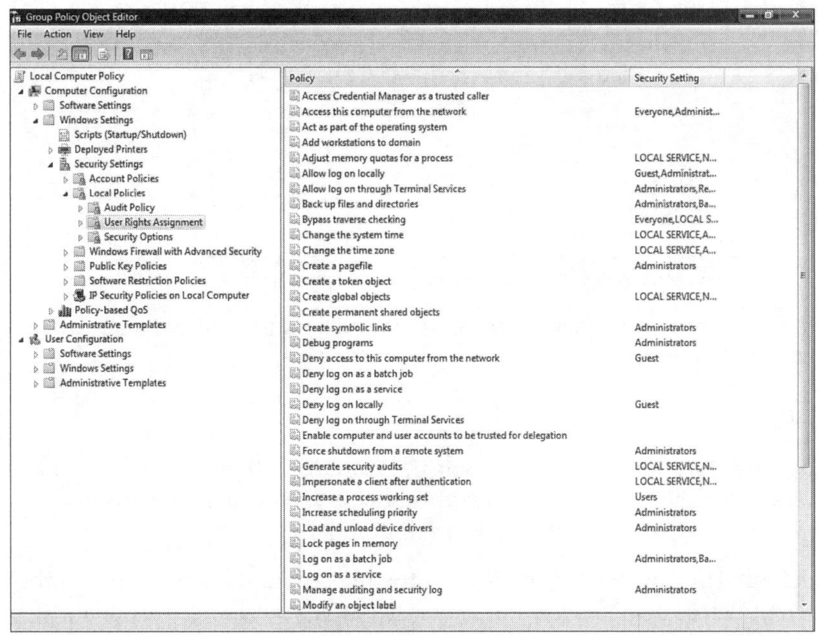

FIGURE 6.8 In the User Rights Assignment branch, use the policies to configure the rights assigned to users or groups.

Each policy is a specific task or action, such as Back Up Files and Directories, Deny Logon Locally, and Shut Down the System. For each task or action, the Security Setting column shows the users and groups who can perform the task or to whom the action applies. To change the setting, double-click the policy. Click Add User or Group to add an object to the policy; or delete an object from the policy by selecting it and clicking Remove.

Setting Account Lockout Policies

Last of all, Windows Vista has a few policies that determine when an account gets **locked out**, which means the user is unable to log on. A lock out occurs when the user fails to log on after a specified number of attempts. This is a good security feature because it prevents an unauthorized user from trying a number of different passwords. Use either of the following methods to view these policies:

- In the Group Policy editor, select Computer Configuration, Windows Settings, Security Settings, Account Policies, Account Lockout Policy, as shown in Figure 6.9.
- In the Local Security Policy snap-in, select Security Settings, Account Policies, Account Lockout Policy.

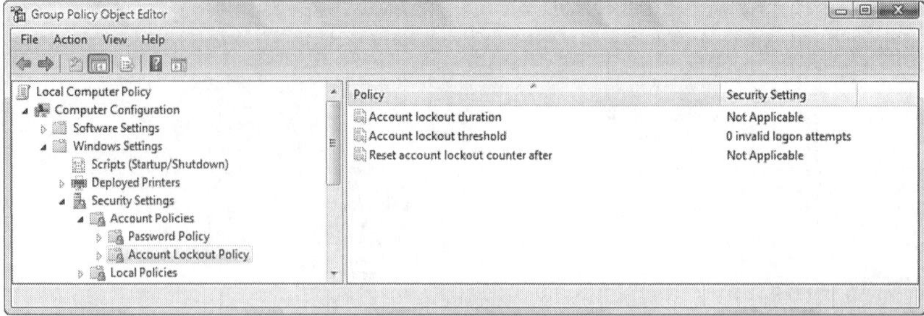

FIGURE 6.9 In the Account Lockout Policy branch, use the policies to configure when an account gets locked out of the system.

There are three policies:

- **Account Lockout Duration**—This policy sets the amount of time, in minutes, that the user is locked out. Note that, to change this policy, you must set the Account Lockout Threshold (described next) to a nonzero number.
- **Account Lockout Threshold**—This policy sets the maximum number of logons the user can attempt before being locked out. Note that after you change this to a nonzero value, Windows Vista offers to set the other two policies to 30 minutes.
- **Reset Account Lockout Counter After**—This policy sets the amount of time, in minutes, after which the counter that tracks the number of invalid logons is reset to 0.

Working with Users and Groups from the Command Line

You can script your user and group chores by taking advantage of the `NET USER` and `NET LOCALGROUP` commands. These commands enable you to add users, change passwords, modify accounts, add users to groups, and remove users from groups. Note that you must run these commands under the Administrator account, so first follow these steps to open a command prompt session:

1. Select Start, All Programs, Accessories.
2. Right-click Command Prompt and then click Run as Administrator.
3. Enter your User Account Control credentials.

The `NET USER` Command

You use the `NET USER` command to add users, set account passwords, disable accounts, set account options (such as the times of day the user is allowed to log on), and remove accounts. For local users, the `NET USER` command has the following syntax:

```
NET USER [username [password ¦ * ¦ /RANDOM] [/ADD] [/DELETE] [options]]
```

username	The name of the user you want to add or work with. If you run `NET USER` with only the name of an existing user, the command displays the user's account data.
password	The password you want to assign to the user. If you use `*`, Windows Vista prompts you for the password; if you use the `/RANDOM` switch, Windows Vista assigns a random password (containing eight characters, consisting of a random mix of letters, numbers, and symbols), and then displays the password on the console.
`/ADD`	Creates a new user account.
`/DELETE`	Deletes the specified user account.
options	These are optional switches you can append to the command:

`/ACTIVE:{YES ¦ NO}`	Specifies whether the account is active or disabled.
`/EXPIRES:{`*date*` ¦ NEVER}`	The date (expressed in the system's Short Date format) on which the account expires.
`/HOMEDIR:`*path*	The home folder for the user, which should be a subfolder within `%SystemDrive%\Users` (make sure that the folder exists).
`/PASSWORDCHG:{YES ¦ NO}`	Specifies whether the user is allowed to change his password.
`/PASSWORDREQ:{YES ¦ NO}`	Specifies whether the user is required to have a password.
`/PROFILEPATH:`*path*	The folder that contains the user's profile.
`/SCRIPTPATH:`*path*	The folder that contains the user's logon script.

`/TIMES:{`*times*` ¦ ALL}`	Specifies the times that the user is allowed to log on to the system. Use single days or day ranges (for example, `Sa` or `M-F`). For times, use 24-hour notation or 12-hour notation with `am` or `pm`. Separate the day and time with a comma, and separate day/time combinations with semicolons. Here are some examples:
	`M-F,9am-5pm`
	`M,W,F,08:00-13:00`
	`Sa,12pm-6pm;Su,1pm-5pm`

9

CAUTION

If you use the /RANDOM switch to create a random password, be sure to make a note of the new password so that you can communicate it to the new user.

Note, too, that if you execute NET USER without any parameters, it displays a list of the local user accounts.

TIP

If you want to force a user to log off when his logon hours expire, open the Group Policy editor and select Computer Configuration, Windows Settings, Security Settings, Local Policies, Security Options. In the Network Security category, enable the Force Logoff When Logon Hours Expire policy.

The NET LOCALGROUP Command

You use the NET LOCALGROUP command to add users to and remove users from a specified security group. NET LOCALGROUP has the following syntax:

```
NET LOCALGROUP [group name1 [name2 ...] {/ADD | /DELETE}
```

group	This is the name of the security group with which you want to work.
name1 [*name2* ...]	One or more usernames that you want to add or delete, separated by spaces.
/ADD	Adds the user or users to the group.
/DELETE	Removes the user or users from the group.

Creating and Enforcing Bulletproof Passwords

Windows Vista sometimes gives the impression that passwords aren't all that important. After all, the user account you specify during setup is supplied with administrative-level privileges *and* a password is optional. That's a dangerous setup, because it means that anyone can start your computer and automatically get administrative rights, and that standard users can elevate permissions without needing a password. However, these problems are easily remedied by supplying a password to *all* local users. This section gives you some pointers for creating strong passwords and runs through Windows Vista's password-related options and policies.

Creating a Strong Password

Ideally, when you're creating a password for a user, you want to pick one that that provides maximum protection without sacrificing convenience. Keeping in mind that the whole point of a password is to select one that nobody can guess, here are some guidelines you can follow when choosing a password:

TIP

Consider submitting a password similar to (but *not* the same as) the one you want to use to an online password complexity checker. I use Microsoft's (www.microsoft.com/athome/security/privacy/password_checker.mspx), but a Google search on "password complexity checker" will reveal any others.

- **Use passwords that are at least eight characters long**—Shorter passwords are susceptible to programs that just try every letter combination. You can combine the 26 letters of the alphabet into about 12 million different five-letter word combinations, which is no big deal for a fast program. If you bump things up to eight-letter passwords, however, the total number of combinations rises to 200 *billion*, which would take even the fastest computer quite a while. If you use 12-letter passwords, as many experts recommend, the number of combinations goes beyond mind-boggling: 90 *quadrillion*, or 90,000 trillion!
- **Don't be too obvious**—Because forgetting a password is inconvenient, many people use meaningful words or numbers so that their password will be easier to remember. Unfortunately, this means that they often use extremely obvious things such as their name, the name of a family member or colleague, their birth date or Social Security number, or even their system username. Being this obvious is just asking for trouble.
- **Don't use single words**—Many crackers break into accounts by using "dictionary programs" that just try every word in the dictionary. So, yes, *xiphoid* is an obscure word that no person would ever guess, but a good dictionary program will figure it out in seconds flat. Using two or more words in your password (or **pass phrase**, as multiword passwords are called) is still easy to remember, and would take much longer to crack by a brute force program.
- **Use a misspelled word**—Misspelling a word is an easy way to fool a dictionary program. (Make sure, of course, that the resulting arrangement of letters doesn't spell some other word.)
- **Mix uppercase and lowercase letters**—Windows Vista passwords are case-sensitive, which means that if your password is, say, *YUMMY ZIMA*, trying *yummy zima* won't work. You can really throw snoops for a loop by mixing the case. Something like *yuMmY zIMa* would be almost impossible to figure out.
- **Add numbers to your password**—You can throw more permutations and combinations into the mix by adding a few numbers to your password.
- **Include a few punctuation marks and symbols**—For extra variety, toss in one or more punctuation marks or special symbols, such as % or #.

- **Try using acronyms**—One of the best ways to get a password that appears random but is easy to remember is to create an acronym out of a favorite quotation, saying, or book title. For example, if you've just read *The Seven Habits of Highly Effective People,* you could use the password T7HoHEP.
- **Don't write down your password**—After going to all this trouble to create an indestructible password, don't blow it by writing it on a sticky note and then attaching it to your keyboard or monitor! Even writing it on a piece of paper and then throwing the paper away is dangerous. Determined crackers have been known to go through a company's trash looking for passwords (this is known in the trade as **Dumpster diving**). Also, don't use the password itself as your Windows Vista password hint.
- **Don't tell your password to anyone**—If you've thought of a particularly clever password, don't suddenly become unclever and tell someone. Your password should be stored in your head alongside all those "wasted youth" things you don't want anyone to know about.
- **Change your password regularly**—If you change your password often (say, once a month or so), even if some skulker does get access to your account, at least he'll have it for only a relatively short period.

User Account Password Options

Each user account has a number of options related to passwords. To view these options, open the Local Users and Groups snap-in (as described earlier in this chapter), and double-click the user with which you want to work. There are three password-related check boxes in the property sheet that appears:

User Must Change Password at Next Logon—If you activate this check box, the next time the user logs on, she will see a dialog box with the message that she is required to change her password. When the user clicks OK, the Change Password dialog box appears and the user enters her new password.

User Cannot Change Password—Activate this check box to prevent the user from changing the password.

Password Never Expires—If you deactivate this check box, the user's password will expire. The expiration date is determined by the Maximum Password Age policy, discussed in the next section.

Taking Advantage of Windows Vista's Password Policies

Windows Vista maintains a small set of useful password-related policies that govern settings such as when passwords expire and the minimum length of a password. There are two methods you can use to view these policies:

- In the Group Policy editor, select Computer Configuration, Windows Settings, Security Settings, Account Policies, Password Policy, as shown in Figure 6.10.
- In the Local Security Policy snap-in, select Security Settings, Account Policies, Password Policy.

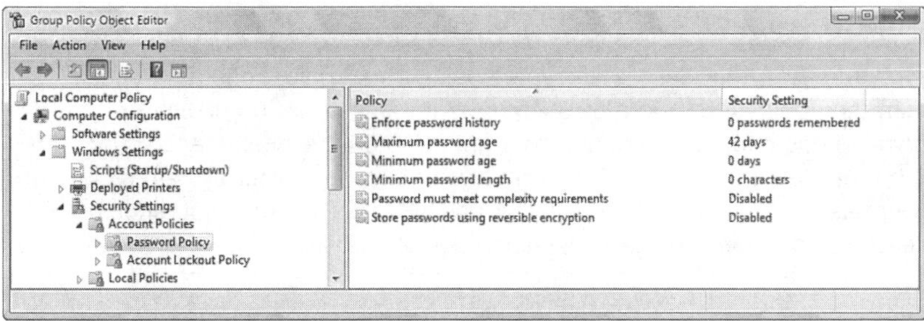

FIGURE 6.10 In the Password Policy branch, use the policies to enforce strong passwords and other protections.

There are six policies:

- **Enforce Password History**—This policy determines the number of old passwords that Windows Vista stores for each user. This is to prevent a user from reusing an old password. For example, if you set this value to 10, the user can't reuse a password until he or she has used at least 10 other passwords. Enter a number between 0 and 24.
- **Maximum Password Age**—This policy sets the number of days after which passwords expire. This applies only to user accounts where the Password Never Expires property has been disabled (refer to the previous section). Enter a number between 1 and 999.
- **Minimum Password Age**—This policy sets the numbers of days that a password must be in effect before the user can change it. Enter a number between 1 and 998 (but less than the Maximum Password Age value).
- **Minimum Password Length**—This policy sets the minimum number of characters for the password. Enter a number between 0 and 14 (where 0 means no password is required).
- **Password Must Meet Complexity Requirements**—If you enable this policy, Windows Vista examines each new password and accepts it only if it meets the following criteria: It doesn't contain all or part of the username; it's at least six characters long; and it contains characters from three of the following four categories: uppercase letters, lowercase letters, digits (0–9), and nonalphanumeric characters (such as $ and #).

- **Store Passwords Using Reversible Encryption**—Enabling this policy tells Windows Vista to store user passwords using reversible encryption. Some applications require this, but they're rare and you should never need to enable this policy because it makes your passwords much less secure.

CAUTION

Reversible encryption means that data is encrypted using a particular code as a seed value, and you can then decrypt the data by applying that same code. Unfortunately, this type of encryption has been cracked, and programs to break reversible encryption are easy to find on the Net. This means that hackers with access to your system can easily decrypt your password store and see all your passwords. Therefore, you should never enable the Store Passwords Using Reversible Encryption policy.

Recovering from a Forgotten Password

Few things in life are as frustrating as a forgotten password. To avoid this headache, Windows Vista offers a couple of precautions that you can take now just in case you forget your password.

The first precaution is called the password hint, discussed earlier (refer to "Creating and Managing User Accounts"), which is a word, phrase, or other mnemonic device that can help you remember your password. To see the hint in the Welcome screen, type any password and press Enter. When Vista tells you the password is incorrect, click OK. Vista redisplays the Password text box with the hint below it.

The second precaution you can take is the Password Reset Disk. This is a floppy disk that enables you to reset the password on your account without knowing the old password. To create a Password Reset Disk, follow these steps:

1. Log on as the user for whom you want to create the disk.
2. Select Start, Control Panel, User Accounts and Family Safety, User Accounts.
3. In the Tasks pane, click Create a Password Reset Disk. This launches the Forgotten Password Wizard.
4. Run through the wizard's dialog boxes. (Note that you'll need a blank, formatted floppy disk.)

The password reset disk contains a single file named `Userkey.psw`, which is an encrypted backup version of your password. Be sure to save this disk in a secure location and, just to be safe, don't label the disk. If you need to use this disk, follow these steps:

1. Start Windows Vista normally.
2. When you get to the Welcome screen, leave your password blank and press the Enter key. Windows Vista will then tell you the password is incorrect.

3. Click OK.
4. Click the Reset Password link.
5. In the initial Password Reset Wizard dialog box, click Next.
6. Insert the password reset disk and click Next.
7. Type a new password (twice), type a password hint, and click Next.
8. Click Finish.

Sharing Files with Other Users

Vista Home Basic

Each user has his or her own profile, which means (in part) his or her own user folders, and Vista requires administrator-level credentials for one user to mess with another user's folders. If you want to share files with other users, Vista gives you two methods: the Public folder and Sharing. The latter is the same as network sharing, so see Chapter 23's "Sharing Resources with the Network" section.

Unfortunately, Vista doesn't make it easy to get to the Public folder, for some reason. The only route is to open any folder window, click the top-level drop-down list in the address bar (as shown in Figure 6.11), and then click Public.

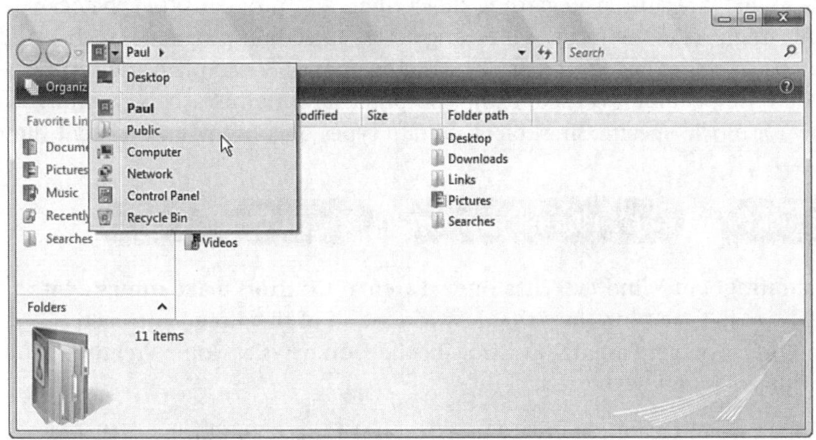

FIGURE 6.11 To get to the hard-to-find Public folder, in any folder window, drop-down the list for the address bar's top-level item and then click Public.

Figure 6.12 shows the Public folder and its subfolders. To share a file with other users, copy (or cut) it from its original folder and paste it in one of the Public subfolders.

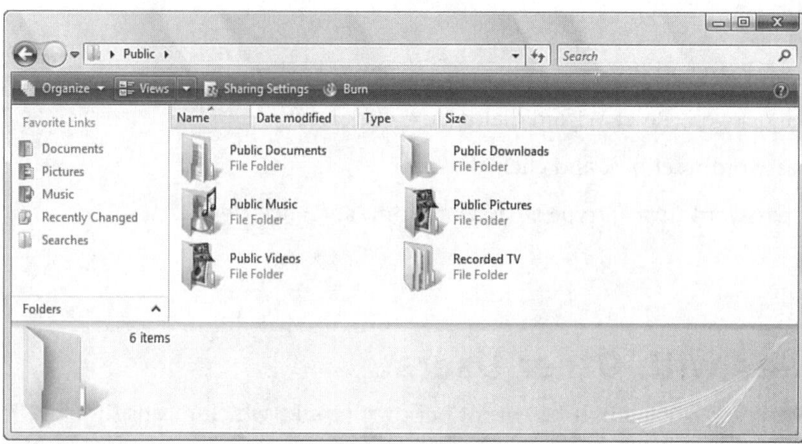

FIGURE 6.12 Copy or move a file to one of the Public subfolders to share the file with other users.

Using Parental Controls to Restrict Computer Usage

If you have children who share your computer, or if you're setting up a computer for the kids' use, it's wise to take precautions regarding the content and programs that they can access. Locally, this might take the form of blocking access to certain programs (such as your financial software), using ratings to control which games they can play, and setting time limits on when the computer is used. If the computer has Internet access, you might also want to allow (or block) specific sites, block certain types of content, and prevent file downloads.

Vista Home Basic Vista Home Premium Vista Ultimate Edition

All this sounds daunting, but Windows Vista's new Parental Controls make things a bit easier by offering an easy-to-use interface that lets you set all of the aforementioned options and lots more. (You get Parental Controls in the Home Basic, Home Premium, and Ultimate editions of Windows Vista.)

Before you begin, be sure to create a standard user account for each child that uses the computer. When that's done, you get to Parental Controls by select Start, Control Panel, Set Up Parental Controls. Enter your credentials to get to the Parental Controls window, and then click the user you want to work with to get to the User Controls window.

Activating Parental Controls and Activity Reporting

You should activate two options here (see Figure 6.13):

- **Parental Controls**—Click On, Enforce Current Settings. This enables the Windows Vista Web Filter, and the Time Limits, Games, and Allow and Block Specific Programs links in the Settings area.
- **Activity Reporting**—Click On, Collect Information About Computer Usage. This tells Vista to track system events such as blocked logon attempts and attempted changes to user accounts, system date and time, and system settings.

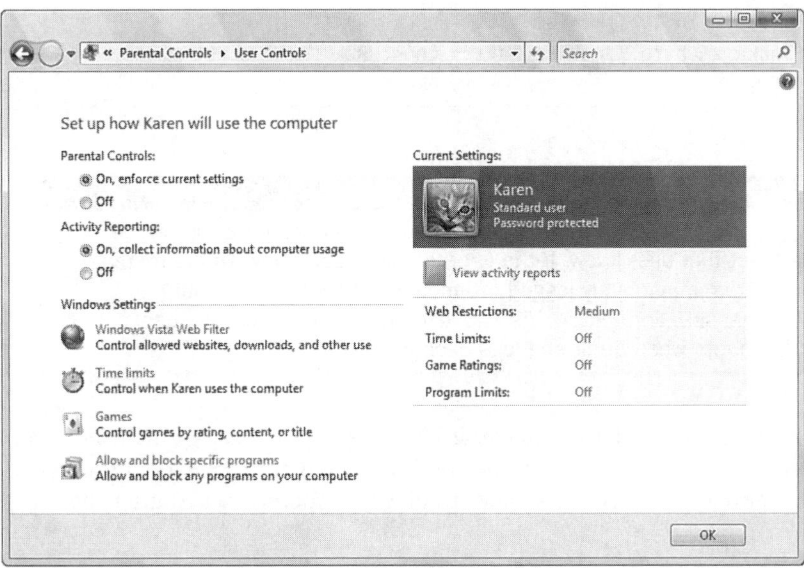

FIGURE 6.13 The User Controls page enables you to set up web, time, game, and program restrictions for the selected user.

The User Controls window gives you four links to use when setting up the controls for this user:

- **Windows Vista Web Filter**—Click this link to display the Web Restrictions page. Here you can allow or block specific websites, set up general site restrictions (High, Medium, None, or Custom), and block file downloads. If you select the Custom Web restriction level, then you can also block specific content categories (such as Pornography, Mature Content, and Bomb Making).

TIP

To make your life easier, you can import lists of allowed or blocked sites. First, create a new text file and change the extension to `Web Allow Block List` (for example, `MyURLs.Web Allow Block List`). Open the file and add the following text to start:

```
<WebAddresses>
</WebAddresses>
```

Between these lines, add a new line for each site using the following format:

```
<URL AllowBlock="n">address</URL>
```

Replace *n* with 1 for a site you want to allow, or 2 for a site you want to block, and replace *address* with the site URL. Here's an example:

```
<WebAddresses>
<URL AllowBlock="1">http://www.goodcleanfun.com</URL>
<URL AllowBlock="1">http://www.wholesomestuff.com</URL>
<URL AllowBlock="2">http://www.smut.com</URL>
<URL AllowBlock="2">http://www.depravity.com</URL>
</WebAddresses>
```

NOTE

If the user is logged on when a restricted time approaches, an icon appears in the notification area to let that user know. If the user is still logged on when the restricted time occurs, the user is immediately logged off and cannot log back on until the restricted time has passed. Fortunately, Vista is kind enough to restore the user's programs and documents when he or she logs back on.

- **Time Limits**—Click this link to display the Time Restrictions page, which shows a grid where each square represents an hour during the day for each day of the week, as shown in Figure 6.14. Click the squares to block computer usage during the selected times.
- **Games**—Click this link to display the Game Controls page. Here you can allow or disallow all games, restrict games based on ratings and contents, and block or allow specific games. You'll see how this works in the next section.
- **Allow and Block Specific Programs**—Click this link to display the Application Restrictions page, which displays a list of the programs on your computer. Activate the *User* Can Only Use the Programs I Allow option and then click the check boxes for the programs you want to allow the person to use.

Example: Setting Up Parental Controls for Games

If you have kids, chances are, they have a computer—either their own or one shared with the rest of the family—and, chances are, they play games on that computer. That's not a problem when they are being supervised, but few of us have the time or energy to sit beside our kids for each and every computer session—and the older the kid, the more likely that a hovering adult will be seen as an interloper. In other words, for all but the youngest users, your children will have some unsupervised gaming time at the computer.

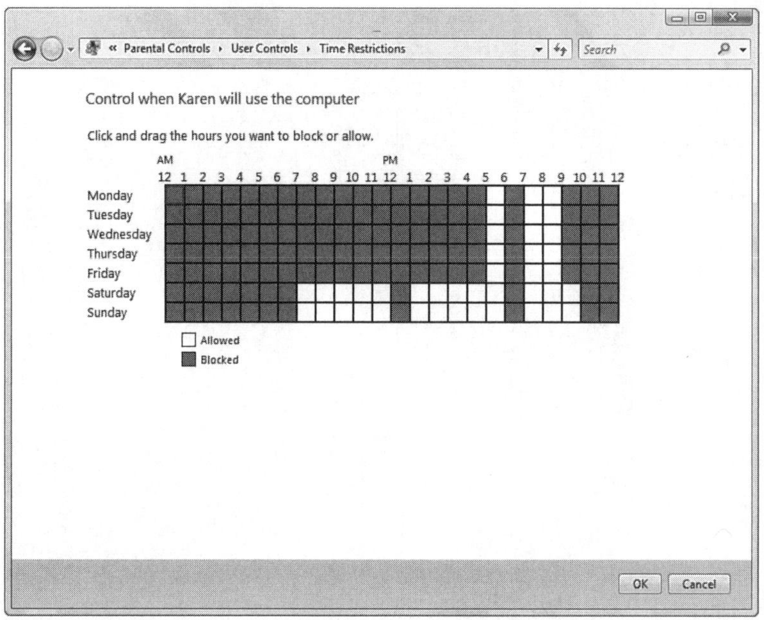

FIGURE 6.14 Use the grid on the Time Restrictions page to block computer access during specified hours.

To avoid worrying about whether your 8-year-old is playing Grand Theft Auto or something equally unsuitable, you can take advantage of the Game Controls section that enables you to control gaming using ratings and content descriptors.

Before setting up the controls, you should select the rating system you want to use. Return to the Parental Controls window and then click the Select a Games Ratings System link to display the Game Rating Systems window shown in Figure 6.15. Select the rating system you prefer and then click OK to return to the Parent Controls window.

Click the user you want to work with to display the User Controls window. Activate the On, Enforce Current Settings option (if you haven't done so already), and then click Games to display the Game Controls window, shown in Figure 6.16.

The next three sections run through the three methods you can use to control game play.

Turn Off Game Play

If your kids are too young to play any games, or if you'd prefer that they spend time on the computer working on more constructive pursuits, you can turn off game playing altogether. In the Can *UserName* Play Games? section, select No to prevent the user named *UserName* from launching any games from the Games Explorer. If you select Yes instead, you can use the techniques in the next two sections to control the games the user can play.

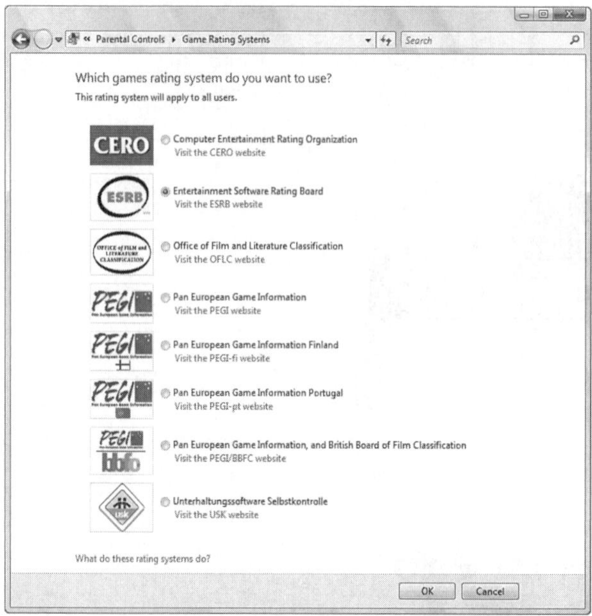

FIGURE 6.15 Use the Game Rating Systems window to choose the rating system you want to use with parental controls.

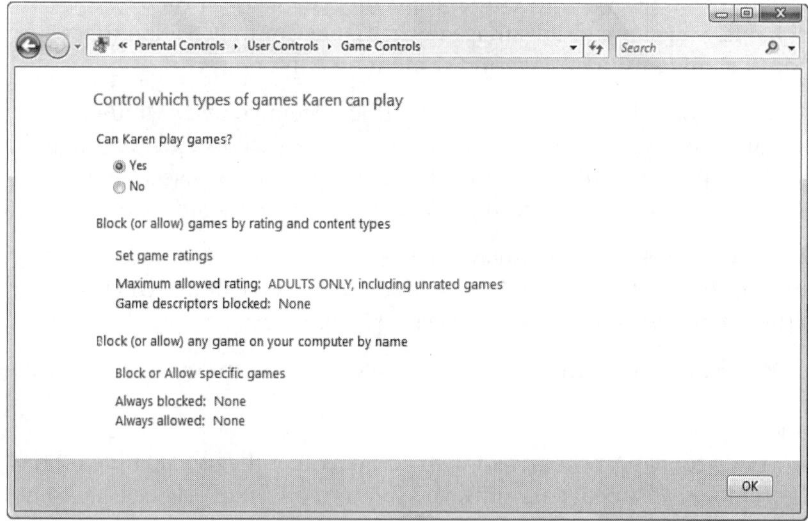

FIGURE 6.16 Use the Game Controls window to set the gaming restrictions for the selected user.

Controlling Games via Ratings and Descriptors

Instead of shutting off all game play, you're more likely to want to prevent each user from playing certain types of games. The easiest way to do that is to use game ratings and content descriptors. In the Game Controls window, click Set Game Ratings to display the Game Restrictions window, shown in Figure 6.17.

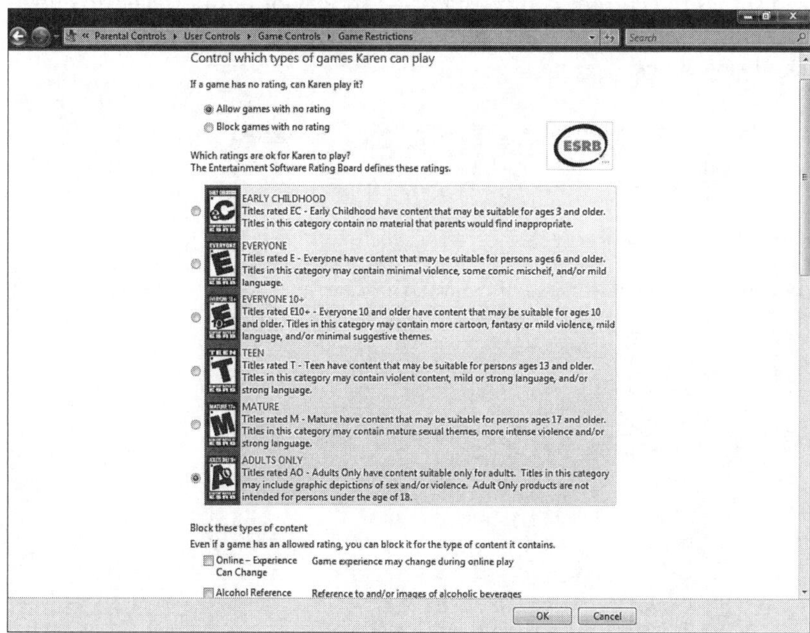

FIGURE 6.17 Use the Game Restrictions window to control game playing using ratings and content descriptors.

Click the rating option that represents the highest rating the user is allowed to play. For example, if you're using the ESRB rating system and you select the Teen option, the user will be able to play games rated as Early Childhood, Everyone, Everyone 10+, and Teen. He or she will not be able to play games rated as Mature or Adults Only.

You can also prevent the user from playing unrated games by selecting the Block Games with No Rating option.

You can also block games based on content descriptors. If you scroll down in the Game Restrictions window, you see the complete set of content descriptors, each with its own check box. For each check box you activate, the user will not be able to run any games that include that content description, even if the game has a rating that you allow.

Blocking and Allowing Specific Games

You might want to fine-tune your game controls by overriding the restrictions you've set up based on ratings and content descriptors. For example, you might have activated the Block Games with No Rating option, but you have an unrated game on your system that you want to allow the kids to play. Similarly, there might be a game that Vista allows based on the ratings and descriptors, but you'd feel more comfortable blocking access to the game.

In the Game Controls window, click Block or Allow Specific Games to display the Game Overrides window, shown in Figure 6.18. The table displays the title and rating of your installed games, and shows the current control status—Can Play or Cannot Play. To allow the user to play a specific game, click Always Allow; to prevent the user from playing a specific game, click Always Block.

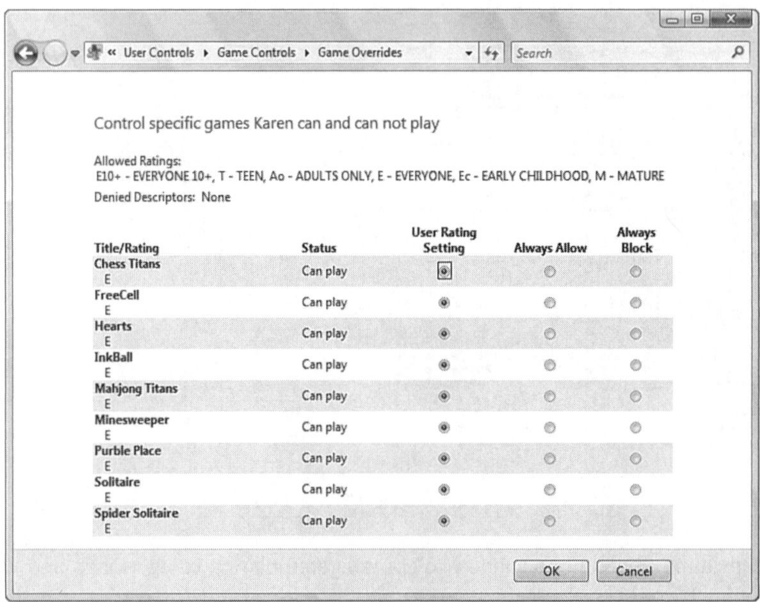

FIGURE 6.18 Use the Game Overrides window to allow or block specific games.

Sharing Your Computer Securely

If you're the only person who uses your computer, you don't have to worry all that much about the security of your user profile—that is, your files and Windows Vista settings. However, if you share your computer with other people, either at home or at the office, you need to set up some kind of security to ensure that each user has his "own" Windows and can't mess with anyone else's (either purposely or accidentally). Here's a list of security precautions to set up when sharing your computer (these techniques have been discussed earlier in this chapter, except where noted):

- **Create an account for each user**—Everyone who uses the computer, even if they use it only occasionally, should have her own user account. (If a user needs to access the computer rarely, or only once, activate the Guest account and let him use that. You should disable the Guest account after the user finishes his session.)

- **Remove unused accounts**—If you have accounts set up for users who no longer require access to the computer, you should delete those accounts.
- **Limit the number of administrators**—Members of the Administrators group can do *anything* in Windows Vista simply by clicking Submit in the User Account Control dialog box. These powerful accounts should be kept to a minimum. Ideally, your system should have just one (besides the built-in Administrator account).
- **Rename the Administrator account**—Renaming the Administrator account ensures that no other user can be certain of the name of the computer's top-level user.
- **Put all other accounts in the Users (Standard users) group**—Most users can perform almost all of their everyday chores with the permissions and rights assigned to the Users group, so that's the group you should use for all other accounts.
- **Use strong passwords on all accounts**—Supply each account with a strong password so that no user can access another's account by logging on with a blank or simple password.
- **Set up each account with a screensaver and be sure the screensaver resumes to the Welcome screen**—To do this, right-click the desktop, click Personalize, and then click Screen Saver. Choose an item in the Screen Saver, and then activate the On Resume, Display Welcome Screen check box.
- **Lock your computer**—When you leave your desk for any length of time, be sure to lock your computer. Either select Start, Lock or press Windows Logo+L. This displays the Welcome screen, and no one else can use your computer without entering your password.
- **Use disk quotas**—To prevent users from taking up an inordinate amount of hard disk space (think MP3 downloads), set up disk quotas for each user. To enable quotas, select Start, Computer, right-click a hard drive, and then click Properties to display the disk's property sheet. Display the Quota tab, click Show Quota Settings, enter your credentials, and then activate the Enable Quota Management check box.

From Here

Here are a few other places in the both to turn to for information related to user accounts and other aspects of this chapter:

- For some logon tips and techniques, see the section in Chapter 2 titled "Useful Windows Vista Logon Strategies."
- To learn more about running a program under the Administrator account, see the section in Chapter 5 titled "Running a Program with the Administrator Account."
- For the details on group policies, see the section in Chapter 10 titled "Implementing Group Policies with Windows Vista."

- To learn how to work with the Registry, see Chapter 11, "Getting to Know the Windows Vista Registry."
- For information on sharing Windows Mail within a single user account, see the section in Chapter 19 titled "Working with Identities."
- You need to set up user accounts for the people with whom you want to share resources in a peer-to-peer network. For the details, see the section in Chapter 23 titled "Sharing Resources with the Network."

CHAPTER 7

Working with Digital Media

IN THIS CHAPTER

- Setting AutoPlay Defaults
- Digital Audio in Windows Vista
- Using Windows Photo Gallery
- Easy Listening in Windows Media Player 11
- Tips for Working with Windows Media Player

The English language is a veritable factory of new words and phrases. Inventive wordsmiths in all fields are constantly forging new additions to the lexicon by blending words, attaching morphemic tidbits to existing words, and creating neologisms out of thin air. Some of these new words strike a chord in popular culture and go through what I call the "cachet-to-cliché" syndrome. In other words, the word is suddenly on the lips of cocktail party participants and water-cooler conversationalists everywhere, and on the fingertips of countless columnists and editorialists. As soon as the word takes root, however, the backlash begins. Rants of the if-I-hear-the-word-*x*-one-more-time-I'll-scream variety start to appear, Lake Superior State University includes the word in its annual list of phrases that should be stricken from the language, and so on.

The word *multimedia* went through this riches-to-rags scenario a few of years ago. Buoyed by the promise of media-rich interactive applications and games, techies and nontechies alike quickly made multimedia their favorite buzzword. It didn't take long, however, for the bloom to come off the multimedia rose.

Part of the problem was that when multimedia first became a big deal in the early 1990s, the average computer just wasn't powerful enough to handle the extra demands made on the system. Not only that, but Windows' support for multimedia was sporadic and half-hearted. That's all changed now, however. The typical PC sold today has more than enough horsepower to handle basic multimedia, and Windows Vista has a number of slick new features that let developers and end-users alike incorporate multimedia seamlessly into their work. Now it doesn't much matter that the word *multimedia* has more or less been replaced by the phrase *digital media* because what really matters is that people can get down to the more practical matter of creating exciting media-enhanced documents.

The basic digital media features of Windows Vista are easy enough to master, but there are plenty of hidden and obscure features that you should know about, and I'll take you through them in this chapter.

Setting AutoPlay Defaults

The AutoPlay feature dictates the program that runs automatically when you insert removable media into a slot in the computer. We've had AutoPlay for CDs since Windows 95, and Windows XP added AutoPlay support for most types of removable media, including DVDs, flash drives, and memory cards.

AutoPlay has become more sophisticated over the years, to the point that XP offered several choices when you inserted removable media, and those choices depended on the contents of the media. For music files, for example, AutoPlay could play or rip the files in Windows Media Player or just open a folder window to view the files. For pictures, AutoPlay could launch the Scanner and Camera Wizard, start a slideshow, launch the Photo Printing Wizard, or view the images. In addition, many third-party programs could tie into the AutoPlay feature and add their own actions to the AutoPlay menu (for example, to play music files in a different program or to edit pictures in an image-editing program).

However, customizing AutoPlay has never been easy. You could always choose a default action when the AutoPlay window appeared, but what if you wanted to change the default? In XP, you configured AutoPlay by opening the property sheet for a drive and then displaying the AutoPlay tab. You then used a drop-down list to choose the content type, clicked the default action, and then clicked Apply. From there you had to repeat this procedure for all the different content types: music files, pictures, video files, mixed content, music CD, DVD movie, and blank CD. Finally, you had to run through all of these steps for all the other removable drives on your system. No doubt sensing that users had better things to do, Microsoft has greatly streamlined the customization of AutoPlay defaults in Windows Vista.

New Before getting to the customization feature, I should point out that Windows Vista also implements an improved AutoPlay window. Figure 7.1 shows an example. As you can see, Vista's AutoPlay window divides the options into two sections: The top section contains actions specific to the dominant content type on the media, and the bottom section—General Options—contains actions not related to content.

To customize the AutoPlay defaults, you have two choices:

- If the AutoPlay window is onscreen, click the Set AutoPlay Defaults in Control Panel link.
- Select Start, Control Panel, Hardware and Sound, AutoPlay (or just launch the AutoPlay icon if you're using Classic view).

FIGURE 7.1 Vista revamped the AutoPlay window and divided the suggested actions into content-related and non-content-related sections.

Either way, you end up at the AutoPlay window shown in Figure 7.2. This page lists 16 different content types, from Audio CD to Super Video CD, and even HD DVD and Blu-ray. Each content type has its own drop-down list, and you use that list to select the default action for each type.

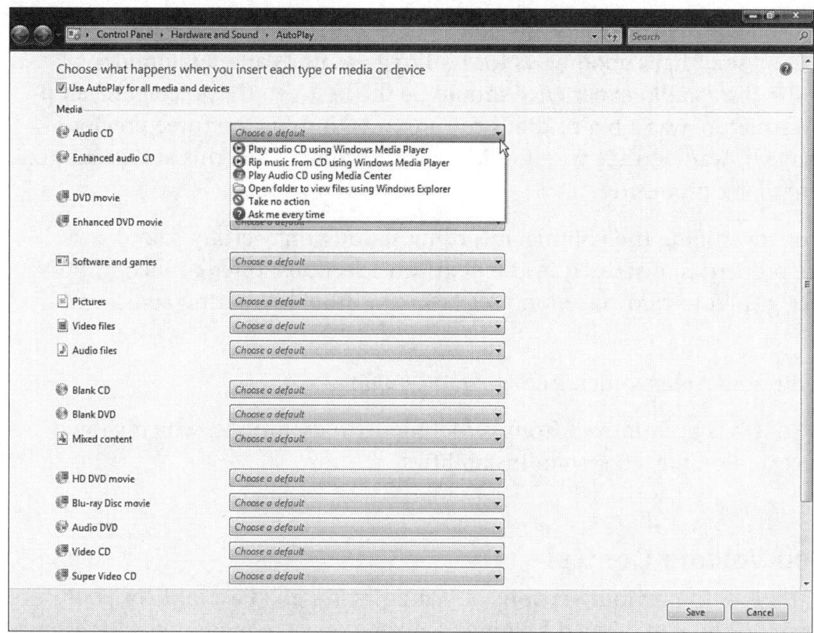

FIGURE 7.2 Use the new AutoPlay page to set the default actions for 14 different content types.

Digital Audio in Windows Vista

The reputation Windows has as an audio playback and editing platform has been, not to put too fine a point on it, abysmal. There have been some improvements over the years. For example, the early audio infrastructure (often called the **audio stack**) seen in Windows 3.1 (16-bit) and Windows 95 (32-bit) supported only one audio stream at a time, but Windows 98 enabled multiple playback streams using the Windows Driver Model architecture. However, Windows audio has always suffered from three major problems:

- **A poor interface for controlling audio and for troubleshooting audio problems**—Tools such as Volume Control, the Sound Recorder, and the Control Panel Sounds and Audio Devices icon had difficult interfaces and limited functionality, and clearly weren't geared for the day-to-day audio tasks that users face.
- **Poor quality playback and recording**—The Windows audio stack has always been merely "good enough." That is, audio in Windows—particularly playback—was constructed to give the average user a reasonable level of quality. However, the default Windows audio had nowhere near the fidelity audiophiles and professional audio users require, so these users spent much of their time working around inherent audio limitations (or giving up on Windows altogether and moving to the Mac).
- **Poor reliability, to the point that audio glitches are one of main causes of system instability**—The problem here has been that much of the audio stack code runs in the sensitive Windows kernel mode, where a buggy driver or process can bring down the entire system.

New To address these problems, the Vista audio team completely rewrote the audio stack from the ground up. That's good news for both regular users and audiophiles because it means the Vista audio experience should be the best yet. Completely revamping the audio infrastructure was a big risk, but the aim was to solve the three previous problems. We'll have to wait and see whether Microsoft accomplished this ambitious goal, but on paper, things look promising:

- New tools for controlling the volume, recording sounds, and setting sound and audio device properties (discussed in the next three sections) offer a much improved user interface geared toward common user tasks and troubleshooting audio problems.
- The new audio stack offers much higher sound quality.
- Most audio code has been moved from kernel mode to user mode, which should greatly reduce audio-induced system instabilities.

Per-Application Volume Control

The Volume Control tool in previous versions of Windows is a good example of poor audio system design. When you opened Volume Control, you were presented with a series of volume sliders labeled Master, Wave, Line In, CD Player, Synthesizer, Aux, and more.

For the average user, most of these labels were, at best, meaningless and, at worst, intimidating. What on earth does the Aux slider control? What's the deal with Line In? Most people ignored all the sliders except Master and just used that slider to control playback volume. However, the Master slider had problems of its own.

For example, suppose that you're waiting for an important email message, so you set up Windows Mail to play a sound when an email message comes in. Suppose further that you're also using Windows Media Player to play music in the background. If you get a phone call, you want to turn down or mute the music. In previous versions of Windows, muting the music playback also meant muting other system sounds, including your email program's audio alerts. So, while you're on the phone, there's a good chance that you'll miss that important message you've been waiting for.

The Windows Vista solution to this kind of program is called **per-application volume control**. This means that Vista gives you a volume control slider for every running program and process that is a dedicated sound application (such as Windows Media Player or Media Center) or is currently producing audio output. In our example, you'd have separate volume controls for Windows Media Player and Windows Mail. When that phone call comes in, you can turn down or mute Windows Media Player while leaving the Windows Mail volume as is, so there's much less chance that you'll miss that incoming message.

Figure 7.3 shows the new Volume window that appears when you click the Volume icon in the notification area, and then click Mixer. The slider on the left controls the speaker volume, so you can use it as a systemwide volume control. The rest of the window contains the **application mixer**—this includes sliders and mute buttons for individual programs, and the program's name and icon.

NOTE

How long an application's slider remains in the Volume Mixer window seems to depend on how often the application accesses the audio stack. If a program just makes the occasional peep, it will appear only briefly in the Volume Mixer and then disappear. If a program makes noise fairly often, then it remains in the Volume Mixer for much longer. So, for example, if you receive email messages all day, you should always see the Windows Mail icon in the Volume Mixer.

In the old Volume Control tool, when you adjusted the Master slider, the other volume sliders remained the same. In the Vista Volume Control tool, when you move the speaker volume slider, the program sliders move along with it. That's a nice touch, but what's even nicer is that the speaker volume slider preserves the relative volume levels of each program. So if you adjust the speaker volume to about half its current level, the sliders in the application mixer also adjust to about half of their current level.

Volume Control also remembers application settings between sessions. So, if you mute Solitaire, for example, it will remain muted the next time you start the program.

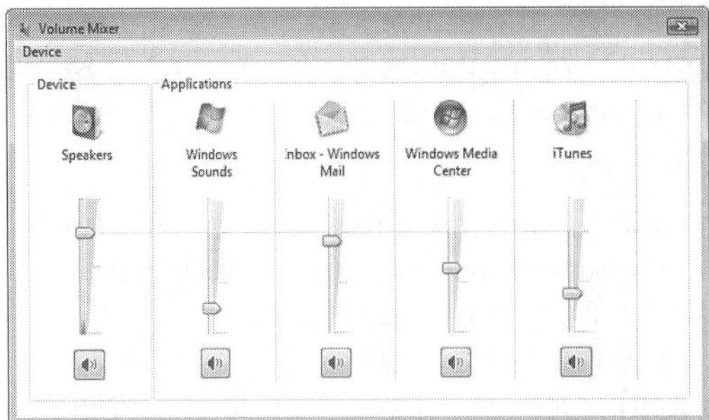

FIGURE 7.3 Windows Vista uses per-application volume control to enable you to set the volume level for each program that outputs audio.

The new volume control also supports metering, in which the current audio output is displayed graphically on each slider (see Figure 7.3). This metering appears as a green wedge that grows taller and wider the louder the sound signal is. This is very useful for troubleshooting audio problems because it tells you whether a particular program is actually producing audio output. If you have no sound from a program but you see the metering in program's volume slider, the problem lies outside of the program (for example, your speakers are turned down or unplugged).

NOTE

Many notebook computers come with volume controls that enable you to physically turn the computer's speaker volume up or down. Microsoft has talked about tying this physical volume control into the Volume Control program so that if you turn down the sound physically, the speaker volume slider would adjust accordingly. This extremely useful feature was not implemented as I wrote this, but it might appear in a later build of Windows Vista.

Sound Recorder

The Sound Recorder accessory first appeared in Windows 95 and has remained a part of Windows ever since. Unfortunately, the Sound Recorder in Windows XP is essentially the same program as the original version, which means the program's annoying limitations haven't changed, either:

- You can save your recording only using the WAV file format.
- You can record only up to one minute of sound.

Windows Vista comes with a completely new version of Sound Recorder that does away with these limitations. For example, you can save your recording using the Windows

Media Audio (**WMA**) format, and there is no limit (other than available hard disk space) to the length of the recording.

Having no recording limit might sound dangerous (long WAV files take up a lot of space), but the new Sound Recorder captures WMA audio at a bit rate of 96Kbps, or about 700KB for a one-minute recording. Compare this to a one-minute CD-quality recording using the old Sound Recorder, which could easily result in a 10MB file!

Figure 7.4 shows the new Sound Recorder window (select Start, All Programs, Accessories, Sound Recorder). Click Start Recording to begin your recording; click Stop Recording when you're done. Sound Recorder displays the Save As dialog box so that you can choose the file location, name, and format.

FIGURE 7.4 The Windows Vista version of Sound Recorder.

Audio Devices and Sound Themes

The Windows Vista replacement for the Control Panel Sound and Audio Devices icon is the Sound dialog box (select Start, Control Panel, Hardware and Sound, Sound), shown in Figure 7.5.

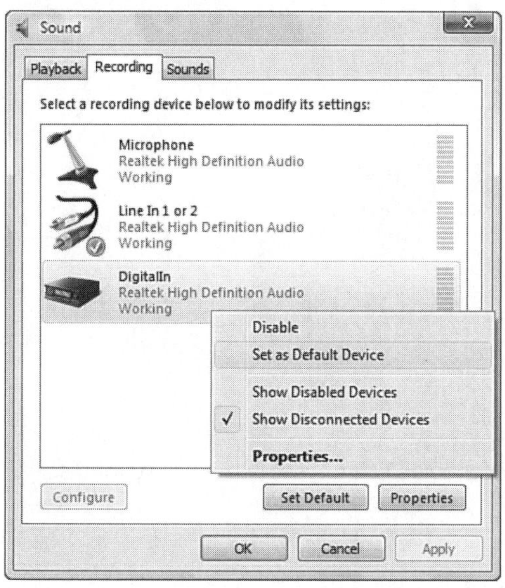

FIGURE 7.5 Open the Sound icon in the Control Panel to control your system's audio properties.

The Playback and Recording tabs show the playback and recording devices on your system. The first thing to notice is that you now have a visual reminder of the default devices for playback and recording in the form of a green check mark icon, shown in Figure 7.5. The check mark means that the device is the default for all uses. However, you can also designate a device as the default. As shown in Figure 7.5, you can right-click a device and then click Set as Default Device.

Windows Vista also implements a more extensive collection of properties for each device. Double-clicking a device displays a property sheet similar to the one shown in Figure 7.6. The properties you see depend on the device. Here's a summary of the tabs you see when you open the default playback device (although note that not all audio playback devices support all of these tabs):

- **General**—Change the name and icon for the device and any jack information disclosed by the driver
- **Levels**—Set the volume levels
- **Advanced**—Set the default playback format and latency and options for allowing applications exclusive control over the device

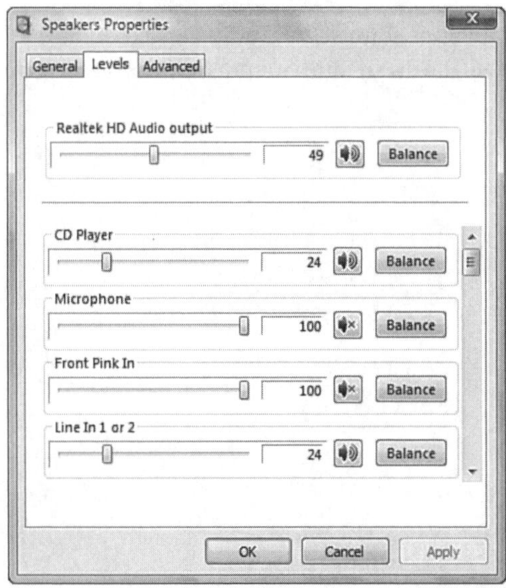

FIGURE 7.6 The audio device Configuration tab enables you to customize how your PC's audio devices work.

Using Windows Photo Gallery

New Over the past few years, digital cameras have become the photography tool of choice for everyone from novices to professionals. And it's no wonder: Digitals give photographers tremendous freedom to shoot at will without having to worry about paying processing costs or running out of film. If there's a downside to all this photographic freedom, it's that most of us end up with huge numbers of photos cluttering our hard drives. The result has been a thriving market for third-party programs to import, view, and manage all those digital images.

Digital-image management seems like the kind of thing that ought to be part of the operating system. However, although Windows has had programs such as the Windows Picture and Fax Viewer, it has never had a program designed to perform the full range of image-management tasks, from importing and viewing to organizing and burning.

Windows Vista changes all that by introducing a new program called Windows Photo Gallery (WPG). This program can import images and videos from a camera, a scanner, removable media, the network, or the Web. You can then view the images, add metadata such as captions and tags, rate the images, search for images, and even apply common fixes to improve the look of photos. You can also burn selected images to a DVD.

You launch the program by selecting Start, All Programs, Windows Photo Gallery. WPG immediately begins gathering the images on your hard disk. You can also import images by hand using the following File menu commands:

- **Add Folder to Gallery**—This command displays the Add Folder to Gallery dialog box, which enables you to import images from a specific folder.
- **Import from Scanner or Camera**—This command launches the Scanner and Camera Wizard, which takes you step by step through the process of importing images from a digital camera, a document scanner, or a removable medium.

Grouping Images

By default, WPG groups the images by date, but you can change that using the View, Group By command, which enables you to group on a number of metadata properties, including Date Taken, File Size, Image Size, and Camera. You can then select View, Table of Contents to see links that take you to each group. For example, Figure 7.7 shows images grouped by File Size with the Table of Contents showing links to each group (Largest, Larger, Medium, and so on).

Image Metadata and Tagging

You can also create your own metadata for each image. WPG enables you to change a number of properties, including `Caption`, `Date Taken`, `Rating`, and `Tags`. The `Tags` property enables you to add one or more descriptive keywords—**tags**—to the image, similar to what you do at photo-sharing websites such as Flickr (www.flickr.com). In WPG, you click the image you want to work with, display the Info pane (click Info or Tags, Create a New Tag), click Add Tags, type the tag, and press Enter. Figure 7.8 shows an image with several tags added. Notice that the tag you create also appears in the Tags list, which enables you to filter the images based on the tag you select. (You can also filter images based on the `Date Taken` and `Ratings` properties, as well on `Recently Imported` and `Folders`.)

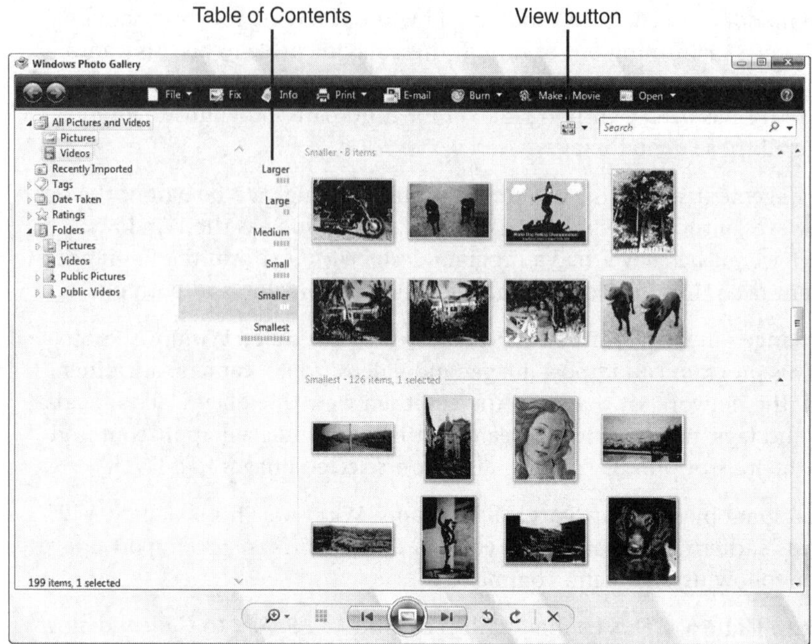

FIGURE 7.7 Vista's new Windows Photo Gallery program enables you to import, view, organize, burn images and videos, and group file via metadata, as shown here.

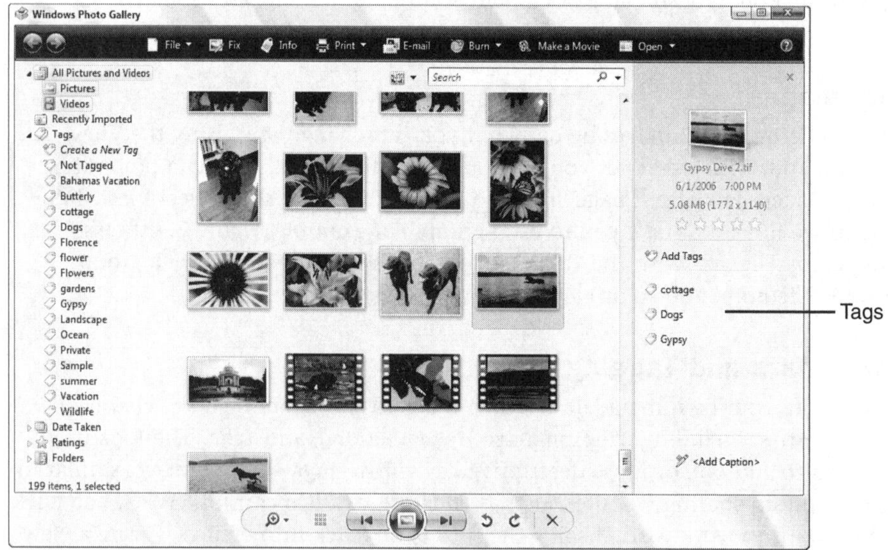

FIGURE 7.8 You can apply descriptive tags to each of your images.

Searching Images with Instant Search

As with so many other Vista windows, WPG comes with an integrated Instant Search box that supports as-you-type searches. After you type text in the Instant Search box, WPG searches filenames and all metadata (including your tags) for matching images and then shows the results in the WPG window. Figure 7.9 shows an example.

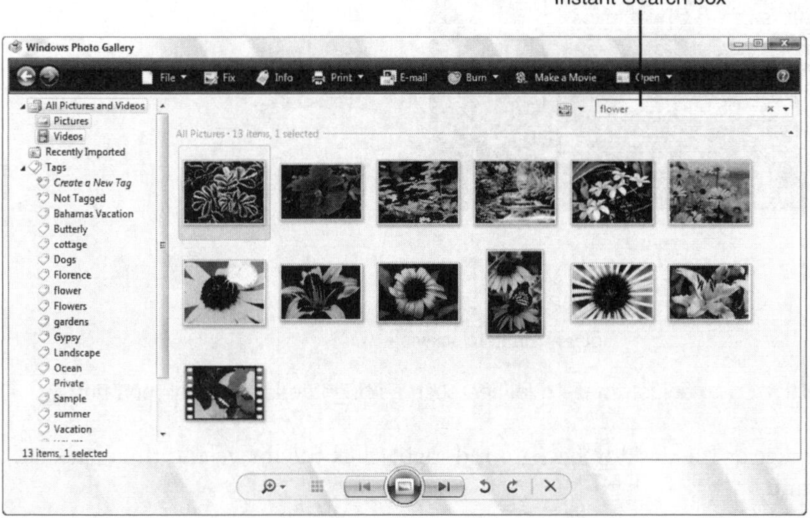

FIGURE 7.9 Windows Photo Gallery supports as-you-type searches on filenames and metadata properties.

Editing an Image

WPG also comes with a limited set of tools for altering images. Click the image you want to work with and then click Fix to display the image in the window shown in Figure 7.10. Here you get sliders to adjust the brightness, contrast, color temperature, and tint. (You can also click Auto Adjust to have WPG make the adjustments for you.) In all WPG windows, you can also rotate the image, as pointed out in Figure 7.10.

More Tools

WPG also supports the following features:

- To preview any image, double-click it. WPG expands the image to take up most of the WPG window.
- To view a slideshow, click the Play Slideshow button (see Figure 7.10) or press F11. Note that the Vista slideshow engine comes with 12 different playback modes. During the slideshow, move the mouse to display the controls, and then click Themes to choose the playback mode you prefer.

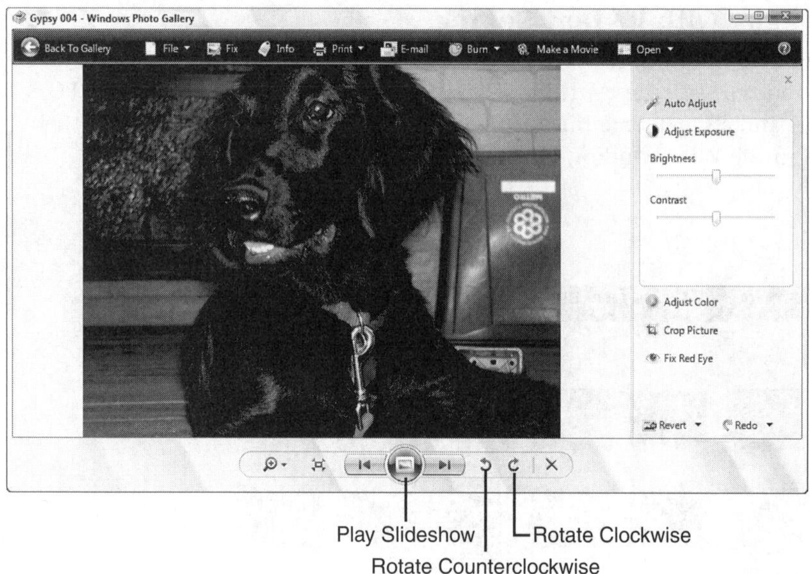

FIGURE 7.10 Click Fix to adjust image qualities such as brightness, contrast, and tint.

- To set an image as the desktop background, right-click the image and then click Set as Background.
- To burn images to a disc, click Burn and then click either Data Disc or Video DVD.

Easy Listening in Windows Media Player 11

Windows Media Player (WMP) is your computer's one-stop media shop, with support for playing digital music, audio CDs, digital videos, DVD movies, Internet radio, and recorded TV shows; ripping music from CDs; burning files to disc; synchronizing with external audio devices; and much more. Vista ships with a new version of this popular program—Windows Media Player 11—that offers a few nice improvements over WMP 10.

The first thing you notice when you launch WMP 11 is that the overall interface is a bit simpler than previous versions (see Figure 7.11). There are still a few too many small, undecipherable icons scattered around the window, but these are small blemishes on an otherwise clean look.

Navigating the Library

One of the things that makes the WMP 11 interface so much simpler than older versions is that you see only one category at a time in the Library. By default, WMP displays the Music category at startup. However, you can change to a different category (Music, Pictures, Video, Recorded TV, or Other Media) using either of the following techniques:

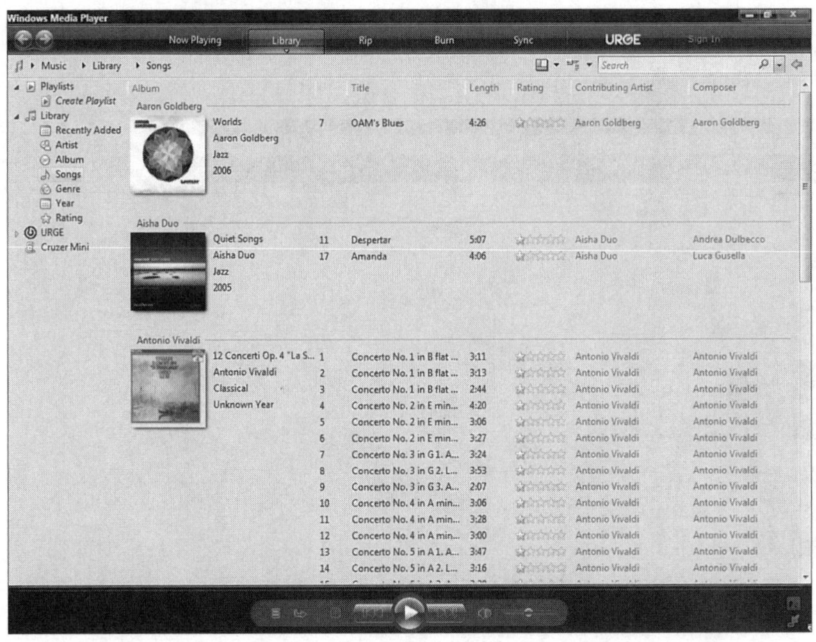

FIGURE 7.11 Windows Media Player 11 offers a simpler, cleaner interface than its predecessors.

- Click the Select a Category list (pointed out in Figure 7.8) and then click the category you want.
- Drop down the Library tab list (see Figure 7.12) and then click the category you want.

The path information beside the Select a Category list tells you the name of the current category, folder, and view, as pointed out in Figure 7.12.

Album Art and the WMP Interface

Another thing you'll notice about the WMP 11 interface is that it features graphics much more predominantly than in older versions of the program. If you've downloaded or scanned album art, it appears throughout the WMP 11 interface. For example, if you select the Artist view, the artist stacks use album art images, as shown in Figure 7.13. Even if you switch to a less specific view, such as Genre, WMP uses album art as part of the stack icons.

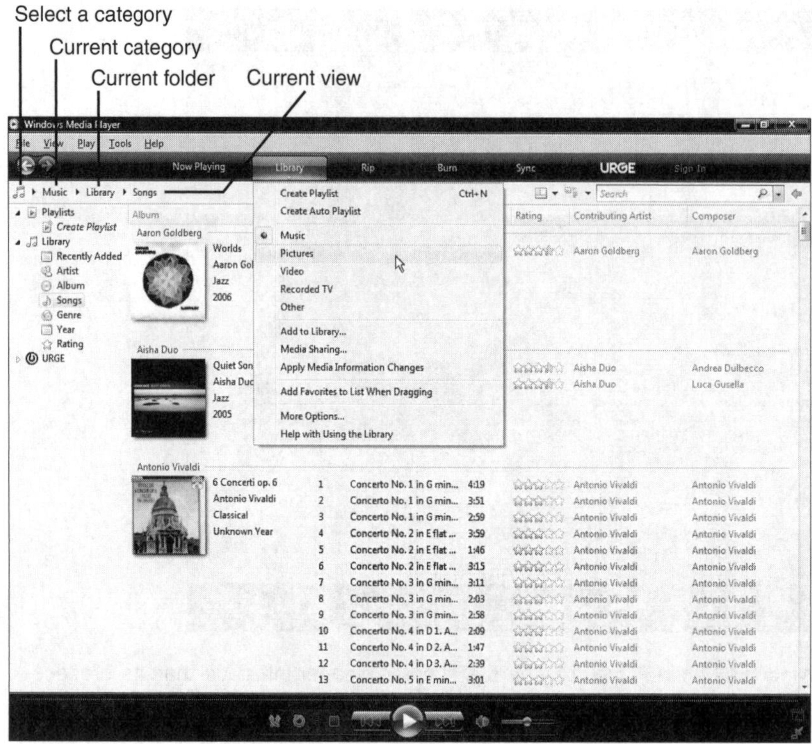

FIGURE 7.12 You navigate to a different category using either the Select a Category list or the Library list.

Grouping and Stacking Media

By default, WMP opens in the Music category's Songs view, which groups songs according to the values in the `Album Artist` property and then by the values in the `Album` property. WMP also offers several other Music views based on media metadata:

- **Artist**—Stacks the albums using the values in the `Album Artist` property (see Figure 7.9)
- **Album**—Groups the albums alphabetically using the values in the `Album` property
- **Genre**—Stacks the albums using the values in the `Genre` property (see Figure 7.14)
- **Year**—Groups the albums by decade using the values in the `Date Released` property
- **Rating**—Stacks the albums using the values in the `Rating` property

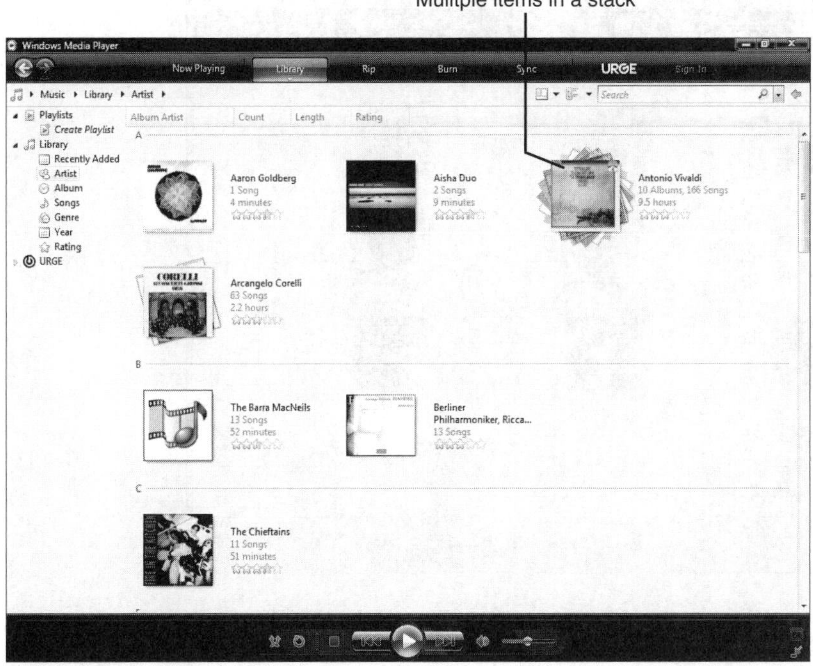

FIGURE 7.13 Album art appears through the Windows Media Player interface, such as the Artist view shown here.

Of course, you get a different set of views for each category. For example, you can view items in the Video category by actors, genre, and rating, and you can view items in the Recorded TV category by series, genre, actors, and rating. In each category, you can see even more views by clicking the Library folder (or by pulling down the Library list in the path data), as shown in Figure 7.15.

Media Metadata and Tagging

Metadata in Windows Media Player is best dealt with by downloading the relevant information from the Internet. However, most WMP metadata is editable, and you can make whatever changes you need by right-clicking the metadata and then clicking Edit.

A new innovation in WMP 11 is the Advanced Tag Editor, which gives you a front-end for much of the metadata available for a particular media file. Right-click the file you want to tag and then click Advanced Tag Editor to display the dialog box shown in Figure 7.16. You can add metadata related to the track and to the artist, and you can also add websites, lyrics (even lyrics synchronized to the music), pictures, and comments.

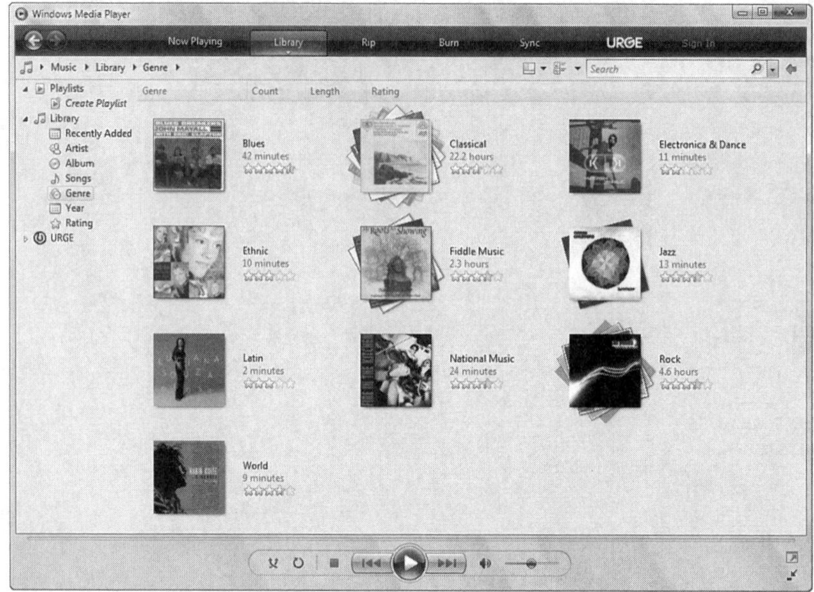

FIGURE 7.14 The Library's Genre folder stacks your albums according to the values in the `Genre` property.

FIGURE 7.15 Click the current category's Library folder to see a complete list of the available views.

Instant Search

By this point in the book, you won't be surprised to learn that WMP 11 comes with an integrated Instant Search box that supports as-you-type searches. After you type your text in the Instant Search box, WMP searches filenames and metadata for matching media files, and then shows the results in the WMP window. Figure 7.17 shows an example.

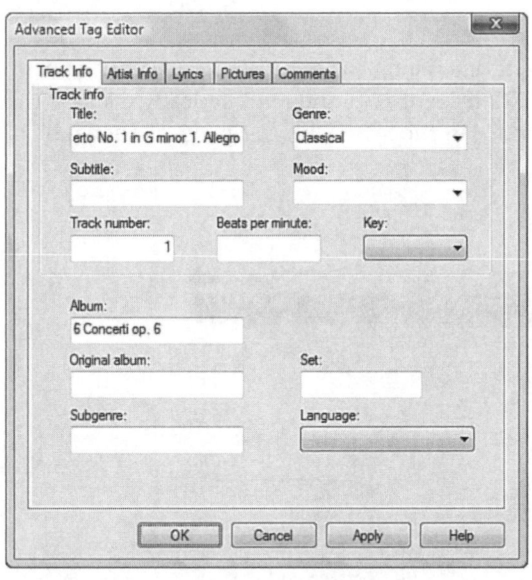

FIGURE 7.16 Use the Advanced Tag Editor to edit the metadata for a media file.

FIGURE 7.17 Windows Media Player supports as-you-type searches on filenames and metadata properties.

Syncing with Media Devices

Syncing items from the Library to a media device is a bit easier in WMP 11. When you insert a WMP-compatible media device, WMP recognizes it and automatically displays the device, its total capacity, and its available space in the Sync tab's List pane, as shown in Figure 7.18.

FIGURE 7.18 When you insert a media device, information about the device appears in the Sync tab's List pane.

To create a list of items to add to the device, display the album, song, or whatever in the Contents pane; click and drag the item; and then drop it inside the Sync List. WMP automatically updates the available storage space in the device as you drop items in the Sync List. When you're ready to add the item, click Start Sync. WMP switches to the device's Sync Status folder to display the progress of the sync.

TIP

You can "preshuffle" the media files before starting the sync. Pull down the Sync List button and click Shuffle List Now.

WMP 11 supports two-way synchronizing, which means that not only can you sync files from your PC to a media device, but you also can sync files from a media device to your PC. This is handy if you've purchased music directly to the device or uploaded media to the device using a different application.

To sync from a media device to your PC, you open a view on the media device, find the files you want to sync, and then click and drag them to the Sync List. Alternatively, just click Start Sync to synchronize everything on the device with WMP.

Media Sharing

It can take quite a while to set up and customize your WMP Library just the way you like it. When you do, however, WMP is a pleasure to use—so much so that you'll probably be tempted to duplicate your efforts on other computers in your home. Unfortunately, previous versions of WMP gave you no easy way to do that. Basically, you had to copy the media files from your original PC to the second PC, and then build your Library from scratch on the second machine.

WMP 11 changes all that by introducing a welcome new feature called Media Sharing. This feature enables you to share your WMP Library with other network users or devices, just as you'd share a folder or a printer.

To get started with Media Sharing, WMP gives you two choices:

- Pull down any tab menu and select More Options; display the Library tab; and then click Configure Media Sharing.
- Right-click the Library folder in any category, and then click Media Sharing.

Either way, you see the Library Sharing dialog box onscreen. Activate the Share My Library check box, click OK, and then enter your credentials when prompted.

When computers or devices connect to your network, Media Player recognizes them and displays the fly-out message shown in Figure 7.19. Click the message and then click either Allow (if you want the computer or device to share your media) or Deny (if you don't).

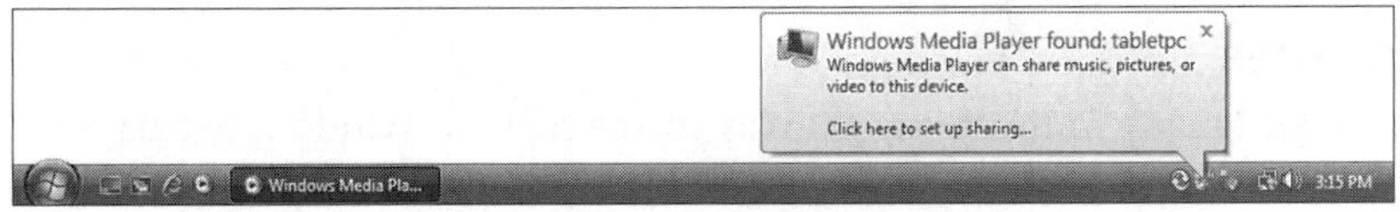

FIGURE 7.19 Media Player displays this message when it detects a new computer or device connected to your network.

To control media sharing, display the Media Sharing dialog box again. This time, you see the configuration shown in Figure 7.20. The large box in the middle lists the network computers and devices that Media Player has detected. In each case, click an icon and then click either Allow or Deny. If you allow an item, you can also click Customize to specify exactly what you want to share based on three criteria: media types, star ratings, and parental ratings. You can also just use the default sharing settings, which you configure by clicking the Settings button in the Media Sharing dialog box.

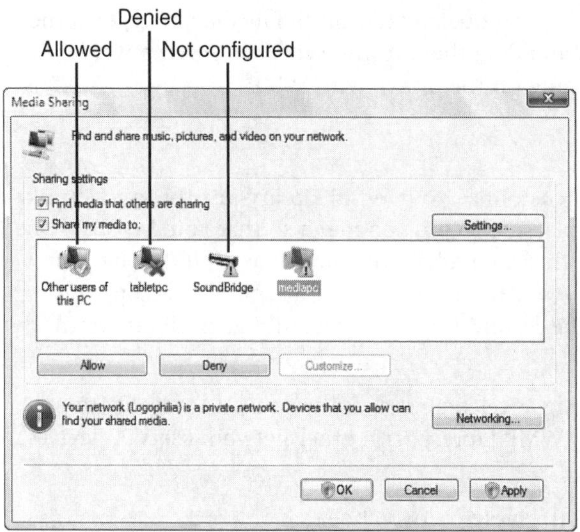

FIGURE 7.20 Use the Media Sharing dialog box to allow or deny other network devices access to your Media Player library.

Tips for Working with Windows Media Player

Outside the new features discussed in the previous few sections, Windows Media Player still performs most of the tasks that we've come to associate with the program, including playing media (of course), ripping music from audio CDs, burning tracks to recordable devices, and so on. The next few sections take you through a few tips and pointers that I hope will help you get more out of this powerful program.

Playing Media Files

Windows Vista gives you many indirect ways to play media files via Windows Media Player. Here's a summary:

- Open Windows Explorer, find the media file you want to play, and then double-click the file.

NOTE

To control the media file types that are associated with Windows Media Player, select Start, Default Programs. In the Default Programs window, click Set Your Default Programs, click Windows Media Player, and then click Choose Defaults for this Program. Activate the check boxes for the file types that you want to open automatically in Windows Media Player. If you don't want Windows Media Player to handle a particular file type, deactivate its check box.

- Insert an audio CD in your CD or DVD drive, or insert a DVD disc in your DVD drive.
- If you have a memory card reader, insert a memory card (such as a CompactFlash card or a MultiMedia Card). If Windows Vista asks what you want to do with this disk, select Play Using Windows Media Player. If you don't want to be bothered with this dialog box each time, activate the Always Do the Selected Action check box. Click OK.
- Download media from the Internet.
- You can also open files directly from Media Player by pressing Alt, pulling down the File menu, and selecting either Open (to launch a media file from your computer or from a network location) or Open URL (to launch a media file from the Internet).

TIP

Many of today's keyboards are media-enhanced, which means they come with extra keys that perform digital media functions such as playing, pausing, and stopping media, adjusting the volume, and changing the track. In addition, here are a few Windows Media Player shortcut keys that you might find useful while playing media files:

Alt+Enter	Toggle Full Screen mode
Ctrl+P	Play or pause the current media
Ctrl+S	Stop the current media
Ctrl+B	Go to the previous track
Ctrl+Shift+B	Rewind to beginning of the media
Ctrl+F	Go to the next track
Ctrl+Shift+F	Fast forward to the end of the media
Ctrl+H	Toggle shuffle playback
Ctrl+T	Toggle repeat playback
Ctrl+1	Switch to Full mode
Ctrl+2	Switch to Skin mode
Alt+1	Display video size at 50%
Alt+2	Display video size at 100%
Alt+3	Display video size at 200%
F7	Mute sound
F8	Decrease volume
F9	Increase volume

Setting Windows Media Player's Playback Options

Windows Media Player comes with several options that you can work with to control various aspects of the playback. To see these options, press Alt and then select Tools, Options. The Player tab, shown in Figure 7.21, contains the following settings:

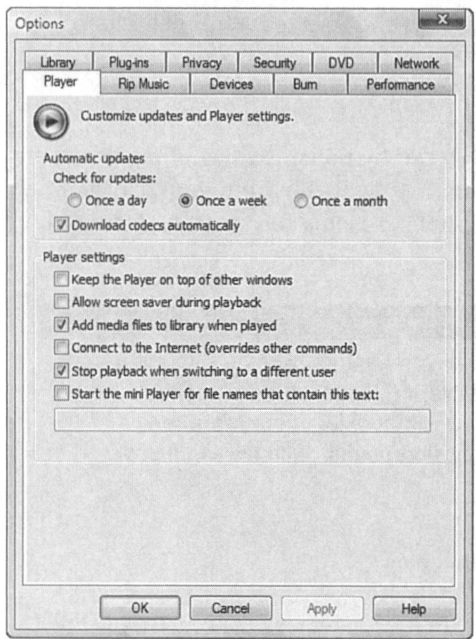

FIGURE 7.21 Use the Player tab to configure Windows Media Player's playback options.

Check for Updates — Use these options to determine how often Windows Media Player checks for newer versions of the program.

TIP

To prevent Windows Media Player from displaying a message that an update is available, create a string setting named `AskMeAgain` in the following Registry key and set its value to `No`:

```
HKLM\SOFTWARE\Microsoft\MediaPlayer\PlayerUpgrade
```

You can also prevent Windows Media Player from automatically updating itself if it detects that a newer version is available. Create the following key, add a `DWORD` value called `DisableAutoUpdate` and set its value to `1`:

```
HKLM\SOFTWARE\Policies\Microsoft\WindowsMediaPlayer
```

Download Codecs Automatically	When this check box is activated, Media Player automatically attempts to download and install a codec for any file type that it doesn't recognize. If you prefer to be prompted before the download occurs, deactivate this check box. You can disable this check box using the Group Policy editor (see Chapter 10, "Using Control Panel and Group Policies"). Select User Configuration, Administrative Templates, Windows Components, Windows Media Player, Playback and enable the Prevent Codec Download policy.
Keep the Player on Top of Other Windows	When this check box is activated, Windows Media Player stays on top of other windows. This is useful if you want to able to access Windows Media Player's playback controls while working in another program.

TIP

Unless you have a large screen running at a high resolution, an always-on-top Windows Media Player window is probably going to get in the way. A better solution is to display the Windows Media Player playback controls in the Windows Vista taskbar. To do that, right-click an empty section of the taskbar and then select Toolbars, Windows Media Player. Minimize the Windows Media Player window and the Windows Media Player toolbar appears in the taskbar.

Allow Screen Saver During Playback	When this check box is activated, the Windows Vista screensaver is allowed to kick in after the system has been idle for the specified number of minutes. If you're watching streaming video content or a DVD movie, leave this check box deactivated to prevent the screensaver from activating.
Add Media Files to Library When Played	When this check box is activated, Windows Media Player adds files that you play to the Library. For example, if you play a downloaded MP3 file, Windows Media Player adds it to the Library. Note that, by default, Windows Media Player doesn't add media from removable media and network shares to the Library (see the next setting).

Connect to the Internet	When this check box is activated, Windows Media Player always connects to the Internet when you select a feature that requires Internet access, such as the Guide (windowsmedia.com) or MSN Music (music.msn.com). This connection occurs even if you have activated the File menu's Work Offline command.
Stop Playback When Switching to a Different User	When this check box is activated, Media Player stops playing when you switch to a different user account.
Start the Mini Player for File Names That Contain This Text	When this check box is activated, Media Player launches the mini Player when it comes upon files that contain the text you specify. For example, if you are sent podcasts or voicemail messages via email, you probably don't want to start up the full Media Player program to hear such files. To hear them using the mini Player, type text that appears consistently in the filenames.

Copying Music from an Audio CD

Windows Media Player comes with the welcome capability to copy (**rip** in the vernacular) tracks from an audio CD to your computer's hard disk. Although this process is straightforward, as you'll see, there are several options that you need to take into account *before* you start copying. These options include the location of the folder in which the ripped tracks will be stored, the structure of the track filenames, the file format to use, and the quality (bit rate) at which you want to copy the tracks. You control all these settings in the Rip Music tab of the Options dialog box (press Alt and then select Tools, Options to get there).

Selecting a Location and Filename Structure

The Rip Music to This Location group displays the name of the folder that will be used to store the copied tracks. By default, this location is `%USERPROFILE%\Music`. To specify a different folder (for example, a folder on a partition with lots of free space), click Change and use the Browse for Folder dialog box to choose the new folder.

The default filenames that Windows Media Player generates for each copied track use the following structure:

`Track_Number Song_Title.ext`

Here, *`Track_Number`* is the song's track number on the CD, *`Song_Title`* is the name of the song, and *`ext`* is the extension used by the recording format (such as WMA or MP3). Windows Media Player can also include additional data in the filename such as the artist name, the album name, the music genre, and the recording bit rate. To control which of these details the name incorporates, click the File Name button in the Rip Music tab to display the File Name Options dialog box, shown in Figure 7.22. Activate the check boxes beside the details you want in the filenames, and use the Move Up and Move Down buttons to determine the order of the details. Finally, use the Separator list to choose which character to use to separate each detail.

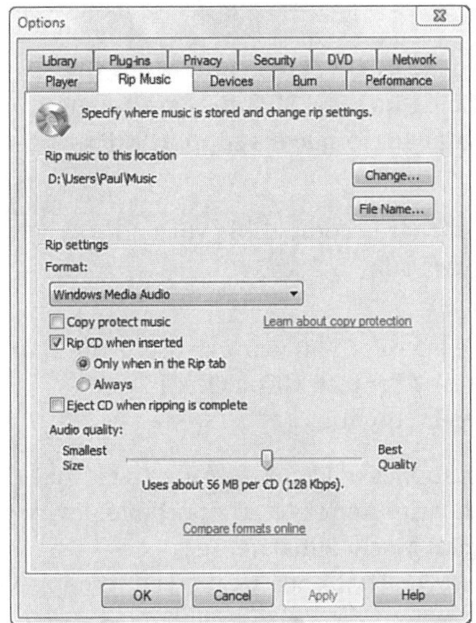

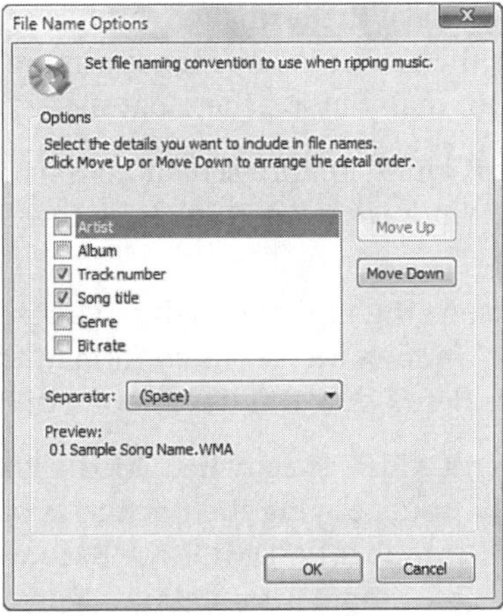

FIGURE 7.22 Use the File Name Options dialog box to specify the details you want in the filename assigned to each copied audio CD track.

Choosing the Recording File Format

Prior to version 10, Windows Media Player supported only a single file format: WMA (Windows Media Audio). This is an excellent music format that provides good quality recordings at high compression rates. If you plan to listen to the tracks only on your computer or on a custom CD, the WMA format is all you need. However, if you have an MP3 player or other device that may not recognize WMA files (although most do, unless you're one of the millions with an iPod), you need to use the MP3 recording format. Windows Media Player 10 provided MP3 encoding support right out of the box, and now Media Player 11 supports

- **Windows Media Audio (WMA)**—This is Windows Media Player's default audio file format. WMA compresses digital audio by removing extraneous sounds that are not normally detected by the human ear. This results in high-quality audio files that are a fraction of the size of uncompressed audio.

- **Windows Media Audio Pro (WMA Pro)**—This version of WMA can create music files that are smaller than regular WMA and so are easier to play on mobile devices that don't have much room.
- **Windows Media Audio (variable bit rate)**—This version of WMA is a bit "smarter" in that it changes the amount of compression depending on the audio data: if the data is more complex, it uses less compression to keep the sound quality high; if the data is less complex, it cranks up the compression.
- **Windows Media Audio Lossless**—This version of WMA doesn't compress the audio tracks at all. This gives you the highest possible audio quality, but it takes up much more space (up to about 400MB per CD).
- **MP3**—This is a popular format on the Internet. Like WMA, MP3 compresses the audio files to make them smaller without sacrificing quality. MP3 files are generally about twice the size of WMA files, but more digital audio players support MP3 (although not many more, these days).
- **WAV**—This is an uncompressed audio file format that is compatible with all versions of Windows, even going back to Windows 3.0.

Use the Format list in the Rip Music tab to choose the encoder you want to use. Note that if you select any Windows Media Audio format, the Copy Protect Music check box becomes enabled. Here's how this check box effects your copying:

- If Copy Protect Music is activated, Media Player applies a license to each track that prevents you from copying the track to another computer or to any portable device that is SDMI-compliant (SDMI is the **Secure Digital Music Initiative**; see www.sdmi.org for more information). Note, however, that you are allowed to copy the track to a writeable CD.
- If Copy Protect Music is deactivated, there are no restrictions on where or how you can copy the track. As long as you're copying tracks for personal use, deactivating this check box is the most convenient route to take.

Specifying the Quality of the Recording

The tracks on an audio CD use the CD Audio Track file format (`.cda` extension), which represents the raw (uncompressed) audio data. You can't work with these files directly because the CDA format isn't supported by Windows Vista and because these files tend to be huge (usually double-digit megabytes, depending on the track). Instead, the tracks need to be converted into a Windows Vista–supported format (such as WMA). This conversion always involves compressing the tracks to a more manageable size. However, because the compression process operates by removing extraneous data from the file (that is, it's a **lossy** compression), there's a tradeoff between file size and music quality. That is, the higher the compression, the smaller the resulting file, but the poorer the sound quality. Conversely, the lower the compression, the larger the file, but the better the sound quality. Generally, how you handle this tradeoff depends on how much hard disk space you have to store the files and how sensitive your ear is to sound quality.

The recording quality is usually measured in kilobits per second (Kbps; this is called the **bit rate**), with higher values producer better quality and larger files, as shown in Table 7.1. To specify the recording quality, use the Audio Quality slider in the Rip Music tab. Move the slider to the right for higher quality recordings, and to the left for lower quality.

TABLE 7.1 Ripping Bit Rates and the Disk Space They Consume

Kbps	KB/Minute	MB/Hour
32	240	14
48	360	21
64	480	28
96	720	42
128	960	56
160	1,200	70
192	1,440	84

TIP

To save a bit of time, Media Player 11 offers a faster way to choose the format and audio quality. Point your mouse at the Rip tab and you'll see a downward-pointing arrow appear. Click the arrow to display a menu, and then select either Format (to select an audio file format) or Bit Rate (to select an audio quality).

Copying Tracks from an Audio CD

After you've made your recording choices, you're ready to start ripping tracks. Here are the steps to follow:

1. Insert the audio CD.
2. Click Rip in the Windows Media Player taskbar. Windows Media Player displays a list of the available tracks. To get the track names, connect to the Internet and then click View Album Info.
3. Activate the check boxes beside the tracks you want to copy.
4. Click Start Rip.

TIP

You can save a step by selecting the Rip tab before inserting the disc. After you insert the disc, Media Player starts ripping the tracks automatically. If there are tracks you don't want ripped, deactivate their check boxes (note that this works even if Media Player has already ripped or is currently ripping a track).

Copying Tracks to a Recordable CD or Device

Windows Media Player can also perform the opposite task: copying media files from your computer to a recordable CD or portable device.

Creating a Playlist

Most people find recording is easiest if it's done from a **playlist**, a customized collection of music files. Here's how to create a new playlist:

1. Click Library in the Windows Media Player taskbar.
2. Click Playlists, Create Playlist. Windows Media Player adds the new playlist.
3. Type a name for the playlist and press Enter. Media Player displays the playlist pane on the right side of the window.
4. For each song you want to include in the new playlist, drag it from the library to the playlist pane.
5. Click Save Playlist.

After your playlist has been created, you can edit the list by highlighting it in the Library's Playlists branch and then right-clicking the tracks.

Recording to a CD or Device

Here are the steps to follow to burn music files to a recordable CD or portable device:

1. Insert the recordable CD or attach the portable device.
2. Click Burn in the Windows Media Player taskbar. The Burn List appears on the right side of the window.
3. For each playlist or song you want to burn, drag it from the library to the Burn List pane.
4. Click Start Burn.

From Here

Here are some places in the book that contain information related to the material presented in this chapter:

- To learn about group policies, see Chapter 10, "Using Control Panel and Group Policies."
- To learn more about hardware and device drivers, see Chapter 17, "Getting the Most Out of Device Manager."
- For the details on configuring a network, see Chapter 22, "Setting Up a Small Network."

CHAPTER 8

Vista's Tools for Business: Contacts, Calendar, and Faxing

IN THIS CHAPTER

- Managing Your Contacts
- Scheduling with Windows Calendar
- Sending and Receiving Faxes

The marketing for Windows Vista often skews strongly towards the "play" side of the operating system: the new graphics tools, Vista's gaming prowess, Media Player, Media Center, and so on. This makes some sense because Microsoft wants to move lots of retail copies of Vista, and home users are the primary retail market. However, Windows Vista also comes with a more sober "business" side. This includes important business must-haves such as networking, security, and backups, of course, but it also includes a few business applications that might prove useful for small shops that can't afford Microsoft Office at a few hundred dollars a pop. In addition to WordPad, the simple-but-functional word processor, and Windows Mail, the surprisingly good email client (see Chapter 19, "Communicating with Windows Mail"), Vista comes with three other programs for which small business types might find uses: Windows Contacts, Windows Calendar, and Windows Fax and Scan. This chapter gives you the details on these three programs. You'll see that with Vista, Windows takes another rather large step toward becoming a standalone system that, if your needs aren't all that lofty, requires little or no third-party software.

Managing Your Contacts

Whether it's working with clients, colleagues, or suppliers, contacting people is a big part of most people's working day. It can also be a time-consuming part of your day if you're constantly looking up information about people, whether it's their phone numbers, physical addresses, email addresses, web addresses, and so on. Streamlining these tasks—a process known as *contact management*—can save you lots of time and make your work more efficient.

New Windows Vista's calls its contact management feature, appropriately enough, Windows Contacts. In previous versions of Windows, you stored contact data in the Address Book, which was a single `.wab` file. Single files can get corrupted, of course, and if that happened with the Address Book, your contacts were toast unless you had a recent backup. Vista removes much of this risk by implementing `Contacts` as a subfolder that resides within your main user account folder (its location is `%UserProfile%\Contacts`). As you can see in Figure 8.1, inside the `Contacts` folder, Vista stores each contact as a separate file that uses the new Contact File (`.contact`) file type.

FIGURE 8.1 Windows Vista's new `Contacts` folder.

The `Contacts` folder gives you a fair amount of flexibility for dealing with your ever-growing network of coworkers, customers, friends, and family. Yes, you can use `Contacts` to store mundane information such as phone numbers and addresses, but with more than three dozen predefined fields available, you can preserve the minutiae of other people's lives: their birthdays and anniversaries, the names of their spouses and children, and even their web page addresses. Even better, `Contacts` enables you to reduce the number of steps it takes to perform many tasks. For example, if you want to send an email to someone in your `Contacts` folder, rather than firing up Windows Mail, creating the email message, and then adding the contact, you can perform all these actions at once by initiating the email directly from the `Contacts` folder.

The next few sections take you inside the `Contacts` folder and show you how to add and edit contacts; create contact groups; import and export contact data; and email and phone contacts. Before getting started, note that Vista gives you six (!) ways to display the `Contacts` folder:

- Select Start, All Programs, Windows Contacts.
- Select Start, click your username, and then double-click Contacts.
- Press Windows Logo+R (or select Start, All Programs, Accessories, Run) to open the Run dialog box, type **wab**, and click OK.
- In Windows Mail, select Tools, Windows Contacts (you can also press Ctrl+Shift+C or click the Contacts button in the toolbar).
- In Windows Calendar, select View, Contacts.
- In Windows Fax and Scan, select Tools, Contacts.

Creating a New Contact

As you'll see a bit later, Vista starts you off with a single file in the `Contacts` folder: a Contact file based on your user account. (See "Filling In Your Own Contact Data," later in this chapter.) To make the `Contacts` folder useful, you have to populate it with your own contacts. Vista gives you four ways to go about this: creating a contact from an email message; creating a contact from scratch; importing contacts from another program or file format; and creating a contact group. The next four sections discuss these methods in detail.

Creating a Contact from a Windows Mail Message

If you have a message in Windows Mail from a person that deserves a spot in your `Contacts` folder, you can use that message to create a bare-bones contact that stores just the sender's name and email address. In Windows Mail, right-click a message from the sender, and then click Add Sender to Contacts. Windows Mail immediately creates a new Contact file for the sender.

8

CAUTION

Windows Mail is configured with a truly annoying default setting: Each person you reply to is automatically added to the `Contacts` folder. Dumb! It's not unusual to have only a minimal connection with some or even most of the people who email us. Think how often an email "relationship" with someone consists of just an initial message and a reply. Putting these relative strangers into your Contacts folder is therefore a waste of space that will only slow you down. Tell Windows Mail to forgo this brain-dead behavior by selecting Tools, Options, displaying the Send tab, and then deactivating the Automatically Put People I Reply to In My Contacts List check box.

TIP

Some people automatically include with their email messages a version of their contact data in an attached file called a vCard (`.vcf`), which acts as a kind of electronic business card. (See "Sending Your Contact Data as an Electronic Business Card," later in this chapter.) If you receive such a message, you can add the person and their contact data to your `Contacts`. Click the vCard icon and then click Open to display the contact data. In the Summary tab, click Add to My Contacts to create a new Contact file for the person.

Creating a Contact from Scratch

If you need to perform your contact creation duties by hand, here are the steps to follow:

1. In the Contacts folder, click New Contact. (You can also right-click the folder and then click New, Contact.) Vista displays a blank contact properties sheet.
2. In the Name and E-mail tab, fill in at least the contact's first name and last name.
3. Use the Full Name list to select how you want the contact's full name displayed: First Last (for example, Paul McFedries); Last First (McFedries Paul); or Last, First (McFedries, Paul).
4. Type the contact's email address and then click Add.
5. Repeat step 4 if the contact has other email addresses.
6. Use the Home, Work, Family, and Notes tabs to add other contact data, as required.
7. Click OK.

Importing Contacts

If you have a large number of contacts, adding them individually by hand is no one's idea of a good time. Fortunately, if you have the contact data in the appropriate format (more on that in a second), Vista enables you to import that data in one operation. Which formats are "appropriate"? Fortunately, Vista supports four common contacts formats:

CSV — This is the Comma Separated Values format, and it consists of a text file with each contact on its own line, and each piece of contact data separated by a comma. In most cases, the first line in the CSV file lists the field names, separated by commas.

LDIF — This is the LDAP (Lightweight Directory Access Protocol) Data Interchange Format. If your contacts reside on an LDAP server and you have client server to access that server, the client should have a feature that exports the contacts to an LDIF file.

vCard This is the vCard format where the data for each contact resides in a .vcf file. A vCard is often used as a kind of electronic business card. Many contact management programs enable you to export contact data as a collection of vCard files.

WAB This the Windows Address Book File format, which is the format used by Outlook Express.

If you have contact data in one of these formats, follow these steps to import that data into Windows Contacts:

1. In Windows Contacts, click Import to display the Import to Windows Contacts dialog box, shown in Figure 8.2.

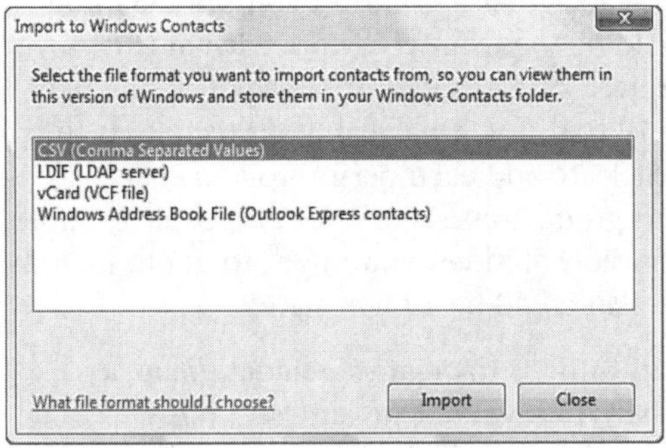

FIGURE 8.2 Use the Import to Windows Contacts dialog box to select a contact file format.

2. Select the contact file format you want to use.
3. Select Import. Vista prompts you to specify the file or files you want to import.
4. How you proceed from here depends on the file format you're using:
   - For LDIF, vCard, and WAB, select the files and then click Open. Skip to step 6.
   - For CSV, type the file path and filename (or click Browse to select it) and then click Next. Proceed with step 5.
5. In the CSV Import dialog box, activate the check box beside each field you want to map, and then click Finish.

NOTE

In the CSV Import dialog box, the Text Field column tells you the names of the fields in the CSV file, and the Contacts Field column tells you the corresponding field that Vista will use to create the contacts. If a field mapping is incorrect, click the field and then click Change Mapping. Use the Change Mapping dialog box to select the correct Contacts field (or deactivate Import This Field to skip it), and then click OK.

6. In the final dialog box, click Close.

NOTE

If you need to use your Windows Contacts entries in another program, Vista enables you to export them. Click Export in the taskbar to open the Export Windows Contacts dialog box. Choose either the CSV or vCard file format, and then click Export. If you choose the CSV format, Vista will ask you to specify which fields you want to export.

Creating a Contact Group

As you probably know, if you need to send an email message to two or more people, you just add everyone's address to the message window, in the To, Cc, or Bcc field (separate each address with a semicolon or comma). However, what if you find yourself emailing the *same* group of people over and over? It could be the team you work with at the office, a collection of people working on the same project, or a group of friends you share jokes and other e-tidbits with. You'll see in Chapter 19 that if you have all your recipients in Windows Contacts, it takes just a few mouse clicks to add each person to a message. That's fine with two or three people, but if your group consists of a dozen people or more, even the handy Contacts list method is just too slow. Besides, you might forget to include someone, and the office politics involved with *that* could be a nightmare.

A better way to go about the whole group email thing is to create a **contact group**: a Contact file that contains two or more contacts. When you create an email message and specify a contact group as the recipient, Windows Mail sends the message to everyone in the group. The members of the group can be either other Contacts or people that you add for the group only.

Follow these steps to create a contact group:

1. In the `Contacts` folder, select New Contact Group. A properties sheet for the contact group appears.
2. Type a group name.
3. Use any of the following three techniques to add members to the group (Figure 8.3 shows a group with a few members added):
    - To add an existing contact, click Add to Contact Group to display the Add Members to Contact Group dialog box. Hold down Ctrl and click each contact you want to add. When you're done, click Add.
    - To add a new contact, click Create New Contact. Use the properties sheet that appears to enter the contact's particulars, and then click OK. Vista creates a new contact for the person and adds the person to the contact group.
    - To add a member without creating a contact, type the contact name and email address, and then click Create for Group Only.

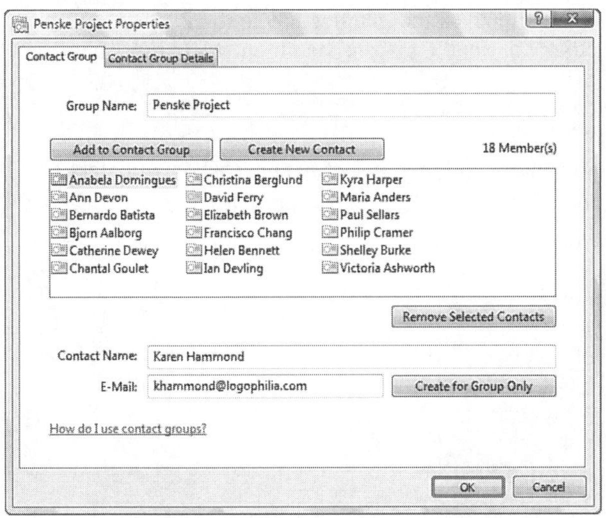

FIGURE 8.3 The properties sheet for a contact group gives you several ways to add members to the group.

4. Display the Contact Group Details tab.
5. In most cases, you won't need to fill in data such as the address and phone number for a contact group. However, you might want to add text to the Notes field or specify a website address, if applicable.
6. Click OK.

Communicating with a Contact

The `Contacts` folder is useful as a repository for contact data that you can refer to as needed. However, `Contacts` is also useful as a shortcut method for communicating with your contacts (as opposed to using Windows Mail). The `Contacts` folder gives you three ways to communicate with a contact:

Emailing a Contact—Select the contact and then click either the E-Mail button in the taskbar or the link to the contact's email address in the Preview pane. (You can also right-click the contact and then select Action, Send E-mail.) Vista displays a New Message window addressed to the contact.

NOTE

If the contact has multiple email addresses, clicking the taskbar's E-Mail button sends the message to the address that you have designated as Preferred. To change the Preferred address, open the contact's properties sheet (select the contact and then click Edit), select the address you prefer to use, and then click Set Preferred. To send a message to a non-Preferred address, either click the address link in the Preview pane or right-click the contact, select Action, Send E-mail To, and then select the address you want to use.

Phoning a Contact—Right-click the contact and then select Action, Call This Contact to open the New Call dialog box, shown in Figure 8.4. Use the Phone Number list to select the number you want to call, and then click Call.

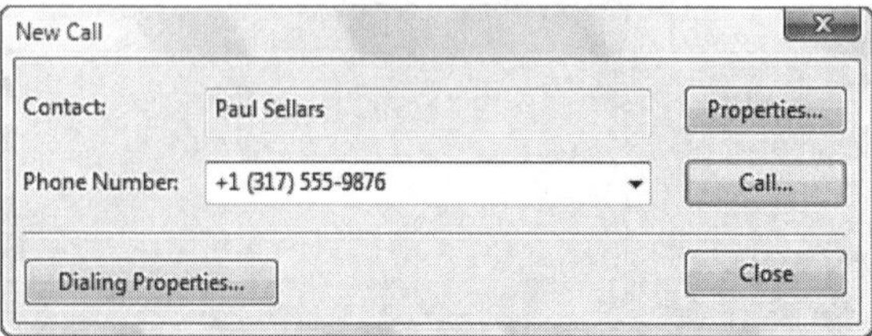

FIGURE 8.4 Use the New Call dialog box to initiate a phone call to a contact.

Visiting a Contact's Web Site—If you've specified either a business or home website for a contact, you can visit that site by selecting the contact and then clicking the website's link in the Preview pane. Alternatively, open the contact's properties sheet, display the tab containing the website address (business or home), and then click Go.

Working with Contacts

If you need to make changes to an existing contact, you have to open the contact's properties sheet, and Vista gives you three ways to do this:

- Select the contact and then click the taskbar's Edit button
- Select the contact and then click the contact's picture in the Preview pane
- Double-click the contact

The next few sections take you through a few more useful techniques for working with contacts.

TIP

By default, Vista sorts the `Contacts` folder by the values in the Name field, which corresponds to the Full Name field in each contact's properties sheet. If for each contact you selected either the Last, First or Last First format in the Full Name field, the Contacts list will be sorted as it should: by last name. However, if you selected the First Last format in the Full Name field, or if you've mixed up the formats, the `Contacts` folder will not sort properly. To work around this problem, right-click a field header and then click Last Name to add the Last Name field to the folder. Click the Last Name header to sort all your contacts by last name.

Changing a Contact's Picture

By default, Vista supplies each new contact with a generic picture. If you have a picture of the contact, you can use that image instead of the generic one. Follow these steps:

1. Open the contact's properties sheet.
2. In the Name and E-mail tab, click the contact's picture and then click Change Picture. The Select a Picture for Contact dialog box appears.
3. Select the picture you want to use and then click Set. Vista adds the picture to the properties sheet, as shown in Figure 8.5.

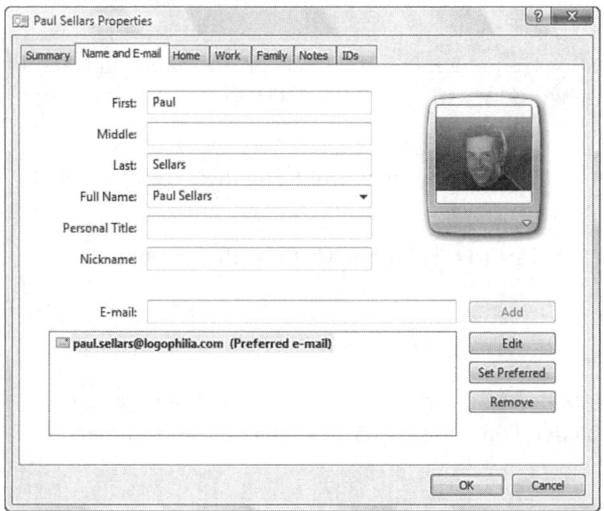

FIGURE 8.5 You can replace the generic contact image with a picture of the contact.

Filling In Your Own Contact Data

I mentioned earlier that Vista automatically creates a contact for your username. This is a bare-bones contact file that contains only your username in the First Name field and your user account picture as the contact picture. You'll see in the next section that you can send your contact data to other people as an electronic business card. Before you do that, of course, you need to fill in your contact data with the data you want others to see:

1. Open the properties sheet for your contact.
2. Fill in the data that you want included in your electronic business card.
3. Click OK.
4. Right-click your contact file.
5. If you see This Is Me in the shortcut menu, it means Vista already knows this contact contains your data, so exit the shortcut menu. Otherwise, click Set As My Contact to tell Vista that the contact file contains your data.

TIP

Even if you don't want to send your contact data electronically, it's still useful to add at least your email address to your contact data. That way, you can easily include your address in an email message or in a contact group.

Sending Your Contact Data as an Electronic Business Card

You saw earlier that if you receive an electronic business card (`.vcf`) file as an attachment, it's very easy to add that person's data to your Contacts list. For that reason, many people set up a contact file for themselves and then routinely send the data as an electronic business card.

If you want to do this only occasionally, right-click your contact file and then click Send Contact. This opens the New Message window with your contact data attached as a `.vcf` file.

If you want to include your electronic business card on all outgoing messages, follow these steps to set this up in Windows Mail:

1. In Windows Mail, select Tools, Options to display the Options dialog box.
2. Display the Compose tab.
3. In the Business Cards section, activate the Mail check box.
4. Use the list beside the Mail check box to select your contact file. (Note that after you select the contact, you can click Edit to open its properties sheet and make changes.)
5. Click OK.

Now every message you send will include your contact data as a `.vcf` file attachment (although you don't see this attachment as you work in the message window). If you don't want Windows Mail to send the business card for a particular message, pull down the Insert menu and click the My Business Card command to deactivate it.

Scheduling with Windows Calendar

New Windows is slowly evolving into a complete computing system in the sense that it contains everything that a user with simple needs could want. It has long had a word processor, text editor, graphics editor, web browser, email client, media player, and backup program. What's missing? On the security side, it's essential to have a bidirectional firewall and antispyware tool, and Vista has both of those. Also, all of us need some way to track appointments and to-do lists, so we need a calendar application; Vista now comes with one of those, too, called Windows Calendar, and it's actually not bad for an operating system freebie. It has a nice, clean interface, and it does all the basic jobs that a calendar should:

- ▶ Create appointments, both one-time and recurring
- ▶ Create all-day events
- ▶ Schedule tasks, with the capability to set a priority flag and a completed flag
- ▶ Set appointment and task reminders
- ▶ View appointments by day, week, or month
- ▶ Publish and subscribe to calendars using the iCal standard
- ▶ Import Calendar (`.ics`) files
- ▶ Create multiple calendars

To start Calendar, use any of the following methods:

- ▶ Select Start, All Programs, Windows Calendar
- ▶ Press Windows Logo+R (or select Start, All Programs, Accessories, Run) to open the Run dialog box, type **`wincal`**, and click OK
- ▶ In Windows Mail, select Tools, Windows Calendar, or press Ctrl+Shift+L

Figure 8.6 shows an empty Calendar window.

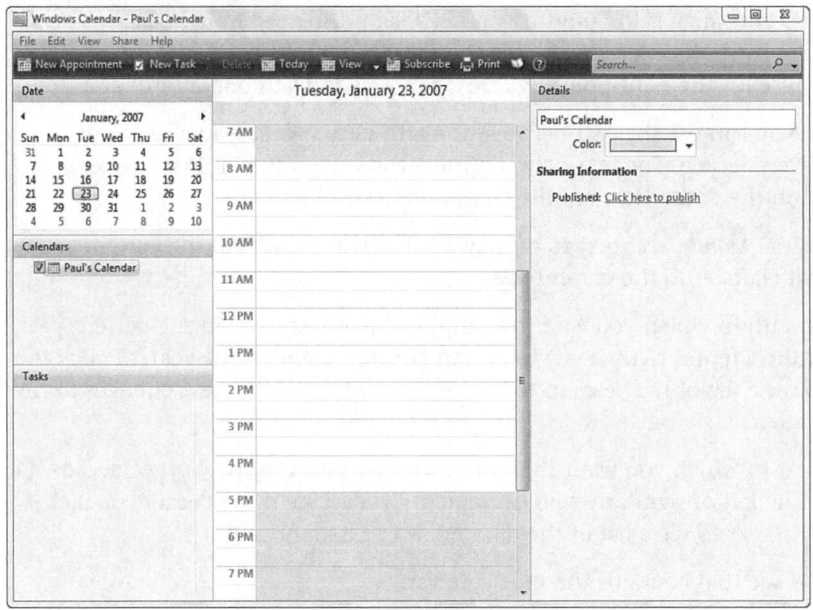

FIGURE 8.6 Use Windows Calendar to track appointments, all-day events, tasks, and more.

As you can see, Calendar is laid out similar to a day planner or desk calendar. There are five main sections:

Date	This area shows one month at a time (usually the current month). You use the Date area to change the date displayed in the Events area. Dates for which you have already scheduled appointments or meetings are shown in bold type. Note that today's date always has a red square around it.
Events	This part of the Calendar window at first shows one day at a time, divided into hour-long intervals (each of which is subdivided into half-hour segments). The appointments and meetings you schedule will appear in this area.
Details	You use this area to add, edit, and view your appointments and tasks.
Calendars	This area displays a list of your calendars. Most people use just a single calendar, but you might want separate calendars for, say, business use and personal use.
Tasks	This area lists the tasks you have set up.

Navigating Dates

Calendar always opens with today's date displayed. However, if you want to work with a different day, the Date area makes it easy. All you have to do is click a date, and Calendar displays it in the Events area. If the month you need isn't displayed in the Date Navigator, click the left-pointing arrow beside the month to move backward one month at a time. Similarly, click the right-pointing arrow to move forward one month at a time.

For larger moves, you can use the text between the arrows to navigate to a different month, year, or even decade. The text between the arrows is a series of links that enable you to zoom out on the dates. Here are the steps to follow:

1. Click the initial *Month, Year* text to display a list of the months in the current year. The link text changes to the current year.
2. Click the month to which you want to jump. If the month isn't in the current year, click either the left and right arrow to decrement or increment the year, or click the *Year* text to see a list of the years in the current decade. The link text changes to the current decade.
3. Click the year to which you want to jump. If the year isn't in the current decade, click either the left or right arrow to decrement or increment the decade, or click the *Year - Year* text to see a list of the decades in the current century.
4. Click the decade that contains the year you want.
5. Click the year that contains the month you want.
6. Click the month.

Here are two other techniques for changing the date:

- To move to today's date, either select View, Today or click the Today button.
- To move to a specific date, select View, Go to Date (or press Ctrl+G) to display the Go to Date dialog box. Enter the date you want in the Date text box, or drop down the box to display a calendar and click the date. You can also use the Show In list to select a different view (see the next section). Click OK to display the date.

Changing the Calendar View

By default, Calendar uses the Day view in the Events area, which shows a single day's worth of appointments and meetings. However, Calendar is quite flexible and has several other views you can use. Here's the complete list:

Day	Select View, Day (or press Ctrl+Shift+1).
Work Week	Displays Monday through Friday for the current week. Select View, Work Week (or press Ctrl+Shift+2).
Week	Displays Sunday through Saturday for the current week. Select View, Week (or press Ctrl+Shift+3).
Month	Displays the current month. Select View, Month (or press Ctrl+Shift+4).

TIP

By default, Calendar uses Sunday as the first day of the week, and Monday as the first day of the work week. To change these days, select File, Options. In the Options dialog box, use the First Day of Week and Start of Work Week lists to specify the days you prefer. Click OK.

Scheduling an Appointment

Calendar helps you keep track of your life by letting you create three kinds of items:

Appointment	This is the most general Calendar item and it refers to any activity for which you set aside a block of time. Typical appointments include a lunch date, a trip to the dentist or doctor, or a meeting. You can also create recurring appointments that are scheduled at regular intervals (such as weekly or monthly).
All-Day Event	This refers to any activity that consumes one or more entire days. Examples include conferences, trade shows, and vacations. In Calendar, events don't occupy blocks of time. Instead, they appear as banners above the affected days. You can also schedule recurring events.

Task	This is a specific chore, action, or project that you want to accomplish. Examples include paying a bill, completing a report, and learning a language. Tasks generally have a start date and a due date, and you can set up Calendar to remind you when the task is due.

The next few sections show you how to create appointments, all-day events, and tasks.

Creating an Appointment

Here are the steps you need to follow to set up a basic appointment:

1. Navigate to the date on which the appointment occurs.
2. Select File, New, Appointment. (You can also press Ctrl+N or click New Appointment.) Calendar creates the new appointment and displays it in the Details area, as shown in Figure 8.7.

NOTE

Calendar creates the new appointment in a block that includes the current time. For example, if it's currently 3:15 p.m., Calendar creates a new hour-long appointment that runs from 3:00 to 4:00. To create the appointment at a specific time, right-click the time in the Events area and then click New Appointment.

TIP

By default, Calendar creates new appointments that are one hour long. If most of your appointments use some other length, you can configure Calendar to use a different default length. Select File, Options to display the Options dialog box. In the Appointments group, use the Default Length list to select the length you prefer (15 minutes, 30 minutes, 1 hour, or 2 hours).

3. Click the title ("New Appointment" is the prosaic default) and then type a new title that describes your appointment.
4. Use the Location text box to specify the location (such as a room number or address) for the appointment.
5. If you have more than one calendar (see "Working with Multiple Calendars," later in this chapter), use the Calendar list to select the one you want to use for the new appointment.
6. If the appointment has an associated page on the web (such as a SharePoint site) or on an intranet, type the address in the URL text box.
7. Use the two Start controls to set the date and time that the appointment starts. Use the left control to change the date, and use the right control to change the time.

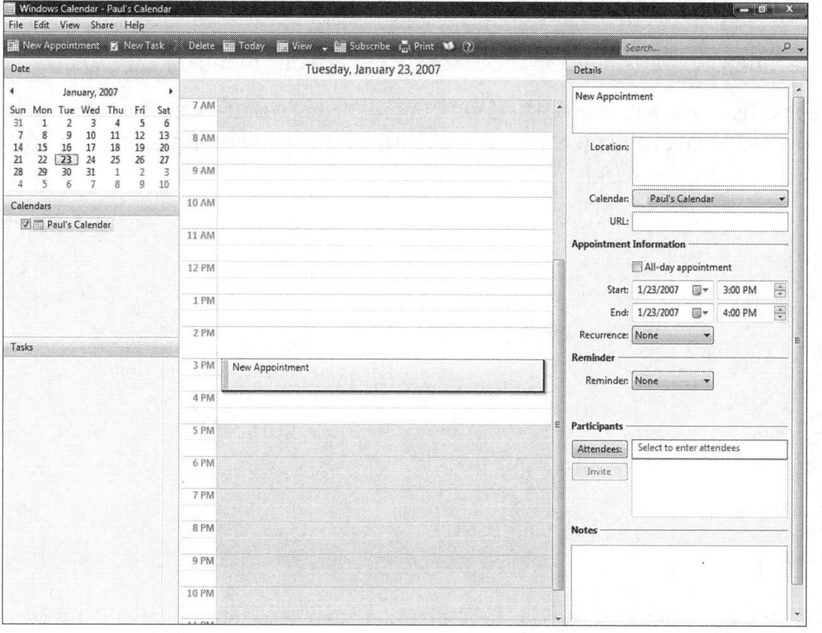

FIGURE 8.7 When you create a new appointment, the Details area displays the controls you use to configure the appointment.

8. Use the two End controls to set the date and time that the appointment ends. Use the left control to change the date, and use the right control to change the time.

TIP

You can also use your mouse to set an appointment's start and end times. To change the start time, click and drag the top edge of the appointment in the Events area; to change the end time, click and drag the bottom edge of the appointment.

9. Use the Notes box to type anything else you can think of regarding the appointment: a longer description, talking points, a few good jokes, and so on.

The steps above enable you to create a simple appointment. I discuss more sophisticated appointment features—specifically, recurrence, reminders, and attendees—in the next few sections.

Creating a Recurring Appointment

If you have an appointment that occurs at a regular interval (say, weekly or monthly), it's a waste of your precious time to enter these as separate appointments. Fortunately, you don't have to do that because Calendar lets you schedule a recurring appointment. For example, if you create a weekly appointment, Calendar fills in that appointment automatically on the same day of the week at the same time for the duration you specify.

To schedule a recurring appointment, follow these steps:

1. Either create a new appointment or click an existing appointment.
2. Use the Repeat list to select one of the following recurrence patterns: Every day, Weekly, Monthly, or Yearly. You can also select Advanced to pop up the Recurrence dialog box, shown in Figure 8.8.

FIGURE 8.8 Use the Recurrence dialog box to set up a custom recurrence interval for the appointment.

3. If you're using the Recurrence dialog box, type a value in the Repeat Every text box and select an interval (Days, Weeks, Months, or Years) in the list beside it.
4. If you chose Weeks or Months, Calendar adds controls to the dialog box to help you clarify your selection:
   - For the Weeks interval, Calendar displays seven buttons, one for each day of the week. Click the button that corresponds to the day of the week you want the appointments scheduled.
   - For the Months interval, Calendar displays several option buttons, the text of which depends on the day and date of the initial appointment. Figure 8.8 shows the recurrence options for a January 23, 2007 initial appointment.
5. Select one of the following options to set a limit on the recurrence:

Forever	Select this option to schedule the appointment indefinitely.
Number of Times	Select this option to schedule the appointment for a specific number of occurrences. Use the text box to type the number of occurrences you want.
Until	Select this option to specify the date of the last appointment. If the date you specify is after an occurrence (for example, if you are scheduling weekly appointments on Tuesdays but the date you specify falls on a Friday), Calendar schedules appointments up to the date that is closest to the one you specified.

6. Click OK.

Adding a Reminder

If you'd like Calendar to remind you that your appointment is coming up, follow these steps:

1. Either create a new appointment or click an existing appointment.
2. Use the Reminder list to specify how soon before the appointment the reminder should be displayed. You can also click On Date to have the reminder appear at a specified date and time.

When the reminder time comes the program displays a dialog box similar to the one shown in Figure 8.9. You have four ways to deal with the reminder:

Snooze	Click this button to have Calendar display the reminder again in five minutes (or whatever time you choose in the Click Snooze to be Reminded Again In list).
Dismiss	Click this button to close the reminder permanently.
Dismiss All	Click this button to close all the displayed reminders permanently.
View Item	Click this button to display the item in the Details area.

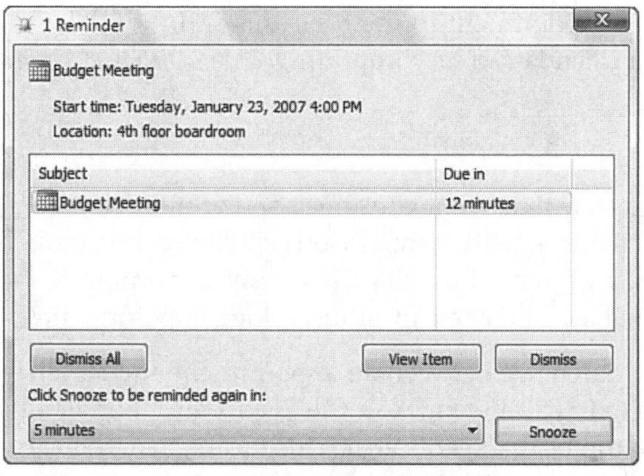

FIGURE 8.9 If you set up your appointment with a reminder, a dialog box such as this one appears when the reminder time comes.

TIP

By default, Calendar does not set up a reminder for new appointments. If you set a reminder for most of your appointments, you can configure Calendar to use a default reminder interval. Select File, Options to display the Options dialog box. In the Appointments group, use the Default Reminder list to select the number of minutes, hours, days, or weeks you want to appear by default in the Details area when you create a new appointment.

Inviting Attendees

If you want other people to attend your appointment, Calendar can send them an email invitation. Here are the steps to follow:

1. Either create a new appointment or click an existing appointment.
2. Specify the attendees by using either of the following techniques:
   - For people who aren't in your Contacts list, use the Attendees text box to type each person's email address, pressing Enter after each one.
   - For people in your Contacts list, click the Attendees button to display your Contacts list. For each person you want to invite, click the person's name and then click To. When you're done, click OK.
3. Click Invite. Calendar creates a new email message addressed to the attendees. The Subject line is INVITE: *Appointment*, where *Appointment* is the title of your appointment. Attached is a file in the iCalendar (`.ics`) format, which includes the specific of the appointment.
4. Add message text, if required, and then click Send.

If the recipients use calendar programs that support the iCalendar format, they can open the attachments to automatically add the appointment to their schedules. (In Windows Calendar, this is the same as importing a calendar, so see "Importing Calendar Files," later in this chapter.)

Creating an All-Day Event

As I mentioned earlier, an allday event is an activity that consumes one or more days (or, at least, the working part of those days). Some activities are obvious all-day events: trade shows, sales meetings, corporate retreats, and so on. But what about, say, a training session that lasts from 9:00 to 4:00? Is that an all-day event or just a long appointment?

From Calendar's point of view, the main difference between an appointment and an all-day event is that an appointment is entered as a time block in the Events area, but an all-day event is displayed as a banner at the top of the Events area. This means that you can also schedule appointments on days that you have all-day events.

A good example that illustrates these differences is a trade show. Suppose the show lasts an entire day and you're a sales rep who will be attending the show. You could schedule the show as a day-long appointment. However, what if you also want to visit with customers who are attending the show? It's possible to schedule conflicting appointments, but having that day-long appointment in there just clutters the Events area. In this case, it makes more sense to schedule the show as an all-day event. This leaves the Events area open for you to schedule appointments with your customers.

Follow these steps to schedule an all-day event:

1. Either create a new appointment or click an existing appointment.
2. Activate the All-Day Appointment check box.
3. Specify the Start and End dates for the event.

Creating a Task

It has become a time-honored tradition for the responsibly forgetful among us to write down reminders of things to do and upcoming activities. The idea behind Calendar's Tasks list is to give you an electronic equivalent of these to-do lists.

Here are the steps you need to follow to set up a task:

1. Select File, New, Task. (You can also press Ctrl+T or click New Task.) Calendar creates the new task and displays it in the Details area, as shown in Figure 8.10.

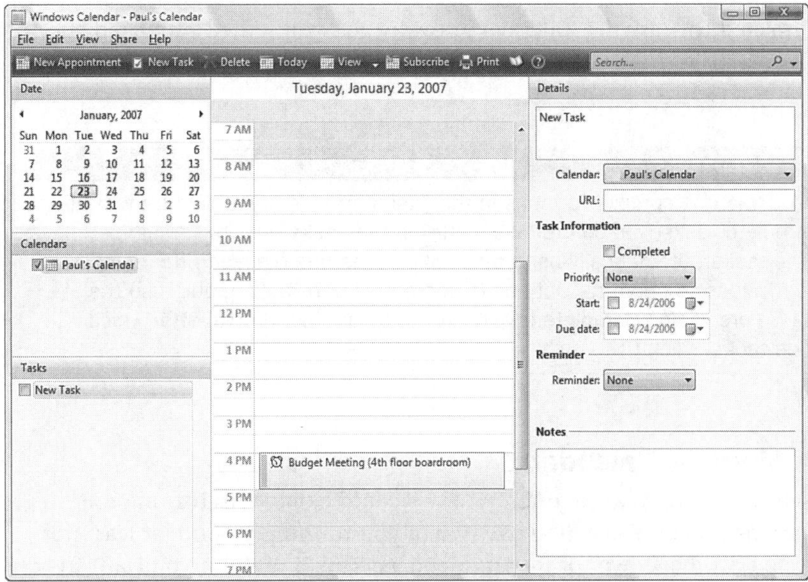

FIGURE 8.10 When you create a new task, the Details area displays the controls you use to configure the task.

When you create a new task, the details appear in, you guessed it, the Details area.

2. Click the title ("New Task" is the default) and then type a new title that describes your task.
3. If you have more than one calendar (see "Working with Multiple Calendars," later in this chapter), use the Calendar list to select the one you want to use for the new task.

4. If the appointment has an associated page on the Web (such as a SharePoint site) or on an intranet, type the address in the URL text box.
5. Use the Priority list to select the importance of the task: Low, Medium, High, or None.
6. Use the Start control to set the date that the task begins.
7. Use the Due Date control to set the date that the task is due to be completed.
8. If you'd like Calendar to remind you that your task is due, click Reminder and use the drop-down list to specify how soon before the appointment the reminder should be displayed. (You can also click On Date to have the reminder appear on a specified date.)
9. Use the Notes box to record anything else you can think of regarding the task: specific actions to perform, task resources, suggested ways to procrastinate, and so on.

When you've completed the task, let Calendar know by activating the Completed check box in the Details area. (Alternatively, click the check box beside the task in the Tasks list.)

TIP

By default, Calendar keeps completed tasks in the Tasks area until you delete them. If you'd rather not delete tasks, you can reduce clutter in the Tasks area by having Calendar hide the tasks automatically once a specified time has elapsed after completion. Select File, Options to open the Options dialog box. In the Tasks group, use the Number of Days Before Hiding Completed Tasks list to select the interval after which Calendar will hide tasks. Click OK.

Working with Multiple Calendars

Life is busy enough these days that we often wish we could clone ourselves in order to get all our tasks and errands done. You can't have two of you running around (at least not yet, anyway), but you can have two (or more) calendars. This is useful if you want to keep appointments and tasks separate. For example, you might want to use one calendar for business items and another for personal items. Similarly, you might want to use different schedules for different projects, clients, departments, and so on.

If you don't like the idea of switching from one calendar to another to view the corresponding appointments and tasks, don't worry because you don't have to do so. Instead, Calendar always shows *all* your appointments and tasks. Calendar helps you keeps things straight by color-coding the items in each calendar (one calendar's items might be red, another's green, and so on).

Follow these steps to create and configure a new calendar:

1. Select File, New Calendar. Calendar displays a new calendar in the Details area.
2. Type a new name for the calendar.
3. Use the Color list to choose the color you want to use for this calendar's appointments and tasks.

Figure 8.11 shows the Calendar window with a couple of calendars in use.

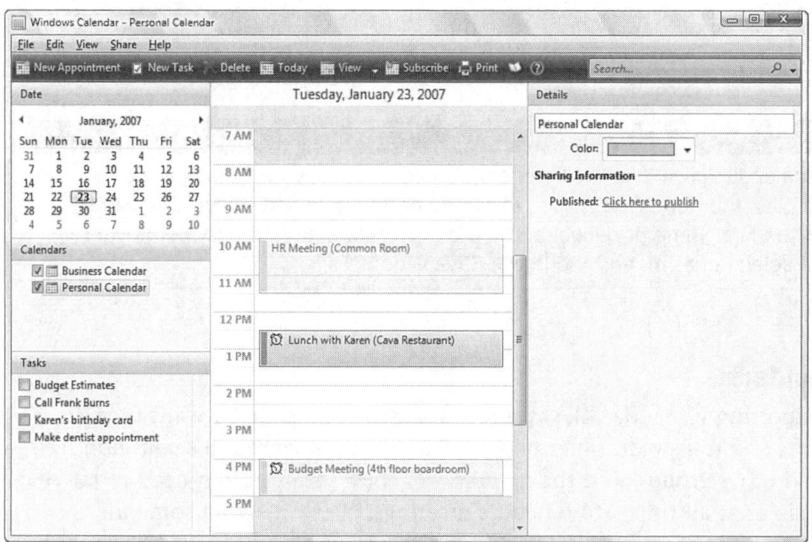

FIGURE 8.11 Windows Calendar with two calendars in use.

TIP

Calendar displays all the items from all your calendars. If you find that the Events area becomes too cluttered, you can hide a calendar's item by deactivating its check box in the Calendars area.

Importing Calendar Files

I mentioned earlier that Windows Mail supports the iCalendar (`.ics`) format, which is the standard calendaring format. Each iCalendar file contains one or more appointments or tasks. If you want to include those items in your version of Calendar, you can import the iCalendar file and then either add the items to your own calendar or display them in a separate calendar. Follow these steps to import an iCalendar file:

1. Select File, Import to display the Import dialog box.
2. Use the Import File text box to specify the location of the calendar file. (Alternatively, click Browse and use the Open dialog box to select the file and click Open.)
3. In the Destination list, you have two choices:
   - Select Create New Calendar to create a separate calendar for the imported items
   - Select the name of an existing calendar to merge the imported items into that calendar
4. Click Import.

NOTE

To export your calendar, click it in the Calendars area; if you only want to export a particular item, click the item. Select File, Export to open the Export dialog box. Select a location, edit the File Name (if necessary; the default filename is the same as your calendar or the selected item), and then click Save.

Sharing Calendars

Importing and exporting iCalendar files is fine if you only occasionally want to share your appointments and tasks with other people. These days, however, it's common to work in teams and other groups, and the members of these groups often need to know each other's schedules at all times (to schedule meetings, check whether someone is in the office, and so on). For these more sophisticated scenarios, you need a more sophisticated sharing method, and Calendar is happy to oblige. The program enables people to **publish** a calendar to an accessible location such as a network share or a website designed to hold calendars. Other people can then **subscribe** to that calendar to add it to their own list of calendars. Once that's done, subscribers can then synchronize with the published calendar to see the most up-to-date information.

Publishing Your Calendar

Here are the steps you need to follow to publish your calendar:

1. In the Calendars list, click the calendar you want to publish.
2. Select Share, Publish to open the Publish Calendar dialog box.
3. Edit the Calendar Name, if necessary.

TIP

After the Calendar publishes, you have the option of sending an email message that includes the address of the shared calendar. Most email clients will display this address as a link. However, if the address includes spaces, the link will stop at the first space. Therefore, consider changing the calendar name to remove any spaces.

4. Use the Location to Publish Calendar to type the address of the network share or website where you want the calendar published (see Figure 8.12).

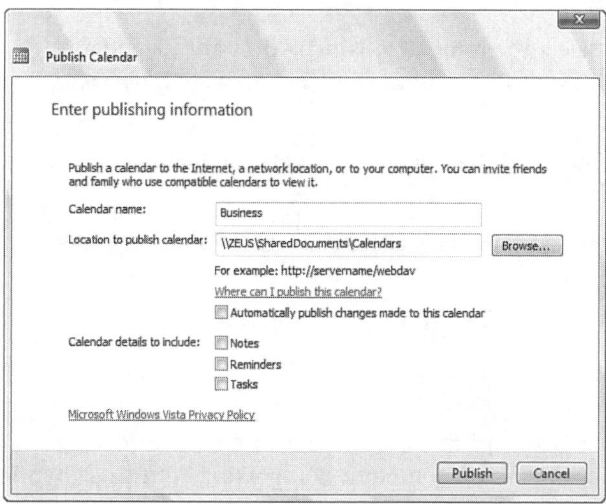

FIGURE 8.12 Use the Publish Calendar dialog box to publish your calendar to a network share or website.

5. If you want Calendar to update your calendar whenever you make changes to it, activate the Automatically Publish Changes Made to This Calendar check box. (If you leave this option deactivated, you can still publish your changes by hand, as described later; see "Working with Shared Calendars.")

6. In the Calendar Details to Include section, activate the check box beside each item you want in your published calendar: Notes, Reminders, and Tasks.

7. Click Publish. Calendar publishes the calendar to the remote location and then displays a dialog box to let you know the operation was successful.

8. To let other people know that your calendar is shared and where it can be found, click Announce. Calendar creates a new email message that includes the following in the body (where *address* is the address of your published calendar):

```
You can subscribe to my calendar at address
```

9. Click Finish.

Subscribing to a Calendar

To add another person's published calendar to your Calendars list, follow these steps:

1. Select Share, Subscribe to open the Subscribe to a Calendar dialog box.

2. Use the Calendar to Subscribe To text box to type the address of the published calendar.

3. Click Next. Calendar subscribes you to the published calendar and then displays the Calendar Subscription Settings dialog box.
4. Edit the calendar name, if necessary.
5. Use the Update Interval list to select the interval at which you want Calendar to update the subscribed calendar: Every 15 Minutes, Every Hour, Every Day, Every Week, or No Update.
6. If you want to receive any reminders in the calendar, activate the Include Reminders check box.
7. If you also want to see the published calendar's tasks, activate the Include Tasks check box.
8. Click Finish. The published calendar appears in your Calendars list.

Working with Shared Calendars

After you publish one or more of your calendars and subscribe to one or more remote calendars, Windows Calendar offers a number of techniques for working with these items. Here's a summary:

- **Changing a calendar's sharing information**—When you select a published or subscribed calendar, the Details pane displays a Sharing Information section, and you use the controls in that section to configure the calendar's sharing options.
- **Publishing calendar changes**—If your published calendar isn't configured to automatically publish changes, you can republish by hand by selecting the calendar and then selecting Share, Sync.
- **Updating a subscribed calendar**—If you didn't configure an update interval for a subscribed calendar, or if you want to see the latest data in that calendar before the next update is scheduled, select the calendar and then select Share, Sync.
- **Synchronizing all shared calendars**—If you have multiple shared calendars (published and subscribed), you can synchronize them all at once by selecting Share, Sync All.
- **Sending a published calendar announcement**—If you didn't send an announcement about your published calendar, or if you want to send the announcement to different people, select the calendar and then select Share, Send Publish E-mail.
- **Stopping a published calendar**—If you no longer want other people to subscribe to your calendar, select it and then select Stop Publishing. When Calendar asks you to confirm, click Unpublish. (Note, however, that if you want your calendar file to remain on the server, you first need to deactivate the Delete Calendar on Server check box.)
- **Stopping a subscribed calendar**—If you no longer want to subscribe to a remote calendar, select it and then press Delete. When Calendar asks you to confirm, click Yes.

Sending and Receiving Faxes

Perhaps I'm dating myself, but I still remember when the fax machine (or the *facsimile machine,* as it was called back then) was the hottest thing around, the new kid on the telecommunications block. How amazing it seemed that we could send a letter or memo or even a picture through the phone lines and have it emerge seconds later across town or even across the country. Sure, the fax that came slithering out the other end was a little fuzzier than the original, and certainly a lot slimier, but it sure beat using the post office.

Vista Business | Vista Enterprise | Vista Ultimate Edition

The faxing fad has come and gone, and with so many other ways to share documents nowadays (email, the Web, SharePoint sites, and so on), faxing is becoming increasingly rare. But reports of the demise of the fax have been greatly exaggerated, which is why Windows Vista continues to provide fax services. The latest incarnation is Windows Fax and Scan, and that name tells you quite a bit about the current state of the faxing world. That is, that although faxing itself stubbornly refuses to leave the business stage, fax machines were for the most part given the hook years ago. After all, what's the point of having a dedicated fax machine when, with the right software, you can perform precisely the same task using a document scanner?

The rest of this chapter shows you how to configure the Fax service and how to use it to send and receive faxes.

Starting Windows Fax and Scan

To launch Windows Fax and Scan, select Start, All Programs, Windows Fax and Scan. (Alternatively, select Start, Control Panel, Printers to open the Printers window, and then double-click the Fax icon.) In the Windows Fax and Scan window, click Fax to display the folders shown in Figure 8.13.

Note first that Fax and Scan looks a lot like Windows Mail—it has a message list, a preview pane, and a folder tree that includes the following five branches:

`Incoming` This folder displays information about the fax that you're currently receiving. For example, during fax reception, the Status column displays `In progress` and the Extended Status column displays `Answered` and then `Receiving`.

`Inbox` This folder stores the incoming faxes that you've received successfully.

`Drafts` This folder stores copies of saved faxes that you're composing but haven't sent yet.

`Outbox` This folder stores data about the fax that you're currently sending. For example, during the send operation, the Status column displays `In progress`, and the Extended Status column displays `Transmitting`.

`Sent Items` This folder stores a copy of each fax that you've sent successfully.

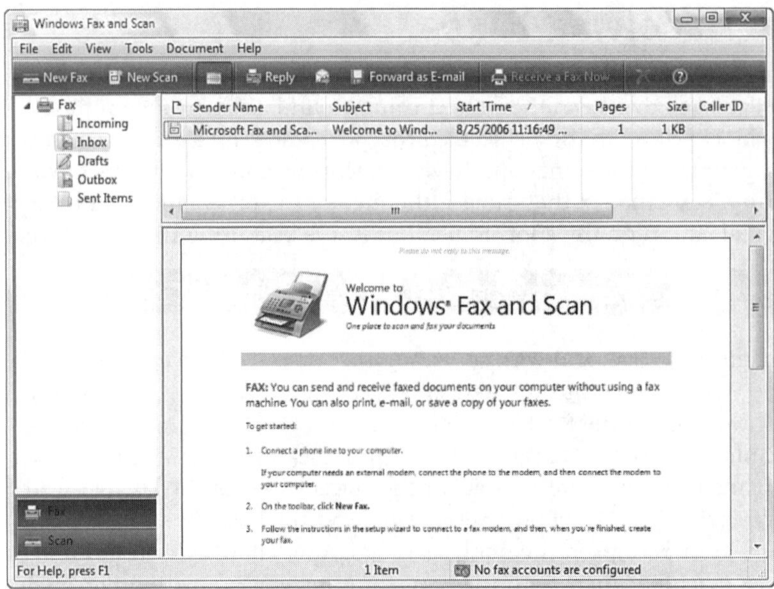

FIGURE 8.13 Windows Fax and Scan is your home base for Windows Vista faxing.

After you first start Windows Fax and Scan, there are two chores you need to perform before going on to more useful pursuits: create a fax account and tell the program a bit about yourself. The next two sections take you through these mundane-but-necessary tasks.

Creating a Fax Account

Before you can do anything useful with Windows Fax and Scan, you have to create a fax account, which the program uses to store your incoming and outgoing faxes. Here are the steps to follow:

1. Select Tools, Fax Accounts to open the Fax Accounts dialog box.
2. Click Add to launch the Fax Setup Wizard.
3. You have two choices right off the bat:

   Connect to a Fax Modem—Click this option to use a fax modem attached to your computer. Type a name for the fax modem and then click Next.

   Connect to a Fax Server on My Network—Click this option to use a network fax server. Type the fax server's network address and then click Next.
4. The wizard next asks how you want to receive faxes:

   Answer Automatically—Click this option to configure Fax and Scan to automatically answer incoming calls after five rings. After you click this option, enter your UAC credentials.

Notify Me—Click this option to configure Fax and Scan to display a message when it detects an incoming call. After you click this option, enter your UAC credentials.

I'll Choose Later; I Want to Create a Fax Now—Click this option if you prefer to set up the receive options later or if you don't have UAC credentials.

5. The Fax Accounts dialog box now displays your account. Click Close.

Entering Some Personal Data

When you send a fax with a cover page, Windows Fax and Scan includes fields for your name, fax number, business phone number, and home phone number. (You can customize these fields; see the "Creating a Cover Page Fax" section later in this chapter.) If you don't want your recipients to see blanks in these fields, follow these steps to add this personal data to your fax account:

1. Select Tools, Sender Information to see the Sender Information dialog box.
2. Type your full name.
3. Type your fax number.
4. Type your work phone.
5. Fill in the other fields as needed.
6. Click OK.

Sending a Fax

To fax something to a friend or colleague (or, heck, even a total stranger), Windows Vista gives you two ways to proceed:

- You can fax a simple note by sending just a cover page.
- You can fax a more complex document either by sending it to the Windows Vista Fax "printer" or by including a file attachment with a fax.

8

Specifying Send Options

Before getting to the specifics of sending a fax, let's take a quick look at the various options that the Fax and Scan service provides for sending. To see these options, follow these steps:

1. Select Tools, Fax Settings and then enter your UAC credentials to display the Fax Settings dialog box.
2. Display the General tab.
3. If you have multiple fax modems installed on your computer, click Select Fax Device to choose the fax modem you want to use to send faxes.

4. Make sure that the Allow the Device to Send Faxes check box is activated.
5. Click More Options to open the More Options dialog box.
6. Edit the TSID setting and then click OK.

NOTE

Windows Vista assigns a name to your fax machine. This is known in the trade as the **TSID—Transmitting Subscriber Identification** (or sometimes **Transmitting Station Identifier**). When the other person receives your fax, your TSID is displayed at the top of each page. If the other person is receiving on a computer, the TSID appears in the TSID line (or some similar field, depending on the program the recipient is using). Unfortunately, the default TSID in Windows Vista is *Fax*, which redefines the word *uninspiring*. To fix this, edit the TSID as described in step 6. For example, it's common to change it to a name—such as your company name, your department name, or your own name—followed by your fax number.

7. Display the Advanced tab to see the following options:

Include Banner in Sent Faxes	When this option is activated, Fax and Scan includes a text banner across the top edge of each page of the outgoing fax. This text includes your TSID, page number, and the recipient's fax number.
Number of Attempts	This value determines the number of times the Fax service attempts to send a fax if it encounters a busy signal or some other error.
Dial Again After	This value determines the number of minutes the Fax service waits between retries.
Discount Rates: Start At	You'll learn later on that you can tell Fax and Scan to send a fax "when discount rates apply," which means when your phone rates are discounted (such as after midnight). Use the Start At spin box to specify the start time for your discounted phone rates.
Discount Rates: End At	Use this spin box to specify the end time for your discounted phone rates.

8. Click OK.

Sending a Cover Page Fax

Let's start with the simple cover page route, which the follow steps describe:

1. Select File, New, Fax, or click the New Fax button. Fax and Scan displays the New Fax window.

2. Use the Cover Page list to select the cover page you want to use. You have four default choices:

confident	This cover page includes the word `confidential`, so use it for faxes that contain sensitive data.
fyi	This cover page includes the phrase `FOR YOUR INFORMATION`, so use it for faxes where you don't require a response or action.
urgent	This cover page includes the word `urgent` in large (52-point) type, so use it for faxes that require immediate attention or action.
generic	This cover page does not contain any special text, so it's useful for regular fax messages.

3. Use the To box to type the recipient's fax number.

TIP

If the recipient is in your `Contacts` folder and you have the Fax field filled in (in either the Work or the Home tab), click To, select the recipient, click To, and then click OK. If the person's name appears in the To box in red type, it means Fax and Scan can't find a fax number. Double-click the recipient to open the contact properties sheet, fill in the Fax number in either the Work or Home tab, and then click OK.

4. Type a subject for the fax.
5. Use the Cover Page Notes text box to type the message you want to appear on the cover page.
6. Select Tools, Options.
7. Choose when you want the fax sent:

Now	Sends the fax right away
When Discount Rates Apply	Sends the fax as soon as possible after your discount rates begin (as you specified in the previous section)
At This Time	Sends the fax at the time you specify use the spin box

8. In the Priority group, use the Send Fax As list to set the fax priority to High, Normal, or Low.
9. Click OK.
10. When you're ready to ship the fax, click Send.

Faxing a Document

The other (and probably more common) method of sending a fax is to send a document directly from an application. You don't need applications with special features to do this, either. That's because Windows Vista comes with a fax printer driver, except that this driver doesn't send a document to the printer. Instead, it renders the document as a fax and sends it to your modem.

To try this, follow these steps:

1. Create the document that you want to ship.
2. Select the program's File, Print command to get to the Print dialog box.
3. Select Fax as the printer and then click Print. The New Fax window appears.
4. Follow the steps outlined in the previous section to set the fax options. With this method, you don't have to bother with a cover page. If you'd still like to include one, use the Cover Page list to select the cover page you prefer.

Fax and Scan gives you two other ways to fax a document:

- Faxing a document as an attachment—The New Fax window looks much like an email message window, so it should come as no surprise that you can "attach" a document to a fax message. Follow the steps from the previous section to configure the fax, and then select Insert, File Attachment (or click the Attach toolbar button). Use the Insert Attachment dialog box to select your document, and then click Attach.
- Faxing a hard-copy document—If the document is a hard copy, you can still fax it by scanning it. In Windows Fax and Scan, select File, New, Fax from Scanner. Place the document in the scanner and then click OK to launch the scanning process. An alternative method is to create a new fax as described in the previous section, and then select Insert, Pages from Scanner.

Working with Fax Cover Pages

I've mentioned fax cover pages a couple of times so far in this chapter, so it's time to take a closer look. In the fax world, a cover page performs the same function as an email message header: It specifies who is supposed to receive the fax and who sent it. Unlike an email message header, which is meant to be read and interpreted by a mail server or gateway, a fax cover sheet is meant for human consumption. In a company or department in which several people share a fax machine, the cover page clarifies who is supposed to get the fax. And when that person does read the message, she can use the rest of the information to see who sent the fax.

As I mentioned earlier, Fax and Scan comes with four prefabricated cover pages. You can use these pages as circumstances dictate, you can modify them to suit your style, or you can create new pages from scratch.

Working with Personal Fax Cover Pages

The four predefined cover pages are **common cover pages** because they're available to all users and to all fax accounts. Any cover pages that you create are **personal cover pages**.

Fax and Scan gives you two ways to create personal cover pages: create a cover page from scratch or modify a copy of a common cover page.

Creating a Personal Cover Page from Scratch To create a personal cover page from scratch, open Windows Fax and Scan, select Tools, Cover Pages to display the Fax Cover Pages dialog box, and then click New. Fax and Scan launches the Fax Cover Page Editor and opens a blank cover page. See "Editing a Cover Page," later in this chapter, to learn how to build your cover page.

Modifying a Copy of a Common Cover Page To create a personal cover page using a copy of a common cover pages, follow these steps:

1. In Windows Fax and Scan, select Tools, Cover Pages to display the Fax Cover Pages dialog box.
2. Click Copy to display the `Common Coverpages` folder.
3. Select the common cover page you want to copy, and then click Open. Fax and Scan adds a copy of the cover page to the Fax Cover Pages dialog box.
4. If you want to rename the copied cover page, select it, click Rename, type the new name, and then press Enter.
5. Make sure that the copied cover page is still selected, and then select Open. Fax and Scan launches the Fax Cover Page Editor and displays the copied cover page. See "Editing a Cover Page," later in this chapter to learn how to modify the cover page.

Figure 8.14 shows the Fax Cover Page Editor with a copy of the `generic` common cover page.

NOTE

To open one of the four common cover pages directly, select File, Open and then navigate to the following folder:

`%SystemDrive%\ProgramData\Windows NT\MSFax\Common Coverpages`

8

Editing a Cover Page

Keeping in mind that cover pages are always sent as bitmaps, the idea behind the Cover Page Editor is to create a template for the bitmap. So, as you might expect, the Cover Page Editor is really a graphics application that specializes in working with fax bitmaps. The templates you work with consist of three types of fields: information, text, and graphics.

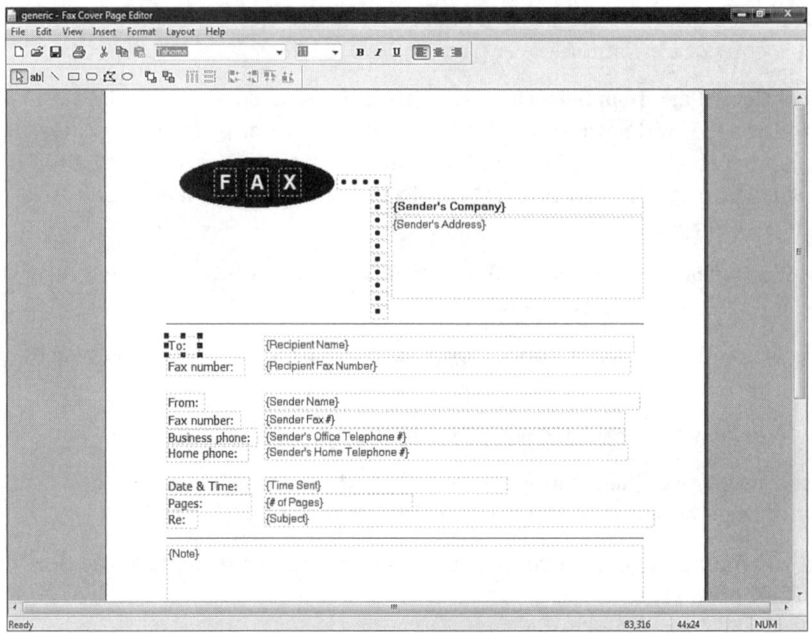

FIGURE 8.14 Windows Fax and Scan provides the Fax Cover Page Editor so that you can edit and create cover pages to use with your faxes.

Inserting Information Fields Information fields are placeholders for data. For example, the {Sender's Company} field (information fields always appear surrounded by braces) tells the Fax service to insert the name of the sender's company each time you use this cover page when you send a fax. With the Cover Page Editor, you can insert fields for recipient, sender, and message data:

- For the recipient, you can insert fields for the person's name and fax number. This information is gleaned from the properties sheet for the recipient's address. Select Insert, Recipient and then click either Name or Fax Number.
- For the sender, you can insert fields for the name, fax number, company, address, telephone numbers, and more. Select Insert, Sender to see the available fields.
- For the message, the available fields include the note text, the Subject line, the date and time the fax was sent, and the number of pages. Selecting Insert, Message displays a menu that lists these fields.

Inserting Text Fields Text fields are text boxes that either describe the contents of each information field or provide titles, subtitles, and headings. To insert a text field, click the Text button on the Drawing toolbar (see Figure 8.14), drag the mouse inside the cover page to create a box for the field, and enter your text. To change the text in an existing field, double-click it. (Note, too, that you can format text fields by using the buttons on the Style toolbar or by selecting Format, Font or Format, Align Text.)

Inserting Graphics Fields Graphics fields are bitmap objects that you can use for logos and separators, or just to add some style to the cover page. The Cover Page Editor's Drawing toolbar enables you to create many kinds of drawing objects, including lines, rectangles, circles, and polygons. Table 8.1 lists the buttons available on this toolbar.

TABLE 8.1 The Cover Page Editor's Drawing Toolbar Buttons

Button	Name	Description
	Line	Creates a straight line.
	Rectangle	Creates a rectangle. (Hold down Shift while dragging to create a square.)
	Rounded Rectangle	Creates a rectangle with rounded corners.
	Polygon	Creates a polygon.
	Ellipse	Creates an ellipse. (Hold down Shift while dragging to create a circle.)
	Bring to Front	Moves the selected object in front of any objects that overlap it. You can also select Layout, Bring to Front or press Ctrl+F.
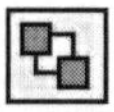	Send to Back	Moves the selected object behind any objects that overlap it. You can also select Layout, Send to Back or press Ctrl+B.
	Space Across	Spaces the selected objects evenly across the page. You can also select Layout, Space Evenly, Across.
	Space Down	Spaces the selected objects evenly down the page. You can also select Layout, Space Evenly, Down.
	Align Left	Aligns the selected objects along their left edges. You can also select Layout, Align Objects, Left.
	Align Right	Aligns the selected objects along their right edges. You can also select Layout, Align Objects, Right.
	Align Top	Aligns the selected objects along their top edges. You can also select Layout, Align Objects, Top.
	Align Bottom	Aligns the selected objects along their bottom edges. You can also select Layout, Align Objects, Bottom.

Receiving Faxes

This section explains how Windows Fax and Scan handles incoming faxes and shows you how to view those faxes when they're sitting in your Inbox.

Specifying Receive Options

Before getting to the specifics of receiving a fax, let's take a quick look at the various options that the Fax service provides for receiving. To see these options, follow these steps:

1. Select Tools, Fax Settings and then enter your UAC credentials to display the Fax Settings dialog box.
2. Display the General tab.
3. If you have multiple fax modems installed on your computer, click Select Fax Device to choose the fax modem you want to use to send faxes.
4. Make sure that the Allow the Device to Receive Fax Calls check box is activated.
5. Select one of the following options:

Manually Answer	Activate this option to answer incoming calls manually (as described in the "Answering Calls Manually" section, later in this chapter).
Automatically Answer After *x* Rings	Activate this option to have Fax and Scan answer incoming calls automatically (as described in the "Answering Calls Automatically" section, later in this chapter). Use the spin box to specify the number of rings after which Fax and Scan answers the call.

6. Click More Options to open the More Options dialog box.
7. Edit the CSID setting.

NOTE

The CSID is your **Called Subscriber Identification**. This identifies your computer to the fax sender.

8. You also have the following options (click OK when you're done):

Print a Copy To	Activate this check box to have Windows Fax and Scan automatically print any received fax. Use the list that becomes activated to choose the printer you want to use.
Save a Copy To	Activate this check box to store a second copy of each fax in the folder that you specify. The original copy of the fax is saved in the Fax and Scan Inbox.

Answering Incoming Calls

How Fax and Scan handles incoming calls from remote fax systems depends on how you set up your fax account to receive calls: manually or automatically. I describe both options in the next two sections.

Answering Calls Automatically Enabling the Automatically Answer After *x* Rings option is the easiest way to handle incoming calls. In this mode, Fax and Scan constantly polls the modem's serial port for calls. When it detects a call coming in, it waits for whatever number of rings you specified (which can be as few as one ring or as many as 99) and then leaps into action. Without any prodding from you, it answers the phone and immediately starts conversing with the remote fax machine. The Fax Status Monitor window appears onscreen so that you can see the progress of the transfer, as shown in Figure 8.15.

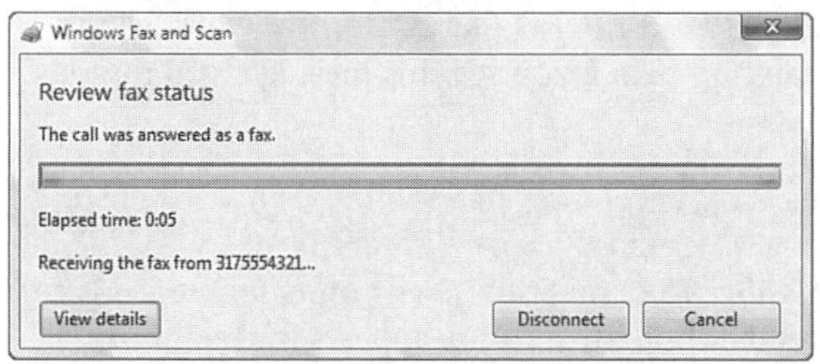

FIGURE 8.15 The Fax Status Monitor appears when Windows Fax and Scan answers the incoming call.

> **TIP**
>
> If you find Fax and Scan's sounds (such as the ringing associated with an incoming call) annoying, you can disable them. Select Tools, Fax Settings, and then display the Tracking tab. Click Sound Options and then deactivate the check boxes for each sound you want to silence.

8

Answering Calls Manually If you work with Fax and Scan in manual mode, when a call comes in you hear a ringing tone and the taskbar's notification area pops up a message that says `Incoming call from fax`, where *fax* is the CSID of the remote fax. To answer the call, you have three choices:

- Click the taskbar message.
- In Windows Fax and Scan, either select Tools, Receive a Fax Now or click the Receive a Fax Now toolbar button.
- If you happen to have the Fax Status Monitor open already, click the Answer Call button.

TIP

You can display the Fax Status Monitor at any time by selecting Tools, Fax Status Monitor.

This mode is ideal if you receive both voice calls and fax calls on the same phone line. Here's the basic procedure you need to follow for incoming calls:

1. When the phone rings, pick up the receiver.
2. If you hear a series of tones, you know that a fax is on its way. In this case, click the notification message or the Answer Call button, as described earlier.
3. Fax and Scan initializes the modem to handle the call. Wait until the Fax and Scan reports `The call was answered as a fax` in the Fax Status Monitor window and then hang up the receiver. If you hang up before you see this message, you disconnect the call.

Working with Received Faxes

Depending on the size of the fax transmission, Fax and Scan takes from a few seconds to a few minutes to process the data. Eventually, though, your fax appears in the inbox. From there, you can perform the following chores:

- **Read the fax**—Double-click the fax in the `Inbox` folder (or select the fax and then press Enter or select File, Open).
- **Print the fax**—Select the fax and then select File, Print.
- **Send a reply to the fax sender**—Select the fax and then select Document, Reply (or click the Reply button). Fax and Scan creates a new fax message with the sender added to the To box.
- **Forward the fax to another fax number**—Select the fax and then select Document, Forward (or click the Forward button). Fax and Scan creates a new fax message with the fax as an attachment.
- **Email the fax as an attachment**—Select the fax and then select Document, Forward as Attachment (or click the Forward as E-mail button). Use the email message window to set up the email message and then click Send.
- **Save the fax as an image**—Select the fax and then select File, Save As. Use the Save As dialog box to choose a name and location for the file and then click Save. Note that the fax is saved as a TIF image.
- **Delete the fax**—Select the fax and then select Edit, Delete (or just press the Delete key).

From Here

Here are some other sections in the book where you'll find information related to the topics in this chapter:

- To learn about User Account Control, see the "User Account Control: Smarter User Privileges" section in Chapter 6, "Getting the Most Out of User Accounts."
- For more on using Windows Mail, see Chapter 19, "Communicating with Windows Mail."
- To learn how to set up a network, see Chapter 22, "Setting Up a Small Network."

CHAPTER 9

Mobile Computing in Windows Vista

IN THIS CHAPTER

- Accessing Notebook Features with the Mobile PC Control Panel
- Monitoring Your Notebook with the Windows Mobility Center
- Managing Notebook Power
- Attaching an External Monitor
- Configuring Presentation Settings
- Understanding Windows SideShow
- Getting the Most Out of Your Tablet PC

Notebook computers used to occupy very specific and unalterable niches in the computing ecology. Sales professionals didn't leave home without them, executives on business trips routinely packed their portables, and corporate employees without a personal machine lugged a laptop home to do some extra work. In each case, though, the notebook computer—with its cramped keyboard, hard-to-read LCD panel, and minuscule hard disk—was always considered a poor substitute for a desktop machine.

For many years, it seemed that notebooks were doomed to remain among the lower castes in the social hierarchy of personal computers. But recent developments have caused notebooks to shed their inferiority complex. Today's luggables have impressive 1024×768 (or better) displays, upward of 100 gigabytes of hard disk real estate, and built-in wireless capabilities. Add a couple of PC card slots, connectors for full-size keyboards and monitors, and maybe even a docking station, and suddenly your desktop system doesn't look so superior.

The notebook community's bid for respectability wasn't lost on the designers of Windows Vista. They've incorporated many new notebook PC features into the operating system, including improved power management, the Mobility Center, Presentation Settings, and Windows SideShow. Vista also supports Tablet PCs in a big way with many more options and settings, a revamped Input Panel, new gestures, and extensive tools for improving handwriting recognition. This chapter takes you through all of these new features.

Accessing Notebook Features with the Mobile PC Control Panel

New Most Windows Vista mobility enhancements are designed with a single purpose in mind: to give you easier access to the notebook-related features that you use most. That makes sense because when you're using a notebook on the go, you might have only a limited amount of battery power, and you don't want to waste it trying to locate some obscure configuration option. And it's still true that most notebook keyboards and pointing devices are harder to use than their full-size desktop counterparts, so the fewer keystrokes and mouse clicks required to perform Windows tasks, the better.

Your first indication that Vista wants to make your mobile computing life easier is the new Mobile PC Control Panel page, shown in Figure 9.1 (select Start, Control Panel, Mobile PC). The idea behind the Mobile PC page is to consolidate in a single spot all the Vista configuration options that are directly or indirectly related to notebooks. Whether you want to change the screen orientation on your Tablet PC, adjust settings before a presentation, or change power options, it's all just a mouse click or two away.

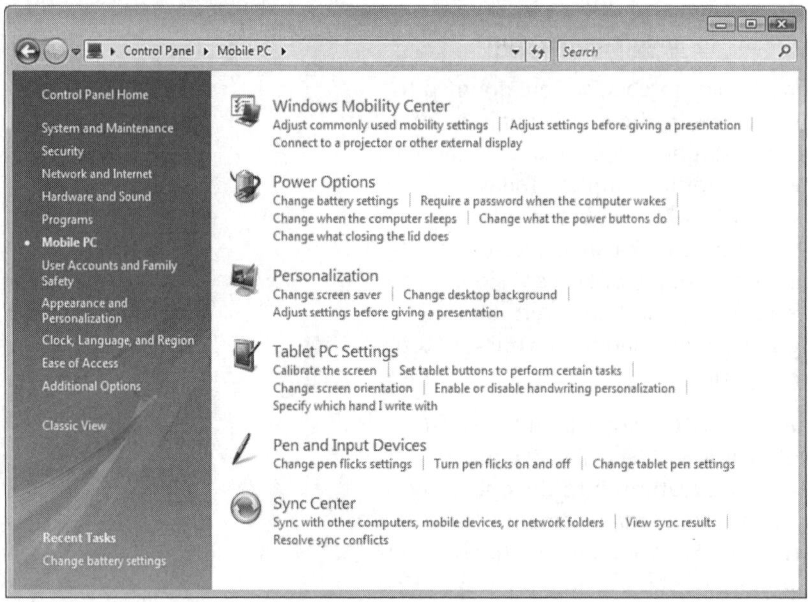

FIGURE 9.1 The Mobile PC Control Panel gives you quick access to most notebook-related configuration options.

Monitoring Your Notebook with the Windows Mobility Center

The Mobile PC Control Panel offers links to a broad range of notebook features. A more targeted approach is the new Vista Windows Mobility Center, which you start by clicking the Windows Mobility Center link in the Mobile PC Control Panel. Figure 9.2 shows the Windows Mobility Center window that appears. (Note that you only see the full Mobility Center in the Business, Enterprise, and Ultimate editions of Vista.)

Vista Business Vista Enterprise Vista Ultimate Edition

FIGURE 9.2 The new Mobility Center offers a selection of information and controls for notebook-related features.

The Mobility Center offers information on eight key notebook areas, as well as controls to adjust these features:

NOTE

If your notebook doesn't support a particular feature, Vista hides the corresponding Mobility Center module. For example, my ThinkPad X41 Tablet PC doesn't support brightness adjustments, so the Brightness module doesn't show up in Figure 9.2. You also don't see the External Display module if your notebook doesn't have a VGA connector for an external monitor.

- **Brightness**—The current brightness setting of your notebook screen (if your machine supports this features). Use the slider to adjust the brightness.
- **Volume**—The current notebook speaker volume. Use the slider to adjust the volume or click Mute to toggle sound off and on.
- **Battery Status**—The current charge level of the notebook battery. Use the drop-down list to select one of three power plans: Balanced, Power Saver, or High Performance (I discuss these plans later; see "Managing Notebook Power").
- **Wireless Network**—The wireless connection status (Connected or Disconnected), and the signal strength, if connected.
- **Screen Orientation**—The current orientation of the Tablet PC screen. Click Rotate Screen to rotate the screen by 90° counterclockwise. See "Changing the Screen Orientation," later in this chapter.

- **External Display**—The current status of the external monitor connected to your notebook or docking station. Click Connect Display to open the Display Settings dialog box and work with the second monitor (see "Attaching an External Monitor," later in this chapter).
- **Sync Center**—The current synchronization status of your offline files. Click the Sync button to synchronize your notebook's offline files. For more information, see "Working with Network Files Offline," in Chapter 23, "Accessing and Administering the Network."
- **Presentation Settings**—The current status of your presentation settings. Click Turn On to activate your presentation settings (see "Configuring Presentation Settings," later in this chapter).

Note, too, that Microsoft is giving PC manufacturers access to the Mobility Center, so we'll likely see the Mobility Center window customized with features that are specific to particular notebooks.

Managing Notebook Power

If you must run your notebook without AC (on an airplane, for example), maximizing battery life is crucial. Like most of its predecessors, Windows Vista supports various power schemes—Vista calls them *power plans*—that specify different time intervals for when the notebook is plugged in and when it's on batteries. However, it's equally important to monitor the current state of the battery to avoid a shutdown while you're working.

NOTE

One way that Windows Vista helps preserve battery power is through its new ReadyDrive technology, which takes advantage of a new storage medium called the **hybrid hard drive**. This is a hard drive that also comes a with non-volatile flash memory chip, typically with a capacity of 1GB. The size of the flash memory means that ReadyDrive can write most data to and from the flash memory, which means much less work for the hard drive and so less of a drain on the battery. ReadyDrive also enables Vista to enter into and resume from Sleep mode faster because it can write and restore the notebook's current state more quickly by using the flash memory.

Monitoring Battery Life

To help you monitor battery life, Windows Vista displays the Power icon in the notification area. When you're running on AC power, the Power icon also includes a plug, as shown in Figure 9.3. When you're on batteries, the Power icon is completely green and displays without the plug, as shown in Figure 9.4. As your notebook uses up battery power, the amount of green decreases accordingly.

To see the exact level of battery power remaining, you have three choices:

- Open the Mobility Center (as described in the previous section) and examine the Battery Status display.

- Hover the mouse pointer over the Power icon. After a second or two, Windows Vista displays a fly-out that tells you the approximate time left on battery power and percentage of battery life remaining (see Figure 9.5).

FIGURE 9.3 On AC power, the Power icon includes a plug.

FIGURE 9.4 On batteries, the amount of green in the Power icon tells you how much battery power is left.

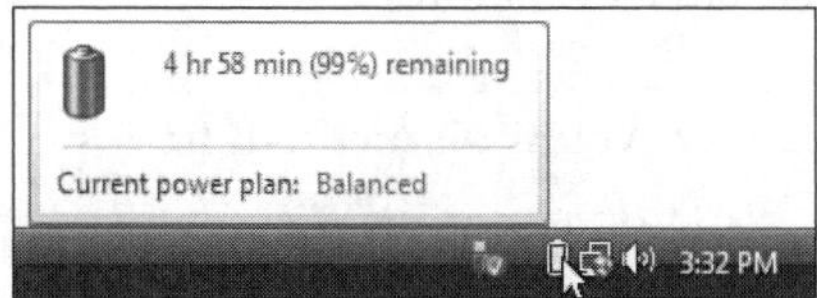

FIGURE 9.5 Hover the mouse pointer over the Power icon to see this fly-out.

- Click the Power icon. Windows Vista displays a larger fly-out, shown in Figure 9.6, that not only shows you the approximate time left on battery power and percentage of battery life remaining, but also enables you to change the current power plan (Balanced, Power Saver, or High Performance).

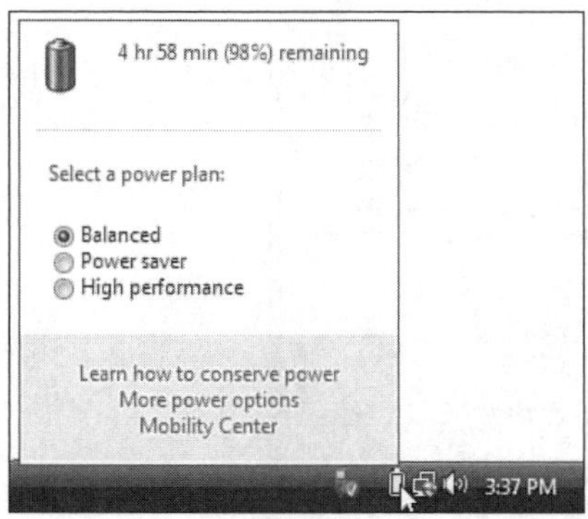

FIGURE 9.6 Click the Power icon to see this fly-out.

Specifying a Power Plan

New Windows Vista shuts down some system components in an effort to keep your battery running longer. This is controlled by your current **power plan**, a power-management configuration that specifies which components shut down and when Windows Vista does so. Windows Vista has three power plans:

- **Power Saver**—Devices such as the screen and hard disk are powered down after a short idle interval. For example, on battery power, Windows Vista turns off the notebook screen after 3 minutes and the hard disk after 5 minutes.
- **High Performance**—Devices are powered down only after a longer idle interval, which improves performance because you're less likely to have to wait for them to start up again. For example, on battery power, Windows Vista turns off the notebook screen and hard disk after 20 minutes.
- **Balanced**—This is the middle road (more or less) between the Power Saver and High Performance plans. For example, on battery power, Windows Vista turns off the notebook screen after 5 minutes and the hard disk after 10 minutes.

The default power plan is Balanced, but Windows Vista gives you three methods to change it:

- **Using the Mobility Center**—In the Battery Status section, use the drop-down list to select a power plan.
- **Using the Power icon**—Click the Power icon to see the banner shown in Figure 9.6, and then click the power plan you prefer.
- **Using the Power Options window**—Click the Power icon and then click More Power Options (or select Start, Control Panel, Mobile PC, Power Options) to display the Power Options window shown in Figure 9.7; then click a power plan option.

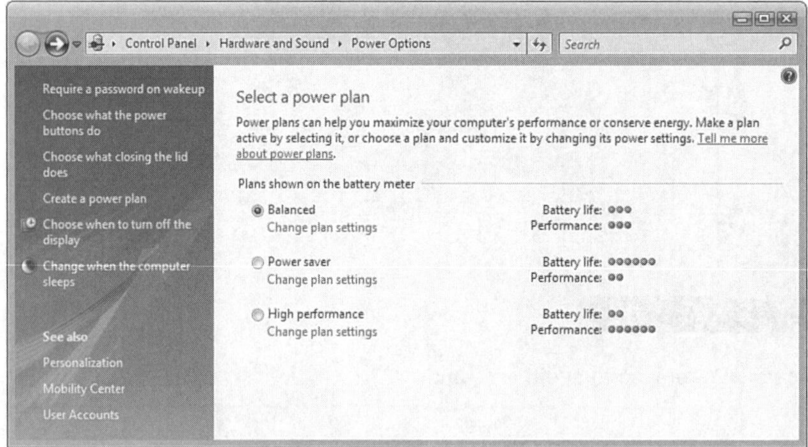

FIGURE 9.7 Double-click the Power icon to display the Power Options window.

Creating a Custom Power Plan

New Vista's preset power plans are probably fine for most uses, but you might want to tweak some plan characteristics. For example, you might want a plan that never turns off the hard disk or that waits longer before turning off the display when the notebook is on AC power. For these and other custom plan settings, Vista gives you two choices: creating your own plan and customizing an existing plan.

Creating Your Own Power Plan

You can set up a new plan that specifies the intervals when Vista turns off the display and puts the computer to sleep both while on battery power and while plugged in. Here are the steps to follow:

1. In the Power Options window, click Create a Power Plan. Vista displays the Create a Power Plan window.
2. Click the built-in power plan that you want to use as a starting point.

CAUTION

The custom plan you create becomes one of Vista's default plans, meaning it appears in the fly-out when you click the Power icon and in the plan list in the Mobility Center. However, Vista *replaces* whatever built-in plan you use to get started on your custom plan. (You can still activate the original built-in plan using the Power Options window.) Therefore, don't base a new custom plan off an existing plan that you activate frequently.

3. Type a Plan Name and click Next. Vista displays the Edit Plan Settings window, shown in Figure 9.8.

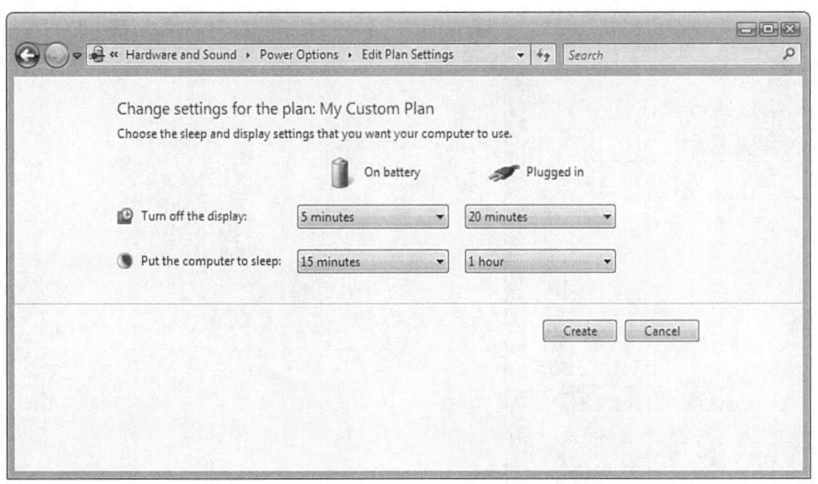

FIGURE 9.8 Use the Edit Plan Settings window to specify the sleep and display settings for your custom power plan.

9

4. In both the On Battery and Plugged In columns, select an idle interval after which Vista will turn off the display and put the computer to sleep.
5. Click Create. Vista creates your custom power plan.

TIP

To delete a custom power plan, open the Power Options window and select a different plan, if you haven't already done so. Click the Change Plan Settings link below your custom plan. In the Edit Plan Settings window, click Delete This Plan. When Vista asks you to confirm, click OK.

Customizing an Existing Power Plan

Just because you saw in the previous section that Windows Vista gave only you two measly power settings—turning off the display and putting the computer to sleep—for your custom plan, that doesn't mean that's the extent of Vista's power options, far from it. You can customize any plan (including a custom plan) with a large number of settings. To work with these settings, follow these steps:

1. In the Power Options window, click the Change Plan Settings link under the plan you want to customize. You see the Edit Plan Settings window (shown in Figure 9.8).
2. Specify your idle intervals for Turn Off the Display and Put the Computer to Sleep.
3. Click the Change Advanced Power Settings link. This displays the Advanced Settings tab, shown in Figure 9.9, which offers a wide range of power-management settings.

FIGURE 9.9 Customizing an existing power plan gives you a much wider range of power-management options.

4. Use the branches in the Advanced Settings tab to set your power management options.

TIP

To see all the available settings, click the Change Settings That Are Currently Unavailable link, and then enter your UAC credentials.

5. Click OK.
6. Click Save Changes. Vista updates the power plan.

Configuring Your Notebook's Power Buttons

New Most newer notebooks enable you to configure three "power buttons": closing the lid, using the on/off button, and using the sleep button. When you activate these buttons, they put your system into sleep mode, hibernate mode, or turn it off altogether. On some notebooks, there isn't a separate sleep button; you simply tap the on/off button quickly.

To configure these buttons for power management in Vista, follow these steps:

1. In the Power Options window, click the Choose What the Power Buttons Do link to see the System Settings window, shown in Figure 9.10. Use the lists to configure the power button, sleep button, and lid switch for battery power and AC power.

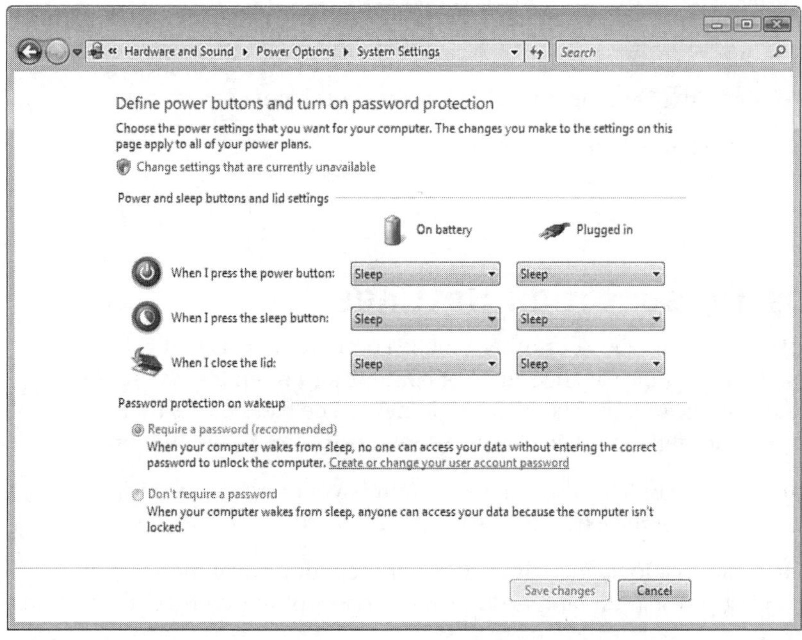

FIGURE 9.10 Use this window to configure what Vista does when you press the power button, the sleep button, or close the notebook lid.

2. Use the lists to configure the power button, sleep button, and lid switch for battery power and AC power.

TIP

By default, Vista disables the options in the Password Protection on Wakeup group. This means that you always have to enter your user account password when Vista wakes from Sleep or Hibernate mode. If you prefer not to enter your password each time, you can enable these options by clicking the Change Settings That Are Currently Unavailable link, and then entering your UAC credentials. Once you've done that, you can click the Don't Require a Password option.

3. Click Save Changes.

Attaching an External Monitor

If you have a second monitor nearby and your notebook or its docking station has a VGA port, you can connect the monitor and extend your notebook's desktop onto the second monitor. This is a great way to expand a small notebook screen. Here's how it works:

1. Attach the external monitor.
2. Right-click the desktop and then click Personalize. (If your desktop is nowhere in sight, click Start, Control Panel, Adjust Screen Resolution.)
3. Click the icon that represents the external monitor (it's the rectangle showing the large 2).
4. Activate the Extend the Desktop onto this Monitor check box.
5. Adjust the resolution and colors, if necessary.
6. Click OK.

Configuring Presentation Settings

New The portability of a notebook or other mobile computer means that these machines are now the first choice as the source of content for presentations, from the boardroom to the conference room. That's the good news. The bad news is that you always need to (or should) tend to a few chores before starting your presentation:

- Turn off your screensaver. The last thing you want is your screensaver kicking in while you're spending some extra time explaining a point.
- Turn off system notifications, including alerts for incoming email messages and instant-messaging posts. Your viewers don't want interruptions by these distractions.
- Adjust the speaker volume to an acceptable level.

- Select an appropriate desktop wallpaper image. Your desktop could be visible before or after the presentation, if only briefly. Even so, you probably want a wallpaper that invokes a professional image, or you might prefer a blank desktop.

If you're a regular presenter, changing all these settings before each presentation and reversing them afterward is a time-consuming chore. However, Windows Vista comes with a new feature called Presentation Settings that promises to take most of the drudgery out of this part of presenting. The Presentation Settings feature is a collection of configuration options, including screen blanking, system notifications, speaker volume, and desktop wallpaper. You use Presentation Settings to specify the configuration options you want to use during a presentation. After you've done that once, you can use Presentation Settings to turn those options on and off with just a few mouse clicks. Presentation Settings is available for all versions of Vista except Home Basic.

To configure the Presentation Settings, follow these steps:

1. Select Start, Control Panel, Mobile PC.
2. Under the Windows Mobility Center icon, click Adjust Settings Before Giving a Presentation. Windows Vista displays the Presentation Settings dialog box shown in Figure 9.11.

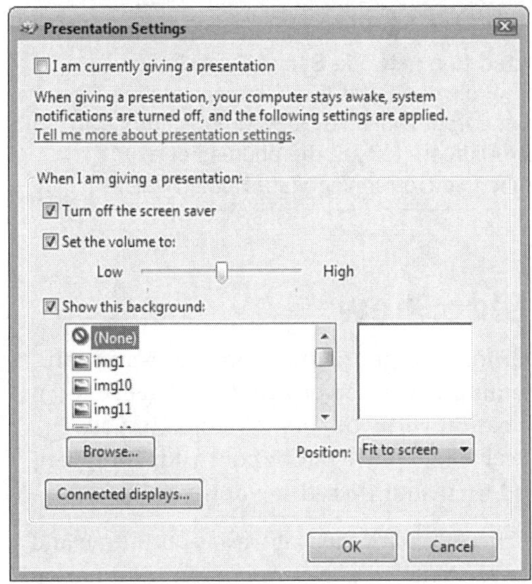

FIGURE 9.11 Use the Presentation Settings dialog box to configure the Vista settings you want to use while you give a presentation.

3. Use the following controls to set up your notebook for presentations:
    - **Turn Off the Screen Saver**—Activate this check box to prevent the screensaver from kicking in
    - **Set the Volume To**—Activate this check box and then use this slider to set the volume level you want
    - **Show this Background**—Activate this check box and then select a background or (None)
4. Click OK.

When it's time to make your presentation, you have two ways to switch to your saved settings:

- Open the Mobility Center and select Turn On in the Presentation Settings section. Select Turn Off when you're done.
- Open the Presentation Settings dialog box, activate the I Am Currently Giving a Presentation check box, and click OK. Deactivate this check box when you finish.

NOTE

Another new presentation-related feature in Vista is Network Projection, which enables you run a presentation on a projector connected to a network. Select Start, All Programs, Accessories, Connect to a Network Projector. Enter your User Account Control credentials and then click either Choose from Available Network Projectors (to see a list of projectors) or Enter the Projector Address (to type the address of a specific projector). This feature is not available if you're running Vista Home Basic.

Understanding Windows SideShow

New Here's a scenario that's all too familiar for a lot of us: You're on your way to an offsite meeting, and when you arrive at the building, you forget which conference room you're supposed to go to. You have the information with you, but it's stored in your calendaring program on your notebook. You have no choice but to boot your computer, load your calendar, get the info you need, and then shut everything down again.

No one likes to power up a computer just to check a quick fact—it wastes both time and battery power. To avoid this, many people simply write whatever important information they need on a sticky note and attach it to the outside of the notebook, but how low-tech can you get?

Here's another scenario: You're waiting in an airport lounge and want to listen to music or catch up on some podcasts, but there's no AC outlet available. How do you listen to the audio without draining your battery entirely? One solution is to configure Windows not to go into sleep mode when you shut the notebook lid. The computer remains running, but the screen turns off automatically when you close the lid, so you save quite a bit of power. However, to control the media playback, you have to open the lid anyway.

One of the most intriguing innovations in Windows Vista is a feature that lets you view information without starting up your computer or resorting to sticky notes, and lets you manipulate a program such as Windows Media Player without having to open the notebook lid. Windows SideShow is a new technology that does two things:

- It enables a notebook manufacturer to add a small display—called a **secondary display** or an **auxiliary display**—to the outside of a notebook case.
- It enables Windows Vista to display information on the secondary display no matter what power state the notebook is in: on, off, or sleep.

If you use a clamshell-style cell phone, you've seen a similar idea: when the phone is closed, a screen on the outside of the phone shows you the current time, battery state, and other data.

With Windows SideShow, however, you get a much more powerful interface that can display a wider variety of content:

- Developers of existing programs can choose to send data to the secondary display.
- Developers can build new gadgets designed for SideShow.

Microsoft created an application programming interface for SideShow, so third-party developers should create a lot of programs and gadgets that you can add to your SideShow menu.

Using the Windows SideShow window (select Start, Control Panel, Hardware and Sound, Windows SideShow; see Figure 9.12), you decide which programs or gadgets you want to appear in the SideShow secondary display. The list of possible gadgets was not finalized as I wrote this, but examples include a calendar (for example, Windows Calendar or the Outlook Calendar), email (such as Windows Mail or the Outlook Inbox), and Windows Media Player. Depending on the layout of the secondary display, you choose which program or gadget you want to work with.

NOTE

Windows SideShow isn't strictly for notebooks. Microsoft has shown images of secondary displays running on keyboards, remote controls, and cell phones. Almost any device that can wirelessly connect to a Vista machine can transform into a SideShow-ready device with the addition of a secondary display.

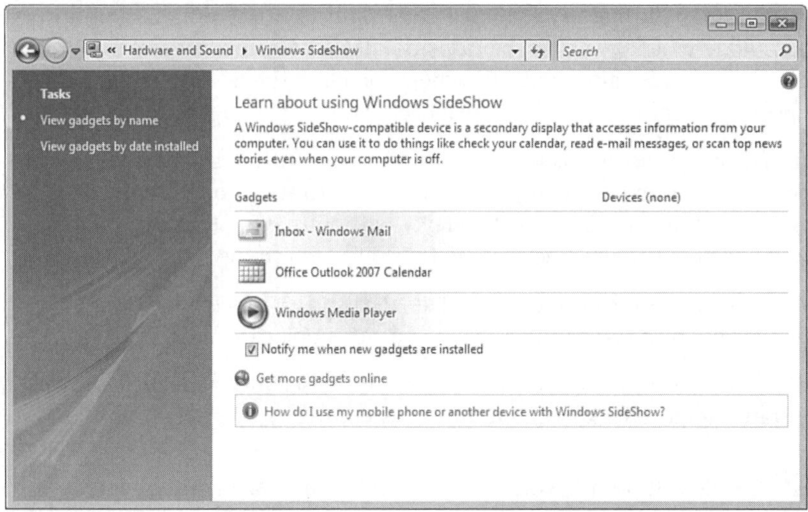

FIGURE 9.12 Use the Windows SideShow Control Panel to decide which programs and gadgets you want to appear in the SideShow secondary display.

Getting the Most Out of Your Tablet PC

In the "old days," working on a document usually meant pulling out a blank sheet of paper, taking up a pen (or some other writing instrument), and then writing out your thoughts in longhand. Nowadays, of course, electronic document editing supersedes this pen-and-paper approach almost entirely. However, there are still plenty of situations when people still write things out in longhand:

- Jotting down an address or other data while on the phone
- Taking notes at a meeting
- Recording a list of things to do while visiting a client
- Creating a quick map or message for faxing
- Sketching out ideas or blueprints in a brainstorming session

Unfortunately, for all but the most trivial notes, writing on paper is inefficient because you eventually have to put the writing into electronic form, either by entering the text by hand or by scanning the document.

What the world has needed for a long time is a way to bridge the gap between purely digital and purely analog writing. We've needed a way to combine the convenience of the electronic format with the simplicity of pen-based writing. After several aborted attempts (think of the Apple Newton), that bridge was built in recent years: the Tablet PC. At first glance, many Tablet PCs look just like small notebook computers, and they certainly can be used just like any notebook. However, a Tablet PC boasts three hardware innovations that make it unique:

- A touch screen (usually pressure-sensitive) that replaces the usual notebook LCD screen. Some Tablet PC screens respond to touch, but most respond to only a specific type of pen (discussed next).
- A **digital pen** or stylus that acts as an all-purpose input device: You can use the pen to click, double-click, click-and-drag, and tap out individual characters using an onscreen keyboard. In certain applications, you can also use the pen to "write" directly on the screen, just as though it were a piece of paper, thus enabling you to jot notes, sketch diagrams, add proofreader marks, or just doodle your way through a boring meeting.
- The ability to reorient the screen physically so that it lies flat on top of the keyboard, thus making the screen's orientation like a tablet or pad of paper. (Note, however, that there are now some Tablet PCs that don't support this feature and have lids like regular notebooks.)

NOTE

Some Tablet PCs come with a screen that's sensitive to finger touches. Windows Vista supports these screens.

The first Tablet PCs came with their own unique operating system: Windows XP Tablet PC Edition. With Windows Vista, the Tablet PC–specific features are now built into the regular operating system, although they are activated only when Vista is installed on a Tablet PC (and you're running any Vista edition except Home Basic).

Before moving on to the new Tablet PC, I should note that Vista comes with a couple of tools that were also part of the XP version: Windows Journal and Sticky Notes. These programs are identical to the XP versions.

Changing the Screen Orientation

New The first Tablet PC feature to mention is one that you've already seen. The new Mobility Center comes with a Screen Orientation section that tells you the current screen orientation (refer to Figure 9.2 earlier in this chapter). There are four settings in all:

- **Primary Landscape**—This is the default orientation, with the taskbar at the bottom of the display and the top edge of the desktop at the top of the display.
- **Secondary Portrait**—This orientation places the taskbar at the right edge of the display, and the top edge of the desktop at the left of the display.
- **Secondary Landscape**—This orientation places the taskbar at the top of the display, and the top edge of the desktop at the bottom of the display.

- **Primary Portrait**—This orientation places the taskbar at the left edge of the display, and the top edge of the desktop at the right of the display.

Setting Tablet PC Options

Before you start inking with Vista, you'll probably want to configure a few settings, and Vista offers quite a few more than XP. Your starting point is the Control Panel's Mobile PC window—specifically, the renamed Tablet PC Settings icon (formerly named *Tablet and Pen Settings*). Select Start, Control Panel, Mobile PC, Tablet PC Settings.

In the Tablet PC Settings dialog box that appears, the General tab is basically the same as the old Settings tab (you can switch between right-handed or left-handed menus and calibrate the pen), and the Display tab is identical to its predecessor (it offers another method to change the screen orientation).

However, the new Handwriting Recognition tab has two sections (as shown in Figure 9.13):

- **Personalization**—Later in this chapter (see "Personalizing Handwriting Recognition"), you'll see that you can provide Vista with samples of your handwriting. This increases the accuracy of the **handwriting recognizer** (the feature that converts handwritten text into typed text), but only when the Use the Personalized Recognizer check box is activated.
- **Automatic Learning**—This feature collects information about your writing, including the words you write and the style in which you write them. Note that this applies not only to your handwriting—the ink you write in the Input Panel, the recognized text, and the corrected text—but also to your typing, including email messages and web addresses typed into Internet Explorer. To use this feature, activate the Use Automatic Learning option.

CAUTION

It's understandable that some people have privacy concerns about the Automatic Learning feature because it is sure to collect proprietary and sensitive data typed into email messages. However, Microsoft notes that the information stays on your computer and is stored in a proprietary format that a text editor or word processor can't read. It seems inevitable that someone will hack this new format, however, so if you do not want sensitive data stored via Automatic Learning, you should turn off this feature.

Working with the Tablet PC Input Panel

As with XP Tablet PC Edition, Windows Vista comes with the Tablet PC Input Panel tool that you use to enter text and other symbols with the digital pen instead of the keyboard. You have two ways to display the Input Panel:

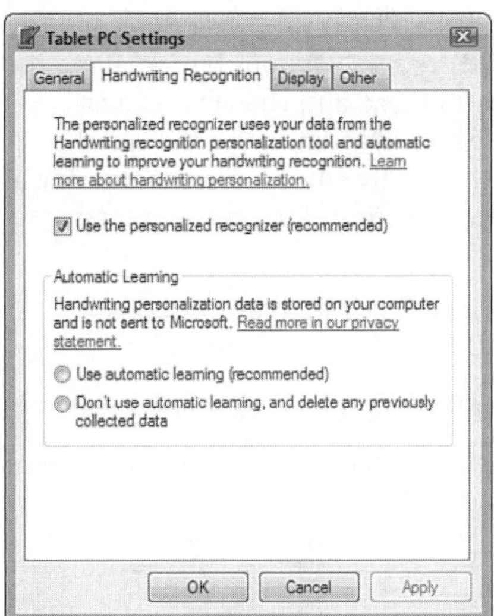

FIGURE 9.13 Use the Handwriting Recognition tab to activate new Vista features for improving handwriting recognition.

- In Vista, an icon for the Input Panel appears in a small tab docked on the left edge of the screen. Hover the mouse pointer over the tab to display it, and then click the icon or any part of the tab.
- Move the pen over any area in which you can enter text (such as a text box). In most cases, the Input Panel icon appears near the text entry area. Click the icon when it appears.

Figure 9.14 shows the Input Panel.

TIP

You can also add an icon for the Input Panel to the Vista taskbar. Right-click the taskbar and then click Toolbars, Tablet PC Input Panel.

FIGURE 9.14 Use the Writing Pad to write words or short phrases by hand.

The layout of the Input Panel is slightly different from the XP version, with the icons for the writing pad, character pad, and onscreen Keyboard, and the Options button along the top. The miniature keyboard that appears with the writing pad and character pad is slightly different as well, with the notable difference being the addition of the Web key full time. (In XP Tablet PC Edition, the Web key appeared only when you were entering a web address.) This makes sense because users often need to write URLs in email messages and other correspondence.

The Vista Input Panel also comes with quite a few more options than its predecessor. Vista gives you two ways to see them:

- In the Input Panel, click Tools and then click Options in the menu that appears.
- In the Tablet PC Settings dialog box, display the Other tab and click the Go to Input Panel Settings link.

Here's a list of some of the more significant new settings:

- **AutoComplete** (Settings tab)—When this check box is activated, the Input Panel automatically completes your handwriting if it recognizes the first few characters. For example, if you're writing an email address that you've entered (via handwriting or typing) in the past, Input Panel recognizes it after a character or two and displays a banner with the completed entry. You need only click the completed entry to insert it. This also works with web addresses and filenames.
- **Show the Input Panel Tab** (Opening tab)—Use this check box to toggle the Input Panel tab on and off. For example, if you display the Tablet PC Input Panel toolbar in the taskbar, you might prefer to turn off the Input Panel tab.
- **You Can Choose Where the Input Panel Tab Appears** (Opening tab)—Choose either On the Left Edge of the Screen (the default) or On the Right Edge of the Screen.
- **New Writing Line** (Writing Pad tab)—Use this slider to specify how close to the end of the writing line you want to write to before starting a new line automatically.
- **Gestures** (Gestures tab)—In XP Tablet PC Edition, you could delete handwritten text by "scratching it out" using a Z-shape gesture. Many people found this hard to master and a bit unnatural, so Vista offers several new scratch-out gestures, which you turn on by activating the All Scratch-Out and Strikethrough Gestures option.

NOTE

Vista offers four new scratch-out gestures:

Strikethrough—A horizontal line (straight or wavy) through the text.

Vertical scratch-out—An M- or W-shaped gesture through the text.

Circular scratch-out—A circle or oval around the text.

Angled scratch-out—An angled line (straight or wavy) through the text. The angle can be from top left to bottom right, or from bottom left to top right.

- **Password Security** (Advanced tab)—This slider (see Figure 9.15) controls the security features that Vista uses when you use the pen to enter a password into a password text box. At the High setting, Vista automatically switches to the onscreen keyboard (and doesn't allow you to switch to the writing pad or character pad) and doesn't show the pen pointer or highlight the keys that you tap while entering the password.

FIGURE 9.15 The Input Panel Options dialog box offers many new features, including security settings that protect password entries.

Using Pen Flicks

New The Input Panel onscreen keyboard has keys that you can tap with your pen to navigate a document and enter program shortcut keys. However, if you just want to scroll through a document or navigate web pages, having the keyboard onscreen is a hassle because it takes up so much room. An alternative is to tap-and-drag the vertical or horizontal scroll box, or tap the program's built-in navigation features (such as the Back and Forward buttons in Internet Explorer).

Vista gives you a third choice for navigating a document: **pen flicks**. Pen flicks are gestures that you can use in any application to scroll up and down in a document, or to navigate backward or forward in Internet Explorer or Windows Explorer:

- **Scroll up** (about one screenful)—Move the pen up in a straight line
- **Scroll down** (about one screenful)—Move the pen down in a straight line
- **Navigate back**—Move the pen to the left in a straight line
- **Navigate forward**—Move the pen right in a straight line

TIP

For a pen flick to work, you need to follow these techniques:

- Move the pen across the screen for about half an inch (at least 10mm)
- Move the pen very quickly
- Move the pen in a straight line
- Lift your pen off the screen quickly at the end of the flick

You can also set up pen flicks for other program features:

- **Copy**—Move the pen up and to the left in a straight line
- **Paste**—Move the pen up and to the right in a straight line
- **Delete**—Move the pen down and to the right in a straight line
- **Undo**—Move the pen down and to the left in a straight line

To activate and configure flicks, follow these steps:

1. Select Start, Control Panel, Mobile PC, Pen and Input Devices. The Pen and Input Devices dialog box appears.
2. Display the Flicks tab, shown in Figure 9.16.
3. Activate the Use Flicks to Perform Common Actions Quickly and Easily check box.
4. Select the flicks you want to use:
    - **Navigational Flicks**—Activate this option to use the Scroll Up, Scroll Down, Back, and Forward flicks.
    - **Navigational Flicks and Editing Flicks**—Activate this option to also use the Copy, Paste, Delete, and Undo flicks in any program.

If you activate the Navigational Flicks and Editing Flicks option, the Customize button enables. Click this button to display the Customize Flicks dialog box shown in Figure 9.17. You use this dialog box to apply one of Vista's built-in actions (such as Cut, Open, Print, or Redo) to a flick. Alternatively, click (add) to create a custom action by specifying a key or key combination to apply to the flick.

TIP

If you forget which flick performs which action, you can easily find out by displaying the Pen Flicks icon in the taskbar's notification area. In the Flicks tab, activate the Display Flicks Icon in the Notification Area check box. (Note that the icon doesn't show up until you attempt at least one flick.) Clicking this icon displays the Current Pen Flicks Settings fly-out that shows your current flick setup.

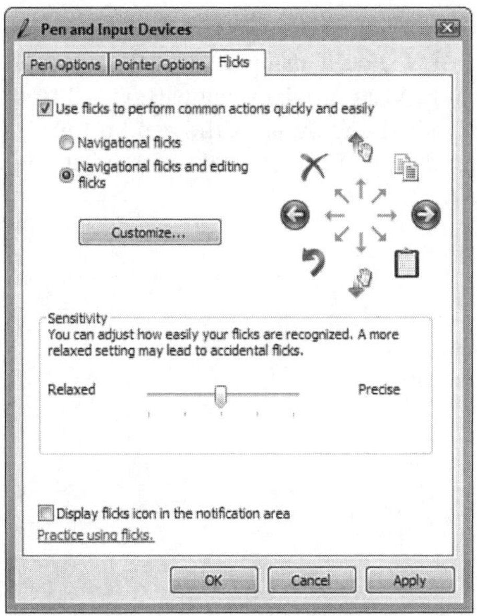

FIGURE 9.16 Use the Flicks tab to activate and configure pen flicks.

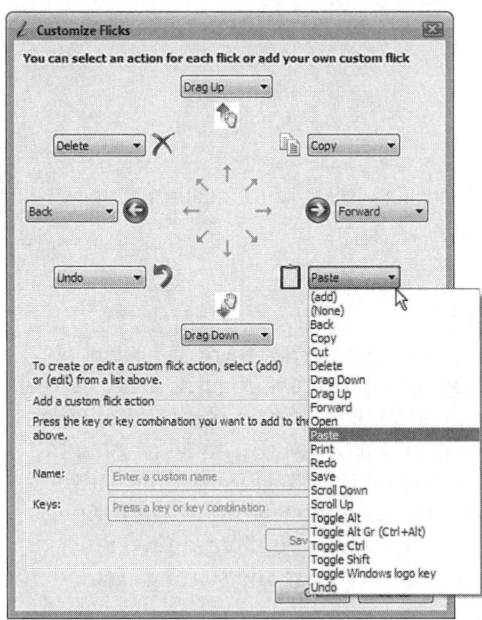

FIGURE 9.17 Use the Customize Flicks dialog box to apply different actions or key combinations to a flick gesture.

Setting Pointer Options

While we're in the Pen and Input Devices dialog box, I should also point out the new Pointer Options tab, shown in Figure 9.18. By default, Vista provides you with visual feedback when you single-tap and double-tap the pen and when you press the pen button. I find that this visual feedback helps when I'm using the pen for mouse-like actions. If you don't, you can turn them off by deactivating the check boxes.

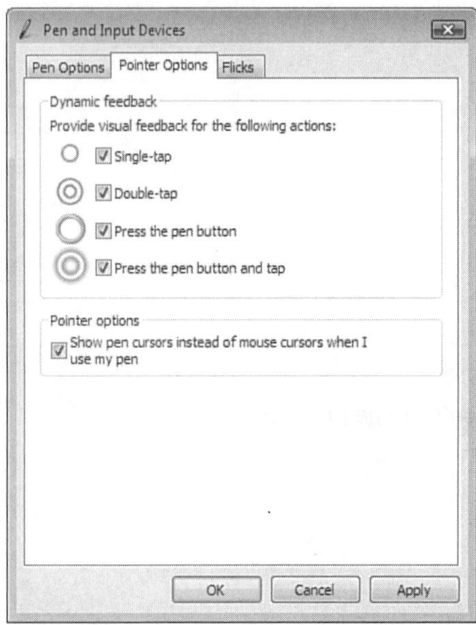

FIGURE 9.18 Use the new Pointer Options tab to toggle Vista's visual feedback for pen actions such as tapping and double-tapping.

Personalizing Handwriting Recognition

New When you use a Tablet PC's digital pen as an input device, there will often be times when you don't want to convert the writing into typed text. A quick sticky note or journal item might be all you need for a given situation. However, in plenty of situations, you need your handwriting converted into typed text. Certainly, when you're using the Input Panel, you always want the handwriting converted to text. However, the convenience and usefulness of handwritten text directly relates to how well the handwriting recognizer does its job. If it misinterprets too many characters, you'll spend too much time either correcting the errors or scratching out chunks of text and starting again.

Rather than just throwing up their hands and saying "That's life with a Tablet PC," Microsoft's developers are doing something to ensure that you get the most out of the handwriting recognizer. Windows Vista comes with a new tool called Handwriting Personalization (select Start, All Programs, Tablet PC, Personalize Handwriting Recognition), shown in Figure 9.19.

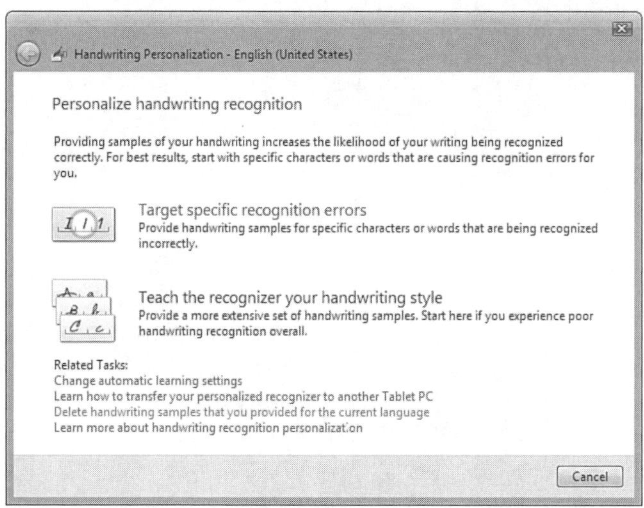

FIGURE 9.19 Use the new Handwriting Personalization tool to improve the Tablet PC's capability to recognize your handwriting.

This feature gives you two methods that improve the Tablet PC's capability to recognize your handwriting (you can run separate recognition chores for each user on the computer):

- **Target Specific Recognition Errors**—With this method you teach the handwriting recognizer to handle specific recognition errors. This is the method to use if you find that the Tablet PC does a pretty good job of recognizing your handwriting, but often incorrectly recognizes certain characters or words. By providing handwritten samples of those characters or words and specifying the correct conversion for them, you teach the handwriting recognizer to avoid those errors in the future.
- **Teach the Recognizer Your Handwriting Style**—With this method, you teach the handwriting recognizer to handle your personal style of handwriting. This is the method to use if you find that the Tablet PC does a poor job of recognizing your handwriting in general. In this case, you provide a more comprehensive set of handwritten samples to give the handwriting recognizer an overall picture of your writing style.

If you select Target Specific Recognition Errors, you next get a choice of two wizards:

- **Character or Word You Specify**—Run this wizard if a character or word is consistently being recognized incorrectly. For a character, you type the character and then provide several samples of the character in handwritten form, as shown in Figure 9.20 (for the lowercase letter u, in this case). The wizard then asks you to provide handwritten samples for a few characters that are similarly shaped. Finally, the wizard asks for handwritten samples of words that contain the character. For a word, the wizard asks you to type the word; then it asks you to write two samples of the word by hand.

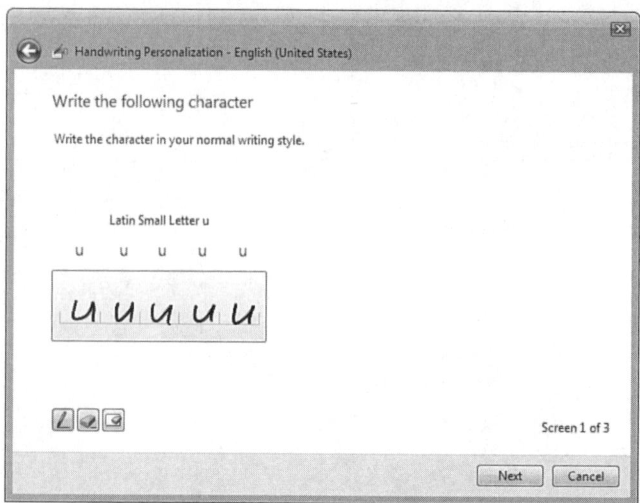

FIGURE 9.20 The wizard asks you to provide several handwritten samples of the character being recognized incorrectly.

- **Characters with Similar Shapes**—Run this wizard if a particular group of similarly shaped characters is causing you trouble. The wizard gives you a list of the six sets of characters that most commonly cause recognition problems, as shown in Figure 9.21. After you choose a set, the wizard goes through each character and asks you to write by hand several samples of the character and of the character in context.

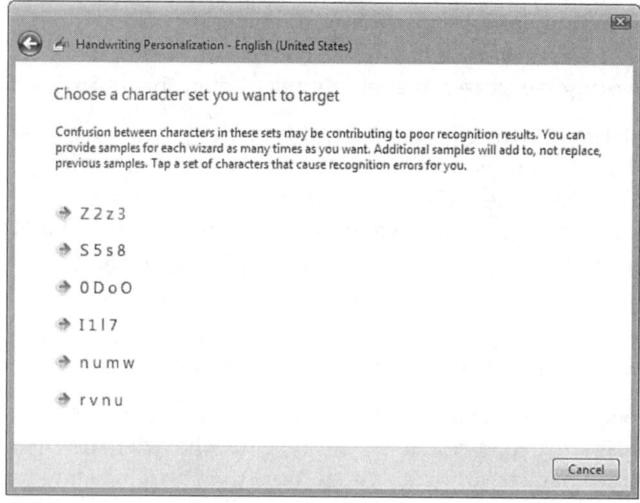

FIGURE 9.21 The wizard asks you to choose from a list of six sets of characters that are commonly confused when handwritten.

If you select Teach the Recognizer Your Handwriting Style, you get a choice of two wizards:

- **Sentences**—This wizard displays a series of sentences, and you provide a handwritten sample for each. Note that there are 50 (!) sentences in all, so wait until you have a lot of spare time before using this wizard. (The wizard does come with a Save for Later button that you can click at any time to stop the wizard and still preserve your work. When you select Sentences again, the program takes you automatically to the next sentence in the sequence.)
- **Numbers, Symbols, and Letters**—This wizard consists of eight screens that take you through the numbers 0 to 9; common symbols such as !, ?, @, $, &, +, #, <, and >; and all the uppercase and lowercase letters. You provide a handwritten sample for each number, symbol, and letter.

When you're done, click Update and Exit to apply your handwriting samples to the recognizer. Note that this takes a few minutes, depending on the number of samples you provided.

Using the Snipping Tool

Windows Vista includes a feature called the *Snipping Tool* that enables you to use your pen to capture ("snip") part of the screen and save it as an image or HTML file. Here's how it works:

1. Select Start, All Programs, Accessories, Snipping Tool. When you first launch the program, it asks if you want the Snipping Tool on the Quick Launch toolbar.
2. Click Yes or No, as you prefer. Vista washes out the screen to indicate that you're in snipping mode and displays the Snipping Tool window.
3. Pull down the New list and select one of the following snip types:
    - **Free-Form Snip**—Choose this type to draw a freehand line around the screen area you want to capture
    - **Rectangular Snip**—Choose this type to draw a rectangular line around the screen area you want to capture
    - **Window Snip**—Choose this type to capture an entire window by tapping it
    - **Full-Screen Snip**—Choose this type to capture the entire screen by tapping anywhere on the screen
4. Use your pen to define the snip, according to the snip type you chose. The snipped area then appears in the Snipping Tool window, as shown in Figure 9.22. From here, you save the snip as an HTML file or a GIF, JPEG, or PNG graphics file.

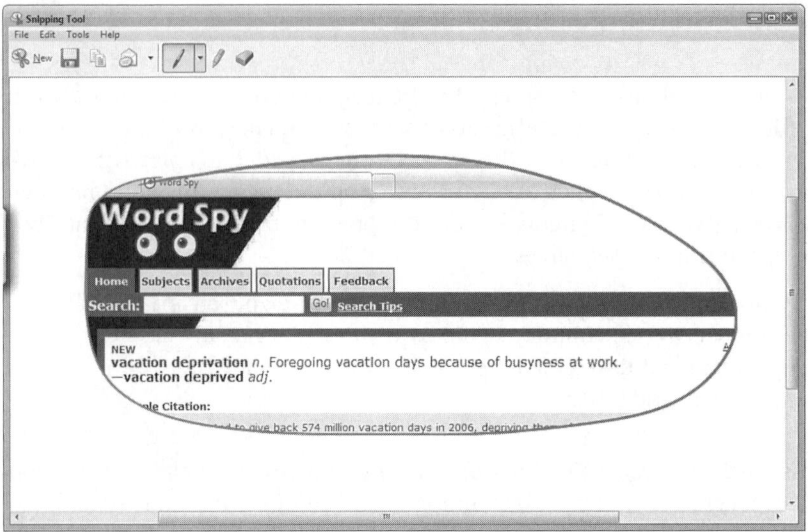

FIGURE 9.22 Use the new Snipping Tool to use your pen to capture part of the screen.

From Here

Here are some other sections in the book where you'll find information related to the topics in this chapter:

- For tips on working with Control Panel, see Chapter 10's "Operating Control Panel" section.
- To learn how to use the Group Policy Editor, see "Implementing Group Policies with Windows Vista" in Chapter 10.
- You learn how to use the Registry Editor in Chapter 11, "Getting to Know the Windows Vista Registry."
- For more information on offline files, see Chapter 23's "Working with Network Files Offline" section.

PART II

Unleashing Essential Windows Vista Power Tools

CHAPTER 10

Using Control Panel and Group Policies

IN THIS CHAPTER

- Operating Control Panel
- Implementing Group Policies with Windows Vista

My goal in this book is to help you unleash the true power of Windows Vista, and my premise is that this goal can't be met by toeing the line and doing only what the manual or Help system tells you. Rather, I believe you can reach this goal only by taking various off-the-beaten track routes that go beyond Windows orthodoxy.

This chapter is a perfect example. The two tools that I discuss—Control Panel and group policies—aren't difficult to use, but they put an amazing amount of power and flexibility into your hands. I discuss them in this early chapter because you'll be using these important tools throughout the rest of the book. However, you can scour the Windows Vista manual and Help system all day long and you'll find only a few scant references to Control Panel and group policies. To be sure, Microsoft is just being cautious because these *are* powerful tools, and the average user can wreak all kinds of havoc if these features are used incorrectly. However, your purchase of this book is proof that you are not an average user; so, by following the instructions in this chapter, I'm sure you'll have no trouble at all using these tools.

Operating Control Panel

Control Panel is a folder that contains a large number of icons—there are more than 50 icons in the Classic View (depending on your version of Vista) of a default Windows Vista setup, but depending on your system configuration, even more icons could be available. Each of these icons deals with a specific area of the Windows Vista configuration: hardware, applications, fonts, printers, multimedia, and much more.

Opening an icon displays a window or dialog box containing various properties related to that area of Windows. For example, launching the Add or Remove Programs icon enables you to install or uninstall third-party applications and Windows Vista components.

To display the Control Panel folder, use any of the following techniques:

- Select Start, Control Panel
- In Windows Explorer, display the Folders list and select the `Desktop\Control Panel` folder
- Press Windows Logo+R (or select Start, All Programs, Accessories, Run) to open the Run dialog box, type **control**, and click OK

TIP

To learn how to convert the Start menu's Control Panel link to a menu of Control Panel icons, see "Putting Control Panel on the Start Menu," later in this chapter.

By default, Windows Vista displays the Control Panel Home page, shown in Figure 10.1, which displays icons for 11 different categories (System and Maintenance, Security, and so on), as well as two or three links to common tasks under each category icon. Windows XP's version of Control Panel offered a similar Category View, which was designed to help novice users, but it just delayed the rest of us unnecessarily and I always counseled my students to switch to Classic View as soon as possible.

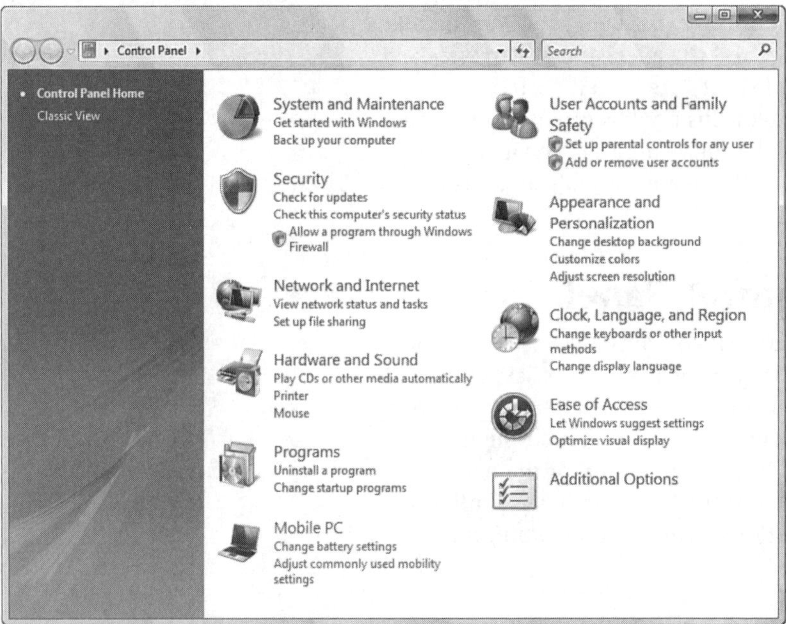

FIGURE 10.1 Switch Control Panel to the Classic View to see all the icons in one window.

I don't do that with Windows Vista, however. After I got used to the layout of the Home page and its offshoots, I can find what I want quite quickly. However, when I switch to Classic View, I find that trying to pick out the one icon I want out of 50-plus icons (see Figure 10.2) is frustrating and time-consuming. Therefore, I recommend sticking with the Home page view until you get used to it.

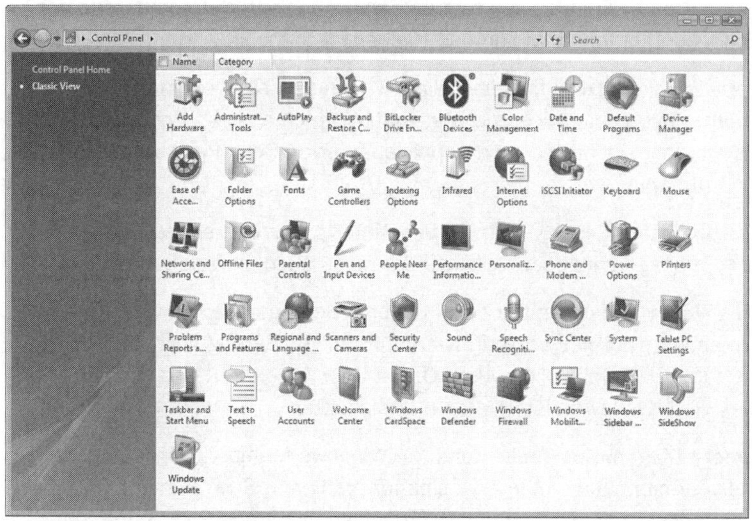

FIGURE 10.2 Switch Control Panel to the Classic View to see all the icons in one window.

Reviewing the Control Panel Icons

To help you familiarize yourself with what's available in Control Panel, this section offers summary descriptions of the Control Panel icons found in a standard Windows Vista installation. Note that your system might have extra icons, depending on your computer's configuration and the programs you have installed.

Add Hardware—Launches the Add Hardware Wizard, which searches for new Plug and Play devices on your system, and can run a more in-depth hardware detection to look for non–Plug and Play devices. You can also use this wizard to install device drivers by hand by choosing the one you want from a list or from a disc that came with your device. See "Tips and Techniques for Installing Devices" in Chapter 17, "Getting the Most Out of Device Manager."

Administrative Tools—Displays a window with more icons, each of which enables you to administer a particular aspect of Windows Vista:

- **Computer Management**—Enables you to manage a local or remote computer. You can examine hidden and visible shared folders, set group policies, access Device Manager, manage hard disks, and much more.
- **Data Sources (ODBC)**—Enables you to create and work with **data source names**, which are connection strings that you use to connect to local or remote databases.
- **Event Viewer**—Enables you to examine Windows Vista's list of **events**, which are unusual or noteworthy occurrences on your system, such as a service that doesn't start, the installation of a device, or an application error. See "Reviewing Event Viewer Logs" in Chapter 15.
- New **iSCSI Initiator**—Displays the iSCSI Initiator properties sheet, which enables you to manage connections to iSCSI devices such as tape drives.
- **Local Security Policy**—Displays the Local Security Settings snap-in, which enables you to set up security policies on your system. Refer to "Setting Account Security Policies" in Chapter 6, "Getting the Most Out of User Accounts," and "Implementing Group Policies with Windows Vista" later in this chapter.
- New **Memory Diagnostics Tool**—Runs the Windows Memory Diagnostics Tool, which checks your computer's memory chips for problems. See "Running the Memory Diagnostics Tool" in Chapter 16, "Troubleshooting and Recovering from Problems."
- New **Print Management**—Displays the Print Management console, which enables you to manage, share, and deploy printers and print servers.
- New **Reliability and Performance Monitor**—Enables you to monitor the performance of your system using Performance Monitor and Reliability Monitor. See "Monitoring Performance" in Chapter 14, "Tuning Windows Vista's Performance."
- **Services**—Displays a list of the system services available with Windows Vista. System services are background routines that enable the system to perform tasks such as network logon, disk management, Plug and Play, Internet Connection Sharing, and much more. You can pause, stop, and start services, as well as configure how service load at startup.
- **System Configuration**—Opens the System Configuration utility. In Chapter 2, refer to the "Using the System Configuration Utility to Modify the BCD" and "Troubleshooting Startup Using the System Configuration Utility" sections.
- **Task Scheduler**—Runs the Task Scheduler console, which enables you to runs programs or scripts on a schedule. In Chapter 15, see "Automating Tasks with the Task Scheduler."
- New **Windows Firewall with Advanced Security**—Enables you to control every aspect of Vista's bi-directional firewall. See "Configuring Windows Firewall" in Chapter 21, "Implementing Windows Vista's Internet Security and Privacy Features."

New AutoPlay—Opens the AutoPlay window, which enables you to configure AutoPlay defaults for various media. Refer to "Setting AutoPlay Defaults" in Chapter 7, "Working with Digital Media."

New Backup and Restore Center—Operates as a front-end for Windows Backup (see Backing Up Your Files" in Chapter 15.

New BitLocker Drive Encryption—Turns on and configures BitLocker, which encrypts your Vista system drive to protect it from unauthorized viewing.

Bluetooth Devices—Enables you to add, configure, and manage devices that use the Bluetooth wireless networking standard. This icon appears only if you've installed a Bluetooth device on your system.

New Color Management—Enables you to configure the colors of your monitor and printer to optimize color output.

Date and Time—Enables you to set the current date and time, select your time zone, and set up an Internet time server to synchronize your system time. You can also display extra clocks to monitor other time zones (see "Displaying Multiple Clocks for Different Time Zones" in Chapter 13, "Customizing the Windows Vista Interface").

New Default Programs—Displays the Default Programs window, which enables you to change the programs that are associated with Vista's file types (refer to Chapter 4, "Mastering File Types") and AutoPlay defaults (refer to "Setting AutoPlay Defaults" in Chapter 7).

Device Manager—Launches Device Manager, which enables you to view and work with your system devices and their drivers. See Chapter 17 for more information.

New Ease of Access Center—Enables you to customize input—the keyboard and mouse—and output—sound and display—for users with special mobility, hearing, or vision requirements.

Folder Options—Enables you to customize the display of Windows Vista's folders, set up whether Windows Vista uses single- or double-clicking, work with file types, and configure offline files.

Fonts—Displays the Fonts folder, from which you can view, install, and remove fonts.

Game Controllers—Enables you to calibrate joysticks and other game devices.

New Indexing Options—Enables you to configure the index used by Vista's new search engine. In Chapter 3, refer to "Desktop Searching with the Windows Search Engine."

Infrared—Enables you to configure infrared settings, file transfers, and photo downloads from digital cameras with infrared support.

Internet Options—Displays a large collection of settings for modifying Internet properties (how you connect, the Internet Explorer interface, and so on).

New iSCSI Initiator—Displays the iSCSI Initiator property sheet, which enables you to manage connections to iSCSI devices such as tape drives.

Keyboard—Enables you to customize your keyboard, work with keyboard languages, and change the keyboard driver.

New Mouse—Enables you to set various mouse options and to install a different mouse device driver.

New Network and Sharing Center—Displays general information about your network connections and sharing settings. See "Using the Network and Sharing Center" in Chapter 23.

New Offline Files—Enables you to enable and configure working with network files offline. In Chapter 23, see "Working with Network Files Offline."

New Parental Controls—Enables you to restrict computer usage for other users of the computer. See "Using Parental Controls to Restrict Computer Usage" in Chapter 6.

Pen and Input Devices—Displays the Pen and Input Devices dialog box, which enables you to configure your Tablet PC's digital pen. In Chapter 9, see "Using Pen Flicks" and "Setting Pointer Options."

New People Near Me—Identifies people nearby on your network so that you can collaborate with them using a program such as Windows Meeting Space. In Chapter 23, see "Collaborating with Windows Meeting Space."

New Performance Information and Tools—Displays the performance rating for your computer (see "Viewing Your Computer's Performance Rating" in Chapter 14) and lets you know if your system has performance problems (see "Checking for Performance Issues" in Chapter 16).

New Personalization—Offers a large number of customization options for the current Vista theme: glass effects, colors, desktop background, screensaver, sounds, mouse pointers, and display settings.

Phone and Modem Options—Enables you to configure telephone dialing rules (see "Working with Different Dialing Locations" in Chapter 24, "Making Remote Network Connections") and to install and configure modems.

Power Options—Enables you to configure power management properties for powering down system components (such as the monitor and hard drive), defining low-power alarms for notebook batteries, enabling sleep and hibernation modes, and configuring notebook power buttons. Refer to "Managing Notebook Power" in Chapter 9.

Printers—Enables you to install and configure printers and the Windows Vista Fax service.

New Problem Reports and Solutions—Enables you to search for and implement solutions that Microsoft has found for problems on your computer. See "Checking for Solutions to Problems" in Chapter 16, "Troubleshooting and Recovering from Problems."

New Programs and Features—Enables you to install and uninstall applications, add and remove Windows Vista components, and view installed updates.

Regional and Language Options—Enables you to configure international settings for country-dependent items such as numbers, currencies, times, and dates.

Scanners and Cameras—Enables you to install and configure document scanners and digital cameras.

Security Center—Displays the Security Center window, which shows the current status of Windows Firewall, Windows Update, virus protection, and Windows Defender. You can also manage your computer's security settings.

Sound—Enables you to control the system volume, map sounds to specific Windows Vista events (such as closing a program or minimizing a window), specify settings for audio, voice, and other multimedia devices.

Speech Recognition Options—Enables you to configure Windows Vista's speech recognition feature.

New Sync Center—Enables you to set up and maintain synchronization with other devices and with offline files.

System—Displays basic information about your system including the Vista edition, system rating, processor type, memory size, computer and workgroup names, and whether Vista is activated. Also gives you access to Device Manager and settings related to performance, startup, System Protection, Remote Assistance, and the Remote Desktop.

Tablet PC Settings—Displays settings for configuring handwriting and other aspects of your Tablet PC. See "Getting the Most Out of Your Tablet PC" in Chapter 9.

Taskbar and Start Menu—Enables you to customize the taskbar and Start menu. See Chapter 13 for more information.

New Text to Speech—Enables you to select a voice and voice speed for text-to-speech translation.

User Accounts—Enables you to set up and configure user accounts.

New Welcome Center—Displays general information about your computer and icons to common Vista tasks.

TIP

The Welcome Center window appears by default each time you start your computer. This window is clearly aimed at novice users and is of no earthly use for anyone with even a bit of computer experience. Fortunately, you can disable the Welcome Center by deactivating the Run at Startup check box at the bottom of the window.

New Windows CardSpace—Enables you to use Microsoft's new CardSpace system to manage your personal online data.

Windows Defender—Launches Windows Defender, Vista's antispyware program. See "Thwarting Spyware with Windows Defender" in Chapter 21.

Windows Firewall—Enables you to configure Windows Firewall. See "Configuring Windows Firewall" in Chapter 21.

New Windows Mobile Device Center—Enables you to connect with a Windows Mobile device for synchronizing files and Outlook data.

New Windows Mobility Center—Displays Vista's new Mobility Center for notebooks. See "Monitoring Your Notebook with the Windows Mobility Center" in Chapter 9, "Mobile Computing in Widows Vista."

Windows Sidebar—Displays the property sheet for Windows Sidebar.

New Windows SideShow—Displays a list of gadgets installed for use with a Windows SideShow-compatible notebook. See "Understanding Windows SideShow" in Chapter 9.

Windows Update—Enables you to configure Vista's Windows Update feature, check for updates, view update history, and set up a schedule for the download and installation of updates.

Understanding Control Panel Files

Many of the Control Panel icons represent by **Control Panel extension** files, which use the `.cpl` extension. These files reside in `the %SystemRoot%\System32` folder. When you open Control Panel, Windows Vista scans the System32 folder looking for CPL files, and then displays an icon for each one.

The CPL files offer an alternative method for launching individual Control Panel dialog boxes. The idea is that you run `control.exe` and specify the name of a CPL file as a parameter. This bypasses the Control Panel folder and opens the icon directly. Here's the syntax:

```
control CPLfile [,option1 [, option2]]
```

`CPLfile`—The name of the file that corresponds to the Control Panel icon you want to open (see Table 10.1 later in this chapter).

`option1`—This option is obsolete and is included only for backward compatibility with batch files and scripts that use `Control.exe` for opening Control Panel icons.

`option2`—The tab number of a multitabbed dialog box. Many Control Panel icons open a dialog that has two or more tabs. If you know the specific tab you want to work with, you can use the *`option2`* parameter to specify an integer that corresponds to the tab's relative position from the left side of the dialog box. The first (leftmost) tab is `0`, the next tab is 1, and so on.

NOTE

If the dialog box has multiple rows of tabs, count the tabs from left to right and from bottom to top. For example, if the dialog box has two rows of four tabs each, the tabs in the bottom row are numbered 0 to 3 from left to right, and the tabs in the top row are numbered 4 to 7 from left to right.

Also, note that even though you no longer use the *`option1`* parameter, you must still display its comma in the command line.

For example, to open Control Panel's System icon with the Hardware tab displayed, run the following command:

```
control sysdm.cpl,,2
```

Table 10.1 lists the various Control Panel icons and the appropriate command line to use. (Note, however, that some Control Panel icons—such as Taskbar and Start Menu—can't be accessed by running `Control.exe`.)

TABLE 10.1 Command Lines for Launching Individual Control Panel Icons

Control Panel Icon	Command	Dialog Box Tabs
Add Hardware	`control hdwwiz.cpl`	N/A
Administrative Tools	`control admintools`	N/A
Bluetooth Devices	`control bthprops.cpl`	4
Date and Time	`control timedate.cpl`	3
Personalization (Display Settings)	`control desk.cpl`	1
Ease of Access Center	`control access.cpl`	N/A
Folder Options	`control folders`	N/A
Fonts	`control fonts`	N/A
Game Controllers	`control joy.cpl`	N/A
Internet Options	`control inetcpl.cpl`	7
Infrared	`control irprops.cpl`	3
iSCSI Initiator	`control iscsicpl.cpl`	N/A
Keyboard	`control keyboard`	N/A
Mouse	`control mouse`	N/A
Network Connections	`control ncpa.cpl`	N/A
People Near Me	`control collab.cpl`	2
Pen and Input Devices	`control tabletpc.cpl`	N/A
Phone and Modem Options	`control telephon.cpl`	N/A
Power Options	`control powercfg.cpl`	N/A
Printers	`control printers`	N/A
Programs and Features	`control appwiz.cpl`	N/A
Regional and Language Options	`control intl.cpl`	4
Scanners and Cameras	`control scannercamer`	N/A

TABLE 10.1 Continued

Control Panel Icon	Command	Dialog Box Tabs
Security Center	`control wscui.cpl`	N/A
Sound	`control mmsys.cpl`	3
System	`control sysdm.cpl`	5
TabletPC	`control tabletpc.cpl`	3
User Accounts	`control nusrmgr.cpl`	N/A
Windows CardSpace	`control infocardcpl.cpl`	N/A
Windows Firewall	`control firewall.cpl`	N/A
Windows Security Center	`control wscui.cpl`	N/A

NOTE

If you find your Control Panel folder is bursting at the seams, you can trim it down to size by removing those icons you never use. There are a number of ways you can do this in Windows Vista, but the easiest is probably via group policies. I discuss group policies in detail later in this chapter, and I include a sample technique that shows you how to use policies to configure access to Control Panel. See "Example: Controlling Access to Control Panel," later in this chapter.

Easier Access to Control Panel

Control Panel is certainly a useful and important piece of the Windows Vista package. It's even more useful if you can get to it easily. I'll close this section by looking at a few methods for gaining quick access to individual icons and the entire folder.

Alternative Methods for Opening Control Panel Icons

Access to many Control Panel icons is scattered throughout the Windows Vista interface, meaning that there's more than one way to launch an icon. Many of these alternative methods are faster and more direct than using the Control Panel folder. Here's a summary:

Date and Time—Right-click the clock in the notification area and then click Adjust Date/Time.

Personalization—Right-click the desktop and then click Personalize.

Folder Options—In Windows Explorer, select Organize, Folder and Search Options.

Fonts—In Windows Explorer, open the `%SystemRoot%\Fonts` folder.

Internet Options—In Internet Explorer, select Tools, Internet Options. Alternatively, click Start, right-click Internet, and then click Internet Properties.

Network and Sharing Center—Click (or right-click) the Network icon in the notification area and then click Network and Sharing Center.

Power Options—Double-click the Power icon in the notification area.

Default Programs—Select Start, Default Programs.

Sound—Right-click the Volume icon in the notification area and then click Audio Devices.

System—Click Start, right-click Computer, and then click Properties.

Taskbar and Start Menu—Right-click the Start button or an empty section of the taskbar, and then click Properties.

Windows Update—Click Start, All Programs, Windows Update.

Putting Control Panel on the Start Menu

You can turn the Start menu's Control Panel command into a menu that displays the Control Panel icons by following these steps:

1. Select Start, Control Panel, Appearance and Personalization, Taskbar and Start menu.
2. Display the Start Menu tab, ensure that the Start Menu option is activated, and then click Customize. The Customize Start Menu dialog box appears.
3. In the list of Start menu items, find the Control Panel item and activate the Display as a Menu option.

TIP

To add the Administrative Tools icon directly to the Start menu, find the System Administrative Tools item and activate the Display on the All Programs Menu and the Start Menu option.

4. Click OK.

Figure 10.3 shows the Start menu with the Control Panel item configured as a menu. Depending on the screen resolution you are using, not all the Control Panel icons might fit on the screen. In that case, hover the mouse pointer over the downward-pointing arrow at the bottom of the menu to scroll through the rest of the icons. (To scroll up, hover the pointer over the upward-pointing arrow that appears at the top of the menu.)

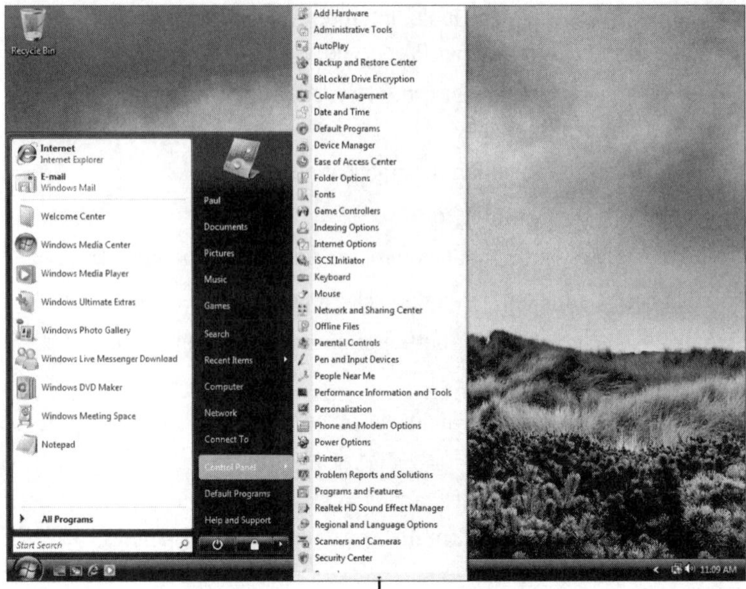

FIGURE 10.3 The Start menu's Control Panel item configured as a menu.

Implementing Group Policies with Windows Vista

Group policies are settings that control how Windows Vista works. You can use them to customize the Windows Vista interface, restrict access to certain areas, specify security settings, and much more.

Group policies are mostly used by system administrators who want to make sure that novice users don't have access to dangerous tools (such as the Registry Editor), or who want to ensure a consistent computing experience across multiple machines. Group policies are also ideally suited to situations in which multiple users share a single computer. However, group policies are also useful on single-user standalone machines, as you'll see throughout this book.

Working with Group Policies

You implement group policies using the Group Policy editor, a Microsoft Management Console snap-in. To start the Group Policy editor, follow these steps:

1. Press Windows Logo+R (or select Start, All Programs, Accessories, Run) to open the Run dialog box.
2. Type **`gpedit.msc`**.
3. Click OK.

4. If the User Account Control dialog box appears, click Continue or type an administrator's password and click Submit.

The Group Policy window that appears is divided into two sections:

Left pane—This pane contains a treelike hierarchy of policy categories, which is divided into two main categories: Computer Configuration and User Configuration. The Computer Configuration policies apply to all users and are implemented before the logon. The User Configuration policies apply only to the current user and, therefore, are not applied until that user logs on.

Right pane—This pane contains the policies for whichever category is selected in the left pane.

The idea, then, is to open the tree's branches to find the category you want. When you click the category, its policies appear in the right pane. For example, Figure 10.4 shows the Group Policy window with the Computer Configuration, Administrative Templates, System, Logon category highlighted.

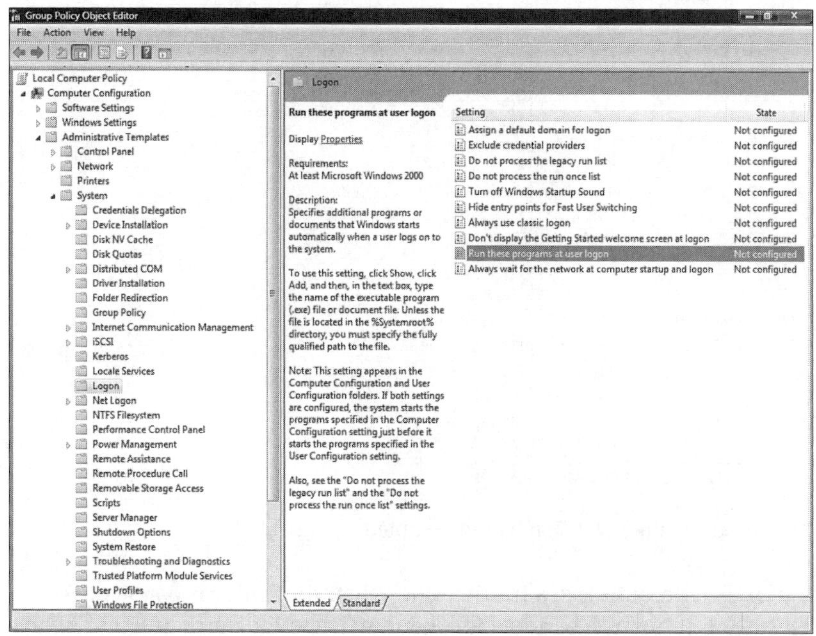

FIGURE 10.4 When you select a category in the left pane, the category's policies appear in the right pane.

TIP

Windows Vista comes with another tool called the Local Security Policy editor, which displays only the policies found in the Group Policy editor's Computer Configuration, Windows Settings, Security Settings branch. To launch the Local Security Policy editor, open the Run dialog box, type **secpol.msc**, and click OK.

In the right pane, the Setting column tells you the name of the policy, and the State column tells you the current state of the policy. Click a policy to see its description on the left side of the pane. To configure a policy, double-click it. The type of window you see depends on the policy:

- For simple policies, you see a window similar to the one shown in Figure 10.5. These kinds of policies take one of three states: Not Configured (the policy is not in effect), Enabled (the policy is in effect and its setting is enabled), and Disabled (the policy is in effect but its setting is disabled).

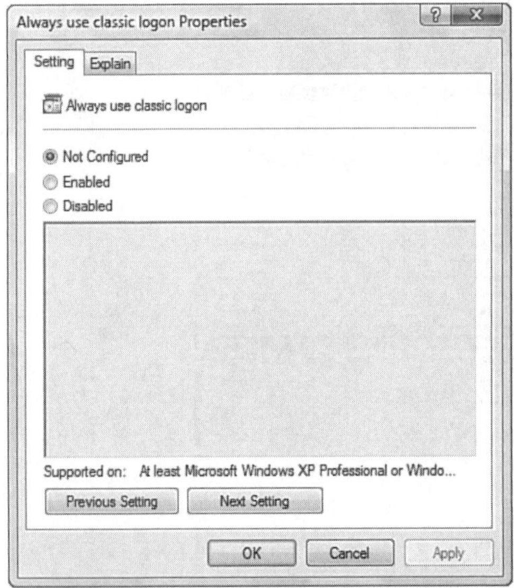

FIGURE 10.5 Simple policies are Not Configured, Enabled, or Disabled.

- Other kinds of policies require extra information when the policy is enabled. For example, Figure 10.6 shows the window for the Run These Programs at User Logon policy. When Enabled is activated, the Show button appears; you use it to specify one or more programs that run when the computer starts.

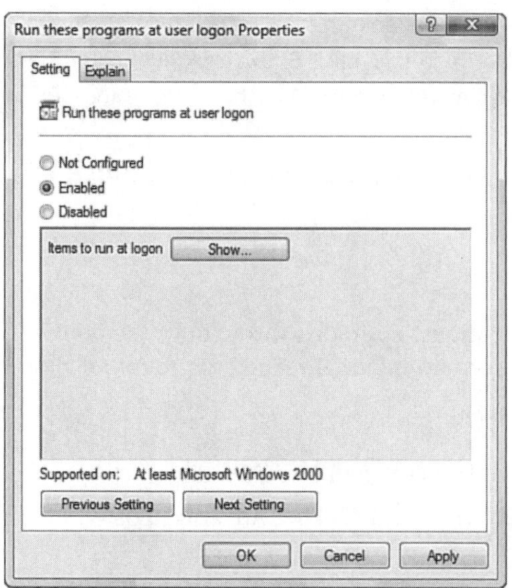

FIGURE 10.6 More complex policies also require extra information such as, in this case, a list of programs to run at logon.

Example: Controlling Access to Control Panel

You can use group policies to hide and display Control Panel icons and to configure other Control Panel access settings. To see how this works, follow these steps:

1. In the Group Policy editor, select User Configuration, Administrative Templates, Control Panel.
2. Configure one or more of the following policies:

   Hide Specified Control Panel Items—If you enable this policy, you can hide specific Control Panel icons. To do this, click Show, click Add, enter the name of the icon you want to hide (such as Game Controllers) or the name of the CPL file (such as `Joy.cpl`), and then click OK.

   Force Classic Control Panel View—If you enable this policy, Control Panel is always displayed in the Classic View and the user can't change to the Home Page view. If you disable this policy, Control Panel is always displayed in the Home Page view and the user can't change to the Classic View.

   Prohibit Access to the Control Panel—If you enable this policy, users can't access Control Panel using the Start menu, Windows Explorer, or the `control.exe` executable.

Show Only Specified Control Panel Applets—If you enable this policy, you hide all Control Panel icons except the ones that you specify. To do this, click Show, click Add, enter the name of the icon you want to show (such as Game Controllers) or the name of the CPL file (such as `Joy.cpl`), and then click OK.

3. When you've finished with a policy, click OK or Apply to put the policy into effect.

From Here

You'll find Control Panel and Group Policy techniques sprinkled throughout the book. Here are some other sections in the book that contain material related to group policies:

- In Chapter 2, refer to "Setting Logon Policies."
- In Chapter 5, refer to "Launching Applications and Scripts at Startup."
- In Chapter 6, refer to "Setting Account Policies" and "Taking Advantage of Windows Vista's Password Policies."
- In Chapter 13, see "Modifying the Start Menu and Taskbar with Group Policies."
- In Chapter 17, see "Working with Device Security Policies."
- In Chapter 23, see "Connecting to Remote Group Policies."

CHAPTER 11

Getting to Know the Windows Vista Registry

IN THIS CHAPTER

As you learn throughout this book, a big part of unleashing Windows Vista involves customizing the interface and the accessories either to suit your personal style or to extract every last ounce of performance from your system. For the most part, these customization options are handled via the following mechanisms:

- Control Panel
- Group policies
- Property sheets for individual objects
- Program menu commands and dialog boxes
- Command-line switches

But there is another, even more powerful mechanism you can use to customize Windows Vista: the Registry. No, it doesn't have a pretty interface like most of the other customization options, and many aspects of the Registry give new meaning to the word arcane, but it gives you unparalleled access to facets of Windows Vista that would be otherwise out of reach. This chapter introduces you to the Registry and its structure, and it shows you how to make changes to the Registry by wielding the Registry Editor.

A Synopsis of the Registry

When you change the desktop wallpaper using Control Panel's Display icon, the next time you start your computer, how does Windows Vista know which wallpaper you selected? If you change your video display driver, how does Windows Vista know to use that driver at startup and not the original driver loaded during Setup? In other words, how does Windows Vista remember the various settings and options either that you've selected yourself or that are appropriate for your system?

The secret to Windows Vista's prodigious memory is the Registry. The Registry is a central repository Windows Vista uses to store anything and everything that applies to the configuration of your system. This includes all the following:

- Information about all the hardware installed on your computer
- The resources those devices use
- A list of the device drivers that Windows Vista loads at startup
- Settings that Windows Vista uses internally
- File type data that associates a particular type of file with a specific application
- Wallpaper, color schemes, and other interface customization settings
- Other customization settings for things such as the Start menu and the taskbar
- Settings for accessories such as Windows Explorer and Internet Explorer
- Internet and network connections and passwords
- Settings and customization options for many applications

It's all stored in one central location, and, thanks to a handy tool called the Registry Editor, it's yours to play with (carefully!) as you see fit.

A Brief History of Configuration Files

It wasn't always this way. In the early days of DOS and Windows (version 1!), system data was stored in two humble files: `CONFIG.SYS` and `AUTOEXEC.BAT`, those famous (or infamous) Bobbsey twins of configuration files.

When Windows 2.0 was born (to little or no acclaim), so too were born another couple of configuration files: `WIN.INI` and `SYSTEM.INI`. These so-called **initialization files** were also simple text files. It was `WIN.INI`'s job to store configuration data about Windows and about Windows applications; for `SYSTEM.INI`, life consisted of storing data about hardware and system settings. Not to be outdone, applications started creating their own INI files to store user settings and program options. Before long, the Windows directory was festooned with dozens of these INI garlands.

The air became positively thick with INI files when Windows 3.0 rocked the PC world. Not only did Windows use `WIN.INI` and `SYSTEM.INI` to store configuration tidbits, but it also created new INIs for Program Manager (`PROGMAN.INI`), File Manager (`WINFILE.INI`), Control Panel (`CONTROL.INI`), and more.

It wasn't until Windows 3.1 hit the shelves that the Registry saw the light of day, albeit in a decidedly different guise from its Windows Vista descendant. The Windows 3.1 Registry was a database used to store registration information related to OLE (object linking and embedding) applications.

Finally, Windows for Workgroups muddied the configuration file waters even further by adding a few new network-related configuration files, including `PROTOCOL.INI`.

The Registry Puts an End to INI Chaos

This INI inundation led to all kinds of woes for users and system administrators alike. Because they were just text files in the main Windows directory, INIs were accidents waiting for a place to happen. Like sitting ducks, they were ripe for being picked off by an accidental press of the Delete key from a novice's fumbling fingers. There were so many of the darn things that few people could keep straight which INI file contained which settings. There was no mechanism to help you find the setting you needed in a large INI file. And the linear, headings-and-settings structure made it difficult to maintain complex configurations.

To solve all these problems, the Windows 95 designers decided to give the old Windows 3.1 Registry a promotion, so to speak. Specifically, they set it up as the central database for all system and application settings. The Registry essentially maintains this structure in Windows Vista.

Here are some of the advantages you get with this revised Registry:

- The Registry files (discussed in the next section) have their Hidden, System, and Read-Only attributes set, so it's much tougher to delete them accidentally. Even if a user somehow managed to blow away these files, Windows Vista maintains backup copies for easy recovery.
- Not only does the Registry serve as a warehouse for hardware and operating system settings, but applications are free to use the Registry to store their own configuration morsels, instead of using separate INI files.
- If you need to examine or modify a Registry entry, the Registry Editor utility gives you a hierarchical, treelike view of the entire Registry database (more on this topic later).
- The Registry comes with tools that enable you to search for specific settings and to query the Registry data remotely.

That's not to say that the Registry is a perfect solution. Many of its settings are totally obscure, it uses a structure that only a true geek could love, and finding the setting you need is often an exercise in guesswork. Still, most of these problems can be overcome with a bit of practice and familiarity, which is what this chapter is all about.

Understanding the Registry Files

As you'll see a bit later, the Registry's files are binary files, so you can't edit them directly. Instead, you use a program called the Registry Editor, which enables you to view, modify, add, and delete any Registry setting. It also has a search feature to help you find settings, and export and import features that enable you to save settings to and from a text file.

To launch the Registry Editor, press Windows Logo+R (or select Start, All Programs, Accessories, Run) to open the Run dialog box, type **regedit**, click OK, and then enter your User Account Control credentials. Figure 11.1 shows the Registry Editor window that appears. (Your Registry Editor window might look different if someone else has used the program previously. Close all the open branches in the left pane to get the view shown in Figure 11.1.)

TIP

Another way to launch the Registry Editor is to select Start, type **regedit** in the Search box, and then click the regedit link that appears.

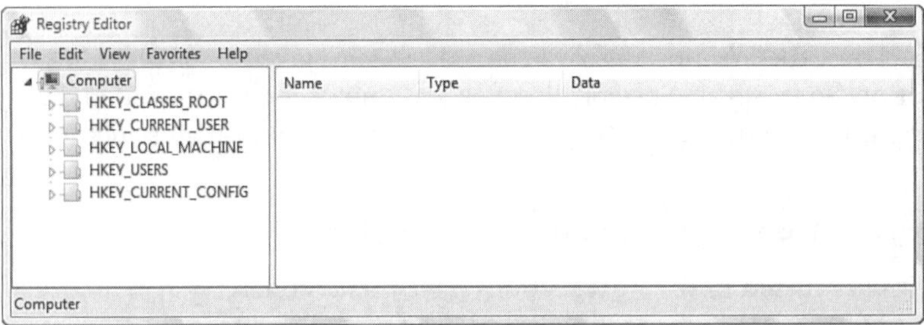

FIGURE 11.1 Running the REGEDIT command launches the Registry Editor, a front-end that enables you to work with the Registry's data.

The Registry Editor is reminiscent of Windows Explorer, and it works in basically the same way. The left side of the Registry Editor window is similar to Explorer's Folders pane, except that rather than folders, you see **keys**. For lack of a better phrase, I'll call the left pane the **Keys pane**.

CAUTION

The Registry Editor is arguably the most dangerous tool in the Windows Vista arsenal. The Registry is so crucial to the smooth functioning of Vista, that a single imprudent change to a Registry entry can bring your system to its knees. Therefore, now that you have the Registry Editor open, don't start tweaking settings willy-nilly. Instead, read the section titled "Keeping the Registry Safe," later in this chapter, for some advice on protecting this precious and sensitive resource.

Navigating the Keys Pane

The Keys pane, like Explorer's Folders pane, is organized in a treelike hierarchy. The five keys that are visible when you first open the Registry Editor are special keys called **handles** (which is why their names all begin with HKEY). These keys are collectively referred to as the Registry's **root keys**. I'll tell you what to expect from each of these keys later (see the section called "Getting to Know the Registry's Root Keys," later in this chapter).

These keys all contain subkeys, which you can display by clicking the plus sign (+) to the left of each key, or by highlighting a key and pressing the plus-sign key on your keyboard's numeric keypad. When you open a key, the plus sign changes to a minus sign (–). To close a key, click the minus sign or highlight the key and press the minus-sign key on the numeric keypad. Again, this is just like navigating folders in Explorer.

You often have to drill down several levels to get to the key you want. For example, Figure 11.2 shows the Registry Editor after I've opened the `HKEY_CURRENT_USER` key, and then the `Control Panel` subkey, and then clicked the `Mouse` subkey. Notice how the status bar tells you the exact path to the current key, and that this path is structured just like a folder path.

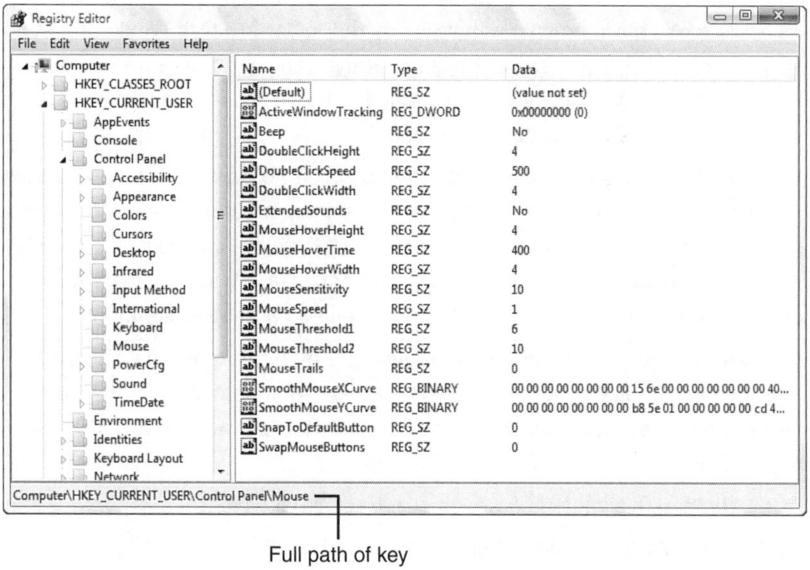

FIGURE 11.2 Open the Registry's keys and subkeys to find the settings you want to work with.

NOTE

To see all the keys properly, you likely will have to increase the size of the Keys pane. To do this, use your mouse to click and drag the split bar to the right. Alternatively, select View, Split, use the Right Arrow key to adjust the split bar position, and then press Enter.

Understanding Registry Settings

If the left side of the Registry Editor window is analogous to Explorer's Folders pane, the right side is analogous to Explorer's Contents pane. In this case, the right side of the Registry Editor window displays the settings contained in each key (so I'll call it the **Settings pane**). The Settings pane is divided into three columns:

Name — This column tells you the name of each setting in the currently selected key (analogous to a filename in Explorer).

Type — This column tells you the data type of the setting. There are six possible data types:

- `REG_SZ`—This is a string value.
- `REG_MULTI_SZ`—This is a series of strings.
- `REG_EXPAND_SZ`—This is a string value that contains an environment variable name that gets "expanded" into the value of that variable. For example, the `%SystemRoot%` environment variable holds the folder in which Windows Vista was installed. So, if you see a Registry setting with the value `%SystemRoot%\System32\`, and Windows Vista is installed in `C:\Windows`, the settings expanded value is `C:\Windows\System32\`.
- `REG_DWORD`—This is a double word value: a 32-bit hexadecimal value arranged as eight digits. For example, 11 hex is 17 decimal, so this number would be represented in `DWORD` form as 0x00000011 (17). (Why "double word"? A 32-bit value represents four bytes of data, and because a **word** in programming circles is defined as two bytes, a four-byte value is a **double word**.)
- `REG_QWORD`—This is a quadruple word value: a 64-bit hexadecimal value arranged as 16 digits. Note that leading zeros are suppressed for the high 8 digits. Therefore, 11 hex appears as 0x00000011 (17) and 100000000 hex appears as 0x1000000000 (4294967296).
- `REG_BINARY`—This value is a series of hexadecimal digits.

Data — This column displays the value of each setting.

Getting to Know the Registry's Root Keys

The root keys are your Registry starting points, so you need to become familiar with what kinds of data each key holds. The next few sections summarize the contents of each key.

`HKEY_CLASSES_ROOT`

`HKEY_CLASSES_ROOT`—usually abbreviated as `HKCR`—contains data related to file extensions and their associated programs, the objects that exist in the Windows Vista system, as well as applications and their Automation information. There are also keys related to shortcuts and other interface features.

The top part of this key contains subkeys for various file extensions. You see `.bmp` for BMP (Paint) files, `.doc` for DOC (Word or WordPad) files, and so on. In each of these subkeys, the `Default` setting tells you the name of the registered file type associated with the extension. (I discussed file types in more detail in Chapter 4, "Mastering File Types.") For example, the `.txt` extension is associated with the `txtfile` file type.

These registered file types appear as subkeys later in the `HKEY_CLASSES_ROOT` branch, and the Registry keeps track of various settings for each registered file type. In particular, the shell subkey tells you the actions associated with this file type. For example, in the `shell\open\command` subkey, the `Default` setting shows the path for the executable file that opens. Figure 11.3 shows this subkey for the `txtfile` file type.

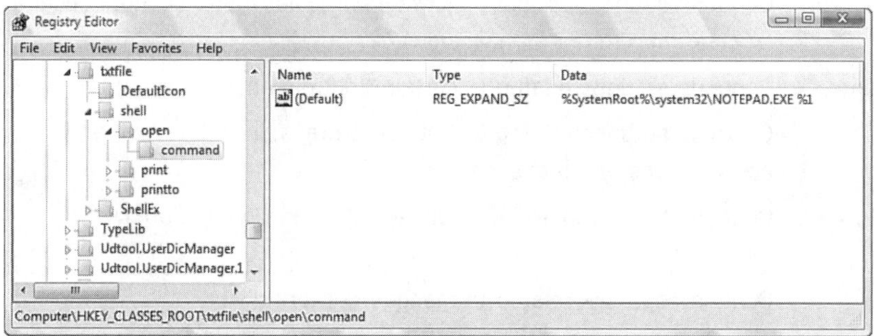

FIGURE 11.3 The registered file type subkeys specify various settings associated with each file type, including its defined actions.

`HKEY_CLASSES_ROOT` is actually a copy (or an **alias**, as these copied keys are called) of the following `HKEY_LOCAL_MACHINE` key:

```
HKEY_LOCAL_MACHINE\Software\Classes
```

The Registry creates an alias for `HKEY_CLASSES_ROOT` to make these keys easier for applications to access and to improve compatibility with legacy programs.

HKEY_CURRENT_USER

`HKEY_CURRENT_USER`—usually abbreviated as `HKCU`—contains data that applies to the user that's currently logged on. It contains user-specific settings for Control Panel options, network connections, applications, and more. Note that if a user has group policies set on his account, his settings are stored in the `HKEY_USERS\sid` subkey (where *`sid`* is the user's security ID). When that user logs on, these settings are copied to `HKEY_CURRENT_USER`. For all other users, `HKEY_CURRENT_USER` is built from the user's profile file, `ntuser.dat`.

TIP

How do you find out each user's SID? First, open the following Registry key:

`HKLM\SOFTWARE\Microsoft\Windows NT\CurrentVersion\ProfileList\`

Here you'll find a list of SIDs. The ones that begin `S-1-5-21` are the user SIDs. Highlight one of these SIDs and then examine the `ProfileImagePath` setting, which will be of the form `%SystemDrive%\Users\`*`user`*, where *user* is the username associated with the SID.

Here's a summary of the most important `HKEY_CURRENT_USER` subkeys:

`AppEvents`	Contains sound files that play when particular system events occur (such as maximizing of a window)
`Control Panel`	Contains settings related to certain Control Panel icons
`Identities`	Contains settings related to Outlook Express, including mail and news options and message rules
`Keyboard Layout`	Contains the keyboard layout as selected via Control Panel's Keyboard icon
`Network`	Contains settings related to mapped network drives
`Software`	Contains user-specific settings related to installed applications and Windows

HKEY_LOCAL_MACHINE

`HKEY_LOCAL_MACHINE` (`HKLM`) contains non-user-specific configuration data for your system's hardware and applications. You'll use the following three subkeys most often:

`Hardware`	Contains subkeys related to serial ports and modems, as well as the floating-point processor.
`Software`	Contains computer-specific settings related to installed applications. The `Classes` subkey is aliased by `HKEY_CLASSES_ROOT`. The `Microsoft` subkey contains settings related to Windows (as well as any other Microsoft products you have installed on your computer).
`System`	Contains subkeys and settings related to Windows startup.

HKEY_USERS

`HKEY_USERS` (`HKU`) contains settings that are similar to those in `HKEY_CURRENT_USER`. `HKEY_USERS` is used to store the settings for users with group policies defined, as well as the default settings (in the `.DEFAULT` subkey) which get mapped to a new user's profile.

HKEY_CURRENT_CONFIG

HKEY_CURRENT_CONFIG (HKCC) contains settings for the current hardware profile. If your machine uses only one hardware profile, HKEY_CURRENT_CONFIG is an alias for HKEY_LOCAL_MACHINE\SYSTEM\ControlSet001. If your machine uses multiple hardware profiles, HKEY_CURRENT_CONFIG is an alias for HKEY_LOCAL_MACHINE\SYSTEM\ControlSet*nnn*, where *nnn* is the numeric identifier of the current hardware profile. This identifier is given by the Current setting in the following key:

```
HKLM\SYSTEM\CurrentControlSet\Control\IDConfigDB
```

Understanding Hives and Registry Files

The Registry database actually consists of a number of files that contain a subset of the Registry called a **hive**. A hive consists of one or more Registry keys, subkeys, and settings. Each hive is supported by several files that use the extensions listed in Table 11.1.

TABLE 11.1 Extensions Used by Hive Supporting Files

Extension	File Contains
None	A complete copy of the hive data
.log1	A log of the changes made to the hive data
.sav	A copy of the hive data as of the end of the text mode portion of the Windows Vista setup

There are also files without extensions that have the suffix _previous appended to the hive name, and these act as backup copies of the hive data. Table 11.2 shows the supporting files for each hive (note that not all of these files might appear on your system).

TABLE 11.2 Supporting Files Used by Each Hive

Hive	Files
HKLM\BCD00000000	%SystemRoot%\System32\config\BCD-Template
	%SystemRoot%\System32\config\BCD-Template.LOG1
HKLM\COMPONENTS	%SystemRoot%\System32\config\COMPONENTS
	%SystemRoot%\System32\config\COMPONENTS.LOG1
	%SystemRoot%\System32\config\COMPONENTS.SAV
	%SystemRoot%\System32\config\components_previous
HKLM\SAM	%SystemRoot%\System32\config\SAM
	%SystemRoot%\System32\config\SAM.LOG1
	%SystemRoot%\System32\config\SAM.SAV
	%SystemRoot%\System32\config\sam_previous
HKLM\SECURITY	%SystemRoot%\System32\config\SECURITY
	%SystemRoot%\System32\config\SECURITY.LOG1
	%SystemRoot%\System32\config\SECURITY.SAV
	%SystemRoot%\System32\config\security_previous

LISTING 11.2 Continued

Hive	Files
HKLM\SOFTWARE	%SystemRoot%\System32\config\SOFTWARE
	%SystemRoot%\System32\config\SOFTWARE.LOG1
	%SystemRoot%\System32\config\SOFTWARE.SAV
	%SystemRoot%\System32\config\software_previous
HKLM\SYSTEM	%SystemRoot%\System32\config\SYSTEM
	%SystemRoot%\System32\config\SYSTEM.LOG1
	%SystemRoot%\System32\config\SYSTEM.SAV
	%SystemRoot%\System32\config\system_previous
HKU\.DEFAULT	%SystemRoot%\System32\config\DEFAULT
	%SystemRoot%\System32\config\DEFAULT.LOG1
	%SystemRoot%\System32\config\DEFAULT.SAV
	%SystemRoot%\System32\config\default_previous

Also, each user has his or her own hive, which maps to `HKEY_CURRENT_USER` during logon. The supporting files for each user hive are stored in `\Users\`*`user`*, where *user* is the username. In each case, the `ntuser.dat` file contains the hive data, and the `ntuser.log` file tracks the hive changes. (If a user has group policies set on her account, the user data is stored in an `HKEY_USERS` subkey.)

NOTE

You can also work with a Registry on a remote computer over a network. See the "Connecting to a Remote Registry" section in Chapter 23, "Accessing and Administering the Network."

Keeping the Registry Safe

The sheer wealth of data stored in one place makes the Registry convenient, but it also makes it very precious. If your Registry went missing somehow, or if it got corrupted, Windows Vista simply would not work. With that scary thought in mind, let's take a moment to run through several protective measures. The techniques in this section should ensure that Windows Vista never goes down for the count because you made a mistake while editing the Registry.

TIP

If you share your computer with other people, you might not want to give them access to the Registry Editor. In Windows Vista, User Account Control automatically blocks Standard users unless they know an administrator's password. Also, you can prevent any user from using this tool by running the Group Policy editor (refer to Chapter 10, "Using Control Panel and Group Policies"). Open User Configuration, Administrative

Templates, System, and then enable the Prevent Access to Registry Editing Tools policy. Note that *you* won't be able to use the Registry Editor, either. However, you can overcome that by temporarily disabling this policy prior to running the Registry Editor.

Backing Up the Registry

New Windows Vista maintains what is known as the **system state**: the crucial system files that Windows Vista requires to operate properly. Included in the system state are the files used during system startup, the Windows Vista–protected system files, and, naturally, the Registry files. Windows Vista's Backup utility has a feature called Complete PC Backup that enables you to easily back up the current system state, so it's probably the most straightforward way to create a backup copy of the Registry should anything go wrong. See the "Backing Up Your Files" section in Chapter 15, "Maintaining Your Windows Vista System," for the details.

Saving the Current Registry State with System Restore

Another easy way to save the current Registry configuration is to use Windows Vista's System Restore utility. This program takes a snapshot of your system's current state, including the Registry. If anything should go wrong with your system, the program enables you to restore a previous configuration. It's a good idea to set a system restore point before doing any work on the Registry. I show you how to work with System Restore in Chapter 15 (see "Setting System Restore Points").

TIP

Another way to protect the Registry is to ensure that its keys have the appropriate permissions. By default, Windows Vista gives members of the Administrators group full control over the Registry. A Standard user gets Full Control permission only over the `HKCU` key when that user is logged on and Read permissions over the rest of the Registry. (Refer to Chapter 6, "Getting the Most Out of User Accounts," for more information on users, groups, and permissions.) To adjust the permissions, right-click the key in the Registry Editor, and then click Permissions. Make sure that only administrators have the Full Control check box activated.

Protecting Keys by Exporting Them to Disk

If you're just making a small change to the Registry, backing up all of its files might seem like overkill. Another approach is to back up only the part of the Registry that you're working on. For example, if you're about to make changes within the `HKEY_CURRENT_USER` key, you could back up just that key, or even a subkey within `HKCU`. You do that by exporting the key's data to a registration file, which is a text file that uses the `.reg` extension. That way, if the change causes a problem, you can import the `.reg` file back into the Registry to restore things the way they were.

Exporting the Entire Registry a `.reg` File

The easiest way to protect the entire Registry is to export the whole thing to a `.reg` file on a separate hard drive or network share. Note that the resulting file will be 90 to 100MB, and possible larger, so make sure the target destination has enough free space. Here are the steps to follow:

1. Open the Registry Editor.
2. Select File, Export to display the Export Registry File dialog box.
3. Select a location for the file.
4. Use the File Name text box to type a name for the file.
5. Activate the All option.
6. If you'll be importing this file into a system running Windows 9x, Windows Me, or Windows NT, use the Save As Type list to choose the Win9x/NT 4 Registration Files (*.reg) item.
7. Click Save.

Exporting a Key to a `.reg` File

Here are the steps to follow to export a key to a registration file:

1. Open the Registry Editor and select the key you want to export.
2. Select File, Export to display the Export Registry File dialog box.
3. Select a location for the file.
4. Use the File Name text box to type a name for the file.
5. Activate the Selected Branch option.
6. If you'll be importing this file into a system running Windows 9x, Windows Me, or Windows NT, use the Save As Type list to choose the Win9x/NT 4 Registration Files (*.reg) item.
7. Click Save.

Finding Registry Changes

One common Registry scenario is to make a change to Windows Vista using a tool such as the Group Policy editor, and then try and find which Registry setting (if any) was affected by the change. However, because of the sheer size of the Registry, this is usually a needle-in-a-haystack exercise that ends in frustration. One way around this is to export some or all the Registry before making the change and then export the same key or keys after making the change. You can then use the FC (file compare) utility at the command prompt to find out where the two files differ. Here's the FC syntax to use for this:

```
FC /U pre_edit.reg post-edit.reg > reg_changes.txt
```

Here, change *pre_edit.reg* to the name of the registration file you exported before editing the Registry; change *post_edit.reg* to the name of the registration file you exported after editing the Registry; and change *reg_changes.txt* to the name of a text file to which the FC output is redirected. Note that the /U switch is required since registration files use the Unicode character set.

Importing a .reg File

If you need to restore the key that you backed up to a registration file, follow these steps:

1. Open the Registry Editor.
2. Select File, Import to display the Import Registry File dialog box.
3. Find and select the file you want to import.
4. Click Open.
5. When Windows Vista tells you the information has been entered into the Registry, click OK.

NOTE

You also can import a .reg file by locating it in Windows Explorer and then double-clicking the file.

CAUTION

Many applications ship with their own .reg files for updating the Registry. Unless you're sure that you want to import these files, avoid double-clicking them. They might end up overwriting existing settings and causing problems with your system.

Working with Registry Entries

Now that you've had a look around, you're ready to start working with the Registry's keys and settings. In this section, I'll give you the general procedures for basic tasks, such as modifying, adding, renaming, deleting, and searching for entries, and more. These techniques will serve you well throughout the rest of the book when I take you through some specific Registry modifications.

Changing the Value of a Registry Entry

Changing the value of a Registry entry is a matter of finding the appropriate key, displaying the setting you want to change, and editing the setting's value. Unfortunately, finding the key you need isn't always a simple matter. Knowing the root keys and their main subkeys, as described earlier, will certainly help, and the Registry Editor has a Find feature that's invaluable (I'll show you how to use it later).

To illustrate how this process works, let's work through an example: changing your registered owner name and company name. In previous versions of Windows, the installation process probably asked you to enter your name and, optionally, your company name. These registered names appear in several places as you work with Windows:

- If you select Help, About in most Windows Vista programs, your registered names appear in the About dialog box.
- If you install a 32-bit application, the installation program uses your registered names for its own records (although you usually get a chance to make changes).

Unfortunately, if you install a clean version of Windows Vista, Setup doesn't ask you for this data, and it takes your username as your registered owner name. (If you upgraded to Windows Vista, the owner name and company name were brought over from your previous version of Windows.) With these names appearing in so many places, it's good to know that you can change either or both names (for example, to put in your proper names if Vista doesn't have them or if you give the computer to another person). The secret lies in the following key:

```
HKLM\SOFTWARE\Microsoft\WindowsNT\CurrentVersion
```

To get to this key, you open the branches in the Registry Editor's tree pane: `HKEY_LOCAL_MACHINE`, and then `SOFTWARE`, and then `Microsoft`, and then `Windows NT`. Finally, click the `CurrentVersion` subkey to select it. Here you see a number of settings, but two are of interest to us (see Figure 11.4):

TIP

If you have keys that you visit often, you can save them as favorites to avoid trudging through endless branches in the keys pane. To do this, navigate to the key and then select Favorites, Add to Favorites. In the Add to Favorites dialog box, edit the Favorite Name text box, if desired, and then click OK. To navigate to a favorite key, pull down the Favorites menu and select the key name from the list that appears at the bottom of the menu.

`RegisteredOrganization`	This setting contains your registered company name.
`RegisteredOwner`	This setting contains your registered name.

Now you open the setting for editing by using any of the following techniques:

- Select the setting name and either select Edit, Modify or press Enter
- Double-click the setting name
- Right-click the setting name and click Modify from the context menu

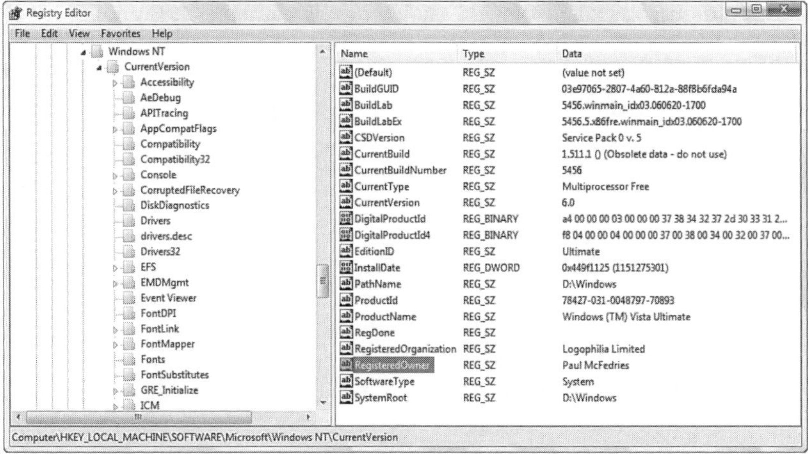

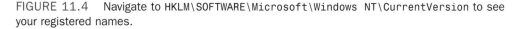

FIGURE 11.4 Navigate to `HKLM\SOFTWARE\Microsoft\Windows NT\CurrentVersion` to see your registered names.

The dialog box that appears depends on the value type you're dealing with, as discussed in the next few sections. Note that edited settings are written to the Registry right away, but the changes might not go into effect immediately. In many cases, you need to exit the Registry Editor and then either log off or restart Windows Vista.

Editing a String Value

If the setting is a `REG_SZ` value (as it is in our example), a `REG_MULTI_SZ` value, or a `REG_EXPAND_SZ` value, you see the Edit String dialog box, shown in Figure 11.5. Use the Value Data text box to enter a new string or modify the existing string, and then click OK. (For a `REG_MULTI_SZ` multistring value, Value Data is a multiline text box. Type each string value on its own line. That is, after each string, press Enter to start a new line.)

FIGURE 11.5 You see the Edit String dialog box if you're modifying a string value.

Editing a `DWORD` or `QWORD` Value

If the setting is a `REG_DWORD`, you see the Edit DWORD (32-Bit) Value dialog box shown in Figure 11.6. In the Base group, select either Hexadecimal or Decimal, and then use the Value Data text box to enter the new value of the setting. (If you chose the Hexadecimal option, enter a hexadecimal value; if you chose Decimal, enter a decimal value.) Note that editing a `QWORD` value is identical, except that the dialog box is named Edit QWORD (64-Bit) Value, instead.

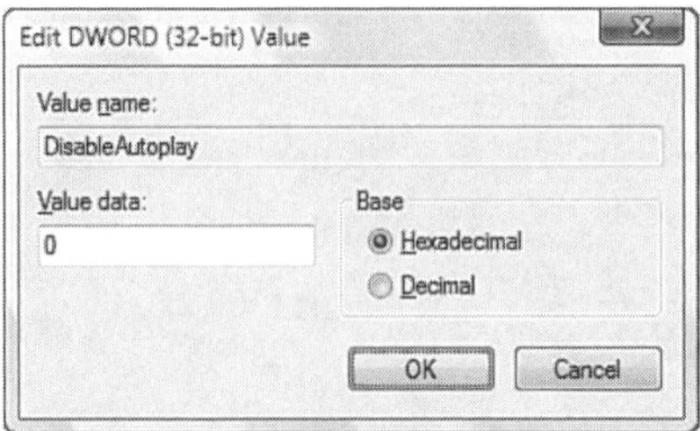

FIGURE 11.6 You see the Edit DWORD Value dialog box if you're modifying a double word value.

Editing a Binary Value

If the setting is a `REG_BINARY` value, you see an Edit Binary Value dialog box like the one shown in Figure 11.7.

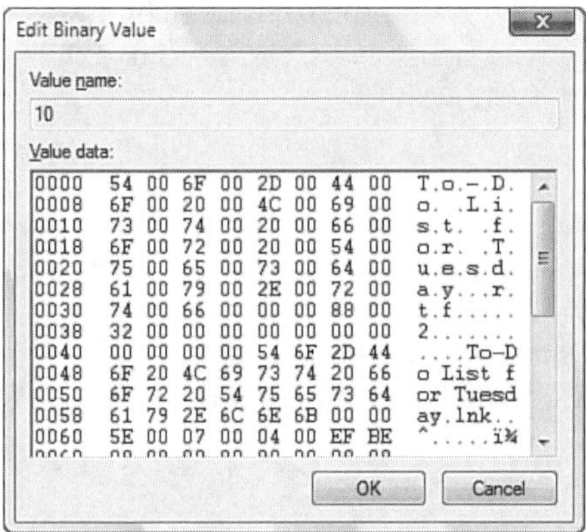

FIGURE 11.7 You see the Edit Binary Value dialog box if you're modifying a binary value.

For binary values, the Value Data box is divided into three vertical sections:

Starting Byte Number — The four-digit values on the left of the Value Data box tell you the sequence number of the first byte in each row of hexadecimal numbers. This sequence always begins at 0, so the sequence number of the first byte in the first row is 0000. There are eight bytes in each row, so the sequence number of the first byte in the second row is 0008, and so on. You can't edit these values.

Hexadecimal Numbers (Bytes)	The eight columns of two-digit numbers in the middle section display the setting's value, expressed in hexadecimal numbers, where which each two-digit number represents a single byte of information. You can edit these values.
ANSI Equivalents	The third section on the right side of the Value Data box shows the ANSI equivalents of the hexadecimal numbers in the middle section. For example, the first byte of the first row is the hexadecimal value 54, which represents the uppercase letter T. You can also edit the values in this column.

Editing a `.reg` File

If you exported a key to a registration file, you can edit that file and then import it back into the Registry. To make changes to a registration file, find the file in Windows Explorer, right-click the file, and then click Edit. Windows Vista opens the file in Notepad.

TIP

If you need to make global changes to the Registry, export the entire Registry and then load the resulting registration file into WordPad or some other word processor or text editor. Use the application's Replace feature (carefully!) to make changes throughout the file. If you use a word processor for this, be sure to save the file as a text file when you're done. You can then import the changed file back into the Registry.

Creating a `.reg` File

You can create registration files from scratch and then import them into the Registry. This is a handy technique if you have some customizations that you want to apply to multiple systems. To demonstrate the basic structure of a registration file and its entries, Figure 11.8 shows two windows. The top window is the Registry Editor with a key named Test highlighted. The settings pane contains six sample settings: the (`Default`) value and one each of the five types of settings (binary, DWORD, expandable string, multistring, and string). The bottom window shows the Test key in Notepad as an exported registration file (`Test.reg`).

Windows Vista registration files always start with the following header:

```
Windows Registry Editor Version 5.00
```

TIP

If you're building a registration file for a Windows 9x, Me, or NT 4 system, change the header to the following:

```
REGEDIT4
```

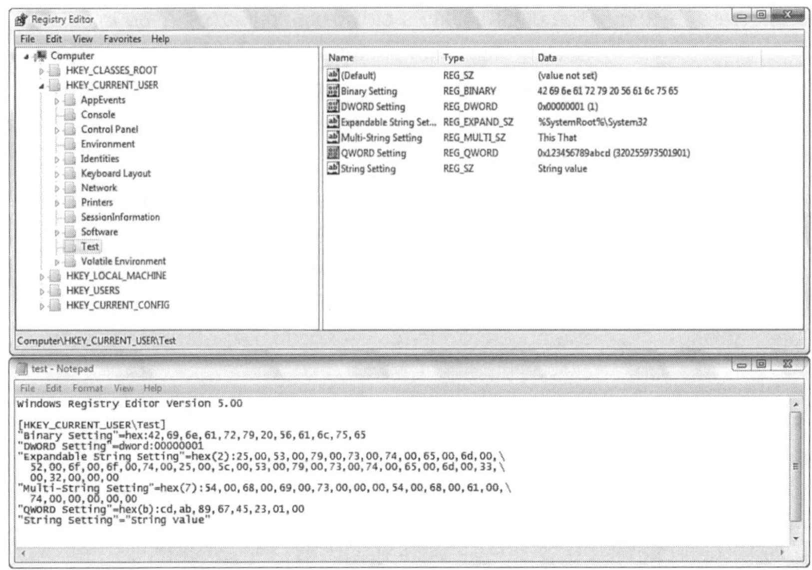

FIGURE 11.8 The settings in the Test key shown in the Registry Editor correspond to the data shown in `Test.reg` file shown in Notepad.

Next is an empty line followed by the full path of the Registry key that will hold the settings you're adding, surrounded by square brackets:

```
[HKEY_CURRENT_USER\Test]
```

Below the key are the setting names and values, which use the following general form:

```
"SettingName"=identifier:SettingValue
```

TIP

If you want to add a comment to a `.reg` file, start a new line and begin the line with a semicolon (`;`).

`SettingName` The name of the setting. Note that you use the `@` symbol to represent the key's `Default` value.

`identifier` A code that identifies the type of data. `REG_SZ` values don't use an identifier, but the other four types do:

`dword`	Use this identifier for a `DWORD` value.
`hex(b)`	Use this identifier for a QWORD value.
`hex`	Use this identifier for a binary value.
`hex(2)`	Use this identifier for an expandable string value.
`hex(7)`	Use this identifier for a multistring value.

SettingValue	This is the value of the setting, which you enter as follows:	
	String	Surround the value with quotation marks.
	DWORD	Enter an eight-digit `DWORD` value.
	QWORD	Enter eight two-digit hexadecimal pairs, separated by commas, with the pairs running from highest order to lowest. For example, to enter the QWORD value 123456789abcd, you would use the following value: `cd,ab,89,67,45,23,01,00`
	Binary	Enter the binary value as a series of two-digit hexadecimal numbers, separating each number with a comma.
	Expandable string	Convert each character to its hexadecimal equivalent and then enter the value as a series of two-digit hexadecimal numbers, separating each number with a comma, and separating each character with 00.
	Multistring	Convert each character to its hexadecimal equivalent and then enter the value as a series of two-digit hexadecimal numbers, separating each number with a comma, and separating each character with 00, and separating each string with space (00 hex).

TIP

To delete a setting using a `.reg` file, set its value to a hyphen (-), as in this example:

```
Windows Registry Editor Version 5.00

[HKEY_CURRENT_USER\Test]
"BinarySetting"=-
```

To delete a key, add a hyphen to the start of the key name, as in this example:

```
Windows Registry Editor Version 5.00

[-HKEY_CURRENT_USER\Test]
```

Renaming a Key or Setting

You won't often need to rename existing keys or settings. Just in case, though, here are the steps to follow:

1. In the Registry Editor, find the key or setting you want to work with, and then highlight it.
2. Select Edit, Rename, or press F2.
3. Edit the name and then press Enter.

CAUTION

Rename only those keys or settings that you created yourself. If you rename any other key or setting, Windows Vista might not work properly.

Creating a New Key or Setting

Many Registry-based customizations don't involve editing an existing setting or key. Instead, you have to create a new setting or key. Here's how you do it:

1. In the Registry Editor, select the key in which you want to create the new subkey or setting.
2. Select Edit, New. (Alternatively, right-click an empty section of the Settings pane and then click New.) A submenu appears.
3. If you're creating a new key, select the Key command. Otherwise, select the command that corresponds to the type of setting you want: String Value, Binary Value, DWORD Value, Multi-String Value, or Expandable String Value.
4. Type a name for the new key or setting.
5. Press Enter.

Deleting a Key or Setting

Here are the steps to follow to delete a key or setting:

1. In the Registry Editor, select the key or setting that you want to delete.
2. Select Edit, Delete, or press Delete. The Registry Editor asks whether you're sure.
3. Click Yes.

CAUTION

Again, to avoid problems, you should delete only those keys or settings that you created yourself. If you're not sure about deleting a setting, try renaming it instead. If a problem arises, you can also return the setting back to its original name.

Finding Registry Entries

The Registry contains only five root keys, but they contain hundreds of subkeys. The fact that some root keys are aliases for subkeys in a different branch only adds to the confusion. If you know exactly where you're going, the Registry Editor's treelike hierarchy is a reasonable way to get there. If you're not sure where a particular subkey or setting resides, however, you could spend all day poking around in the Registry's labyrinthine nooks and crannies.

To help you get where you want to go, the Registry Editor has a Find feature that enables you to search for keys, settings, or values. Here's how it works:

1. In the Keys pane, select Computer at the top of the pane (unless you're certain of which root key contains the value you want to find; in this case, you can highlight the appropriate root key instead).
2. Select Edit, Find or press Ctrl+F. The Registry Editor displays the Find dialog box, shown in Figure 11.9.

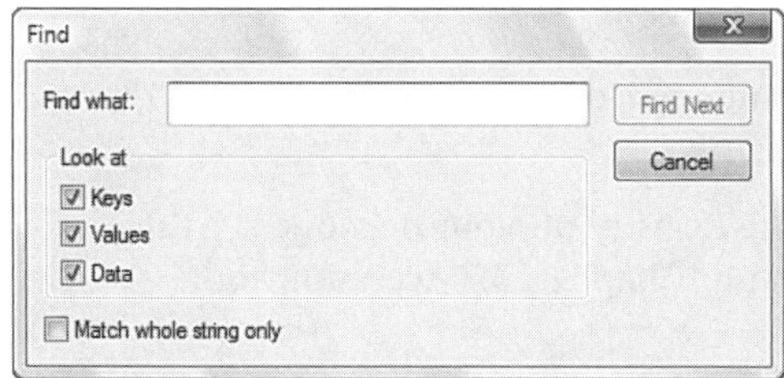

FIGURE 11.9 Use the Find dialog box to search for Registry keys, settings, or values.

3. Use the Find What text box to enter your search string. You can enter partial words or phrases to increase your chances of finding a match.
4. In the Look At group, activate the check boxes for the elements you want to search. For most searches, you want to leave all three check boxes activated.
5. If you want to find only those entries that exactly match your search text, activate the Match Whole String Only check box.
6. Click the Find Next button. The Registry Editor highlights the first match.
7. If this isn't the item you want, select Edit, Find Next (or press F3) until you find the setting or key you want.

When the Registry Editor finds a match, it displays the appropriate key or setting. Note that if the matched value is a setting name or data value, Find doesn't highlight the current key. This is a bit confusing, but remember that the current key always appears at the bottom of the Keys pane.

From Here

Here's a list of a some chapters and sections of the book that contain information related to what you learned about the Registry in this chapter:

- For the details on file types and how they relate to the HKEY_CLASSES_ROOT key, refer to Chapter 4, "Mastering File Types."
- Windows Vista has three main programs that serve as front-ends for the Registry, and I discuss them in Chapter 10, "Using Control Panel and Group Policies."
- To learn how to read, add, and modify Registry entries programmatically, see the section "Working with Registry Entries" in Chapter 12.
- Many of the Registry values are generated by Windows Vista's customization features. I discuss many of these features in Chapter 13, "Customizing the Windows Vista Interface."
- For a broad look at Windows Vista memory features, as well as how to use the System Monitor, see Chapter 14, "Tuning Windows Vista's Performance."
- To learn how to use System Restore and Backup, see Chapter 15, "Maintaining Your Windows Vista System."
- To better understand the Registry's hardware-related keys, head for Chapter 17, "Getting the Most Out of Device Manager."
- For information on connecting to a remote Registry on your network, see the "Connecting to a Remote Registry" section in Chapter 23, "Accessing and Administering the Network."

CHAPTER 12

Programming the Windows Script Host

IN THIS CHAPTER

- WSH: Your Host for Today's Script
- Scripts and Script Execution
- Programming Objects
- Programming the `WScript` Object
- Programming the `WshShell` Object
- Programming the `WshNetwork` Object
- Example: Scripting Internet Explorer

In Appendix C, "Automating Windows Vista with Batch Files," you learn how to tame the command prompt by creating **batch files**—small, executable text files that run one or more commands. You'll see that with a little ingenuity and a dash of guile, it's possible to make batch files perform some interesting and useful tasks. Indeed, for many years, batch files were the only way to automate certain kinds of tasks. Unfortunately, the batch file world is relentlessly command-line–oriented. So, with the exception of being able to launch Windows programs, batch files remain ignorant of the larger Windows universe.

If you're looking to automate a wider variety of tasks in Windows, you need to supplement your batch file knowledge with scripts that can deal with the Registry, shortcuts, files, and network drives, and that can even interact with Windows programs via Automation. The secret to these powerful scripts is the **Windows Script Host** (**WSH**). This chapter introduces you to the Windows Script Host, shows you how to execute scripts, and runs through the various elements in the Windows Script Host object model.

WSH: Your Host for Today's Script

As you might know, Internet Explorer is really just an empty container application that's designed to host different data formats, including ActiveX controls, various file formats (such as Microsoft Word documents and Microsoft Excel worksheets), and several ActiveX scripting engines. A **scripting engine** is a dynamic link library (DLL) that provides programmatic support for a particular scripting language. Internet Explorer supports two such scripting engines: VBScript (`VBScript.dll`) and JavaScript (`JSscript.dll`). This enables web programmers to write small programs—**scripts**—that interact with the user, control the browser, set cookies, open and close windows, and more. Although these scripting engines don't offer full-blown programmability (you can't compile scripts, for example), they do offer modern programming structures such as loops, conditionals, variables, objects, and more. In other words, they're a huge leap beyond what a mere batch file can do.

The Windows Script Host is also a container application, albeit a scaled-down application in that its only purpose in life is to host scripting engines. Right out of the box, the Windows Script Host supports both the VBScript and JavaScript engines. However, Microsoft designed the Windows Script Host to be a universal host that can support any ActiveX-based scripting engine. Therefore, there are also third-party vendors offering scripting engines for languages such as Perl, Tcl, and Rexx.

The key difference between Internet Explorer's script hosting and the Windows Script Host is the environment in which the scripts run. Internet Explorer scripts are web page–based, so they control and interact with either the web page or the web browser. The Windows Script Host runs scripts within the Windows Vista shell or from the command prompt, so you use these scripts to control various aspects of Windows. Here's a sampling of the things you can do:

- Execute Windows programs
- Create and modify shortcuts
- Use Automation to connect and interact with Automation-enabled applications such as Microsoft Word, Outlook, and Internet Explorer
- Read, add, and delete Registry keys and items
- Access the VBScript and JavaScript object models, which give access to the file system, runtime error messages, and more
- Use pop-up dialog boxes to display information to the user, and determine which button the user clicked to dismiss the dialog box
- Read environment variables, which are system values that Vista keeps in memory, such as the folder into which Vista is installed—the `%SystemRoot%` environment variable—and the name of the computer—the `%ComputerName%` environment variable
- Deal with network resources, including mapping and unmapping network drives, accessing user data (such as the username and user domain), and connecting and disconnecting network printers

Clearly, we've gone *way* beyond batch files!

What about speed? After all, you wouldn't want to load something that's the size of Internet Explorer each time you need to run a simple script. That's not a problem because, as I've said, the Windows Script Host does nothing but host scripting engines, so it has much less memory overhead than Internet Explorer. That means that your scripts run quickly. For power users looking for a Windows-based batch language, the Windows Script Host is a welcome tool.

NOTE

This chapter does not teach you how to program in either VBScript or JavaScript and, in fact, assumes that you're already proficient in one or both of these languages. If you're looking for a programming tutorial, my *Absolute Beginner's Guide to VBA* (Que, 2004) is a good place to start (VBScript is a subset of VBA—Visual Basic for Applications). For JavaScript, try my *Special Edition Using JavaScript* (Que, 2001).

Scripts and Script Execution

Scripts are simple text files that you create using Notepad or some other text editor. You can use a word processor such as WordPad to create scripts, but you must make sure that you save these files using the program's Text Only document type. For VBScript, a good alternative to Notepad is the editor that comes with either Visual Basic or any program that supports VBA (such as the Office suite). Just remember that VBScript is a subset of VBA (which is, in turn, a subset of Visual Basic), so it does not support all objects and features.

In a web page, you use the `<script>` tag to specify the scripting language you're using, as in this example:

```
<SCRIPT LANGUAGE="VBScript">
```

With the Windows Script Host, the script file's extension specifies the scripting language:

- For VBScript, save your text files using the `.vbs` extension (which is registered as the following file type: VBScript Script File).
- For JavaScript, use the `.js` extension (which is registered as the following file type: JScript Script File).

As described in the next three sections, you have three ways to run your scripts: by launching the script files directly, by using `WSscript.exe`, or by using `CScript.exe`.

Running Script Files Directly

The easiest way to run a script from within Windows is to launch the `.vbs` or `.js` file directly. That is, you either double-click the file in Windows Explorer or type the file's path and name in the Run dialog box. Note, however, that this technique does not work at the command prompt. For that, you need to use the CScript program described a bit later.

Using WScript for Windows-Based Scripts

The .vbs and .js file types have an open method that's associated with WScript (WScript.exe), which is the Windows-based front-end for the Windows Script Host. In other words, launching a script file named MyScript.vbs is equivalent to entering the following command in the Run dialog box:

```
wscript myscript.vbs
```

The WScript host also defines several parameters that you can use to control how the script executes. Here's the full syntax:

```
WSCRIPT filename arguments //B //D //E:engine //H:host //I //Job:xxxx
➥//S //T:ss //X
```

filename	Specifies the filename, including the path of the script file, if necessary.
arguments	Specifies optional arguments required by the script. An **argument** is a data value that the script uses as part of its procedures or calculations.
//B	Runs the script in batch mode, which means script errors and Echo method output lines are suppressed. (I discuss the Echo method later in this chapter.)
//D	Enables Active Debugging. If an error occurs, the script is loaded into the Microsoft Script Debugger (if it's installed) and the offending statement is highlighted.
//E:*engine*	Executes the script using the specified scripting *engine*, which is the scripting language to use when running the script.
//H:*host*	Specifies the default scripting host. For *host*, use either CScript or WScript.
//I	Runs the script in interactive mode, which displays script errors and Echo method output lines.
//Job:*xxxx*	In a script file that contains multiple jobs, executes only the job with id attribute equal to *xxxx*.
//S	Saves the specified WScript arguments as the default for the current user; uses the following Registry key to save the settings: HKCU\Software\Microsoft\Windows Script Host\Settings
//TT:*ss*	Specifies the maximum time in seconds (*ss*) that the script can run before it shuts down automatically.
//X	Executes the entire script in the Microsoft Script Debugger (if it's installed).

For example, the following command runs `MyScript.vbs` in batch mode with a 60-second maximum execution time:

```
wscript myscript.vbs //B //TT:60
```


Creating Script Jobs

A script **job** is a section of code that performs a specific task or set of tasks. Most script files contain a single job. However, it's possible to create a script file with multiple jobs. To do this, first surround the code for each job with the `<script>` and `</script>` tags, and then surround those with the `<job>` and `</job>` tags. In the `<job>` tag, include the `id` attribute and set it to a unique value that identifies the job. Finally, surround all the jobs with the `<package>` and `</package>` tags. Here's an example:

```
<package>
<job id="A">
<script language="VBScript">
    WScript.Echo "This is Job A."
</script>
</job>

<job id="B">
<script language="VBScript">
      WScript.Echo "This is Job B."
</script>
</job>
</package>
```

Save the file using the `.wsf` (Windows Script File) extension.

NOTE

If you write a lot of script, the Microsoft Script Debugger is an excellent programming tool. If there's a problem with a script, the debugger can help you pinpoint its location. For example, the debugger enables you to step through the script's execution one statement at a time. If you don't have the Microsoft Script Debugger, you can download a copy from msdn.microsoft.com/scripting.

Using CScript for Command-Line Scripts

The Windows Script Host has a second host front-end application called CScript (`CScript.exe`), which enables you to run scripts from the command line. In its simplest form, you launch CScript and use the name of the script file (and its path, if required) as a parameter, as in this example:

```
cscript myscript.vbs
```

The Windows Script Host displays the following banner and then executes the script:

```
Microsoft (R) Windows Script Host Version 5.7 for Windows
Copyright (C) Microsoft Corporation. All rights reserved.
```

As with WScript, the CScript host has an extensive set of parameters you can specify:

```
CSCRIPT filename arguments //B //D //E:engine //H:host //I //Job:xxxx
➥//S //T:ss //X //U //LOGO //NOLOGO
```

This syntax is almost identical to that of WScript, but adds the following three parameters:

`//LOGO`	Displays the Windows Script Host banner at startup
`//NOLOGO`	Hides the Windows Script Host banner at startup
`//U`	Uses Unicode for redirected input/output from the console

Script Properties and `.wsh` Files

In the last two sections, you saw that the WScript and CScript hosts have a number of parameters you can specify when you execute a script. It's also possible to set some of these options by using the properties associated with each script file. To see these properties, right-click a script file and then click Properties. In the properties sheet that appears, display the Script tab, shown in Figure 12.1. You have two options:

Stop Script After Specified Number of Seconds—If you activate this check box, Windows shuts down the script after it has run for the number of seconds specified in the associated spin box. This is useful for scripts that might hang during execution. For example, a script that attempts to enumerate all the mapped network drives at startup might hang if the network is unavailable.

Display Logo When Script Executed in Command Console—As you saw in the previous section, the CScript host displays some banner text when you run a script at the command prompt. If you deactivate this check box, the Windows Script Host suppresses this banner (unless you use the `//LOGO` parameter).

When you make changes to these properties, the Windows Script Host saves your settings in a new file that has the same name as the script file, except with the `.wsh` (Windows Script Host Settings) extension. For example, if the script file is `MyScript.vbs`, the settings are stored in `MyScript.wsh`. These `.wsh` files are text files organized into sections, much like `.ini` files. Here's an example:

```
[ScriptFile]
Path=C:\Users\Paul\Documents\Scripts\Popup1.vbs
[Options]
Timeout=0
DisplayLogo=1
```

FIGURE 12.1 In a script file's properties sheet, use the Script tab to set some default options for the script.

To use these settings when running the script, use either WScript or CScript and specify the name of the `.wsh` file:

```
wscript myscript.wsh
```

NOTE

Rather than setting properties for individual scripts, you might prefer to set global properties that apply to the WScript host itself. Those global settings then apply to every script that runs using the WScript host. To do this, run `WScript.exe` without any parameters. This displays the properties sheet for WScript, which contains only the Script tab shown in Figure 12.1. The settings you choose in the properties sheet are stored in the following Registry key:

```
HKLM\Software\Microsoft\Windows Script Host\Settings
```

Programming Objects

Although this chapter isn't a programming primer per se, I'd like to take some time now to run through a few quick notes about programming objects. This will serve you well throughout the rest of the chapter as I take you on a tour of the Windows Script Host object model.

The dictionary definition of an object is "anything perceptible by one or more of the senses, especially something that can be seen and felt." In scripting, an **object** is an application element that exposes an interface to the programmer, who can then perform the programming equivalent of seeing and feeling:

- You can make changes to the object's *properties* (this is the seeing part).
- You can make the object perform a task by activating a *method* associated with the object (this is the feeling part).

Working with Object Properties

Every programmable object has a defining set of characteristics. These characteristics are the object's **properties**, and they control the appearance and position of the object. For example, the `WScript` object (the top-level Windows Script Host object) has an `Interactive` property that determines whether the script runs in interactive mode or batch mode.

When you refer to a property, you use the following syntax:

```
Object.Property
```

`Object`	The name of the object
`Property`	The name of the property with which you want to work

For example, the following expression refers to the `Interactive` property of the `WScript` object:

```
WScript.Interactive
```

Setting the Value of a Property

To set a property to a certain value, you use the following syntax:

```
Object.Property = value
```

Here, *`value`* is an expression that specifies the value to which you want to set the property. As such, it can be any of the scripting language's recognized data types, which usually include the following:

- A numeric value
- A string value, enclosed in double quotation marks (such as `"My Script Application"`)
- A logical value (in VBScript: `True` or `False`; in JavaScript: `true` or `false`)

For example, the following VBScript statement tells the Windows Script Host to run the script using interactive mode:

```
WScript.Interactive = True
```

Returning the Value of a Property

Sometimes you need to know the current setting of a property before changing the property or performing some other action. You can find out the current value of a property by using the following syntax:

```
variable = Object.Property
```

Here, *variable* is a variable name or another property. For example, the following statement stores the current script mode (batch or interactive) in a variable named `currentMode`:

```
currentMode = WScript.Interactive
```

Working with Object Methods

An object's properties describe what the object is, whereas its **methods** describe what the object *does*. For example, the `WScript` object has a `Quit` method that enables you to stop the execution of a script.

How you refer to a method depends on whether the method requires any arguments. If it doesn't, the syntax is similar to that of properties:

```
Object.Method
```

Object	The name of the object
Method	The name of the method you want to run

For example, the following statement shuts down a script:

```
WScript.Quit
```

If the method requires arguments, you use the following syntax:

```
Object.Method(Argument1, Argument2, ...)
```

NOTE

In VBScript, the parentheses around the argument list are necessary only if you'll be storing the result of the method in a variable or object property. In JavaScript, the parentheses are always required.

For example, the `WshShell` object has a `RegWrite` method that you use to write a key or value to the Registry. (I discuss this object and method in detail later in this chapter; see "Working with Registry Entries.") Here's the syntax:

```
WshShell.RegWrite strName, anyValue[, strType]
```

strName	The name of the Registry key or value
anyValue	The value to write, if *strName* is a Registry value
strType	The data type of the value

ARGUMENT NAMING CONVENTIONS

When presenting method arguments in this chapter, I'll follow Microsoft's naming conventions, including the use of the following prefixes for the argument names:

Prefix	*Data Type*
any	Any type
b	Boolean
int	Integer
nat	Natural numbers
obj	Object
str	String

For many object methods, not all the arguments are required. In the `RegWrite` method, for example, the *strName* and *anyValue* arguments are required, but the *strType* argument is not. Throughout this chapter, I differentiate between required and optional arguments by surrounding the optional arguments with square brackets—for example, [*strType*].

For example, the following statement creates a new value named `Test` and sets it equal to `Foo`:

```
WshShell.RegWrite "HKCU\Software\Microsoft\Windows Script Host\Test",
➥"Foo", "REG_SZ"
```

Assigning an Object to a Variable

If you're using JavaScript, you assign an object to a variable using a standard variable assignment:

```
var variableName = ObjectName
```

variableName	The name of the variable
ObjectName	The object you want to assign to the variable

In VBScript, you assign an object to a variable by using the `Set` statement. `Set` has the following syntax:

```
Set variableName = ObjectName
```

variableName	The name of the variable
ObjectName	The object you want to assign to the variable

You'll see later on that you must often use Automation to access external objects. For example, if you want to work with files and folders in your script, you must access the scripting engine object named `FileSystemObject`. To get this access, you use the `CreateObject` method and store the resulting object in a variable, like so:

```
Set fs = CreateObject("Scripting.FileSystemObject")
```

Working with Object Collections

A **collection** is a set of similar objects. For example, `WScript.Arguments` is the set of all the arguments specified on the script's command line. Collections are objects, too, so they have their own properties and methods, and you can use these properties and methods to manipulate one or more objects in the collection.

The members of a collection are **elements**. You can refer to individual elements by using an **index**. For example, the following statement refers to the first command-line argument (collection indexes always begin at 0):

```
WScript.Arguments(0)
```

If you don't specify an element, the Windows Script Host assumes that you want to work with the entire collection.

VBScript: Using `For Each...Next` Loops for Collections

As you might know, VBScript provides the `For...Next` loop that enables you to cycle through a chunk of code a specified number of times. For example, the following code loops 10 times:

```
For counter = 1 To 10
    Code entered here is repeated 10 times
Next counter
```

A useful variation on this theme is the `For Each...Next` loop, which operates on a collection of objects. You don't need a loop counter because VBScript loops through the individual elements in the collection and performs on each element whatever operations are inside the loop. Here's the structure of the basic `For Each...Next` loop:

```
For Each element In collection
    [statements]
Next
```

element	A variable used to hold the name of each element in the collection
collection	The name of the collection
statements	The statements to execute for each element in the collection

The following code loops through all the arguments specified on the script's command line and displays each one:

```
For Each arg In WScript.Arguments
    WScript.Echo arg
Next
```

JavaScript: Using Enumerators and `for` Loops for Collections

To iterate through a collection in JavaScript, you must do two things: create a new `Enumerator` object and use a `for` loop to cycle through the enumerated collection.

To create a new `Enumerator` object, use the `new` keyword to set up an object variable (where *`collection`* is the name of the collection you want to work with):

```
var enum = new Enumerator(collection)
```

Then set up a special `for` loop:

```
for (; !enumerator.atEnd(); enumerator.moveNext())
{
    [statements];
}
```

enumerator	The `Enumerator` object you created
statements	The statements to execute for each element in the collection

The `Enumerator` object's `moveNext` method runs through the elements in the collection, whereas the `atEnd` method shuts down the loop after the last item has been processed. The following code loops through all the arguments specified on the script's command line and displays each one:

```
var args = new Enumerator(WScript.Arguments);
for (; !args.atEnd(); args.moveNext())
{
   WScript.Echo(args.item());
}
```

Programming the `WScript` Object

The `WScript` object represents the Windows Script Host applications (`WScript.exe` and `CScript.exe`). You use this object to get and set certain properties of the scripting host, as well as to access two other objects: `WshArguments` (the `WScript` object's `Arguments` property) and `WshScriptEngine` (accessed via the `WScript` object's `GetScriptEngine` method). `WScript` also contains the powerful `CreateObject` and `GetObject` methods, which enable you to work with Automation-enabled applications.

Displaying Text to the User

The `WScript` object method that you'll use most often is the `Echo` method, which displays text to the user. Here's the syntax:

```
WScript.Echo [Argument1, Argument2,...]
```

Here, *`Argument1`*, *`Argument2`*, and so on, are any number of text or numeric values that represent the information you want to display to the user. In the Windows-based host (`WScript.exe`), the information displays in a dialog box; in the command-line host (`CScript.exe`), the information displays at the command prompt (much like the command-line `ECHO` utility).

Shutting Down a Script

You use the `WScript` object's `Quit` method to shut down the script. You can also use `Quit` to have your script return an error code by using the following syntax:

```
WScript.Quit [intErrorCode]
```

`intErrorCode`	An integer value that represents the error code you want to return

You could then call the script from a batch file and use the `ERRORLEVEL` environment variable to deal with the return code in some way. (See Appendix C for more information on `ERRORLEVEL`.)

Scripting and Automation

Applications such as Internet Explorer and Word come with (or **expose**, in the jargon) a set of objects that define various aspects of the program. For example, Internet Explorer has an `Application` object that represents the program as a whole. Similarly, Word has a `Document` object that represents a Word document. By using the properties and methods that come with these objects, it's possible to programmatically query and manipulate the applications. With Internet Explorer, for example, you can use the `Application` object's `Navigate` method to send the browser to a specified web page. With Word, you can read a `Document` object's `Saved` property to see whether the document has unsaved changes.

This is powerful stuff, but how do you get at the objects that these applications expose? You do that by using a technology called **Automation**. Applications that support Automation implement object libraries that expose the application's native objects to Automation-aware programming languages. Such applications are **Automation servers**, and the applications that manipulate the server's objects are **Automation controllers.** The Windows Script Host is an Automation controller that enables you to write script code to control any server's objects.

This means that you can use an application's exposed objects more or less as you use the Windows Script Host objects. With just a minimum of preparation, your script code can refer to and work with the Internet Explorer `Application` object, or the Microsoft Word `Document` object, or any of the hundreds of other objects exposed by the applications on your system. (Note, however, that not all applications expose objects. Outlook Express and most of the built-in Windows Vista programs—such as WordPad and Paint—do not expose objects.)

Creating an Automation Object with the `CreateObject` Method

The `WScript` object's `CreateObject` method creates an Automation object (specifically, what programmers call an **instance** of the object). Here's the syntax:

```
WScript.CreateObject(strProgID)
```

`strProgID` — A string that specifies the Automation server application and the type of object to create. This string is a **programmatic identifier**, which is a label that uniquely specifies an application and one of its objects. The programmatic identifier always takes the following form:

`AppName.ObjectType`

Here, *`AppName`* is the Automation name of the application and *`ObjectType`* is the object class type (as defined in the Registry's `HKEY_CLASSES_ROOT` key). For example, here's the programmatic ID for Word:

`Word.Application`

Note that you normally use `CreateObject` within a `Set` statement, and that the function serves to create a new instance of the specified Automation object. For example, you could use the following statement to create a new instance of Word's `Application` object:

```
Set objWord = CreateObject("Word.Application")
```

You need to do nothing else to use the Automation object. With your variable declared and an instance of the object created, you can use that object's properties and methods directly. Listing 12.1 shows a VBScript example (you must have Word installed for this to work).

LISTING 12.1 A VBScript Example That Creates and Manipulates a Word `Application` Object

```
' Create the Word Application object
'
Set objWord = WScript.CreateObject("Word.Application")
'
' Create a new document
'
objWord.Documents.Add
'
```

LISTING 12.1 Continued

```
' Add some text
'
objWord.ActiveDocument.Paragraphs(1).Range.InsertBefore "Automation test."
'
' Save the document
'
objWord.ActiveDocument.Save
'
' We're done, so quit Word
'
objWord.Quit
```

This script creates and saves a new Word document by working with Word's `Application` object via Automation. The script begins by using the `CreateObject` method to create a new Word `Application` object, and the object is stored in the `objWord` variable. From there, you can wield the `objWord` variable just as though it were the Word `Application` object.

For example, the `objWord.Documents.Add` statement uses the `Documents` collection's `Add` method to create a new Word document, and the `InsertBefore` method adds some text to the document. The `Save` method then displays the Save As dialog box so that you can save the new file. With the Word-related chores complete, the `Application` object's `Quit` method runs to shut down Word. For comparison, Listing 12.2 shows a JavaScript procedure that performs the same tasks.

LISTING 12.2 A JavaScript Example That Creates and Manipulates a Word `Application` Object

```
// Create the Word Application object
//
var objWord = WScript.CreateObject("Word.Application");
//
// Create a new document
//
objWord.Documents.Add();
//
// Add some text
//
objWord.ActiveDocument.Paragraphs(1).Range.InsertBefore("Automation test.");
//
// Save the document
//
objWord.ActiveDocument.Save();
//
```

LISTING 12.2 Continued

```
// We're done, so quit Word
//
objWord.Quit();
```

Making the Automation Server Visible

The `CreateObject` method loads the object, but doesn't display the Automation server unless user interaction is required. For example, you see Word's Save As dialog box when you run the `Save` method on a new document (as in Listings 12.1 and 12.2). Not seeing the Automation server is the desired behavior in most Automation situations. However, if you *do* want to see what the Automation server is up to, set the `Application` object's `Visible` property to `True`, as in this example:

```
objWord.Visible = True
```

Working with an Existing Object Using the `GetObject` Method

If you know that the object you want to work with already exists or is already open, the `CreateObject` method isn't the best choice. In the example in the previous section, if Word is already running, the code will start a second copy of Word, which is a waste of resources. For these situations, it's better to work directly with the existing object. To do that, use the `GetObject` method:

```
WScript.GetObject(strPathname, [strProgID])
```

`strPathname`	The pathname (drive, folder, and filename) of the file you want to work with (or the file that contains the object you want to work with). If you omit this argument, you have to specify the *`strProgID`* argument.
`strProgID`	The programmatic identifier that specifies the Automation server application and the type of object to work with (that is, the *`AppName.ObjectType`* class syntax).

Listing 12.3 shows a VBScript procedure that puts the `GetObject` method to work.

LISTING 12.3 A VBScript Example That Uses the `GetObject` Method to Work with an Existing Instance of a Word `Document` Object

```
' Get the Word Document object
'
Set objDoc = WScript.GetObject("C:\GetObject.doc", "Word.Document")
'
' Get the word count
'
WScript.Echo objDoc.Name & " has " & objDoc.Words.Count & " words."
'
```

LISTING 12.3 Continued

```
' We're done, so quit Word
'
objDoc.Application.Quit
```


The `GetObject` method assigns the Word `Document` object named `GetObject.doc` to the `objDoc` variable. After you've set up this reference, you can use the object's properties and methods directly. For example, the `Echo` method uses `objDoc.Name` to return the filename and `objDoc.Words.Count` to determine the number of words in the document.

Note that although you're working with a `Document` object, you still have access to Word's `Application` object. That's because most objects have an `Application` property that refers to the `Application` object. In the script in Listing 12.3, for example, the following statement uses the `Application` property to quit Word:

```
objDoc.Application.Quit
```

Exposing VBScript and JavaScript Objects

One of the most powerful uses for scripted Automation is accessing the object models exposed by the VBScript and JavaScript engines. These models expose a number of objects, including the local file system. This enables you to create scripts that work with files, folders, and disk drives, read and write text files, and more. You use the following syntax to refer to these objects:

Scripting.*ObjectType*

`Scripting` is the Automation name of the scripting engine, and *`ObjectType`* is the class type of the object.

NOTE

This section just gives you a brief explanation of the objects associated with the VBScript and JavaScript engines. For the complete list of object properties and methods, please see the following site: msdn.microsoft.com/scripting.

Programming the `FileSystemObject`

`FileSystemObject` is the top-level file system object. For all your file system scripts, you begin by creating a new instance of `FileSystemObject`:

In VBScript:

```
Set fs = WScript.CreateObject("Scripting.FileSystemObject")
```

In JavaScript:

```
var fs = WScript.CreateObject("Scripting.FileSystemObject");
```

Here's a summary of the file system objects you can access via Automation and the top-level `FileSystemObject`:

`Drive`—This object enables you to access the properties of a specified disk drive or UNC network path. To reference a `Drive` object, use either the `Drives` collection (discussed next) or the `FileSystemObject` object's `GetDrive` method. For example, the following VBScript statement references drive C:

```
Set objFS = WScript.CreateObject("Scripting.FileSystemObject")
Set objDrive = objFS.GetDrive("C:")
```

`Drives`—This object is the collection of all available drives. To reference this collection, use the `FileSystemObject` object's `Drives` property:

```
Set objFS = WScript.CreateObject("Scripting.FileSystemObject")
Set objDrives = objFS.Drives
```

`Folder`—This object enables you to access the properties of a specified folder. To reference a `Folder` object, use either the `Folders` collection (discussed next) or the `FileSystemObject` object's `GetFolder` method:

```
Set objFS = WScript.CreateObject("Scripting.FileSystemObject")
Set objFolder = objFS.GetFolder("C:\My Documents")
```

`Folders`—This object is the collection of subfolders within a specified folder. To reference this collection, use the `Folder` object's `Subfolders` property:

```
Set objFS = WScript.CreateObject("Scripting.FileSystemObject")
Set objFolder = objFS.GetFolder("C:\Windows")
Set objSubfolders = objFolder.Subfolders
```

`File`—This object enables you to access the properties of a specified file. To reference a `File` object, use either the `Files` collection (discussed next) or the `FileSystemObject` object's `GetFile` method:

```
Set objFS = WScript.CreateObject("Scripting.FileSystemObject")
Set objFile = objFS.GetFile("c:\autoexec.bat")
```

`Files`—This object is the collection of files within a specified folder. To reference this collection, use the `Folder` object's `Files` property:

```
Set objFS = WScript.CreateObject("Scripting.FileSystemObject")
Set objFolder = objFS.GetFolder("C:\Windows")
Set objFiles = objFolder.Files
```

`TextStream`—This object enables you to use sequential access to work with a text file. To open a text file, use the `FileSystemObject` object's `OpenTextFile` method:

```
Set objFS = WScript.CreateObject("Scripting.FileSystemObject")
Set objTS= objFS.OpenTextFile("C:\Boot.ini")
```

Alternatively, you can create a new text file by using the FileSystemObject object's CreateTextFile method:

```
Set objFS = WScript.CreateObject("Scripting.FileSystemObject")
Set objTS= objFS.CreateTextFile("C:\Boot.ini")
```


Either way, you end up with a TextStream object, which has various methods for reading data from the file and writing data to the file. For example, the following script reads and displays the text from C:\Boot.ini:

```
Set objFS = WScript.CreateObject("Scripting.FileSystemObject")
Set objTS = objFS.OpenTextFile("C:\Boot.ini")
strContents = objTS.ReadAll
WScript.Echo strContents
objTS.Close
```

Programming the WshShell Object

WshShell is a generic name for a powerful object that enables you to query and interact with various aspects of the Windows shell. You can display information to the user, run applications, create shortcuts, work with the Registry, and control Windows' environment variables. The next few sections discuss each of those useful tasks.

Referencing the WshShell Object

WshShell refers to the Shell object exposed via the Automation interface of WScript. Therefore, you must use CreateObject to return this object:

```
Set objWshShell = WScript.CreateObject("WScript.Shell")
```

From here, you can use the objWshShell variable to access the object's properties and methods.

Displaying Information to the User

You saw earlier that the WScript object's Echo method is useful for displaying simple text messages to the user. You can gain more control over the displayed message by using the WshShell object's Popup method. This method is similar to the MsgBox function used in Visual Basic and VBA in that it enables you to control both the dialog box title and the buttons displayed, as well as to determine which of those buttons the user pressed. Here's the syntax:

WshShell.Popup(*strText*, [*nSecondsToWait*], [*strTitle*], [*intType*])

WshShell	The WshShell object.
strText	The message you want to display in the dialog box. You can enter a string up to 1,024 characters long.

nSecondsToWait	The maximum number of seconds the dialog box will be displayed.
strTitle	The text that appears in the dialog box title bar. If you omit this value, `Windows Script Host` appears in the title bar.
intType	A number or constant that specifies, among other things, the command buttons that appear in the dialog box (see the next section). The default value is `0`.

For example, the following statements display the dialog box shown in Figure 12.2:

```
Set objWshShell = WScript.CreateObject("WScript.Shell")
objWshShell.Popup "Couldn't find Memo.doc!", , "Warning"
```

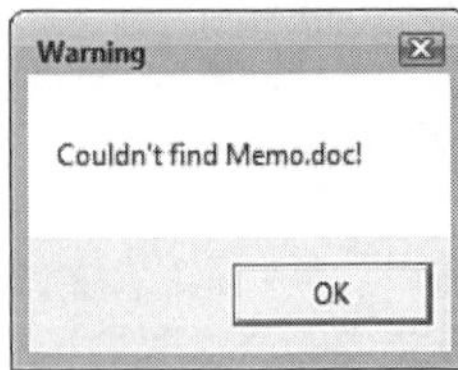

FIGURE 12.2 A simple message dialog box produced by the `Popup` method.

TIP

For long messages, VBScript wraps the text inside the dialog box. If you prefer to create your own line breaks, use VBScript's `Chr` function and the carriage return character (ASCII 13) between each line:

```
WshShell.Popup "First line" & Chr(13) & "Second line"
```

For JavaScript, use `\n` instead:

```
WshShell.Popup("First line" + "\n" + "Second line");
```

Setting the Style of the Message

The default `Popup` dialog box displays only an OK button. You can include other buttons and icons in the dialog box by using different values for the *intType* parameter. Table 12.1 lists the available options.

TABLE 12.1 The `Popup` Method's *intType* Parameter Options

VBScript Constant	Value	Description
Buttons		
`vbOKOnly`	0	Displays only an OK button. This is the default.
`vbOKCancel`	1	Displays the OK and Cancel buttons.
`vbAbortRetryIgnore`	2	Displays the Abort, Retry, and Ignore buttons.
`vbYesNoCancel`	3	Displays the Yes, No, and Cancel buttons.

TABLE 12.1 Continued

VBScript Constant	Value	Description
vbYesNo	4	Displays the Yes and No buttons.
vbRetryCancel	5	Displays the Retry and Cancel buttons.
Icons		
vbCritical	16	Displays the Critical Message icon.
vbQuestion	32	Displays the Warning Query icon.
vbExclamation	48	Displays the Warning Message icon.
vbInformation	64	Displays the Information Message icon.
Default Buttons		
vbDefaultButton1	0	The first button is the default (that is, the button selected when the user presses Enter).
vbDefaultButton2	256	The second button is the default.
vbDefaultButton3	512	The third button is the default.

You derive the *intType* argument in one of two ways:

- By adding the values for each option
- By using the VBScript constants separated by plus signs (+)

The script in Listing 12.4 shows an example and Figure 12.3 shows the resulting dialog box.

LISTING 12.4 A VBScript Example That Uses the Popup Method to Display the Dialog Box Shown in Figure 12.3

```
' First, set up the message
'
strText = "Are you sure you want to copy" & Chr(13)
strText = strText & "the selected files to drive A?"
strTitle = "Copy Files"
intType = vbYesNoCancel + vbQuestion + vbDefaultButton2
'
' Now display it
'
Set objWshShell = WScript.CreateObject("WScript.Shell")
intResult = objWshShell.Popup(strText, ,strTitle, intType)
```

Here, three variables—strText, strTitle, and intType—store the values for the Popup method's *strText*, *strTitle*, and *intType* arguments, respectively. In particular, the following statement derives the *intType* argument:

```
intType = vbYesNoCancel + vbQuestion + vbDefaultButton2
```

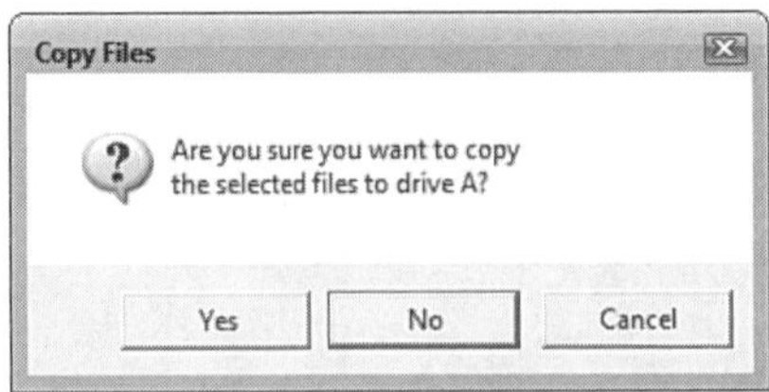

FIGURE 12.3 The dialog box that's displayed when you run the script.

You also could derive the *intType* argument by adding up the values that these constants represent (3, 32, and 256, respectively), but the script becomes less readable that way.

Getting Return Values from the Message Dialog Box

A dialog box that displays only an OK button is straightforward. The user either clicks OK or presses Enter to remove the dialog from the screen. The multibutton styles are a little different, however; the user has a choice of buttons to select, and your script should have a way to find out which button the user chose, which enables it to decide what to do next, based on the user's selection. You do this by storing the `Popup` method's return value in a variable. Table 12.2 lists the seven possible return values.

TABLE 12.2 The `Popup` Method's Return Values

VBScript Constant	Value	Button Selected
`vbOK`	1	OK
`vbCancel`	2	Cancel
`vbAbort`	3	Abort
`vbRetry`	4	Retry
`vbIgnore`	5	Ignore
`vbYes`	6	Yes
`vbNo`	7	No

To process the return value, you can use an `If...Then...Else` or `Select Case` structure to test for the appropriate values. For example, the script shown earlier used a variable called `intResult` to store the return value of the `Popup` method. Listing 12.5 shows a revised version of the script that uses a VBScript `Select Case` statement to test for the three possible return values.

LISTING 12.5 A Script That Uses a `Select Case` Statement to Process the `Popup` Method's Return Value

```
' First, set up the message
'
strText = "Are you sure you want to copy" & Chr(13)
strText = strText & "the selected files to drive A?"
strTitle = "Copy Files"
```

LISTING 12.5 Continued

```
intType = vbYesNoCancel + vbQuestion + vbDefaultButton2
'
' Now display it
'
Set objWshShell = WScript.CreateObject("WScript.Shell")
intResult = objWshShell.Popup(strText, ,strTitle, intType)
'
' Process the result
'
Select Case intResult
    Case vbYes
        WScript.Echo "You clicked ""Yes""!"
    Case vbNo
        WScript.Echo "You clicked ""No""!"
    Case vbCancel
        WScript.Echo "You clicked ""Cancel""!"
End Select
```


Running Applications

When you need your script to launch another application, use the `Run` method:

`WshShell``.Run` *`strCommand`*`, [`*`intWindowStyle`*`], [`*`bWaitOnReturn`*`]`

`WshShell` The `WshShell` object.

`strCommand` The name of the file that starts the application. Unless the file is in the Windows folder, you should include the drive and folder to make sure that the script can find the file.

`intWindowStyle` A constant or number that specifies how the application window will appear:

intWindowStyle	Window Appearance
0	Hidden
1	Normal size with focus
2	Minimized with focus (this is the default)
3	Maximized with focus
4	Normal without focus
6	Minimized without focus

`bWaitOnReturn` A logical value that determines whether the application runs asynchronously. If this value is `True`, the script halts execution until the user exits the launched application; if this value is `False`, the script continues running after it has launched the application.

Here's an example:

```
Set objWshShell = WScript.CreateObject("WScript.Shell")
objWshShell.Run "Control.exe Inetcpl.cpl", 1, True
```

This `Run` method launches Control Panel's Internet Properties dialog box.

NOTE

To learn more about launching individual Control Panel icons using `Control.exe`, refer to "Operating Control Panel" in Chapter 10, "Using Control Panel and Group Policies."

Working with Shortcuts

The Windows Script Host enables your scripts to create and modify shortcut files. When writing scripts for other users, you might want to take advantage of this capability to display shortcuts for new network shares, Internet sites, instruction files, and so on.

Creating a Shortcut

To create a shortcut, use the `CreateShortcut` method:

```
WshShell.CreateShortcut(strPathname)
```

`WshShell`	The `WshShell` object.
`strPathname`	The full path and filename of the shortcut file you want to create. Use the `.lnk` extension for a file system (program, document, folder, and so on) shortcut; use the `.url` extension for an Internet shortcut.

The following example creates and saves a shortcut on a user's desktop:

```
Set WshShell = objWScript.CreateObject("WScript.Shell")
Set objShortcut = objWshShell.CreateShortcut("C:\Users\
➥Paul\Desktop\test.lnk")
objShortcut.Save
```

Programming the `WshShortcut` Object

The `CreateShortcut` method returns a `WshShortcut` object. You can use this object to manipulate various properties and methods associated with shortcut files.

This object contains the following properties:

`Arguments`—Returns or sets a string that specifies the arguments used when launching the shortcut. For example, suppose that the shortcut's target is the following:

```
C:\Windows\Notepad.exe C:\Boot.ini
```

In other words, this shortcut launches Notepad and loads the `Boot.ini` file. In this case, the `Arguments` property would return the following string:

```
C:\Boot.ini
```

`Description`—Returns or sets a string description of the shortcut.

`FullName`—Returns the full path and filename of the shortcut's target. This will be the same as the *`strPathname`* value used in the `CreateShortcut` method.

`Hotkey`—Returns or sets the hotkey associated with the shortcut. To set this value, use the following syntax:

```
WshShortcut.Hotkey = strHotKey
```

`WshShortcut`	The `WshShortcut` object.
`strHotKey`	A string value of the form *`Modifier+Keyname`*, where *`Modifier`* is any combination of Alt, Ctrl, and Shift, and *`Keyname`* is one of A through Z or 0 through 12.

For example, the following statement sets the hotkey to Ctrl+Alt+7:

```
objShortcut.Hotkey = "Ctrl+Alt+7"
```

`IconLocation`: Returns or sets the icon used to display the shortcut. To set this value, use the following syntax:

```
WshShortcut.IconLocation = strIconLocation
```

`WshShortcut`	The `WshShortcut` object.
`strIconLocation`	A string value of the form *`Path,Index`*, where *`Path`* is the full pathname of the icon file and *`Index`* is the position of the icon within the file (where the first icon is `0`).

Here's an example:

```
objShortcut.IconLocation = "C:\Windows\System32\Shell32.dll,21"
```

`TargetPath`	Returns or sets the path of the shortcut's target.
`WindowStyle`	Returns or sets the window style used by the shortcut's target. Use the same values outlined earlier for the `Run` method's *`intWindowStyle`* argument.
`WorkingDirectory`	Returns or sets the path of the shortcut's working directory.

NOTE

If you're working with Internet shortcuts, bear in mind that they support only two properties: `FullName` and `TargetPath` (the URL target).

The `WshShortcut` object also supports two methods:

`Save`	Saves the shortcut file to disk.
`Resolve`	Uses the shortcut's `TargetPath` property to look up the target file. Here's the syntax: `WshShortcut.Resolve = intFlag`
`WshShortcut`	The WshShortcut object.
`intFlag`	Determines what happens of the target file is not found:

`intFlag`	**What Happens**
1	Nothing
2	Windows continues to search subfolders for the target file
4	Updates the `TargetPath` property if the target file is found in a new location

Listing 12.6 shows a complete example of a script that creates a shortcut.

LISTING 12.6 A Script That Creates a Shortcut File

```
Set objWshShell = WScript.CreateObject("WScript.Shell")
Set objShortcut = objWshShell.CreateShortcut("C:\Users\Paul
➥\Desktop\Edit BOOT.INI.lnk")
With objShortcut
    .TargetPath = "C:\Windows\Notepad.exe"
    .Arguments = "C:\Boot.ini"
    .WorkingDirectory = "C:\"
    .Description = "Opens BOOT.INI in Notepad"
    .Hotkey = "Ctrl+Alt+7"
    .IconLocation = "C:\Windows\System32\Shell32.dll,21"
    .WindowStyle = 3
    .Save
End With
```

Working with Registry Entries

You've seen throughout this book that the Registry is one the most crucial data structures in Windows. However, the Registry isn't a tool that only Windows yields. Most 32-bit applications make use of the Registry as a place to store setup options, customization values the user selected, and much more. Interestingly, your scripts can get in on the act as well. Not only can your scripts read the current value of any Registry setting, but they can also use the Registry as a storage area. This enables you to keep track of user settings, recently used files, and any other configuration data that you'd like to save between sessions. This section shows you how to use the `WshShell` object to manipulate the Registry from within your scripts.

Reading Settings from the Registry

To read any value from the Registry, use the WshShell object's `RegRead` method:

```
WshShell.RegRead(strName)
```

WshShell The `WshShell` object.

strName The name of the Registry value or key that you want to read. If *strName* ends with a backslash (\), `RegRead` returns the default value for the key; otherwise, `RegRead` returns the data stored in the value. Note, too, that *strName* must begin with one of the following root key names:

Short Name	Long Name
HKCR	HKEY_CLASSES_ROOT
HKCU	HKEY_CURRENT_USER
HKLM	HKEY_LOCAL_MACHINE
N/A	HKEY_USERS
N/A	HKEY_CURRENT_CONFIG

The script in Listing 12.7 displays the name of the registered owner of this copy of Windows Vista.

LISTING 12.7 A Script That Reads the `RegisteredOwner` Setting from the Registry

```
Set objWshShell = WScript.CreateObject("WScript.Shell")
strSetting = "HKLM\SOFTWARE\Microsoft\Windows NT\CurrentVersion\RegisteredOwner"
strRegisteredUser = objWshShell.RegRead(strSetting)
WScript.Echo strRegisteredUser
```

Storing Settings in the Registry

To store a setting in the Registry, use the `WshShell` object's `RegWrite` method:

```
WshShell.RegWrite strName, anyValue [, strType]
```

WshShell The `WshShell` object.

strName The name of the Registry value or key that you want to set. If *strName* ends with a backslash (\), `RegWrite` sets the default value for the key; otherwise, `RegWrite` sets the data for the value. *strName* must begin with one of the root key names detailed in the `RegRead` method.

anyValue The value to be stored.

strType The data type of the value, which must be one of the following: `REG_SZ` (the default), `REG_EXPAND_SZ`, `REG_DWORD`, or `REG_BINARY`.

The following statements create a new key named `ScriptSettings` in the `HKEY_CURRENT_USER` root:

```
Set objWshShell = WScript.CreateObject("WScript.Shell")
objWshShell.RegWrite "HKCU\ScriptSettings\", ""
```

The following statements create a new value named `NumberOfReboots` in the `HKEY_CURRENT_USER\ScriptSettings` key, and set this value to `1`:

```
Set objWshShell = WScript.CreateObject("WScript.Shell")
objWshShell.RegWrite "HKCU\ScriptSettings\NumberOfReboots", 1, "REG_DWORD"
```

Deleting Settings from the Registry

If you no longer need to track a particular key or value setting, use the `RegDelete` method to remove the setting from the Registry:

```
WshShell.RegDelete(strName)
```

WshShell	The `WshShell` object.
strName	The name of the Registry value or key that you want to delete. If *strName* ends with a backslash (`\`), `RegDelete` deletes the key; otherwise, `RegDelete` deletes the value. *strName* must begin with one of the root key names detailed in the `RegRead` method.

To delete the `NumberOfReboots` value used in the previous example, you would use the following statements:

```
Set objWshShell = WScript.CreateObject("WScript.Shell")
objWshShell.RegDelete "HKCU\ScriptSettings\NumberOfReboots"
```

Working with Environment Variables

Windows Vista keeps track of a number of **environment variables** that hold data such as the location of the Windows folder, the location of the temporary files folder, the command path, the primary drive, and much more. Why would you need such data? One example would be for accessing files or folders within the main Windows folder. Rather than guessing that this folder is `C:\Windows`, it would be much easier to just query the `%SystemRoot%` environment variable. Similarly, if you have a script that accesses files in a user's My Documents folder, hard-coding the username in the file path is inconvenient because it means creating custom scripts for every possible user. Instead, it would be much easier to create just a single script that references the `%UserProfile%` environment variable. This section shows you how to read environment variable data within your scripts.

The defined environment variables are stored in the `Environment` collection, which is a property of the `WshShell` object. Windows Vista environment variables are stored in the `"Process"` environment, so you reference this collection as follows:

```
WshShell.Environment("Process")
```

Listing 12.8 shows a script that runs through this collection, adds each variable to a string, and then displays the string.

LISTING 12.8 A Script That Displays the System's Environment Variables

```
Set objWshShell = WScript.CreateObject("WScript.Shell")
'
' Run through the environment variables
'
strVariables = ""
For Each objEnvVar In objWshShell.Environment("Process")
    strVariables = strVariables & objEnvVar & Chr(13)
Next
WScript.Echo strVariables
```

Figure 12.4 shows the dialog box that appears (your mileage may vary).

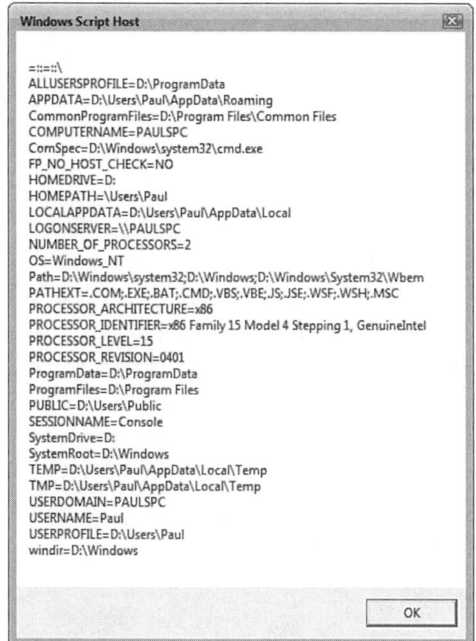

FIGURE 12.4 A complete inventory of a system's environment variables.

If you want to use the value of a particular environment variable, use the following syntax:

```
WshShell.Environment("Process")("strName")
```

WshShell	The WshShell object
strName	The name of the environment variable

Listing 12.9 shows a revised version of the script from Listing 12.6 to create a shortcut. In this version, the `Environment` collection is used to return the value of the `%UserProfile%` variable, which is used to contrast the path to the current user's Desktop folder.

LISTING 12.9 A Script That Creates a Shortcut File Using an Environment Variable

```
Set objWshShell = WScript.CreateObject("WScript.Shell")
strUserProfile = objWshShell.Environment("Process")("UserProfile")
Set objShortcut = objWshShell.CreateShortcut(strUserProfile & _
                  "\Desktop\Edit BOOT.INI.lnk")
With objShortcut
    .TargetPath = "C:\Windows\Notepad.exe"
    .Arguments = "C:\Boot.ini"
    .WorkingDirectory = "C:\"
    .Description = "Opens BOOT.INI in Notepad"
    .Hotkey = "Ctrl+Alt+7"
    .IconLocation = "C:\Windows\System32\Shell32.dll,21"
    .WindowStyle = 3
    .Save
End With
```

Programming the `WshNetwork` Object

`WshNetwork` is a generic name for an object that enables you to work with various aspects of the Windows network environment. You can determine the computer name and username, you can enumerate the mapped network drives, you can map new network drives, and more. The next couple of sections show you how to work with this object.

Referencing the `WshNetwork` Object

`WshNetwork` refers to the `Network` object exposed via the Automation interface of WScript. This means you use `CreateObject` to return this object, as shown here:

```
Set objWshNetwork = WScript.CreateObject("WScript.Network")
```

From here, you use the `WshNetwork` variable to access the object's properties and methods.

WshNetwork Object Properties

The WshNetwork object supports three properties:

ComputerName	Returns the network name of the computer
UserDomain	Returns the network domain name of the current user
UserName	Returns the username of the current user

Mapping Network Printers

The WshNetwork object supports several methods for working with remote printers. For example, to map a network printer to a local printer resource, use the WshNetwork object's AddWindowsPrinterConnection method:

```
WshNetwork.AddPrinterConnection strPrinterPath
```

WshNetwork	The WshNetwork object
strPrinterPath	The UNC path to the network printer

Here's an example:

```
Set objWshNetwork = WScript.CreateObject("WScript.Network")
objWshNetwork.AddWindowsPrinterConnection "\\ZEUS\printer"
```

To remove a remote printer mapping, use the WshNetwork object's RemovePrinterConnection method:

```
WshNetwork.RemovePrinterConnection strPrinterPath [, bForce] [, bUpdateProfile]
```

WshNetwork	The WshNetwork object
strPrinterPath	The UNC path to the network printer
bForce	If True, the resource is removed even if it is currently being used
bUpdateProfile	If True, the printer mapping is removed from the user's profile

Here's an example:

```
Set objWshNetwork = WScript.CreateObject("WScript.Network")
objWshNetwork.RemovePrinterConnection "\\ZEUS\inkjet"
```

Mapping Network Drives

The WshNetwork object supports several methods for mapping network drives. To map a shared network folder to a local drive letter, use the WshNetwork object's MapNetworkDrive method:

```
WshNetwork.MapNetworkDrive strLocalName, strRemoteName,
➥[bUpdateProfile], [strUser], [strPassword]
```

WshNetwork	The `WshNetwork` object
strLocalName	The local drive letter to which the remote share will be mapped (for example, `F:`)
strRemoteName	The UNC path for the remote share
bUpdateProfile	If `True`, the drive mapping is stored in the user's profile
strUser	Use this value to enter a username that might be required to map the remote share (if you're logged on as a user who doesn't have the proper permissions, for example)
strPassword	Use this value to enter a password that might be required to map the remote drive

Here's an example:

```
Set objWshNetwork = WScript.CreateObject("WScript.Network")
objWshNetwork.MapNetworkDrive "Z:", "\\ZEUS\SharedDocs"
```

To remove a mapped network drive, use the `WshNetwork` object's `RemoveNetworkDrive`:

```
WshNetwork.RemoveNetworkDrive strName, [bForce], [bUpdateProfile]
```

WshNetwork	The `WshNetwork` object.
strName	The name of the mapped network drive you want removed. If you use a network path, all mappings to that path are removed; if you use a local drive letter, only that mapping is removed.
bForce	If `True`, the resource is removed even if it is currently being used.
bUpdateProfile	If `True`, the network drive mapping is removed from the user's profile.

Here's an example:

```
Set objWshNetwork = WScript.CreateObject("WScript.Network")
objWshNetwork.RemoveNetworkDrive "Z:"
```

Example: Scripting Internet Explorer

To give you a taste of the power and flexibility of scripting—particularly Automation programming—I'll close this chapter by showing you how to program a specific Automation server: Internet Explorer. You'll see that your scripts can control just about everything associated with Internet Explorer:

- The position and dimensions of the window
- Whether the menu bar, toolbar, and status bar are displayed

- The current URL
- Sending the browser backward and forward between navigated URLs

Displaying a Web Page

To get started, I'll show you how to use the `InternetExplorer` object to display a specified URL. You use the `Navigate` method to do this, and this method uses the following syntax:

```
InternetExplorer.Navigate URL [, Flags,] [ TargetFramename] [, PostData]
 [ ,Headers]
```

InternetExplorer	A reference to the `InternetExplorer` object with which you're working.
URL	The address of the web page you want to display.
Flags	One of (or the sum of two or more of) the following integers that control various aspects of the navigation:
	1 Opens the *URL* in a new window
	2 Prevents the *URL* from being added to the history list
	4 Prevents the browser from reading the page from the disk cache
	8 Prevents the *URL* from being added to the disk cache
TargetFrameName	The name of the frame in which to display the *URL*.
PostData	Specifies additional `POST` information that HTTP requires to resolve the hyperlink. The most common uses for this argument are to send a web server the contents of a form, the coordinates of an imagemap, or a search parameter for an ASP file. If you leave this argument blank, this method issues a `GET` call.
Headers	Specifies header data for the HTTP header.

Here's an example:

```
Set objIE = CreateObject("InternetExplorer.Application")
objIE.Navigate "http://www.microsoft.com/"
```

Navigating Pages

Displaying a specified web page isn't the only thing the `InternetExplorer` object can do. It also has quite a few methods that give you the ability to navigate backward and forward through visited web pages, refresh the current page, stop the current download, and more. Here's a summary of these methods:

`GoBack`	Navigates backward to a previously visited page
`GoForward`	Navigates forward to a previously visited page
`GoHome`	Navigates to Internet Explorer's default Home page
`GoSearch`	Navigates to Internet Explorer's default Search page
`Refresh`	Refreshes the current page
`Refresh2`	Refreshes the current page using the following syntax: `Refresh2(`*`Level`*`)` *`Level`* A constant that determines how the page is refreshed: `0` Refreshes the page with a cached copy 1 Refreshes the page with a cached copy only if the page has expired 3 Performs a full refresh (doesn't use a cached copy)
`Stop`	Cancels the current download or shuts down dynamic page objects, such as background sounds and animations.

Using the `InternetExplorer` Object's Properties

Here's a summary of many of the properties associated with the `InternetExplorer` object:

`Busy`	Returns `True` if the `InternetExplorer` object is in the process of downloading text or graphics. This property returns `False` when a download of the complete document has finished.
`FullScreen`	A Boolean value that toggles Internet Explorer between the normal window and a full-screen window in which the title bar, menu bar, toolbar, and status bar are hidden.
`Height`	Returns or sets the window height.
`Left`	Returns or sets the position of the left edge of the window.
`LocationName`	Returns the title of the current document.
`LocationURL`	Returns the URL of the current document.
`MenuBar`	A Boolean value that toggles the menu bar on and off.
`StatusBar`	A Boolean value that toggles the status bar on and off.
`StatusText`	Returns or sets the status bar text.
`ToolBar`	A Boolean value that toggles the toolbar on and off.
`Top`	Returns or sets the position of the top edge of the window.
`Type`	Returns the type of document currently loaded in the browser.
`Visible`	A Boolean value that toggles the object between hidden and visible.
`Width`	Returns or sets the window width.

Running Through a Sample Script

To put some of the properties and methods into practice, Listing 12.10 shows a sample script.

LISTING 12.10 A Script That Puts the `InternetExplorer` Object Through Its Paces

```
Option Explicit
Dim objIE, objWshShell, strMessage, intResult

' Set up the Automation objects
Set objIE = WScript.CreateObject("InternetExplorer.Application")
Set objWshShell = WScript.CreateObject("WScript.Shell")

' Navigate to a page and customize the browser window
objIE.Navigate "http://www.wordspy.com/"
objIE.Toolbar = False
objIE.StatusBar = False
objIE.MenuBar = False

' Twiddle thumbs while the page loads
Do While objIE.Busy
Loop

' Get the page info
strMessage = "Current URL:  " & objIE.LocationURL & vbCrLf & _
    "Current Title: " & objIE.LocationName & vbCrLf & _
    "Document Type: " & objIE.Type & vbCrLf & vbCrLf & _
    "Would you like to view this document?"

' Display the info
intResult = objWshShell.Popup(strMessage, , "Scripting IE", vbYesNo + vbQuestion)

' Check the result
If intResult = vbYes Then

    ' If Yes, make browser visible
    objIE.Visible = True
Else

    ' If no, bail out
    objIE.Quit
End If
Set objIE = Nothing
Set objWshShell = Nothing
```

The script begins by creating instances of the `InternetExplorer` and WScript `Shell` objects. The `Navigate` method displays a page, and then turns off the toolbar, status bar, and menu bar. A `Do...Loop` checks the `Busy` property and loops while it's `True`. In other words, this loop won't exit until the page is fully loaded. A string variable is used to store the URL, the title, and type of the page, and this string is then displayed in a `Popup` box, which also asks whether the user wants to see the page. If the user clicks the Yes button, the browser is made visible; if the user clicks the No button, the `Quit` method shuts down the browser.

From Here

Here are some sections of the book that contain information related to the scripting techniques you learned in this chapter:

- To learn how to run scripts when you start your Windows Vista system, see the section "Specifying Startup and Logon Scripts" in Chapter 5, "Installing and Running Applications."
- To learn more about the Registry, see Chapter 11, "Getting to Know the Windows Vista Registry."
- I show you a script that displays the available free space on all your drives in the "Checking Free Disk Space" section of Chapter 15, "Maintaining Your Windows Vista System."
- For some examples of security-related scripts, see Chapter 21, "Implementing Windows Vista's Internet Security and Privacy Features."
- You can also "program" Windows Vista using batch files. See Appendix C, "Automating Windows Vista with Batch Files."

PART III

Unleashing Windows Vista Customization and Optimization

CHAPTER 13

Customizing the Windows Vista Interface

IN THIS CHAPTER

- Customizing the Start Menu for Easier Program and Document Launching
- Customizing the Taskbar for Easier Program and Document Launching
- Controlling Taskbar Grouping
- Modifying the Start Menu and Taskbar with Group Policies
- Using Screen Space Efficiently

Microsoft spent countless hours and untold millions of dollars testing and retesting the Windows Vista user interface (UI) in its usability labs. It's important, however, to remember that Windows Vista is an operating system designed for the masses. With an installed base running in the hundreds of millions, it's only natural that the Windows UI would incorporate lots of lowest-common-denominator thinking. So, in the end, you have an interface that most people find easy to use most of the time; an interface that skews toward accommodating neophytes and the newly digital; an interface designed for a typical computer user, whoever the heck that is.

In other words, unless you consider yourself a typical user (and your purchase of this book proves otherwise), Windows Vista in its right-out-of-the-box getup won't be right for you. Fortunately, you'll find no shortage of options and programs that will help you remake Windows Vista in your own image, and that's just what this chapter shows you how to do. After all, you weren't produced by a cookie cutter, so why should your operating system look like it was?

Having said that, I should also point out that it's my philosophy that the litmus test of any interface customization is a simple question: Does it improve productivity? I've seen far too many tweaks that fiddle uselessly with some obscure setting, resulting in little or no improvement to the user's day-to-day Windows experience. This may be fine for people with lots of time to kill, but most of us don't have that luxury, so efficiency and productivity must be the goals of the customization process. (Note that this does not preclude aesthetic improvements to the Windows

Vista interface. A better-looking Windows provides a happier computing experience, and a happier worker is a more productive worker.)

To that end, I devote most of this chapter to the most common of computing tasks: launching programs and documents. I packed this chapter with useful tips and techniques for rearranging Windows Vista to help you get your programs and documents up and running as quickly and as easily as possible.

Customizing the Start Menu for Easier Program and Document Launching

The whole purpose of the Start menu is, as its name implies, to start things, particularly programs and documents. Yes, you can also launch these objects via shortcut icons on the desktop, but that's not a great alternative because windows cover the desktop most of the time. So, if you want to get something going in Windows Vista, the vast majority of the time you're going to have to do it via the Start menu. The good news is that Windows Vista's Start menu is wonderfully flexible and geared, in fact, to launching objects with as few mouse clicks or keystrokes as possible. To get to that state, however, you have to work with a few relatively obscure options and settings, which you'll learn about in the next few sections.

Getting More Favorite Programs on the Start Menu

The Start menu is divided vertically into two sections, as shown in Figure 13.1:

- Favorite programs—This is the left side of the Start menu, which appears by default with a white background. This side includes the fixed Internet and E-mail icons at the top, and below them are shortcut icons for the nine programs that you've used most frequently.
- Built-in features—This is the right side of the Start menu, which appears by default with a black or gray background. It contains icons for various Windows Vista folders and features.

The list of favorite programs is one of the best features in Windows Vista because it ensures that the programs you use most often are always just a couple of mouse clicks away. If there's a downside to this feature, it's that it displays only nine icons, so the list omits many frequently used programs. However, if you have enough room, you can tell Windows Vista to display up to 30 icons in this area. Here's how:

1. Right-click the Start menu and then click Properties. The Taskbar and Start Menu Properties dialog box appears.
2. Select the Start Menu tab.
3. Make sure that the Start Menu option is activated and then click the Customize button to its right. The Customize Start Menu dialog box appears, as shown in Figure 13.2.

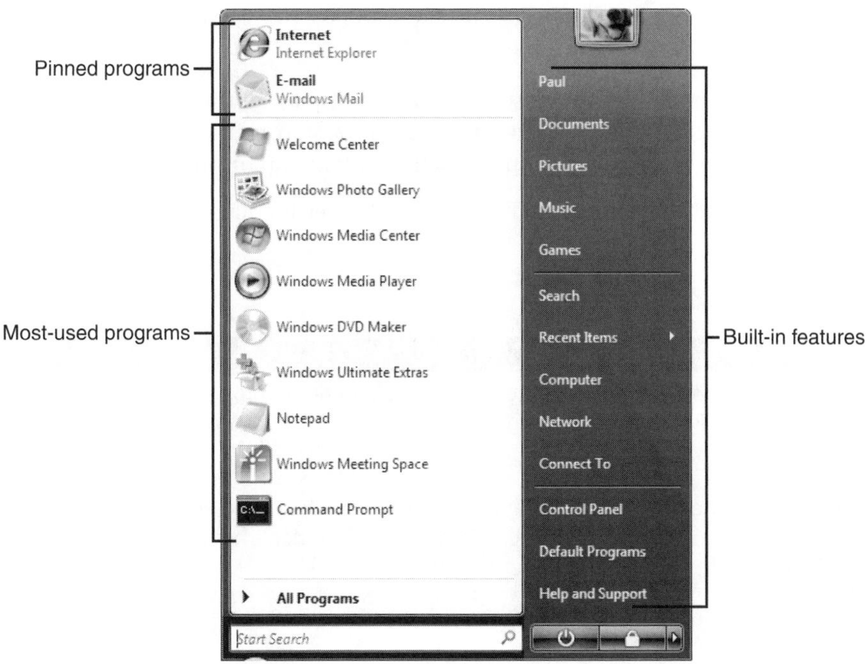

FIGURE 13.1 The Start menu lists favorite programs on the left and built-in icons for Vista features on the right.

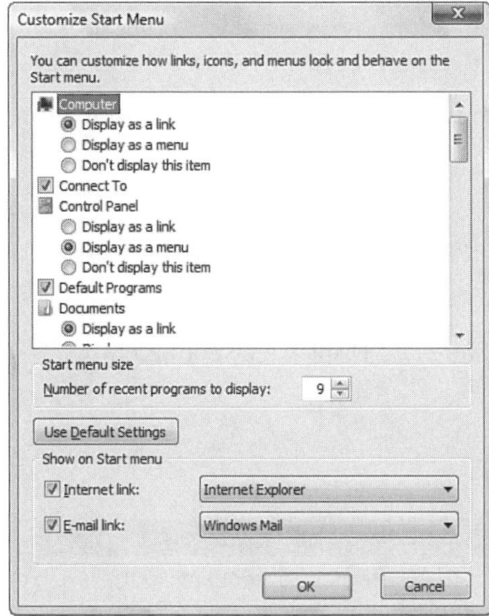

FIGURE 13.2 Use the Customize Start Menu dialog box to set the maximum number of shortcut icons that appear in the Start menu's list of favorite programs.

4. Use the Number of Recent Programs to Display spin box to specify the number of favorite programs you want to display.
5. If you don't think you have enough screen space to display all the icons, deactivate the Large Icons option (it's at the bottom of the list of Start menu features). This significantly reduces the amount of space each icon takes up on the Start menu.
6. Click OK to return to the Taskbar and Start Menu Properties dialog box.
7. Click OK.

TIP

To prevent a program from appearing on the Start menu's frequent programs list, open the Registry Editor and display the following key:

```
HKCR\Applications\program.exe
```

Here, *program.exe* is the name of the program's executable file. (If the key doesn't exist, create it.) Create a string value called `NoStartPage` (you don't need to assign a value to it). Restart Vista to put the new setting into effect.

Clearing the Recent Programs List

Windows Vista allows you to clear the Start menu list of recent programs. Why would you want to do this? You might want to start over with an empty list of frequent programs so that you can populate it with the programs you will use over the next few days. Alternatively, you might want to keep the list cleared for privacy reasons if other people have access to your computer. Follow these steps to clear the list:

1. Right-click the Start menu and then click Properties. The Taskbar and Start Menu Properties dialog box appears.
2. Select the Start Menu tab.
3. Deactivate the Store and Display a List of Recently Opened Programs check box.
4. Click Apply. Windows Vista clears the list.
5. If you want to start a new list, activate the Store and Display a List of Recently Opened Programs check box.
6. Click OK.

TIP

If you need to get rid of only one or two icons from the Start menu's frequent programs list, click Start, right-click an icon you want to delete, and then click Remove from This List.

Customizing the Internet and E-mail Icons

Above the Start menu's favorite programs list is the **pinned programs** list (pointed out in Figure 13.1), which contains two icons that appear permanently on the Start menu:

Internet—By default, this icon launches the Internet Explorer web browser.

E-mail—By default, this icon launches the Windows Mail email client.

NOTE

If your computer's manufacturer or reseller preinstalled Windows Vista, you might notice that the manufacturer or reseller altered the default Internet and email programs to support other software packaged with your computer. Similarly, third-party programs might mess with these icons. Microsoft Office, for example, will associate Outlook with the E-mail icon. However, you should be able to modify the defaults further to reflect your own preferences.

If you have multiple web browsers or email clients installed on your computer, you can customize these icons to launch a different program. Here are the steps to follow:

1. Right-click the Start menu and then click Properties to display the Taskbar and Start Menu Properties dialog box.
2. Select the Start Menu tab, make sure that the Start Menu option is activated, and then click the Customize button to its right to open the Customize Start Menu dialog box.
3. If you want the Internet icon to appear on the Start menu, leave the Internet Link check box activated; otherwise, deactivate it and continue with step 5.
4. If the Internet Link check box is activated, use the list to its right to choose the web browser you want associated with the icon.
5. If you want the E-mail icon to appear on the Start menu, leave the E-mail Link check box activated; otherwise, deactivate it and continue with step 7.
6. If the E-mail Link check box is activated, use the list to its right to choose the email client you want associated with the icon.
7. Click OK.

It's also possible to change the text and icon used for the Internet item on the Start menu. You do this by first displaying the following key in the Registry Editor:

```
HKLM\SOFTWARE\Clients\StartMenuInternet\client\
```

Here, `client` is the name of the executable file of the program associated with the icon (such as `Iexplorer.exe` for Internet Explorer). The (Default) setting controls the icon text, and the (Default) setting of the `DefaultIcon` subkey controls the icon.

Customizing the text and icon for the email item is similar. You'll find the necessary settings here:

```
HKLM\Software\Clients\Mail\client\
```

Here `client` is the name of the program associated with the icon (such as Windows Mail). The (Default) setting controls the icon text, and the (Default) setting of the `DefaultIcon` subkey controls the icon. Note that you might have to create this subkey.

Setting Program Access and Defaults

You can modify Windows Vista to use other programs as the default for activities such as web browsing, email, instant messaging, and media playing. This enables you to have your favorite programs available in more convenient locations and to have those programs launch automatically in certain situations.

Your version of Windows Vista is most likely set up to use Internet Explorer, Windows Mail, Windows Messenger, and Windows Media Player as the default programs for web browsing, email, instant messaging, and media playing, respectively. This means that Internet Explorer and Windows Mail are associated with the Start menu's Internet and E-mail items. In addition, it means these programs launch automatically in response to certain events. For example, when you right-click a media file and then click Play, the media plays in Windows Media Player.

You can set up as defaults any other programs you have installed for web browsing, email, instant messaging, and media playing. You can also disable access to programs so that other users cannot launch them on your computer. Here are the steps to follow:

1. Select Start, Default Programs to display the Default Programs window.
2. Click Set Program Access and Computer Defaults and then enter your User Account Control credentials when prompted. Windows Vista displays the Set Program Access and Computer Defaults dialog box.
3. Click the configuration you want to start with:

   Computer Manufacturer—This configuration appears if your computer vendor defined its own program defaults.

   Microsoft Windows—This configuration is the Windows default as defined by Microsoft.

   Non-Microsoft—This configuration is generated by Windows Vista if you have one or more non-Microsoft programs available in any of the categories (such as a web browser or email program).

   Custom—Use this item to configure your own default programs.
4. If you activated the Custom configuration, you see options similar to those shown in Figure 13.3. You can do two things with this configuration:

   - Activate the option buttons of the programs you prefer to use as the system defaults.

- Deactivate the Enable Access to This Program check box for any program that you don't want other users to have access to.

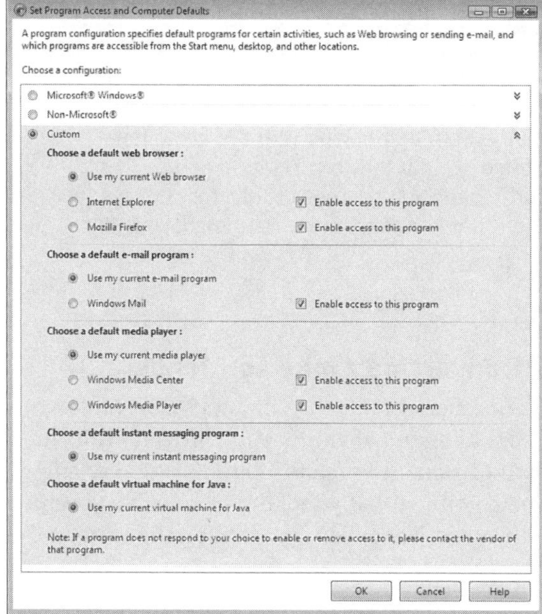

FIGURE 13.3 Use the Set Program Access and Computer Defaults feature to set up a custom program configuration for your system.

5. Click OK to put the new defaults into effect.

Pinning a Favorite Program Permanently to the Start Menu

The Start menu's list of favorite programs is such a time-saving feature that it can be frustrating if a program drops off the list. Another aggravation is that the icons often change position because Windows Vista displays the programs in order of popularity. When you display the Start menu, this constant shifting of icons can result in a slight hesitation while you look for the icon you want. (This is particularly true if you've expanded the maximum number of icons.) Contrast both of these problems with the blissfully static nature of the pinned programs list's Internet and E-mail icons, which are always where you need them, when you need them.

You can get the same effect with other shortcuts by adding—or **pinning**—them to the pinned programs list. To do this, first open the Start menu and find the shortcut you want to work with. Then you have two choices:

- Right-click the shortcut and then click Pin to Start Menu
- Drag the shortcut and drop it in the pinned programs list

You can also use this technique to pin shortcuts residing on the desktop to the pinned programs lists. If you decide later that you longer want a shortcut pinned to the Start menu, right-click the shortcut and then click Unpin from Start Menu.

TIP

When you display the Start menu, you can select an item quickly by pressing the first letter of the item's name. If you add several shortcuts to the pinned programs list, however, you might end up with more than one item that begins with the same letter. To avoid conflicts, rename each of these items so that they begin with a number. For example, renaming "Backup" to "1 Backup" means you can select this item by pressing 1 when the Start menu is displayed. (To rename a Start menu item, right-click the item and then click Rename.)

Streamlining the Start Menu by Converting Links to Menus

The right side of the Start menu contains a number of built-in Windows Vista features, which are set up as links. That is, you click an item and a window or a program runs in response. That's fine for items such as Search or Default Programs, but it's not very efficient for an item such as Control Panel where you're usually looking to launch a specific icon. It seems wasteful to have to open the Control Panel window, launch the icon, and then close Control Panel.

A better approach is to convert a link into a menu of items that would normally display in a separate window. For example, the Control Panel item could display a menu of its icons. One of the nicer features in Windows Vista is that it's easy to convert many of the Start menu links into menus. Here are the required steps:

1. Right-click the Start menu and then click Properties to display the Taskbar and Start Menu Properties dialog box appears.
2. Select the Start Menu tab, make sure the Start Menu option is activated, and then click the Customize button to its right to open the Customize Start Menu dialog box.
3. In the list of Start menu items, find the following items and activate the Display as a Menu option:

    Computer

    Control Panel

    Documents

    Games

    Music

    Personal folder (your user name)

    Pictures

NOTE

To see an example of the Start menu with the Control Panel displayed as a menu, see Figure 10.3 on page 294.

4. Activate the Favorites Menu check box to add a menu of your Internet Explorer favorites to the Start menu.
5. In the Start Menu Items group, find the System Administrative Tools item and activate the Display on the All Programs Menu and the Start Menu option. This gives you an Administrative Tools menu that offers shortcuts to features such as Computer Management, Device Manager, System Configuration, and the Local Security Policy editor.
6. Click OK to return to the Taskbar and Start Menu Properties dialog box.
7. Make sure that the Store and Display a List of Recently Opened Files check box is activated. This adds the Recent Items menu to the Start menu, which displays the last 15 documents that you worked with.
8. Click OK.

Adding, Moving, and Removing Other Start Menu Icons

In addition to the main Start menu, you can also customize the icons on the All Programs menu and submenus to suit the way you work. Using the techniques I discuss in this section you can perform the following Start menu productivity boosts:

- Move important features closer to the beginning of the All Programs menu hierarchy
- Remove features you don't use
- Add new commands for features not currently available on the All Programs menu (such as the Registry Editor)

Windows Vista offers three methods for adding and removing Start menu shortcuts, and I explain each of them in the next three sections.

Dragging and Dropping onto the Start Button

The quickest way to add a shortcut is to drag an executable file from Windows Explorer and then do either of the following:

Drop it on the Start button—This pins the shortcut to the Start menu.

Hover over the Start button—After a second or two, the main Start menu appears. Now hover the file over All Programs until the menu appears, and then drop the file where you want the shortcut to appear.

Working with the Start Menu Folder

The All Programs shortcuts are stored in two places:

- `%AppData%\Microsoft\Windows\Start Menu\Programs`—Shortcuts in this subfolder appear only in the current user's Start menu. Here, `%AppData%` is `%SystemDrive%\Users\`*`user`*`\AppData\Roaming`, where *`user`* is the name of the current user.
- `%AllUsersProfile%\Microsoft\Windows\Start Menu\Programs`—The `All Users\Start Menu\Programs` subfolder. Shortcuts in this folder appear to all users. Here, `%AllUsersProfile%` is `%SystemDrive%\ProgramData`.

> **TIP**
>
> A quick way to get to the current user's Start Menu folder is to right-click the Start button and then click Explore.

By working with these folders, you get the most control over not only where your Start menu shortcuts appear, but also the names of those shortcuts. Here's a summary of the techniques you can use:

- Within the Programs folder and its subfolders, you can drag existing shortcuts from one folder to another.
- To create a new shortcut, drag the executable file and drop it inside the folder you want to use. Remember that if you want to create a shortcut for a document or other nonexecutable file, right-drag the file and then select Create Shortcuts Here when you drop the file.
- You can create your own folders within the Programs folder hierarchy and they'll appear as submenus within the All Programs menu.
- You can rename a shortcut the same way you rename any file.
- You can delete a shortcut the same way you delete any file.

Working with All Programs Menu Shortcuts Directly

Many of the chores listed in the previous section are more easily performed by working directly within the All Programs menu itself. That is, you open the All Programs menu, find the shortcut you want to work with, and then use any of these techniques:

- Drag the shortcut to another section of its current menu
- Drag the shortcut to another menu or to the Recycle Bin
- Right-click the shortcut and then select a command (such as Delete) from the context menu

Customizing the Taskbar for Easier Program and Document Launching

In Windows Vista, the taskbar acts somewhat like a mini-application. The purpose of this "application" is to display a button for each running program and to enable you to switch from one program to another. Like most applications these days, the taskbar also has its own toolbars that, in this case, enable you to launch programs and documents.

Displaying the Built-In Taskbar Toolbars

Windows Vista taskbar comes with six default toolbars:

Address—This toolbar contains a text box into which you can type a local address (such as a folder or file path), a network address (a UNC path), or an Internet address. When you press Enter or click the Go button, Windows Vista loads the address into Windows Explorer (if you entered a local or network folder address), an application (if you entered a file path), or Internet Explorer (if you entered an Internet address). In other words, this toolbar works just like the Address Bar used by Windows Explorer and Internet Explorer.

TIP

If you create an application-specific path for a program, then you can launch that program just by typing the name of its executable file. See "Creating Application-Specific Paths" in Chapter 5.

Windows Media Player—This toolbar contains controls for playing media. When you activate this toolbar, it appears when you minimize the Windows Media Player window.

Links—This toolbar contains several buttons that link to predefined Internet sites. This is the same as the Links toolbar that appears in Internet Explorer.

Tablet PC Input Panel—This toolbar contains just a single icon: the Tablet PC Input Panel icon, which, when clicked, displays the Tablet PC Input Panel.

Desktop—This toolbar contains all the desktop icons, as well as an icon for Internet Explorer and submenus for your user folder and the following folders: Public, Computer, Network, Control Panel, and Recycle Bin.

Quick Launch—This is a collection of one-click icons that launch Internet Explorer or Media Player, clear the desktop, or activate the 3-D Window Switcher. Other applications—such as Microsoft Office—also add icons to this toolbar.

NOTE

You can adjust the size of a toolbar by clicking and dragging the toolbar's left edge. However, this won't work if the taskbar is locked. To unlock the taskbar, right-click an empty section of the taskbar and then click Lock the Taskbar to deactivate it. Also, make sure that the desktop is visible by minimizing all open windows (click Show Desktop in the Quick Launch toolbar, or right-click the taskbar and then click Show the Desktop).

To toggle these toolbars on and off, right-click an empty spot on the taskbar and then use either of the following techniques:

- Click Toolbars and then click the toolbar you want to work with.
- Click Properties, click the Toolbars tab, activate the check box of the toolbar you want to work with, and then click OK.

Setting Some Taskbar Toolbar Options

After you've displayed a toolbar, there are a number of options you can set to customize the look of the toolbar and to make the toolbars easier to work with. Right-click an empty section of the toolbar and then click one of the following commands:

View—This command displays a submenu with two options: Large Icons and Small Icons. These commands determine the size of the toolbar's icons. For example, if a toolbar has more icons than can be shown given its current size, switch to the Small Icons view.

Show Text—This command toggles the icon titles on and off. If you turn on the titles, it makes it easier to decipher what each icon does, but you'll see fewer icons in a given space.

Show Title—This command toggles the toolbar title (displayed to the left of the icons) on and off.

Creating New Taskbar Toolbars

In addition to the predefined taskbar toolbars, you can also create new toolbars that display the contents of any folder on your system. For example, if you have a folder of programs or documents that you launch regularly, you can get one-click access to those items by displaying that folder as a toolbar. Here are the steps to follow:

1. Right-click an empty spot on the toolbar, and then click Toolbars, New Toolbar. Windows Vista displays the New Toolbar dialog box.
2. Select the folder you want to display as a toolbar. (Or click New Folder to create a new subfolder within the currently selected folder.)
3. Click Select Folder. Windows Vista creates the new toolbar.

Improving Productivity by Setting Taskbar Options

The taskbar comes with a few options that can help you be more productive either by saving a few mouse clicks or by giving you more screen room to display your applications. Follow these steps to set these taskbar options:

1. Right-click the taskbar and then click Properties. (Alternatively, open Control Panel's Taskbar and Start Menu icon.) The Taskbar and Start Menu Properties dialog box appears with the Taskbar tab displayed, as shown in Figure 13.4.

FIGURE 13.4 Use the Taskbar tab to set up the taskbar for improved productivity.

2. Activate or deactivate the following options, as required to boost your productivity:

   Lock the Taskbar—When this check box is activated, you can't resize the taskbar and you can't resize or move any taskbar toolbars. This is useful if you share your computer with other users and you don't want to waste time resetting the taskbar if it's changed by someone else.

   Auto-Hide the Taskbar—When this check box is activated, Windows Vista reduces the taskbar to a thin, blue line at the bottom of the screen when you're not using it. This is useful if you want a bit more screen room for your applications. To redisplay the taskbar, move the mouse to the bottom of the screen. Note, however, that you should consider leaving this option deactivated if you use the taskbar frequently; otherwise, auto-hiding it will slow you down because it takes Windows Vista a second or two to restore the taskbar when you hover the mouse over it.

   Keep the Taskbar on Top of Other Windows—If you deactivate this option, Windows Vista hides the taskbar behind any window that's either maximized or moved over the taskbar. To get to the taskbar, you need to either minimize or move the window or you need to press the Windows logo key. This isn't a very efficient way to work, so I recommend leaving this option activated.

   Group Similar Taskbar Buttons—See the next section, "Controlling Taskbar Grouping," for more information on this setting.

Show Quick Launch—Leave this check box activated to display the Quick Launch toolbar, discussed earlier (refer to "Displaying the Built-In Taskbar Toolbars"). Quick Launch is a handy way to access Internet Explorer, the desktop, Windows Media Player, and the 3-D Window Switcher (as well as any other shortcuts you add to the Quick Launch folder), so I recommend leaving this option activated.

Show Window Previews (Thumbnails)—Leave this check box activated to see thumbnail views of your open windows when you hover the mouse pointer over the taskbar buttons. This can help you find the window you want among all the taskbar buttons, so it offers a small productivity boost. (Note, however, that you don't see thumbnails for grouped buttons.)

3. Click the Notification Area tab, shown in Figure 13.5.

FIGURE 13.5 Use the Notification Area tab to customize the notification area.

4. To help reduce notification area clutter and make this part of the taskbar more useful, you can do two things:

    - Activate the Hide Inactive Icons check box. When this check box is activated, Windows Vista hides notification area icons that you haven't used for a while. This gives the taskbar a bit more room to display program buttons, so leave this option activated if you don't use the notification area icons all that often. If you do use the icons frequently, deactivate this option to avoid having to click the arrow to display the hidden icons.
    - In the System Icons group, deactivate the check box for each icon you don't use.

NOTE

If your notification area is crowded with icons, it's inefficient to display all the icons if you use only a few of them. Instead of showing them all, activate the Hide Inactive Icons check box and click Customize. For the icons you use often, click the item's Behavior column and then click Show in the list that appears. This tells Windows Vista to always display the icon in the notification area. For icons you never use, click Hide, instead, which tells Vista to never display the icon in the notification area.

5. Click OK.

Displaying Multiple Clocks for Different Time Zones

New If you have colleagues, friends, or family members who work or live in a different time zone, it is often important to know the correct time in that zone. For example, you would not want to call someone at home at 9 a.m. your time if that person lives in a time zone that is three hours behind you. Similarly, if you know that a business colleague leaves work at 5 p.m. and that person works in a time zone that is seven hours ahead of you, you know that any calls you place to that person must occur before 10 a.m. your time.

If you need to be sure about the current time in another time zone, you can customize Windows Vista's date and time display to show not only your current time, but also the current time in the other time zone. Follow these steps:

1. Click the Clock icon and then click Change Date and Time Settings to display the Date and Time dialog box.
2. Click the Additional Clocks tab. Figure 13.6 shows a completed version of this tab.
3. Activate the first Show This Clock check box.
4. Use the Select Time Zone list to click the time zone you want to display in the additional clock.
5. Use the Enter Display Name text box to type a name for the clock.
6. Repeat steps 4–6 for the second clock.
7. Click OK.

To see the clocks, click the time to display a fly-out similar to the one shown in Figure 13.7.

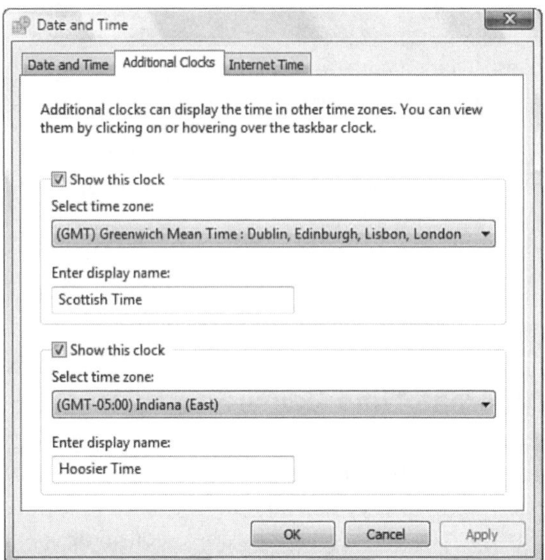

FIGURE 13.6 Use the Additional Clocks tab to add one or two more clocks for different time zones in Windows Vista.

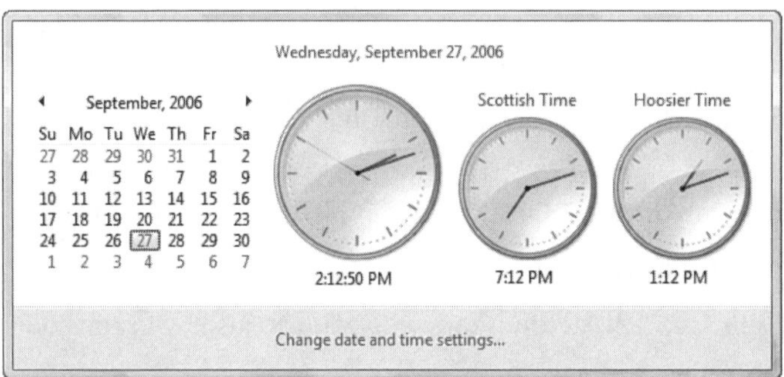

FIGURE 13.7 Click the time to see your additional clocks.

TIP

After you customize Windows Vista with the extra clocks, you normally click the time in the notification area to see the clocks. However, if you just hover the mouse pointer over the time, Windows Vista displays a banner that shows the current date, your current local time, and the current time in the other time zones.

Controlling Taskbar Grouping

Taskbar grouping means that when the taskbar fills up with buttons, Windows Vista consolidates icons from the same program into a single button, as shown in Figure 13.8. To access one of these grouped windows, you click the button and then click the window you want.

TIP

You can close all of a group's windows at once by right-clicking the group button and then clicking Close Group.

FIGURE 13.8 When the taskbar gets filled with buttons, Windows Vista groups similar windows into a single button, as shown here with Windows Explorer and Internet Explorer.

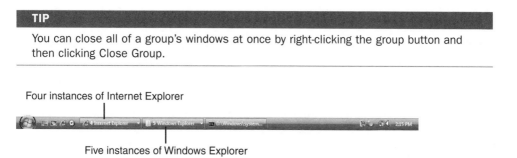

The grouping feature makes it easier to read the name of each taskbar button, but the price is a slight efficiency drop because it takes two clicks to activate a window instead of one. If you don't like this tradeoff, you can disable the grouping feature by right-clicking the taskbar, clicking Properties, and then deactivating the Group Similar Taskbar Buttons check box.

TIP

Another way to prevent grouping is to give the taskbar more room to display buttons. The easiest way to do that is to resize the taskbar by dragging its top edge up until the taskbar expands. If this doesn't work, the taskbar is probably locked. Unlock it by right-clicking the taskbar and then clicking Lock the Taskbar.

Alternatively, you can tweak the grouping feature to suit the way you work. To do this, open the Registry Editor and head for the following key:

```
HKCU\Software\Microsoft\Windows\CurrentVersion\Explorer\Advanced\
```

Add a `DWORD` value called `TaskbarGroupSize` and set it to one of the following values:

`0`—When the grouping kicks in (that is, when the taskbar gets full), Windows Vista groups the buttons from only the applications that you have used the least.

`1`—When the grouping kicks in, Windows Vista groups the buttons from only the application that has the most windows open. If a second application surpasses the number of open windows in the first application, the second application's windows are grouped as well (that is, the first application's windows remained grouped).

x—Windows Vista will group any application that has at least *x* windows open, where *x* is a number between 2 and 99. Note that the grouping occurs even if the taskbar is not full.

Note that you must log off or restart Windows Vista to put the new setting into effect. You can change this setting via Tweak UI: simply display the Taskbar, Grouping item.

Modifying the Start Menu and Taskbar with Group Policies

You've seen throughout this book that the group policies offer unprecedented control over the Windows Vista interface without having to modify the Registry directly. This is particularly true of the Start menu and taskbar, which boast more than 60 policies that do everything from removing Start menu links such as Run and Help to hiding the taskbar's notification area. To see these policies, launch the Group Policy editor (refer to Chapter 10, "Using Control Panel and Group Policies") and select User Configuration, Administrative Templates, Start Menu and Taskbar.

Most of the policies are straightforward: By enabling them, you remove a feature from the Start menu or taskbar. For example, enabling the Remove Run Menu from Start Menu policy prevents the user from adding the Run command to the Start menu (or hides the Run command if the user has already added it) and disables the Windows Logo+R shortcut key. This is handy if you're trying to restrict a user to using only those programs and documents that appear on the Start menu.

Here are a few policies that I think are the most useful:

Clear History of Recently Opened Documents on Exit—Enable this policy to remove all documents from the current user's Recent Items list whenever Windows Vista exits.

Remove Drag-and-Drop Context Menus on the Start Menu—Enable this policy to prevent the current user from rearranging the Start menu using drag-and-drop techniques.

Do Not Keep History of Recently Opened Documents—Enable this policy to prevent Windows Vista from tracking the current user's recently opened documents.

Prevent Changes to Taskbar and Start Menu Settings—Enable this policy to prevent the current user from accessing the Taskbar and Start Menu Properties dialog box.

Remove Access to the Context Menus for the Taskbar—Enable this policy to prevent the current user from seeing the taskbar's shortcut (also called **context**) menus by right-clicking the taskbar.

Do Not Display Any Custom Toolbars in the Taskbar—Enable this policy to prevent the current user from adding custom toolbars to the taskbar.

Hide the Notification Area—Enable this policy to prevent the current user from seeing the taskbar's notification area.

Remove User Name from Start Menu—Enable this policy to prevent the current user's name from appearing at the top of the Start menu. This is a good idea if you need more room on the Start menu for the pinned or frequent program lists.

Turn Off All Balloon Notifications—Enable this policy to prevent the current user from seeing the balloon tips that Windows Vista displays when it prompts you about new hardware being detected, downloading automatic updates, and so on.

Using Screen Space Efficiently

How images appear on your monitor and how efficiently you use the monitor's viewable area is a function of two measurements: the color quality and the screen resolution. The **color quality** is a measure of the number of colors available to display images on the screen. Color quality is usually expressed in either bits or total colors. For example, a 4-bit display can handle up to 16 colors (2 to the power of 4 equals 16). The most common values are 16-bit (65,536 colors), 24-bit (16,777,216 colors), and 32-bit (16,777,216 colors).

The **screen resolution** is a measure of the density of the pixels used to display the screen image. The pixels are arranged in a row-and-column format, so the resolution is expressed as rows by columns, where **rows** is the number of pixel rows and **columns** is the number of pixel columns. For example, an 800 by 600 resolution means screen images are displayed using 800 rows of pixels and 600 columns of pixels.

How does all this effect productivity?

- In general, the greater the number of colors, the sharper your screen image will appear. Sharper images, especially text, are easier to read and put less strain on the eyes.

SHARPENING TEXT WITH CLEARTYPE

If you read a lot of onscreen text, particularly if you use a notebook or an LCD screen, activate Windows Vista's ClearType feature, which drastically reduces the jagged edges of screen fonts and makes text super-sharp and far easier to read than regular screen text. ClearType is activated by default in Windows Vista. To be sure, right-click the desktop and then click Personalize. In the Personalization window, click Window Color and Appearance and then Open Classic Appearance Properties for More Color Options. In the Appearance Settings dialog box, click Effects to open the Effects dialog box. Make sure that the Use the Following Method to Smooth Edges of Screen Fonts check box is activated and then select ClearType from the list below it. Click OK in each open dialog box to put the new setting into effect.

- At higher resolutions, individual screen items—such as icons and dialog boxes—appear smaller because these items tend to have a fixed height and width, expressed in pixels. For example, a dialog box that's 400 pixels wide will appear half as wide as the screen at 800 by 600. However, it will appear to be only one quarter of the screen width at 1,600 by 1,200 (a common resolution for very larger monitors).

This means that at higher resolutions your maximized windows will appear larger, so you'll get a larger work area.

The key thing to bear in mind about all this is that there's occasionally a tradeoff between color quality and resolution. That is, depending on how much video memory is installed on your graphics adapter, you might have to trade higher resolution for lower color quality, or vice versa.

Rather than eking out the most from a single monitor, you can attach a second monitor to your system and extend your desktop onto that monitor. This enables you to display your work on one monitor and windows that you want to keep an eye on—such as your email client or your web browser—on the second monitor. To make this happen, you either need to add a second video card to your system (preferably the same type as your existing card) or you need to use a single video card that offers two VGA ports.

To change the screen resolution and color quality, and to activate a second monitor, follow these steps:

1. Select Start, Control Panel, Appearance and Personalization.
2. Under Personalization, click the Adjust Screen Resolution link to get the Display Settings dialog box onscreen, as shown in Figure 13.9.

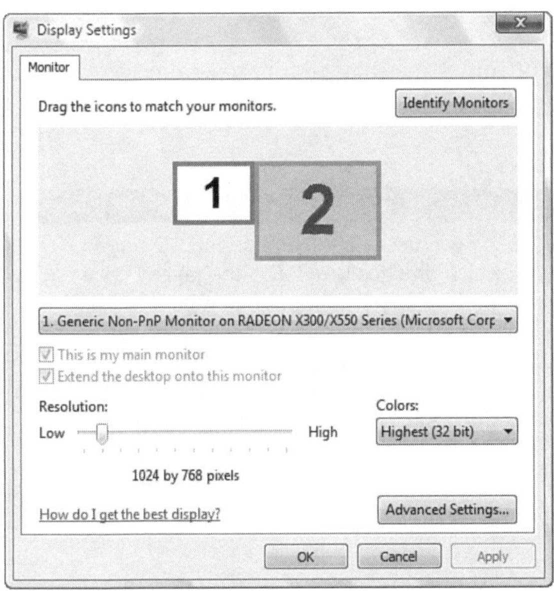

FIGURE 13.9 Use the Display Settings dialog box to set the screen resolution and color quality.

3. To set the resolution, drag the Resolution slider left or right.
4. To set the color quality, choose an item from the Colors list.
5. If you have a second monitor attached to your computer, click the monitor icon labeled 2 and then activate the Extend the Desktop onto This Monitor check box. You can then repeat steps 3 and 4 to set the resolution and colors for the second monitor.
6. Click OK. Windows Vista performs the adjustment and then displays a dialog box asking if you want to keep the new setting.
7. Click Yes.

NOTE

If your graphics adapter or monitor can't handle the new resolution or color quality, you'll end up with a garbled display. In this case, just wait for 15 seconds and Windows Vista will restore the resolution to its original setting.

From Here

Here's a list of sections in this book where you'll find information related to the topics in this chapter:

- To learn how to personalize Windows Explorer, refer to "Customizing Windows Explorer" in Chapter 3.
- For the details on customizing the New menu and the Open With list, refer to the "Customizing the New Menu" and "Customizing Windows Vista's Open With List" sections in Chapter 4.
- For the details on group policies, refer to Chapter 10, "Using Control Panel and Group Policies."
- To learn more about the Registry, refer to Chapter 11, "Getting to Know the Windows Vista Registry."
- To learn how to personalize Internet Explorer, see "Customizing Internet Explorer" in Chapter 18.

CHAPTER 14

Tuning Windows Vista's Performance

IN THIS CHAPTER

- Vista's Performance Improvements
- Monitoring Performance
- Optimizing Startup
- Optimizing Applications
- Optimizing the Hard Disk
- Optimizing Virtual Memory

We often wonder why our workaday computer chores seem to take just as long as they ever did, despite the fact that hardware is generally more reliable and more powerful than ever. The answer to this apparent riddle relates to Parkinson's Law of Data, which I mentioned back in Chapter 1, "An Overview of Windows Vista." On a more general level, a restatement of Parkinson's Law is as follows: *The increase in software system requirements is directly proportional to the increase in hardware system capabilities*. For example, imagine that a slick new chip is released that promises a 30% speed boost; software designers, seeing the new chip gain wide acceptance, add 30% more features to their already bloated code to take advantage of the higher performance level. Then another new chip is released, followed by another software upgrade—and the cycle continues *ad nauseum* as these twin engines of computer progress lurch co-dependently into the future.

So, how do you break out of the performance deadlock created by the immovable object of software code bloat meeting the irresistible force of hardware advancement? By optimizing your system to minimize the effects of overgrown applications and to maximize the native capabilities of your hardware. Of course, it helps if your operating system gives you a good set of tools to improve and monitor performance, diagnose problems, and keep your data safe. Windows XP came with a decent set of client tools, and Vista improves on them, although not with anything radically new or earth-shattering. Vista's performance and maintenance improvements are evolutionary, not revolutionary, but they're definitely better than anything we've seen in a Microsoft client operating system.

Vista's Performance Improvements

Certain computer pastimes—hardcore gaming, software development, database administration, and digital video editing, to name just a few—require hardware help to maximize performance. Whether it's scads of system RAM, a mountain of hard drive storage space, or a state-of-the-art graphics card, these intense computer tasks require the best hardware that users can afford.

Those of us who are not into those intense computing pursuits generally don't need the fastest machine on the market to write memos, build spreadsheet models, or design web pages. What we really need is a system that doesn't get in our way by making us wait for seemingly routine tasks. For example, in Windows XP, I often right-click a document in Explorer with the intention of clicking a command such as Cut, Copy, or Rename. Along the way, however, my mouse pointer has to pass over the Send To command. XP populates the Send To menu by going to the Registry and searching for items that it can add to this menu. For some reason, that sometimes takes several seconds, so my mouse pointer remains stuck on Send To, even though that's not the command I want.

This kind of interface annoyance must have bugged the Windows programmers one too many times also because they've rewritten the interface code from the ground up to make actions such as choosing menu options (including displaying the Send To menu) much faster. Even the in-place All Programs menu (refer to Chapter 2, "Customizing and Troubleshooting the Windows Vista Startup") is a huge improvement over XP and enables you to launch items much more quickly from deeply nested folders such as System Tools and Ease of Access.

Besides these fit-and-finish performance improvements, Vista comes with a host of new features and updated technologies designed to make Vista the fastest Windows ever. The next few sections take you through the most important of these performance enhancements.

Faster Startup

New The first thing you'll notice about Windows Vista is that it starts up *much* faster than any previous version of Windows. I don't mean that it's a second or two faster, either. My own testing reveals that Vista starts up in approximately *half* the time of an equivalent XP setup. For example, on an XP machine that takes 60 seconds from power-up to the point that you can actually start working with the interface, the equivalent Vista system would take 25 to 30 seconds. Remember, too, that I was testing with a beta version of Vista, so the release version you'll use should be even faster.

NOTE

One Microsoft document claimed that Vista startups would take "typically 2 to 3 seconds." This seems *extremely* unlikely, but it sure would be nice if it was true! (But see my discussion of the new sleep mode, later in this chapter.)

Where does the startup speed boost come from? Some of it comes from optimizing the startup code. However, most of the improvement comes from Vista's asynchronous startup script and application launching. Older versions of Windows were hobbled at startup because they had to wait for each startup script, batch file, and program to launch before Windows handed the desktop over to the user.

Vista handles startup jobs asynchronously, which means they run in the background, whereas Vista devotes most of its startup energies to getting the desktop onscreen. This means that it's not unusual to notice startup scripts or programs running well after the desktop has made its appearance. Because all startup items run in the background, theoretically it shouldn't matter how many script or programs you run at startup; Vista should start up just as fast as if you had *no* startup items.

CAUTION

The Vista team was right to give the user top startup priority because it's frustrating to wait forever for startup items to execute. However, asynchronous startup could lead to problems if a script or program that you require for your work has not finished its chores before you're ready. In most cases, this should just mean enduring the usual waiting game, but it's something to bear in mind whenever you or one of your programs adds a script, program, or service to the startup.

Sleep Mode: The Best of Both Worlds

New In the last few versions of Windows, you had a number of options at your disposal for turning off your computer. You could use the Shut Down option to turn off the system entirely, which saved power but forced you to close all your documents and applications. You could put the system into Standby mode, which preserved your work and enabled you to restart quickly, but didn't entirely shut off the machine's power. Or you could go into Hibernate mode, which preserved your work and completely shut off the machine, but also took a relatively long time to restart (faster than Shut Down, but slower than Standby).

I think it's safe to say that these options confused most users, particularly the (subtle) difference between the Standby and Hibernate modes. By far the most common power-management complaint I've heard over the past few years is, "Why can't Windows be more like a Mac?" That is to say, why can't we turn off our machines instantly, and have them resume instantly with our windows and work still intact, as Apple has done with OS X?

The new answer to these questions is that Vista is heading in that direction with a new Sleep state that combines the best of the old Standby and Hibernate modes:

- As in Standby, you enter Sleep mode within just a few seconds.
- As in both Standby and Hibernate, Sleep mode preserves all your open documents, windows, and programs.

- As in Hibernate, Sleep mode shuts down your computer (although, as you'll see, it doesn't quite shut down everything).
- As in Standby, you resume from Sleep mode within just a few seconds.

How can Vista preserve your work *and* restart in just a few seconds? The secret is that Vista doesn't really shut off your computer when you initiate Sleep mode. Instead, it shuts down everything except a few crucial components such as the CPU and RAM. By preserving power to the RAM chips, Vista can keep your work intact and redisplay it instantly on waking. Don't worry, though: Vista *does* make a copy of your work to the hard disk, so if your computer completely loses power, your work is still preserved.

To use Sleep mode, open the Start menu and click the Sleep button, shown in Figure 14.1. (Notice that Microsoft has designed the Sleep button to look like a power button. This is no coincidence because Microsoft would greatly prefer that we "shut down" using Sleep mode instead of actually powering off.) Vista saves the current state and shuts off the computer in a few seconds. To resume, press your computer's power button; the Vista Welcome screen appears almost immediately.

FIGURE 14.1 Click the new Sleep button to quickly shut down your computer and save your work.

SuperFetch with ReadyBoost: The Faster Fetcher

New **Prefetching** was a performance feature introduced in Windows XP that monitored your system and anticipated the data that you might use in the near future. It then loaded (prefetched) that data into memory ahead of time. If that data was indeed what your system required, performance would increase because XP wouldn't have to fetch the data from your hard disk.

Windows Vista introduces a new and improved version of the Prefetcher: SuperFetch. This technology tracks the programs and data you use over time to create a kind of profile of your disk usage. Using the profile, SuperFetch can then make a much more educated guess about the data that you'll require and, like the Prefetcher, can then load that data into memory ahead of time for enhanced performance.

However, SuperFetch goes even further by taking advantage of Vista's new ReadyBoost technology. If you insert a 512MB (or larger) USB 2.0 Flash drive into your system, Vista displays the AutoPlay dialog box shown in Figure 14.2. If you click Speed Up My System Using Windows ReadyBoost, SuperFetch uses that drive's capacity as storage for the SuperFetch cache. This frees up the system RAM that SuperFetch would otherwise use, which should result in an automatic (and probably quite dramatic) performance boost. Not only that, but you still get an extra performance nudge from SuperFetch itself because even though data access via the Flash drive is slower than with system RAM, it's still many times faster than even the fastest hard drive.

FIGURE 14.2 If you insert a USB Flash drive into your system, SuperFetch can use it as its cache to improve system performance.

You can also control the amount of storage space that SuperFetch uses on the Flash drive:

1. Select Start, Computer to open the Computer window.
2. Right-click the Flash drive and then click Properties to open the device's properties sheet.
3. Select the ReadyBoost tab, shown in Figure 14.3.
4. Click Use This Device to let SuperFetch access the Flash memory.

5. Use the slider to set the maximum amount of memory SuperFetch can use.
6. Click OK.

NOTE

SuperFetch usually sets the maximum memory it can use to a value less than the total capacity of the Flash drive. That's because most Flash drives contain both fast and slow Flash memory, and SuperFetch can use only the fast variety.

NOTE

As I write this, an interesting rumor was circulating—started by, of all people, Jim Allchin, Microsoft's President of Platforms and Services (that is, the Windows Vista head honcho; at least until he retires when Vista ships)—that claimed ReadyBoost was also going to be configured to take advantage of memory on unused computers on your network. It was not clear when Vista would incorporate this eyebrow-raising idea.

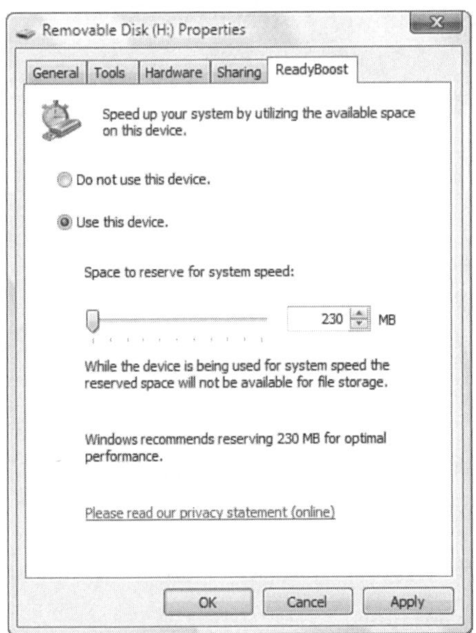

FIGURE 14.3 In the Flash drive's properties sheet, use the ReadyBoost tab to set the maximum amount of memory that SuperFetch can use.

Restart Manager

New In the old days, "updating" an operating system or program meant installing an entirely new version of the software. Then Microsoft and some software vendors started posting "patches" on bulletin boards, then FTP sites, and eventually on the Web. Strangely, they didn't actually *tell* anyone that those patches were there, but they assumed that intrepid power users would unearth them and somehow get them installed.

This primitive state of affairs ended a few Windows versions ago when Microsoft introduced Windows Update, a service that made it much easier to find, download, and install security patches, bug fixes, software and certified driver updates, and service packs. Software vendors followed suit, and it soon become common to have a "Check for Updates" feature in a software package so that you could remain up-to-date.

Having the latest Windows updates and the latest versions of programs is a real boon because it makes computers more secure and more robust. However, it doesn't come without a cost. One of the biggest productivity killers today is the "Reboot Required" message you see all too often after installing even what seems like a minor patch. This dreaded message means that you have to save all your work, shut down your running programs, restart the system, and then open all your programs, windows, and documents all over again. It's frustrating, and it usually seems so unnecessary. Why is there so often a need for a restart after patching Windows or a program?

The short answer is that it's not possible to overwrite a running executable file or dynamic link library (DLL), which the operating system locks while the program is in use. If the update includes a new version of a running executable or DLL, and that executable or DLL can't be shut down, the only way to perform the update is with a reboot, which ensures that *all* executables and DLLs are unloaded.

Why can't you just close the running program? It's not that easy, unfortunately. For one thing, you can't be sure these days when you shut down a program that you're shutting down *all* instances of the program in memory. Consider Microsoft Word, for example, which can be running not only in the Word window, but also in Outlook as the email editor, in Internet Explorer when it displays a `.doc` file, and so on. For another thing, many executable files operate in the background, and you don't even know they're running, so there's no interface for shutting them down.

Of course, it's silly to unload the entire system just to patch what could be a single running file. Fortunately, Windows Vista is tackling this absurdity with the new Restart Manager technology. Restart Manager does three things:

1. It looks for all the processes that are using the file that needs to be updated.
2. It shuts down all those processes.
3. After the updates are applied, it restarts those processes.

The real trick here is the *way* that Restart Manager performs these restarts in programs designed to work with it. Restart Manager doesn't just start up the program and leave you to fend for yourself by reopening all your documents. Instead, it preserves the *exact* state of each running process and then restores that state upon restarting the process. If you're working in Word on a document named `Budget.doc` and the cursor was in line 10, column 20, Restart Manager not only restarts Word, but it also opens `Budget.doc` *and* restores the cursor to line 10, column 20. (Microsoft calls saving the program state in this way **freeze-drying**.) Note that the full functionality of Restart Manager is available only to applications written to take advantage of it. Office 2007 is the only program I know of that has this capability, but expect most major applications to become Restart Manager–aware in their next versions.

For programs that don't support Restart Manager, Windows Vista introduces a new idea called **side-by-side compliant** DLLs. This technology enables an installation program to write a new version of a DLL to the hard disk, even if the old version is still in use. When you shut down the program, Vista replaces the old version of the DLL with the new one, so the next time you start the application, the update will be complete.

All of this means that updates should require far fewer reboots in Vista than in XP. Not that reboots will never be required, however. In particular, there will always be patches that must update one or more core operating system files. By definition, core operating system files run at startup and remain running as long as the system is on, and it's not possible to shut them down without shutting down the entire operating system. (Technically, you *can* rename the file and then install the new version under the old name, but that could lead to all kinds of system problems.) In those situations, there will be no choice but to reboot to apply the patch. Hopefully, however, Vista's faster shutdown and startup times will make this less of a headache as well.

Monitoring Performance

Performance optimization is a bit of a black art in that every user has different needs, every configuration has different operating parameters, and every system can react in a unique and unpredictable way to performance tweaks. That means if you want to optimize your system, you have to get to know how it works, what it needs, and how it reacts to changes. You can do this by just using the system and paying attention to how things look and feel, but a more rigorous approach is often called for. To that end, the next few sections take you on a brief tour of Windows Vista's performance monitoring capabilities.

Viewing Your Computer's Performance Rating

New From a high-level perspective, each version of Windows XP was the same no matter what hardware it ran on. Yes, the set of device drivers running on each system could be vastly different, but from the user's perspective, it didn't matter whether you were running a bare-bones budget PC or a 64-bit behemoth: The look and feel of XP, and the programs and features that were available, didn't change. On the surface, that seems more than a little strange because there's a huge performance gulf between a box that meets only the minimal requirements for running Windows and a top-end machine with a fast 64-bit processor, scads of RAM, and a state-of-the-art **GPU** (graphics processing unit). Unfortunately, this situation meant that all too often the system opted for lowest common denominator settings that worked for low-end machines but did nothing to take advantage of high-end hardware.

Fortunately, this one-size-fits-all approach to Windows is history in Windows Vista. That's because Vista tailors certain aspects of itself to the capabilities of the system on which you're installing it. I mentioned in Chapter 1 that the Vista interface changes depending on the graphics hardware on the machine, with low-end machines getting the straightforward Classic interface, midrange adapters getting the Vista Basic theme, and high-end GPUs getting the full Aero treatment.

But Vista also scales other aspects up or down to suit its hardware home. With games, for example, Vista enables certain features only if the hardware can support them. Other features scaled for the computer's hardware are TV recording (for example, how many channels can it record at once?) and video playback (for example, what is the optimal playback size and frame rate that doesn't result in dropped frames?).

The tool that handles all of this, not only for Vista itself but also for third-party programs, is the Windows System Assessment Tool, or **WinSAT**. This tool runs during setup, and again whenever you make major performance-related hardware changes to your system. It focuses on four aspects of your system performance: graphics, memory, processor, and storage. For each of these subsystems, WinSAT maintains a set of metrics stored as an **assessment** in XML format. Vista needs to examine only the latest assessment to see what features the computer can support. Note, too, that third-party programs can use an application programming interface that gives them access to the assessments, so developers can tune program features depending on the WinSAT metrics.

Five metrics are used:

- **Processor**—This metric determines how fast the system can process data. The Processor metric measures calculations per second processed.
- **Memory (RAM)**—This metric determines how quickly the system can move large objects through memory. The Memory metric measures memory operations per second.
- **Graphics**—This metric determines the computer's capability to run a composited desktop like the one created by the Desktop Window Manager. The Graphics metric expresses frames per second.
- **Gaming Graphics**—This metric determines the computer's capability to render 3D graphics, particularly those used in gaming. The Gaming Graphics metric expresses effective frames per second.
- **Primary Hard Disk**—This metric determines how fast the computer can write to and read from the hard disk. The Storage metric measures megabytes per second.

In addition to WinSAT, Windows Vista comes with the Performance Rating tool that rates your system based on its processor, RAM, hard disk, regular graphics, and gaming graphics. The result is the Windows Experience Index base score.

To launch this tool, select Start, Control Panel, System and Maintenance, Performance Information and Tools. As you can see in Figure 14.4, Vista supplies a subscore for each of the five categories and calculates an overall base score. You can get a new rating (for example, if you change performance-related hardware) by clicking the Update My Score link.

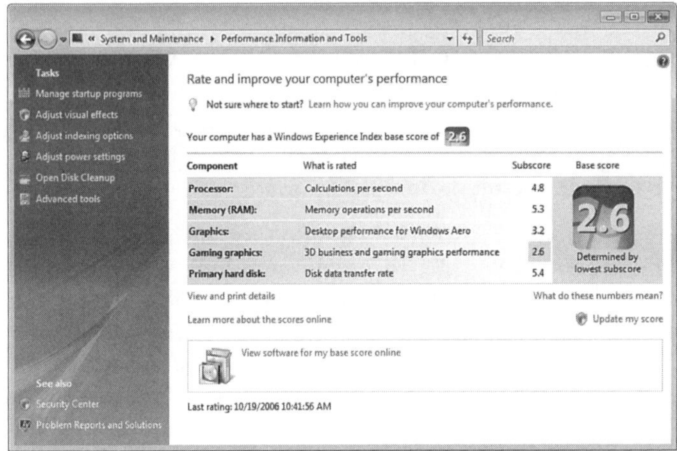

FIGURE 14.4 Vista calculates a Windows System Performance Rating based on five categories.

Interpreting the ratings is a bit of a black art, but I can tell you the following:

- In general, the higher the rating, the better the performance.
- The lowest possible value is 1.0.
- There doesn't seem to be a highest possible value, which I assume is a reflection of the simple fact that hardware will improve over time. (Microsoft has said, however, that it will attempt to keep the ratings constant over time. So, for example, a machine rated 3.0 today will have the same relative performance as a machine rated 3.0 two years ago or two years from now.) I've seen ratings as high as 5.3—this was a Memory (RAM) subscore given to a machine with 2GB RAM.
- The base score takes a weakest-link-in-the-chain approach. That is, you could have nothing but 5.0 scores for everything else, but if you get just 1.0 because your notebook can't do gaming graphics, your base score will be 1.0.

Monitoring Performance with Task Manager

The Task Manager utility is excellent for getting a quick overview of the current state of the system. To get it onscreen, press Ctrl+Alt+Delete to open the Windows Security screen and then click the Start Task Manager link.

> **TIP**
>
> To bypass the Windows Security screen, either press Ctrl+Shift+Esc, or right-click an empty section of the taskbar and click Task Manager.

The Processes tab, shown in Figure 14.5, displays a list of the programs, services, and system components currently running on your system. (By default, Windows Vista shows just the process you have started. To see all the running processes, click Show Processes from All Users.) The processes display in the order in which they were started, but you can change the order by clicking the column headings. (To return to the original, chronological order, you must shut down and restart Task Manager.)

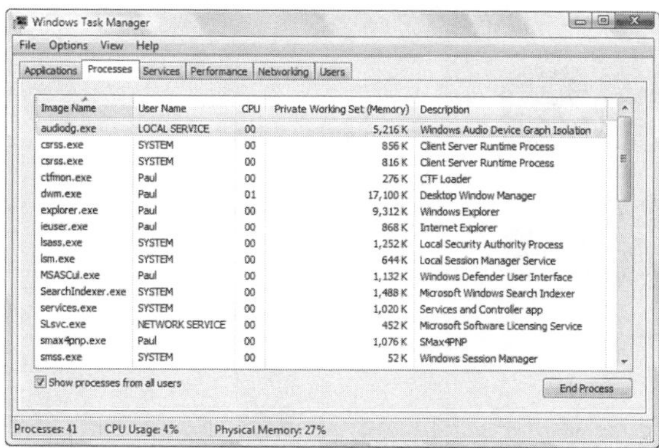

FIGURE 14.5 The Processes tab lists your system's running programs and services.

In addition to the image name of each process and the user who started the process, you also see two performance measures:

CPU The values in this column tell you the percentage of CPU resources that each process is using. If your system seems sluggish, look for a process consuming all or nearly all the resources of the CPU. Most programs will monopolize the CPU occasionally for short periods, but a program that is stuck at 100 (percent) for a long time most likely has some kind of problem. In that case, try shutting down the program. If that doesn't work, click the program's process and then click End Process. Click the Yes button when Windows Vista asks whether you're sure that you want to do this.

Memory	This value tells you approximately how much memory a process is using. This value is less useful because a process might genuinely require a lot of memory to operate. However, if this value is steadily increasing for a process that you're not using, it could indicate a problem and you should shut down the process.

TIP

The four default columns in the Processes tab aren't the only data available to you. Select the View, Select Columns command to see a list of more than two dozen items that you can add to the Processes tab.

The Performance Tab, shown in Figure 14.6, offers a more substantial collection of performance data, particularly for that all-important component, your system's memory.

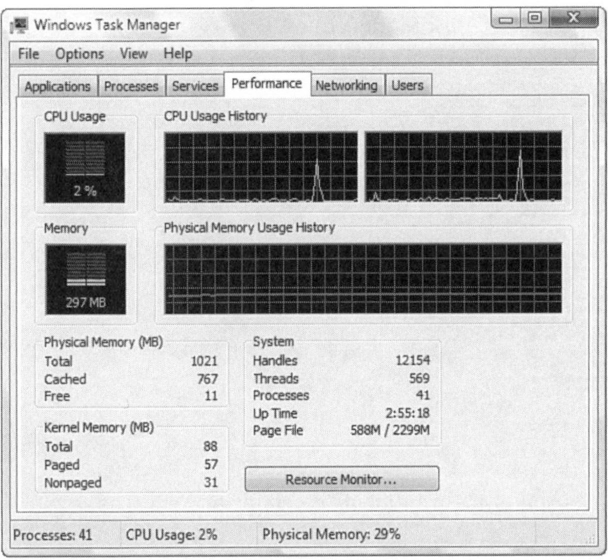

FIGURE 14.6 The Performance tab lists various numbers related to your system's memory components.

The graphs show you both the current value and the values over time for the CPU usage (the total percentage of CPU resources that your running processes are using) and the physical memory usage. Below the graphs are various numbers. Here's what they mean:

Physical Memory Total	The total amount of physical RAM in your system.
Physical Memory Cached	The amount of physical RAM that Windows Vista has set aside to store recently used programs and documents.

Physical Memory Free	The amount of physical RAM that Windows Vista has available for your programs. Note that Windows Vista does not include the system cache (refer to the previous item) in this total.
Kernel Memory Total	The total amount of RAM used by the Windows Vista system components and device drivers.
Kernel Memory Paged	The amount of kernel memory mapped to pages in virtual memory.
Kernel Memory Nonpaged	The amount of kernel memory that cannot map to pages in virtual memory.
System Handles	The number of object handles used by all running processes. A **handle** is a pointer to a resource. For example, if a process wants to use a particular service offered by a particular object, the process asks the object for a handle to that service.
System Threads	The number of threads used by all running processes. A **thread** is a single processor task executed by a process, and most processes can use two or more threads at the same time to speed up execution.
System Processes	The number of processes currently running (that is, the number of items you see in the Processes tab if you activate the Show Processes from All Users control).
System Up Time	The number of days, hours, minutes, and seconds that you have been logged on to Windows Vista in the current session.
System Page File	The minimum and maximum values of the page file. What is a page file? Your computer can address memory beyond the amount physically installed on the system. This nonphysical memory is **virtual memory** implemented by setting up a piece of your hard disk to emulate physical memory. This hard disk storage is actually a single file called a **page file** (or sometimes a **paging file** or a **swap file**). When physical memory is full, Windows Vista makes room for new data by taking some data that's currently in memory and swapping it out to the page file.

Here are two notes related to these values that will help you monitor memory-related performance issues:

- If the Physical Memory Free value approaches zero, it means your system is starving for memory. You might have too many programs running or a large program is using lots of memory.

- If the Physical Memory Caches value is much less than half the Physical Memory Total value, it means your system isn't operating as efficiently as it could because Windows Vista can't store enough recently used data in memory. Because Windows Vista gives up some of the system cache when it needs RAM, close down programs you don't need.

In all of these situations, the quickest solution is to reduce the system's memory footprint by closing either documents or applications. For the latter, use the Processes tab to determine which applications are using the most memory and shut down the ones you can live without for now. The better, but more expensive, solution is to add more physical RAM to your system. This decreases the likelihood that Windows Vista will need to use the paging file, and it enables Windows Vista to increase the size of the system cache, which greatly improves performance.

TIP

If you're not sure which process corresponds to which program, display the Applications tab, right-click a program, and then click Go to Process. Task Manager displays the Processes tab and selects the process that corresponds to the program.

Using the Reliability and Performance Monitor

New Windows Vista comes with a new tool for monitoring your system yourself: the Reliability and Performance Monitor. You load this Microsoft Management Console snap-in by pressing Windows Logo+R (or selecting Start, All Programs, Accessories, Run), typing **`perfmon.msc`**, and clicking OK. After you enter your Use Account Control credentials, Figure 14.7 shows the console window that appears.

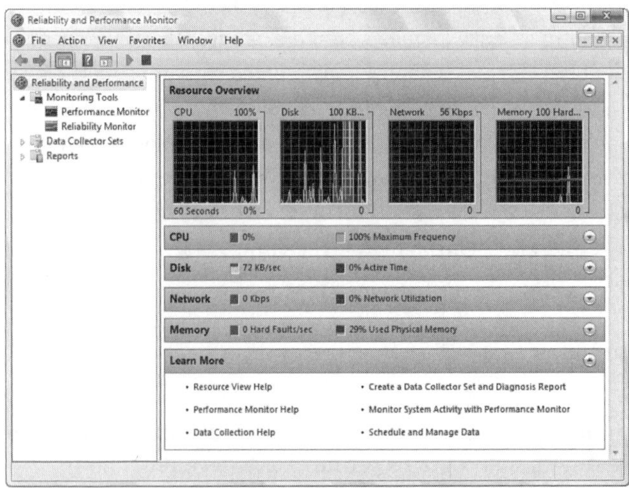

FIGURE 14.7 The new Reliability and Performance Monitor enables you to monitor various aspects of your system.

The console root—Reliability and Performance—displays the Resource Monitor, which is divided into six sections:

- **Resource Overview**—This section shows graphs of the data in the CPU, Disk, Network, and Memory sections.
- **CPU**—This section shows the percentage of CPU resources that your system is using. Click the downward-pointing arrow to expand the section and show the percentage of resources that each running process is using.
- **Disk**—This section shows the total hard disk I/O transfer rate (disk reads and writes in kilobytes per second). Expand the section to see the files involved in the current disk I/O operations.
- **Network**—This section shows the total network **data-transfer rate** (data sent and received in megabits per second). Expand the section to see the remote computers involved in the current network transfers.
- **Memory**—This section shows the average number of hard memory faults per second and the percentage of physical memory used. Expand the section to view the individual processes in memory, as well as the hard faults and memory used for each.

NOTE

A memory fault does not refer to a physical problem. Instead, it means that the system could not find the data it needed in the file system cache. If it finds the data elsewhere in memory, it is a **soft fault**; if the system has to go to the hard disk to retrieve the data, it is a **hard fault**.

- **Learn More**—This section contains links to the Reliability and Performance Monitor help files.

The Reliability and Performance Monitor tree has three branches: Monitoring Tools—which includes the Performance Monitor (discussed next) and the Reliability Monitor (discussed in Chapter 15, "Maintaining Your Windows Vista System")—Data Collector Sets, and Reports.

Performance Monitor

The Performance Monitor branch displays the Performance Monitor, which provides you with real-time reports on how various system settings and components are performing (see Figure 14.8). Each item is a **counter**, and the displayed counters are at the bottom of the window. A different-colored line represents each counter, and that color corresponds to the colored lines shown in the graph. Note, too, that you can get specific numbers for a counter—the most recent value, the average, the minimum, and the maximum—by clicking a counter and reading the boxes just below the graphs. The idea is that you should configure Performance Monitor to show the processes you're interested in (page file size, free memory, and so on) and then keep it running while you perform your normal chores. By examining the Performance Monitor readouts from time to time, you gain an appreciation of what is typical on your system. If you run into performance problems, you can check Performance Monitor to see whether you've run into any bottlenecks or anomalies.

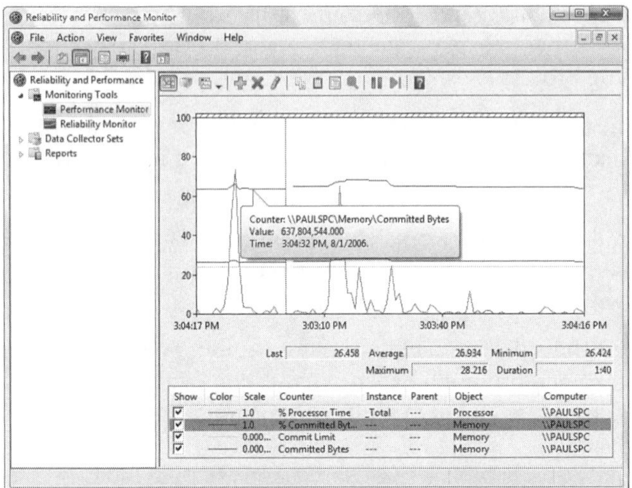

FIGURE 14.8 Use Performance Monitor to keep an eye on various system settings and components.

By default, Performance Monitor shows only the % Processor Time setting, which tells you the percentage of time the processor is busy. To add another setting to the Performance Monitor window, follow these steps:

1. Right-click anywhere inside the Performance Monitor and then click Add Counters. The Add Counters dialog box appears.
2. To use the Available Counters list, click the downward-pointing arrow beside a counter category (such as Memory, Paging File, or Processor). A list of available counters appears.
3. Select the counter you want to use. (If you need more information about the item, activate the Show Description check box.)
4. Click Add.
5. Repeat steps 2–4 to add any other counters you want to monitor.
6. Click OK.

Performance Monitor was System Monitor in previous versions of Windows, and it has been around for a while. However, Vista's version has a few new features that make it easier to use and a more powerful diagnostics tool:

- If you're using a counter with a significantly different scale, you can scale the output so that the counter appears within the graph. For example, the graph's vertical axis runs from `0` to `100`; if you're displaying a percentage counter, the Scale value is `1.0`, which means the graph numbers correspond directly to the percentages (`50` on the graph corresponds to 50%). If you're also showing, say, the Commit Limit counter, which shows values in bytes, the numbers can run in the billions. The Commit Limit counter's `Scale` value is `0.00000001`, so the value `20` on the graph corresponds to 2 billion bytes.
- You can save the current graph as a GIF image file.
- You can toggle the display of individual counters on and off.
- You can change the duration of the sample (the number of seconds of data that appear on the chart). You can specify a value between 2 and 1,000 seconds.
- You can see individual data points by hovering the mouse over a counter. After a second or two, Performance Monitor displays the counter name, the time and date of the sample, and the counter value at that time (refer to Figure 14.12).
- The horizontal (time) axis now has labels that tell you the beginning and end times of the current sample.

Data Collector Sets

A **data collector** is a custom set of performance counters, event traces, and system-configuration data that you define and save so that you can run and view the results any time you need them. You can configure a data collector set to run for a preset length of time or until the set reaches a specified size. You can also configure a data collector to run on a schedule. For example, you could run the data collector every hour for 15 minutes from 9 a.m. to 5 p.m. This enables you to benchmark performance and analyze the results not only intraday (to compare performance at different times of the day), but also interday (to see whether performance is slowing over time).

Reports

This section holds the reports created by each data collector set. These are `.blg` files, and you can see the results by clicking the report and then switching to Sysmon view (click the Chart icon in the toolbar). Alternatively, open the folder that contains the report file in Windows Explorer (the default save location is `%SystemDrive%\perflogs`) and double-click the report file.

Optimizing Startup

One of the longest-running debates in computer circles involves the question of whether to turn off the computer when you're not using it. The "off" camp believes that shutting down the computer reduces hard disk wear and tear (because the disk's platters spin full-time, even when the computer is idle), prevents damage from power surges or power failures that occur while the machine is off, and saves energy. The "on" camp believes that cold starts are hard on many computer components, that energy can be saved by taking advantage of power-saving features, and that leaving the computer running is more productive because it avoids the lengthy startup process.

In the end, I believe the overall boot time is what usually determines which of these camps you belong to. If your startup time is unbearably long, you'll certainly be more inclined to leave your computer running all the time. Fortunately, Windows Vista has made great strides on improving startup times, which now routinely measure in seconds instead of minutes. However, if you're convinced that turning off the computer is a sensible move but you hate waiting even for Windows Vista's faster startup process, the next few sections provide a few tips for improving startup performance even more.

Reducing or Eliminating BIOS Checks

Many computers run through one or more diagnostic checks at system startup. For example, it's common for machines to check the integrity of the system memory chips. That seems like a good idea, but it can take an interminable amount of time to complete on a system with a great deal of memory. Access your system's BIOS settings and turn off these checks to reduce the overall time of the computer's Power-On Self Test (POST).

NOTE

How you access your computer's BIOS settings (also called the **CMOS setup**) depends on the manufacturer. You usually have to press a function key (normally F1, F2, or F10), a key such as Delete or Esc, or a key combination. During the POST, you should see some text on the screen that tells you what key or key combination to press.

Reducing the OS Choices Menu Timeout

If you have two or more operating systems on your computer, you see Windows Vista's OS Choices menu at startup. If you're paying attention to the startup, you can press the Enter key as soon as this menu appears and your system will boot the default operating system. If your mind is elsewhere, however, the startup process waits 30 seconds until it automatically selects the default choice. If this happens to you frequently, you can reduce that 30-second timeout to speed up the startup. There are three ways to do this:

- Press Windows Logo+R (or select Start, All Programs, Accessories, Run), type **`msconfig -2`**, click OK, and enter your UAC credentials. In the System Configuration tool's Boot tab, modify the value in the Timeout text box.
- Select Start, right-click Computer, and then click Properties. In the System window, click Advanced System Settings and enter your UAC credentials to open the System Properties dialog box and display the Advanced tab. In the Startup and Recovery group, click Settings and then adjust the value of the Time to Display List of Operating Systems spin box.

- Click Start, All Programs, Accessories, right-click Command Prompt, and then click Run as Administrator. At the command prompt, enter the following command (replace **ss** with the number of seconds you want to use for the timeout):

  ```
  BCDEDIT /timeout ss
  ```

Turning Off the Startup Splash Screen

You can prevent the Windows Vista splash screen from appearing, which will shave a small amount of time from the startup. Press Windows Logo+R (or select Start, All Programs, Accessories, Run), type **msconfig -2**, click OK, and then enter your UAC credentials. In the System Configuration tool's Boot tab, activate the No GUI Boot check box.

CAUTION

Activating the No GUI Boot option means that you won't see any startup blue-screen errors. In other words, if a problem occurs, all you'll know for sure is that your system has hung, but you won't know why. For this reason, the small performance improvement represented by activating the No GUI Boot option is likely not enough to offset the lack of startup error messages.

Upgrading Your Device Drivers

Device drivers designed to work with Windows Vista will generally load faster than older drivers. Therefore, you should check each of your device drivers to see whether a Windows Vista–compatible version exists. If one is available, upgrade to that driver as described in Chapter 17, "Getting the Most Out of Device Manager" (see the section "Updating a Device Driver").

Using an Automatic Logon

One of the best ways to reduce startup time frustration is to ignore the startup altogether by doing something else (such as getting a cup of coffee) while the boot chores occur. However, this strategy fails if the logon process interrupts the startup. If you're the only person who uses your computer, you can overcome this problem by setting up Windows Vista to log you on automatically. I discussed this in Chapter 2; see the section "Setting Up an Automatic Logon."

Configuring the Prefetcher

Prefetching is a Windows Vista performance feature that analyzes disk usage and then reads into memory the data that you or your system accesses most frequently. The prefetcher can speed up booting, application launching, or both. You configure the prefetcher using the following Registry setting:

```
HKLM\SYSTEM\CurrentControlSet\Control\SessionManager\Memory Management\
➥PrefetchParameters\EnablePrefetcher
```

There's also a SuperFetch setting:

```
HKLM\SYSTEM\CurrentControlSet\Control\SessionManager\Memory Management\
➥PrefetchParameters\EnableSuperfetch
```

In both cases, set the value to 1 for application-only fetching, 2 for boot-only fetching, or 3 for both application and boot fetching (this is the default for both settings). You can try experimenting with boot-only fetching to see whether it improves your startup times, but my own testing shows only minimal startup improvements. The more programs you run at startup, the more your startup performance should improve with boot-only fetching.

Optimizing Applications

Running applications is the reason we use Windows Vista, so it's a rare user who doesn't want his applications to run as fast as possible. The next few sections offer some pointers for improving the performance of applications under Windows Vista.

Adding More Memory

All applications run in RAM, of course, so the more RAM you have, the less likely it is that Windows Vista will have to store excess program or document data in the page file on the hard disk, which is a real performance killer. In Task Manager or System Monitor, watch the Available Memory value. If it starts to get too low, you should consider adding RAM to your system.

Installing to the Fastest Hard Drive

If your system has multiple hard drives that have different performance ratings, install your applications on the fastest drive. This enables Windows Vista to access the application's data and documents faster.

Optimizing Application Launching

As I mentioned in the previous section, Windows Vista's fetching components can optimize disk files for booting, application launching, or both. It probably won't make much difference, but experiment with setting the Registry's `EnablePrefetcher` and `EnableSuperfetch` values to 1 to optimize application launching.

Getting the Latest Device Drivers

If your application works with a device, check with the manufacturer or Windows Update to see whether a newer version of the device driver is available. In general, the newer the driver, the faster its performance. I show you how to update device drivers in Chapter 17; see the section titled "Updating a Device Driver."

Optimizing Windows Vista for Programs

You can set up Windows Vista so that it's optimized to run programs. This involves adjusting the **processor scheduling**, which determines how much time the processor allocates to the computer's activities. In particular, processor scheduling differentiates between the **foreground program**—the program in which you are currently working—and **background programs**—programs that perform tasks, such as printing or backing up, while you work in another program.

Optimizing programs means configuring Vista so that it gives more CPU time to your programs. This is the default in Vista, but it's worth your time to make sure that this default configuration is still the case on your system. Here are the steps to follow:

1. Select Start, right-click Computer, and then click Properties to display the System window.
2. Click the Advanced System Settings link and then enter your UAC credentials to open the System Properties dialog box with the Advanced tab displayed.
3. In the Performance group, click Settings to display the Performance Options dialog box.
4. Display the Advanced tab, shown in Figure 14.9.

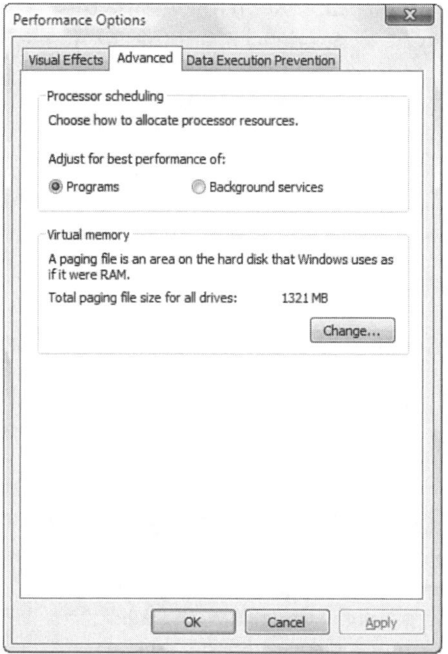

FIGURE 14.9 In the Performance Options dialog box, use the Advanced tab to optimize Windows Vista for programs.

5. In the Processor Scheduling group, activate the Programs option.
6. Click OK.
7. When Windows Vista tells you the changes require a restart, click OK to return to the System Properties dialog box.
8. Click OK. Windows Vista asks whether you want to restart your system.
9. Click Yes.

Setting the Program Priority in Task Manager

You can improve the performance of a program by adjusting the priority given to the program by your computer's processor. The processor enables programs to run by doling out thin slivers of its computing time to each program. These time slivers are called **cycles** because they are given to programs cyclically. For example, if you have three programs running—A, B, and C—the processor gives a cycle to A, one to B, another to C, and then another to A again. This cycling happens quickly, appearing seamless when you work with each program.

The **base priority** is the ranking that determines the relative frequency with which a program gets processor cycles. A program given a higher frequency gets more cycles, which improves the program's performance. For example, suppose that you raise the priority of program A. The processor might give a cycle to A, one to B, another to A, one to C, another to A, and so on.

Follow these steps to change a program's priority:

1. Launch the program you want to work with.
2. Open Task Manager, as described earlier in this chapter (refer to "Monitoring Performance with Task Manager").
3. Display the Processes tab.
4. Right-click your application's process to display its shortcut menu.
5. Click Set Priority, and then click (from highest priority to lowest) Realtime, High, or AboveNormal.

TIP

After you've changed the priority of one or more programs, you might forget the values that you have assigned to each one. To help, you can view the priority for all the items in the Processes tab. Click View and then click Select Columns to display the Select Columns dialog box. Activate the Base Priority check box and click OK. This adds a Base Priority column to the Processes list.

Optimizing the Hard Disk

Windows Vista uses the hard disk to fetch application data and documents as well as to store data in the page file temporarily. Therefore, optimizing your hard disk can greatly improve Windows Vista's overall performance, as described in the next few sections.

Examining Hard Drive Performance Specifications

If you're looking to add another drive to your system, your starting point should be the drive itself: specifically, its theoretical performance specifications. Compare the drive's average seek time with other drives (the lower the value, the better). In addition, pay attention to the rate at which the drive spins the disk's platters. A 7,200 RPM (or higher) drive will have noticeably faster performance than, say, a 5,400 RPM drive. Many notebook hard drives are even slower than that!

Performing Hard Drive Maintenance

For an existing drive, optimization is the same as maintenance, so you should implement the maintenance plan I discuss in Chapter 15. For a hard disk, this means doing the following:

- Keeping an eye on the disk's free space to make sure that it doesn't get too low
- Periodically cleaning out any unnecessary files on the disk
- Uninstalling any programs or devices you no longer use
- Checking all partitions for errors frequently
- Defragmenting partitions on a regular schedule

Disabling Compression and Encryption

If you use NTFS on a partition, Windows Vista enables you to compress files to save space, as well as to encrypt files for security. (See "Converting FAT16 and FAT32 Partitions to NTFS," later in this chapter.) From a performance point of view, however, you shouldn't use compression and encryption on a partition if you don't have to. Both technologies slow down disk accesses because of the overhead involved in the compression/decompression and encryption/decryption processes.

Turning Off the Indexer

The Indexer is a Windows Vista background process that indexes the contents of a drive on-the-fly as you add or delete data. This greatly speeds up Vista's new search features (including Instant Search) because Vista knows the contents of each file. However, you should consider turning off the Indexer for a drive if you don't do much file searching. To do this, follow these steps:

1. Select Start, Computer.
2. Right-click the drive you want to work with and then click Properties. Windows Vista display's the drive's properties sheet.
3. On the General tab, deactivate the Index This Drive for Faster Searching check box.
4. Click OK.

Enabling Write Caching

You should also make sure that your hard disk has write caching enabled. **Write caching** means that Windows Vista doesn't flush changed data to the disk until the system is idle, which improves performance. The downside of write caching is that a power outage or system crash means that the data never gets written, so the changes are lost. The chances of this happening are minimal, so I recommend leaving write caching enabled, which is the Windows Vista default. To make sure, follow these steps:

1. Select Start, right-click Computer, and then click Manage. After you enter your User Account Control credentials, Vista displays the Computer Management window.
2. Click Device Manager.
3. Open the Disk Drives branch.
4. Double-click your hard disk to display its properties sheet.
5. In the Policies tab, make sure that the Enable Write Caching on the Disk check box is activated.
6. For maximum performance, activate the Enable Advanced Performance check box. (Note that this option is available only with certain hard drives that support it.)

CAUTION

Activating the Enable Advanced Performance option tells Vista to use an even more aggressive write-caching algorithm. However, an unscheduled power shutdown means you will almost certainly lose some data. Activate this option only if your system is running off an uninterruptible power supply (UPS).

7. Click OK.

Converting FAT16 and FAT32 Partitions to NTFS

The NTFS file system is your best choice if you want optimal hard disk performance because, in most cases, NTFS outperforms both FAT16 and FAT32. (This is particularly true with large partitions and with partitions that that have lots of files.) Note, however, that for best NTFS performance you should format a partition as NTFS and then add files to it. If this isn't possible, Windows Vista offers the `CONVERT` utility for converting a FAT16 or FAT32 drive to NTFS:

```
CONVERT volume /FS:NTFS [/V] [/CvtArea:filename] [/NoSecurity] [/X]
```

`volume`	Specifies the drive letter (followed by a colon) or volume name you want to convert.
`/FS:NTFS`	Specifies that the file system is to be converted to NTFS.
`/V`	Uses verbose mode, which gives detailed information during the conversion.
`/CvtArea:`*`filename`*	Specifies a contiguous placeholder file in the root directory that will be used to store the NTFS system files.
`/NoSecurity`	Specifies that the default NTFS permissions are not to be applied to this volume. All the converted files and folders will be accessible by everyone.
`/X`	Forces the volume to dismount first if it currently has open files.

For example, running the following command at the command prompt converts drive C to NTFS:

```
convert c: /FS:NTFS
```

Note, however, that if Windows Vista is installed on the partition you're trying to convert, you'll see the following message:

```
Convert cannot gain exclusive access to the C: drive, so it cannot
convert it now. Would you like to schedule it to be converted the
next time the system restarts? <Y/N>
```

In this case, press **Y** to schedule the conversion.

If you make the move to NTFS, either via formatting a partition during Setup or by using the `CONVERT` utility, you can implement a couple of other tweaks to maximize NTFS performance. I cover these tweaks in the next two sections.

Turning Off 8.3 Filename Creation

To support legacy applications that don't understand long filenames, for each file, NTFS keeps track of a shorter name that conforms to the old 8.3 standard used by the original DOS file systems. The overhead involved in tracking two names for one file isn't much for a small number of files, but it can become onerous if a folder has a huge number of files (300,000 or more).

To disable the tracking of an 8.3 name for each file, enter the following statement at the command prompt:

```
FSUTIL BEHAVIOR SET DISABLE8DOT3 1
```

Note, too, that you can do the same thing by changing the value of the following Registry setting to 1 (note that the default value is 0):

```
HKLM\SYSTEM\CurrentControlSet\Control\FileSystem\NtfsDisable8dot3NameCreation
```

NOTE

The FSUTIL program requires Administrator account privileges. Click Start, All Programs, Accessories, right-click Command Prompt, and then click Run as Administrator.

Disabling Last Access Timestamp

For each folder and file, NTFS stores an attribute called Last Access Time that tells you when the user last accessed the folder or file. If you have folders that contain a large number of files and if you use programs that frequently access those files, writing the Last Access Time data can slow down NTFS. To disable writing of the Last Access Time attribute, enter the following statement at the command prompt:

```
FSUTIL BEHAVIOR SET DISABLELASTACCESS 1
```

You can achieve the same effect by changing the value of the following Registry setting to 1 (note that the default value is 0):

```
HKLM\SYSTEM\CurrentControlSet\Control\FileSystem\NtfsDisableLastAccessUpdate
```

Optimizing Virtual Memory

No matter how much main memory your system boasts, Windows Vista still creates and uses a page file for virtual memory. To maximize page file performance, you should make sure that Windows Vista is working optimally with the page file. The next few sections present some techniques that help you do just that.

Storing the Page File Optimally

The location of the page file can have a major impact on its performance. There are three things you should consider:

- **If you have multiple physical hard disks, store the page file on the hard disk that has the fastest access time**—You'll see later in this section that you can tell Windows Vista which hard disk to use for the page file.

- **Store the page file on an uncompressed partition**—Windows Vista is happy to store the page file on a compressed NTFS partition. However, as with all file operations on a compressed partition, the performance of page file operations suffers because of the compression and decompression required. Therefore, you should store the page file on an uncompressed partition.
- **If you have multiple hard disks, store the page file on the hard disk that has the most free space**—Windows Vista expands and contracts the page file dynamically depending on the system's needs. Storing the page file on the disk with the most space gives Windows Vista the most flexibility.

See "Changing the Paging File's Location and Size," later in this chapter, for the details on moving the page file.

Splitting the Page File

If you have two or more physical drives (not just two or more partitions on a single physical drive), splitting the page file over each drive can improve performance because it means that Windows Vista can extract data from each drive's page file simultaneously. For example, if your current initial page file size is 384MB, you'd set up a page file on a drive with a 192MB initial size, and another page file on a second drive with a 192MB initial size.

See "Changing the Paging File's Location and Size" to learn how to split the page file.

Customizing the Page File Size

By default, Windows Vista sets the initial size of the page file to 1.5 times the amount of RAM in your system, and it set the maximum size of the page file to 3 times the amount of RAM. For example, on a system with 256MB RAM, the page file's initial size will be 384MB and its maximum size will be 768MB. The default values work well on most systems, but you might want to customize these sizes to suit your own configuration. Here are some notes about custom page file sizes:

- The less RAM you have, the more likely it is that Windows Vista will use the page file, so the Windows Vista default page file sizes make sense. If your computer has less than 1GB RAM, you should leave the page file sizes as is.
- The more RAM you have, the less likely it is that Windows Vista will use the page file. Therefore, the default initial page file size is too large and the disk space reserved by Windows Vista is wasted. On systems with 512MB RAM or more, you should set the initial page file size to half the RAM size, but leave the maximum size at three times the amount of RAM, just in case.
- If disk space is at a premium and you can't move the page file to a drive with more free space, set the initial page file size to 2MB (the minimum size supported by Windows Vista). This should eventually result in the smallest possible page file, but you'll see a bit of a performance drop because Windows Vista will often have to increase the size the page file dynamically as you work with your programs.

- You might think that setting the initial size and the maximum size to the same relatively large value (say, two or three times RAM) would improve performance because it would mean that Windows Vista would never resize the page file. In practice, however, it has been shown that this trick does *not* improve performance, and in some cases actually decreases performance.
- If you have a large amount of RAM (at least 1GB), you might think that Windows Vista would never need virtual memory, so it would be okay to turn off the page file. This won't work, however, because Windows Vista needs the page file anyway, and some programs might crash if no virtual memory is present.

See "Changing the Paging File's Location and Size" to learn how to customize the page file size.

Watching the Page File Size

Monitor the page file performance to get a feel for how it works under normal conditions, where *normal* means while running your usual collection of applications and your usual number of open windows and documents.

Start up all the programs you normally use (and perhaps a few extra, for good measure) and then watch Performance Monitor's Process\Page File Bytes and Process\Page File Bytes Peak counters.

Changing the Paging File's Location and Size

The page file is named `Pagefile.sys` and it's stored in the root folder of the `%SystemDrive%`. Here's how to change the hard disk that Windows Vista uses to store the page file as well as the page file sizes:

NOTE

The `Pagefile.sys` file is a hidden system file. To see it, open any folder window and select Organize, Folder and Search Options. In the Folder Options dialog box, click the View tab, activate the Show Hidden Files and Folders option, and deactivate the Hide Protected Operating System Files check box. When Vista asks you to confirm the display of protected operating system files, click Yes, and then click OK.

1. If necessary, defragment the hard disk that you'll be using for the page file. See Chapter 15's "Defragmenting Your Hard Disk" section.
2. Select Start, right-click Computer, and then click Properties to display the System window.
3. Click Advanced System Settings and enter your User Account Control credentials to open the System Properties dialog box with the Advanced tab displayed.
4. In the Performance group, click Settings to display the Performance Options dialog box.

5. In the Advanced tab's Virtual Memory group, click Change. Windows Vista displays the Virtual Memory dialog box.
6. Deactivate the Automatically Manage Paging File Size for All Drives check box. Vista enables the rest of the dialog box controls, as shown in Figure 14.10.

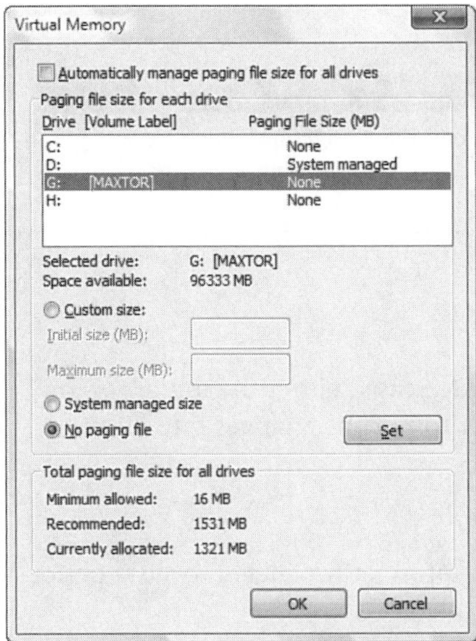

FIGURE 14.10 Use the Virtual Memory dialog box to select a different hard disk to store the page file.

7. Use the Drive list to select the hard drive you want to use.
8. Select a page file size option:

Custom Size	Activate this option to set your own page file sizes using the Initial Size (MB) and Maximum Size (MB) text boxes. Ensure that Windows Vista is able to resize the page file dynamically, as needed, by entering a maximum size that's larger than the initial size.
System Managed Size	Activate this option to let Windows Vista manage the page file sizes for you.
No Paging File	Activate this option to disable the page file on the selected drive.

TIP

If you want to move the page file to another drive, first select the original drive and then activate the No Paging File option to remove the page file from that drive. Select the other drive and choose either Custom Size or System Managed Size to add a new page file to that drive.

TIP

If you want to split the page file over a second drive, leave the original drive as is, select the second drive, and choose either Custom Size or System Managed Size to create a second page file on that drive.

9. Click Set.

Exit all the dialog boxes. If you changed the drive or decreased either the initial size or the maximum size, you need to restart your computer to put the changes into effect.

From Here

Here's a list of sections in this book where you'll find information related to Vista performance tuning:

- To learn how to logon automatically, see the "Setting Up an Automatic Logon" section in Chapter 2.
- To learn about the Ctrl+Alt+Delete logon requirement, see the "Requiring Ctrl+Alt+Delete at Startup" section in Chapter 2.
- To learn more about the Indexer Service, see the "Desktop Searching with the Windows Search Engine" section in Chapter 3.
- To control the number of applications that load at startup, see the "Launching Applications and Scripts at Startup" section in Chapter 5.
- To learn about hard drive maintenance, see Chapter 15, "Maintaining Your Windows Vista System."
- To learn how to update to a newer device driver, see the "Updating a Device Driver" section in Chapter 17.

CHAPTER 15

Maintaining Your Windows Vista System

IN THIS CHAPTER

- Vista's Stability Improvements
- Checking Your Hard Disk for Errors
- Checking Free Disk Space
- Deleting Unnecessary Files
- Defragmenting Your Hard Disk
- Setting System Restore Points
- Backing Up Your Files
- Checking For Updates and Security Patches
- Reviewing Event Viewer Logs
- Setting Up a 10-Step Maintenance Schedule

Computer problems, like the proverbial death and taxes, seem to be one of those constants in life. Whether it's a hard disk giving up the ghost, a power failure that trashes your files, or a virus that invades your system, the issue isn't *whether* something will go wrong, but rather *when* it will happen. Instead of waiting to deal with these difficulties after they've occurred (what I call **pound-of-cure mode**), you need to become proactive and perform maintenance on your system in advance (**ounce-of-prevention mode**). This will not only reduce the chances that something will go wrong, but it will also set up your system to recover more easily from any problems that do occur. This chapter shows you various Windows Vista utilities and techniques that can help you do just that. At the end of the chapter, I give you a step-by-step plan for maintaining your system and checking for the first signs of problems.

Vista's Stability Improvements

Few things in this life are as frustrating as an operating system that won't operate, either because Windows itself has given up the ghost or because some program has locked up solid and taken Windows down with it. Fortunately, each new version of Windows seems to be a little more stable and a little better at handling misbehaving programs than its predecessor, so at least we're heading in the right direction.

It's still early, but it looks as though Windows Vista continues this positive trend. Vista comes with a passel of new tools and technologies designed to prevent crashes and to recover from them gracefully if they do occur. The next few sections take you through the most important of these stability improvements.

I/O Cancellation

If you've used Windows for a while, you've probably come across a Windows Error Reporting dialog box similar to the one shown in Figure 15.1. This error message is generated by the Windows Dr. Watson debugging tool, and it includes not only a description of the error, but also the option to send an error report to Microsoft. This report includes information such as the problem type, what program or device caused the problem and where within the program or device the problem occurred, system data such as the OS version, RAM size, and device data, and associated files that might aid troubleshooting, such as system-generated listings that detail software behavior before the problem occurred.

NOTE

Many people who have clicked Send Error Report have wondered why they've never heard back from Microsoft—not even a simple "Thank you." That's not surprising because Microsoft has probably received hundreds of thousands, perhaps even millions, of these reports. Even token responses are out of the question.

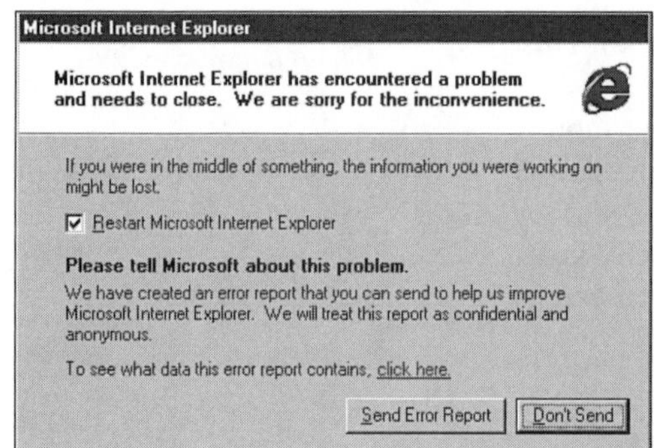

FIGURE 15.1 If Windows handles a program error, it displays a Windows Error Reporting dialog box similar to this one.

This program continues with Vista's new Windows Error Reporting service. This is an opt-in error-reporting service designed to provide Microsoft and program developers with much more detailed information about program crashes.

TIP

Vista offers a limited set of customization options that control the behavior of the Windows Error Reporting service as well as the contents of the reports. Select Start, Control Panel, System and Maintenance, Problem Reports and Solutions, and then click the Change Settings link. For more option, run the Group Policy Editor and open the Computer Configuration, Administrative Templates, Windows Components, Windows Error Reporting branch.

That can only be a good thing because it's clear that these kinds of reports are useful. Microsoft has received and studied many such reports over the years, and we're starting to see the fruits of this labor in Windows Vista, which comes with built-in fixes for many of the most common causes of program crashes. The most common of these by far is when a program has made an input/output (I/O) request to a service, resource, or another program, but that process is busy or otherwise incommunicado. In the past, the requesting program would often simply wait forever for the I/O data, thus resulting in a hung program and requiring a reboot to get the system running again.

To prevent this all-too-common scenario, Windows Vista implements an improved version of a technology called **I/O cancellation**, which can detect when a program is stuck waiting for an I/O request and then can cancel that request to help the program recover from the problem. Microsoft is also making I/O cancellation available to developers via an API, so programs, too, can cancel their own unresponsive requests and automagically recover themselves.

Reliability Monitor

In previous versions of Windows, the only way you could tell whether your system was stable was to think about how often in the recent past you were forced to reboot. If you couldn't remember the last time your system required a restart, you could assume that your system was stable. Not exactly a scientific assessment!

Windows Vista changes all that by introducing the Reliability Monitor. This new feature is part of the Reliability and Performance Monitor, which I discussed in more detail in Chapter 14 (see "Using the Reliability and Performance Monitor"). You load this Microsoft Management Console snap-in by pressing Windows Logo+R, typing `perfmon.msc`, and clicking OK. In the console window that appears, click Reliability Monitor.

Reliability Monitor keeps track of the overall stability of your system, as well as **reliability events**, which are either changes to your system that could affect stability or occurrences that might indicate instability. Reliability events include the following:

- Windows updates
- Software installs and uninstalls
- Device driver installs, updates, rollbacks, and uninstalls
- Application hangs and crashes
- Device drivers that fail to load or unload
- Disk and memory failures
- Windows failures, including boot failures, system crashes, and sleep failures

Reliability Monitor graphs these changes and generates a measure of system stability over time so that you can graphically see whether any changes affected system stability (see

Figure 15.2). The System Stability Chart shows the overall stability index. A score of 10 indicates a perfectly reliable system, and lower scores indicate decreasing reliability.

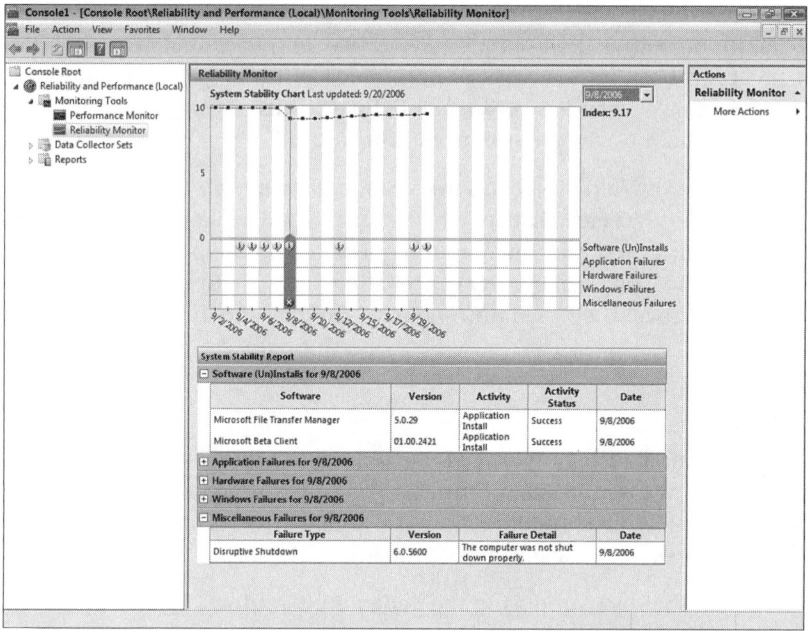

FIGURE 15.2 Reliability Monitor compares system stability with reliability events over time.

Service Recovery

A **service** is a program or process that works in the background to perform a specific, low-level support function for the operating system. You can see all the services on your system by following these steps:

1. Click Start.
2. Right-click Computer and then click Manage.
3. Enter your User Account Control credentials. Vista displays the Computer Management window.
4. Select Services and Applications, Services. On most systems, you'll see more than 125 different services listed.

Many services are mission-critical, and if any one of these crucial services fails, it almost always means that the only way to recover your system is to shut down and restart your computer. With Windows Vista, however, every service has a recovery policy that enables Vista to restart not only the service, but also any other service or process that is dependent on the failed service.

Startup Repair Tool

When your computer won't start, it's bad enough that you can't get to your programs and data and that your productivity nosedives. What's even worse is that you can't get to your normal troubleshooting and diagnostics tools to see what the problem might be. Yes, there are startup troubleshooting techniques, but they can often be time-consuming, hit-or-miss affairs. If Windows is in its own partition, or if there's a solid backup ready, many people would prefer to simply reinstall Windows than spend an entire day tracking down a startup problem.

Such drastic solutions could be a thing of the past, thanks to Vista's new Startup Repair Tool (SRT), which is designed to fix many common startup problems automatically. When a startup failure occurs, Vista starts the SRT immediately. The program then analyzes the startup logs and performs a series of diagnostic tests to determine the cause of the startup failure. The SRT looks for a number of possible problems, but three are the most common:

- Incompatible or corrupted device drivers
- Missing or corrupted startup configuration files
- Corrupted disk metadata

If the SRT determines that one of these problems or some other common snag caused the startup failure, the SRT attempts to fix the problem automatically. If it's successful, it lets you know what repairs it made and writes all changes to a log file so you can see exactly what transpired.

If the SRT can't fix the problem, it tries the system's last known good configuration. If that doesn't work, it writes all of its diagnostic data to a log and offers you support options to try to fix the problem yourself.

Checking Your Hard Disk for Errors

Our hard disks store our programs and, most importantly, our precious data, so they have a special place in the computing firmament. They ought to be pampered and coddled to ensure a long and trouble-free existence, but that's rarely the case, unfortunately. Just consider everything that a modern hard disk has to put up with:

- **General wear and tear**—If your computer is running right now, its hard disk is spinning away at between 5,400 and 10,000 revolutions per minute. That's right, even though you're not doing anything, the hard disk is hard at work. Because of this constant activity, most hard disks simply wear out after a few years.
- **The old bump-and-grind**—Your hard disk includes **read/write heads** that are used to read data from and write data to the disk. These heads float on a cushion of air just above the spinning hard disk platters. A bump or jolt of sufficient intensity can send them crashing onto the surface of the disk, which could easily result in trashed data. If the heads happen to hit a particularly sensitive area, the entire hard disk could crash. Notebook computers are particularly prone to this problem.

- **Power surges**—The current supplied to your PC is, under normal conditions, relatively constant. It's possible, however, for massive power surges to assail your computer (for example, during a lightning storm). These surges can wreak havoc on a carefully arranged hard disk.

So, what can you do about it? Windows Vista comes with a program called Check Disk that can check your hard disk for problems and repair them automatically. It might not be able to recover a totally trashed hard disk, but it can at least let you know when a hard disk might be heading for trouble.

Check Disk performs a battery of tests on a hard disk, including looking for invalid filenames, invalid file dates and times, bad sectors, and invalid compression structures. In the hard disk's file system, Check Disk also looks for the following errors:

- Lost clusters
- Invalid clusters
- Cross-linked clusters
- File system cycles

The next few sections explain these errors in more detail.

Understanding Clusters

Large hard disks are inherently inefficient. Formatting a disk divides the disk's magnetic medium into small storage areas called **sectors**, which usually hold up to 512 bytes of data. A large hard disk can contain tens of millions of sectors, so it would be too inefficient for Windows Vista to deal with individual sectors. Instead, Windows Vista groups sectors into **clusters**, the size of which depends on the file system and the size of the partition, as shown in Table 15.1.

TABLE 15.1 Default Cluster Sizes for Various File Systems and Partition Sizes

Partition Size	FAT16 Cluster Size	FAT32 Cluster Size	NTFS Cluster Size
7MB–16MB	2KB	N/A	512 bytes
17MB–32MB	512 bytes	N/A	512 bytes
33MB–64MB	1KB	512 bytes	512 bytes
65MB–128MB	2KB	1KB	512 bytes
129MB–256MB	4KB	2KB	512 bytes
257MB–512MB	8KB	4KB	512 bytes
513MB–1,024MB	16KB	4KB	1KB
1,025MB–2GB	32KB	4KB	2KB
2GB–4GB	64KB	4KB	4KB
4GB–8GB	N/A	4KB	4KB

TABLE 15.1 Continued

Partition Size	FAT16 Cluster Size	FAT32 Cluster Size	NTFS Cluster Size
8GB–16GB	N/A	8KB	4KB
16GB–32GB	N/A	16KB	4KB
32GB–2TB	N/A	N/A	4KB

Still, each hard disk has many thousands of clusters, so it's the job of the file system to keep track of everything. In particular, for each file on the disk, the file system maintains an entry in a **file directory**, a sort of table of contents for your files. (On an NTFS partition, this is the **Master File Table**, or **MFT**.)

Understanding Lost Clusters

A **lost cluster** (also sometimes called an **orphaned cluster**) is a cluster that, according to the file system, is associated with a file, but that has no link to any entry in the file directory. Program crashes, power surges, or power outages are some typical causes of lost clusters.

If Check Disk comes across lost clusters, it offers to convert them to files in either the file's original folder (if Check Disk can determine the proper folder) or in a new folder named `Folder.000` in the root of the `%SystemDrive%`. (If that folder already exists, Check Disk creates a new folder named `Folder.001` instead.) In that folder, Check Disk converts the lost clusters to files with names like `File0000.chk` and `File0001.chk`.

15

You can look at these files (using a text editor) to see whether they contain any useful data and then try to salvage it. Most often, however, these files are unusable and most people just delete them.

Understanding Invalid Clusters

An **invalid cluster** is one that falls under one of the following three categories:

- A file system entry with an illegal value. (In the FAT16 file system, for example, an entry that refers to cluster 1 is illegal because a disk's cluster numbers start at 2.)
- A file system entry that refers to a cluster number larger than the total number of clusters on the disk.
- A file system entry that is marked as unused, but is part of a cluster chain.

In this case, Check Disk asks whether you want to convert these lost file fragments to files. If you say yes, Check Disk truncates the file by replacing the invalid cluster with an **EOF** (**end of file**) marker and then converts the lost file fragments to files. These are probably the truncated portion of the file, so you can examine them and try to piece everything back together. More likely, however, you just have to trash these files.

Understanding Cross-Linked Clusters

A **cross-linked cluster** is a cluster assigned to two different files (or twice in the same file). Check Disk offers to delete the affected files, copy the cross-linked cluster to each affected file, or ignore the cross-linked files altogether. In most cases, the safest bet is to copy the cross-linked cluster to each affected file. That way, at least one of the affected files should be usable.

Understanding Cycles

In an NTFS partition, a **cycle** is a corruption in the file system whereby a subfolder's parent folder is listed as the subfolder itself. For example, a folder named `C:\Data` should have `C:\` as its parent; if `C:\Data` is a cycle, `C:\Data`—the same folder—is listed as the parent instead. This creates a kind of loop in the file system that can cause the cycled folder to "disappear."

Running the Check Disk GUI

Check Disk has two versions: a GUI version and a command-line version. See the next section to learn how to use the command-line version. Here are the steps to follow to run the GUI version of Check Disk:

1. In Windows Explorer, right-click the drive you want to check and then click Properties. The drive's properties sheet appears.
2. Display the Tools tab.
3. Click the Check Now button and enter your User Account Control credentials. The Check Disk window appears, as shown in Figure 15.3.

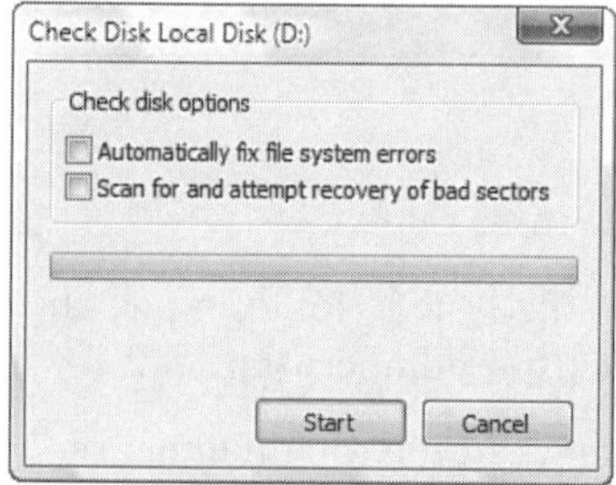

FIGURE 15.3 Use Check Disk to scan a hard disk partition for errors.

4. Activate one or both of the following options, if desired:

   Automatically Fix File System Errors—If you activate this check box, Check Disk automatically repairs any file system errors that it finds. If you leave this option deactivated, Check Disk just reports on any errors it finds.

   Scan for and Attempt Recovery of Bad Sectors—If you activate this check box, Check Disk performs a sector-by-sector surface check of the hard disk surface. If Check Disk finds a bad sector, it automatically attempts to recover any information stored in the sector and it marks the sector as defective so that no information can be stored there in the future.

5. Click Start.
6. If you activated the Automatically Fix File System Errors check box and are checking a partition that has open system files, Check Disk will tell you that it can't continue because it requires exclusive access to the disk. It will then ask whether you want to schedule the scan to occur the next time you boot the computer. Click Schedule Disk Check.
7. When the scan is complete, Check Disk displays a message letting you know and a report on the errors it found, if any.

The AUTOCHK Utility

If you click Schedule Disk Check when Check Disk asks whether you want to schedule the scan for the next boot, the program adds the AUTOCHK utility to the following Registry setting:

```
HKLM\SYSTEM\CurrentControlSet\Control\Session Manager\BootExecute
```

This setting specifies the programs that Windows Vista should run at boot time when the Session Manager is loading. AUTOCHK is the automatic version of Check Disk that runs at system startup. If you want the option of skipping the disk check, you need to specify a timeout value for AUTOCHK. You change the timeout value by adding the `AutoChkTimeOut` setting as a DWORD value in the same Registry key:

```
HKLM\SYSTEM\CurrentControlSet\Control\Session Manager\
```

Set this to the number of seconds that you want to use for the timeout. Another way to set the timeout value is to use the `CHKNTFS /T:[`*`time`*`]` command, where *`time`* is the number of seconds to use for the timeout. (If you exclude *`time`*, CHKNTFS returns the current timeout setting.) For example, the following command sets the timeout to 60 seconds:

```
CHKNTFS /T:60
```

When AUTOCHK is scheduled with a timeout value greater than 0, you see the following the next time you restart the computer:

```
A disk check has been scheduled.
To skip disk checking, press any key within 60 second(s).
```

You can bypass the check by pressing a key before the timeout expires.

15

Running Check Disk from the Command Line

Here's the syntax for Check Disk's command-line version:

```
CHKDSK [volume [filename]] [/F] [/V] [/R] [/X] [/I] [/C] [/L:[size]]
```

volume	The drive letter (followed by a colon) or volume name.
filename	On FAT16 and FAT32 disks, the name of the file to check. Include the path if the file isn't in the current folder.

`/F`	Tells Check Disk to fix errors automatically. This is the same as running the Check Disk GUI with the Automatically Fix File System Errors option activated.
`/V`	Runs Check Disk in verbose mode. On FAT16 and FAT32 drives, Check Disk displays the path and name of every file on the disk; on NTFS drives, displays cleanup messages, if any.
`/R`	Tells Check Disk to scan the disk surface for bad sectors and recover data from the bad sectors, if possible. This is the same as running the Check Disk GUI with the Scan for and Attempt Recovery of Bad Sectors option activated.
`/X`	On NTFS nonsystem disks that have open files, forces the volume to dismount, invalidates the open file handles, and then runs the scan (the `/F` switch is implied).
`/I`	On NTFS disks, tells Check Disk to check only the file system's index entries.
`/C`	On NTFS disks, tells Check Disk to skip the checking of cycles within the folder structure. This is a rare error, so using `/C` to skip the cycle check can speed up the disk check.
`/L:[`*`size`*`]`	On NTFS disks, tells Check Disk to set the size of its log file to the specified number of kilobytes. The default size is 65,536, which is big enough for most systems, so you should never need to change the size. Note that if you include this switch without the *`size`* parameter, Check Disk tells you the current size of the log file.

Checking Free Disk Space

Hard disks with capacities measured in the tens of gigabytes are commonplace even in low-end systems nowadays, so disk space is much less of a problem than it used to be. Still, you need to keep track of how much free space you have on your disk drives, particularly the `%SystemDrive%`, which usually stores the virtual memory page file.

One way to check disk free space is to view the Computer folder using either the Tiles view—which includes the free space and total disk space with each drive icon—or the Details view—which includes columns for Total Size and Free Space, as shown in Figure 15.4. Alternatively, right-click the drive in Windows Explorer and then click Properties. The disk's total capacity, as well as its current used and free space, appear in the General tab of the disk's properties sheet.

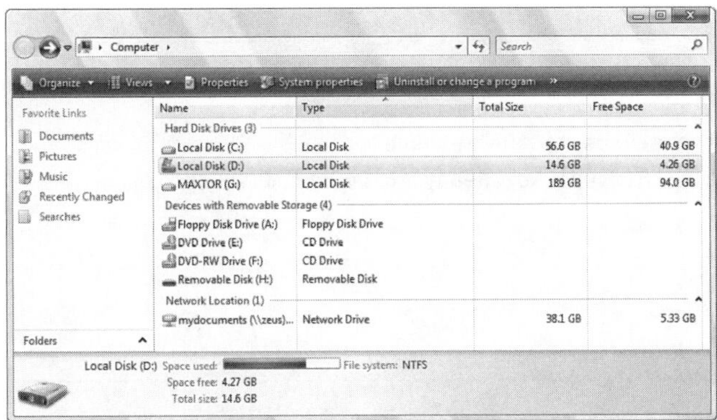

FIGURE 15.4 Display the Computer folder in Details view to see the total size and free space on your system's disks.

Listing 15.1 presents a VBScript procedure that displays the status and free space for each drive on your system.

LISTING 15.1 A VBScript Example That Displays the Status and Free Space for Your System's Drives

```
Option Explicit
Dim objFSO, colDiskDrives, objDiskDrive, strMessage

' Create the File System Object
Set objFSO = CreateObject("Scripting.FileSystemObject")

' Get the collection of disk drives
Set colDiskDrives = objFSO.Drives

' Run through the collection
strMessage = "Disk Drive Status Report" & vbCrLf & vbCrLf
For Each objDiskDrive in colDiskDrives

    ' Add the drive letter to the message
    strMessage = strMessage & "Drive: " & objDiskDrive.DriveLetter & vbCrLf

    ' Check the drive status
    If objDiskDrive.IsReady = True Then

        ' If it's ready, add the status and the free space to the message
        strMessage = strMessage & "Status: Ready" & vbCrLf
        strMessage = strMessage & "Free space: " & objDiskDrive.FreeSpace
        strMessage = strMessage & vbCrLf & vbCrLf
```

LISTING 15.1 Continued

```
    Else

        ' Otherwise, just add the status to the message
        strMessage = strMessage & "Status: Not Ready" & vbCrLf & vbCrLf
    End If
Next

' Display the message
Wscript.Echo strMessage
```

This script creates a `FileSystemObject` and then uses its `Drives` property to return the system's collection of disk drives. Then a `For Each...Next` loop runs through the collection, gathering the drive letter, the status, and, if the disk is ready, the free space. It then displays the drive data as shown in Figure 15.5.

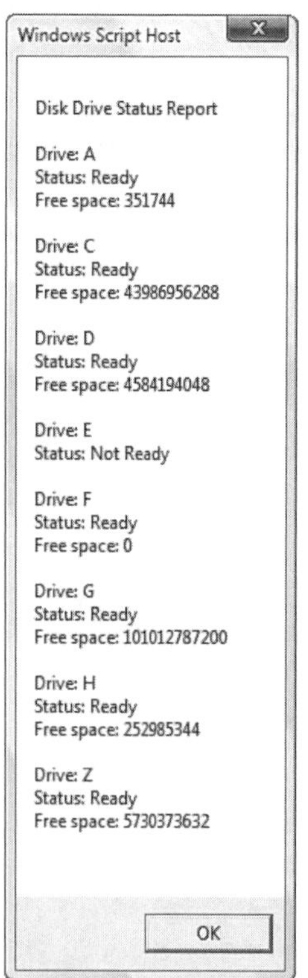

FIGURE 15.5 The script displays the status and free space for each drive on your system.

Deleting Unnecessary Files

If you find that a hard disk partition is getting low on free space, you should delete any unneeded files and programs. Windows Vista comes with a Disk Cleanup utility that enables you to remove certain types of files quickly and easily. Before discussing this utility, let's look at a few methods you can use to perform a spring cleaning on your hard disk by hand:

- **Uninstall programs you don't use**—If you have an Internet connection, you know it's easier than ever to download new software for a trial run. Unfortunately, that also means it's easier than ever to have unused programs cluttering your hard disk. Use the Control Panel's Add or Remove Programs icon to uninstall these and other rejected applications.
- **Delete downloaded program archives**—Speaking of program downloads, your hard disk is also probably littered with ZIP files or other downloaded archives. For those programs you use, you should consider moving the archive files to a removable medium for storage. For programs you don't use, you should delete the archive files.
- **Archive documents you don't need very often**—Our hard drives are stuffed with ancient documents that we use only rarely, if at all: old projects, business records from days gone by, photos and videos from occasions held long ago, and so on. You probably don't want to delete any of this, but you can free up hard disk space by archiving those old documents to removable media such as recordable CD or DVD disks, or a flash drive.
- **Remove Windows Vista components that you don't use**—If you don't use some Windows Vista components, remove them from your system. To do this, select Start, Control Panel, Programs, Turn Windows Features On or Off. Enter your UAC credentials to see the Windows Features dialog box. Deactivate the check box for each feature you don't use, and then click OK.
- **Delete application backup files**—Applications often create backup copies of existing files and name the backups using either the `bak` or `.old` extension. Use Windows Explorer's Search utility to locate these files and delete them.

After you've performed these tasks, you should next run the Disk Cleanup utility, which can automatically remove some of the preceding file categories, as well as several other types of files, including downloaded programs, Internet Explorer cache files, the hibernation files, Recycle Bin deletions, temporary files, file system thumbnails, and offline files. Here's how it works:

1. Select Start, All Programs, Accessories, System Tools, Disk Cleanup. The Disk Cleanup Options dialog box appears.

2. Click one of the following options and then enter your UAC credentials when prompted:

   My Files Only—Click this option to delete only those disposable files that you have generated yourself.

   Files from All Users on This Computer—Click this option to delete disposable files generated by every user on your computer

3. In the Drive Selection dialog box that appears, select the disk drive you want to work with and then click OK. Disk Cleanup scans the drive to see which files can be deleted, and then displays a window similar to the one in Figure 15.6.

TIP

Windows Vista enables you to bypass the Drive Selection dialog box. Press Windows Logo+R (or select Start, All Programs, Accessories, Run) to open the Run dialog box. Type **`cleanmgr /ddrive`**, where *`drive`* is the letter of the drive you want to work with (for example, `cleanmgr /dc`), and then click OK.

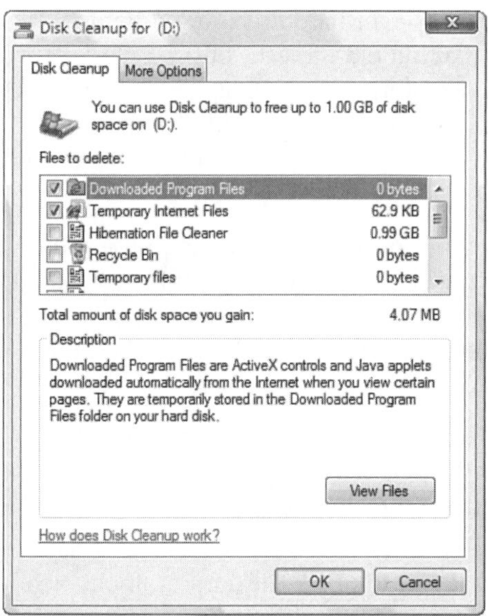

FIGURE 15.6 Disk Cleanup can automatically and safely remove certain types of files from a disk drive.

4. In the Files to Delete list, activate the check box beside each category of file you want to remove. If you're not sure what an item represents, select it and read the text in the Description box. Note, too, that for most of these items you can click View Files to see what you'll be deleting.

5. Click OK. Disk Cleanup asks whether you're sure that you want to delete the files.
6. Click Yes. Disk Cleanup deletes the selected files.

SAVING DISK CLEANUP SETTINGS

It's possible to save your Disk Cleanup settings and run them again at any time. This is handy if, for example, you want to delete all your downloaded program files and temporary Internet files at shutdown. Launch the command prompt and then enter the following command:

```
cleanmgr /sageset:1
```

Note that the number 1 in the command is arbitrary: you can enter any number between 0 and 65535. This launches Disk Cleanup with an expanded set of file types to delete. Make your choices and click OK. What this does is save your settings to the Registry; it doesn't delete the files. To delete the files, open the command prompt and enter the following command:

```
cleanmgr /sagerun:1
```

You can also create a shortcut for this command, add it to a batch file, or schedule it with the Task Scheduler.

Defragmenting Your Hard Disk

Windows Vista comes with a utility called Disk Defragmenter that's an essential tool for tuning your hard disk. Disk Defragmenter's job is to rid your hard disk of file fragmentation.

File fragmentation is one of those terms that sounds scarier than it actually is. It simply means that a file is stored on your hard disk in scattered, noncontiguous bits. This is a performance drag because it means that when Windows Vista tries to open such a file, it must make several stops to collect the various pieces. If a lot of files are fragmented, it can slow even the fastest hard disk to a crawl.

Why doesn't Windows Vista just store files contiguously? Recall that Windows Vista stores files on disk in clusters, and that these clusters have a fixed size, depending on the disk's capacity. Recall too that Windows Vista uses a file directory to keep track of each file's whereabouts. When you delete a file, Windows Vista doesn't actually clean out the clusters associated with the file. Instead, it just marks the deleted file's clusters as unused.

To see how fragmentation occurs, let's look at an example. Suppose that three files — `FIRST.TXT`, `SECOND.TXT`, and `THIRD.TXT`—are stored on a disk and that they use up four, three, and five clusters, respectively. Figure 15.5 shows how they might look on the disk.

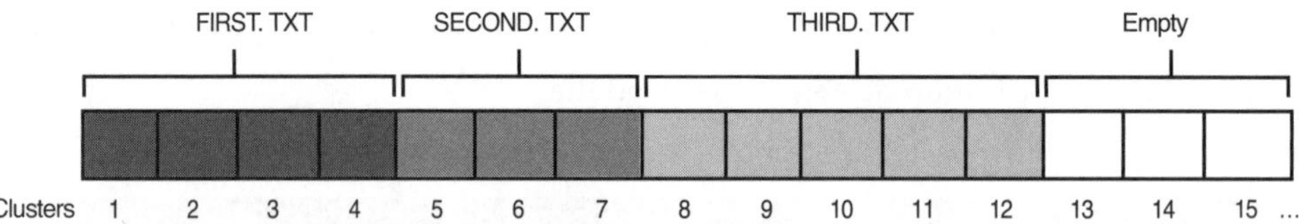

FIGURE 15.7 Three files before fragmentation.

If you now delete `SECOND.TXT`, clusters 5, 6, and 7 become available. But suppose that the next file you save—call it `FOURTH.TXT`—takes up five clusters. What happens? Well, Windows Vista looks for the first available clusters. It finds that 5, 6, and 7 are free, so it uses them for the first three clusters of `FOURTH.TXT`. Windows continues and finds that clusters 13 and 14 are free, so it uses them for the final two clusters of `FOURTH.TXT`. Figure 15.8 shows how things look now.

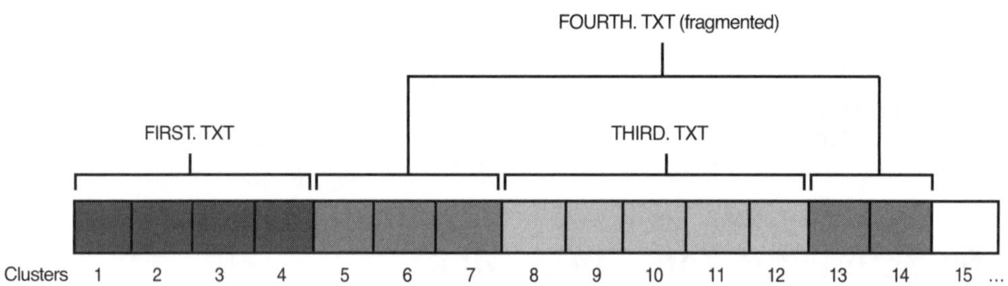

FIGURE 15.8 A fragmented file.

As you can see, `FOURTH.TXT` is stored noncontiguously—in other words, it's fragmented. Although a file fragmented in two pieces isn't that bad, it's possible for large files to split into dozens of blocks.

Running the Disk Defragmenter Tool

New The good news with Windows Vista is that it configures Disk Defragmenter to run automatically—the default schedule is weekly: every Sunday at 4:00 a.m. This means that you should never need to defragment your system manually. However, you might want to run a defragment before loading a particularly large software program.

Before using Disk Defragmenter, you should perform a couple of housekeeping chores:

- Delete any files from your hard disk that you don't need, as described in the previous section. Defragmenting junk files only slows down the whole process.
- Check for file system errors by running Check Disk as described earlier in this chapter (refer to "Checking Your Hard Disk for Errors").

Follow these steps to use Disk Defragmenter:

1. Select Start, All Programs, Accessories, System Tools, Disk Defragmenter. Alternatively, in Windows Explorer, right-click the drive you want to defragment, click Properties, and then display the Tools tab in the dialog box that appears. Click the Defragment Now button. Either way, the Disk Defragmenter window appears, as shown in Figure 15.9.

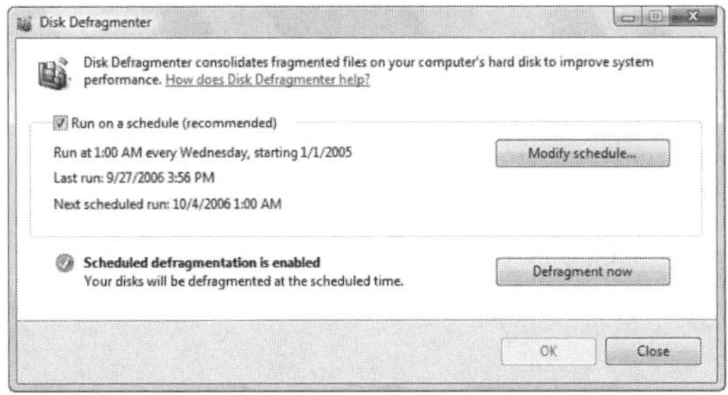

FIGURE 15.9 Use Disk Defragmenter to eliminate file fragmentation and improve hard disk performance.

2. Click Defragment Now. Windows Vista defragments your hard drives.

3. When the defragment is complete, click Close.

TIP

In some cases, you can defragment a drive even further by running Disk Defragmenter on the drive twice in a row. (That is, run the defragment, and when it's done immediately run a second defragment.)

Changing the Disk Defragmenter Schedule

If you want to run Disk Defragmenter on a different day, at a different time, more often or less often, follow these steps to change the default schedule:

1. Select Start, All Programs, Accessories, System Tools, Disk Defragmenter.
2. Make sure that the Run On a Schedule check box is activated.
3. Click Modify Schedule to display the Disk Defragmenter: Modify Schedule dialog box.
4. Use the How Often list to select the defragment frequency: Daily, Weekly, or Monthly.

5. For a Weekly schedule, use the What Day list to select the day of the week on which to run the defragment; for a Monthly schedule, use the What Day list to select the day of the month on which to run the defragment.
6. Use the What Time list to select the time of day to run the defragment.
7. Click OK to return to the Disk Defragmenter window.
8. Click Close.

Defragmenting from the Command Line

If you want to schedule a defragment or perform this chore from a batch file, you have to use the DEFRAG command-line utility. (You need an Administrator command line to run DEFRAG. Select Start, All Programs, Accessories, right-click Command Prompt, and then click Run as Administrator.) Here's the syntax:

```
DEFRAG volume [-c] [-a] [-f] [-v]
```

volume	Specifies the drive letter (followed by a colon) of the disk you want to defragment.
-c	Tells DEFRAG to defragment all the system's drives.
-a	Tells DEFRAG only to analyze the disk.
-f	Forces DEFRAG to defragment the disk, even if it doesn't need defragmenting or if the disk has less than 15% free space. (DEFRAG normally requires at least that much free space because it needs an area in which to sort the files.)
-v	Runs DEFRAG in verbose mode, which displays both the analysis report and the defragmentation report.

Setting System Restore Points

One of the biggest causes of Windows instability in the past was the tendency of some newly installed programs simply to not get along with Windows. The problem could be an executable file that didn't mesh with the Windows system or a Registry change that caused havoc on other programs or on Windows. Similarly, hardware installs often caused problems by adding faulty device drivers to the system or by corrupting the Registry.

To help guard against software or hardware installations that bring down the system, Windows Vista offers the System Restore feature. Its job is straightforward, yet clever: to take periodic snapshots—called **restore points** or **protection points**—of your system, each of which includes the currently installed program files, Registry settings, and other crucial system data. The idea is that if a program or device installation causes problems on your system, you use System Restore to revert your system to the most recent restore point before the installation.

System Restore automatically creates restore points under the following conditions:

- **Every 24 hours**—This is called a **system checkpoint** and it's set once a day as long as your computer is running. If your computer isn't running, the system checkpoint is created the next time you start your computer, assuming that it has been at least 24 hours since that previous system checkpoint was set.

NOTE

The system checkpoint interval is governed by a task in the Task Scheduler (select Start, All Programs, Accessories, System Tools, Task Scheduler). Open the Task Scheduler Library, Microsoft, Windows branch, and then click the SystemRestore task. To make changes to the task, click Properties in the Action pane to display the SR Properties dialog box. To change the schedule that Vista uses to create system checkpoints, display the Triggers tab, click the trigger you want to change (Daily or At Startup), and then click Edit.

- **Before installing certain applications**—Some newer applications—notably Office 2000 and later—are aware of System Restore and will ask it to create a restore point prior to installation.
- **Before installing a Windows Update patch**—System Restore creates a restore point before you install a patch either by hand via the Windows Update site or via the Automatic Updates feature.
- **Before installing an unsigned device driver**—Windows Vista warns you about installing unsigned drivers. If you choose to go ahead, the system creates a restore point before installing the driver.
- **Before restoring backed-up files**—When you use the Windows Vista Backup program to restore one or more backed-up files, System Restore creates a restore point just in case the restore causes problems with system files.
- **Before reverting to a previous configuration using System Restore**—Sometimes reverting to an earlier configuration doesn't fix the current problem or it creates its own set of problems. In these cases, System Restore creates a restore point before reverting so that you can undo the restoration.

It's also possible to create a restore point manually using the System Protection feature. Here are the steps to follow:

1. Select Start, right-click Computer, and then click Properties to open the System Window.
2. Click System Protection and then enter your UAC credentials to open the System Properties dialog box with the System Protection tab displayed, as shown in Figure 15.10.

FIGURE 15.10 Use the System Protection tab to set a restore point.

3. By default, Vista creates automatic restore points for just the system drive. If you have other drives on your system and you want to create automatic restore points for them, as well, use the Automatic Restore Points list to activate the check box beside each drive you want to protect.

4. Click Create to display the Create a Restore Point dialog box.

5. Type a description for the new restore point and then click Create. System Restore creates the restore point and displays a dialog box to let you know.

6. Click OK.

NOTE

In Windows XP you could adjust the amount of disk space System Restore used, but you can't do that in Windows Vista. Instead, Vista always reserves a minimum of about 300MB (on the system drive) to hold restore point data, but it might use more disk space if your system has lots of restore points and if the system drive has enough free space. If the drive runs out of free space, System Restore deletes the oldest restore points to free up some room. Note, however, that there doesn't seem to be a limit on the number of restore points, so on a massive hard disk with lots of free space you could easily end up with tens of gigabytes worth of restore points. If you want to free up that disk space, run Disk Cleanup as described earlier, select the More Options tab, and then click Clean Up in the System Restore group. This will delete all but the most recent restore point.

Backing Up Your Files

In theory, theory and practice are the same thing; in practice, they're not. That old saw applies perfectly to data backups. In theory, backing up data is an important part of everyday computing life. After all, we know that our data is valuable to the point of being irreplaceable, and you saw earlier that there's no shortage of causes that can result in a hard disk crashing: power surges, rogue applications, virus programs, or just simple wear and tear. In practice, however, backing up our data always seems to be one of those chores we'll get to "tomorrow." After all, that old hard disk seems to be humming along just fine, thank you—and anyway, who has time to work through the few dozen floppy disks you need for even a small backup?

When it comes to backups, theory and practice don't usually converge until that day you start your system and you get an ugly `Invalid system configuration` or `Hard disk failure` message. Believe me: Losing a hard disk that's crammed with unarchived (and now lost) data brings the importance of backing up into focus real quick. To avoid this sorry fate, you have to find a way to take some of the pain out of the practice of backing up.

Unfortunately, in previous versions of Windows, backing up files was never as easy as it should have been. The Microsoft Backup program from the past few versions of Windows seemed, at best, an afterthought, a token thrown in because an operating system should have *some* kind of backup program. Most users who were serious about backups immediately replaced Microsoft Backup with a more robust third-party alternative.

That might not happen in Windows Vista because the new backup program—now called Windows Backup—is quite an improvement on its predecessors:

- You can back up to a writeable optical disc, USB Flash drive, external hard disk, or other removable medium.
- You can back up to a network share.
- After you set up the program, backing up is completely automated, particularly if you back up to a resource that has plenty of room to hold your files (such as a hard disk or roomy network share).
- You can create a system image backup—which Microsoft calls a *Complete PC backup*—that saves the exact state of your computer and thus enables you to completely restore your system if your computer dies or is stolen.

If there's a downside to Windows Backup, it's that it's not very friendly to power users. It's completely wizard-driven, and there's no way to configure a backup manually.

As a measure of how important automated backups are in Windows Backup, when you first launch the program (select Start, All Programs, Accessories, System Tools, Backup Status and Configuration), it displays the page shown in Figure 15.11.

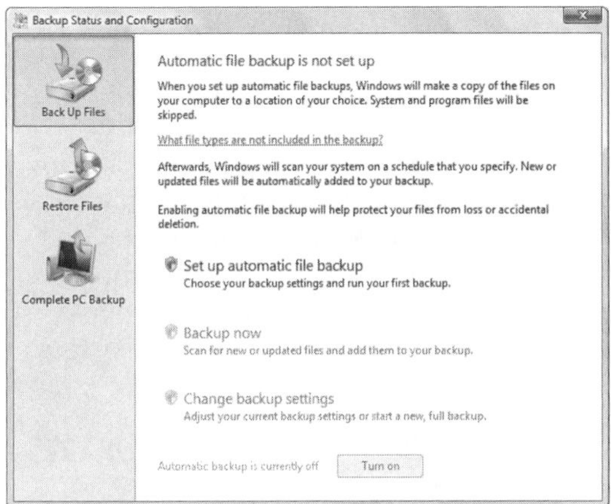

FIGURE 15.11 When you first launch Windows Backup, the program prompts you to configure and start the Automatic Backups feature.

Configuring Automatic File Backups

Vista Home Premium | Vista Business | Vista Enterprise | Vista Ultimate Edition

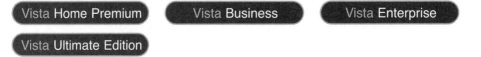

Follow these steps to configure and activate Vista's Automatic File Backup feature:

1. Click Set Up Automatic File Backup and then enter your UAC credentials to load the Back Up Files Wizard.
2. The wizard first wants to know the backup destination. You have two choices (click Next when you're ready to continue):

   On a Hard Disk, CD, or DVD—Select this option if you want to use a disk drive on your computer. If you have multiple drives, use the list to select the one you want to use.

   On a Network—Select this option if you want to use a shared network folder. Either type the UNC address of the share or click Browse to use the Browse for Folder dialog box to select the shared network folder.

3. If your system has multiple hard drives, the wizard asks you to select which of them you want to include in the backup. Deactivate the check box beside any drive you don't want to include in the backup (you can't exclude the system drive, however), and then click Next.
4. The next dialog box provides you with a long list of file types to back up, including documents, pictures, videos, and e-mail, as shown in Figure 15.12. Leave the check boxes activated for those document types you want to include in the backup and then click Next.

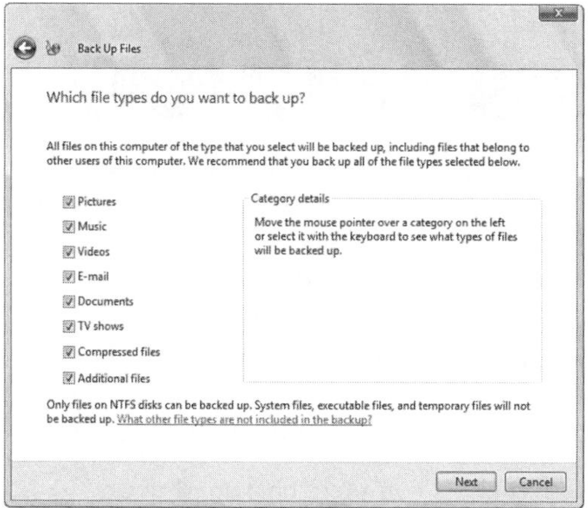

FIGURE 15.12 Use this wizard dialog box to specify the file types you want to include in the backup.

5. The next dialog box asks you to set up a backup schedule:

   How Often—Select Daily, Weekly, or Monthly.

   What Day—If you chose Weekly, select the day of the week you want the backups to occur; if you chose Monthly, select the day of the month you want the backups to occur.

   What Time—Select the time of day you want the backup to run. (Choose a time when you won't be using your computer.)

6. Click Save Settings and Start Backup to save your configuration and launch the backup. Windows Backup lets you know that it will perform a full backup of your system now.
7. Click Yes.
8. Follow any instructions that appear on screen, particularly if Windows Backup asks you to insert or format a disc. After the backup starts, click the File Backup is Running icon in the notification area to watch the progress.
9. When the backup is done, click Close.

The next time you run Windows Backup, the initial window shows you the backup status, when your system was last backed up, and when the next backup will occur. The window also sprouts several new options:

Back Up Now—Click this option to rerun the entire backup.

Change Backup Settings—Click this option to change your backup configuration by running through the Back Up Files Wizard's dialog boxes again.

Automatic Backup is Currently On—Click the Turn Off button to disable the automatic backup feature.

Creating a System Image Backup

Vista Business | Vista Enterprise | Vista Ultimate Edition

The worst-case scenario for PC problems is a system crash that renders your hard disk or system files unusable. Your only recourse in such a case is to start from scratch with either a reformatted hard disk or a new hard disk. This usually means that you have to reinstall Windows Vista and then reinstall and reconfigure all your applications. In other words, you're looking at the better part of a day or, more likely, a few days, to recover your system. However, Windows Vista has a feature that takes most of the pain out of recovering your system. It's called Complete PC Backup, and it's part of the System Recovery Options that I discuss in Chapter 16, "Troubleshooting and Recovering from Problems."

The safety net used by Complete PC Backup is actually a complete backup of your Windows Vista installation; this is a **system image**. It takes a long time to create a system image (at least several hours, depending on how much stuff you have), but it's worth it for the peace of mind. Here are the steps to follow to create the system image:

1. Select Start, All Programs, Accessories, System Tools, Backup Status and Configuration.
2. Select Complete PC Backup.
3. Click Create a Backup Now and enter your UAC credentials to launch the Windows Complete PC Backup Wizard.
4. The wizard asks you to specify a backup destination. You have two choices (click Next when you're ready to continue):

   On a Hard Disk—Select this option if you want to use a disk drive on your computer. If you have multiple drives, use the list to select the one you want to use.

   On One or More DVDs—Select this option if you want to use DVDs to hold the backup.
5. Windows Complete PC Backup automatically includes your internal hard disk in the system image, and you can't change that. However, if you also have external hard drives, you can add them to the backup by activating their check boxes. Click Next. Windows Complete PC Backup asks you to confirm your backup settings.
6. Click Start Backup. Windows Complete PC Backup creates the system image.
7. When the backup is complete, click Close.

Checking for Updates and Security Patches

Microsoft is constantly working to improve Windows Vista with bug fixes, security patches, new program versions, and device driver updates. All of these new and improved components are available online, so you should check for updates and patches often.

Checking the Windows Update Website

The main online site for Windows Vista updates is the Windows Update website, which you load into Internet Explorer by selecting Start, All Programs, Windows Update. You should visit this site regularly to look for crucial new components that can make Windows Vista more reliable and more secure.

Windows Vista also comes with a vastly improved automatic updating feature, which can download and install updates automatically. If you prefer to know what's happening with your computer, it's possible to control the automatic updating by following these steps:

1. Select Start, Control Panel, Security, Windows Update. This displays the Windows Update window, which shows you the current update status and enables you to view installed updates.

> **NOTE**
>
> To view the updates installed on your computer, click the View Update History link.

2. Click the Change Settings link to display the Change Settings window, shown in Figure 15.13.

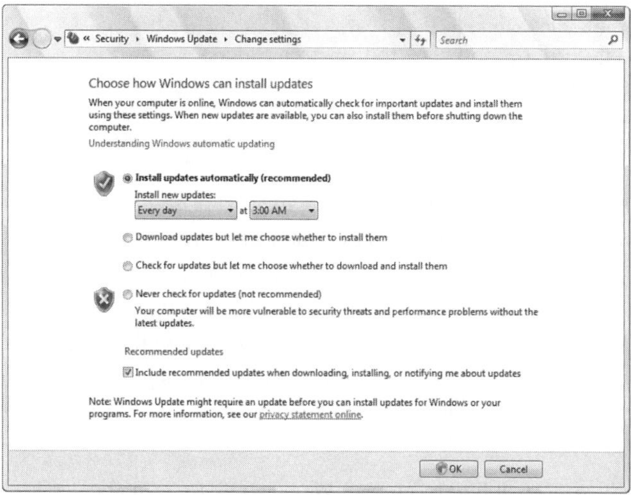

FIGURE 15.13 Use the Change Settings window to configure Vista's automatic updating.

3. Activate one of the following options to determine how Windows Vista performs the updating:

   Install Updates Automatically—This option tells Windows Vista to download and install updates automatically. Windows Vista checks for new updates on the date (such as Every Day or Every Sunday) and time you specify. For example, you might prefer to choose a time when you won't be using your computer.

CAUTION

To go into effect, some updates require your computer to reboot. In such cases, if you activate the Automatic option, Windows Vista will automatically reboot your system. This could lead to problems if you have open documents with unsaved changes or if you need a particular program to be running at all times. You can work around these problems by saving your work constantly, by setting up an automatic logon (refer to "Setting Up an Automatic Logon" in Chapter 2, "Customizing and Troubleshooting the Windows Vista Startup"), and by putting any program you need running in your Startup folder (refer to "Using the Startup Folder" in Chapter 5, "Installing and Running Applications").

Download Updates, but Let Me Choose Whether to Install Them—If you activate this option, Windows Vista checks for new updates and then automatically downloads any updates that are available. Windows Vista then displays an icon in the notification area to let you know that the updates are ready to install. Click the icon to see the list of updates. If you see an update that you don't want to install, deactivate its check box.

TIP

An update that you choose not to install still appears in the View Available Updates window. If you'd prefer not to see that update, right-click the update, click Hide Update, enter your UAC credentials, and then click Cancel. If you later want to unhide the update, display the Windows Update window and click the Restore Hidden Updates link. In the Restore Hidden Updates window, activate the update's check box, click Restore, and then enter your UAC credentials.

Check for Updates but Let Me Choose Whether to Download and Install Them—If you activate this option, Windows Vista checks for new updates and then, if any are available, displays an icon in the notification area to let you know that the updates are ready to download. Click the icon to see the list of updates. If you see an update that you don't want to download, deactivate its check box. Click Start Download to initiate the download. When the download is complete, Windows Vista displays an icon in the notification area to let you know that the updates are ready to install. Click the icon and then click Install to install the updates.

Never Check for Updates—Activate this option to prevent Windows Vista from checking for new updates.

4. Click OK and enter your UAC credentials to put the new settings into effect.

Checking for Security Vulnerabilities

Microsoft regularly finds security vulnerabilities in components such as Internet Explorer and Windows Media Player. Fixes for these problems are usually available via Windows Update.

However, to ensure that your computer is safe, you should download and regularly run the Microsoft Baseline Security Analyzer. This tool not only scans your system for missing security patches, but it also looks for things such as weak passwords and other Windows vulnerabilities. Download the tool here: www.microsoft.com/technet/security/tools/mbsahome.mspx.

After you've installed the tool, follow these steps to use it:

1. Select Start, All Programs, Microsoft Baseline Security Analyzer 2.0. The program's Welcome screen appears.
2. Click Scan a Computer.
3. Your computer should be in the Computer Name list. If not, choose it from that list. Alternatively, use the IP Address text boxes to enter your computer's IP address.
4. Use the Options check boxes to specify the security components you want to check. For most scans, you should leave all the options activated.
5. Click Start Scan. The program checks your system and displays a report on your system's security (and usually offers remedies for any vulnerability it finds). Figure 15.14 shows a sample report.

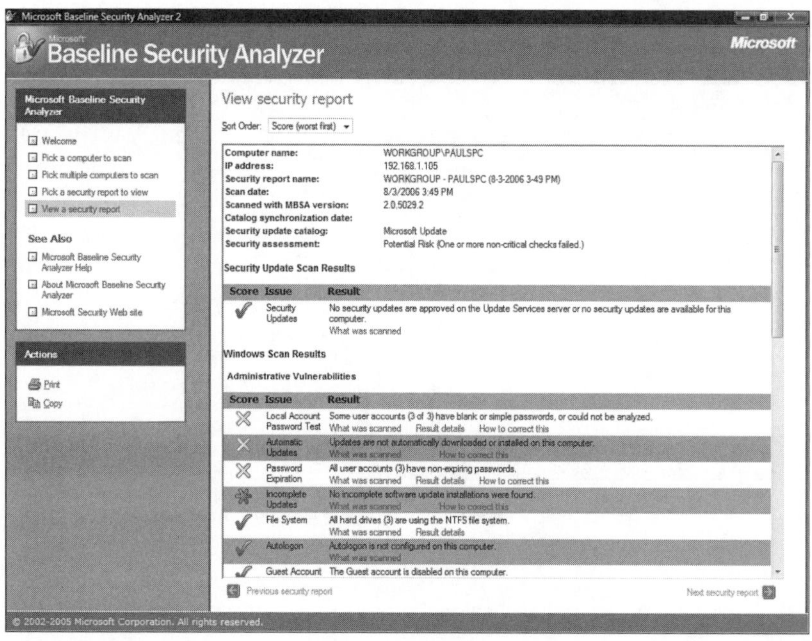

FIGURE 15.14 A sample report generated by Microsoft Baseline Security Analyzer.

Reviewing Event Viewer Logs

Windows Vista constantly monitors your system for unusual or noteworthy occurrences. It might be a service that doesn't start, the installation of a device, or an application error.

Vista tracks these occurrences, called **events**, in several different event logs. For example, the Application log stores events related to applications, including Windows Vista programs and third-party applications. The System log stores events generated by Windows Vista and components such as system services and device drivers.

To examine these logs, you use the Event Viewer snap-in, which has a much-improved interface in Windows Vista. You get to the Event Viewer by using any of the following techniques (in each case you must also enter your UAC credentials):

- Select Start, right-click Computer, click Manage, and then click Event Viewer.
- Press Windows Logo+R (or select Start, All Programs, Accessories, Run), type **`eventvwr.msc`**, and then click OK.
- Select Start, Control Panel, System and Maintenance, and under Administrative Tools, click the View Event Logs link.

Figure 15.15 shows the home page of the Event Viewer, which offers a summary of events, recent views, and available actions. (If you don't see the Action pane, click the Show/Hide Action Pane toolbar button, pointed out in Figure 15.15.)

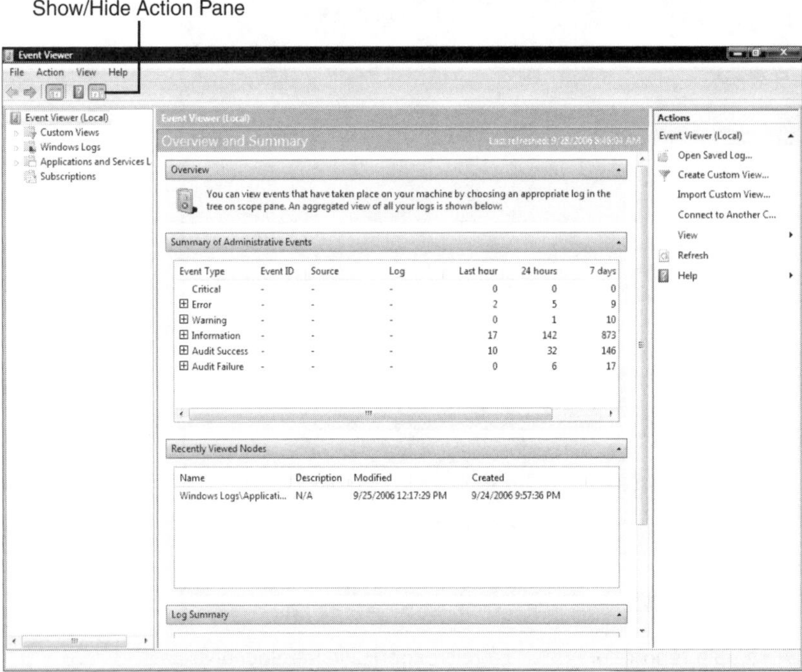

FIGURE 15.15 The Event Viewer is much improved in Windows Vista, with a new interface and new features.

The scope pane offers three branches: Custom Views, Windows Logs, and Applications and Services Logs.

The Custom Views branch lists the event views defined on your system (as described later). If you filter an event log or create a new event view, the new view is stored in the Custom Views branch.

The Windows Logs branch displays several sub-branches, four of which represent the main logs that the system tracks (see Figure 15.16):

- **Application**—Stores events related to applications, including Windows Vista programs and third-party applications
- **Security**—Stores events related to system security, including logons, user accounts, and user privileges
- **Setup**—Stores events related to Windows setup
- **System**—Stores events generated by Windows Vista and components such as system services and device drivers

You should scroll through the Application and System event logs regularly to look for existing problems or for warnings that could portend future problems. The Security log isn't as important for day-to-day maintenance. You need to use it only if you suspect a security issue with your machine; for example, if you want to keep track of who logs on to the computer.

NOTE

The System log catalogs device driver errors, but Windows Vista has other tools that make it easier to see device problems. As you'll see in Chapter 17, "Getting the Most Out of Device Manager" (see "Troubleshooting with Device Manager"), Device Manager displays an icon on devices that have problems, and you can view a device's properties sheet to see a description of the problem. Also, the System Information utility (`Msinfo32.exe`) reports hardware woes in the System Summary, Hardware Resources, Conflicts/Sharing branch and the System Summary, Components, Problem Devices branch.

When you select a log, the middle pane displays the available events, including the event's date, time, and source; its type (Information, Warning, or Error); and other data. Here's a summary of the major interface changes and new features that you get when viewing a log in Vista's Event Viewer:

- The Preview pane shows you the basic event data in the General tab, and more specific data in the Details tab. You can toggle the Preview pane on and off by selecting View, Preview Pane.
- Event data is now stored in XML format. To see the schema, click XML View in the Preview pane's Details tab.
- The Filter command now generates queries in XML format.

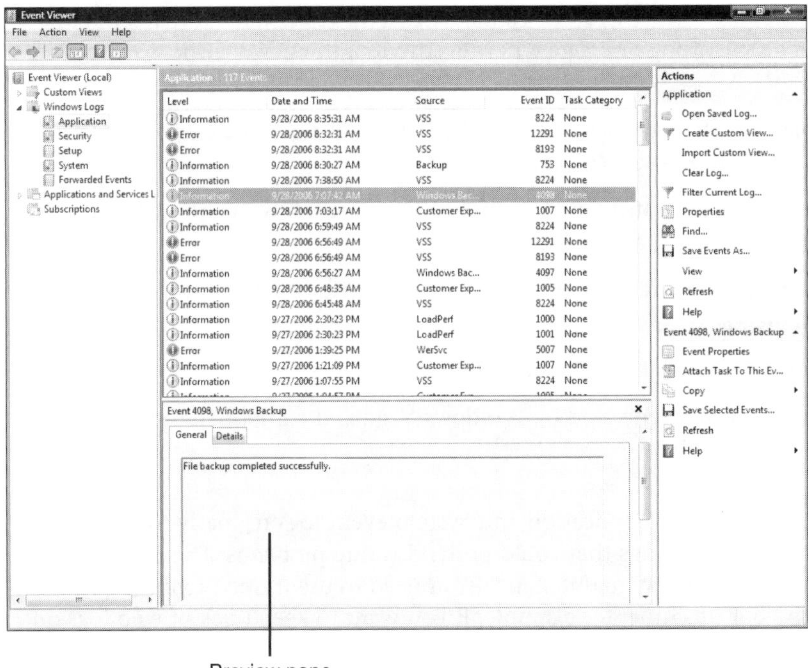

FIGURE 15.16 Click a log to see a list of the events in that log.

- You can click Create Custom View to create a new event view based on the event log, event type, event ID, and so on.
- You can attach tasks to events. Click the event you want to work with and then click Attach Task to This Event in the Action pane. This launches the Scheduled Tasks Wizard, which enables you to either run a program or script or have an email sent to you each time the event fires.
- You can save selected events to a file using the Event File (`.elf`) format.

The Applications and Services Logs branch lists the programs, components, and services that support the standard event-logging format that is new to Windows Vista. All the items in this branch formerly stored their logs in separate text files that were unavailable in older versions of Event Viewer unless you specifically opened the log file.

Setting Up a 10-Step Maintenance Schedule

Maintenance is effective only if it's done regularly, but there's a fine line to be navigated. If maintenance is performed too often, it can become a burden and interfere with more interesting tasks; if it's performed too seldom, it becomes ineffective. How often should you perform the 10 maintenance chores listed in this chapter? Here's a 10-step maintenance plan:

1. Check your hard disk for errors. Run a basic scan about once a week. Run a more thorough disk surface scan once a month. The surface scan takes a long time, so run it when you won't be using your computer for a while.

2. Check free disk space. Do this once about once a month. If the free space is getting low on a drive, check it approximately once a week.

3. Delete unnecessary files. If free disk space isn't a problem, run this chore once every two or three months.

4. Defragment your hard disk. How often you defragment your hard disk depends on how often you use your computer. If you use it every day, you should run Disk Defragmenter about once a week. If your computer doesn't get heavy use, you probably need to run Disk Defragmenter only once a month or so.

5. Set restore points. Windows Vista already sets regular system checkpoints, so you need to create your own restore points only when you're installing a program or device or making some other major change to your system.

6. Back up your files. If you use your computer frequently and generate a lot of data each day, use the Daily automatic backup. For a computer you use infrequently, a Monthly backup is sufficient.

7. Create a system image backup. You should create a system image backup once a month or any time you make major changes to your system.

8. Check Windows Update. If you've turned off automatic updating, you should check in with the Windows Update website about once a week.

9. Check for security vulnerabilities. Run the Microsoft Baseline Security Analyzer once a month. You should also pay a monthly visit to Microsoft's Security site to keep up to date on the latest security news, get security and virus alerts, and more: `www.microsoft.com/security/`.

10. Review Event Viewer logs. If your system appears to be working fine, you need only check the Application and System log files weekly or every couple of weeks. If the system has a problem, check the logs daily to look for Warning or Error events.

Remember that Windows Vista offers a couple of options for running most of these maintenance steps automatically:

- If you want to run a task every day, set it up to launch automatically at startup, as described in Chapter 5.

- Use the Task Scheduler (Start, All Programs, Accessories, System Tools, Task Scheduler) to set up a program on a regular schedule.

From Here

Here's a list of sections in the book where you'll find related information on Windows Vista maintenance:

- To learn how to log on automatically, see the "Setting Up an Automatic Logon" section in Chapter 2.
- For the details on launching programs automatically at system startup, see the "Launching Applications and Scripts at Startup" section in Chapter 5.
- For more about scripting Windows Vista, see Chapter 12, "Programming the Windows Script Host."
- If, despite your diligent maintenance, you run into problems, see Chapter 16, "Troubleshooting and Recovering from Problems." Also, see the section titled "Troubleshooting Device Problems" in Chapter 17.

CHAPTER 16

Troubleshooting and Recovering from Problems

IN THIS CHAPTER

- Troubleshooting Strategies: Determining the Source of a Problem
- General Troubleshooting Tips
- More Troubleshooting Tools
- Troubleshooting Using Online Resources
- Recovering from a Problem

A long time ago, somebody proved mathematically that it was impossible to make any reasonably complex software program problem-free. As the number of variables increase, as the interactions of subroutines and objects become more complex, and as the underlying logic of a program grows beyond the ability of a single person to grasp all at once, errors inevitably creep into the code. Given Windows Vista's status as possibly the most complex software ever created, the bad news is that there are certainly problems lurking in the weeds. However, the good news is that the overwhelming majority of these problems are extremely obscure and appear only under the rarest circumstances.

This doesn't mean that you're guaranteed a glitch-free computing experience—far from it. Third-party programs and devices cause the majority of computer woes, either because they have inherent problems themselves or because they don't get along well with Windows Vista. Using software, devices, and device drivers designed for Windows Vista can help tremendously, as can the maintenance program I outlined in Chapter 15, "Maintaining Your Windows Vista System." But computer problems, like the proverbial death and taxes, are certainties in life, so you need to know how to troubleshoot and resolve the problems that will inevitably come your way. In this chapter I help you do just that by showing you my favorite techniques for determining problem sources, and by taking you through all of Windows Vista's recovery tools.

The Origins of the Word "Bug"

Software glitches are traditionally called **bugs**, although many developers shun the term because it comes with too much negative baggage these days. Microsoft, for example, prefers the euphemistic term **issues**. There's a popular and appealing tale of how this sense of the word *bug* came about. As the story goes, in 1947 an early computer pioneer named Grace Hopper was working on a system called the Mark II. While investigating a problem, she found a moth among the machine's vacuum tubes, so from then on glitches were called *bugs*. A great story, to be sure, but this tale was *not* the source of the "computer glitch" sense of "bug." In fact, engineers had already been referring to mechanical defects as "bugs" for at least 60 years before Ms. Hopper's discovery. As proof, the *Oxford English Dictionary* offers the following quotation from an 1889 edition of the *Pall Mall Gazette*:

Mr. Edison, I was informed, had been up the two previous nights discovering 'a bug' in his phonograph—an expression for solving a difficulty, and implying that some imaginary insect has secreted itself inside and is causing all the trouble.

Troubleshooting Strategies: Determining the Source of a Problem

One of the ongoing mysteries that all Windows Vista users experience at one time or another is what might be called the "now-you-see-it-now-you-don't" problem. This is a glitch that plagues you for a while and then mysteriously vanishes without any intervention on your part. (This also tends to occur when you ask a nearby user or someone from the IT department to look at the problem. Like the automotive problem that goes away when you take the car to a mechanic, computer problems will often resolve themselves as soon as a knowledgeable user sits down at the keyboard.) When this happens, most people just shake their heads and resume working, grateful to no longer have to deal with the problem.

Unfortunately, most computer ills aren't resolved so easily. For these more intractable problems, your first order of business is to track down the source of the glitch. This is, at best, a black art, but it can be done if you take a systematic approach. Over the years, I've found that the best approach is to ask a series of questions designed to gather the required information and/or to narrow down what might be the culprit. The next few sections take you through these questions.

Did You Get an Error Message?

Unfortunately, most computer error messages are obscure and do little to help you resolve a problem directly. However, error codes and error text can help you down the road, either by giving you something to search for in an online database (see "Troubleshooting Using Online Resources," later in this chapter) or by providing information to a tech support person. Therefore, you should always write down the full text of any error message that appears.

TIP

If the error message is lengthy and you can still use other programs on your computer, don't bother writing down the full message. Instead, while the message is displayed, press Print Screen to place an image of the current screen on the clipboard. Then open Paint or some other graphics program, paste the screen into a new image, and save the image. If you think you'll be sending the image via email to a tech support employee or someone else that can help with the problem, consider saving the image as a monochrome or 16-color bitmap or, if possible, a JPEG file, to keep the image size small.

TIP

If the error message appears before Windows Vista starts, but you don't have time to write it down, press the Pause Break key to pause the startup. After you record the error, press Ctrl+Pause Break to resume the startup.

Does an Error or Warning Appear in the Event Viewer Logs?

Open the Event Viewer and examine the Application and System logs. (Refer to the "Reviewing Event Viewer Logs" section in Chapter 15 for more information on the Event Viewer.) In particular, look in the Level column for Error or Warning events. If you see any, double-click each one to read the event description. Figure 16.1 shows an example.

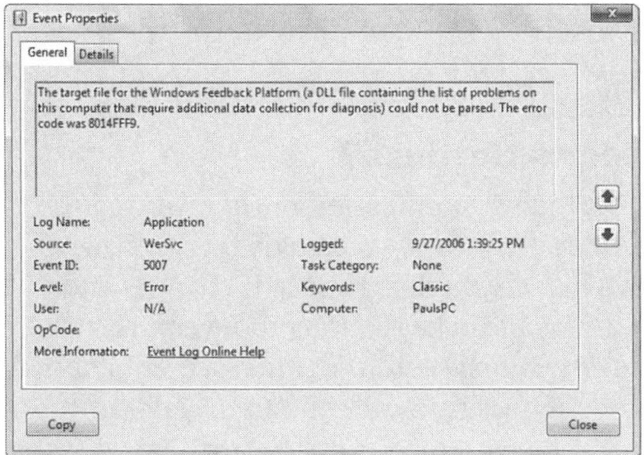

FIGURE 16.1 In the Event Viewer, look for Error and Warning events in the Application and System logs.

Does an Error Appear in System Information?

Select Start, All Programs, Accessories, System Tools, System Information to launch the System Information utility. (Alternatively, press Windows Logo+R, type **msinfo32**, and click OK.) In the Hardware Resources branch, check the Conflicts/Sharing sub-branch for device conflicts. Also, see whether the Components\Problem Devices category lists any devices, as shown in Figure 16.2.

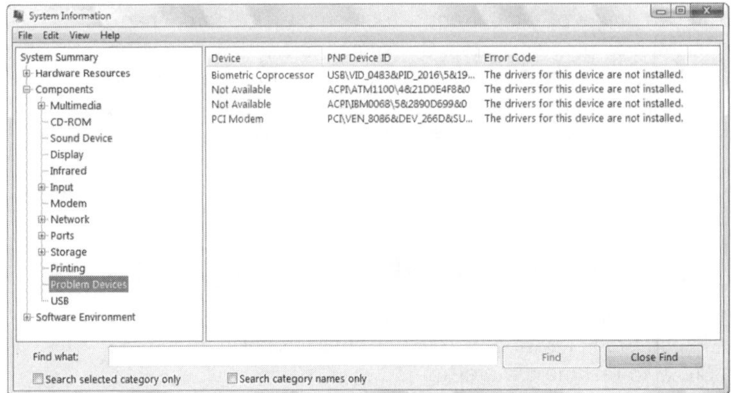

FIGURE 16.2 You can use the System Information utility to look for device conflicts and problems.

Did You Recently Edit the Registry?

Improper Registry modifications can cause all kinds of mischief. If the problem occurred after editing the Registry, try restoring the changed key or setting. Ideally, if you exported a backup of the offending key, you should import the backup. I showed you how to back up the Registry in Chapter 11, "Getting to Know the Windows Vista Registry." Refer to the "Keeping the Registry Safe" section.

Did You Recently Change Any Windows Settings?

If the problem started after you changed your Windows configuration, try reversing the change. Even something as seemingly innocent as activating a screensaver can cause problems, so don't rule anything out. If you've made a number of recent changes and you're not sure about everything you did, or if it would take too long to reverse all the changes individually, use System Restore to revert your system to the most recent checkpoint before you made the changes. See "Recovering Using System Restore," later in this chapter.

Did Windows Vista "Spontaneously" Reboot?

When certain errors occur, Windows Vista will reboot itself. This apparently random behavior is actually built into the system in the event of a system failure (also called a **stop error** or a **blue screen of death**—BSOD). By default, Windows Vista writes an error event to the system log, dumps the contents of memory into a file, and then reboots the system. So, if your system reboots, check the Event Viewer to see what happened.

You can control how Windows Vista handles system failures by following these steps:

1. Select Start, Control Panel, System and Maintenance, System.
2. Click the Advanced System Settings link and then enter your UAC credentials to open the System Properties dialog box with the Advanced tab displayed.
3. In the Startup and Recovery group, click Settings. Figure 16.3 shows the Startup and Recovery dialog box that appears.

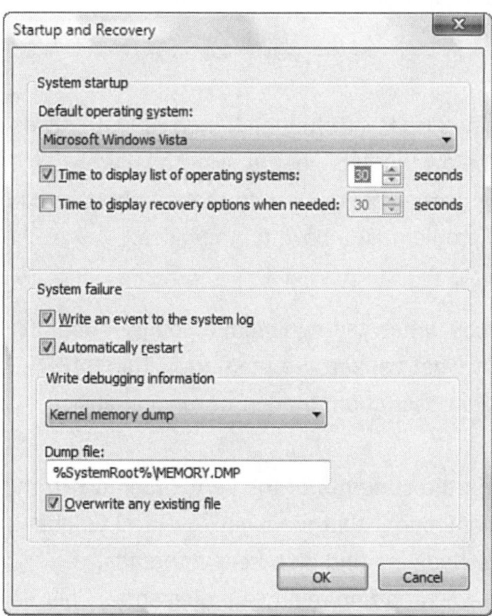

FIGURE 16.3 Use the Startup and Recovery dialog box to configure how Windows Vista handles system failures.

4. Configure how Windows Vista handles system failures using the following controls in the System Failure group:

   Write an Event to the System Log—Leave this check box activated to have the system failure recorded in the system log. This enables you to view the event in the Event Viewer.

   Automatically Restart—This is the option that, when activated, causes your system to reboot when a stop error occurs. Deactivate this check box if you want to avoid the reboot. This is useful if an error message appears briefly before Vista reboots. By disabling the automatic restart, you give yourself time to read and write down the error message.

16

TIP

If the BSOD problem occurs during startup, your computer windows up in an endless loop: you reboot, the problem occurs, the BSOD appears, and then your computer reboots. Unfortunately, the BSOD appears only fleetingly, so you never have enough time to read (much less record) the error message. If this happens, display the Windows Boot Manager menu (refer to Chapter 2, "Customizing and Troubleshooting the Windows Vista Startup"), press F8 to display the Advanced Boot Options menu, and then select the Disable Automatic Restart On System Failure item. This tells Vista not to reboot after the BSOD appears, so you can then write down the error message and, hopefully, successfully troubleshoot the problem.

Write Debugging Information—This list determines what information Windows Vista saves to disk (in the folder specified in the text box below the list) when a system failure occurs. This information—it's called a **memory dump**—contains data that can help a tech support employee determine the cause of the problem. You have four choices:

- **None**—No debugging information is written.
- **Small Memory Dump (64 KB)**—This option writes the minimum amount of useful information that could be used to identify what caused the stop error. This 64KB file includes the stop error number and its description, the list of running device drivers, and the processor state.
- **Kernel Memory Dump**—This option writes the contents of the kernel memory to the disk. (The **kernel** is the Windows Vista component that manages low-level functions for processor-related activities such as scheduling and dispatching threads, handling interrupts and exceptions, and synchronizing multiple processors.) This dump includes memory allocated to the kernel, the hardware abstraction layer, and the drivers and programs used by the kernel. Unallocated memory and memory allocated to user programs are not included in the dump. This information is the most useful for troubleshooting, so I recommend using this option.
- **Complete Memory Dump**—This option writes the entire contents of RAM to the disk.

CAUTION

Windows Vista first writes the debugging information to the paging file—`Pagefile.sys` in the root folder of the `%SystemDrive%`. When you restart the computer, Windows Vista then transfers the information to the dump file. Therefore, you must have a large enough paging file to handle the memory dump. This is particularly true for the Complete Memory Dump option, which requires the paging file to be as large as the physical RAM, plus one megabyte. The file size of the Kernel Memory Dump is typically about a third of physical RAM, although it may be as large as 800MB. If the paging file isn't large enough to handle the dump, Vista only writes as much information as can fit into the paging file. I showed you how to check and adjust the size of the paging file in Chapter 14, "Tuning Windows Vista's Performance"; see the section titled "Changing the Paging File's Location and Size."

Overwrite Any Existing File—When this option is activated, Windows Vista overwrites any existing dump file with the new dump information. If you deactivate this check box, Windows Vista creates a new dump file with each system failure. Note that this option is enabled only for the Kernel Memory Dump and the Complete Memory Dump (which by default write to the same file: `%SystemRoot%\Memory.dmp`).

Did You Recently Change Any Application Settings?

If so, try reversing the change to see whether doing so solves the problem. If that doesn't help, here are three other things to try:

- Check the developer's website to see whether an upgrade or patch is available.
- Run the application's Repair option (if it has one), which is often useful for fixing corrupted or missing files. To see whether a program as a Repair option, select Start, Control Panel, Programs, Programs and Feature to display a list of your installed applications. Click the problematic application and then look for a Repair item in the task bar.
- Reinstall the program.

NOTE

If a program freezes, you won't be able to shut it down using conventional methods. If you try, you might see a dialog box warning you that the program is not responding. If so, click End Now to force the program to close. If that doesn't work, right-click the taskbar and then click Task Manager. When you display the Applications tab, you should see your stuck application listed, and the Status column will likely say `Not responding`. Click the program and then click End Task.

16

Did You Recently Install a New Program?

If you suspect a new program is causing system instability, restart Windows Vista and try operating the system for a while without using the new program. (If the program has any components that load at startup, be sure to deactivate them, as I described in Chapter 2; refer to the "Custom Startups Using the Boot Configuration Data" section.) If the problem doesn't reoccur, the new program is likely the culprit. Try using the program without any other programs running.

You should also examine the program's readme file (if it has one) to look for known problems and possible workarounds. It's also a good idea to check for a Windows Vista-compatible version of the program. Again, you can also try the program's Repair option or you can reinstall the program.

Similarly, if you recently upgraded an existing program, try uninstalling the upgrade.

TIP

One common cause of program errors is having one or more program files corrupted because of bad hard disk sectors. Before you reinstall a program, run a surface check on your hard disk to identify and block off bad sectors. I showed you how to do a hard disk surface scan in Chapter 15; refer to the "Checking Your Hard Disk for Errors" section.

TIP

When a program crashes, Windows Vista displays a dialog box asking if you want to see if a solution to the problem is available. You can control the behavior of this prompt. See "Checking for Solutions to Problems," later in this chapter.

Did You Recently Install a New Device?

If you recently installed a new device or if you recently updated an existing device driver, the new device or driver might be causing the problem. Check Device Manager to see whether there's a problem with the device. Follow my troubleshooting suggestions in Chapter 17, "Getting the Most Out of Device Manager"; see the section titled "Troubleshooting Device Problems."

Did You Recently Install an Incompatible Device Driver?

As you'll see in Chapter 17, Windows Vista allows you to install drivers that aren't Windows Vista–certified, but it also warns you that this is a bad idea. Incompatible drivers are one of the most common sources of system instability, so whenever possible, you should uninstall the driver and install one designed for Windows Vista. If you can't uninstall the driver, Windows Vista automatically set a system restore point before it installed the driver, so you should use that to restore the system to its previous state. (See "Recovering Using System Restore," later in this chapter.)

Did You Recently Apply an Update from Windows Update?

It's an unfortunate fact of life that occasionally updates designed to fix one problem end up causing another problem. Fortunately, Vista offers a couple of solutions for problems caused by updates:

- Select Start, Control Panel, Programs, View Installed Updates. In the Installed Updates window, click the update you want to remove and then click Uninstall.
- Before you install an update from the Windows Update site, Windows Vista creates a system restore point—usually named *(Install) Windows Update*. If your system becomes unstable after installing the update, use System Restore to revert to the preupdate configuration.

TIP

If you have Windows Vista set up to perform automatic updating, you can keep tabs on the changes made to your system by select Start, System and Maintenance, Windows Update. Click the View Update History link to see a list of the installed updates, which includes the update Name, Status (such as Successful), Type (such as Important or Optional), and Date Installed.

General Troubleshooting Tips

Figuring out the cause of a problem is often the hardest part of troubleshooting, but by itself it doesn't do you much good. When you know the source, you need to parlay that information into a fix for the problem. I discussed a few solutions in the previous section, but here are a few other general fixes you need to keep in mind:

- **Close all programs**—You can often fix flaky behavior by shutting down all your open programs and starting again. This is a particularly useful fix for problems caused by low memory or low system resources.
- **Log off Windows Vista**—Logging off clears the RAM and so gives you a slightly cleaner slate than merely closing all your programs.
- **Reboot the computer**—If there are problems with some system files and devices, logging off won't help because these objects remain loaded. By rebooting the system, you reload the entire system which is often enough to solve many computer problems.
- **Turn off the computer and restart**—You can often solve a hardware problem by first shutting your machine off. Wait for 30 seconds to give all devices time to spin down, and then restart.
- **Check connections, power switches, and so on**—Some of the most common (and some of the most embarrassing) causes of hardware problems are the simple physical things: making sure that a device is turned on; checking that cable connections are secure; and ensuring that insertable devices are properly inserted.
- **Use the Help and Support Center**—Microsoft has greatly improved the quality of the Help system in Windows Vista. The Help and Support Center (select Start, Help and Support) is awash in articles and advice on using Windows Vista. However, the real strength of Help and Support is, in my opinion, the Support side. In the Help and Support Center home page, click Troubleshooting to see links for general troubleshooting and for fixing specific problems related to hardware, email, networking, and more. Note, too, that the Help and Support Center offers a number of **Troubleshooters**—guides that take you step-by-step through troubleshooting procedures.

More Troubleshooting Tools

Windows Vista comes with new diagnostic tools—together, they're called the **Windows Diagnostic Infrastructure (WDI)**—that not only do a better job of finding the source of many common disk, memory, and network problems, but can detect impending failures and alert you to take corrective or mitigating action (such as backing up your files). The next few sections describe these new tools.

Understanding Disk Diagnostics

New A hard disk can suddenly bite the dust thanks to a lightning strike, an accidental drop from a decent height, or an electronic component shorting out. However, most of the time hard disks die a slow death. Along the way, hard disks almost always show some signs of decay, such as the following:

- Spin-up time gradually slows
- Drive temperature increases
- The seek error rate increases
- The read error rate increases
- The write error rate increases
- The number of reallocated sectors increases
- The number of bad sectors increases
- The cyclic redundancy check (CRC) produces an increasing number of errors

Other factors that might indicate a potential failure are the number of times that the hard drive has been powered up, the number of hours in use, and the number of times the drive has started and stopped spinning.

Since about 1996, almost all hard-disk manufacturers have built into their drives a system called **Self-Monitoring, Analysis, and Reporting Technology**, or **SMART**. This system monitors the parameters just listed (and usually quite a few more highly technical hard disk attributes) and uses a sophisticated algorithm to combine these attributes into a value that represents the overall health of the disk. When that value goes beyond some predetermined threshold, SMART issues an alert that hard-disk failure might be imminent.

Although SMART has been around for a while and is now standard, taking advantage of SMART diagnostics has, until now, required third-party programs. However, Windows Vista comes with a new Diagnostic Policy Service (*DPS*) that includes a Disk Diagnostics component that can monitor SMART. If the SMART system reports an error, Vista displays a message that your hard disk is at risk. It also guides you through a backup session to ensure that you don't lose any data before you can have the disk replaced.

Understanding Resource Exhaustion Detection

New Your system can become unstable if it runs low on virtual memory, and there's a pretty good chance it will hang if it runs out of virtual memory. Older versions of Windows displayed one warning when they detected low virtual memory and another warning when the system ran out of virtual memory. However, in both cases, users were simply told to shut down some or all of their running programs. That often solved the problem, but shutting *everything* down is usually overkill because it's often the case that just one running program or process is causing the virtual memory shortage.

Vista takes this more subtle point of view into account with its new Windows Resource Exhaustion Detection and Resolution tool (*RADAR*), which is part of the Diagnostic Policy Service. This tool also monitors virtual memory and issues a warning when resources run low. However, RADAR also identifies which programs or processes are using the most virtual memory, and it includes a list of these resource hogs as part of the warning. This enables you to shut down just one or more of these offending processes to get your system in a more stable state.

Microsoft is also providing developers with programmatic access to the RADAR tool, thus enabling vendors to build resource exhaustion detection into their applications. When such a program detects that it is using excessive resources, or if it detects that the system as a whole is low on virtual memory, the program can free resources to improve overall system stability.

NOTE

The Resource Exhaustion Detection and Recovery tool divides the current amount of committed virtual memory by the **commit limit**, the maximum size of the virtual memory paging file. If this percentage approaches 100, RADAR issues its warning. If you want to track this yourself, run the Reliability and Performance Monitor (refer to "Using the Reliability and Performance Monitor," in Chapter 14), select Performance Monitor and add the % Committed Bytes In Use counter in the `Memory` object. If you want to see the exact commit numbers, add the Committed Bytes and Commit Limit counters (also in the `Memory` object).

Running the Memory Diagnostics Tool

New Few computer problems are as maddening as those related to physical memory defects because they tend to be intermittent and they tend to cause problems in secondary systems, forcing you to waste time on wild goose chases all over your system.

Therefore, it is welcome news indeed that Vista ships with a new Windows Memory Diagnostics tool that works with Microsoft Online Crash Analysis to determine whether defective physical memory is the cause of program crashes. If so, Windows Memory Diagnostics lets you know about the problem and schedules a memory test for the next time you start your computer. If it detects actual problems, the system also marks the affected memory area as unusable to avoid future crashes.

Windows Vista also comes with a Memory Leak Diagnosis tool that's part of the Diagnostic Policy Service. If a program is leaking memory (using up increasing amounts of memory over time), this tool will diagnose the problem and take steps to fix it.

To run the Memory Diagnostics Tool yourself, follow these steps:

1. Select Start, Control Panel, System and Maintenance, Administrative Tools to open the Administrative Tools window.
2. Double-click Memory Diagnostics Tool and enter your UAC credentials to display the Windows Memory Diagnostics Tool window.
3. Click one of the following options:

   Restart Now and Check for Problems—Click this option to force an immediate restart and schedule a memory test during startup. Be sure to save your work before clicking this option.

   Check for Problems the Next Time I Start My Computer—Click this option to schedule a memory test to run the next time you boot.

After the test runs (it takes 10 or 15 minutes, depending on how much RAM is in your system), Vista restarts and you see (for a short time) the Windows Memory Diagnostic Tool icon in the taskbar's notification area. This icon displays the results of the memory test.

TIP

If you're having trouble starting Windows Vista and you suspect memory errors might be the culprit, boot your machine to the Windows Boot Manager menu (refer to Chapter 2). When the menu appears, press Tab to select the Windows Memory Diagnostic item, and then press Enter. If you can't get to the Windows Boot Manager, you can also run the Memory Diagnostic Tool using Vista's new System Recovery Options. See "Recovering Using the System Recovery Options," later in this chapter.

Checking for Solutions to Problems

New Microsoft constantly collects information about Vista from users. When a problem occurs, Vista usually asks whether you want to send information about the problem to Microsoft and, if you do, it stores these tidbits in a massive database. Engineers then tackle the "issues" (as they euphemistically call them) and hopefully come up with solutions.

One of Vista's most promising new features is Problem Reports and Solutions, and it's designed to make solutions available to anyone who goes looking for them. Vista keeps a list of problems your computer is having, so you can tell it to go online and see if a solution is available. If there's a solution waiting, Vista will download it, install it, and fix your system.

Here are the steps to follow to check for solutions to problems:

1. Select Start, Control Panel, System and Maintenance, Problem Reports and Solutions.
2. In the Problem Reports and Solutions window, click the Check for New Solutions link. Windows Vista begins checking for solutions.
3. If you see a dialog box asking whether you want to send more information about your problems, click Send Information.
4. If a solution exists for your computer, you'll see it listed in the Solutions to Install section of the Problem Reports and Solutions window. Click the solution to install it.

By default, when a problem occurs, Vista does two things:

- It automatically checks for a solution to the problem.
- It asks whether you want to send more information about the problem to Microsoft.

You can control this behavior by configuring a few settings:

1. In the Problem Reports and Solutions window, click Change Settings.
2. In the Choose How to Check for Solutions to Computer Problems window, click Advanced Settings to display the Advanced Settings for Problem Reporting window shown in Figure 16.4.

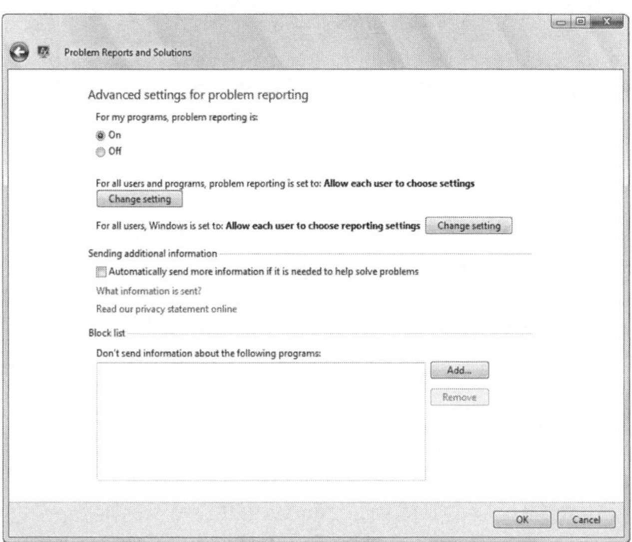

FIGURE 16.4 Use the Advanced Settings for Problem Reporting window to configure the Problem Reports and Solutions feature.

3. If you don't want to report problems at all on your user account, activate the Off option. Alternatively, you can configure problem reporting for all users of your computer. Click Change Setting beside the For All Users and Programs, Problem Reporting Is Set To, and then click one of the following options (when you're done, click OK and enter your UAC credentials):

   On—Activate this option to force all users to report problems

   Off—Activate this option to force all user not to report problems

   Allow Each User to Choose Settings—Activate this option (it's the default) to enable each user to turn problem reporting on or off

4. To configure problem reporting, click Change Setting beside For All Users, Windows Is Set To, and then click one of the following options (when you're done, click OK and enter your UAC credentials):

   Allow Each User to Choose Reporting Settings—Activate this options to enable the Automatically Send More Information If It Is Need to Help Solve Problems check box.

   Ask Each Time a Problem Occurs—Activate this option to have Vista prompt each user to check box solutions and to send additional information about the problem.

   Automatically Check for Solutions—Activate this option (it's the default) to have Vista automatically check online for an existing solution to a problem.

   Automatically Check for Solutions and Send Additional Information, If Needed—Activate this option to have Vista automatically check online for an existing solution to a problem and to automatically send extra information about the problem.

5. If you want Vista to always send the extra troubleshooting information, activate the Automatically Send More Information If It Is Needed To Help Solve Problems check box.

6. If you don't want Vista to send information about a specific program, click Add, locate and select the program's executable file, and then click Open.

7. Click OK.

Troubleshooting Using Online Resources

The Internet is home to an astonishingly wide range of information, but its forte has always been computer knowledge. Whatever problem you have, there's a good chance that someone out there has run into the same thing, knows how to fix it, and has posted the solution on a website or newsgroup, or would be willing to share it with you if asked. True, finding what you need is sometimes difficult, and you often can't be sure how accurate some of the solutions are. However, if you stick to the more reputable sites and if you get second opinions on solutions offered by complete strangers, you'll find the online world an excellent troubleshooting resource. Here's my list of favorite online resources:

Microsoft Product Support Services—This is Microsoft's main online technical support site. Through this site you can access frequently asked questions about Windows Vista, see a list of known problems, download files, and send questions to Microsoft support personnel: support.microsoft.com/.

Microsoft Knowledge Base—The Microsoft Product Support Services site has links that enable you to search the Microsoft Knowledge Base, which is a database of articles related to all Microsoft products including, of course, Windows Vista. These articles provide you with information about Windows Vista and instructions on using Windows Vista features. But the most useful aspect of the Knowledge Base is for troubleshooting problems. Many of the articles were written by Microsoft support personnel after helping customers overcome problems. By searching for error codes or keywords, you can often get specific solutions to your problems.

Microsoft TechNet—This Microsoft site is designed for IT professionals and power users. It contains a huge number of articles on all Microsoft products. These articles give you technical content, program instructions, tips, scripts, downloads, and troubleshooting ideas: www.microsoft.com/technet/.

Windows Update—Check this site for the latest device drivers, security patches, Service Packs, and other updates: windowsupdate.microsoft.com/.

Microsoft Security—Check this site for the latest information on Microsoft's security and privacy initiatives, particularly security patches: www.microsoft.com/security/.

Vendor websites—All but the tiniest hardware and software vendors maintain websites with customer support sections that you can peruse for upgrades, patches, workarounds, frequently asked questions, and sometimes chat or bulletin board features.

Newsgroups—There are computer-related newsgroups for hundreds of topics and products. Microsoft maintains its own newsgroups via the msnews.microsoft.com server (an account for which is automatically set up in Windows Mail), and Usenet has a huge list of groups in the alt and comp hierarchies. Before asking a question in a newsgroup, be sure to search Google Groups to see whether your question has been answered in the past: groups.google.com/.

TIP

You can also access Microsoft's Vista newsgroups via the Web: http://windowshelp.microsoft.com/communities/newsgroups/en-us/default.mspx

Recovering from a Problem

Ideally, solving a problem will require a specific tweak to the system: a Registry setting change, a driver upgrade, a program uninstall. But sometimes you need to take more of a "big picture" approach to revert your system to some previous state in the hope that you'll leap past the problem and get your system working again. Windows Vista offers three ways to try such an approach—last known good configuration, System Restore, and System Recovery Options—which you should use in that order. The next three sections discuss these tools.

Booting Using the Last Known Good Configuration

Each time Windows Vista starts successfully in Normal mode, the system makes a note of which **control set**—the system's drivers and hardware configuration—was used. Specifically, it enters a value in the following Registry key:

```
HKLM\SYSTEM\Select\LastKnownGood
```

For example, if this value is `1`, it means that control set 1 was used to start Windows Vista successfully:

```
HKLM\SYSTEM\ControlSet001
```

If you make driver or hardware changes and then find that the system won't start, you can tell Windows Vista to load using the control set that worked the last time. (That is, the control set that doesn't include your most recent hardware changes.) This is the **last known good configuration**, and the theory is that by using the previous working configuration, your system should start because it's bypassing the changes that caused the problem. Here's how to start Windows Vista using the last known good configuration:

1. Restart your computer.
2. At the Windows Boot Manager menu (refer to Chapter 2), press F8 to display the Advanced Boot Options menu.
3. Select the Last Known Good Configuration option.

Recovering Using System Restore

The Last Known Good Configuration option is most useful when your computer won't start and you suspect that a hardware change is causing the problem. You might think that you can also use the last known good configuration if Windows Vista starts but is unstable, and you suspect a hardware change is causing the glitch. Unfortunately, that won't work because when you start Windows Vista successfully in Normal mode, the hardware change is added to the last known good configuration. To revert the system to a previous configuration when you can start Windows Vista successfully, you need to use the System Restore feature.

I showed you how to use System Restore to set restore points in Chapter 15 (refer to the "Setting System Restore Points" section). Remember, too, that Windows Vista creates automatic restore points each day and when you perform certain actions (such as installing an uncertified device driver). To revert your system to a restore point, follow these steps:

1. Select Start, All Programs, Accessories, System Tools, System Restore and then enter your UAC credentials to display the System Restore dialog box.
2. The first System Restore dialog box offers two options:

   Recommended Restore—Activate this option to restore Windows Vista to the restore point shown (which is usually the most recent restore point). Skip to Step 4.

   Choose a Different Restore Point—Activate this option to select from a list of restore points. Click Next to display the Chose a Restore Point dialog box, shown in Figure 16.5, and continue with step 3.
3. Click the restore point you want to use. There are five common types of restore points:

   System—A restore point that Windows Vista creates automatically. For example, the System Checkpoint is the restore point that Vista creates each day or when you boot your computer.

   Install—A restore point set prior to installing a program or update.

   Manual—A restore point you create yourself.

   Undo—A restore point set prior to a previous use of System Restore to revert the system to an earlier state.

   Unknown—Any restore point that doesn't fit in the above categories.

NOTE

By default, Windows Vista displays only the restore points from the previous five days. If you need to restore to an earlier date, activate the Show Restore Points Older Than 5 Days check box. Note that this check box only appears if you have at least one restore point that is more than five days old.

4. Click Next. If other hard disks are available in the restore point, Vista displays a list of the disks. Activate the check box beside each disk you want to include in the restore, and then click Next.
5. Click Finish. Vista asks you to confirm that you want your system restored.
6. Click Yes. System Restore begins reverting to the restore point. When it's done, it restarts your computer and displays a message telling you the results of the restore.
7. Click Close.

TIP

System Restore is available in Safe mode. So, if Windows Vista won't start properly, and if using the last known good configuration doesn't work, perform a Safe mode startup and run System Restore from there. If you can't start Vista at all, you can also run System Restore using the System Recovery Options, discussed in the next section.

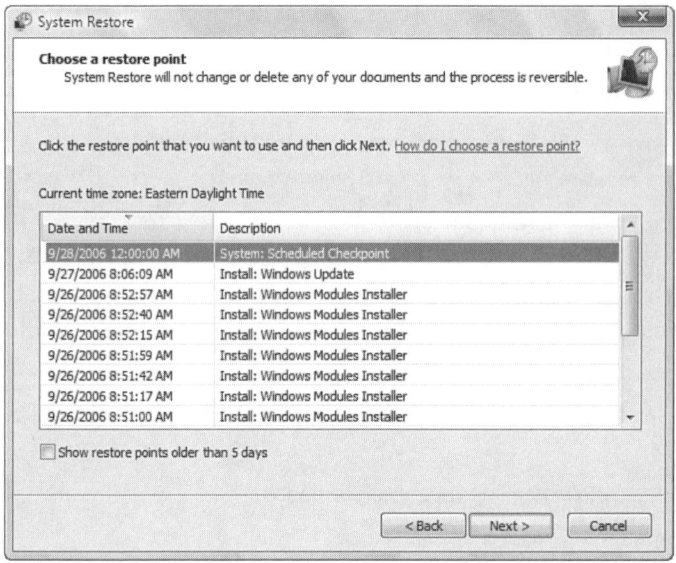

FIGURE 16.5 Use the Choose a Restore Point window to choose the restore point you want to revert to.

Recovering Using the System Recovery Options

If Windows Vista won't start normally, your first troubleshooting step is almost always to start the system in Safe mode. When you make it to Windows Vista, you can investigate the problem and make the necessary changes (such as disabling or rolling back a device driver). But what if your system won't even start in Safe mode?

Your next step should be booting with the last known good configuration. And if that doesn't work either? Don't worry, there's still hope in the form of the System Recovery Options, a utility that enables you to launch recovery tools or access the command line. Here's how to use it:

1. Insert the Windows Vista DVD.
2. Restart your computer. If your system prompts you to boot from the DVD, press the required key or key combination.

TIP

If your system won't boot from the Windows Vista DVD, you need to adjust the system's BIOS settings to allow this. Restart the computer and look for a startup message that prompts you to press a key or key combination to modify the BIOS settings (which might be called *Setup* or something similar). Find the boot options and either enable a DVD drive-based boot or make sure that the option to boot from the DVD drive comes before the option to boot from the hard disk. If you use a USB keyboard, you may also need to enable an option that lets the BIOS recognize keystrokes after the POST but before the OS starts.

3. In the initial Install Windows screen, click Next.
4. Click Repair Your Computer. If your system has multiple Vista partitions, you see a list of them.
5. Click the Vista partition you want to repair and click Next. The System Recovery Options window appears, as shown in Figure 16.6.

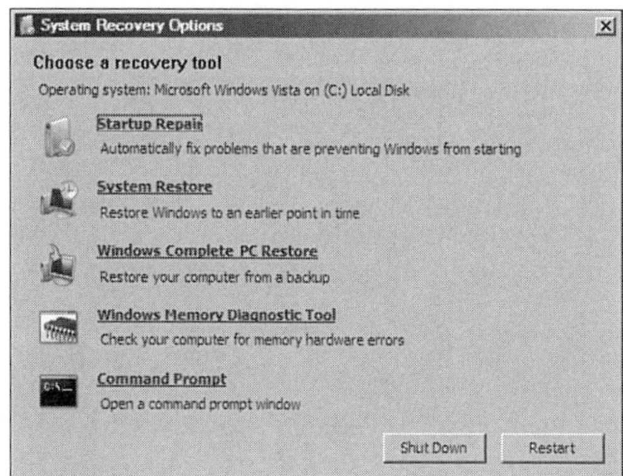

FIGURE 16.6 The System Recovery Options window offers several tools to help you get your system back on its feet.

The System Recovery Options window offers you the following five tools to help get your system back up and running:

Startup Repair—This tool checks your system for problems that might be preventing it from starting. If it finds any, it attempts to fix them automatically.

System Restore—This tool runs System Restore so that you can revert your system to a protection point (refer to "Recovering Using System Restore" earlier in this chapter).

Windows Complete PC Restore—This tool restores your system using a system image backup, which you learned how to create in Chapter 15 (refer to "Creating a System Image Backup").

Windows Memory Diagnostic Tool—This tool checks your computer's memory chips for faults, as described earlier (see "Running the Memory Diagnostics Tool").

Command Prompt—This tool takes you to the Windows Vista command prompt, where you can run commands such as CHKDSK. (See Appendix B, "Using the Windows Vista Command Prompt.")

From Here

Here's a list of other places in the book where you'll find information related to troubleshooting:

- In Chapter 2, refer to the "Troubleshooting Windows Vista Startup" section.
- In Chapter 5, refer to the "Practicing Safe Setups" section.
- In Chapter 11, refer to the "Keeping the Registry Safe" section.
- Refer to Chapter 15, "Maintaining Your Windows Vista System."
- In Chapter 17, see the "Troubleshooting Device Problems" section.
- In Chapter 24, see the "Repairing a Network Connection" section.

CHAPTER 17

Getting the Most Out of Device Manager

IN THIS CHAPTER

- Tips and Techniques for Installing Devices
- Managing Your Hardware with Device Manager
- Working with Device Security Policies
- Troubleshooting Device Problems

Man is a shrewd inventor, and is ever taking the hint of a new machine from his own structure, adapting some secret of his own anatomy in iron, wood, and leather, to some required function in the work of the world.

—Ralph Waldo Emerson

Emerson's concept of a machine was decidedly low-tech ("iron, wood, and leather"), but his basic idea is still apt in these high-tech times. Man has taken yet another "secret of his own anatomy"—the brain—and used it as the "hint of a new machine"—the computer. And although even the most advanced computer is still a mere toy compared to the breathtaking complexity of the human brain, some spectacular advancements have been made in the art of hardware in recent years.

One of the hats an operating system must wear is that of an intermediary between you (or your software) and your hardware. Any operating system worth its salt has to translate incomprehensible "device-speak" into something you can make sense out of, and it must ensure that devices are ready, willing, and able to carry out your commands. Given the sophistication and diversity of today's hardware market, however, that's no easy task.

The good news is that Windows Vista brings to the PC world support for a broad range of hardware, from everyday devices such as keyboards, mice, printers, monitors, and video, sound, memory, and network cards, to more exotic hardware fare such as IEEE 1394 (FireWire) controllers and infrared devices. However, although this hardware support is broad, it's not all that deep, meaning that Windows Vista doesn't have built-in support for many older devices. So, even though lots of hardware vendors have taken at least some steps toward upgrading their devices and drivers, managing hardware is still one of Windows Vista's trickier areas. This chapter should help as I take you through lots of practical techniques for installing, updating, and troubleshooting devices in Windows Vista.

Tips and Techniques for Installing Devices

When working with Windows 2000 and Windows NT, there was one cardinal rule for choosing a device to attach to your Windows XP system: Check the hardware compatibility list! This was a list of devices known to work with Windows. Like its operating system ancestors, Windows Vista also maintains a list of compatible hardware, only now it's called the **Windows Marketplace**. You can get to this website by using either of the following methods:

- Select Start, All Programs, Extras and Upgrades, Windows Marketplace
- Enter the following address in your web browser: `www.windowsmarketplace.com`

If you see your device (and, in some cases, the correct device version) in the hardware list, you can install it secure in the knowledge that it will work properly with Windows Vista. If you don't see the device, all is not lost because you still have two other options:

- Check the box for some indication that the device works with Windows Vista or contains drivers for Windows Vista. Seeing the Designed for Windows Vista logo on the box is the best way to be sure that the device works with Windows Vista.
- Check the manufacturer's website to see whether an updated Windows Vista driver or device setup program is available.

Installing Plug and Play Devices

There was a time when the Holy Grail of device configuration was a setup in which you need only to insert or plug in a peripheral and turn it on (if necessary), and your system configured the device automatically. In other words, the system not only recognized that a new device was attached to the machine, but it also gleaned the device's default resource configuration and, if required, resolved any conflicts that might have arisen with existing devices. And, of course, it could be able to perform all this magic without your ever having to flip a DIP switch, fiddle with a jumper, or fuss with various IRQ, I/O port, and DMA combinations.

Plug and Play was an attempt by members of the PC community to reach this Zen-like hardware state. Did they succeed? Since its initial support in Windows 95, it has taken time to get right, but yes, Plug and Play works like a charm. But only if your Windows Vista system meets the following criteria:

- **It has a Plug and Play BIOS**—One of the first things that happens inside your computer when you turn it on (or do a hardware reboot) is the ROM BIOS (basic input/output system) code performs a Power-On Self Test to check the system hardware. If you have a system with a Plug and Play BIOS (and any system capable of running Vista should have one), the initial code also enumerates and tests all the Plug and Play–compliant devices on the system. For each device, the BIOS not only activates the device, but also gathers the device's resource configuration (IRQ, I/O ports, and so forth). When all the Plug and Play devices have been isolated, the BIOS then checks for resource conflicts and, if there are any, takes steps to resolve them.

- **It uses Plug and Play devices**—Plug and Play devices are the extroverts of the hardware world. They're only too happy to chat with any old Plug and Play BIOS or operating system that happens along. What do they chat about? The device essentially identifies itself to the BIOS (or the operating system if the BIOS isn't Plug and Play–compliant) by sending its **configuration ID**, which tells the BIOS what the device is and which resources it uses. The BIOS then configures the system's resources accordingly.

Plug and Play is built in to every device that connects via a USB or IEEE 1394 port, and it comes with all PC Card devices and almost all interface cards that connect to the PCI, AGP, or PCI Express buses. Other devices that connect via the serial, parallel, or PS/2 ports aren't necessarily Plug and Play–compliant, but almost all of these devices manufactured in the past few years are. Interface cards that connect to the legacy ISA bus are not Plug and Play–compliant.

Before you install a Plug and Play device, check to see whether the hardware came with a setup program on a floppy disk, a CD, or as part of the downloaded package. If it did, run that program and, if you're given any setup options, be sure to install at least the device driver. Having the driver loaded on the system helps Windows Vista install the device automatically.

How Windows reacts when you install a Plug and Play device designed for Windows Vista depends on how you installed the device:

- If you **hot-swapped** a device such as a USB device, a PC Card, or flash drive, Windows Vista recognizes the device immediately and installs the driver for it.
- If you turned your computer off to install the device, Windows Vista recognizes it the next time you start the machine, and installs the appropriate driver.

Either way, an icon appears in the notification area and a balloon tip titled Installing Device Drivers Software appears. When the installation is complete, you see another balloon that says Your Devices Are Ready to Use.

If Windows Vista did not find a device driver for the new hardware, it automatically runs the Found New Hardware wizard. The wizard first gives you three choices, as shown in Figure 17.1:

Locate and Install Driver Software—Click this option to begin the device driver installation process.

Ask Me Again Later—Click this option to avoid installing the device driver now (for example, you might be waiting for the drivers to arrive via the mail or a lengthy download). Vista will prompt you again the next time you plug in the device (or the next time you log on to Vista if you leave the device plugged in).

Don't Show This Message Again for This Device—Click this option to bypass the driver installation. For example, this is the path to choose if the device comes with a separate installation CD.

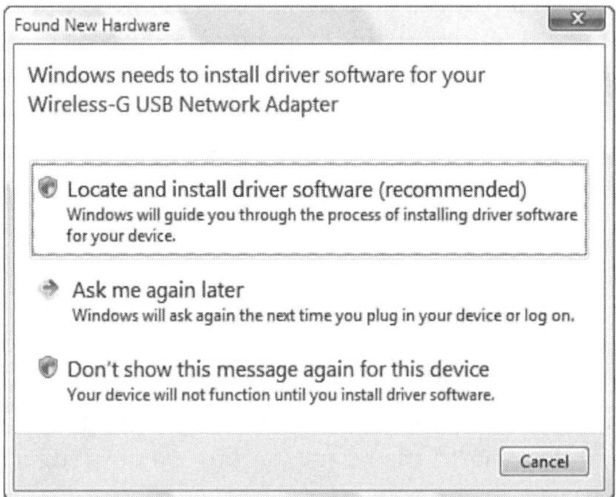

FIGURE 17.1 The Found New Hardware Wizard appears if Windows Vista can't install the device's driver automatically.

In most cases, you'll click the Locate and Install Driver Software option. After you enter your User Account Control credentials, Vista checks Windows Update for a driver. If it finds one, it installs the driver automatically.

NOTE

If you want total control over the driver installation process, you can tell Vista not to install Windows Update drivers automatically. See "Checking Windows Update for Drivers," later in this chapter.

If Vista can't find a driver on Windows Update, it prompts you to insert the disc that came with your device, as shown in Figure 17.2. If you insert a CD, in most cases Vista will recognize the CD and search it automatically for drivers. If Vista doesn't start checking the CD automatically, or if you have a floppy disk instead, click Next to prod Vista into checking for drivers.

If you don't have a disc, follow these steps to continue:

1. Click the I Don't Have the Disc. Show Me Other Options link.
2. The Found New Hardware Wizard now gives you two choices:

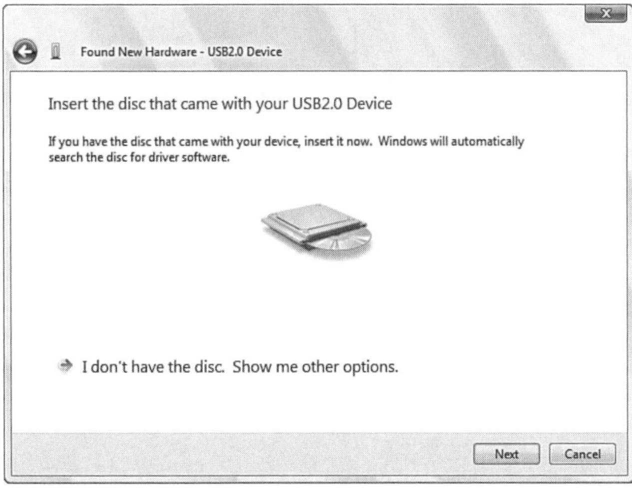

FIGURE 17.2 If Vista can't install a driver from Windows Update, it prompts you to insert the disc that came with your device.

Check for a Solution—Click this option if you think a problem is preventing Windows Vista from installing the device driver. The wizard will check to see whether the problem has a solution. If you select this option, follow the instructions that appear onscreen and skip the rest of these steps.

Browse My Computer for Driver Software—Click this option to install a driver that resides on your computer or in a shared network folder. If you select this option, continue with step 3.

CAUTION

If the downloaded driver is contained within a compressed file (such as a ZIP file), be sure to decompress the file before moving on to the next wizard step.

3. In the Browse for Driver Software on Your Computer dialog box, shown in Figure 17.3, type the location of the driver files and click Next. Windows Vista installs the driver software.
4. When the installation is complete, click Close.

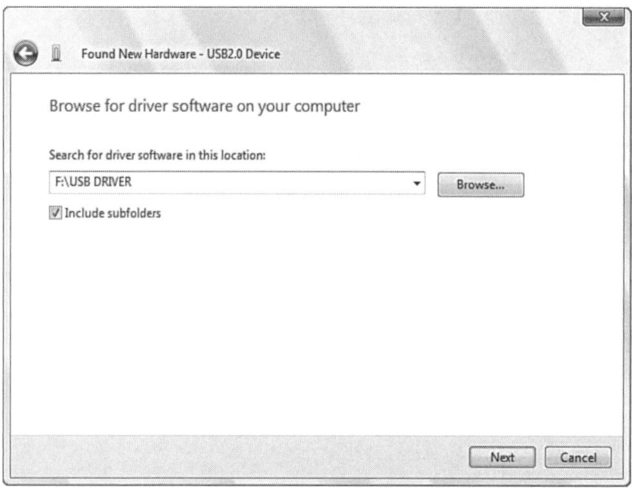

FIGURE 17.3 This dialog box appears if you elected to install the device driver from a location on your computer.

Installing Legacy Devices

When it comes to installing legacy devices (that is, devices that don't support Plug and Play), your best bet by far is to run the setup program that the manufacturer supplies either on a floppy disk, a CD, or as part of the driver download. If asked, choose the Windows Vista driver, if one is available. If no Windows Vista driver is available, the Windows XP driver will work in most cases. If the device has drivers only for Windows 2000, NT, Windows 9x, or Windows Me, they probably will not work with Windows Vista, so there's no point in installing them. Go to the manufacturer's website and look for a Windows Vista (or, at worst, a Windows XP) driver to download.

If you don't have a setup program for the device, Windows Vista might still be able to support the hardware using one of its legacy device drivers. To do this, you need to run one of Windows Vista's hardware wizards. Some of these wizards are device-specific, so you should use those where appropriate:

- **Modem**—Select Start, Control Panel. Hardware and Sound, Phone and Modem Options icon, display the Modems tab, and click Add
- **Printer**—Select Start, Control Panel, Printers and then click the Add a Printer link
- **Scanner or digital camera**—Select Start, Control Panel. Hardware and Sound, Scanners and Cameras icon, and then click Add Device

For all other devices, connect the device and then run the Add Hardware Wizard:

1. Launch Device Manager as described later in this chapter (see "Managing Your Hardware with Device Manager").

2. Click any item in the Device Manager tree.
3. Select Action, Add Legacy Hardware. Vista starts the Add Hardware Wizard.
4. In the wizard's initial dialog box, click Next.
5. You now have two choices:

   Search for and Install the Hardware Automatically—Activate this option if you have a device that the wizard is capable of locating using hardware detection. This route often works with modems, printers, video cards, and network cards. Click Next to start the detection process. If the detection fails, the wizard will let you know. In this case, click Next and proceed with step 6.

   Install the Hardware That I Manually Select from a List—Activate this option to pick out the device by hand. Click Next.

6. Select the hardware category that applies to your device. If you don't see an appropriate category, select Show All Devices. Click Next.
7. Depending on the hardware category you selected, a new wizard might appear. (For example, if you chose the Modems category, the Install New Modem Wizard appears.) In this case, follow the wizard's dialog boxes. Otherwise, a dialog box appears with a list of manufacturers and models. You have two choices:
   - Specify your device by first selecting the device's manufacturer in the Manufacturers list and then selecting the name of the device in the Models list.
   - If you have a manufacturer's floppy disk, CD, or downloaded file, click Have Disk, enter the appropriate path and filename in the Install from Disk dialog box, and click OK.
8. Click Next. Windows Vista installs the device.
9. Click Finish to complete the wizard.

Controlling Driver Signing Options

Device drivers that meet the Designed for Windows Vista specifications have been tested for compatibility with Microsoft and then given a digital signature. This signature tells you that the driver works properly with Windows Vista and that it hasn't been changed since it was tested. (For example, the driver hasn't been infected by a virus or Trojan horse program.) When you're installing a device, if Windows Vista comes across a driver that has not been digitally signed, it displays a dialog box similar to the one shown in Figure 17.4.

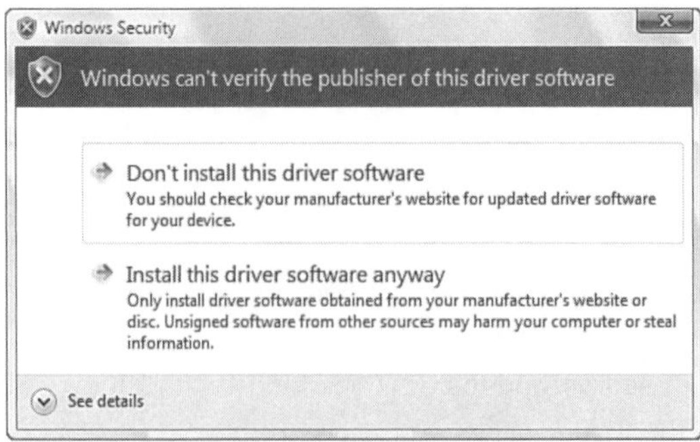

FIGURE 17.4 Windows Vista displays a dialog box similar to this one when it comes across a device driver that does not have a digital signature.

If you click Don't Install this Driver Software, Windows Vista aborts the driver installation and you won't be able to use the device. This is the most prudent choice in this situation because an unsigned driver can cause all kinds of havoc, including lock-ups, **BSODs** (Blue Screens of Death), and other system instabilities. You should check the manufacturer's website for a Windows Vista–compatible driver, or upgrade to newer hardware that's supported by Windows Vista.

Having said all that, although not installing an unsigned driver is the *prudent* choice, it's not the most *convenient* choice because in most cases you probably want to use the device now rather than later. The truth is that *most* of the time these unsigned drivers cause no problems and work as advertised, so it's probably safe to continue with the installation. In any case, Windows Vista always sets a restore point prior to the installation of an unsigned driver, so you can always restore your system to its previous state should anything go wrong.

NOTE

Test your system thoroughly after installing the driver: Use the device, open and use your most common applications, and run some disk utilities. If anything seems awry, use the restore point to roll back the system to its previous configuration.

By default, Windows Vista gives you the option of either continuing or aborting the installation of the unsigned driver. You can change this behavior to automatically accept or reject all unsigned drivers by following these steps:

1. Press Windows Logo+R (or select Start, All Programs, Accessories, Run) to open the Run dialog box, type **gpedit.msc**, and click OK to launch the Group Policy Object Editor.

2. Open the User Configuration\Administrative Templates\System\Driver Installation branch.

3. Double-click the Code Signing for Device Drivers policy. Windows Vista displays the Code Signing for Device Drivers Properties dialog box.
4. Click Enable.
5. Use the When Windows Detects a Driver File Without a Digital Signature list to select one of the following items:

   Ignore—Choose this option if you want Windows Vista to install all unsigned drivers.

   Warn—Choose this option if you want Windows Vista to warn you about an unsigned driver by displaying the dialog box in Figure 17.4.

   Block—Choose this option if you want Windows Vista not to install any unsigned drivers.
6. Click OK.

TIP

There are some device drivers that Windows Vista knows will cause system instabilities. Windows Vista will simply refuse to load these problematic drivers, no matter which action you choose in the Driver Signing Options dialog box. In this case, you'll see a dialog box similar to the one in Figure 17.4, except this one tells you that the driver will not be installed and your only choice is to cancel the installation.

Managing Your Hardware with Device Manager

Windows Vista stores all its hardware data in the Registry, but it provides Device Manager to give you a graphical view of the devices on your system. To display Device Manager, first use any of the following techniques:

- Select Start, Control Panel, Hardware and Sound, Device Manager.
- Select Start, Control Panel, System and Maintenance, System (or click Start, right-click Computer, and then click Properties), and then click Device Manager.
- Select Start, right-click Computer, and click Manage. In the Computer Management window, click the Device Manager branch.
- Select Start, Control Panel, System and Maintenance, System (or click Start, right-click Computer, and then click Properties), and then click Advanced System Settings. In the System Properties dialog box that appears, display the Hardware tab and then click Device Manager.

Note that in all cases Vista at some point prompts you to enter your UAC credentials.

TIP

A quick way to go directly to the Device Manager snap-in is to press Windows Logo+R (or select Start, All Programs, Accessories, Run) to open the Run dialog box, type **devmgmt.msc**, and click OK. Note, too, that you can display the System window quickly by pressing Windows Logo+Pause/Break.

Device Manager's default display is a tree-like outline that lists various hardware types. To see the specific devices, click the plus sign (+) to the left of a device type. For example, opening the DVD/CD-ROM Drives branch displays all the DVD and CD-ROM drives attached to your computer, as shown in Figure 17.5.

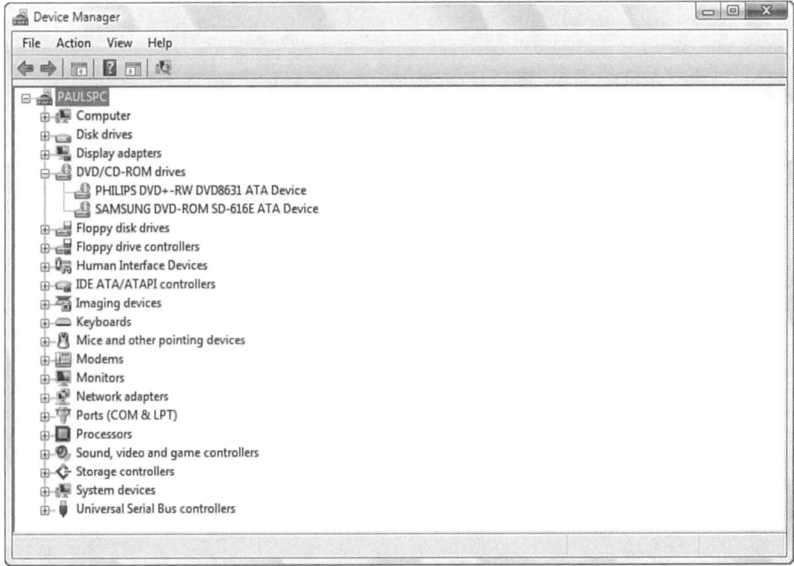

FIGURE 17.5 Device Manager organizes your computer's hardware in a tree-like hierarchy organized by hardware type.

Controlling the Device Display

Device Manager's default view is by hardware type, but it also offers several other views, all of which are available on the snap-in's View menu:

Devices by Connection	This view displays devices according to what they are connected to within your computer. For example, to see which devices connect to the PCI bus, on most systems you'd open the ACPI branch, and then the Microsoft ACPI-Compliant System branch, and finally the PCI Bus branch.

Resources by Type	This view displays devices according to the **hardware resources** they require. Your computer's resources are the communications channels by which devices communicate back and forth with software. There are four types: Interrupt Request (IRQ), Input/Output (IO), Direct memory access (DMA), and Memory (a portion of the computer's memory that's allocated to the device and is used to store device data).
Resources by Connection	This view displays the computer's allocated resources according to how they're connected within the computer.
Show Hidden Devices	When you activate this command, Device Manager displays those non–Plug and Play devices that you normally don't need to adjust or troubleshoot. It also displays **nonpresent devices**, which are those that have been installed but aren't currently attached to the computer.

Viewing Device Properties

Each device listed in Device Manager has its own properties sheet. You can use these properties not only to learn more about the device (such as the resources it's currently using), but also to make adjustments to the device's resources, change the device driver, alter the device's settings (if it has any), and make other changes.

To display the properties sheet for a device, double-click the device or click the device and then select Action, Properties. The number of tabs you see depends on the hardware, but most devices have at least the following:

General	This tab gives you general information such as the name of the device, its hardware type, and the manufacturer's name. The Device Status group tells you whether the device is working properly, and gives you status information if it's not (see "Troubleshooting with Device Manager," later in this chapter).
Driver	This tab gives you information about the device driver and offers several buttons to managing the driver. See "Working with Device Drivers," next.
Resources	This tab tells you the hardware resources used by the device.

Working with Device Drivers

For most users, device drivers exist in the nether regions of the PC world, shrouded in obscurity and the mysteries of assembly language programming. As the middlemen brokering the dialogue between Windows Vista and our hardware, however, these complex chunks of code perform a crucial task. After all, it's just not possible to unleash the full potential of your system unless the hardware and the operating system coexist harmoniously and optimally. To that end, you need to ensure that Windows Vista is using appropriate drivers for all your hardware. You do that by updating to the latest drivers and by rolling back drivers that aren't working properly.

Checking Windows Update for Drivers

Before getting to the driver tasks that Vista offers, recall that earlier in this chapter I told you that if Vista can't find drivers when you initially attach a device, it automatically checks Windows Update to see whether any drivers are available. If Vista finds a driver, it installs the software automatically. In most cases, this is desirable behavior because it requires almost no input from you. However, lots of people don't like to use Windows on automatic pilot all the time because doing so can lead to problems. In this case, it could be that you've downloaded the driver you actually want to use from the manufacturer's website, so you don't want whatever is on Windows Update to be installed.

To gain control over Windows Update driver downloads, follow these steps:

1. Select Start, right-click Computer, and then click Properties to open the System window.
2. Click Advanced System Settings and then enter your UAC credentials to display the System Properties dialog box.
3. Display the Hardware tab.
4. Click Windows Update Driver Settings. Vista displays the Windows Update Driver Settings dialog box, shown in Figure 17.6.

FIGURE 17.6 Use the Windows Update Driver Settings dialog box to control how Vista uses Windows Update to locate and install device drivers.

5. You have three choices:

   Check for Drivers Automatically—This is the default setting and it tells Vista to go ahead and locate and install Windows Update drivers each time you attach a new device.

Ask Me Each Time I Connect a New Device Before Checking for Drivers—Activate this option to tell Vista to prompt you before it connects to Windows Update for drivers. If you want to control Windows Update driver installation, this is the ideal setting because it enables you to prevent those installs when you don't need them, and to approve those installs when you do.

Never Check for Drivers When I Connect a Device—Activate this option to tell Vista to bypass Windows Update for all new devices. Use this option if you always use the manufacturer's device driver, whether it's on a disc that comes with the device or via the manufacturer's website.

6. Click OK.

If you activated the Ask Me Each Time I Connect a New Device Before Checking for Drivers option, the next time you attach a device for which Vista can't install drivers automatically, you see a Found New Hardware dialog box similar to the one shown in Figure 17.7. You have three choices:

Yes, Always Search Online—Click this option to restore the automatic Windows Update driver installation. (This is the same as choosing the Check for Drivers Automatically option in the Windows Update Driver Settings dialog box.)

Yes, Search Online This Time Only—Click this option to have Vista search Windows Update for drivers only for the current device. (This is the same as choosing the Ask Me Each Time I Connect a New Device Before Checking for Drivers option in the Windows Update Driver Settings dialog box.)

Don't Search Online—Click this option to bypass Windows Update for this device.

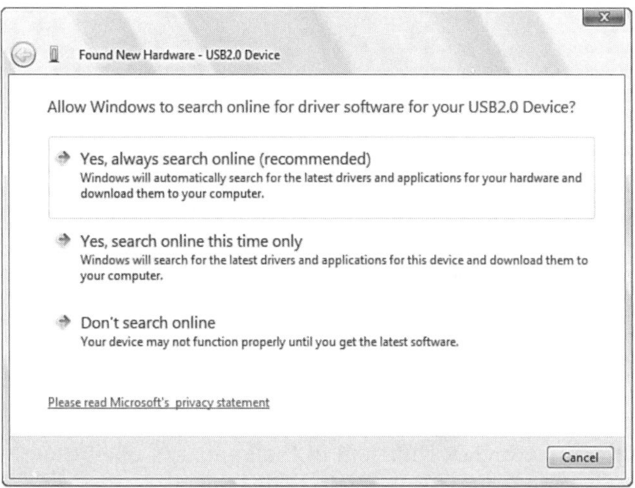

FIGURE 17.7 You see this dialog box if you opted to have Vista prompt you to check for drivers on Windows Update.

Updating a Device Driver

Follow these steps to update a device driver:

1. If you have a disc with the updated driver, insert it. If you downloaded the driver from the Internet, decompress the driver file, if necessary.
2. In Device Manager, click the device with which you want to work.
3. Select Action, Update Driver Software. (You can also click the Update Driver Software button in the toolbar or open the device's properties sheet, display the Driver tab, and click Update Driver.) The Update Driver Software wizard appears.
4. This wizard works the same way as the Found New Hardware Wizard discussed earlier in this chapter, so follow the instructions given in the "Installing Plug and Play Devices" section.

Rolling Back a Device Driver

If an updated device driver is giving you problems, you have two ways to fix things:

- If updating the driver was the last action you performed on the system, restore the system to most recent restore point.
- If you've updated other things on the system in the meantime, a restore point might restore more than you need. In that case, you need to roll back just the device driver that's causing problems.

Follow these steps to roll back a device driver:

1. In Device Manager, open the device's properties sheet.
2. Display the Driver tab.
3. Click Roll Back Driver.

Uninstalling a Device

When you remove a Plug and Play device, the BIOS informs Windows Vista that the device is no longer present. Windows Vista, in turn, updates its device list in the Registry, and the peripheral no longer appears in the Device Manager display.

If you're removing a legacy device, however, you need to tell Device Manager that the device no longer exists. To do that, follow these steps:

1. Click the device in the Device Manager tree.
2. Select Action, Uninstall. (Alternatively, click Uninstall in the toolbar or open the device's properties sheet, display the Driver tab, and click Uninstall.)
3. When Windows Vista warns you that you're about to remove the device, click OK.

Working with Device Security Policies

The Group Policy editor offers several device-related policies. To see them, open the Group Policy editor and select Local Computer Policy, Computer Configuration, Windows Settings, Security Settings, Local Policies, Security Options. Here are the policies in the Devices category:

Policy	Description
Allow Undock Without Having to Log On	When this policy is enabled, users can undock a notebook computer without having to log on to Windows Vista (that is, they can undock the computer by pressing the docking station's eject button). If you want to restrict who can do this, disable this policy.

TIP

To control who can undock the computer, display Local Computer Policy, Computer Configuration, Windows Settings, Security Settings, Local Policies, User Rights Assignment. Use the Remove Computer from Docking Station policy to assign the users or groups who have this right.

Policy	Description
Allowed to Format and Eject Removable Media	Use this policy to determine the groups allowed to format floppy disks and eject CDs and other removable media.
Prevent Users from Installing Printer Drivers	Enable this policy to prevent users from installing a network printer. Note that this doesn't affect the installation of a local printer.
Restrict CD-ROM Access to Locally Logged-On User Only	Enable this policy to prevent network users from operating the computer's CD-ROM or DVD drive at the same time as a local user. If no local user is accessing the drive, the network user can access it.
Restrict Floppy Access to Locally Logged-On User Only	Enable this policy to prevent network users from operating the computer's floppy drive at the same time as a local user. If no local user is accessing the drive, the network user can access it.

Troubleshooting Device Problems

Windows Vista has excellent support for most newer devices, and most major hardware vendors have taken steps to update their devices and drivers to run properly with Windows Vista. If you use only recent, Plug and Play–compliant devices that qualify for the Designed for Windows Vista logo, you should have a trouble-free computing experience (at least from a hardware perspective). Of course, putting *trouble-free* and *computing* next to each other is just asking for trouble. Hardware is not foolproof; far from it. Things still can, and will, go wrong, and, when they do, you'll need to perform some kind of troubleshooting. (Assuming, of course, that the device doesn't have a physical fault that requires a trip to the repair shop.) Fortunately, Windows Vista also has some handy tools to help you both identify and rectify hardware ills.

Troubleshooting with Device Manager

Device Manager not only provides you with a comprehensive summary of your system's hardware data, it also doubles as a decent troubleshooting tool. To see what I mean, check out the Device Manager tab shown in Figure 17.8. See how the icon for the Atheros AR5006X Wireless Network Adapter device has an exclamation mark superimposed on it? This tells you that there's a problem with the device.

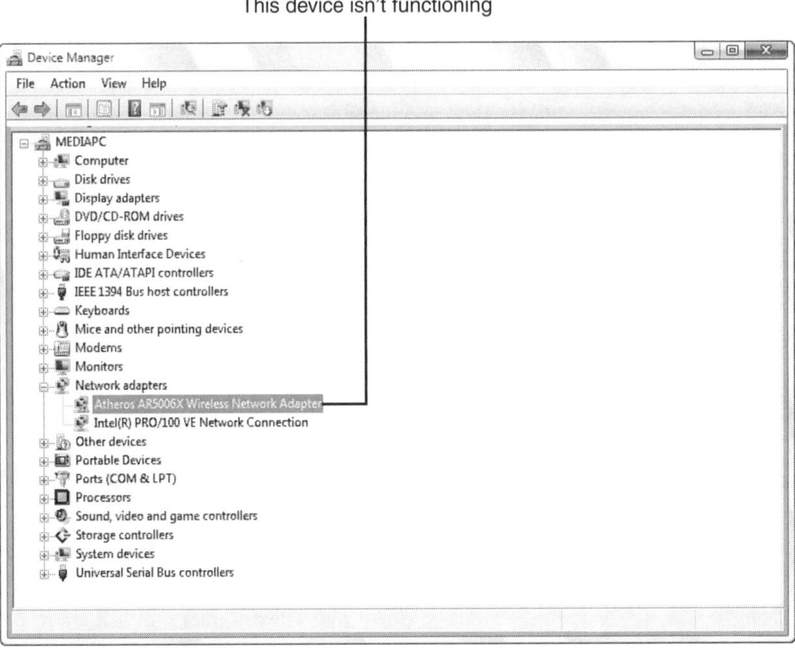

FIGURE 17.8 The Device Manager uses icons to warn you there's a problem with a device.

If you examine the device's properties, as shown in Figure 17.9, the Device Status area tells you a bit more about what's wrong. As you can see in Figure 17.9, the problem here is that the device won't start. Either try Device Manager's suggested remedy or click the Check for Solutions button to see whether Microsoft has a fix for the problem.

NOTE

Device Manager has several dozen error codes. See the following Microsoft Knowledge Base article for a complete list of the codes as well as solutions to try in each case: support.microsoft.com/default.aspx?scid=kb;en-us;Q310123.

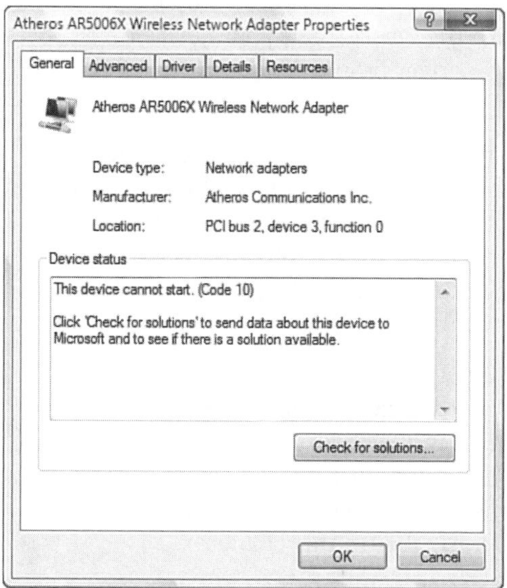

FIGURE 17.9 The Device Status area tells you if the device isn't working properly.

Device Manager uses three different icons to give you an indication of the device's current status:

- A black exclamation mark (!) on a yellow field tells you that there's a problem with the device.
- A red X tells you that the device is disabled or missing.
- A blue i on a white field tells you that the device's Use Automatic Settings check box (on the Resources tab) is deactivated and that at least one of the device's resources was selected manually. Note that the device might be working just fine, so this icon doesn't indicate a problem. If the device isn't working properly, however, the manual setting might be the cause. (For example, the device might have a DIP switch or jumper set to a different resource.)

If your system flags a device, but you don't notice any problems, you can usually get away with just ignoring the flag. I've seen lots of systems that run perfectly well with flagged devices, so this falls under the "If it ain't broke..." school of troubleshooting. The danger here is that tweaking your system to try and get rid of the flag can cause other—usually more serious—problems.

Troubleshooting Device Driver Problems

Other than problems with the hardware itself, device drivers are the cause of most device woes. This is true even if your device doesn't have one of the problem icons that I mentioned in the previous section. That is, if you open the device's properties sheet, Vista may tell you that the device is "working properly," but all that means is that Vista can establish a simple communications channel with the device. So if your device isn't working right, but Vista says otherwise, suspect a driver problem. Here are a few tips and pointers for correcting device driver problems:

- **Reinstall the driver**—A driver might be malfunctioning because one or more of its files have become corrupted. You can usually solve this by reinstalling the driver. Just in case a disk fault caused the corruption, you should check the partition where the driver is installed for errors before reinstalling. (In Chapter 15, "Maintaining Your Windows Vista System," see the "Checking Your Hard Disk for Errors" section for instructions on checking a disk for errors.)

- **Upgrade to a signed driver**—Unsigned drivers are accidents waiting for a place to happen in Windows Vista, so you should upgrade to a signed driver, if possible. How can you tell whether an installed driver is unsigned? Open the device's properties sheet, and display the Driver tab. Signed driver files display a name beside the Digital Signer label, whereas unsigned drivers display `Not digitally signed` instead. Refer to "Updating a Device Driver," earlier in this chapter.

- **Disable an unsigned driver**—If an unsigned driver is causing system instability and you can't upgrade the driver, try disabling it. In the Driver tab of the device's properties sheet, click Disable.

- **Use the Signature Verification Tool**—This program checks your entire system for unsigned drivers. To use it, press Windows Logo+R (or select Start, All Programs, Accessories, Run) to open the Run dialog box, type **`sigverif`**, and click OK. In the File Signature Verification window, click Start. When the verification is complete, the program displays a list of the unsigned driver files (if any). The results for all the scanned files are written to the log file `Sigverif.txt`, which is copied to the `%SystemRoot%` folder when you close the window that shows the list of unsigned drivers. In the Status column of `Sigverif.txt`, look for files listed as `Not Signed`. If you find any, consider upgrading these drivers to signed versions.

- **Try the manufacturer's driver supplied with the device**—If the device came with its own driver, try either updating the driver to the manufacturer's or running the device's setup program.

- **Download the latest driver from the manufacturer**—Device manufacturers often update drivers to fix bugs, add new features, and tweak performance. Go to the manufacturer's website to see whether an updated driver is available. (See "Tips for Downloading Device Drivers," next.)
- **Try Windows Update**—The Windows Update website often has updated drivers for downloading. Select Start, All Programs, Windows Update and let the site scan your system. Then click the Driver Updates link to see which drivers are available for your system.
- **Roll back a driver**—If the device stops working properly after you update the driver, try rolling it back to the old driver. (Refer to "Rolling Back a Device Driver," earlier in this chapter.)

Tips for Downloading Device Drivers

Finding device drivers on the World Wide Web is an art in itself. I can't tell you how much of my life I've wasted rooting around manufacturer websites trying to locate a device driver. Most hardware vendor sites seem to be optimized for sales rather than service, so although you can purchase, say, a new printer with just a mouse click or two, downloading a new driver for that printer can take a frustratingly long time. To help you avoid such frustration, here are some tips from my hard-won experience:

- If the manufacturer offers different sites for different locations (such as different countries), always use the company's "home" site. Most mirror sites aren't true mirrors, and (Murphy's Law still being in effect) it's usually the driver you're looking for that a mirror site is missing.
- The temptation when you first enter a site is to use the search feature to find what you want. This works only sporadically for drivers, and the site search engines almost always return marketing or sales material first.
- Instead of the search engine, look for an area of the site dedicated to driver downloads. The good sites will have links to areas called Downloads or Drivers, but it's far more common to have to go through a Support or Customer Service area first.
- Don't try to take any shortcuts to where you *think* the driver might be hiding. Trudge through each step the site provides. For example, it's common to have to select an overall driver category, and then a device category, and then a line category, and then the specific model you have. This is tedious, but it almost always gets you where you want to go.
- If the site is particularly ornery, the preceding method might not lead you to your device. In that case, try the search engine. Note that device drivers seem to be particularly poorly indexed, so you might have to try lots of search text variations. One thing that usually works is searching for the exact filename. How can you possibly know that? A method that often works for me is to use Google (www.google.com) or Google Groups (groups.google.com) or some other web search engine to search for your driver. Chances are someone else has looked for your file

and will have the filename (or, if you're really lucky, a direct link to the driver on the manufacturer's site).

- When you get to the device's download page, be careful which file you choose. Make sure that it's a Vista driver, and make sure that you're not downloading a utility program or some other nondriver file.
- When you finally get to download the file, be sure to save it to your computer rather than opening it. If you reformat your system or move the device to another computer, you'll be glad you have a local copy of the driver so that you don't have to wrestle with the whole download rigmarole all over again.

Troubleshooting Resource Conflicts

On modern computer systems that support the Advanced Configuration and Power Interface (ACPI), use PCI cards, and external Plug and Play–compliant devices, resource conflicts have become almost nonexistent. That's because the ACPI is capable of managing the system's resources to avoid conflicts. For example, if a system doesn't have enough IRQ lines, ACPI will assign two or more devices to the same IRQ line and manage the devices so that they can share the line without conflicting with each other. (To see which devices share an IRQ line, activate Device Manager's View, Resources by Connection command, and then double-click the Interrupt Request (IRQ) item.)

ACPI's success at allocating and managing resources is such that Windows Vista doesn't allow you to change a device's resources, even if you'd want to do such a thing. If you open a device's properties sheet and display the Resources tab, you'll see that none of the settings can be changed.

If you use legacy devices in your system, however, conflicts could arise because Windows Vista is unable to manage the device's resources properly. If that happens, Device Manager will let you know there's a problem. To solve it, first display the Resources tab on the device's properties sheet. The Resource Settings list shows you the resource type on the left and the resource setting on the right. If you suspect that the device has a resource conflict, check the Conflicting Device List box to see whether it lists any devices. If the list displays only `No conflicts`, the device's resources aren't conflicting with another device.

If there is a conflict, you need to change the appropriate resource. Some devices have multiple configurations, so one easy way to change resources is to select a different configuration. To try this, deactivate the Use Automatic Settings check box and then use the Setting Based On drop-down list to select a different configuration. Otherwise, you need to play around with the resource settings by hand. Here are the steps to follow to change a resource setting:

1. In the Resource Type list, select the resource you want to change.
2. Deactivate the Use Automatic Settings check box, if it's activated.

3. For the setting you want to change, either double-click it or select it and then click the Change Setting button. (If Windows Vista tells you that you can't modify the resources in this configuration, select a different configuration from the Setting Based On list.) A dialog box appears that enables you to edit the resource setting.
4. Use the Value spin box to select a different resource. Watch the Conflict Information group to make sure that your new setting doesn't step on the toes of an existing setting.
5. Click OK to return to the Resources tab.
6. Click OK. If Windows Vista asks whether you want to restart your computer, click Yes.

TIP

An easy way to see which devices are either sharing resources or are conflicting is via the System Information utility. Select Start, Run, type **`msinfo32`**, and click OK. (Alternatively, select Start, All Programs, Accessories, System Tools, System Information.) Open the Hardware Resources branch and then click Conflicts/Sharing.

From Here

Here's a list of places elsewhere in the book where you'll find information related to devices:

- For hard disk techniques, refer to "Optimizing the Hard Disk" in Chapter 14, "Tuning Windows Vista's Performance," and "Checking Your Hard Disk for Errors" in Chapter 15, "Maintaining Your Windows Vista System."
- For other troubleshooting techniques, refer to Chapter 16, "Troubleshooting and Recovering from Problems."
- For information on networking hardware, see the "Hardware: NICs and Other Network Knickknacks" section in Chapter 22, "Setting Up a Small Network."

PART IV

Unleashing Windows Vista for the Internet

CHAPTER 18

Exploring the Web with Internet Explorer

IN THIS CHAPTER

- Understanding Web Page Addresses
- Tips and Techniques for Better Web Surfing
- Searching the Web
- The Favorites Folder: Sites to Remember
- Working with RSS Feeds
- Customizing Internet Explorer

As I write this, Internet Explorer is by far the most dominant web browser with, depending on which source you use, anywhere from 80% to 85% of the market. (This is down about 10% since the release of the Firefox browser in late 2004.) And because most computer-savvy people have also been on the Internet for a number of years, it's safe to say that Internet Explorer is probably one of the most familiar applications available today. Or perhaps I should say that the *basics* of Internet Explorer are familiar to most people. However, as with any complex program, there are hidden pockets of the browser that most people don't know about. Significantly, many of these seldom-seen areas are not as obscure as you might think. You can put many of these features to good use immediately to make your web surfing easier, more efficient, and more productive. In this chapter, I take you on a tour of a few of my favorite Internet Explorer nooks and crannies and I show you how they can improve your web experience. You also learn about several of the new features that come with Internet Explorer 7, the latest version of Microsoft's Web browser, which comes with all versions of Windows Vista.

Understanding Web Page Addresses

Let's begin by examining that strange creature, the World Wide Web address, officially known as a **Uniform Resource Locator** (**URL**). A web page's address usually takes the following form:

http://*host.domain*/*directory*/*file.name*

host.domain	The domain name of the host computer where the page resides.
directory	The host computer directory that contains the page.
file.name	The page's filename. Note that most web pages use the extensions `.html` and `.htm`.

Here are some notes about URLs:

- The *http* part of the URL signifies that **HTTP** (**Hypertext Transfer Protocol**) is the TCP/IP protocol to use for communication between the web browser and the web server. HTTP is the protocol for standard web pages. Other common protocols are **https** (**Secure Hypertext Transfer Protocol**; secure web pages), **ftp** (**File Transfer Protocol**; file downloads), and **file** (for opening local files within the browser).
- Most web domains use the www prefix and the com suffix (for example, www.mcfedries.com). Other popular suffixes are edu (educational sites), gov (government sites), net (networking companies), and org (not-for-profit sites). Note, too, that most servers don't require the www prefix (for example, mcfedries.com).
- Directory names and filenames are case sensitive on most web hosts (those that run UNIX servers, anyway).

NOTE

Most websites use one or more default filenames, the most common of which are `index.html` and `index.htm`. If you omit the filename from the URL, the web server displays the default page.

Tips and Techniques for Better Web Surfing

Surfing web pages with Internet Explorer is straightforward and easy, but even experienced users might not be aware of all the ways that they can open and navigate pages. Here's a review of all the techniques you can use to open a web page in Windows Vista:

- **Type a URL in any Address bar**—Internet Explorer and all Windows Vista folder windows have an Address bar. To open a page, type the URL in the Address bar and press the Enter key.
- **Type a URL in the Run dialog box**—Press Windows Logo+R (or select Start, All Programs, Accessories, Run), type the URL you want in the Run dialog box, and click OK.

CAUTION

When you type a URL in the Run dialog box, you must include the "www" portion of the address. For example, typing **microsoft.com** won't work, but typing **www.microsoft.com** will. If the URL doesn't have a "www" component—for example, support.microsoft.com—you must include add "http://" to the front of the address.

- **Select a URL from the Address bar**—Internet Explorer's Address bar doubles as a drop-down list that holds the last 25 addresses you entered.
- **Use the Open dialog box for remote pages**—Press Ctrl+O to display the Open dialog box, type the URL, and click OK.
- **Use the Open dialog box for local pages**—If you want to view a web page that's on your computer, display the Open dialog box, enter the full path (drive, folder, and filename), and click OK. Alternatively, click Browse, find the page, click Open, and then click OK.
- **Select a favorite**—Press Alt+C to open the Favorites Center, click the Favorites button, and then click the site you want to open.
- **Click a Links bar button**—If you've added buttons to the Links bar, click a button to navigate to that site. See "Customizing the Links Bar for One-Click Surfing," later in this chapter.)
- **Click a web address in a Windows Mail message**—When Windows Mail recognizes a web address in an email message (that is, an address that begins with http://, https://, ftp://, www., and so on), it converts the address into a link. Clicking the link opens the address in Internet Explorer. Note, too, that many other programs are URL-aware, including the Microsoft Office suite of programs.

After you opened a page, you usually move to another page by clicking a link: either a text link or an imagemap. However, there are more techniques you can use to navigate to other pages:

- **Open a link in another window**—If you don't want to leave the current page, you can force a link to open in another Internet Explorer window by right-clicking the link and then clicking Open in New Window. You can open a new window for the current page by selecting File, New, Window, or by pressing Ctrl+N.

TIP

You can also hold down the Shift key and click a link to open that link in a new browser window.

- **Retrace the pages you've visited**—To return to a page you visited previously in this session, either click Internet Explorer's Back button or press Alt+Left arrow. After you go back to a page, you move ahead through the visited pages by clicking the Forward button or pressing Alt+Right arrow. Note, too, that an arrow appears to the right of the Forward button, as pointed out in Figure 18.1. This is the Recent Pages arrow and clicking this arrow displays a list of pages you've visited in the current session.

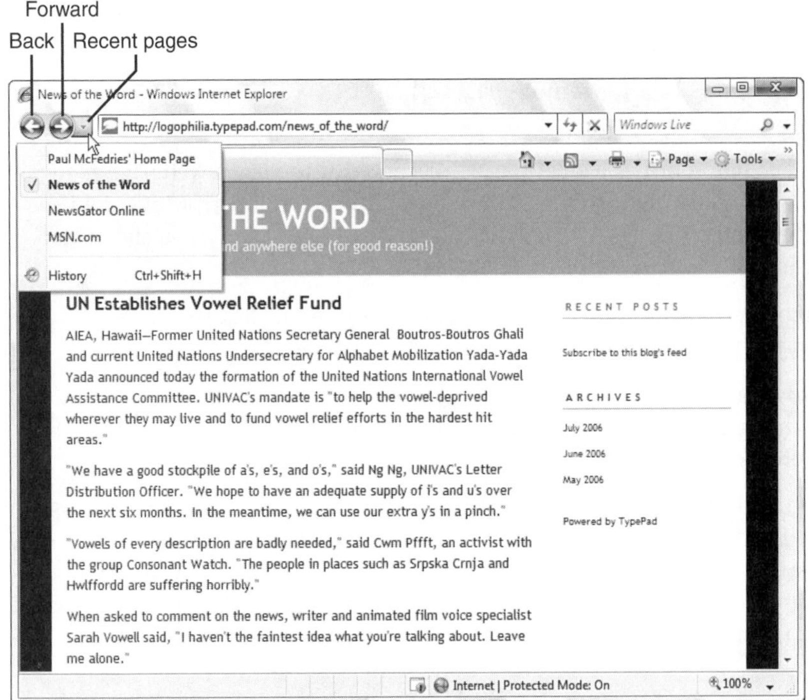

FIGURE 18.1 Click the Recent Pages arrow to see a list of the pages you've visited in the current session.

- **Return to the start page**—When you launch Internet Explorer without specifying a URL, you usually end up at MSN, the default start page (http://www.msn.com/; note, however, that many computer manufacturers change the default start page). You can return to this page at any time by clicking the Home button in the toolbar or by pressing Alt+Home.
- **Use the History list**—Press Alt+C to open the Favorites Center and click the History button to see a list of the sites you've visited over the past 20 days. Just click a URL to go to a site. The items you see in the History list are based on the contents of the `%UserProfile%\AppData\Local\Microsoft\Windows\History` folder. See "Using the Handy History List," later in this chapter, for more on the History list.

Taking Advantage of the Address Bar

Internet Explorer's Address bar (and the Address bars that appear in all Windows Vista folder windows) appears to be nothing more than a simple type-and-click mechanism. However, it's useful for many things, and comes with its own bag of tricks for making it even easier to use. Here's a rundown:

- Internet Explorer maintains a list of the last 25 URLs you typed into the Address bar. To access this list, press F4 and then use the Up Arrow and Down Arrow keys to select an item from the list.

Clearing the Address Bar List

One way to clear the Address bar list is to clear the history files. You do this by selecting Tools, Delete Browsing History, and then clicking Delete History. If you prefer to preserve the history files, note that Internet Explorer stores the last 15 typed URLs in the following Registry key:

```
HKCU\Software\Microsoft\Internet Explorer\TypedURLs
```

You can therefore clear the Address bar list by closing all Internet Explorer windows and deleting the settings `url1` through `url15` in this key. Here's a script that does so:

```
Option Explicit
Dim objWshShell, i
Set objWshShell = WScript.CreateObject("WScript.Shell")
For i = 1 to 25
    objWshShell.RegDelete "HKCU\Software\Microsoft\Internet Explorer\
➥TypedURLs\url" & i
Next 'i
objWshShell.Popup "Finished deleting typed URLs", , "Delete Typed URLs"
```

Note that if there are fewer than 25 addresses in the history list, you will get a Windows Script Host error stating the following:

```
Unable to remove registry key "HKCU\Software\Microsoft\Internet
➥\Explorer\TypedURLs\urln,
```

Here, *n* is one greater than the number of history items found in the list. You can safely ignore the message; the script removed all the history items from the list.

- To edit the Address bar text, press Alt+D to select it.
- The Address bar's AutoComplete feature monitors the address as you type. If any previously entered addresses match your typing, they appear in a list. To choose one of those addresses, use the Down Arrow key to select it and then press the Enter key. The quickest way to use AutoComplete is to begin typing the site's domain name. For example, if you want to bring up http://www.microsoft.com/, start typing the *microsoft* part. If you start with the full address, you have to type http://www. or just www., and then one other character.
- Internet Explorer assumes that any address you enter is for a website. Therefore, you don't need to type the http:// prefix because Internet Explorer adds it for you automatically.
- Internet Explorer also assumes that most web addresses are in the form http://www.*something*.com. Therefore, if you simply type the *something* part and press Ctrl+Enter, Internet Explorer will automatically add the http://www. prefix and

the .com suffix. For example, you can get to the Microsoft home page (http://www.microsoft.com) by typing **`microsoft`** and pressing Ctrl+Enter.

- Some websites use frames to divide a web page into multiple sections. Some of these sites offer links to other websites but, annoyingly, those pages appear within the first site's frame structure. To break out of frames, drag a link into the Address bar.
- To search from the Address bar (AutoSearch), first type your search text. As you type, Internet Explorer adds `Search for "`*`text`*`"` below the Address bar, where *`text`* is your search text. When you've finished your search text, press Tab to select the `Search for` item and then press Enter. Alternatively, precede your search text with the word `go`, `find`, or `search`, or with a question mark (`?`), as in these examples:

```
go vbscript
find autosearch
search neologisms
? registry
```

Creating a Shortcut to a URL

Another way to navigate websites via Internet Explorer is to create shortcuts that point to the appropriate URLs. To do this, use either of the following techniques:

- Copy the URL to the Clipboard, create a new shortcut (open the folder in which you want to store the shortcut and then select File, New, Shortcut), and then paste the URL into the Type the Location of the Item text box.
- You can create a shortcut for the currently displayed page by using the page icon that appears to the left of the address in the Address bar. Drag this icon and drop it on the desktop or on whatever folder you want to use to store the shortcut.
- You can create a shortcut for any hypertext link by dragging the link text from the page.

After your shortcut is in place, you can open the website by launching the shortcut's icon.

TIP

If you have a site that you use frequently, create a shortcut for it in the taskbar's Quick Launch toolbar. The easiest way to do this is to navigate to the site, click and drag the site's icon from the Address bar, and then drop it inside the Quick Launch toolbar. To increase the size of the Quick Launch toolbar so that you can see all the icons, right-click the taskbar and then click to deactivate the Lock the Taskbar command. Click and drag the move handle that appears just to the right of the Quick Launch toolbar.

TIP

Internet shortcuts are simple text files that use the URL extension. They contain only the address of the Internet site, as in the following example:

```
[InternetShortcut]
URL=http://www.microsoft.com/
```

If you need to make changes to that address, it's possible to edit the shortcut by opening the URL file in Notepad.

Working with Tabs

New It's a rare Internet Explorer user who doesn't usually have half a dozen or more browser windows open at the same time. You might have several sites that you check for updated content throughout the day; a few sites that you use for current research; another site that streams a radio station or other music; your favorite search engine site; and an extra browser window or two for random surfing.

It's convenient to have all these sites ready for action, but having all those windows open makes it harder to navigate to your other windows, and it's a drain on resources because the full Internet Explorer interface is repeated in each window. (Depending on your system, each open Internet Explorer window can consume up to 20MB in RAM.) Many of us who would like to have 12 or 15 sites at our fingertips have learned to make do with far fewer.

Fortunately, that might all change with Internet Explorer 7. Like Firefox, Opera, Safari, and quite a few other browsers, Internet Explorer 7 finally has **tabbed browsing**, in which each open page appears in its own tab within a single Internet Explorer window. You can open up to about 50 tabs in each window, which ought to be enough for anybody. One of the nicest features of tabs is that Internet Explorer supplies each tab with its own execution thread, which means that you can start a page loading in one tab while reading downloaded page text in another tab. You can also specify multiple home pages that load in their own tabs when you start Internet Explorer (see "Changing the Home Page," later in this chapter).

Opening a Page in a New Tab

Tabs are only as useful as they are easy to use, and Internet Explorer does a good job of smoothing the transition to tabbed browsing. One way that it does this is by giving you a satisfyingly wide variety of methods to use for opening a page in a new tab. There are six in all:

- **Hold down Ctrl and click a link in a web page**—This creates a new tab and loads the linked page in the background.

TIP

Opening a page in the background in a new tab when you Ctrl+click a link is useful if you want to keep reading the current page. However, I find that most of the time I want to read the new page right away. If you have a fast connection, the page loads quickly enough that the delay between clicking and reading is usually minimal. In such cases, you can tell Internet Explorer to switch to the new tab automatically when you Ctrl+click a link. Select Tools, Internet Options to open the Internet Options dialog box, display the General tab, and then click Settings in the Tabs group. In the Tabbed Browsing Settings dialog box, activate the Always Switch to New Tabs When They Are Created check box, and then click OK in the open dialog boxes.

- **Use the middle mouse button (if you have one) to click a link in a web page—** This creates a new tab and loads the linked page in the background.
- **Type the page URL in the Address bar and then press Alt+Enter—**This creates a new tab and loads the page in the foreground.
- **Click the New Tab button (or press Ctrl+T) to display a blank tab—**Type the page URL in the Address bar and then press the Enter key. This loads the page in the foreground.
- **Click and drag a web page link or the current Address bar icon and drop it on the New Tab button—**This creates a new tab and loads the page in the foreground.
- **Click a link in another program—**This creates a new tab and loads the linked page in the foreground.

Figure 18.2 shows Internet Explorer with several tabs open.

To close a tab, Internet Explorer gives you five choices:

- Click the tab's Close Tab button.
- Select the tab and then press Ctrl+W.
- Right-click the tab and then click Close.
- To close every tab except one, right-click the tab you want to keep open and then click Close Other Tabs.
- Click the tab using the middle mouse button.

Navigating Tabs

When you have two or more tabs open, navigating them is straightforward:

- With your mouse, click the tab of the page you want to use.
- With your keyboard, press Ctrl+Tab to navigate the tabs from left-to-right (and from the last tab to the first tab); press Ctrl+Shift+Tab to navigate the tabs from right-to-left (and from the first tab to the last tab).

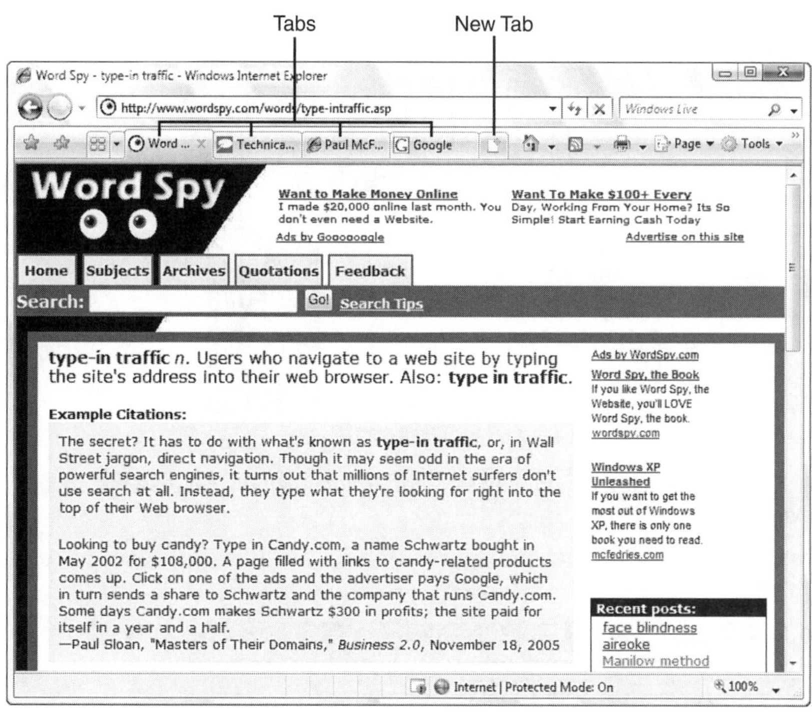

FIGURE 18.2 Internet Explorer 7 supports tabbed browsing to enable you to display multiple pages in a single browser window.

Unfortunately, Internet Explorer has only so much room to the right of the command bar, so it can display only a limited number of tabs. Internet Explorer does reduce the tab width as you add more tabs, but the width can shrink only so far if the tabs are to remain useable. On a 1024×768 screen, Internet Explorer can display a maximum of nine tabs. If you open more tabs than Internet Explorer can display, Internet Explorer adds two new buttons to the tab strip, as shown in Figure 18.3. Click « to display the previous unseen tab and click » to display the next unseen tab.

Internet Explorer also maintains a Tab list that shows you all the pages currently open in tabs. Click the Tab List button (shown in Figure 18.3) to display the list.

Working with Quick Tabs

Internet Explorer ups the tab ante a bit compared to other tabbed browsers with a new feature called *Quick Tabs* that displays a live thumbnail of each tabbed page. As shown in Figure 18.4, click the Quick Tabs button (or press Ctrl+Q) to see the Quick Tabs. From there you can click a thumbnail to open that tab.

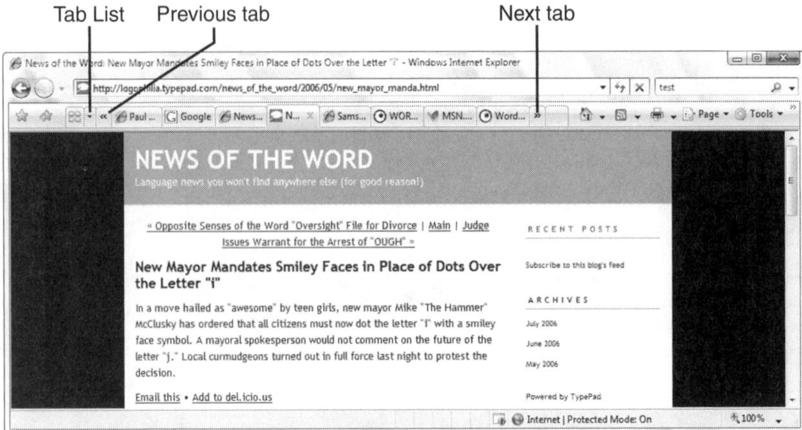

FIGURE 18.3 If you have more tabs open than Internet Explorer can display, use the double-arrow buttons to display the unseen tabs.

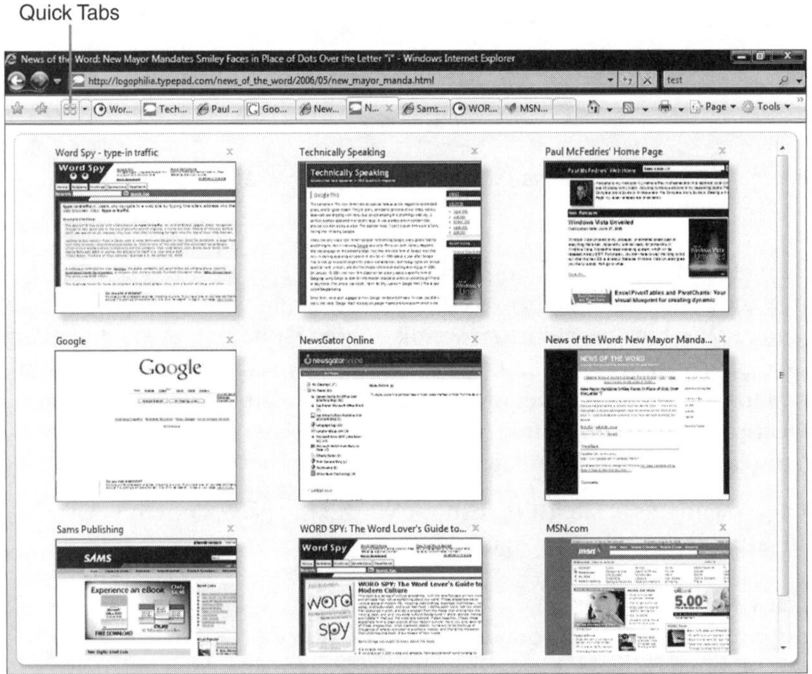

FIGURE 18.4 Click the Quick Tabs button to display thumbnails of your open tabs.

Using the Handy History List

You saw earlier (refer to "Tips and Techniques for Better Web Surfing") how you can click the Back and Forward buttons to follow your own footsteps on the World Wide Web. However, Internet Explorer wipes those lists clean when you exit the program. What do you do when you want to revisit a site from a previous session? Happily, Internet Explorer keeps track of the addresses of all the pages you perused for the last 20 days.

The names and addresses of these pages are stored in the History list, and you can view it by clicking the Favorites Center button (see Figure 18.5) and then clicking History (alternatively, you can press Ctrl+H). To bring a site into view, follow these steps:

1. Click the day or week you want to work with. Internet Explorer displays a list of the domains you visited on that day or during that week.
2. Click the domain of the website that contains the page you want to see. Internet Explorer opens the domain to reveal all the pages you visited within that site, as shown in Figure 18.5.
3. Click the name of the page you want.

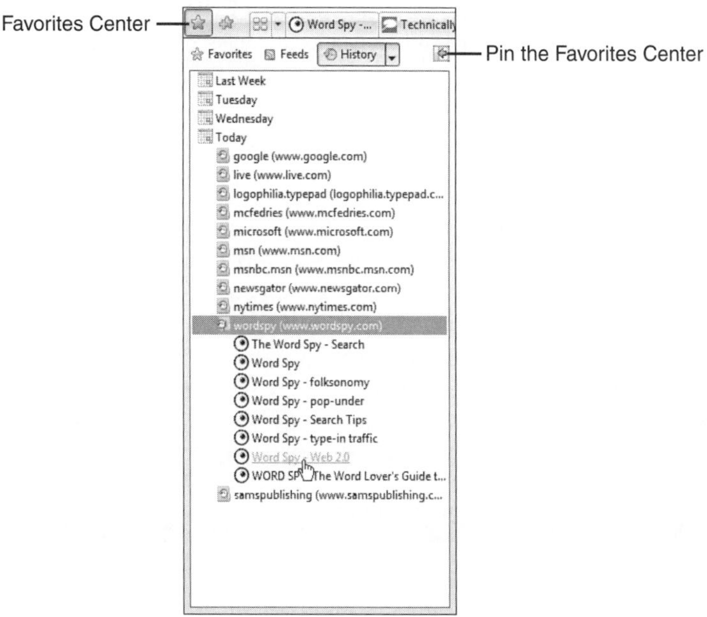

FIGURE 18.5 The History list keeps track of all the web addresses you called on in the last 20 days.

TIP

If you want to revisit a number of sites, it's a hassle to reopen the Favorites Center repeatedly. You can tell Internet Explorer to leave the Favorites Center open by clicking the Pin the Favorites Center button, pointed out in Figure 18.5.

If you have a large History list, you might have trouble finding the page you want. To help, click the drop-down arrow beside the History button to display a menu with the following choices:

By Date—Click this item to sort the History list by the date you visited each page (this is the default sort order).

By Site—Click this item to sort by the site names.

By Most Visited—Click this item to sort the History list by popularity, with the pages you visited most often at the top.

By Order Visited Today—Click this item to show only the pages you visited today, sorted in the order you visited them (with the most recent at the top).

Search History—Click this item to search the History list. Internet Explorer searches not only the site and page names, but also the page text (via local copies of each page stored in the Temporary Internet Files folder).

Searching the Web

Veteran surfers, having seen a wide range of what the Web has to offer, usually prefer to tackle it using a targeted approach that enables them to find information quickly, and do research. This means using one or more of the Web's many search engines. It's usually best to deal with a search engine site directly, but Internet Explorer offers some default searching options. For example, you saw earlier in this chapter (refer to "Taking Advantage of the Address Bar") that you can run searches directly from the Address bar. You can also run searches from the Search box, which appears to the right of the Address bar.

TIP

You can press Ctrl+E to activate the Search box.

TIP

In some cases you may only want to search for text within the currently displayed Web page. To do that, first display the menu bar by selecting Tools, Menu Bar, and then select Edit, Find On This Page (or you can bypass the menu bar by pressing Ctrl+F). Use the Find dialog box to enter your search text and then click Next.

Enter your search terms in the Search box and then press Enter or click Search (you can also press Alt+Enter to open the results in a new tab).

Adding More Search Engines

By default, Internet Explorer initially submits the search text to the Windows Live search engine. (The default search engine is also the one that Internet Explorer uses for the Address bar AutoSearch.) If you want access to other search engines—or *search providers*, as Internet Explorer insists on calling them—via the Search box, follow these steps:

1. Click the drop-down arrow to the right of the Search box.
2. Click Find More Providers. Internet Explorer displays a web page with links to various search engines, including AOL, Ask.com, and Google.
3. Click the link for the search engine you want to add. The Add Search Provider dialog box appears.
4. If you want Internet Explorer to use this search engine as the default, activate the Make This My Default Search Provider check box.
5. Click Add Provider.

To use the new search engine, drop down the Search box list to see a list of the search engines, and then click the one you want to use.

TIP

You can change the default search engine at any time. Drop down the Search box list and then click Change Search Defaults. In the Change Search Defaults dialog box, click the search engine you want to use and then click Set Default. Click OK to put the new setting into effect.

Setting Up Other Search Engines for Address Bar Searching

Address bar–based searching with the search text preceded by a keyword such as `go` or `?` is often the quickest route for simple searches. Unfortunately, you're limited to using Internet Explorer's default search engine. But what if you regularly use several search engines, depending on the search text or the results you get? In that case, it's still possible to set up an AutoSearch for any number of other search engines. Here are a few sample steps that create an AutoSearch URL for Google searches:

1. Run the Registry Editor and display the following key:

```
HKCU\Software\Microsoft\Internet Explore\SearchURL
```

2. Create a new subkey. The name of this subkey will be the text that you enter into the Address bar before the search text. For example, if you name this subkey `google`, you'll initiate an Address bar search by typing **`google`** ***`text`***, where ***`text`*** is your search text.
3. Highlight the new subkey and open its (Default) value for editing.
4. Type the URL that initiates a search for the search engine, and specify **`%s`** as a placeholder for the search text. For Google, the URL looks like this

   `http://www.google.com/search?q=%s`

5. You also have to specify the characters or hexadecimal values that Internet Explorer substitutes for characters that have special meaning within a query string: space, pound sign (#), percent (%), ampersand (&), plus (+), equal (=), and question mark (?). To do this, add the following settings to the new subkey:

Name	Type	Data
<space>	REG_SZ	+
#	REG_SZ	%23
%	REG_SZ	%25
&	REG_SZ	%26
+	REG_SZ	%2B
=	REG_SZ	%3D
?	REG_SZ	%3F

Figure 18.6 shows a completed example. The text that you type in the Address bar before the search string—that is, the name of the new subkey—is called the **search prefix**. Although I used `google` as the search prefix in my example, ideally it should be a single character (such as `g` for Google or `a` for AltaVista) to minimize typing.

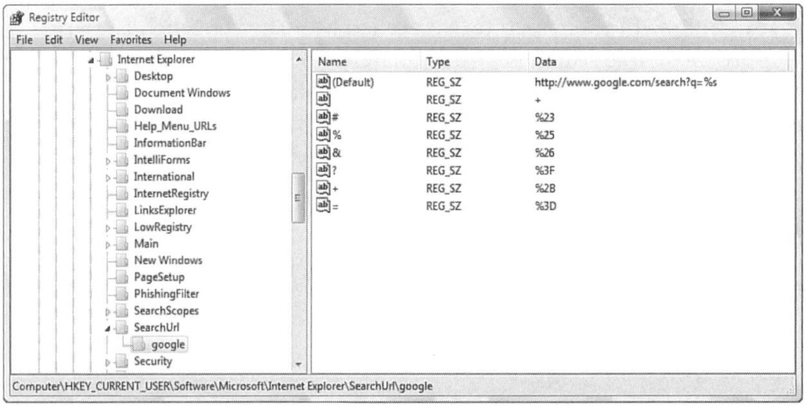

FIGURE 18.6 A sample search prefix for the Google search engine.

How do you know the proper URL to use for a search engine? Go to the search engine site and run a search with a single word. When the results appear, examine the URL in the Address bar, which usually takes the following general form:

ScriptURL?QueryString

Here, *ScriptURL* is the address of the site's search script and *QueryString* is the data sent to the script. In most cases, you can just copy the URL and substitute %s for your search text when you set up your search prefix. I often experiment with reducing the query string to the minimum necessary for the search to execute properly. For example, a typical Google search might produce a URL such as the following:

```
http://www.google.com/search?hl=en&lr=&q=mcfedries&btnG=Search
```

In the query string, each item is separated by an ampersand (&), so I delete one item at a time until either the search breaks or I'm down to the search text (`q=mcfedries` in the earlier query string). To save you some legwork, these are the minimal search URLs for a number of search sites:

All the Web:

http://www.alltheweb.com/search?query=%s&cat=web

AltaVista:

http://www.altavista.com/web/results?q=%s

AOL Search:

http://search.aol.com/aolcom/search?query=%s

Ask.com:

http://www.ask.com/web?q=%s

Encarta (Dictionary only):

http://encarta.msn.com/encnet/features/dictionary/DictionaryResults.aspx?
➥search=%s

Encarta (General):

http://encarta.msn.com/encnet/refpages/search.aspx?q=%s

Excite:

http://msxml.excite.com/info.xcite/search/web/%s

Live.com

http://www.live.com/?q=%s

Lycos:

http://search.lycos.com/default.asp?query=%s

MSN:

http://search. msn.com/results.asp?q=%s

Yahoo:

http://search.yahoo.com/bin/search?p=%s

The Favorites Folder: Sites to Remember

The sad truth is that much of what you'll see on the Web will be utterly forgettable and not worth a second look. However, there are all kinds of gems out there waiting to be uncovered—sites you'll want to visit regularly. Instead of memorizing the appropriate URLs, jotting them down on sticky notes, or plastering your desktop with shortcuts, you can use Internet Explorer's handy Favorites feature to keep track of your choice sites.

The Favorites feature is really just a folder (you'll find it in your `%UserProfile%` folder) that you use to store Internet shortcuts. The advantage of using the Favorites folder as opposed to any other folder is that you can add, view, and link to the Favorites folder shortcuts directly from Internet Explorer.

Adding a Shortcut to the Favorites Folder

When you find a site that you'd like to declare as a favorite, follow these steps:

1. Click the Add to Favorites button (it's to the right of the Favorites Center button, as shown in Figure 18.7; alternatively, you can press Alt+Z) and then click Add to Favorites. The Add a Favorite dialog box appears.

TIP

The quickest route to the Add a Favorite dialog box is to press Ctrl+D.

2. The Name text box displays the title of the page. The title is the text that will appear when you view the list of your favorites later. Feel free to edit this text if you like.
3. Internet Explorer enables you to set up subfolders to hold related favorites. If you don't want to bother with this, skip to step 4. Otherwise, click the New Folder button to display the Create a Folder dialog box, type a Folder Name, and then click Create.
4. Use the Create In list to select the folder in which you want to store the favorite.
5. Click Add.

Opening an Internet Shortcut from the Favorites Folder

The purpose of the Favorites folder, of course, is to give you quick access to the sites you visit regularly. To link to one of the shortcuts in your Favorites folder, you have three choices:

- In Internet Explorer, the Favorites list contains the complete list of your Favorites folder shortcuts. To link to a shortcut, click the Favorites Center button, click Favorites (see Figure 18.7), and then select the shortcut you want.

TIP

You can quickly display the Favorites list by pressing Ctrl+I.

TIP

Internet Explorer offers two methods for quickly adding a site to the Favorites list:

- If the current page has a link to the site you want to save, click and drag the link to the Favorites list.
- If you want to save the current page instead, click and drag the icon from the Address bar to the Favorites list.

Both techniques work only when you fix the Favorites Center into position on the left side of the Internet Explorer window. Therefore, before using either technique, you have to click the Pin the Favorites Center button.

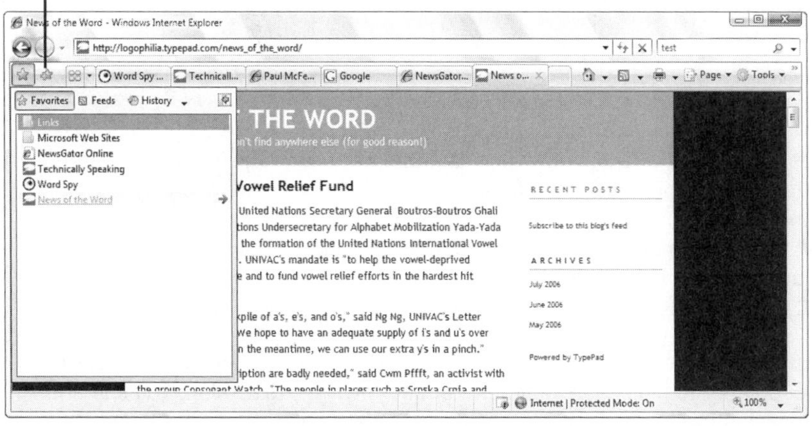

FIGURE 18.7 In the Favorites Center, the Favorites list displays the contents of your Favorites folder.

- Select Start, Favorites and then click the favorite you want from the submenu that appears.

NOTE

If the Favorites submenu doesn't appear on your Start menu, right-click the Start button, click Properties, and then click the Customize button beside the Start Menu option (which should be activated). In the list of Start Menu items, activate the Favorites Menu check box, and then click OK.

Maintaining Favorites

When you have a large number of favorites, you need to do some regular maintenance to keep things organized. This involves creating new subfolders, moving favorites between folders, changing URLs, deleting unused favorites, and more. Here's a summary of a few maintenance techniques you'll use most often:

- To change the URL of a favorite, display the Favorites list, find the item you want to work with, and right-click it. In the contextual menu, click Properties and then use the properties sheet to adjust the URL.
- To move a favorite, display the Favorites list, find the item you want to work with, and then drag the item to another spot on the menu (or into a submenu).
- To delete a favorite, display the Favorites list, find the item you want to work with, right-click it, and then click Delete.
- To sort the favorites alphabetically, pull down the Favorites menu, right-click any favorite or folder, and then click Sort By Name.
- To send a favorite via email, open the Favorites folder, right-click the favorite, and then select Send To, Mail Recipient.

Allowing Internet Shortcut Attachments in Outlook

If you use Microsoft Outlook (2003 or later) as your email client, the program blocks certain types of outgoing attachments, including Internet shortcuts. Therefore, after you select the Mail Recipient command, the message window displays a message telling you that it has blocked access to the `potentially unsafe attachment`. To work around this problem, open the Registry Editor and navigate to the following key (note that you might have to create the Security key):

```
HKCU\Software\Microsoft\Office\11.0\Outlook\Security
```

Create a new string value named `Level1Remove`, open the new value, and type **`.url`**. This tells Outlook not to block attachments that use the `.url` extension. You can add multiple extensions to the `Level1Remove` value; separate each one with a semicolon. This workaround also works with Outlook 2007, except that you use the following key (which, again, you might have to create):

```
HKCU\Software\Microsoft\Office\12.0\Outlook\Security
```

Sharing Favorites with Other Browsers

Many users like to run Internet Explorer along with another browser such as Firefox or Netscape on their machines. Unfortunately, these browsers store saved sites differently: Internet Explorer uses *favorites*, whereas Firefox and Netscape use *bookmarks*. However, Internet Explorer has a feature that enables you to either export favorites to a bookmark file or import bookmarks as favorites. Here's how to do it:

1. In Internet Explorer, press Alt to display the menu bar and then select File, Import and Export. The Import/Export Wizard makes an appearance.
2. Click Next.
3. Select one of the following:

Import Favorites	Select this option to import Firefox or Netscape bookmarks as favorites. When you click Next, the wizard asks you for the path to the `bookmark.htm` file. Click Next when you're done.
Export Favorites	Select this option to export your favorites as Netscape bookmarks. When you click Next, the wizard first asks you which Favorites folder you want to export. Click Next again and the wizard prompts you to enter the path to the bookmark.htm file. Click Next when you've done that.

4. This wizard performs the requested operation and then displays a dialog box to let you know when it's complete. Click Finish.

Working with RSS Feeds

New Some websites—particularly blogs—regularly add new content. That makes for a dynamic and interesting site (depending on the content, of course), but it does mean that you have to check the site often if you want to keep up with the latest information. You can avoid this hassle altogether by turning the tables and having the site tell you when it has posted something new. You can do this if the site supports a feature called *Real Simple Syndication*, or *RSS*, which enables you to subscribe to the feed that the site sends out. That feed usually contains the most recent data posted to the site.

RSS feeds are XML files, so you cannot read them directly. Instead, you need a *feed reader* program or website that can interpret the RSS content. However, Internet Explorer 7 has this capability built in, so you can subscribe to and read RSS feeds from the comfort of your desktop.

Navigating to a site that has one or more feeds available enables the View Feeds icon in Internet Explorer command bar. Pull down the View Feeds list (or press Alt+J) to see a list of the site's feeds, as shown in Figure 18.8.

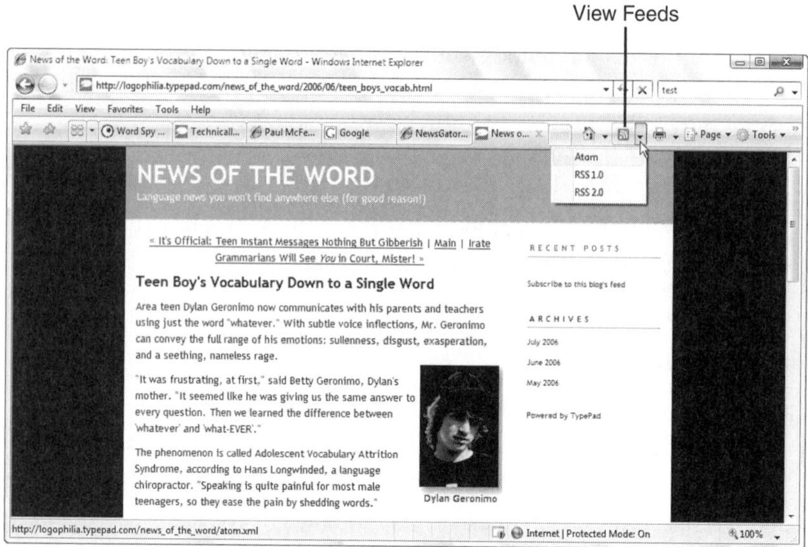

FIGURE 18.8 If a site offers one or more RSS feeds, Internet Explorer's View Feeds button becomes enabled.

Why would a site have multiple feeds? There are two main reasons:

- The site offers a single feed in multiple formats. The three main formats are RSS 1.0, RSS 2.0, and Atom (see Figure 18.8). Internet Explorer supports all three formats, so in this case it doesn't matter which one you choose.
- The site offers multiple content feeds. For example, some blogs offer separate feeds for posts and comments.

Click the feed you want to view, and Internet Explorer displays the feed content, as shown in Figure 18.9.

Subscribing to a Feed

Simply viewing a site's RSS feed is only marginally useful. To get more out of a feed, you need to subscribe to it, which tells Internet Explorer to check the feed for new content automatically and download that content to your computer, which makes the feed part of what Microsoft calls the *RSS Feed Store*. (The default update schedule is once per day.) You then have two ways to view the content of your subscribed feeds (see "Reading Feeds," later in this chapter):

- Use the Feeds list in the Favorites Center
- Use the RSS Feeds gadget in Windows Sidebar

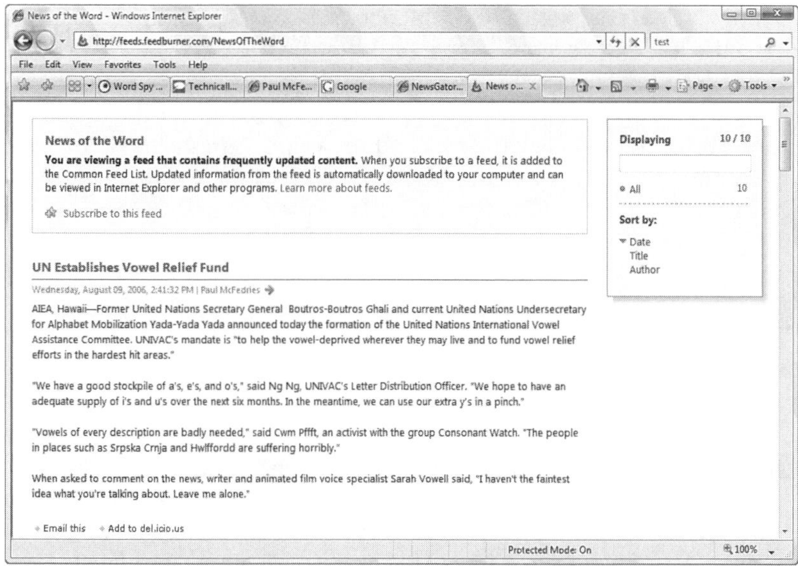

FIGURE 18.9 Select the feed you want and Internet Explorer displays the feed content.

To subscribe to a feed, follow these steps:

1. Display the feed you want to subscribe to.
2. Click the Subscribe to This Feed link. The Subscribe to This Feed dialog box appears.
3. The Name text box displays the title of the feed, which is the text that appears when you later view the Feed list. You can edit this text if you like.
4. Internet Explorer enables you to set up subfolders to hold related feeds. If you don't want to bother with this, skip to step 4. Otherwise, click the New Folder button to display the Create a Folder dialog box, type a folder name, and then click Create.
5. Use the Create In list to select the folder in which you want to store the feed.
6. Click Subscribe.

Reading Feeds

Because, by definition, a feed you contains content that updates regularly, you'll want to stay on top of your feeds and peruse them for new content as often as you can. As I mentioned earlier, you have two ways to view your feeds: the Favorites Center and Windows Sidebar.

To view feeds via the Favorites Center, click the Favorites Center button and then click Feeds. (Immediately after you subscribe to a feed, you can also click the View My Feeds link.) Figure 18.10 shows a Feeds list with a few subscribed feeds. If the feed name appears in bold type, it means the feed has added new content since the last time you read it; feed names that appear in regular text have not added content. To be sure, you can refresh a feed: either click the Refresh This Feed button that appears when you hover the mouse over a feed (see Figure 18.10) or right-click the feed and then click Refresh. To view a feed, click it in the Feeds list. (After you click a feed, Internet Explorer closes the Favorites Center. If you're going through several feeds, be sure to keep the Favorites Center onscreen by first clicking the Pin the Favorites Center button.)

TIP

You can display the Feeds list quickly by pressing Ctrl+J.

TIP

When you view a feed, Internet Explorer assumes that you're going to read the whole thing, so it automatically activates the Mark Feed as Read link (by displaying a blue check mark beside it). If you're only reading part of the feed, click Mark Feed as Read to deactivate it.

FIGURE 18.10 Your subscribed feeds appear in the Favorite Center's Feeds list.

To view feeds in Windows Sidebar, you need to add the RSS Feeds gadget. This is part of the default Windows Sidebar configuration, so your Sidebar should already display it. If not, right-click the Sidebar, click Add Gadgets to open the Gadget Gallery, and then double-click the RSS Feeds gadget to add it to the Sidebar. The RSS Feeds gadget operates by showing you the latest unread posts from your RSS Feed Store. It shows four posts at a time, with each post showing the title, feed name, and post date. To view a post, click the title to display the content in a side window, as shown in Figure 18.11.

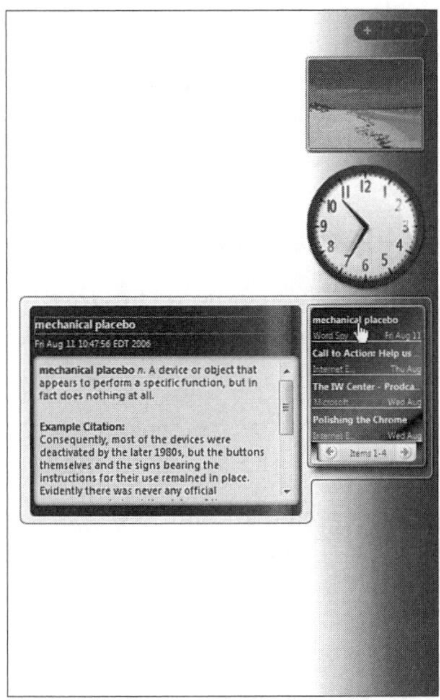

FIGURE 18.11 Click a post title to view the post in the RSS Feeds gadget.

By default, the RSS Feeds gadget shows up to 100 of the unread posts from all your feeds. To control this, right-click the RSS Feeds gadget (if a post is currently displayed, click another part of the Sidebar or desktop to close it), and then click Options. The RSS Feeds dialog box that appears has two lists (click OK when you're done):

- Select a Feed from the Microsoft RSS Feed Store—Select All Feeds or a specific feed
- Select Number of Recent Items—Select the maximum number of recent posts to show in the gadget: 4, 20, 40, or 100

Setting the Feed Update Schedule

Most websites that offer you a feed update it at the same time as, or soon after, the site posts new content. The frequency with which this occurs varies widely: once a day, once a week, several times a day, or even several times an hour.

By default, Internet Explorer checks for an updated feed once per day. Checking once a day is a reasonable schedule for sites that post new content once or twice a day or every couple of days. However, it's not an efficient schedule for feeds that update much more or much less frequently. For example, if a feed updates only once a week, it's wasteful for Internet Explorer to check the feed every day. On the other hand, if a feed updates many times during a day, you might not see a time-sensitive post until it is too late or you might face a daunting number of posts to read. You can make a feed more efficient or easier to read by setting up a custom refresh schedule that suits the feed. Here are the steps to follow:

1. Click Favorites Center and then click Feeds to display the Feeds list.
2. Right-click the feed you want to work with and then click Properties. (If Internet Explorer displays the feed, you can also click the View Feed Properties link.) Internet Explorer displays the Feed Properties dialog box.
3. Click the Use Custom Schedule option. Internet Explorer activates the Frequency list.
4. Use the Frequency list to select the update schedule you prefer: 15 minutes, 30 minutes, 1 hour, 4 hours, 1 day, 1 week, or Never.
5. Click OK.

TIP

If you want to use the same schedule for all your feeds, the easiest way to do so is to change the default schedule. If you have the Feed Properties dialog box open, click Settings. Otherwise, click Tools, and then click Internet Options to display the Internet Options dialog box. Click the Content tab and then click Settings in the Feeds group. Use the Default Schedule list to click the interval you want to use and then click OK in all open dialog boxes. Note that this only affects those feeds where you've selected the Use Default Schedule option. Feeds where you have selected the Use Custom Schedule option are not affected.

Customizing Internet Explorer

Internet Explorer is chock full of customization options that enable you to set up the program for the way you work and surf. The rest of this chapter examines what I think are the most useful of Internet Explorer's long list of customization features.

TIP

You can brand your version of Internet Explorer by setting up a custom window title, a custom browser logo, and custom toolbar buttons. You can do all of this via the Group Policy editor (see Chapter 10). Run the program and select User Configuration, Windows Settings, Internet Explorer Maintenance, Browser User Interface. Use the Browser Title, Custom Logo and Animated Bitmaps, and Browser Toolbar Customizations settings to perform the customizations.

Customizing the Links Bar for One-Click Surfing

The Links bar gives you one-click access to web pages, and so is more convenient than even the Favorites folder (unless you have the Favorites Center pinned). To take full advantage of this convenience, you'll want to redesign the Links bar so that its links and setup are suitable for the way you work. Here's a list of a few techniques and options you can use to work with and customize the Links bar:

NOTE

Before you can perform certain operations on the Links bar, you have to display it! Select Tools, Toolbars, Links. Internet Explorer adds the Links toolbar just below the Address bar.

- **Creating a new link button**—To add a new Links bar button for the current page, drag the page icon from the Address bar and drop it on the Links bar. To add a new button for a hypertext link, drag the link and drop it on the Links bar. If you've already saved the page as a favorite, drag the icon from the Favorites Center and drop it inside the Links bar. (You can also drag-and-drop items from the History list.) If the page title is long, you'll likely want to rename it to something shorter to avoid wasting precious Links bar space.
- **Changing button positions**—The positions of the Links bar buttons are not permanent. To move any button, use your mouse to drag the button left or right along the Links bar.
- **Renaming a button**—Right-click the button and then click Rename. Use the Rename dialog box to edit the name and then click OK.
- **Changing the URL for a button**—Right-click a button and then click Properties. Use the URL text box to edit the URL for the button.
- **Deleting a link**—To remove a button from the Links bar, right-click it and then click Delete.

TIP

The Links bar buttons are URL shortcut files located in the `%UserProfile%\Favorites\Links` folder. You can use this folder to work with the shortcuts directly. Perhaps most importantly, you can also use the folder to create subfolders. When you click a subfolder in the Links bar, it drops down a list of the URL shortcuts that are in that subfolder.

TIP

After you have customized your Links bar to suit your style, you can make it even more convenient by displaying it as part of the taskbar. To do this, right-click an empty section of the taskbar, and then click Toolbars, Links.

Controlling the Web Page Cache

In the same way that a disk cache stores frequently used data for faster performance, Internet Explorer also keeps a cache of files from web pages you've visited recently. The cache is maintained on a per-user basis and is located in the following folder:

```
%UserProfile%\Local\Microsoft\Windows\Temporary Internet Files
```

Internet Explorer uses these saved files to display web pages quickly the next time you ask to see them or while you are offline.

To control the cache, select Tools, Internet Options and display the General tab. Use the following buttons in the Temporary Internet files group:

Delete Files	Clicking this button displays the Delete Browsing History dialog box. (You can also display the dialog box by select Tools, Delete Browsing History.) Click the Delete Files button to clean out the Temporary Internet Files folder.
Settings	Clicking this button displays the Temporary Internet Files and History Settings dialog box, shown in Figure 18.12.

You have the following options:

Check for Newer Versions of Stored Pages	Activate an option in this group to determine when Internet Explorer checks for updated versions of cache files. If you have a fast connection and you want to be certain that you're always seeing the most current data, activate the Every Time I Visit the Webpage option.

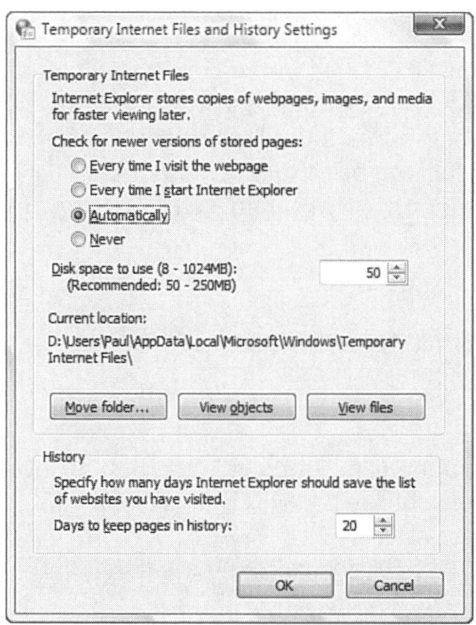

FIGURE 18.12 Use this dialog box to control how the Internet Explorer cache works.

NOTE

No matter which cache update option you choose, you can view the most up-to-date version of a page at any time by pressing F5 or by clicking the Refresh button.

Disk Space to Use Use this spin box to set the size of the cache as a percentage of the hard disk's capacity. A larger cache speeds up website browsing but also uses more hard drive space.

Move Folder Click this button to change the folder used for the cache. For example, you could move the cache to a partition with more free space so that you can increase the cache size, or to a faster hard drive to improve cache performance. Note that you must restart your computer if you move the cache folder.

View Objects Click this button to display the Downloaded Program Files folder, which holds the Java applets and ActiveX controls that have been downloaded and installed on your system.

View Files Click this button to display the Temporary Internet Files folder.

Setting Internet Explorer Options

You had a brief introduction to the Internet Options dialog box in the previous section. However, this dialog box is loaded with useful options and settings that enable you to control dozens of aspects of Internet Explorer's behavior and look. These include cosmetic options such as the fonts and colors used by the program, but also more important concerns, such as your home page and the level of security that Internet Explorer uses. To display these options, you have several ways to proceed:

- In Internet Explorer, select Tools, Internet Options
- Select Start, Control Panel, Network and Internet, Internet Options
- Select Start, right-click the Internet icon, and then click Internet Properties

Which ever method you use, you see the Internet Options (or Internet Properties) dialog box. The next few sections discuss the details of some of the controls in this dialog box.

NOTE

I don't discuss the Security and Privacy tabs here. For the details on these important tabs, see Chapter 21, "Implementing Windows Vista's Internet Security and Privacy Features."

Changing the Home Page

In Internet Explorer, the **home page** is what the browser views when you start a new session. The default home page is usually MSN (msn.com), but most computer manufacturers substitute their own pages.

To change the home page, display the General tab and then click one of the following buttons:

Use Current	For this button, first navigate to the page you want to use. Then open the Internet Options dialog box and click Use Current to change the home page to the current page.
Use Default	Click this button to revert to Internet Explorer's default home page.
Use Blank	Click this button if you'd prefer to launch Internet Explorer without loading a home page.

New Internet Explorer 7 gives you an easier way to set the current page as your home page. Navigate to the page, click the drop-down arrow beside the Home button, and then click Add or Change Home Page. In the Add or Change Home Page dialog box that appears, activate the Use this Webpage as Your Only Home Page option, and then click Yes.

Even better, Internet Explorer 7 enables you to specify *multiple* home pages. When you launch Internet Explorer or click the Home button, Internet Explorer 7 loads each home page in a separate tab. This is a great feature if you regularly open several pages at the start of each browsing session. You can use two methods to specify multiple home pages:

- Display the Internet Options dialog box and click the General tab. In the Home Page list box, type the address of each page on a separate line. (That is, type one address, press Enter to start a new line, and then type the next address.)
- Navigate to the page you want to add, click the drop-down arrow beside the Home button, and then click Add or Change Home Page. In the Add or Change Home Page dialog box that appears, activate the Add this Webpage to Your Home Page Tabs option, and then click Yes.

NOTE

If Internet Explorer currently displays all the tabs that you want to use as your home pages, click the drop-down arrow beside the Home button, and then click Add or Change Home Page. In the Add or Change Home Page dialog box that appears, activate the Use the Current Tab Set as Your Home Page option, and then click Yes.

If you no longer want to use a particular home page, click the drop-down arrow beside the Home button, click Remove, and then click the home page you want to delete. When Internet Explorer asks you to confirm, click Yes.

Configuring the Page History

The General tab's Browsing History group also controls various options related to the History folder (refer to the "Using the Handy History List" section, earlier in this chapter):

Delete Files — Clicking this button displays the Delete Browsing History dialog box. (You can also display the dialog box by selecting Tools, Delete Browsing History.) Click the Delete History button to remove all URLs from the History folder.

Settings — Clicking this button displays the Temporary Internet Files and History Settings dialog box, shown earlier in Figure 18.12. Use the Days to Keep Pages in History spin box to set the maximum number of days that Internet Explorer stores a URL in its History list. Enter a value between 1 and 99. If you do not want Internet Explorer to keep any pages in the History folder, enter **0**.

Setting More General Options

The General tab also boasts four buttons at the bottom:

Colors — Click this button to display the Colors dialog box. There you can deactivate the Use Windows Colors check box to set the default text and background colors used in the Internet Explorer window. If you leave this check box activated, Internet Explorer uses the colors defined in the Display properties sheet. You can also use the Visited and Unvisited buttons to set the default link colors. Finally, activate the Use Hover Color check box to have Internet Explorer change the color of a link when you position the mouse pointer over it. Use the Hover button to set the color.

Languages — Click this button to display the Language Preference dialog box, which enables you to add one or more languages to Internet Explorer. This makes it possible for Internet Explorer to handle pages in foreign languages. You can also use this dialog box to set up relative priorities for the designated languages.

Fonts — Click this button to display the Fonts dialog box, which enables you to determine how web page fonts appear within Internet Explorer.

TIP

To change the size of the fonts Internet Explorer uses, select Page, Text Size, and then choose a relative font size from the cascade menu (for example, Larger or Smaller). If you have a mouse with a wheel button, hold down Ctrl while pressing and turning the wheel. This changes the onscreen text size on the fly.

Accessibility — Click this button to display the Accessibility dialog box. From here, you can tell Internet Explorer to ignore the colors, font styles, and font sizes specified on any web page. You can also specify your own style sheet to use when formatting web pages.

Understanding Internet Explorer's Advanced Options

Internet Explorer has a huge list of customization features found in the Advanced tab of the Internet Properties dialog box (see Figure 18.13). Many of these settings are obscure, but many others are extremely useful for surfers of all stripes. This section runs through all of these settings.

TIP

The advanced options can be set for users via the Group Policy editor. Run the program and open the User Configuration, Windows Settings, Internet Explorer Maintenance branch. Right-click Internet Explorer Maintenance and then click

Preference Mode; click the Advanced branch that is added to the Internet Explorer Maintenance section. Double-click the Internet Settings item to work with the advanced options.

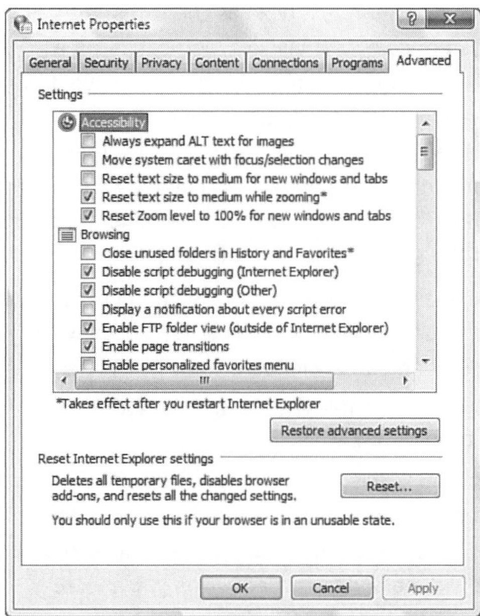

FIGURE 18.13 In the Internet Properties dialog box, the Advanced tab contains a long list of Internet Explorer customization settings.

The Accessibility group has five options:

Always Expand ALT Text for Images — Most webmasters define a text description for each image they include on a page. If you tell Internet Explorer not to show images (see the later discussion of the Show Pictures check box), all you see are boxes where the images should be, and each box contains the text description (known as **alt text**, where *alt* is short for *alternate*). Activating this check box tells Internet Explorer to expand the image box horizontally so that the alt text appears on a single line.

Move System Caret with Focus/Selection Changes	Activating this check box tells Internet Explorer to move the system caret whenever you change the focus. (The **system caret** is a visual indication of what part of the screen currently has the focus. If a text box has the focus, the system caret is a blinking, vertical bar; if a check box or option button has the focus, the system caret is a dotted outline of the control name.) This is useful if you have a screen reader or screen magnifier that uses the position of the system caret to determine what part of the screen to read or magnify.
Reset Text Size to Medium for New Windows and Tabs	Activating this check box tells Internet Explorer to return the Text Size value to Medium when you open a new window or tab. This is useful if you find that you only have to enlarge the text size for a few sites.
Reset Text Size to Medium While Zooming	Activating this check box tells Internet Explorer to return the Text Size value to Medium when you use the Zoom feature (select Page, Zoom). This is helpful because it gives you a more consistent zooming experience—you're always starting the zoom from the same text size.
Reset Zoom Level to 100% for New Windows and Tabs	Activating this check box tells Internet Explorer to return the Zoom value to 100% when you open a new window or tab. This is useful if you find that you have to zoom in on only a few sites.

Here are the options in the Browsing group:

Close Unused Folders in History and Favorites	When you activate this check box, Internet Explorer keeps unused folders closed when you display the History list and the Favorites list. That is, if you open a folder and then open a second folder, Internet Explorer automatically closes the first folder. This makes the History and Favorites lists easier to navigate, so it's usually best to leave this option activated. You need to restart Internet Explorer if you change this setting.

Disable Script Debugging (Internet Explorer)	This check box toggles the script debugger (if one is installed) on and off within Internet Explorer only. You should have to activate this option only if you're a page designer and you have scripts in your pages that you need to debug before uploading them to the Web.
Disable Script Debugging (Other)	This is similar to the Disable Script Debugging (Internet Explorer) option, except that it toggles the script debugger (again, if one is installed) on and off within any application other than Internet Explorer that can display web content (such as Windows Mail).
Display a Notification About Every Script Error	If you activate this check box, press Alt and then select Tools, FTP in Windows Explorer to display a dialog box to alert you to JavaScript or VBScript errors on a page. If you leave this option deactivated, Internet Explorer displays an error message in the status bar. To see the full error message, double-click the status bar message. Only script programmers will need to enable this option and, even then, only when they're debugging scripts. Many websites are poorly programmed and contain script errors. Therefore, enabling this option means that you'll have to deal with lots of annoying dialog boxes as you surf.
Enable FTP Folder View (Outside of Internet Explorer)	When you activate this option and you access an FTP (File Transfer Protocol) site, Internet Explorer displays the contents of the site using the familiar Windows folder view. This makes it easy to drag and drop files from the FTP site to your hard disk, and possibly to perform other file maintenance chores, depending on what permissions you have at the site.
Enable Page Transitions	This check box toggles Internet Explorer's support for page transitions on and off—websites that use a server that supports FrontPage extensions can define various page transitions (such as wipes and fades). However, these transitions often slow down your browsing, so I recommend turning them off.

Enable Personalized Favorites Menu	When you enable this check box, Windows Vista's personalized menu feature applies to Internet Explorer's Favorites menu as well. This means that Internet Explorer hides favorites that you haven't visited in a while. To see the hidden favorites, click the downward-pointing arrow at the bottom of the menu. Personalized menus reduce the command clutter that can confuse novice users, but they just slow down experienced users. I recommend leaving this option turned off.
Enable Third-Party Browser Extensions	With this check box activated, Internet Explorer supports third-party extensions to its interface. For example, the Google toolbar is a third-party extension that integrates the Google search engine into Internet Explorer as a toolbar. If you deactivate this check box, third-party extensions don't appear and can't display. Deactivating this check box is a good way to turn off some (but, unfortunately, not all) of those annoying third-party toolbars that install themselves without permission. You need to restart Internet Explorer if you change this setting.
Enable Visual Styles on Buttons and Controls in Webpages	With this check box activated, Internet Explorer applies the current Windows Vista visual style to all web pages for objects such as form buttons. If you deactivate this check box, Internet Explorer applies its default visual style to all page elements.
Force Offscreen Compositing Even Under Terminal Server	If you activate this check box, Internet Explorer performs all **compositing**—the combining of two or more images—in memory before displaying the result onscreen. This avoids the image flashing that can occur when running Internet Explorer under Terminal Services, but it can reduce performance significantly. I recommend leaving this option unchecked. You have to restart Internet Explorer if you change this setting.

Notify When Downloads Complete	If you leave this check box activated, Internet Explorer leaves its download progress dialog box onscreen after the download finishes (see Figure 18.14). This enables you to click either Open to launch the downloaded file or Open Folder to display the file's destination folder. If you deactivate this check box, Internet Explorer closes this dialog box as soon as the download is complete.

TIP

You can also force Internet Explorer to close the Download Complete dialog box automatically by activating the Close This Dialog Box When Download Completes check box.

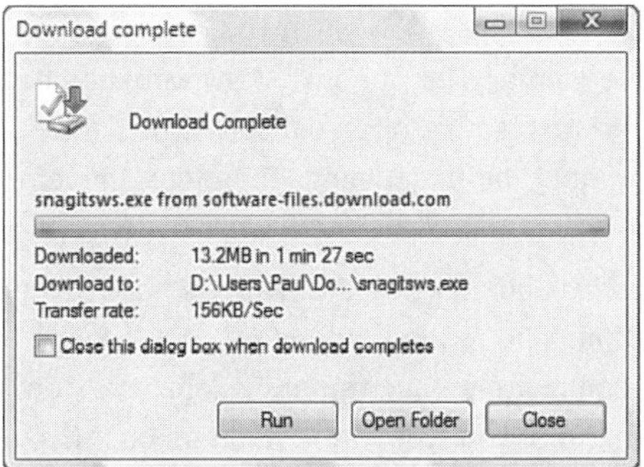

FIGURE 18.14 When Internet Explorer completes a file download, it leaves this dialog box onscreen to help you deal with the file.

Reuse Windows for Launching Shortcuts	With this check box enabled and tabbed browsing turned off, Windows looks for an already-open Internet Explorer window when you click a web page shortcut (such as a web address in a Windows Mail email message). If a window is open, the web page loads there. This is a good idea because it prevents Internet Explorer windows from multiplying unnecessarily. If you deactivate this option, Windows always loads the page into a new Internet Explorer window.

Show Friendly HTTP Error Messages	With this check box enabled, Internet Explorer intercepts the error messages (for, say, pages not found) generated by web servers and replaces them with its own messages that offer more information as well as possible solutions to the problem. If you deactivate this option, Internet Explorer displays the error message generated by the web server. However, I recommend deactivating this option because webmasters often customize the web server error messages to be more helpful than the generic messages reported by Internet Explorer.
Underline Links	Use these options to specify when Internet Explorer should format web page links with an underline. The Hover option means that the underline appears only when you position the mouse pointer over the link. Many websites use colored text, so it's often difficult to recognize a link without the underlining. Therefore, I recommend that you activate the Always option.
Use Inline AutoComplete	This check box toggles the Address bar's inline AutoComplete feature on and off. When inline AutoComplete is on, Internet Explorer monitors the text that you type in the Address bar. If your text matches a previously typed URL, Internet Explorer automatically completes the address by displaying the matching URL in the Address bar. It also displays a drop-down list of other matching URLs. When inline AutoComplete is off, Internet Explorer displays only the drop-down list of matching URLs.

NOTE

If you want to prevent Internet Explorer from displaying the drop-down list of matching URLs, display the Content tab and click the Settings button in the AutoComplete group to display the AutoComplete Settings dialog box. Deactivate the Web Addresses check box. Note that Internet Explorer's AutoComplete feature also applies to web forms. That is, AutoComplete can remember data that you type into a form—including usernames and passwords—and automatically enter that data when you use the form again. You can control the web form portion of AutoComplete by using the other check boxes in the Use AutoComplete For section of the AutoComplete Settings dialog box.

Use Most Recent Order When Switching Tags with Ctrl+Tab	If you activate this check box, press Ctrl+Tab (and Ctrl+Shift+Tab) switches between tabs in the order you most recently viewed them.
Use Passive FTP (for Firewall and DSL Modem Compatibility)	In a normal FTP session, Internet Explorer opens a connection to the FTP server (for commands) and then the FTP server opens a second connection back to the browser (for data). If you're on a network with a firewall, however, it will not allow incoming connections from a server. With passive FTP, the browser establishes the second (data) connection itself. Therefore, if you're on a firewalled network or are using a DSL modem and you can't establish an FTP connection, activate this check box.
Use Smooth Scrolling	This check box toggles a feature called **smooth scrolling** on and off. When you activate this check box to enable smooth scrolling, pressing the Page Down or Page Up key causes the page to scroll down or up at a preset speed. If you deactivate this check box, pressing the Page Down or Page Up key causes the page to jump instantly down or up.

TIP

When reading a web page, you can scroll down one screen by pressing the spacebar. To scroll up one screen, press Shift+spacebar.

The check boxes in the HTTP 1.1 Settings branch determine whether Internet Explorer uses the HTTP 1.1 protocol:

Use HTTP 1.1	This check box toggles Internet Explorer's use of HTTP 1.1 to communicate with web servers. (HTTP 1.1 is the standard protocol used on the Web today.) You should deactivate this check box only if you're having trouble connecting to a website. This tells Internet Explorer to use HTTP 1.0, which might solve the problem.
Use HTTP 1.1 Through Proxy Connections	This check box toggles on and off the use of HTTP 1.1 only when connecting through a proxy server.

The options in the International group relate to security, so see Chapter 21, "Implementing Windows Vista's Internet Security and Privacy Features," for a discussion of them.

The options in the Multimedia branch toggle various multimedia effects on and off:

Always Use ClearType for HTML	When this check box is activated, Internet Explorer displays HTML text using ClearType, which gives text a sharper look on LCD monitors. If you don't have an LCD monitor, you might not like how ClearType renders text, so you should deactivate this check box. You need to restart Internet Explorer if you change this setting.
Enable Automatic Image Resizing	If you activate this check box, Internet Explorer automatically shrinks large images so that they fit inside the browser window. This is useful if you're running Windows Vista with a small monitor or at a relatively low resolution, and you're finding that many website images don't fit entirely into the browser window.
Play Animations in Webpages	This check box toggles animated GIF images on and off. Most animated GIFs are unwelcome annoyances, so you'll probably greatly improve your surfing experience by clearing this check box. If you turn this option off and you want to view an animation, right-click the box and then click Show Picture.
Play Sounds in Webpages	This check box toggles web page sound effects on and off. Because the vast majority of web page sounds are extremely bad MIDI renditions of popular tunes, turning off sounds will save your ears.
Show Image Download Placeholders	If you activate this check box, Internet Explorer displays a box that is the same size and shape as the image it is downloading.
Show Pictures	This check box toggles web page images on and off. If you're using a slow connection, turn off this option and Internet Explorer will show only a box where the image would normally appear. (If the designer has included alt text, that text will appear inside the box.) If you want

	to view a picture when you've toggled images off, right-click the box and select the Show Picture option.
Smart Image Dithering	This check box toggles image dithering on and off. **Dithering** is a technique that slightly alters an image to make jagged edges appear smooth.

In the Printing group, the Print Background Colors and Images check box determines whether Internet Explorer includes the page's background when you print the page. Many web pages use solid colors or fancy images as backgrounds, so you'll print these pages faster if you leave this setting deactivated.

The options in the Search from the Address bar group control Internet Explorer's Address bar searching:

Do Not Search from the Address Bar	Activate this option to disable Address bar searching.
Just Display the Results in the Main Window	Activate this option to display, in the main browser window, a list of the sites that the search engine found.

The Security branch has many options related to Internet Explorer security. I discuss these options in Chapter 21.

From Here

Here's a list of some other places in the book where you'll find information related to what you learned in this chapter:

- To learn how to control Internet Explorer via scripting, refer to the "Example: Scripting Internet Explorer" section in Chapter 12, "Programming the Windows Scripting Host."
- For the details on sending and receiving email using Windows Mail, see Chapter 19, "Communicating with Windows Mail."
- For information on the newsgroup capabilities of Windows Mail, see Chapter 20, "Participating in Internet Newsgroups."
- To learn about the security and privacy features in Internet Explorer, see Chapter 21, "Implementing Windows Vista's Internet Security and Privacy Features."

CHAPTER 19

Communicating with Windows Mail

IN THIS CHAPTER

If software programs can have inferiority complexes, Outlook Express, the email client that shipped with the previous few versions of Windows, would be a prime candidate. After all, Outlook Express was always seen as the poor cousin of Outlook, Microsoft's flagship email client. That might have been a bad rap because Outlook Express 6, the version that shipped with Windows XP, was a mature, full-featured client that did just about everything Outlook does. (The exception was that Outlook Express didn't support scripting. But that was really a mark in its favor because most email virus programmers target Outlook and its capability to run scripts embedded in messages.) More than that, Outlook Express even came with a few unique features of its own. The problem, though, is that many people didn't know what Outlook Express was capable of.

That could all change with Windows Vista because Outlook Express has been given a new moniker—Windows Mail—that should evoke fewer comparisons with the Office version of Outlook. Unfortunately, the name is just about all that's new with Windows Mail. Only three new features are of any significance:

- **Junk Mail Filter**—Borrowed from Microsoft Outlook's excellent spam filter, this does a fine job of detecting incoming spam and relegating it to the new `Junk Email` folder.
- **Instant Search box**—Like the Vista Start menu and folder windows, Windows Mail comes with an Instant Search box in the upper-right corner. You can use the Search box to perform as-you-type searches of the To, Cc, subject, and body text fields of the messages in the current folder.

- **Microsoft Communities**—Windows Mail comes with a preconfigured account for Microsoft's msnews.microsoft.com news server, which hosts more than 2,000 microsoft.public.* newsgroups. If you have a Microsoft Passport ID such as a Hotmail address, you can log in to the news server and rate newsgroup posts as either Useful or Not Useful.

My goal in this chapter is to give you a taste of what Windows Mail can do. I take you through subjects such as setting up accounts, processing messages, customizing columns, setting read and send options, maintaining Windows Mail, and working with identities, all of which will help you perform your email chores faster and more efficiently. (If you want to learn about the new spam filter, head for Chapter 21, "Implementing Windows Vista's Internet Security and Privacy Features.")

Setting Up Mail Accounts

If you haven't yet started Windows Mail—and so haven't yet defined your first mail account—or if you have multiple accounts and need to set up the others, this section shows you how to do it within Windows Mail.

Specifying Basic Account Settings

Here are the steps to follow to set up an email account with just the basic settings (which should be enough to get most accounts up and running):

1. Start the process using one of the following techniques:
   - Start Windows Mail for the first time.
   - In Windows Mail, select Tools, Accounts to display the Internet Accounts dialog box, click Add to open the Select Account Type dialog box, click E-mail Account, and then click Next.
2. Type your **display name**—this is the name that appears in the From field when you send a message—and click Next.
3. Type the email address for the account and click Next.
4. Specify your mail server data (click Next when you're done):

Incoming Mail Server Type	Use this list to select the incoming mail server type: POP3 or IMAP.
Incoming E-mail Server Name	Type the domain name for your incoming mail server.
Outgoing E-mail Server (SMTP) Name	Type the domain name for your outgoing mail server.

Outgoing Server Requires Authentication	Activate this check box if your Simple Mail Transfer Protocol (SMTP) server requires authentication before it will send your messages. (See "Enabling SMTP Authentication," later in this chapter, for more details.)

5. Type your email username and your password, and then click Next.
6. After Windows Mail sets up your account, it connects to your incoming mail server and downloads your waiting messages. If you don't want this to happen (for example, you might prefer to leave the messages on the server), activate the Do Not Download My E-mail at This Time check box.
7. Click Finish.
8. If you started from the Internet Accounts dialog box, click Close.

When the wizard completes its labors, your new account appears in the Mail section of the Internet Accounts dialog box, as shown in Figure 19.1 (note, too, the predefined account for the Microsoft Communities newsgroups). The next few sections use this dialog box, so you might want to leave it open for now. You can always return to it by selecting Tools, Accounts.

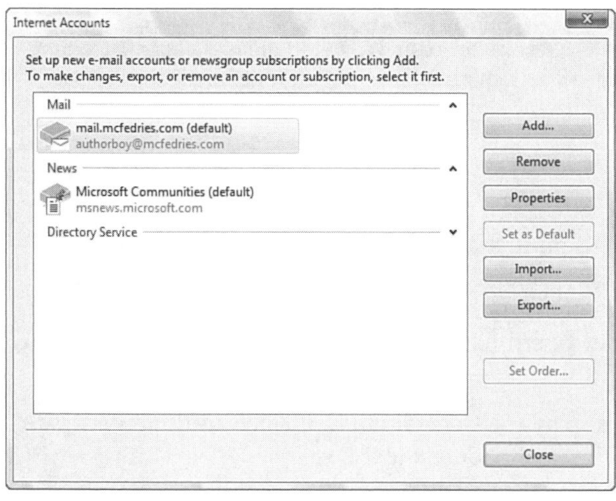

FIGURE 19.1 Your Internet email accounts are listed in the Mail section of the Internet Accounts dialog box.

Setting the Default Account

If you have more than one account, you should specify one of them as the default account. The default account is the one Windows Mail uses automatically when you send a message. To set the default account, select it in the Mail group and then click Set as Default.

NOTE

It *is* possible to send a message using any of your accounts. However, sending a message using anything other than the default account requires an extra step. See "Sending Messages," later in this chapter.

Specifying Advanced Account Settings

Although the basic account settings that you specify during the account setup process suffice in most cases, many accounts require a more advanced setup. For example, your Internet Service Provider (ISP) might require a different SMTP port or you might prefer to leave copies of your messages on the server.

To work with the advanced settings, select an account in the Mail group and then click Properties. The properties sheet that appears contains a number of tabs, and most of the controls in this dialog box are straightforward. The next four sections take you through some of the other options and show how useful they can be.

NOTE

I discuss the options in the Security tab as well as other email security issues in Chapter 21.

Using a Different Reply Address

It's occasionally useful to have replies sent to a different address. For example, if you're sending a message requesting feedback from a number of people, you might prefer that the return messages go to a colleague or assistant for collating or processing. Similarly, if you send a work-related message from a personal account, you might want replies sent to your work account.

To specify a different reply address, display the General tab in the account's properties sheet, and then type the address in the Reply Address text box.

Enabling SMTP Authentication

With spam such a big problem these days, many ISPs now require **SMTP authentication** for outgoing mail, which means that you must log on to the SMTP server to confirm that you are the person sending the mail (as opposed to some spammer spoofing your address). If your ISP uses authentication, display the Servers tab in the account's properties sheet, and then activate the My Server Requires Authentication check box. By default, Windows Mail logs you on using the same username and password as your incoming mail server. If your ISP has given you separate logon data, click Settings, activate the Log On Using option, type your account name and password, and click OK.

Specifying a Different SMTP Port

For security reasons, some ISPs insist that all their customers' outgoing mail route through the ISP's SMTP server. This usually isn't a problem if you're using an email account maintained by the ISP, but it can lead to problems if you're using an account provided by a third party (such as your website host):

- Your ISP might block messages sent using the third-party account because it thinks you're trying to relay the message through the ISP's server (a technique often used by spammers).
- You might incur extra charges if your ISP allows only a certain amount of SMTP bandwidth per month or a certain number of sent messages, whereas the third-party account offers higher limits or no restrictions at all.
- You might have performance problems because the ISP's server takes much longer to route messages than the third-party host.

You might think that you can solve the problem by specifying the third-party host's SMTP server in the account settings. However, this doesn't usually work because outgoing email transmits by default through port 25; when you use this port, you must also use the ISP's SMTP server.

To work around this, many third-party hosts offer access to their SMTP server via a port other than the standard port 25. To configure an email account to use a nonstandard SMTP port, display the Advanced tab in the account's properties sheet, and then use the Outgoing Mail (SMTP) text box to type the port number specified by the third-party host.

Checking the Same Account from Two Different Computers

In today's increasingly mobile world, it's common to have to check the same email account from multiple devices. For example, you might want to check your business account using not only your work computer, but also using your home computer or your notebook while traveling or using a PDA or other portable device while commuting.

Unfortunately, after you download a message, the server deletes it from the server and you can't access it from any other device. If you need to check mail on multiple devices, the trick is to leave a copy of the message on the server after you download it. That way the message will still be available when you check messages using another device.

To tell Windows Mail to leave a copy of each message on the server, display the Advanced tab in the account's properties sheet, and activate the Leave a Copy of Messages on the Server check box. You can also activate the following options:

Remove from Server After *X* Days	If you activate this check box, Windows Mail automatically deletes the message from the server after the number of days specified in the spin box.
Remove from Server When Deleted from 'Deleted Items'	If you activate this check box, Windows Mail deletes the message from the server only when you permanently delete the message from your system.

Here's a good strategy to follow:

- On your main computer, activate the Leave a Copy of Messages on the Server check box *and* the Remove from Server After *X* Days check box. Set the number of days long enough so that you have time to download the messages using your other devices.
- On all your other devices, activate only the Leave a Copy of Messages on the Server check box.

This strategy ensures that you can download messages on all your devices, but it prevents messages from piling up on the server.

NOTE

Other occasions could arise when you prefer to leave messages on the server temporarily. For example, if you're on the road, you might want to download the messages to a notebook or to some other computer that you're using temporarily. By leaving the messages on the server, you can still download them to your main computer when you return to the office or to your home. Similarly, you might want to download your messages into another email client for testing purposes or for taking advantage of features in that client but not found in Windows Mail.

Handling Incoming Messages

Incoming email messages are stored in your mailbox on your ISP's server until you use an email client such as Windows Mail to retrieve them. The easiest way to do that is to let Windows Mail check for and download new messages automatically. Several settings within the Options dialog box control this feature. Select Tools, Options and make sure that the General tab is displaying, as shown in Figure 19.2.

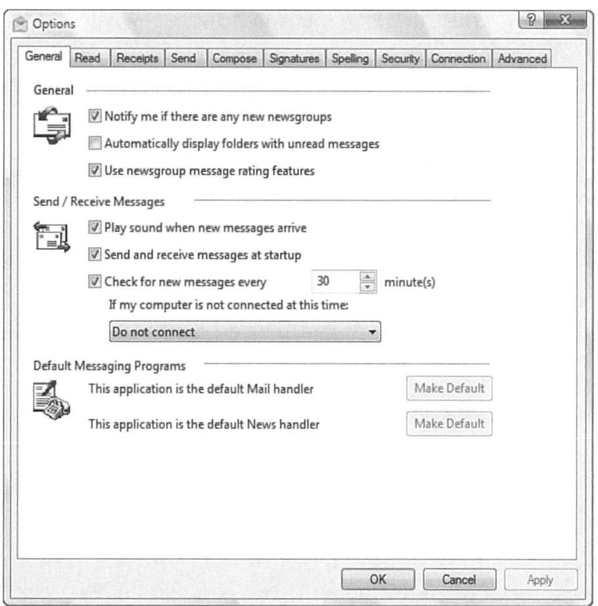

FIGURE 19.2 The General tab contains options related to retrieving messages.

Here are the settings related to retrieving messages:

Play Sound When New Messages Arrive — When you activate this option, Windows Mail plays a sound whenever it downloads one or more messages. If multiple messages arrive, Windows Mail plays the sound only once. This is useful only if you don't get very many messages and if you leave Windows Mail running in the background while maintaining a connection to the Internet. The sound is either annoying or redundant in any other scenario, so consider deactivating this check box.

TIP

It's possible to change the sound that indicates the arrival of a new message. Select Start, Control Panel, Hardware and Sound, Audio Devices and Sound Themes, and then display the Sounds tab. In the Program Events list, select New Mail Notification and then click Browse to choose the sound file you want Windows Mail to play when it delivers new messages.

Send and Receive Messages at Startup	When this check box is activated, Windows Mail connects with the server to check for waiting messages as soon as you start the program. It also sends any messages that are waiting in the Outbox folder. Note that if your computer has no current connection to the Internet, Windows Mail attempts to establish one. This is true even if you select Do Not Connect in the If My Computer Is Not Connected at This Time list (described later). If you prefer to stay offline at startup, deactivate this check box.
Check for New Messages Every *X* Minute(s)	With this option activated, Windows Mail automatically checks for new messages using the interval specified in the spin box. You can enter a time between 1 and 480 minutes.
If My Computer Is Not Connected at This Time	If you activate the Check for New Messages Every *X* Minute(s) check box, use the following list to specify what Windows Mail should do if your computer is not connected to the Internet when the time comes to check for new mesages:

- **Do Not Connect**—Choose this option to prevent Windows Mail from initiating a connection
- **Connect Only When Not Working Offlin**e—Choose this option to tell Windows Mail to connect only when the program is in online mode
- **Connect Only When Working Offline**—Choose this option to tell Windows Mail to connect only when the program is in offline mode

NOTE

To put Windows Mail in offline mode, pull down the File menu and activate the Work Offline command. To return to online mode, deactivate this command.

If you elect not to have Windows Mail check for new mail automatically, you can use any of the following techniques to check the server by hand:

- **To receive messages on all your accounts**—Select Tools, Send and Receive, Receive All, or click the Send/Receive button's arrow to drop down the list and then click Receive All.

- **To receive messages on only a single account**—Select Tools, Send and Receive and then select the account you want to work with, or click the Send/Receive button's arrow to drop down the list and then click the account.
- **To send and receive messages on all your accounts**—If you also have messages waiting in your outbox, select Tools, Send and Receive, Send and Receive All, or click the Send/Receive toolbar button.

TIP

A quick way to send and receive messages on all your accounts is to press Ctrl+M or F5.

Processing Messages

Each new message that arrives is stored in the `Inbox` folder's message list and appears in a bold font. To view the contents of any message, select it in the message list; Windows Mail displays the message text in the preview pane. If you find the preview pane too confining, you can open the selected message in its own window by double-clicking it.

When you have a message selected, you can do plenty of things with it (in addition to reading it, of course). You can print it, save it to a file, move it to another folder, reply to it, delete it, and more. Most of these operations are straightforward, so I'll just summarize the basic techniques here:

- **Dealing with attachments**—If a message has an attachment, you'll see a paper clip icon in the Inbox folder's Attachment column, as well as in the upper-right corner of the preview pane. You have two choices:

Open the attachment	Click the preview pane's paper clip icon and then click the name of the file.
Save the attachment	Click the preview pane's paper clip icon and then click Save Attachments. You can also select the File, Save Attachments command.

- **Moving a message to a different folder**—Later in this chapter, I'll show you how to create new folders you can use for storing related messages. To move a message to another folder, use your mouse to drag the message from the `Inbox` folder and then drop it on the destination folder.
- **Saving a message**—Instead of storing the message in a folder, you might prefer to save it to a file. To do so, select File, Save As and then use the Save As dialog box to select a location, enter a filename, and select a file type.

- **Saving a message as stationery**—If you receive a formatted message and you like the layout, you can save it as stationery for your own use. To do so, select File, Save As Stationery.
- **Printing a message**—To print a copy of the message, select File, Print.
- **Replying to a message**—Windows Mail gives you two reply options:

Reply to message author	This option sends the reply to only the person who sent the original message. Windows Mail ignores any names in the Cc line. To use this option, select Message, Reply to Sender or press Ctrl+R. You can also click the Reply button on the toolbar.
Reply to all message recipients	This option sends the reply not only to the original author, but also to anyone else mentioned in the Cc line. To use this option, select Message, Reply to All or press Ctrl+Shift+R. You can also click the Reply All button on the toolbar.

- **Forwarding a message**—You can forward a message to another address by using either of the following commands:

Forward	Select Message, Forward, press Ctrl+F, or click the Forward toolbar button. Windows Mail inserts the full text of the original message into the body of the new message and appends a greater than sign (>) to the beginning of each line.
Forward as Attachment	Select Message, Forward as Attachment. In this case, Windows Mail packages the original message as an attachment, but it makes no changes to the message. The user who receives the forwarded message can open this attachment and view the original message exactly as you received it.

- **Deleting a message**—To get rid of a message, select it in the folder and then press Delete (or Ctrl+D) or click the toolbar's Delete button. If the message is open, press Ctrl+D or click the Delete button. Note that Windows Mail doesn't really delete the message. Instead, it just moves it to the `Deleted Items` folder. If you change your mind and decide to keep the message, open the `Deleted Items` folder and move the message back to the folder it came from. To remove a message permanently, open the `Deleted Items` folder and delete the message from there.

Customizing the Message Columns

The default columns in Windows Mail tell you the basic information you need for any message. More information is available, however. For example, you might want to know the date and time the message was sent, the size of the message, and to whom the message was sent. You can display these items as columns in the message list. Here are the steps to follow to customize the Windows Mail columns:

1. Select View, Columns. (You can also right-click any column header and then click Columns.) Windows Mail displays the Columns dialog box, shown in Figure 19.3.

FIGURE 19.3 Use the Columns dialog box to customize the columns displayed in the message list.

2. To add a column, either activate its check box or select it and click Show.
3. To remove a column, either deactivate its check box or select it and click Hide.
4. To change the order of the columns, select a column and then use the Move Up and Move Down buttons to position the column where you want it. (Columns listed top to bottom display from left to right in the message list.)
5. To control the width of a column, select it and enter a new value in the The Selected Column Should Be *X* Pixels Wide text box.
6. Click OK.

Here are a few more column customization tricks:

- To change the width of a displayed column, use your mouse to drag the right edge of the column's header to the left or right.
- To change the width of a displayed column to fit its widest entry, double-click the right edge of the column's header.
- To change the position of a column, use your mouse to drag the column's header left or right.

Setting Read Options

To help you work with your correspondence, Windows Mail has a number of options related to reading messages. To view them, select Tools, Options to open the Options dialog box, and display the Read tab, as shown in Figure 19.4.

NOTE

For a discussion of the options in newsgroups, see Chapter 20, "Participating in Internet Newsgroups."

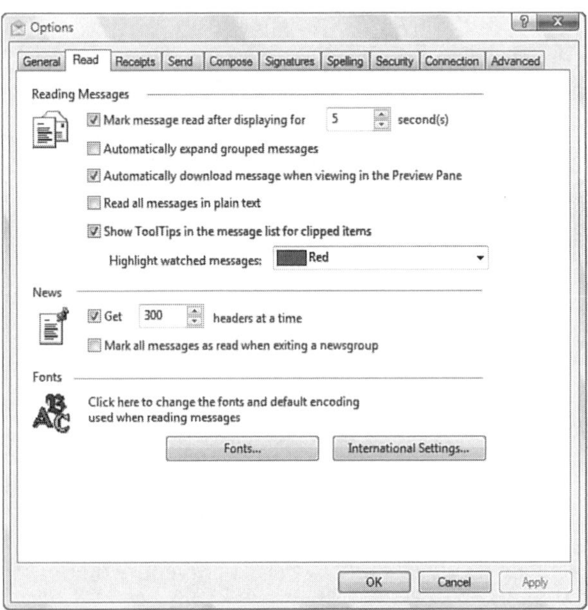

FIGURE 19.4 Use the Read tab to set various properties related to reading messages.

Here's a review of the controls in this tab:

Mark Message Read After Displaying for *X* Second(s)	Deactivate this check box to prevent Windows Mail from removing the boldfacing while you're reading a message. Alternatively, you can use the spin box to adjust how long it takes Windows Mail to remove the bold (the maximum is 60 seconds).

Marking Messages as Read

You can also control the marking of read messages via the Edit menu using the following commands:

Mark as Read—Turns off boldfacing for the current message or messages. Alternatively, press Ctrl+Q or Ctrl+Enter, or right-click the message and then click Mark as Read.

Mark as Unread—Turns on boldfacing for the current message or messages. You can also press Ctrl+Shift+Enter or right-click the message and then click Mark as Unread.

Mark Conversation as Read—Turns off boldfacing for all the messages in the conversation associated with the current message. (A **conversation** or **thread** is a group of messages that have the same subject line, ignoring the Re: and Fw: prefixes added to replies and forwards.) Alternatively, press Ctrl+T. For this command to work, you have to group messages by conversation by selecting the View, Current View, Group Messages by Conversation command.

Mark All Read—Turns off boldfacing on all messages in the current folder. You can also press Ctrl+Shift+A.

NOTE

Note that you can ask Windows Mail to display only unread messages by selecting the View, Current View, Hide Read Messages command. Select View, Current View, Show All Messages to return to the regular view.

Automatically Expand Grouped Messages	When you group messages by conversation (by selecting the View, Current View, Group Messages By Conversation command), Windows Mail displays only the first message in the group and includes a plus sign (+) to its left. You have to click the plus sign to see the other messages in the conversation. If you prefer to see all the messages in the conversation automatically, activate this check box.
Automatically Download Message When Viewing in the Preview Pane	When you're working with a Web-based email account (such as Hotmail) or a newsgroup, deactivate this check box to prevent Windows Mail from downloading message text when the message header is selected. When you're ready to receive the text, press the spacebar.

Read All Messages in Plain Text	Activate this check box to convert all HTML messages to plain text, which helps to thwart web bugs and malicious scripts. I discuss these and other security-related issues in Chapter 21.
Show ToolTips in the Message List for Clipped Items	When this check box is activated, Windows Mail displays clipped information (such as a subject line that's cut off at the end because the Subject column is too narrow) in a ToolTip when you hover the mouse pointer over the item.
Highlight Watched Messages	Use this list to specify the color that Windows Mail uses to display messages marked as watched. To mark a message as watched, you must first display the Watch/Ignore column (refer to the "Customizing the Message Columns" section, earlier in this chapter). Then click inside the column beside the message to add an eyeglasses icon to the column and to format the message in the specified color.
Fonts	Click this button to display the Fonts dialog box, which displays a list of the character sets installed on your computer. For each character set, you can specify a proportional and fixed-width font, as well as a font size and encoding. You can also specify which character set to use as the default.
International Settings	Click this button to display the International Read Settings dialog box. Activate the Use Default Encoding for All Incoming Messages to apply the encoding shown in the Default Encoding box to all your messages.

Sending Messages

Composing a basic message in Windows Mail is straightforward, and it isn't all that much different from composing a letter or memo in WordPad. There are a number of ways to get started, not all of them well known. Here's a summary:

- In Windows Mail, select Message, New Message; press Ctrl+N; or click the Create Mail toolbar button.

- In Internet Explorer, pull down the Page menu and then choose one of the following commands:

Send Page by E-mail	Select this command to create a new message with the current web page as the content of the message.
Send Link by E-mail	Select this command to create a new message with a URL shortcut file attached. This file is a shortcut for the current website that the recipient can click to load that site into Internet Explorer.

- In a web page, click a mailto link. This creates a new message addressed to the recipient specified by the link.
- In Windows Explorer, right-click a file and then click Send To, Mail Recipient. This creates a new message with the file attached.

From here, if you have multiple email accounts, use the From list to select the account from which you want to send the message. Use the To field to enter the address of the recipient; use the Cc field to enter the address of a recipient that you want to receive a copy of the message; use the Bcc field to enter the addresses of any recipients you want to receive blind copies of the message. (By default, Windows Mail does not display the Bcc field. To see it, select the View, All Headers command.) Note that in each field you can specify multiple recipients by separating the addresses with a semicolon (;).

Use the Subject field to enter a brief description of the message, and then use the box below the Subject field to enter your message. To send your message, you have two choices:

- **Select File, Send Message (or press Alt+S)**—This tells Windows Mail to send the message out to the Internet right away.
- **Select File, Send Later**—This command tells Windows Mail to store the message in the `Outbox` folder. If you choose this route, Windows Mail displays a dialog box telling you that your message is stored in the `Outbox` folder. Click OK. When you're ready to send the message, select the Tools, Send and Receive, Send All command in the Windows Mail window.

Taking Control of Your Messages

Windows Mail offers many more options for composing messages than the simple steps outlined in the previous section. Here's a summary of the other features and techniques you can use to modify your outgoing messages:

- **Choosing the message format**—Pull down the Format menu and select either Rich Text (HTML) or Plain Text. If you select the HTML sending format, use any of the formatting options found on the Format menu or the Formatting toolbar. Remember, however, that not all systems will transfer the rich text formatting (although most will).

- **Setting the message priority**—Select Message, Set Priority, and then choose the level—High, Normal, or Low—from the submenu that appears. Alternatively, drop down the Set Priority toolbar list and then click the level you want.
- **Attaching a file**—Select Insert, File Attachment, or click the Attach File to Message toolbar button, use the Open dialog box to select a file, and then click Open. Windows Mail adds an Attach box below the Subject line and displays the name and size of the file. To remove the attachment, click it in the Attach box and then press Delete.

TIP

Another way to attach a file to a message is to drag the file from Windows Explorer and drop it in the body of the message.

- **Inserting a file into the message**—Depending on the type of object you want to work with, Windows Mail gives you two methods of inserting objects (first click the position within the message where you want the file inserted):

Inserting file text	If you have text in a separate file that you want to add to the message, select the Insert, Text from File command. In the Insert Text File dialog box that appears, select the file and click Open. Windows Mail adds the file's contents to the message.
Inserting an image	To insert an image file into the message, select Insert, Picture. In the Picture dialog box that appears, select the image file and click Open. Windows Mail inserts the picture into the message.

- **Applying stationery**—Email stationery is a predefined message format that includes a background image and text. This is essentially a web page to which you can also add your own text. You choose stationery by selecting the Format, Apply Stationery command, and then picking out the stationery you want from the submenu that appears. Note that you can also begin a message with specific stationery by selecting the Message, New Message Using command in Windows Mail and then selecting the stationery. (Alternatively, drop down the Create Mail toolbar list and click the stationery you want.)

Working with Stationery

To set default stationery, select Tools, Options and then display the Compose tab. In the Stationery group, activate the Mail check box and then click the Select button to the right of that check box. Use the Select Stationery dialog box to choose the default stationery and then click OK. Note that the stationery files are HTML files, so if you know how to create your own web pages, you can also create your own stationery. Be sure to store the web page file in the following folder:

```
%UserProfile%\AppData\Local\Microsoft\Windows Mail\Stationery
```

Another way to create stationery is to click the Create New button in the Compose tab. (This button is also available in the Select Stationery dialog box.) This launches the Stationery Setup Wizard that takes you through the steps required to create custom stationery.

- **Inserting a signature**—A **signature** is text that appears at the bottom of a message. Most people use a signature to provide their email and web addresses, their company contact information, and perhaps a snappy quote or epigram that reflects their personality. If you've defined a signature (see the next section), you can insert it into the body of the message at the current cursor position by selecting Insert, Signature. If you've defined multiple signatures, select the one you want from the submenu that appears.
- **Requesting a read receipt**—To ask the recipient to send you a read receipt, select the Tools, Request Read Receipt command. Note that you can also set up Windows Mail to request a read receipt for all outgoing messages. In the Windows Mail window, select Tools, Options and then display the Receipts tab. Activate the Request a Read Receipt for All Sent Messages check box, and click OK. (Of course, *asking* for a read receipt is one thing, but actually *receiving* one is quite another. Unless the recipient's email client is set up to automatically send read receipts when requested, the decision on whether to send a read receipt is up to the recipient, and most people opt not to send them.)
- **Digitally signing or encrypting a message**—I cover these options in Chapter 21.

Creating a Signature

As I mentioned in the previous section, a signature is a few lines of text that provide contact information and other data. Windows Mail enables you to define a signature and append it to the bottom of every outgoing message (you can also insert it by hand in individual messages). Follow these steps to define a signature:

1. In the main Windows Mail window, select Tools, Options to open the Options dialog box.
2. Display the Signatures tab.
3. Click New to add a new signature to the Signatures list.
4. The default name for each new signature (such as Signature #1) is not very informative. To define a new name, click the signature, click Rename, type the new name, and then press Enter.
5. You now have two choices:
    - **Type the signature text by hand**—Activate the Text option and type your signature in the box provided.

- **Get the signature from a text file**—Activate the File option and enter the full path to the file in the box provided. (Alternatively, click Browse to choose the file from a dialog box.) In this case, note that if the file is in HTML format, the recipient might not see your signature correctly if their email client doesn't support HTML or (more likely these days) the recipient has opted to view all messages in plain text.

6. If you want Windows Mail to add the signature to all of your messages, activate the Add Signatures to All Outgoing Messages check box.
7. If you'd rather use the signature only on original messages, leave the Don't Add Signature to Replies and Forwards check box activated.
8. Windows Mail adds the default signature automatically if you activated the Add Signatures to All Outgoing Messages check box. To set a signature as the default, select it in the Signatures list and then click Set as Default.
9. To associate a signature with one or more accounts, select the signature in the Signatures list and then click Advanced. In the Advanced Signature Settings dialog box, activate the check box beside each account with which you want to associate the signature. Click OK.
10. Click OK to put the signature options into effect.

Creating an Email Shortcut for a Recipient

If you don't leave Windows Mail open all day, when you want to send a message it can seem like a lot of work to start the program, compose the new message, send it, and then close Windows Mail. You can save yourself a couple of steps by creating an email shortcut for a particular recipient on your desktop or in a folder such as `Quick Launch`. When you open the shortcut, a new email message window appears, already addressed to the recipient. You fill in the rest of the message and send it, all without starting Windows Mail. Follow these steps to create an email shortcut:

1. Display the desktop or open the folder in which you want to create the shortcut.
2. Right-click the desktop or folder and then select New, Shortcut. The Create Shortcut dialog box appears.
3. In the text box, type the following (where *`address`* is the email address of the recipient; see the example in Figure 19.5):

   `mailto:`*`address`*

4. Click Next.
5. Type a title for the shortcut (such as the person's name or email address).
6. Click Finish.

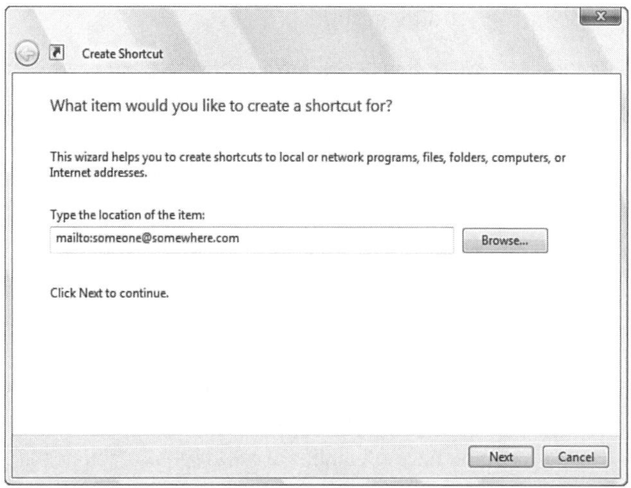

FIGURE 19.5 Type **`mailto:`*`address`*** to create an email shortcut for an email recipient.

Setting Send Options

Windows Mail offers a number of options for sending email. Select Tools, Options, and display the Send tab in the Options dialog box that appears, as shown in Figure 19.6.

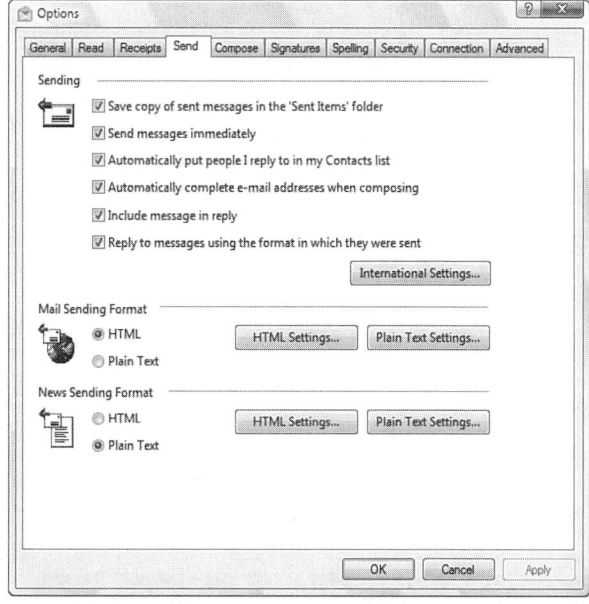

FIGURE 19.6 Windows Mail's options for sending email.

Here's a quick rundown of the options in the Sending group:

Save Copy of Sent Messages In the 'Sent Items' Folder	When this check box is activated, Windows Mail saves a copy of each message you send in the `Sent Items` folder. It's a good idea to leave this option checked because doing so gives you a record of the messages you send.
Send Messages Immediately	When you activate this check box, Windows Mail passes your message to the SMTP server as soon as you click the Send button. If you deactivate this option, clicking the Send button when composing a message only stores that message in the `Outbox` folder. This is useful if you have a number of messages to compose and you use a dial-up connection to the Internet. That is, you could compose all your messages offline and store them in the `Outbox` folder. You could then connect to the Internet and send all your messages at once.
Automatically Put People I Reply to in My Address Book	When you activate this option, each time you reply to a message, Windows Mail adds the recipient's name and email address to your Address Book. This only serves to clutter your Address Book with names you'll never or rarely use, so I recommend deactivating this check box.
Automatically Complete E-Mail Addresses When Composing	If you activate this check box, Windows Mail monitors the email addresses you enter when composing a message. If you've entered a similar address before, the program will automatically complete the rest of the address.
Include Message in Reply	When you enable this check box, Windows Mail includes the original message text as part of the new message when you reply to or forward a message. This is a good idea because including the original message text serves as a reminder to the original author of what you're responding to.

TIP

Including the original message text in replies is useful, but you should rarely have to include the entire reply. It's good email etiquette to delete unnecessary parts of the original message. Keep only the text that directly applies to your response.

Reply to Messages Using the Format in Which They Were Sent — When you activate this check box, Windows Mail automatically selects either the HTML or Plain Text sending format depending on the format used in the original message. If you prefer to always use your default sending format, deactivate this check box.

The Mail Sending Format group contains two option buttons that determine whether your messages contain formatting: HTML and Plain Text. If you activate the HTML button, Windows Mail enables you to apply a number of formatting options to your messages. In effect, your message becomes a miniature web page that you can format in much the same way that you would format a web page. Note, however, that only recipients who have an HTML-enabled mail client can see the formatting. Clicking the HTML Settings button beside the HTML option displays the HTML Settings dialog box, shown in Figure 19.7.

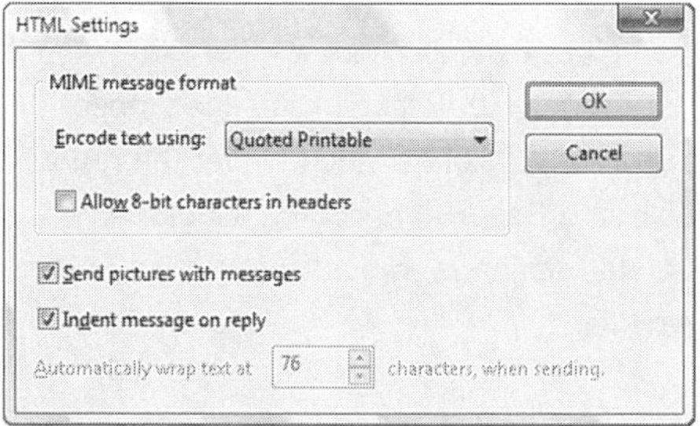

FIGURE 19.7 Use this dialog box to work with settings associated with the HTML sending format.

Here's a synopsis of the available options:

Encode Text Using — SMTP supports only 7-bit ASCII data, so binary messages or messages that include full 8-bit values (such as foreign characters), must be encoded. This list determines how (or whether) Windows Mail encodes message text:

- **None**—Tells Windows Mail not to encode the text.
- **Quoted Printable**—Use this encoding if your messages have full 8-bit values. This encoding converts each of these characters into an equal sign (=) followed by the character's hexadecimal representation. This ensures SMTP compatibility. (Note that most 7-bit ASCII characters are not encoded.)

- **Base 64**—Use this encoding if your message contains binary data. This encoding uses the Base64 alphabet, which is a set of 64 character/value pairs: A through Z is 0 through 25; a through z is 26 through 51; 0 through 9 is 52 through 61; + is 62 and / is 63. All other characters are ignored.

Allow 8-Bit Characters in Headers	When this check box is activated, characters that require eight bits—including ASCII 128 or higher, foreign character sets, and double-byte character sets—will be allowed within the message header without being encoded. If you leave this check box deactivated, these characters are encoded.
Send Pictures with Messages	When you activate this check box, Windows Mail sends pictures embedded in the message or used as the message background with the message text.
Indent Message on Reply	When you enable this check box and reply to a message, Windows Mail displays the original message indented below your reply.
Automatically Wrap Text at *X* Characters, When Sending	This spin box determines the point at which Windows Mail wraps text onto a new line. Many Internet systems can't read lines longer than 80 characters, so you shouldn't select a value higher than that. Note that the Quoted Printable and Base 64 encoding schemes require 76-character lines, so this option is available only if you select None in the Encode Text Using list.

If you activate the Plain Text option instead, Windows Mail sends your message as regular text, without any formatting. Clicking the Plain Text Settings button displays the Plain Text Settings dialog box, shown in Figure 19.8.

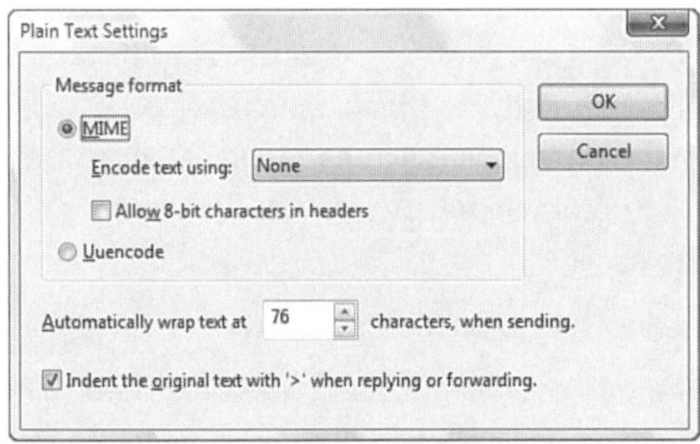

FIGURE 19.8 Use this dialog box to work with settings associated with the Plain Text sending format.

This dialog box includes many of the same options as the HTML Settings dialog box shown earlier. Here's what's different:

MIME	**MIME** stands for **Multipurpose Internet Mail Extensions,** the standard encoding format for text-based messages. Each of the encoding options I discussed earlier is MIME based.
Uuencode	This is an older encoding format used primarily when sending binary files to newsgroups.
Indent the Original Text with > When Replying or Forwarding	On the Internet, it's standard that original message text in a plain text reply be indicated with a greater than sign (>) at the beginning of each line. (Colons are sometimes used instead.) When you activate this check box, Windows Mail prefaces each line of the original message with whatever character you specify in the list.

Maintaining Windows Mail

For the most part, Windows Mail is a set-it-and-forget-it application. After the program and your accounts have been set up, you can go about your email business without worrying about Windows Mail itself. However, to ensure trouble- and worry-free operation, here's a list of a few maintenance chores you should perform from time-to-time:

- **Remove clutter from your inbox**—Few things in business life are more daunting and frustrating than an inbox bursting at the seams with a huge list of new or unprocessed messages. To prevent this from happening, you should regard the `Inbox` folder as a temporary holding area for all your incoming messages. Periodically throughout the day, you should perform the following routine to keep your Inbox clean:

  If a message doesn't require a response, file it or delete it. By *file it,* I mean move the message to another folder. You should have folders set up for all major recipients, projects, customers, and categories that you deal with.

  If a message requires a response and you can answer it without further research or without taking a lot of time, answer it immediately and then either delete or file the message.

  If a message requires a response but you can't send a reply right away, move the message to a folder designated for messages that require further action. You can then handle those messages later in the day when you have some time.

TIP

Before moving the message to whatever you've designated as your "action items" folder, be sure to mark the message as unread. That way you'll be able to see at a glance whether there are items in that folder and how many there are.

- **Clean out your `Deleted Items` folder**—This folder is a good safeguard to help you recover accidentally deleted messages. However, after a while, it's extremely unlikely that you'll need to recover a message from this folder. Therefore, you should regularly delete messages from the `Deleted Items` folder. I recommend leaving the last month's worth of deleted messages and deleting everything older.
- **Look for Windows Mail patches and updates**—Pay a visit to Windows Update to see whether Microsoft has released any security patches or updates for Windows Mail.
- **Back up your messages**—Windows Mail keeps your messages in various folders, the names of which correspond to the names you see in Windows Mail's Local Folders list. For example, the Inbox messages are stored in the `Inbox` folder. Each message uses the Windows Mail E-mail Message file type (`.eml` extension). Together these folders constitute the Windows Mail message store, which you can find in the following folder:

  ```
  %UserProfile%\AppData\Local\Microsoft\Windows Mail\Local Folders
  ```

  You should include the contents of this folder in your backups and run those backups regularly.

TIP

You can change the location of the message store. In Windows Mail, select Tools, Options, display the Advanced tab, and click Maintenance. Click the Store Folder button and, in the Store Location dialog box, click Change. Use the Browse for Folder dialog box to choose the new location and click OK. Note, too, that the following Registry setting holds the Windows Mail store location:

```
HKCU\Software\Microsoft\Windows Mail\Store Root
```

NOTE

The structure of the Windows Mail message store shows two major internal differences between Vista's Windows Mail email client and XP's Outlook Express email client. First, it shows us that Windows Mail no longer supports **identities**: separate mail accounts and folders for individual users. Instead, Windows Mail assumes that you use separate user accounts to maintain email privacy and security, which is indicated by the fact that the message store is located in a `%UserProfile%` subfolder. (This makes sense because having two different methods for maintaining separate email accounts is redundant, and user accounts provide more security and privacy.) Second, it shows us that Windows Mail no longer uses separate `.dbx` files to store the contents of each folder. This is good for a number of reasons. It enables you to access each message as an individual file (for example, you can double-click any `.eml` file to view the message). It brings the messages into the file system (for example, the message store is searchable) and it likely lessens the risk of data loss because `.dbx` files would occasionally become corrupted.

- **Back up your accounts**—If you have multiple accounts, re-creating them on a new system or in the event of a crash can be a lot of work. To lessen the drudgery, make backups of your accounts by saving them to Internet Account Files (`.iaf` extension). In Windows Mail, select Tools, Accounts, select an account, and then click Export. In the Export Internet Account dialog box, choose a location and then click Save. Note that you can also do this with News and Directory Service accounts.

TIP

Windows Mail stores the data for each account in a file named `account{ID}.oeaccount`, where *ID* is a unique 32-digit identifier. An even easier way to back up your accounts is to include these account files in your backup. You can find these files in the same folder as your message store:

```
%UserProfile%\AppData\Local\Microsoft\Windows Mail\Local Folders
```

- **Back up your Windows Mail data**—Your defined Windows Mail rules, signatures, and settings are stored in the following Registry key:

  ```
  HKCU\Software\Microsoft\Windows Mail\
  ```

  Regularly export this key (refer to Chapter 11, "Getting to Know the Windows Vista Registry") to save this important Windows Mail data.

- **Compact your message store database**—Although Windows Mail keeps your email data in regular folders and `.eml` files, it keeps track of those folders and files using a database file named `WindowsMail.MSMessageStore`. When you delete messages, Windows Mail removes the corresponding data from the message store database, which results in gaps within the file. To remove these gaps and reduce the size of the file, Windows Mail is set up to compact the database from time to time. Specifically, Windows Mail compacts the database every hundredth time you shut down the program. If you want the database compacted more often, select Tools, Options, display the Advanced tab, and click Maintenance. Make sure to activate the Compact the Database on Shutdown Every *X* Runs check box, and use the spin box to set the compaction interval you prefer.

19

Filtering Incoming Messages

Just a few years ago, my email chores took up only a few minutes of each workday. Now it takes me up to two or three hours to get through the hundreds of messages I receive every day. What's interesting about this time increase is that it's by no means unusual. Most people find that when they really get into Internet email, the messages start to pile up quickly.

To help ease the crunch, Windows Mail offers **message rules**, and you can set up and configure these rules to handle incoming messages for you automatically. Of course, these rules are limited in what they can do, but what they *can* do isn't bad:

- If you'll be out of the office for a few days or if you'll be on vacation, you can create a rule to send out an automatic reply that lets each sender know you received the message but won't be able to deal with it for a while.
- If you have multiple email accounts, you can set up a rule to redirect incoming messages into separate folders for each account.

NOTE

One of the problems with redirecting messages to other folders is that it's less convenient to read those messages. Windows Mail helps by bolding the name of any folder that contains unread messages. It also tells you how many unread messages are in each folder. Windows Mail opens the folder tree to reveal any folders that have unread messages. To enable this option, select Tools, Options and check that the Automatically Display Folders with Unread Messages setting in the General tab is marked.

- You can create a rule to redirect incoming messages into separate folders for specific people, projects, or mailing lists.
- If you receive unwanted messages from a particular source (such as someone who is harassing you or someone who sends you an excessive number of jokes), you can set up a rule to automatically delete those messages.

Here are the steps to follow to create a message rule:

1. Select the Tools, Message Rules, Mail command. One of two things will happen:
   - If this is the first time you are creating a rule, Windows Mail displays the New Mail Rule dialog box.
   - If you already have at least one rule, the Message Rules dialog box appears with the Mail Rules tab displayed. In this case, click New to open the New Mail Rule dialog box.
2. In the Select the Conditions for Your Rule list, activate the check box beside the rule condition you want to use to pick out a message from the herd. Windows Mail adds the condition to the Rule Description text box. You're free to select multiple conditions.

3. The condition shown in the Rule Description text box will probably have some underlined text. You need to replace that underlined text with the specific criterion you want to use (such as a word or an address). To do that, click the underlined text, type the criterion in the dialog box that appears, and click Add. Most conditions support multiple criteria (such as multiple addresses or multiple words in a Subject line), so repeat this step as necessary. When you're done, click OK. Windows Mail updates the Rule Description text box with the text you entered, as shown in Figure 19.9.

FIGURE 19.9 Click underlined text in the Rule Description text box to edit the text to the criterion you want for your rule.

TIP

If you add multiple words or phrases to a rule criterion, you can make that criterion use Boolean operators such as AND, OR, and NOT. To do this, click the Options button in the dialog box that appears in step 3. To make an AND criterion, activate Message Matches All of the *X* Below (where *X* depends on the condition—for example, *words* or *people*); to make an OR criterion, activate Message Matches Any One of the *X* Below; to make a NOT criterion, activate Message Does Not Contain the *X* Below.

CAUTION

If you've defined multiple rules, problems can occur if you have two or more rules that apply to an incoming message, but the first of those rules moves the message to another folder. In such cases, Windows Mail will often display an error message saying that it can't process more rules. To avoid this error, add the condition Stop Processing More Rules to the initial rule.

4. If you selected multiple conditions, Windows Mail assumes that all the conditions must be true before invoking the rule (Boolean AND). If you need only one of the conditions to be true (Boolean OR), click and in the Rule Description text box, activate the Messages Match Any One of the Criteria option, and click OK.
5. In the Select the Actions for Your Rule list, activate the check box beside the action you want Windows Mail to take with messages that meet your criteria. You might have to click underlined text in the Rule Description text box to complete the action. You can select multiple actions.
6. Use the Name of the Rule text box to type a descriptive name for the rule.
7. Click OK. Windows Mail drops you off at the Mail Rules tab of the Message Rules dialog box.

Whichever method you used, here are a few notes to bear in mind when working with the list of rules:

- **Toggling rules on and off**—Use the check box beside each rule to turn the rule on and off.
- **Setting rule order**—Some rules should be processed before others. For example, if you have a rule that deletes messages from annoying people, you want Windows Mail to process that rule before sending out a vacation reply. To adjust the order of a rule, select it and click either Move Up or Move Down.
- **Modifying a rule**—To make changes to a rule, you have two choices: If you just want to edit the rule's underlined values, select the rule and use the Rule Description box to click the underlined values you want to change; if you want to make more substantial changes to a rule, select it and click Modify.
- **Applying a rule**—If you want to apply a rule to existing `Inbox` folder messages or to messages in a different folder, click Apply Now to open the Apply Mail Rules Now dialog box. Select the rule you want to apply (or click Select All to apply them all). To choose a different folder, click Browse. When you're ready, click Apply Now.
- **Deleting a rule**—Select the rule and click Remove. When Windows Mail asks whether you're sure, click Yes.

Finding a Message

Although you'll delete many of the messages that come your way, it's unlikely that you'll delete all of them. Over time, you'll probably end up with hundreds (or more likely thousands) of messages stored throughout various folders. What happens if you want to find a particular message? Even if you curmudgeonly delete everything that comes your way, your `Sent Items` folder will eventually contain copies of the hundreds or thousands of missives you've sent out. What do you do if you want to find one of those messages?

For both incoming and outgoing messages, Windows Mail offers a decent Find Message feature that can look for messages based on addresses, subject lines, body text, dates, and more.

Simple Searches

Like many other Windows Vista features, Windows Mail comes with an Instant Search box in the upper-right corner. If you're not fussy about what part of the message Find uses to look for a particular word, and if you already know which folder holds the message you want, you can use the Instant Search box for quick-and-dirty searches. Here are the steps to follow:

1. Use the Local Folders list to select the folder in which you want to search.
2. Click inside the Instant Search box (or press Ctrl+E).
3. Type the text that you want to use as the search criteria. Instant Search looks for the search text in the From, To, and Subject fields as well as the body of each message.

NOTE

When entering your search criteria, you can enter partial words, single words, or multiple words. If you include multiple words, Instant Search matches only messages that contain *all* the words. If you want to search for an exact phrase, place quotation marks around the phrase. Finally, note that the search is not case sensitive.

Advanced Searches

If you want to search specific message fields, if you want to specify different criteria for each field, or if you want to include specialized criteria (such as the message date or whether a message has attachments), you have to use the full-fledged Find Message feature. To try it out, select the Edit, Find, Message command. (Alternatively, press Ctrl+Shift+F or click the Find toolbar button.) Figure 19.10 shows the Find Message dialog box that appears. Use the following controls to set the search criteria:

Browse	Select the folder to search. If you want the search to include the subfolders of the selected folder, leave the Include Subfolders check box activated.
From	Type one or more words that specify the email address or display the name of the sender you want to find.

NOTE

As with Instant Search, the individual Find Message criteria match only those messages that contain *all* the words you enter, match only whole words, and are not case sensitive. Note, too, that Find Message looks only for messages that match all the criteria you enter.

FASTER SEARCHING

The Find Message feature in Windows Mail is quite slow, particularly if you have a message store containing thousands of messages. If you frequently search for messages, there are third-party tools available that can search your email much faster. A good choice is Google Desktop Search (desktop.google.com).

To	Type one or more words that specify the email address or display name of the recipient you want to find.
Subject	Type one or more words that specify the Subject line you want to find.
Message	Type one or more words that specify the message body you want to find.
Received Before	Select the latest received date for the message you want to find.
Received After	Select the earliest received date for the message you want to find.
Message Has Attachment(s)	Activate this check box to find only messages that have attached files.
Message Is Flagged	Activate this check box to find only messages that have been flagged.

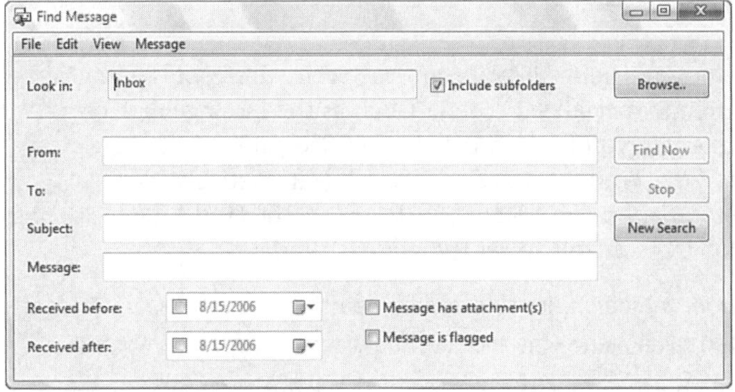

FIGURE 19.10 Use the Find Message dialog box to look for specific messages in a folder.

After you define your search criteria, click Find Now. If Windows Mail finds any matches, it displays them in a message list at the bottom of the dialog box. From there, you can open a message or use any of the commands in the menus to work with the messages (reply, forward, move to another folder, delete, and so on).

From Here

Here's a list of chapters where you'll find related information:

- For information on user accounts, refer to Chapter 6, "Getting the Most Out of User Accounts."
- You can also use Windows Mail as a newsreader. For the details, see Chapter 20, "Participating in Internet Newsgroups."
- For information on Windows Mail security and privacy issues, see Chapter 21, "Implementing Windows Vista's Internet Security and Privacy Features."

CHAPTER 20

Participating in Internet Newsgroups

IN THIS CHAPTER

The vast majority of the attention, buzz, and hype about the Internet is centered on the World Wide Web. That's not surprising because it's the easiest Net service for novices to use, and it's where all the cutting-edge development is taking place. The rest of the Internet services fall into two categories: those that have fallen into disuse (anybody remember Gopher?) and those that just keep on keeping on.

A good example of the latter type of service is Usenet. Usenet is, in essence, a collection of topics available for discussion. These discussion groups (or **newsgroups**, as they're normally called) are open to all and sundry, and they usually won't cost you a dime (aside from the usual connection charges, of course; note, too, that some ISPs charge extra for newsgroup access).

Will you find anything interesting in these discussion groups? Well, let's put it this with way: With more than 100,000 (that's right, one hundred *thousand*) groups to choose from, if you can't find anything that strikes your fancy, you'd better check your pulse. (Not all service providers offer the complete menu of Usenet groups, so the number available to you might be considerably less than 100,000.) On the other hand, most of Usenet has no central control, which means that many newsgroups have degenerated into a collection of rambling, off-topic posts and unsolicited commercial email. (One wag has likened Usenet to a *verbal landfill*.) Not all groups are this bad, but you'll need to be cautious when choosing which discussions you join.

In this chapter, I'll now turn your attention (if I may) to the Usenet service. I'll give you some background about Usenet, and then I'll show you how to wield the newsreader portion of the Windows Mail show.

NOTE

Usenet began its life back in 1979 at Duke University. A couple of resident computer whizzes (James Elliot and Tom Truscott) needed a way to easily share research, knowledge, and smart-aleck opinions among Duke students and faculty. So, in true hacker fashion, they built a program that would do just that. Eventually, other universities joined in, and the thing just mushroomed. Today, tens of millions of people participate in Usenet, sending millions of messages a day.

Some Usenet Basics

To get your Usenet education off on the right foot, this section looks at a few crucial concepts that will serve as the base from which you can explore the rest of Usenet:

hierarchy Usenet divides its discussion groups into several classifications, or ***hierarchies***. There are several so-called **mainstream** hierarchies:

biz	Business
comp	Computer hardware and software
misc	Miscellaneous stuff that doesn't really fit anywhere else
news	Usenet-related topics
rec	Entertainment, hobbies, sports, and more
sci	Science and technology
soc	Sex, culture, religion, and politics
talk	Debates about controversial political and cultural topics

Most Usenet-equipped Internet service providers give you access to all the mainstream hierarchies. In addition, a huge alt (alternative) hierarchy covers just about anything that either doesn't belong in a mainstream hierarchy or is too wacky to be included with the mainstream groups. There are also many smaller hierarchies designed for specific geographic areas. For example, the ba hierarchy includes discussion groups for the San Francisco Bay area, the can hierarchy is devoted to Canadian topics, and so on.

newsgroup This is the official Usenet moniker for a discussion topic. Why are they called *newsgroups*? Well, the original Duke University system was designed to share announcements, research findings, and commentary. In other words, people used this system if they had some news to share with their colleagues. The name stuck, and now you'll often hear Usenet referred to as **Netnews** or simply as **the news**.

newsreader The software you use to read a newsgroup's articles and to post your own articles. In Windows Vista, you can use Windows Mail as a newsreader. Other Windows newsreaders include Agent (www.forteinc.com/agent/) and NewsPro (www.netwu.com/newspro/). For the Mac, you can try Microsoft Entourage, part of the Office 2004 suite, or MT-NewsWatcher (www.smfr.org/mtnw/).

NOTE

Instead of using a newsreader, you can access all the newsgroups through your web browser by using Google Groups (groups.google.com). This is useful if your ISP does not offer newsgroup access or if you would like to read particular newsgroups without having to subscribe to them. However, if you want to post messages to a newsgroup, you must register with Google.

news server (or **NNTP server**) A computer that stores newsgroups and handles requests to post and download newsgroup messages. There are four types of news server:

- **ISP news server**—Most ISPs supply you with an account on their news server in addition to your email account. Your news server username and password are usually the same as your email username and password, but check with your ISP. You should also confirm the Internet name of the ISP's news server. This name usually takes the form news.*ispname*.com or nntp.*ispname*.com, where *ispname* is the name of your ISP.
- **Commercial news server**—If your ISP does not offer newsgroup access, or if your ISP offers only a limited number of groups, consider using a commercial news server, which offers newsgroup access for a fee. Two of the largest commercial news servers are Giganews (www.giganews.com) and Newscene (www.newscene.com).
- **Public news server**—If you are on a limited budget, try a public news server that offers free newsgroup access. Note, however, that most public servers restrict the number of users on the server, offer a limited number of groups, or place a cap on the amount you can download. For a list of public news servers, try Newzbot (www.newzbot.com) or Free Usenet News Servers (freenews.maxbaud.net).

- **Semi-private news server**—Some companies maintain their own news server and their own set of newsgroups. For example, Microsoft maintains a news server at msnews.microsoft.com that runs more than 2,000 groups related to Microsoft products and technologies. Windows Mail sets up an account for this server automatically.

post To send an article to a newsgroup.

subscribe In a newsreader, to add a newsgroup to the list of groups you want to read. If you no longer want to read the group, you unsubscribe from the group.

thread A series of articles related to the same Subject line. A thread always begins with an original article and then progresses through one or more follow-ups. Note that Windows Mail calls a thread a *conversation*.

Figuring Out Newsgroup Names

Newsgroup names aren't too hard to understand, but we need to go through the drill to make sure that you're comfortable with them. In their basic guise, newsgroup names have three parts: the hierarchy to which they belong, followed by a dot, followed by the newsgroup's topic. For example, check out the following name:

rec.boats

Here, the hierarchy is rec (recreation), and the topic is boats. Sounds simple enough so far. But many newsgroups were too broad for some people, so they started breaking the newsgroups into subgroups. For example, the rec.boats people who were into canoeing got sick of speedboat discussions, so they created their own *paddle* newsgroup. Here's how its official name looks:

rec.boats.paddle

You'll see lots of these subgroups in your Usenet travels. (For example, there are also newsgroups named rec.boats.building and rec.boats.racing.) Occasionally, you'll see sub-subgroups, such as soc.culture.african.american, but these are still rare in most hierarchies (the exception is the comp hierarchy, in which you'll find all kinds of these sub-subgroups).

Understanding Articles and Threads

Articles, as you can imagine, are the lifeblood of Usenet. As I mentioned earlier, every day people post hundreds of thousands of articles to the different newsgroups. Some newsgroups might get only one or two articles a day, but many get a dozen or two, on average. (And some very popular groups—rec.humor is a good example—can get a hundred or more postings in a day.)

Happily, Usenet places no restrictions on article content. (However, a few newsgroups have **moderators** who decide whether an article is worth posting.) Unlike, say, the heavily censored America Online chat rooms, Usenet articles are the epitome of free speech. Articles can be as long or short as you like (although extremely long articles are frowned on because they take so long to retrieve) and, within the confines of the newsgroup's subject matter, they can contain whatever ideas, notions, and thoughts you feel like getting off your chest. You're free to be inquiring, informative, interesting, infuriating, or even incompetent—it's entirely up to you. (Although you should read the section "Practicing Newsgroup Etiquette" later in this chapter for hints on how to behave.)

Earlier I told you that newsgroups were *discussion topics*, but that doesn't mean they work like a real-world discussion, where you have immediate conversational give and take. Instead, newsgroup discussions lurch ahead in discrete chunks (articles) and unfold over a relatively long period (sometimes even weeks or months).

To get the flavor of a newsgroup discussion, think of the Letters to the Editor section of a newspaper. Someone writes an article in the paper, and later someone else sends in a letter commenting on the content of the article. A few days after that, more letters might come in, such as a rebuttal from the original author or someone else weighing in with his two cents' worth. Eventually, the discussion dies out either because the topic has been exhausted or because everyone lost interest.

Newsgroups work in just the same way. Someone posts an article, and then the other people who read the group can, if they like, respond to the article by posting a **follow-up** article. Others can then respond to the response, and so on down the line. This entire discussion—from the original article to the last response—is called a **thread**.

Practicing Newsgroup Etiquette

To help make Usenet a pleasant experience for all the participants, there are a few rules of newsgroup etiquette—sometimes called **netiquette**, a blend of *network* and *etiquette*—you should know. Here's a summary:

- **Don't SHOUT**—Use the normal rules of capitalization in your message text. In particular, AVOID LENGTHY PASSAGES OR ENTIRE MESSAGES WRITTEN IN CAPITAL LETTERS, WHICH ARE DIFFICULT TO READ AND MAKE IT APPEAR THAT YOU ARE SHOUTING.
- **Write good subjects**—Busy newsgroup readers often use a message's subject line to decide whether to read the message. This is particularly true if the recipient does not know you. Therefore, do not use subject lines that are either vague or overly general—for example, Info Required or A Newsgroup Post. Make your subject line descriptive enough that the reader can tell at a glance what your message is about.

TIP

When you reply to a post, the newsreader adds *Re:* to the subject line. However, it's common for the topic under discussion to change after a while. If you're changing the topic in a reply, be sure to change the subject line, too. If you think other readers of the original subject will also be interested in this reply, quote the original subject line as part of your new subject, as in this example:

```
Dog food suggestions needed (was Re: Canine nutrition)
```

- **Quote appropriately**—When posting a follow-up, you can make sure that other group readers know what you are responding to by including quotes from the original message in your reply. However, quoting the entire message is usually wasteful, especially if the message is lengthy. Just include enough of the original to put your response into context.
- **Be patient**—If you post an article and it doesn't show up in the newsgroup five seconds later, don't resend the article. A posted article goes on quite a journey as it wends its way through the highways and byways of the Internet. As a result, it could take several minutes or even as long as an hour before your article appears in the newsgroup. (This is why it's bad Usenet form to post articles "announcing" some current news event. By the time the article appears, the event is likely to be old news to most readers, and you'll end up looking just plain silly. If you're aching to discuss it with someone, try the misc.headlines group.)
- **Don't send flames**—If you receive a message with what appears to be a thoughtless or insulting remark, your immediate reaction might be to compose an emotionally charged, scathing reply. Such a message is a **flame**, and it will probably only make matters worse. If you feel the message merits a response (and very often, it doesn't), allow yourself at least 24 hours to cool down before responding to the message.
- **Ask questions**—If you are just starting out with newsgroups, you might have questions about how they work or what kinds of groups are available. There is a newsgroup devoted to these kinds of questions: news.newusers.questions.
- **Read the FAQ**—After you've subscribed to a newsgroup and before you post your first message, read through the group's list of Frequently Asked Questions (FAQ). Some newsgroups post their own FAQs regularly, usually monthly. You can also find FAQs in the answers topic under each mainstream hierarchy: comp.answers, rec.answers, and so on. Alternatively, the news.answers group contains periodic FAQ postings from most groups that have FAQs.
- **Search existing posts**—If you have a question that isn't in the FAQ, there's still a good chance that someone has asked it before and received an answer. Before posting, search the newsgroup to see if your question has popped up in the past.
- **Post something**—Newsgroups thrive on participation and the constant give and take of post and follow-up. Merely reading posts adds no value to a group, so every subscriber is expected to post at least occasionally.

- **Post appropriately**—When you want to post a message, think carefully about which newsgroup is appropriate so that you do not send a message that other people see as off-topic or even offensive. Also, unless it is absolutely necessary, do not post your message to two or more groups—a practice called **cross-posting**—even if they cover closely related topics.
- **Read existing follow-ups**—Before posting a reply to an existing message, check to see whether the post already has any follow-ups. If so, read them to make sure that your follow-up does not simply repeat something that was already said.
- **Don't advertise**—For the most part, Usenet is not an advertising medium, so do not post ads to newsgroups. If you really want to advertise, use the appropriate group in the biz hierarchy. For example, if you have property you want to sell, you can post an ad on biz.marketplace.real-estate. Including the address of your website in your signature is perfectly acceptable, however.
- **Use summaries**—Posts that act as surveys or that ask for suggestions can often generate lots of responses, many of which are repeats. If you want to post such a message, tell the respondents to send their replies to you via email and offer to summarize the results. When all the follow-ups are in, post your own follow-up that includes a summary of the responses you received.

Setting Up a News Account

Now that you know a bit about Usenet, it's time to get down to more practical matters. Specifically, the rest of this chapter will show you how to use Windows Mail to subscribe to, read, and post to newsgroups.

First, however, you need to know how to set up an account for the new server you want to use. I mentioned earlier that Windows Mail automatically adds an account for the Microsoft Communities groups (msnews.microsoft.com). If you want to set up an account for another server, here are the steps to follow:

1. In Windows Mail, select Tools, Accounts to display the Internet Accounts dialog box.
2. Click Add to display the Select Account Type dialog box.
3. Click Newsgroup Account and then click Next.
4. Type your **display name**—this is the name that will appear in the From field when you post a message—and click Next.
5. Type an email address and click Next. The Internet News Server Name dialog box appears.

CAUTION

Why do you need to specify an email address for Usenet? Because people might want to respond to one of your posts privately, rather than to the newsgroup itself. Unfortunately, many spammers harvest the email addresses of Usenet participants for their nefarious ends, so it's not a good idea to use a legitimate address in your news account. I'll discuss this in more detail when I discuss spam avoidance in Chapter 21, "Implementing Windows Vista's Internet Security and Privacy Features."

6. Type the name of your server in the News (NNTP) Server text box. If you must log on to the server, activate the My News Server Requires Me to Log On check box. Click Next.
7. If your news server requires a logon, type your account name (your username) and your password and click Next.
8. Click Finish. Your new account appears in the News tab of the Internet Accounts dialog box, as shown in Figure 20.1.

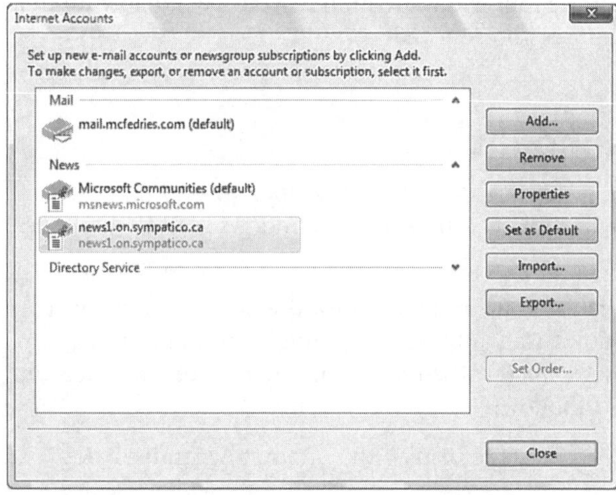

FIGURE 20.1 Your Internet news accounts are listed in the News tab.

9. Click Close. Windows Mail asks whether you want to download newsgroups from the news account.
10. Click Yes. Windows Mail downloads the groups (note that this might take quite a while, depending on the speed of your connection), and then displays the Newsgroup Subscriptions dialog box.

I show you how to use the Newsgroup Subscriptions dialog box in the next section, so keep it open for now.

Working with Newsgroups in Windows Mail

With your news account defined, your next chore is to subscribe to one or more newsgroups. If you don't have the Newsgroup Subscriptions window open from the previous section, use any of the following techniques to display it:

- Select Tools, Newsgroups
- Press Ctrl+W
- Click the news account in the Folders list and then click the Newsgroups toolbar button

If you have multiple news accounts, click the one you want to work with in the Account(s) list. (If you elected not to download the account's newsgroups from the server during the account setup, Windows Mail automatically downloads the newsgroups now.) Windows Mail displays the account's newsgroups, as shown in Figure 20.2.

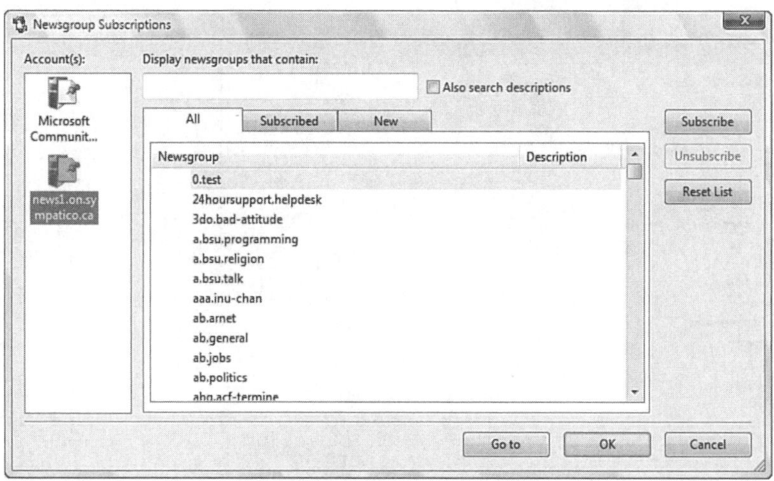

FIGURE 20.2 Use this dialog box to work with newsgroups in Windows Mail.

Newsgroups are at the heart of Usenet, so you'll need to become comfortable with basic newsgroup chores such as subscribing and unsubscribing. The next two sections take you through the basics.

Subscribing to a Newsgroup

Before you can read or post articles, you have to add a newsgroup or two to your news server account. You have two ways of doing this: You can subscribe to a newsgroup or you can open a newsgroup without committing to a subscription.

Either way, you must first display the group you want in the Newsgroup list. You can either scroll through the groups or type all or part of the newsgroup name in the Display

Newsgroups That Contain text box. Note that Windows Mail looks for group names that contain the text you type. If you type **wine**, for example, Windows Mail will match alt.food.wine, rec.crafts.winemaking, and so on. Figure 20.3 shows this example.

Downloading Newsgroup Descriptions

Some newsgroups have descriptions that give you a brief overview of what the group is about. By default, Windows Mail doesn't download these descriptions because it slows down the group retrieval process. However, if you have a fast connection, you should tell Windows Mail to download the descriptions. To do that, return to Windows Mail and select Tools, Accounts. In the News tab, click the news account you want to work with and then click Properties (or just double-click the account) to open the account's properties sheet. In the Advanced tab, activate the Use Newsgroup Descriptions check box and then click OK. Open the Newsgroup Subscriptions window again, click the new server, and then click Reset List. Windows Mail downloads the newsgroup names and their descriptions. To include the descriptions when searching newsgroup names, activate the Also Search Descriptions check box.

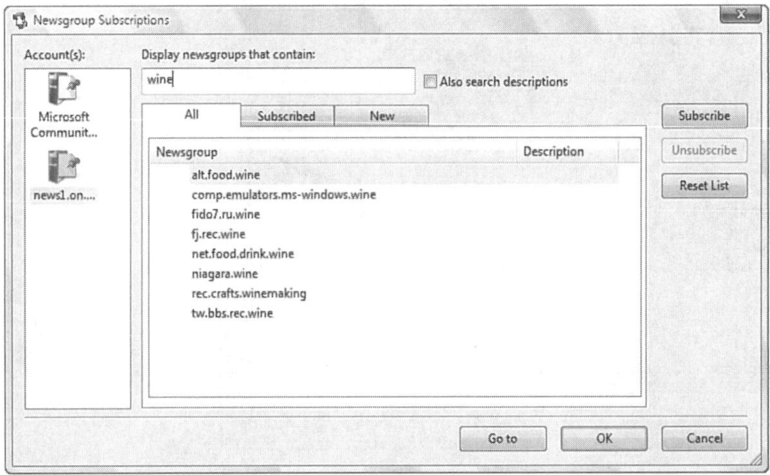

FIGURE 20.3 Windows Mail matches newsgroup names that contain the text you type.

After you've selected a newsgroup, use either of the following techniques:

- **If you just want to view the group without subscribing, click Go To**—You'll be returned to the Windows Mail window with the newsgroup displayed. If you later want to subscribe to this group, right-click the group name in the Local Folders list and then click Subscribe.
- **If you want to subscribe to the group, click the Subscribe button**—You can repeat this process for any other newsgroup subscriptions. In each case, Windows Mail adds the name of the group to the Subscribed tab. (To subscribe to multiple groups at once, hold down Ctrl, click each group, and then click Subscribe.) When you're done, click OK to return to the main Windows Mail window.

Unsubscribing from a Newsgroup

If you get tired of a newsgroup, you can unsubscribe at any time by using either of the following techniques:

- In the Newsgroup Subscriptions dialog box, display the Subscribed tab, select the newsgroup, and click Unsubscribe.
- In the Windows Mail window, right-click the group name in the Local Folders list and then click Unsubscribe.

Downloading Messages

With some newsgroups selected, you're now ready to start grabbing messages to read. With Windows Mail, you have two ways to proceed:

- **Online**—Working online means you're connected to the news server. You can download message headers at any time, and highlighting a message downloads the message text immediately.
- **Offline**—Working offline means that you connect briefly to get the available headers in a group. While you're not connected, you examine the subject lines of the messages and mark those that you want to retrieve. You then connect again and tell Windows Mail to download the marked messages.

In Windows Mail, you switch between offline and online mode by activating and deactivating the File, Work Offline command.

Downloading Message Headers

When you're in online mode, Windows Mail offers the following methods for downloading a newsgroup's message headers (this known as **synchronizing** the headers):

- **Click the newsgroup in the Folders list**—Windows Mail will download the headers for you automatically. For busy groups, the default download limit of 300 might not grab every header. To get more headers, select Tools, Get Next 300 Headers. (As you'll see later, you can adjust this header limit to your liking.)
- **Click the newsgroup and then select the Tools, Synchronize Newsgroup command**—In the Synchronize Newsgroup dialog box, activate the Get the Following Items check box, activate the Headers Only option, and then click OK.
- **To synchronize all the newsgroups at once, select the news server in the Local Folders list**—Select all the groups, right-click any selected group, click Synchronization Settings, and then click Headers Only. Now select Tools, Synchronize All. Windows Mail downloads all the available headers for the newsgroups.

If you're on a dial-up connection, you might want to switch to offline mode at this point so that you can review the headers.

Downloading Messages

To view the contents (the message body) of any message while you're online, just select it in the message list. Windows Mail then downloads the message body and displays it in the preview pane.

Working Offline: Marking Messages for Downloading

While working offline, you have to mark those messages that you want to download. Here are the techniques you can use:

- **Marking a single message for download**—Right-click the message and click Download Message Later.

> **TIP**
>
> An easier way to mark messages for downloading is to the use the Mark for Offline column. To display this column, right-click any column header and then click Columns (or select View, Columns). In the Columns dialog box, activate the Mark for Offline check box and then click OK. To mark a message for download, click inside the Mark for Offline column. Windows Mail adds an arrow to the column.

- **Marking a thread for download**—Right-click a message in the thread and then click Download Conversation Later.

If you change your mind about downloading a message, repeat the techniques just mentioned.

Working Offline: Getting the Message Bodies

To get the message bodies, follow these steps:

1. Switch to online mode.
2. Select the Tools, Synchronize Newsgroup command to display the Synchronize Newsgroup dialog box.
3. Make sure that you enable the Get Messages Marked for Download check box, as shown in Figure 20.4.
4. You can also leave the Get the Following Items check box activated and then select one of the following options:

All Messages	This option downloads every available header and body.
New Messages Only	This option looks for new messages and downloads both the headers and the bodies.
Headers Only	This option looks for new headers and downloads them.

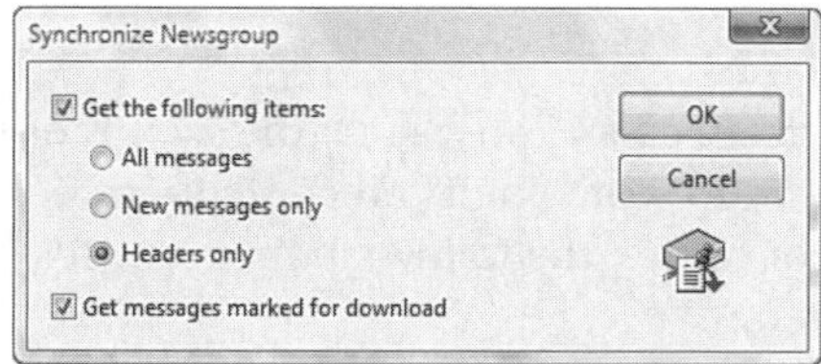

FIGURE 20.4 Use this dialog box to tell Windows Mail what you want to download.

5. Click OK. Windows Mail starts downloading the messages.
6. When the download is complete, switch to offline mode.

Notes on Working with Newsgroup Messages

You can treat newsgroup messages in much the same way that you treat email messages. That is, you can view the message text in the preview pane, open the message in its own window, save the message, copy it to another folder, and so on. I discussed all of these message techniques and quite a few others in Chapter 19, "Communicating with Windows Mail." Here are a few notes on tasks that are specific to newsgroup messages:

- **Dealing with threads**—If you see a plus sign (+) beside a message header, it means that replies exist for this header. To see the other messages in the thread, click the plus sign or highlight the message and press plus sign (+) on your numeric keypad.
- **Unscrambling ROT13 messages**—Some messages are encoded using a scheme called **ROT13**. This scheme encodes the message by shifting the letters of the alphabet 13 positions to the right, and wrapping around to the front of the alphabet when it reaches the end. (The *ROT* part is short for *rotate*.) If you come across a message encoded using ROT13, you can use Windows Mail's built-in decoder. To use it, select Message, Unscramble (ROT13).
- **Canceling one of your messages**—If you post a message and then have second thoughts, you can remove it from the newsgroup by highlighting it and selecting Message, Cancel Message. (This command is available only for messages you've sent. People who have downloaded your message will still see it.)
- **Combining and decoding multiple attachments**—Some multimedia groups post large binary files that are split into multiple posts. To extract the original binary file from these posts, first select all the posts. Then select Message, Combine and Decode to display the Order for Decoding dialog box. Use the Move Up and Move Down buttons to order the posts (the subject lines usually tell you the proper order), and then click OK.

Following Up a Message

Usenet is at its best when it's interactive: questions are asked and answered; the swords of conflicting opinions are crossed; debaters cut and parry to score points on contentious issues. The engine behind all this verbal jousting is, of course, the follow-up message. To post a follow-up with Windows Mail, follow these steps:

1. Select the original message in the message list.
2. Select Message, Reply to Group. (You can also press Ctrl+G or click the Reply Group toolbar button.) Windows Mail opens a message composition window and fills it with the text from the original article.
3. Cut out any unnecessary text from the original article.
4. Type your own text in the article body.
5. Select File, Send Message. (Alternatives for faster service: Alt+S or click the Send button.) Windows Mail displays a dialog box telling you that your message has been sent to the news server and that it might not appear immediately.
6. Click OK.

TIP

Instead of posting a follow-up message, you might prefer to reply directly to the author via email. To do this, select the message and select Message, Reply to Author (or else press Ctrl+R or click the Reply button). Take a look at the address to make sure it has not been *munged*—altered slightly so that if a spam bot picks it up, the address will be unusable. If so, delete the extra characters that the user has inserted in the address.

If you want to send a message to both the group and the author, select Message, Reply to All, or press Ctrl+Shift+R.

Posting a New Message

As I've said before, original messages are the lifeblood of Usenet because they get the discussions off the ground and give the rest of us something to read (as well as laugh at, sneer at, and hurl verbal abuse at). If you're feeling creative, you can take advantage of this section, which shows you how to post a new message from Windows Mail.

To get started, select the newsgroup to which you want to post, and then use any of the following techniques:

- Select Message, New Message
- Press Ctrl+N
- Click the Write Message button on the toolbar

Whichever method you choose, the New Message window appears. This window is almost identical to the New Message window I discussed in the previous chapter. There are three main differences:

- If you have multiple news server accounts, you see a News Server list from which you select the server you want to use.
- The To field is replaced by a Newsgroups field.
- For Microsoft Communities newsgroups, you see a Post Type section with the following three options: Comment, Question, and Suggestion. Select the option that describes your post.

The Newsgroups field should show the name of the current newsgroup. If you want to send your message to more than one newsgroup, separate the newsgroup names with a comma (,). Alternatively, click Newsgroups and then choose a newsgroup from the dialog box that appears.

To post your message, select File, Send Message (or press Alt+S, or click the Send button in the toolbar).

Filtering Newsgroup Messages

I mentioned at the top of this chapter that many newsgroups are riddled with **spam** (unsolicited commercial email) and off-topic rants and raves. Such groups are said to have a bad **signal-to-noise ratio**. To help improve this ratio, Windows Mail has a newsgroup filter feature that enables you to set up criteria for messages you don't want to see. Here are the steps to follow to set up a newsgroup filter:

1. Select the Tools, Message Rules, News command. One of two things will happen:
    - If this is the first time you are creating a rule, Windows Mail displays the New News Rule dialog box.
    - If you already have at least one rule, the Message Rules dialog box appears with the News Rules tab displayed. In this case, click New to open the New News Rule dialog box.
2. In the Select the Conditions for Your Rule list, activate the check box beside the rule condition you want to use to pick out a message from the herd. Windows Mail adds the condition to the Rule Description text box. Note that you're free to select multiple conditions.
3. The condition shown in the Rule Description text box will probably have some underlined text. You need to replace that underlined text with the specific criterion you want to use (such as a word or an address). To do that, click the underlined text, type the criterion in the dialog box that appears, and click Add. Most conditions support multiple criteria (such as multiple addresses or multiple words in a subject line), so repeat this step as necessary. When you're done, click OK.

4. If you selected multiple conditions, Windows Mail assumes that all the conditions must be true before invoking the rule (Boolean AND). To change this, click and in the Rule Description text box, activate the Messages Match Any One of the Criteria option, and click OK.
5. In the Select the Actions for Your Rule list, activate the check box beside the action you want Windows Mail to take with messages that meet your criteria. You might have to click underlined text in the Rule Description text box to complete the action. In addition, you can select multiple actions.
6. Use the Name of the Rule text box to type a descriptive name for the rule.
7. Click OK. Windows Mail drops you off at the News Rules tab of the Message Rules dialog box.

Rating Posts

Most newsgroups are busy places frequented by a wide range of people. Some posts are extremely informative, interesting, and some people routinely make meaningful contributions to the group. Other posts are not so useful, whether they are off-topic or part of the flame wars that erupt in most newsgroups.

Unfortunately, separating the good posts from the bad is a difficult task. After you spend time in a group, you learn who the competent users are and which users are not worth reading. For every other post, however, there is no way to know in advance whether the content is worth your time to read it.

New Windows Mail aims to reduce that uncertainty by enabling you to rate any post in a Windows Communities group using a simple scale: Useful or Not Useful. By rating posts, you help others decide which posts to read and which to ignore.

Note that to rate a post, you must have an account on the Microsoft Passport Network—for example, an MSN Hotmail or Windows Live Mail account. If you have such an account, your first step is to sign in to Windows Communities by following these steps:

1. Select any newsgroup in the Windows Communities server.
2. Select Tools, Microsoft Communities: Sign In. (Alternatively, click any message in the group and then click the Sign In button that appears in the message header.)
3. Type your Passport Network E-mail Address and Password.
4. Click Sign In.

After you sign in, you see a Rate this Post section in the header of each message, as shown in Figure 20.5. Drop down the list and then click either Useful or Not Useful. Note that Windows Mail doesn't give you any way to change the rating, so make sure that you click the correct choice.

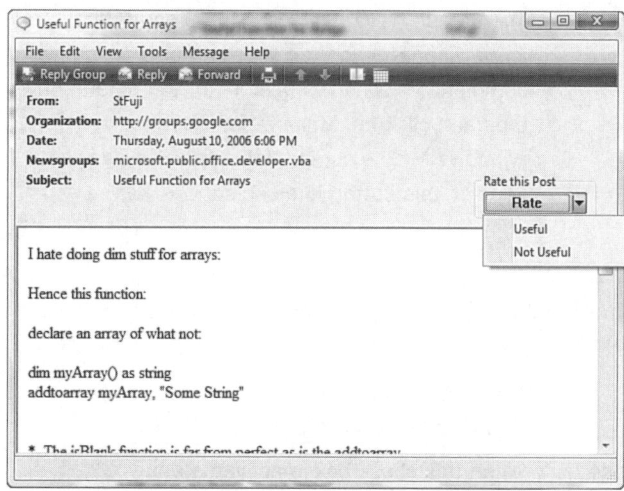

FIGURE 20.5 After you sign in to Microsoft Communities, you can rate posts on the server's newsgroups.

Setting News Options

You saw in the last chapter that Windows Mail has all kinds of options and settings that enable you to customize many aspects of the Windows Mail email client. There are also quite a few options related to newsgroups, and this section runs through them all.

Options for Newsgroups and Messages

The options related to newsgroups and messages are in the Options dialog box, which you can get to by selecting the Tools, Options command.

Setting General Options

The General tab contains three group-related settings (refer to Chapter 19 for explanations of the other options in this tab):

Notify Me If There Are Any New Newsgroups	With this check box activated, Windows Mail polls the server for the names of newsgroups added since you last connected. If there are any, Windows Mail displays a dialog box to let you know. (A list of the new groups appears in the New tab of the Newsgroup Subscriptions dialog box.)
Use Newsgroup Communities Support Features	If you deactivate this check box, you cannot rate Microsoft Communities posts, and the Post Type options don't appear in the post composition window.

This Application Is NOT the Default News Handler	The default news handler is the program that loads whenever you run your web browser's news command. If Windows Mail is not the default news program, click the Make Default button. If Windows Mail is currently the default news handler, this button is disabled.

Setting Read Options

The Read tab boasts the following message-related settings (refer to Chapter 19 to learn about the other options in this tab):

Automatically Expand Grouped Messages	Activating this check box tells Windows Mail to expand all downloaded threads.
Automatically Download Message When Viewing in the Preview Pane	When this check box is activated and you're online, Windows Mail downloads and displays a message when you highlight its header. If you'd prefer not to have messages downloaded automatically, deactivate this check box.
Get *X* Headers at a Time	Use this spin box to specify the maximum number of newsgroup headers that Windows Mail downloads when you select the Tools, Get Next *X* Headers command. Increase this value if you read busy newsgroups with lots of messages. (The maximum value is 1,000.) If you want to always download every message in a newsgoup, deactivate this check box.
Mark All Messages as Read When Exiting a Newsgroup	Activate this check box to force Windows Mail to mark all the messages in the current newsgroup as read when you select a different newsgroup or folder.

Setting Maintenance Options

You'll find a few more message-related options in the Maintenance dialog box, shown in Figure 20.6. To display this dialog box, select the Advanced tab and then click Maintenance. Most of these options affect the local storage that Windows Mail uses for downloaded messages. Here's a summary:

Purge Newsgroup Messages in the Background	Activate this check box to have Windows Mail automatically delete newsgroup messages according to the following two settings.
Delete Read Message Bodies in Newsgroups	If you activate this check box, each time you exit Windows Mail, the program deletes from local storage the bodies of those posts that you've read.
Delete News Messages *X* Days After Being Downloaded	When you activate this check box, Windows Mail deletes any downloaded message the specified number of days after you downloaded it.
Clean Up Now	Click this button to force Windows Mail to compact its local storage space immediately.
News	Activate this check box to have Windows Mail maintain a log of commands sent to and from the news server. This log is stored in a text file named `account`, where `account` is the name of the news account. The log file is saved in your user account's Windows Mail folder: `%UserProfile%\AppData\Local\Microsoft\Windows Mail`

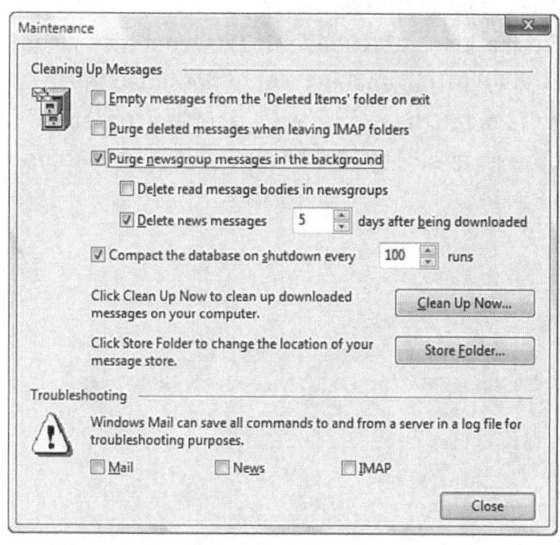

FIGURE 20.6 The Maintenance tab contains various options related to the local storage of downloaded messages.

Options for Individual Newsgroups

Windows Mail also maintains a few properties related to individual newsgroups. To view these settings, right-click a newsgroup and then click Properties. The properties sheet that appears contains three tabs: General, Synchronize, and Local File. The General tab tells you the name of the newsgroup, the total number of available messages, and the number of those messages that are unread.

The Synchronize tab enables you to set the default download setting for this newsgroup. These are the same options that appear when you select the Tools, Synchronize this Newsgroup command, discussed earlier in this chapter.

The Local File tab, shown in Figure 20.7, contains settings that control the newsgroup's local message store, which is a subfolder (with the same name as the newsgroup) in the server's folder, which appears in your user's account's Windows Mail folder. For example, each Windows Communities group you subscribe to has a subfolder in the following location:

```
AppData\Local\Microsoft\Windows Mail\Microsoft Communities
```

You can adjust the group storage by using the following buttons:

Remove Messages	Click this button to remove all the downloaded message bodies from the local storage file.
Delete	Click this button to clean out all the downloaded headers and message bodies from the local storage file.
Reset	Click this button to clean out all the downloaded headers and message bodies from the local storage file and to reset messages marked as read or watched. This enables you to download these headers again, which is useful if you're having trouble accessing the newsgroup or if the local storage file becomes slow or inaccessible due to its large size.

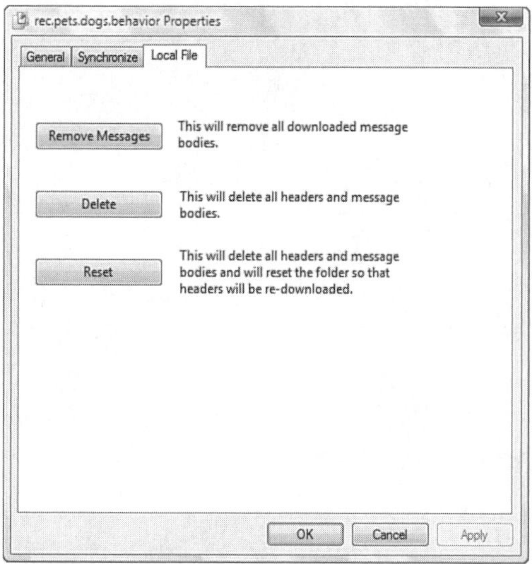

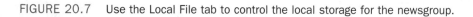

FIGURE 20.7 Use the Local File tab to control the local storage for the newsgroup.

From Here

Here's a list of chapters where you'll find related information:

- To learn how to wield Windows Mail for Internet email, refer to Chapter 19, "Communicating with Windows Mail."
- For information on Windows Mail security and privacy issues, see Chapter 21, "Implementing Windows Vista's Internet Security and Privacy Features."

CHAPTER 21

Implementing Windows Vista's Internet Security and Privacy Features

IN THIS CHAPTER

- Control Panel's Security Settings
- New Security Center Features
- Windows Firewall: Bidirectional Protection
- Thwarting Spyware with Windows Defender
- Surfing the Web Securely
- Working with Email Safely and Securely
- Security and Privacy Options for Windows Media Player
- More New Security Features

As more people, businesses, and organizations establish a presence online, the world becomes an increasingly connected place. And the more connected the world becomes, the more opportunities arise for communicating with others, doing research, sharing information, and collaborating on projects. The flip side to this new connectedness is the increased risk of connecting with a remote user whose intentions are less than honorable. The person at the other end of the connection could be a fraud artist who sets up a legitimate-looking website to steal your password or credit card number, or a cracker who breaks into your Internet account. It could be a virus programmer who sends a Trojan horse attached to an email, or a website operator who uses web browser security holes to run malicious code on your machine. While this was happening, Microsoft's operating systems seemed to become less secure. It's difficult to say whether overall operating system security got worse with each new release, but it's not hard to see that a perfect security storm was brewing:

- Thanks to the Internet, news of vulnerabilities spread quickly and efficiently.
- An increasing number of malicious users online worked to exploit those vulnerabilities.
- An increasing number of Windows users got online, most of whom didn't keep up with the latest security patches from Microsoft.

- An increasing number of online users had always-on broadband connections, which give malicious users more time to locate and break into poorly patched machines.

So, even though it might have been the case that each new version of Windows was no less secure than it predecessors, it *appeared* that Windows was becoming increasingly vulnerable to attack.

To combat not only this perception but also the fundamental design flaws that were causing these security holes, Microsoft began its Trustworthy Computing Initiative (**TCI**) in 2003. The goal was to make people "as comfortable using devices powered by computers and software as they are today using a device that is powered by electricity." How is Microsoft going about this? It's a broad initiative, but it really comes down to two things:

- **Reduce the "attack surface area."**—This means reducing the number of places where an attacker can get a foothold on the system. For example, why run any ActiveX controls that the user or system doesn't require, particularly if that object is potentially exploitable?
- **Help the user to avoid making "bad trust decisions."**—If the user lands on a phishing website, why not have the web browser warn the user that the site is probably not trustworthy?

Windows Vista is Microsoft's first major opportunity to put these and other TCI ideas into effect. You've already seen some of those ideas implemented in new features such as User Account Control and Parental Controls. This chapter takes you on a tour of the new and improved Internet security features in Windows Vista.

Control Panel's Security Settings

New With so many new security features, it's a good thing that Windows Vista does a better job of organizing security-related tasks than previous versions of Windows. Vista's one-stop security shop is, appropriately, the Control Panel, which has a Security icon in the Home folder that has four links:

- **Security**—Click this link to open the `Security` folder and see Vista's main security settings, as shown in Figure 21.1. I discuss many of these features in this chapter.
- **Check for Updates**—Click this link to open the `Windows Update` folder, which shows when you last checked for updates, your current Windows Update status, and a link for checking updates.
- **Check This Computer's Security Status**—Click this link to open the Security Center. The next section covers the Security Center.
- **Allow a Program Through Windows Firewall**—Displays the Windows Firewall Settings dialog box so that you specify a program or port as a firewall exception (see "Windows Firewall: Bidirectional Protection").

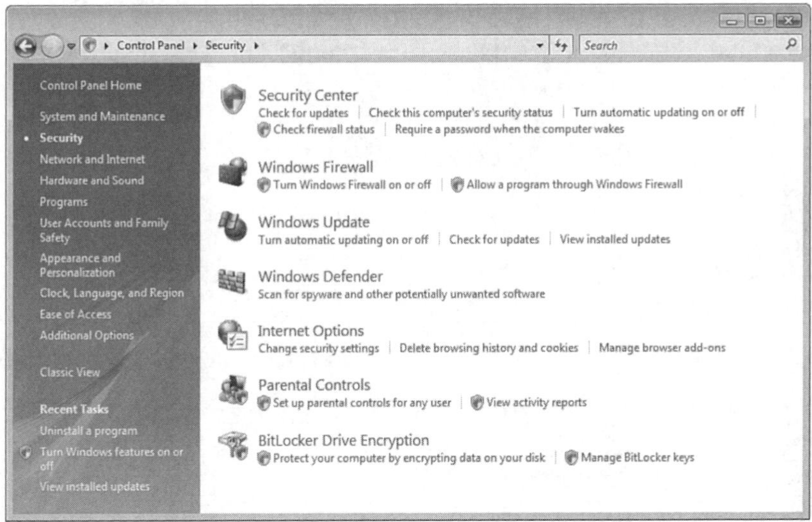

FIGURE 21.1 Click the Control Panel's Security link to see this list of Vista's main security settings.

New Security Center Features

New Windows XP Service Pack 2 introduced the world to the Security Center, which enabled you to see the status of the Windows Firewall, Automatic Updates, and virus protection. It also offered links to various security settings.

The Security Center in Windows Vista (select Start, Control Panel, Security, Security Center) remains pretty much the same, except that it now offers two new items in the Security Essentials area, as shown in Figure 21.2:

- **Malware Protection**—This item tells you the current status of Virus Protection (*still* not included in Windows) and Spyware and Other Malware Protection. Windows Defender handles the latter (see "Thwarting Spyware with Windows Defender," later in this chapter).

TIP

As in XP, if you have an antivirus program installed that Windows doesn't recognize, you can tell Vista that you'll monitor the program yourself. Click the Show Me Other Available Options link, and then click I Have an Antivirus Program That I'll Monitor Myself.

- **Other Security Settings**—This item checks your Internet Security Settings and User Account Control status. If you have Internet Explorer's Protected mode enabled (see "Protected Mode: Reducing Internet Explorer's Privileges," later in this chapter), and if you have User Account Control enabled, this item's status shows as OK. If you have Protected mode disabled, or if you have User Account Protection disabled, this item's status shows as Not OK.

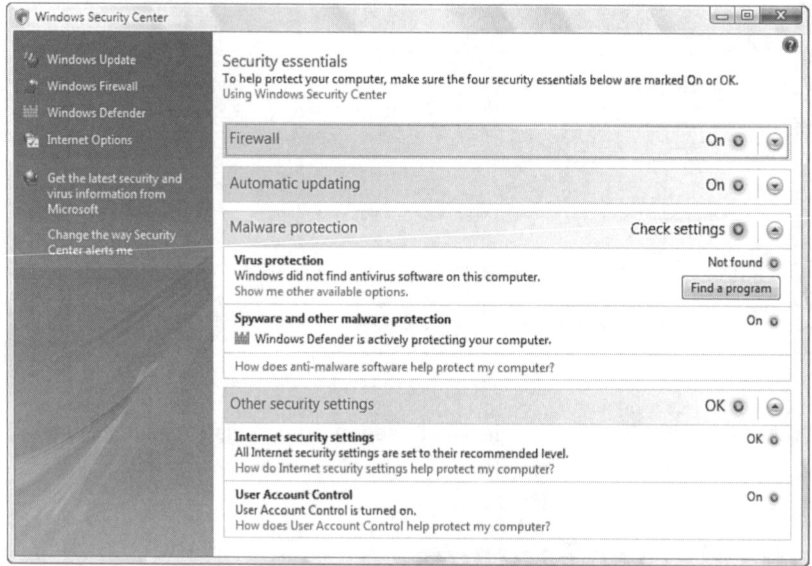

FIGURE 21.2 Windows Vista's version of the Security Center.

Windows Firewall: Bidirectional Protection

If you access the Internet using a **broadband**—cable modem or DSL—service, chances are, you have an always-on connection, which means there's a much greater chance that a malicious hacker could find your computer and have his way with it. You might think that with millions of people connected to the Internet at any given moment, there would be little chance of a "script kiddy" finding you in the herd. Unfortunately, one of the most common weapons in a black-hat hacker's arsenal is a program that runs through millions of IP addresses automatically, looking for live connections. The fact that many cable systems and some DSL systems use IP addresses in a narrow range compounds the problem by making it easier to find always-on connections.

When a cracker finds your address, he has many avenues from which to access your computer. Specifically, your connection uses many different ports for sending and receiving data. For example, the File Transfer Protocol (FTP) uses ports 20 and 21, web data and commands typically use port 80, email uses ports 25 and 110, the domain name system (DNS) uses port 53, and so on. In all, there are dozens of these ports, and every one is an opening through which a clever cracker can gain access to your computer.

As if that weren't enough, attackers can check your system for the installation of some kind of Trojan horse or virus. (Malicious email attachments sometimes install these programs on your machine.) If the hacker finds one, he can effectively take control of your machine (turning it into a **zombie computer**) and either wreak havoc on its contents or use your computer to attack other systems.

Again, if you think your computer is too obscure or worthless for someone else to bother with, think again. Hackers probe a typical computer connected to the Internet all day long for vulnerable ports or installed Trojan horses at least a few times every day. If you want to see just how vulnerable your computer is, several good sites on the Web will test your security:

- Gibson Research (Shields Up): grc.com/default.htm
- DSL Reports: www.dslreports.com/secureme_go
- HackerWhacker: www.hackerwhacker.com

New The good news is that Windows Vista includes an updated version of the Windows Firewall tool that debuted in Windows XP. This program is a personal firewall that can lock down your ports and prevent unauthorized access to your machine. In effect, your computer becomes invisible to the Internet (although you can still surf the Web and work with email normally).

The main change in Vista's version of Windows Firewall is that the program is now *bidirectional*. This means that it blocks not only unauthorized *incoming* traffic, but also unauthorized *outgoing* traffic. If your computer has a Trojan horse installed (it might have been there before you installed Vista, or someone with physical access to your computer might have installed it), it might attempt to send data out to the Web. For example, it might attempt to contact a controlling program on another site to get instructions, or it might attempt to send sensitive data from your computer to the Trojan's owner. A bidirectional firewall can put a stop to that.

The Windows Firewall in Vista also supports the following new features:

- The IP Security (IPSec) protocol
- Environments that use only Internet Protocol version 6 (IPv6)
- Both incoming and outgoing firewall exceptions
- Exceptions applied to specific computers and users
- Exceptions applied to many different protocols (not just TCP and UDP)
- Exceptions applied to both local and remote ports
- Exceptions applied to specific interface types: location area network, remote access, or wireless
- Exceptions applied to specific Vista services
- Command-line support for controlling the firewall

From this list, you can see that Vista's firewall is a far more sophisticated tool than any of the versions that shipped with XP or its service packs. A powerful new interface for working with Windows Firewall settings, exceptions, and monitoring reflects that sophistication. It's Windows Firewall with Advanced Security (**WFAS**), and it's a Microsoft Management Console snap-in. To load it, press Windows Logo+R, type **`wf.msc`**, click OK, and then enter your User Account Control credentials. Figure 21.3 shows the WFAS snap-in.

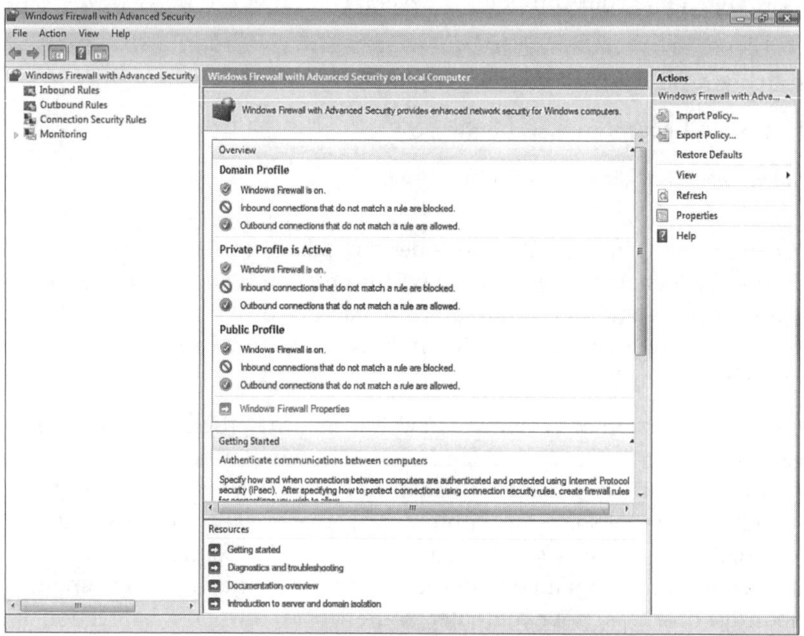

FIGURE 21.3 The new Windows Firewall with Advanced Security snap-in offers sophisticated firewall-management features.

The home page of the snap-in presents an overview of the current firewall settings, as well as a number of links to configure and learn about WFAS. This snap-in configures the firewall by setting policies and storing them in three profiles. The domain profile is used when your computer is connected to a network domain; the private profile is used when your computer is connected to a private network; and the public profile is used when your computer is connected to a public network. To change the settings for the profiles, click the Windows Firewall Properties link, and then use the Domain Profile, Private Profile, and Public Profile tabs to modify the settings (although the defaults should be fine for most people).

The scope pane contains four main sub-branches:

- **Inbound Rules**—This branch presents a list of defined rules for inbound connections. In most cases, the rules aren't enabled. To enable a rule, you right-click it and then click Enable Rule (or you can click the rule and then click Enable Rule in the

Action pane). You can create your own rule by right-clicking Inbound Rules and then clicking New Rule (or clicking New Rule in the Action pane). This launches the New Inbound Rule Wizard.

- **Outbound Rules**—This branch presents a list of defined rules for outbound connections. As with inbound connections, you can enable the rules you want to use and create your own rules. Note, too, that you can customize any rule by double-clicking it to display its properties sheet (see Figure 21.4). With this properties sheet, you can change the program executable to which the exception is applied, allow or block a connection, set the computer and user authorization, change the ports and protocols, and specify the interface types and services.

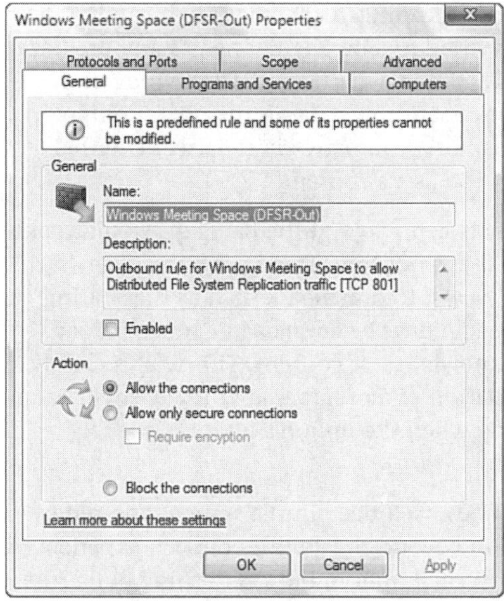

FIGURE 21.4 Use an exception's properties sheet to customize all aspects of the exception.

- **Connection Security Rules**—This branch is where you create and manage **authentication rules**, which determine the restrictions and requirements that apply to connections with remote computers. Right-click Computer Connection Security and then click New Rule (or click New Rule in the Action pane) to launch the New Connection Security Rule Wizard.

- **Monitoring**—This branch shows the enabled firewall settings. For example, the Firewall sub-branch shows the enabled inbound and outbound firewall rules, and the Connection Security, Rules sub-branch shows the enabled authentication rules.

Thwarting Spyware with Windows Defender

I've been troubleshooting Windows PCs for many years. It used to be that users accidentally deleting system files or making ill-advised attempts to edit the Registry or some other important configuration file caused most problems. Recent versions of Windows (particularly XP) could either prevent these kinds of PEBCAK (**Problem Exists Between Chair and Keyboard**) issues or recover from them without a lot of trouble. However, I think we're all too well aware of the latest menace to rise in the past few years, and it has taken over as the top cause of desperate troubleshooting calls I receive: **malware**, the generic term for malicious software such as viruses and Trojan horses. The worst malware offender by far these days is **spyware**, a plague upon the earth that threatens to deprive a significant portion of the online world of its sanity. As often happens with new concepts, the term *spyware* has become encrusted with multiple meanings as people attach similar ideas to a convenient and popular label. However, spyware is generally defined as any program that surreptitiously monitors a user's computer activities—particularly the typing of passwords, PINs, and credit card numbers—or harvests sensitive data on the user's computer, and then sends that information to an individual or a company via the user's Internet connection (the so-called *back channel*) without the user's consent.

You might think that having a robust firewall between you and the bad guys would make malware a problem of the past. Unfortunately, that's not true. These programs piggyback on other legitimate programs that users actually *want* to download, such as file-sharing programs, download managers, and screen savers. A **drive-by download** is the download and installation of a program without a user's knowledge or consent. This relates closely to a **pop-up download**—the download and installation of a program after the user clicks an option in a pop-up browser window, particularly when the option's intent is vaguely or misleadingly worded.

To make matters even worse, most spyware embeds itself deep into a system, and removing it is a delicate and time-consuming operation beyond the abilities of even experienced users. Some programs actually come with an Uninstall option, but it's nothing but a ruse, of course. The program appears to remove itself from the system, but what it actually does is a **covert reinstall**—it reinstalls a fresh version of itself when the computer is idle.

All this means that you need to buttress your firewall with an antispyware program that can watch out for these unwanted programs and prevent them from getting their hooks into your system. In previous versions of Windows, you needed to install a third-party program. However, Windows Vista comes with an antispyware program named Windows Defender (formerly *Microsoft AntiSpyware*).

You can open Windows Defender using any of the following methods:

- Select Start, All Programs, Windows Defender
- Select Start, Control Panel, Security, Windows Defender
- Double-click the Windows Defender icon in the taskbar's notification area (although this icon usually appears only when Windows Defender needs your attention)

Whichever method you use, you end up at the Windows Defender Home screen, shown in Figure 21.5. This window shows you the date, time, and results of your last scan, as well as the current Windows Defender status.

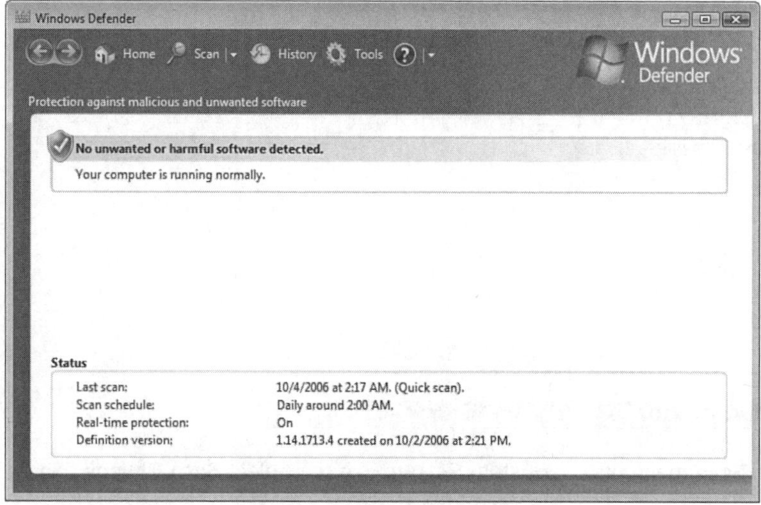

FIGURE 21.5 Windows Defender removes spyware from your system and keeps your system safe by preventing spyware installations.

Spyware Scanning

Windows Defender protects your computer from spyware in two ways. It can scan your system for evidence of installed spyware programs (and remove or disable those programs, if necessary), and it can monitor your system in real time to watch for activities that indicate the presence of spyware (such as a drive-by download or data being sent via a back channel).

For the scanning portion of its defenses, Windows Defender supports three different scan types:

- **Quick Scan**—This scan checks just those areas of your system where it is likely to find evidence of spyware. This scan usually takes just a couple of minutes. This scan is the default, and you can initiate one at any time by clicking the Scan link.
- **Full Scan**—This scan checks for evidence of spyware in system memory, all running processes, and the system drive (usually drive C:), and it performs a deep scan on all folders. This scan might take 30 minutes or more, depending on your system. To run this scan, pull down the Scan menu and click Full Scan.
- **Custom Scan**—This scan checks just the drives and folders that you select. The length of the scan depends on the number of locations you select and the number of objects in those locations. To run this scan, pull down the Scan menu and click

Custom Scan, which displays the Select Scan Options page shown in Figure 21.6. Click Select, activate the check boxes for the drives you want scanned, and then click OK. Click Scan Now to start the scan.

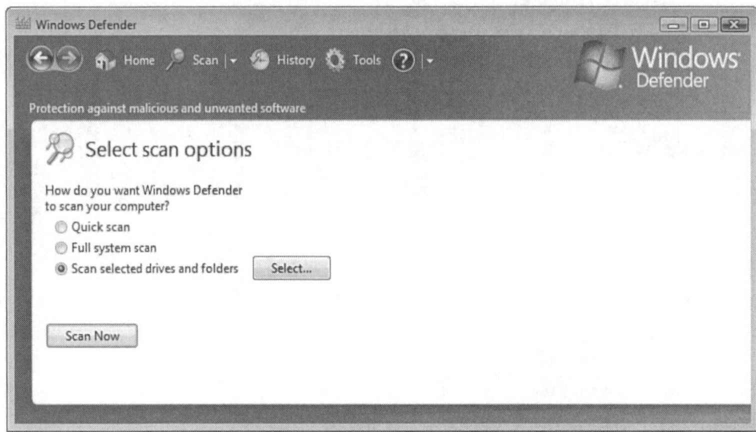

FIGURE 21.6 In the Scan menu, select Custom Scan to see the Select Scan Options page.

Windows Defender Settings

By default, Windows Defender is set up to perform a Quick Scan of your system every morning at 2:00 a.m. To change this, click Tools and then click Options to display the Options page shown (partially) in Figure 21.7. Use the controls in the Automatic Scanning section to specify the scan frequency time and type.

The rest of the Options page offers options for customizing Windows Defender. There are four more groups:

- **Default Actions**—Set the action that Windows Defender should take if it finds alert items (potential spyware) in the High, Medium, and Low categories: Definition Recommended Action (Windows Defender's default action for the detected spyware), Ignore, or Remove.

- **Real-Time Protection Options**—Enables and disables real-time protection. You can also toggle security agents on and off. **Security agents** monitor Windows components that are frequent targets of spyware activity. For example, activating the Auto Start security agent tells Windows Defender to monitor the list of startup programs to ensure that spyware doesn't add itself to this list and run automatically at startup.

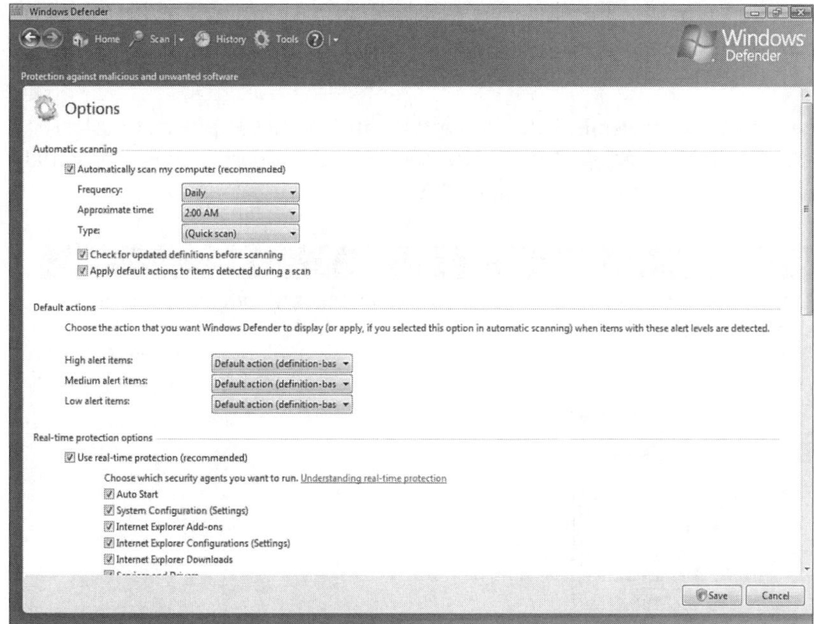

FIGURE 21.7 Use the Options page to set up a spyware scan schedule.

TIP

Windows Defender will often warn you that a program might be spyware and ask whether you want to allow the program to operate normally or to block it. If you accidentally allow an unsafe program, click Tools, Allowed Items; select the program in the Allowed Items list and then click Remove from List. Similarly, if you accidentally blocked a safe program, click Tools, Quarantined Items; select the program in the Quarantined Items list; and then click Remove.

- **Advanced Options**—Use these options to enable scanning inside compressed archives and to prevent Windows Defender from scanning specific folders.
- **Administrator Options**—This section has a check box that toggles Windows Defender on and off, and another that, when activated, allows non-Administrators to use Windows Defender.

Surfing the Web Securely

When implementing security for Internet Explorer, Microsoft realized that different sites have different security needs. For example, it makes sense to have stringent security for Internet sites, but you can probably scale the security back a bit when browsing pages on your corporate intranet.

To handle these different types of sites, Internet Explorer defines various **security zones**, and you can customize the security requirements for each zone. The status bar displays the current zone.

To work with zones, either select Tools, Internet Options in Internet Explorer, or select Start, Control Panel, Security, Internet Options. In the Internet Properties dialog box that appears, select the Security tab, shown in Figure 21.8.

TIP

Another way to get to the Security tab is to double-click the security zone shown in the Internet Explorer status bar.

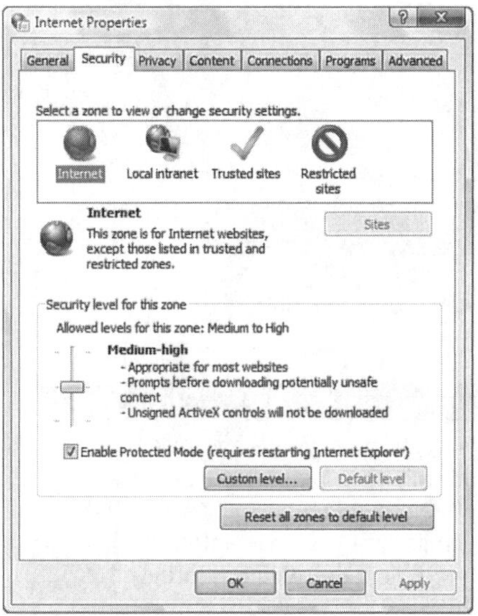

FIGURE 21.8 Use the Security tab to set up security zones and customize the security options for each zone.

The list at the top of the dialog box shows icons for the four types of zones available:

Internet	Websites that aren't in any of the other three zones. The default security level is Medium.
Local Intranet	Web pages on your computer and your network (intranet). The default security level is Medium-Low.
Trusted Sites	Websites that implement secure pages and that you're sure have safe content. The default security level is Low.
Restricted Sites	Websites that don't implement secure pages or that you don't trust, for whatever reason. The default security level is High.

TIP

You can use the Group Policy editor to hide the Security and Privacy tabs in the Internet Options dialog box. Select User Configuration, Administrative Templates, Windows Components, Internet Explorer, Internet Control Panel, and then enable the Disable the Privacy Page and Disable the Security Page policies. The Security Page sub-branch enables you to set policies for the settings in each zone.

Adding and Removing Zone Sites

Three of these zones—Local Intranet, Trusted Sites, and Restricted Sites—enable you to add sites. To do so, follow these steps:

1. Select the zone you want to work with and then click Sites.
2. If you selected Trusted Sites or Restricted Sites, skip to step 4. Otherwise, if you selected the Local Intranet zone, you see a dialog box with four check boxes. The Automatically Detect Intranet Network check box activates by default, and this tells Vista to detect intranets automatically, which should be fine in most cases. If you want more detailed control, deactivate that check box to enable the other three:

Include All Local (Intranet) Sites Not Listed in Other Zones	When activated, this option includes all intranet sites in the zone. If you add specific intranet sites to other zones, those sites aren't included in this zone.
Include All Sites That Bypass the Proxy Server	When this check box is activated, sites that you've set up to bypass your proxy server (if you have one) are included in this zone.
Include All Network Paths (UNCs)	When this check box is activated, all network paths that use the Universal Naming Convention are included in this zone. (UNC is a standard format used with network addresses. They usually take the form `\\server\resource`, where *server* is the name of the network server and *resource* is the name of a shared network resource.)

3. To add sites to the Local Intranet zone, click Advanced.
4. Type the site's address in the Add This Website to the Zone text box and then click Add.

NOTE

When typing an address, you can include an asterisk as a wildcard character. For example, the address http://*.microsoft.com adds every microsoft.com domain, including www.microsoft.com, support.microsoft.com, windowsupdate.microsoft.com, and so on.

5. If you make a mistake and enter the wrong site, select it in the Websites list and then click Remove.
6. Two of these dialog boxes (Local Intranet and Trusted Sites) have a Require Server Verification (https:) for All Sites In This Zone check box. If you activate this option, each site you enter must use the secure HTTPS protocol.
7. Click OK.

Changing a Zone's Security Level

To change the security level for a zone, select the zone and then use the Security Level for This Zone slider to set the level. To set up your own security settings, click Custom Level. This displays the Security Settings dialog box shown in Figure 21.9.

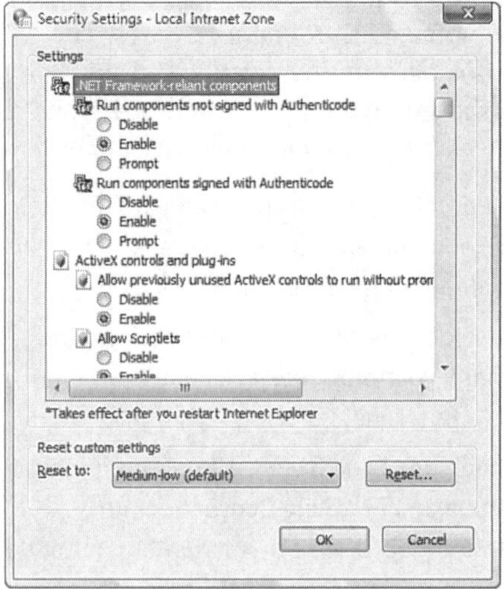

FIGURE 21.9 Use this dialog box to set up customized security levels for the selected zone.

The Security Settings dialog box provides you with a long list of possible security issues, and your job is to specify how you want Internet Explorer to handle each issue. You usually have three choices:

Disable	Security is on. For example, if the issue is whether to run an ActiveX control, the control does not run.
Enable	Security is off. For example, if the issue is whether to run an ActiveX control, the control runs automatically.
Prompt	Internet Explorer asks how you want to handle the issue. For example, whether you want to accept or reject an ActiveX control.

Protected Mode: Reducing Internet Explorer's Privileges

New Windows Vista's antispyware initiatives aren't restricted to Windows Defender. Because spyware often leeches onto a system through a drive-by or pop-up download, it makes sense to set up the web browser as the first line of defense. Microsoft has done just that by introducing **Protected mode** for Internet Explorer. Protected mode builds on Vista's new User Account Control feature that I discussed earlier in this book (in Chapter 6, see "User Account Control: Smarter User Privileges"). User Account Control means that Internet Explorer runs with a privilege level that's high enough to surf the Web, but that's about it. Internet Explorer can't install software without your permission (see Figure 21.10), modify the user's files or settings, add shortcuts to the Startup folder, or even change its own settings for the default home page and search engine. The Internet Explorer code is completely isolated from any other running application or process on your system. In fact, Internet Explorer can write data only to the `Temporary Internet Files` folder. If it needs to write elsewhere (during a file download, for example), it must get your permission. Therefore, Internet Explorer blocks any add-ons or other malware that attempts a covert install via Internet Explorer before they can even get to Windows Defender.

NOTE

If you don't want to run Internet Explorer 7 in Protected mode for some reason, you can turn it off. Select Tools, Internet Options, and then select the Security tab. Click the Enable Protected Mode check box to deactivate it, click OK, and then click OK again in the Warning! dialog box. Internet Explorer displays a message in the information bar telling you that your security settings are putting you at risk.

FIGURE 21.10 Internet Explorer 7 implements Protected mode to prevent covert spyware installs.

Total Security: Internet Explorer Without Add-Ons

New For the ultimate in browsing security, Windows Vista ships with an alternative Internet Explorer shortcut that loads the browser without any third-party add-ons, extensions, toolbars, or ActiveX controls. This is useful if you suspect your computer is infected with spyware that has hijacked your browser. This often means not only that the spyware has changed your home page, but in many cases the spyware also prevents you from accessing antispyware or antivirus sites. By running Internet Explorer without any add-ons, you effectively disable the spyware and you can then surf to whatever site you need. Internet Explorer without add-ons is also completely safe from being infected with spyware, so running this version of Internet Explorer is useful if you'll be surfing in darker areas of the web were you suspect the possibility of infection is very high.

Select Start, All Programs, Accessories, System Tools, Internet Explorer (No Add-Ons). Internet Explorer starts and displays the Add-Ons Disabled page. Click the Home button or enter an address to continue browsing.

Thwarting Phishers with the Phishing Filter

New **Phishing** refers to creating a replica of an existing web page to fool a user into submitting personal, financial, or password data. The term comes from the fact that Internet scammers are using increasingly sophisticated lures as they "fish" for users' financial information and password data. The most common ploy is to copy the web page code from a major site—such as AOL or eBay—and use it to set up a replica page that appears to be part of the company's site. (This is why another name for phishing is **spoofing**.) Phishers send out a fake email with a link to this page, which solicits the user's credit card data or password. When a recipient submits the form, it sends the data to the scammer and leaves the user on an actual page from the company's site so that he or she doesn't suspect a thing.

A phishing page looks identical to a legitimate page from the company because the phisher has simply copied the underlying source code from the original page. However, no spoof page can be a perfect replica of the original. Here are five things to look for:

- **The URL in the Address bar**—A legitimate page will have the correct domain—such as aol.com or ebay.com—whereas a spoofed page will have only something similar—such as aol.whatever.com or blah.com/ebay.

NOTE

With some exceptions (see the following discussion of domain spoofing), the URL in the Address bar is usually the easiest way to tell whether a site is trustworthy. For this reason, Internet Explorer 7 makes it impossible to hide the Address bar in all browser windows, even simple pop-ups.

- **The URLs associated with page links**—Most links on the page probably point to legitimate pages on the original site. However, some links might point to pages on the phisher's site.
- **The form-submittal address**—Almost all spoof pages contain a form into which you're supposed to type whatever sensitive data the phisher seeks from you. Select View, Source, and look at the value of the `<form>` tag's `action` attribute—the form

submits your data to this address. Clearly, if the form is not sending your data to the legitimate domain, you're dealing with a phisher.

- **Text or images that aren't associated with the trustworthy site**—Many phishing sites are housed on free web hosting services. However, many of these services place an advertisement on each page, so look for an ad or other content from the hosting provider.
- **Internet Explorer's lock icon in the status bar and Security Report area**—A legitimate site would transmit sensitive financial data only using a secure HTTPS connection, which Internet Explorer indicates by placing a lock icon in the status bar and in the Address bar's new Security Report area. If you don't see the lock icon on a page that asks for financial data, the page is almost certainly a spoof.

If you watch for these things, you'll probably never be fooled into giving up sensitive data to a phisher. However, it's often not as easy as it sounds. For example, some phishers employ easily overlooked domain-spoofing tricks such as replacing the lowercase letter L with the number 1, or the uppercase letter O with the number 0. Still, phishing sites don't fool most experienced users, so this isn't a big problem for them.

Novice users, on the other hand, need all the help they can get. They tend to assume that if everything they see on the Web looks legitimate and trustworthy, it probably is. And even if they're aware that scam sites exist, they don't know how to check for telltale phishing signs. To help these users, Internet Explorer 7 comes with a new tool called the *Phishing Filter*. This filter alerts you to potential phishing scams by doing two things each time you visit a site:

- Analyzes the site content to look for known phishing techniques (that is, to see whether the site is *phishy*). The most common of these is a check for domain spoofing. This common scam also goes by the names *homograph spoofing* and the *lookalike attack*. Internet Explorer 7 also supports Internationalized Domain Names (IDN), which refers to domain names written in languages other than English, and it checks for *IDN spoofing*, domain name ambiguities in the user's chosen browser language.
- Checks a global database of known phishing sites to see whether it lists the site. This database is maintained by a network of providers such as Cyota, Inc., Internet Identity, and MarkMonitor, as well as by reports from users who find phishing sites while surfing. According to Microsoft, this "URL reputation service" updates several times an hour with new data.

It's a sign of the phishing times that Internet Explorer comes with the Phishing Filter activated by default. The Phishing Filter rarely gets in the way, but you can turn it off if you'd rather not use it. Select Tools, Phishing Filter, Turn Off Automatic Website Checking. In the Microsoft Phishing Filter dialog box (see Figure 21.11), make sure the Turn Off Automatic Phishing Filter option is activated, and then click OK.

NOTE

If you turn off the automatic Phishing Filter checks, you can still check for phishing site by site. After you navigate to a site that you want to check, select Tools, Phishing Filter, Check This Website.

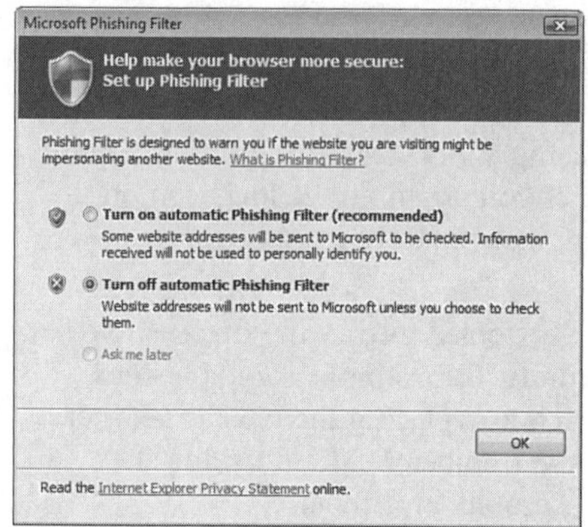

FIGURE 21.11 Internet Explorer 7 immediately asks whether you want to turn on the Phishing Filter.

Here's how the Phishing Filter works:

- If you visit a site that Internet Explorer knows is a phishing scam, it changes the background color of the Address bar to red and displays a `Phishing Website` message in the Security Report area. It also blocks navigation to the site by displaying a separate page telling you that the site is a known phishing scam. A link is provided to navigate to the site, if you so choose.

NOTE

The Security Report area is another Internet Explorer 7 security innovation. Clicking whatever text or icon appears in this area produces a report on the security of the site. For example, if you navigate to a secure site, you see the lock icon in this area. Click the lock to see a report that shows the site's digital certificate information.

- If you visit a site that Internet Explorer thinks is a potential phishing scam, it changes the background color of the Address bar to yellow and displays a `Suspicious Website` message in the Security Report area.

Figure 21.12 shows Internet Explorer 7 displaying a warning about a known phishing site.

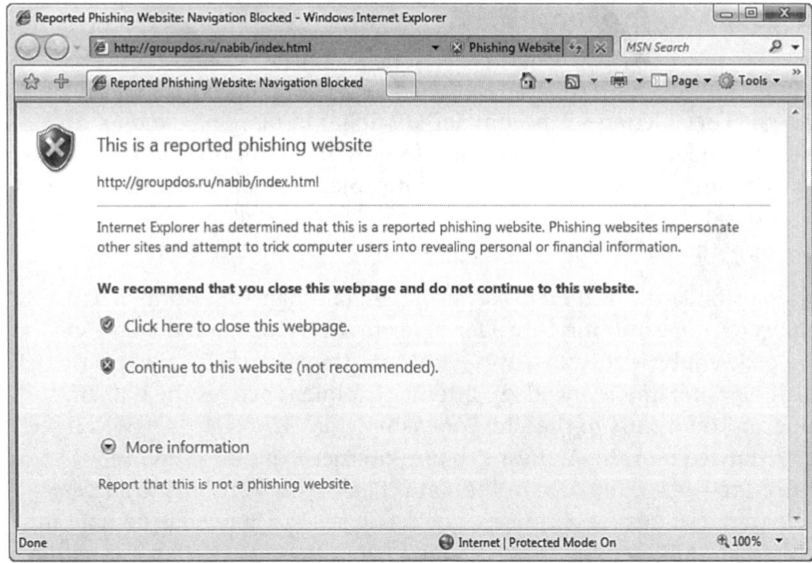

FIGURE 21.12 If Internet Explorer 7 detects a known phishing site, it displays "Phishing Website" in the Security Report area and blocks access to the site.

For a suspected phishing site, click the `Suspicious Website` text, and Internet Explorer displays the security report shown in Figure 21.13. If you're sure that this is a scam site, report it to improve the database of phishing sites and prevent others from giving up sensitive data. You should also send a report if you're sure that the site is *not* being used for phishing, because that improves the database as well. To report a site, either click the Report link in the security report or select Tools, Phishing Filter, Report This Website. This opens the Phishing Filter Feedback page.

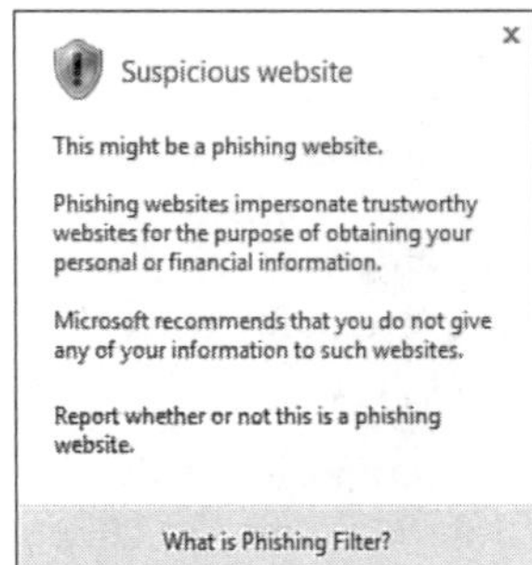

FIGURE 21.13 This report appears when you click the Suspicious Website warning.

Encoding Addresses to Prevent IDN Spoofing

I mentioned earlier that phishers often resort to IDN spoofing to fool users into thinking an address is legitimate. For example, instead of the address ebay.com, a phisher might use εbαy.com (with the Greek letters ε (epsilon) and α (alpha) in place of e and a). Almost all the world's characters have a Unicode value, but Internet Explorer is usually set up to recognize only a single language (such as English). If it comes across a character it doesn't recognize, it works around the problem by converting all Unicode values into an equivalent value that uses only the ASCII characters supported by the domain name system.

This conversion uses a standard called *Punycode*. If the domain name uses only ASCII characters, the Punycode value and the Unicode value are the same. For a domain such as εbαy.com, the Punycode equivalent is xn—by—c9b0.com (the xn— prefix always appears; it tells you that the domain name is encoded). Internet Explorer encodes the domain to this Punycode value and then surfs to the site. For example, in Figure 21.14, you can see that I entered http://εbαy.com in the Address bar, but Internet Explorer shows the Punycode value http://xn—by—c9b0.com in the status bar. If you were able to successfully surf to this site (it doesn't exist, of course), you'd also see the Punycode domain in the Address bar. (Internet Explorer also displays a message in the Information Bar telling you that the address contains characters it doesn't recognize.) In other words, an IDN spoofing site is less likely to fool users because the URL that appears in the status bar and the address no longer looks similar to the URL of the legitimate site.

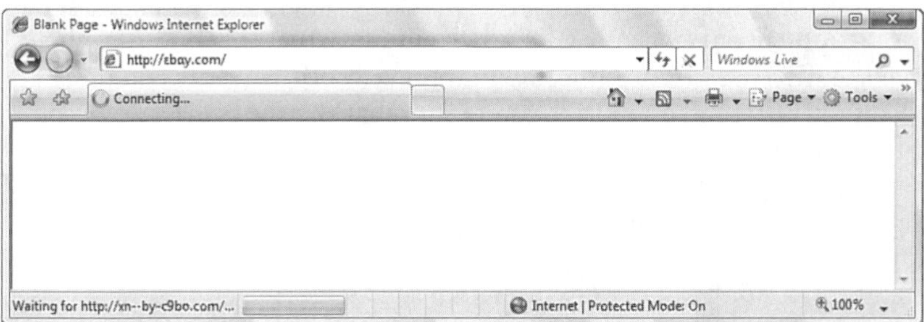

FIGURE 21.14 Internet Explorer encodes IDN domain names to their Punycode equivalents before surfing to the site.

Note that Internet Explorer doesn't always display Punycode. There are actually three instances where you see Punycode instead of Unicode:

- The address contains characters that don't appear in any of the languages you've added to Internet Explorer. (To add a language, select Tools, Internet Options, click Languages in the General tab, and then click Add.)
- The address contains characters from two or more different languages (for example, it contains a Greek character and an Arabic character).
- The address contains one or more characters that don't exist in any language.

With Internet Explorer 7 IDN spoofs can work in only a single language, and will work only if the user has added that single language to Internet Explorer.

Internet Explorer comes with a few options that enable you to control aspects of this encoding process and related features. Select Tools, Internet Options, click the Advanced tab, and scroll down the International section, which contains the following check boxes (you need to restart Internet Explorer if you change any of these settings):

Always Show Encoded Addresses	Activate this check box to tell Internet Explorer to display the encoded Punycode web addresses in the status bar and Address bar. If you're not worrying about IDN spoofing, you can deactivate this check box to see the Unicode characters instead.
Send IDN Server Names	When activated, this check box tells Internet Explorer to encode addresses into Punycode before sending them for domain resolution.
Send IDN Server Names for Intranet Addresses	When activated, this check box tells Internet Explorer to encode intranet addresses into Punycode before sending them for resolution. Some intranet sites don't support Punycode, so this setting is off by default.
Send UTF-8 URLs	When activated, this check box tells Internet Explorer to send web page addresses using the UTF-8 standard, which is readable in any language. If you're having trouble accessing a page that uses non-English characters in the URL, the server might not be able to handle UTF-8, so deactivate this check box.
Show Information Bar for Encoded Addresses	When activated, this check box tells Internet Explorer to display the following Information bar message when it encodes an address into Punycode: `This Web address contains letters or symbols that cannot be displayed with the current language settings.`
Use UTF-8 for Mailto Links	When activated, this check box tells Internet Explorer to use UTF-8 for the addresses in `mailto` links.

Managing Add-Ons

New Internet Explorer 7 gives you a much better interface for managing all your browser add-ons, including ActiveX controls, toolbars, helper objects, and more. Select Tools, Manage Add-Ons, Enable or Disable Add-Ons to display the Manage Add-Ons dialog box shown in Figure 21.15. Select the add-on you want to work with and then click Enable or Disable. (You can also click Delete to remove the add-on from your system.) Click OK when you're done, and then restart Internet Explorer.

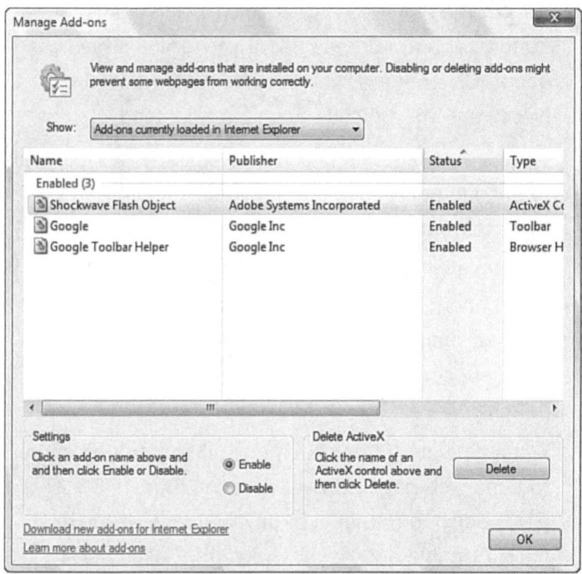

FIGURE 21.15 Use the Manage Add-Ons dialog box to view, enable, disable, and delete Internet Explorer add-ons.

Deleting Browser History

New Internet Explorer 7 makes it much easier to delete your browsing history. In previous versions, you had to make separate deletions for cache files, cookies, visited URLs, saved form data, and saved passwords. In Internet Explorer 7, you select Tools, Delete Browsing History to display the Delete Browsing History dialog box shown in Figure 21.16. From here, you can delete the browser history by category:

Temporary Internet Files — Click Delete Files to remove all files from the Internet Explorer cache, located in the following folder:

```
%UserProfile%\AppData\Local\Microsoft\Windows\
Temporary Internet Files
```

Cookies	Click Delete Cookies to remove all the cookies files (see the next section for details on cookies) from the following folder: `%UserProfile%\AppData\Roaming\Microsoft\Windows\Cookies`

TIP

If you just want to delete certain cookies—for example, those from advertisers—open the Cookies folder and delete the files individually.

History	Click Delete History to remove the list of websites you've visited, which resides as files in the following folder: `%UserProfile%\AppData\Local\Microsoft\Windows\History`

TIP

If you just want to delete history from a certain site, day, or week, click Favorites Center (or press Alt+C), and click History to display the History list. If you want to delete just a few sites, open the appropriate History branch, and then, for each site, right-click the site and then click Delete. If you want to delete a number of sites, right-click the appropriate day or week and then click Delete. Click Yes when Internet Explorer asks you to confirm.

Form Data	Click Delete Forms to remove your saved form data.
Passwords	Click Delete Passwords to remove your saved passwords.

Alternatively, you can click Delete All to erase everything in one shot.

NOTE

If you don't want Internet Explorer to save your form data, passwords, or both, select Tools, Internet Options, select the Content tab, and then click Settings in the AutoComplete group. In the AutoComplete Settings dialog box, deactivate the Forms check box to stop saving form data. If you no longer want to save form passwords, deactivate the User Name and Passwords on Forms check box. Click OK in all open dialog boxes.

Enhancing Online Privacy by Managing Cookies

A **cookie** is a small text file that's stored on your computer. Websites use them to "remember" information about your session at that site: shopping cart data, page customizations, passwords, and so on.

FIGURE 21.16 Use the Delete Browsing History dialog box to delete some or all of your Internet Explorer 7 browsing history.

NOTE

The term *cookie* derives from the old programming term **magic cookie**, which means something passed between routines or programs and that enables the receiver to perform some operation. It's this idea of passing data from one thing to another (in this case, from a page to your computer) that inspired the original cookie creators.

No other site can access your cookies, so they're generally safe and private under most—but definitely not all—circumstances. To understand why cookies can sometimes compromise your privacy, you have to understand the different cookie types that exist:

- **Temporary cookie**—This type of cookie lives just as long as you have Internet Explorer running. IE deletes all temporary cookies when you shut down the program.
- **Persistent cookie**—This type of cookie remains on your hard disk through multiple Internet Explorer sessions. The cookie's duration depends on how it's set up, but it can be anything from a few seconds to a few years.
- **First-party cookie**—This is a cookie set by the website you're viewing.
- **Third-party cookie**—This is a cookie set by a site other than the one you're viewing. Advertisers that have placed an ad on the site you're viewing create and store most third-party cookies.

These cookie types can compromise your privacy in two ways:

- A site might store **personally identifiable information**—your name, email address, home address, phone number, and so on—in a persistent first- or third-party cookie and then use that information in some way (such as filling in a form) without your consent.
- A site might store information about you in a persistent third-party cookie and then use that cookie to track your online movements and activities. The advertiser can do this because it might have (for example) an ad on dozens or hundreds of websites, and that ad is the mechanism that enables the site to set and read their cookies. Such sites are supposed to come up with **privacy policies** stating that they won't engage in surreptitious monitoring of users, they won't sell user data, and so on.

To help you handle these scenarios, Windows Vista implements a privacy feature that gives you extra control over whether sites can store cookies on your machine. To check out this feature, select Internet Explorer's Tools, Internet Options command, and then display the Privacy tab. You set your cookie privacy level by using the slider in the Settings group. First, let's look at the two extreme settings:

- **Accept All Cookies**—This setting (it's at the bottom of the slider) tells Internet Explorer to accept all requests to set and read cookies.
- **Block All Cookies**—This setting (it's at the top of the slider) tells Internet Explorer to reject all requests to set and read cookies.

CAUTION

Blocking all cookies might sound like the easiest way to maximize your online privacy. However, many sites rely on cookies to operate properly, so if you block all cookies you might find that your web surfing isn't as convenient or as smooth as it used to be.

In between are four settings that offer more detailed control. Table 21.1 shows you how each setting affects the three types of privacy issues.

TABLE 21.1 Cookie Settings and Their Effect on Surfing Privacy

	Third-Party Cookies with No Compact Privacy Policy	Third-Party Cookies Using Personally Identifiable Information Without the Type of Consent	First-Party Cookies Using Personally Identifiable Information Without the Type of Consent
Low	Restricted	Restricted (implicit)	OK
Medium (the default)	Blocked	Blocked (implicit)	Restricted (implicit)
Medium High	Blocked	Blocked (explicit)	Blocked (implicit)
High	Blocked	Blocked (explicit)	Blocked (explicit)

Here are some notes about the terminology in this table:

- **Restricted** means that Internet Explorer doesn't allow the site to set a persistent cookie, just a temporary one.
- A **compact** privacy policy is a shortened form of a privacy policy that can be sent along with the cookie and that can be read by the browser.
- **Implicit consent** means that one or more pages leading up to the cookie warned you that your personally identifiable information would be used and you agreed that it was okay.
- **Explicit consent** means that the page that reads the cookie warned you that your personally identifiable information would be used and you agreed that it was okay.

NOTE

If you decide to change the privacy setting, you should first delete all your cookies because the new setting won't apply to any cookies already on your computer. See "Deleting Browser History," earlier in this chapter.

Blocking Pop-Up Windows

Among the most annoying things on the Web are those ubiquitous pop-up windows that infest your screen with advertisements when you visit certain sites. (A variation on the theme is the **pop under**, a window that opens under your current browser window, so you don't know it's there until you close the window.) Pop-up windows can also be dangerous because some unscrupulous software makers have figured out ways to use them to install software on your computer without your permission. They're nasty things, any way you look at them.

Fortunately, Microsoft has given us a way to stop most pop-ups before they start. Internet Explorer comes with a feature called the *Pop-up Blocker* that looks for pop-ups and prevents them from opening. It's not perfect (the occasional pop-under still breaks through the defences), but it make surfing sites much more pleasant. Follow these steps to use and configure the Pop-up Blocker:

1. In Internet Explorer, select Tools, Internet Options to display the Internet Options dialog box.
2. Display the Privacy tab.
3. Activate the Turn On Pop-Up Blocker check box.
4. To set options for this feature, click Settings to display the Pop-Up Blocker Settings dialog box. You have the following options (click Close when you're done):

TIP

You can also display the Pop-Up Blocker Settings dialog box by selecting Tools, Pop-up Blocker, Popup Blocker Settings.

Address of Web Site to Allow	Use this option when you have a site that displays pop-ups you want to see. Type the address and then click Add.
Play a Sound When a Pop-up Is Blocked	When this check box is activated, Internet Explorer plays a brief sound each time is blocks a pop-up. If this gets annoying after a while, deactivate this check box.
Show Information Bar When a Pop-up Is Blocked	When this check box is activated, Internet Explorer displays a yellow bar below the Address bar each time it blocks a pop-up so that you know it's working on your behalf.

5. Click OK.

With the Pop-Up Blocker on the case, it monitors your surfing and steps in front of any pop-up window that tries to disturb your peace. A yellow Information bar appears under the Address bar to let you know that Pop-Up Blocker thwarted a pop-up. Clicking the Information bar displays a menu with the following choices:

Temporarily Allow Pop-Ups	Click this command to enable pop-ups on the site only during the current session.
Always Allow Pop-Ups from This Site	Click this command to allow future pop-ups for the current domain.
Settings	Click this command to see a submenu with three commands: click Turn Off Pop-Up Blocker to turn off the feature entirely; click Show Information Bar for Pop-Ups to tell Internet Explorer to stop displaying the Information bar for each blocked pop-up; and click Settings to display the Pop-Up Blocker Settings dialog box.

Understand Internet Explorer's Advanced Security Options

To close our look at Windows Vista's web security features, this section takes you through Internet Explorer's Advanced security options. Select Tools, Internet Options, display the Advanced tab, and then scroll down to the Security section to see the following options:.

Allow Active Content from CDs to Run on My Computer	Leave this check box deactivated to prevent active content such as scripts and controls located in CD-based web pages to execute on your computer. However, if you have a CD-based program that won't function, you might need to activate this check box to enable the program to work properly.
Allow Active Content to Run in Files on My Computer	Leave this check box deactivated to prevent active content such as scripts and controls located in local web pages to execute on your computer. If you're testing a web page that includes active content, activate this check box so that you can test the web pages locally.
Allow Software to Run or Install Even If the Signature Is Invalid	Leave this check box deactivated to avoid running or installing software that doesn't have a valid digital signature. If you can't get a program to run or install, consider activating this check box.
Check for Publisher's Certificate Revocation	When this option is activated, Internet Explorer examines a site's digital security certificates to see whether they have been revoked.
Check for Server Certificate Revocation	If you activate this option, Internet Explorer also checks the security certificate for the web page's server.
Check for Signatures on Downloaded Programs	If you activate this check box, Internet Explorer checks for a digital signature on any program that you download.
Do Not Save Encrypted Pages to Disk	If you activate this option, Internet Explorer won't store encrypted files in the Temporary Internet Files folder.
Empty Temporary Internet Files Folder When Browser Is Closed	With this option activated, Internet Explorer removes all files from the Temporary Internet Files folder when you exit the program.

Enable Integrated Windows Authentication	With this check box activated, Internet Explorer uses Integrated Windows Authentication (formerly known as Windows NT Challenge/Response Authentication) to attempt to log on to a restricted site. This means the browser attempts to log on using the current credentials from the user's network domain logon. If this doesn't work, Internet Explorer displays a dialog box prompting the user for a username and password.
New Enable Memory Protection to Help Mitigate Online Attacks	Activate this check box to enable Data Execution Prevention (DEP) for Internet Explorer. DEP prevents malicious code from executing in protected memory locations.
New Enable Native XMLHTTP Support	With this check box activated, Internet Explorer works properly with sites that use the XMLHTTPRequest API to transfer XML data between the browser and a server. This API is most commonly used in Ajax-powered sites. Ajax (Asynchronous JavaScript and XML) is a web development technique that creates sites that operate much like desktop programs. In particular, the XMLHTTPRequest API enables the browser to request and accept data from the server without reloading the page.
New Phishing Filter	This item offers three option buttons: ▶ **Disable Phishing Filter**—Click this option to shut off the Phishing Filter. ▶ **Turn Off Automatic Website Checking**—Click this option to tell Internet Explorer not to check each site to determine whether it's a suspicious or a known phishing site. Internet Explorer displays a Phishing Filter icon in the status bar, and you can click that icon to check the current site. ▶ **Turn On Automatic Website Checking**—Click this option to tell Internet Explorer to check each site to determine whether it's a suspicious or a known phishing site.
Use SSL 2.0	This check box toggles support for the Secure Sockets Layer Level 2 security protocol on and off. This version of SSL is currently the Web's standard security protocol.

Use SSL 3.0	This check box toggles support for SSL Level 3 on and off. SSL 3.0 is more secure than SSL 2.0 (it can authenticate both the client and the server), but isn't currently as popular as SSL 2.0.
Use TLS 1.0	This check box toggles support for **Transport Layer Security** (**TLS**) on and off. This is a relatively new protocol, so few websites implement it.
Warn About Certificate Address Mismatch	When activated, this option tells Internet Explorer to display a warning dialog box if a site is using an invalid digital security certificate.
Warn If Changing Between Secure and Not Secure Mode	When activated, this option tells Internet Explorer to display a warning dialog box whenever you enter and leave a secure site.
Warn If POST Submittal Is Redirected to a Zone That Does Not Permit Posts	When activated, this option tells Internet Explorer to display a warning dialog box if a form submission is sent to a site other than the one hosting the form.

Working with Email Safely and Securely

Email is by far the most popular online activity, but it can also be the most frustrating in terms of security and privacy. Email viruses are legion; spam gets worse every day; and messages that should be secret are really about as secure as if they were written on the back of a postcard. Fortunately, it doesn't take much to remedy these and other email problems, as you'll see over the next few sections.

Protecting Yourself Against Email Viruses

Until just a few years ago, the primary method that computer viruses used to propagate themselves was the floppy disk. A user with an infected machine would copy some files to a floppy, and the virus would surreptitiously add itself to the disk. When the recipient inserted the disk, the virus copy came to life and infected yet another computer. When the Internet became a big deal, viruses adapted and began propagating either via malicious websites or via infected program files downloaded to users' machines.

Over the past couple of years, however, by far the most productive method for viruses to replicate has been the humble email message. Melissa; I Love You; BadTrans; Sircam; Klez. The list of email viruses and Trojan horses is a long one but they all operate more or less the same way: They arrive as a message attachment, usually from someone you know. When you open the attachment, the virus infects your computer and then, without your knowledge, uses your email client and your address book to ship out messages with more copies of itself attached. The nastier versions also mess with your computer by deleting data or corrupting files.

You can avoid infection by one of these viruses by implementing a few common sense procedures:

- Never open an attachment that comes from someone you don't know.
- Even if you know the sender, if the attachment isn't something you're expecting, assume that the sender's system is infected. Write back and confirm that the sender emailed the message.
- Some viruses come packaged as scripts hidden within messages that use the Rich Text (HTML) format. This means that the virus can run just by viewing the message! If a message looks suspicious, don't open it; just delete it. (Note that you'll need to turn off the Windows Mail Preview pane before deleting the message. Otherwise, when you highlight the message, it appears in the Preview pane and sets off the virus. Select View, Layout, deactivate the Show Preview Pane check box, and click OK.)

CAUTION

It's particularly important to turn off the Preview pane before displaying Windows Mail's Junk E-mail folder. Since many junk messages also carry a virus payload, your chances of initiating an infection are highest when working with messages in this folder.

- Install a top-of-the-line antivirus program, particularly one that checks incoming email. In addition, be sure to keep your antivirus program's virus list up to date. As you read this, there are probably dozens, maybe even hundreds, of morally challenged scumnerds designing even nastier viruses. Regular updates will help you keep up.

In addition to these general procedures, Windows Mail also comes with its own set of virus protection features. Here's how to use them:

1. In Windows Mail, select Tools, Options.
2. Display the Security tab.
3. In the Virus Protection group, you have the following options:

Select the Internet Explorer Security Zone to Use	Earlier in this chapter I described the security zone model used by Internet Explorer (refer to "Surfing the Web Securely"). From the perspective of Windows Mail, you use the security zones to determine whether to allow active content inside an HTML-format message to run: ▶ **Internet Zone**—If you choose this zone, active content is allowed to run. ▶ **Restricted Sites Zone**—If you choose this option, active content is disabled. This is the default setting and the one I recommend.

Warn Me When Other Applications Try to Send Mail as Me	As I mentioned earlier, it's possible for programs and scripts to send email messages without your knowledge. This happens by using Simple MAPI (**Messaging Application Programming Interface**) calls, which can send messages via your computer's default mail client—and it's all hidden from you. With this check box activated, Windows Mail displays a warning dialog box when a program or script attempts to send a message using Simple MAPI.

Sending Messages Via CDO

Activating the Warn Me When Other Applications Try to Send Mail as Me option protects you against scripts that attempt to send surreptitious messages using Simple MAPI calls. However, there's another way to send messages behind the scenes. It's **Collaboration Data Objects** (**CDO**), and Windows Vista installs it by default. Here's a sample script that uses CDO to send a message:

```
Dim objMessage
Dim objConfig
strSchema = "http://schemas.microsoft.com/cdo/configuration/"

Set objConfig = CreateObject("CDO.Configuration")
With objConfig.Fields
    .Item(strSchema & "sendusing") = 2
    .Item(strSchema & "smtpserver") = "mail.mcfedries.com"
    .Item(strSchema & "smtpserverport") = 25
    .Item(strSchema & "smtpauthenticate") = 1
    .Item(strSchema & "sendusername") = "your_user_name"
    .Item(strSchema & "sendpassword") = "your_password"
    .Update
End With

Set objMessage = CreateObject("CDO.Message")
With objMessage
    Set .Configuration = objConfig
    .To = "you@there.com"
    .From = "me@here.com"
    .Subject = "CDO Test"
    .TextBody = "Just testing..."
    .Send
End With
Set objMessage = Nothing
Set objConfig = Nothing
```

The Warn Me When Other Applications Try to Send Mail as Me option does *not* trap this kind of script, so bear in mind that your system is still vulnerable to Trojan horses that send mail via your Windows Vista accounts. However, in the preceding example

I've included code to handle SMTP authentication (just in case you want to try out the script and your ISP requires authentication). In practice, a third-party script wouldn't know your SMTP password, so a CDO script will fail on any account that requires authentication.

Do Not Allow Attachments to Be Saved or Opened That Could Potentially Be a Virus	With this check box activated, Windows Mail monitors attachments to look for file types that could contain viruses or destructive code. If it detects such a file, it disables your ability to open and save that file, and it displays a note at the top of the message to let you know about the unsafe attachment, as shown in Figure 21.17.

File Types Disabled by Windows Mail

Internet Explorer's built-in unsafe-file list defines the file types that Windows Mail disables. That list includes file types associated with the following extensions: `.ad`, `.ade`, `.adp`, `.bas`, `.bat`, `.chm`, `.cmd`, `.com`, `.cpl`, `.crt`, `.exe`, `.hlp`, `.hta`, `.inf`, `.ins`, `.isp`, `.js`, `.jse`, `.lnk`, `.mdb`, `.mde`, `.msc`, `.msi`, `.msp`, `.mst`, `.pcd`, `.pif`, `.reg`, `.scr`, `.sct`, `.shb`, `.shs`, `.url`, `.vb`, `.vbe`, `.vbs`, `.vsd`, `.vss`, `.vst`, `.vsw`, `.wsc`, `.wsf`, `.wsh`.

TIP

What do you do if you want to send a file that's on the Windows Mail unsafe file list and you want to make sure that the recipient will be able to open it? The easiest workaround is to compress the file into a `.zip` file—a file type not blocked by Windows Mail, Outlook, or any other mail client that blocks file types.

4. Click OK to put the new settings into effect.

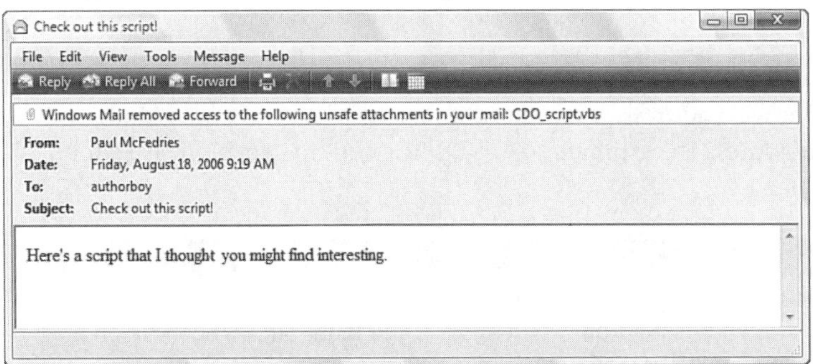

FIGURE 21.17 If Windows Mail detects an unsafe file attachment, it displays a notice at the top of the message to let you know that you do not have access to the file.

Thwarting Spam with Windows Mail's Junk Filter

New **Spam**—unsolicited commercial messages—has become a plague upon the earth. Unless you've done a masterful job at keeping your address secret, you probably receive at least a few spam emails every day, and it's more likely that you receive a few dozen. The bad news is that most experts agree that it's only going to get worse. And why not? Spam is one of the few advertising media for which the costs are substantially borne by the users, not the advertisers.

The best way to avoid spam is to avoid getting on a spammer's list of addresses in the first place. That's hard to do these days, but here are some steps you can take:

- Never use your actual email address in a newsgroup account. The most common method that spammers use to gather addresses is to harvest them from newsgroup posts. One common tactic you can use is to alter your email address by adding text that invalidates the address but is still obvious for other people to figure out:

  ```
  user@myisp.remove_this_to_email_me.com
  ```

- When you sign up for something online, use a fake address, if possible. If you need or want to receive email from the company and so must use your real address, make sure that you deactivate any options that ask if you want to receive promotional offers. Alternatively, enter the address from an easily disposable free web-based account (such as a Hotmail account) so that any spam you receive will go there instead of to your main address. If your free email account overflows with junk mail, remove it and create a new one. (You can also do this through your ISP if it allows you to create multiple email accounts.)
- Never open suspected spam messages because doing so can sometimes notify the spammer that you've opened the message, thus confirming that your address is legit. For the same reason, you should never display a spam message in the Windows Mail Preview pane. Shut off the Reading pane (select View, Layout, deactivate Show Preview Pane, and click OK) before selecting any spam messages that you want to delete.
- Never—I repeat, *never*—respond to spam, even to an address within the spam that claims to be a "removal" address. By responding to the spam, all you're doing is proving that your address is legitimate, so you'll just end up getting *more* spam.

TIP

If you create web pages, never put your email address on a page because spammers use **crawlers** that harvest addresses from web pages. If you must put an address on a page, hide it using some simple JavaScript code:

```
<script language="JavaScript" type="text/javascript">
<!--
var add1 = "webmaster"
var add2 = "@"
```

```
var add3 = "whatever.com"
document.write(add1 + add2 + add3)
//-->
</script>
```

If you do get spam despite these precautions, the good news is that Windows Mail comes with a Junk Email feature that can help you cope. Junk Email is a **spam filter**, which means that it examines each incoming message and applies sophisticated tests to determine whether the message is spam. If the tests determine that the message is probably spam, Windows Mail exiles the email to a separate `Junk E-mail` folder. The basis for the Windows Mail spam filter is the much-admired filter that comes with Outlook 2003, which was voted best spam filter by *Consumer Reports* in September 2005. It's not perfect (no spam filter is), but with a bit of fine-tuning as described in the next few sections, it can be a very useful weapon against spam.

Setting the Junk Email Protection Level

Filtering spam is always a trade-off between protection and convenience. That is, the stronger the protection you use, the less convenient the filter becomes, and vice versa. This inverse relationship is the result of a filter phenomenon called a **false positive**—a legitimate message that the filter has pegged as spam and so (in Windows Mail's case) moved the message to the `Junk E-mail` folder. The stronger the protection level, the more likely it is that false positives will occur, so the more time you must spend checking the `Junk E-mail` folder for legitimate messages that need to be rescued.

Fortunately, Windows Mail gives you several junk email levels to choose from, so you can choose a level that gives the blend of protection and convenience that suits you. To set the junk email level, select Tools, Junk E-mail Options. Windows Mail displays the Junk E-mail Options dialog box. The Options tab gives you four options for the Junk E-mail protection level:

- **No Automatic Filtering**—This option turns off the junk email filter. However, Windows Mail still moves messages from blocked senders to the `Junk E-mail` folder (see "Blocking Senders," later in this chapter). Choose this option only if you use a third-party spam filter or if you handle spam using your own message rules.

- **Low**—This is the default protection level, and it's designed to move only messages with obvious spam content to the `Junk E-mail` folder. This is a good level to start with—particularly if you get only a few spams a day—because it catches most spam and has only a minimal risk of false positives.

- **High**—This level handles spam aggressively and so only rarely misses a junk message. On the downside, the High level also occasionally catches legitimate messages in its nets, so you need to check the `Junk E-mail` folder regularly to look for false positives. Use this level if you get a lot of spam—a few dozen messages or more each day.

NOTE

If you get a false positive in your `Junk E-mail` folder, click the message and then select Message, Junk E-mail, Mark as Not Junk.

- **Safe List Only**—This level treats all incoming messages as spam, except for those messages that come from people or domains in your Safe Senders list (see "Specifying Safe Senders," later in this chapter) or that are sent to addresses in your Safe Recipients list. Use this level if your spam problem is out of control (a hundred or more spams each day) and if most of your nonspam email comes from people you know or from mailing lists you subscribe to.

If you hate spam so much that you never want to even *see* it, much less deal with it, activate the Permanently Delete Suspected Junk E-mail check box.

CAUTION

Spam is so hair-pullingly frustrating that you might be tempted to activate the Permanently Delete Suspected Junk E-mail check box out of sheer spite. I don't recommend this, however. The danger of false positives is too great, even with the Low level, and it's not worth missing a crucial message.

You can improve the performance of the junk email filter by giving Windows Mail a bit more information. Specifically, you can specify safe senders and you can block senders and countries.

Specifying Safe Senders

If you use the Low or High junk email protection level, you can reduce the number of false positives by letting Windows Mail know about the people or institutions that regularly send you mail. By designating these addresses as Safe Senders, you tell Windows Mail to leave their incoming messages in your Inbox automatically and never redirect them to the `Junk E-mail` folder. Certainly if you use the Safe Lists Only protection level, you must specify some Safe Senders because Windows Mail treats everyone else as a spammer (unless someone sends mail to an address in your Safe Recipients list—see the next section).

Your Safe Senders list can consist of three types of addresses:

- **Individual email addresses of the form *`someone@somewhere.com`***—All messages from those addresses are not treated as spam.
- **Domain names of the form *`@somewhere.com`***—All messages from any address within that domain are not treated as spam.
- **Your Contacts list**—You can tell Windows Mail to treat everyone in your Contacts list as a Safe Sender, which makes sense because you're unlikely to be spammed by someone you know.

You can specify a Safe Sender contact in two ways. You can either enter the address by hand by displaying the Safe Senders tab in the Junk E-mail Options dialog box and then clicking Add, or use an existing message from the sender by clicking the message, selecting Message, Junk E-mail, and then selecting either Add Sender to Safe Senders List or Add Sender's Domain to Safe Senders List.

Blocking Senders

If you notice that a particular address is the source of much spam or other annoying email, the easiest way to block the spam is to block all incoming messages from that address. You can do this using the Blocked Senders list, which watches for messages from a specific address and relegates them to the `Junk E-mail` folder.

As with the Safe Senders list, you can specify a Blocked Sender address in two ways. You can either enter the address by hand by displaying the Blocked Senders tab in the Junk E-mail Options dialog box and then clicking Add, or use an existing message from the sender by selecting the message you want to work with and then selecting Message, Junk E-mail, Add Sender to Blocked Senders List.

Blocking Countries and Languages

Windows Mail also has two features that enable you to handle spam with an international flavor:

- **Spam that comes from a particular country or region**—If you receive no legitimate messages from that country or region, you can treat all messages from that location as spam. Windows Mail does this by using the **top-level domain** (**TLD**), which is the final suffix that appears in a domain name. There are two types: a generic top-level domain, such as `com`, `edu`, or `net`; and a country code top-level domain, such as `ca` (Canada) and `fr` (France). Windows Mail uses the latter to filter spam that comes from certain countries.

- **Spam that comes in a foreign language**—If you don't understand a language, you can safely treat all messages that appear in that language as spam. The character set of a foreign language always appears using a special encoding unique to that language. (An **encoding** is a set of rules that establishes a relationship between the characters and their representations.) Windows Mail uses that encoding to filter spam in a specified language.

In the Junk E-mail Options dialog box, display the International tab and use the following techniques:

- To filter spam based on one or more countries, click the Blocked Top-Level Domain List, activate the check box beside each of the countries you want to filter, and then click the OK button.

- To filter spam based on one or more languages, click the Blocked Encodings List, activate the check box beside each of the languages you want to filter, and then click the OK button.

Email Phishing Protection

Internet Explorer's Phishing Filter works well if you stumble into a phishing site while surfing the Web. However, most phishing "lures" are email messages that appear to be from legitimate businesses, and they include links that send you to phishing sites where they hope to dupe you into giving up confidential information. To help prevent you from falling into that trap, Windows Mail includes an antiphishing feature of its own: If it detects a potential phishing email, it blocks that message from appearing. The Phishing tab in the Junk E-mail Options dialog box controls this feature. Make sure that you activate the Protect My Inbox from Messages with Potential Phishing Links check box. Note, too, that you can also redirect potential phishing messages to the `Junk E-mail` folder by activating the Move Phishing E-mail to the Junk Mail Folder check box.

If Windows Mail detects a potential phishing message, it displays a message to let you know and it displays the message header in red text. If you open the suspicious message, Windows Mail displays the message shown in Figure 21.18 and disables the message's images and links. If you're sure that the message is not a phishing attempt, click Unblock.

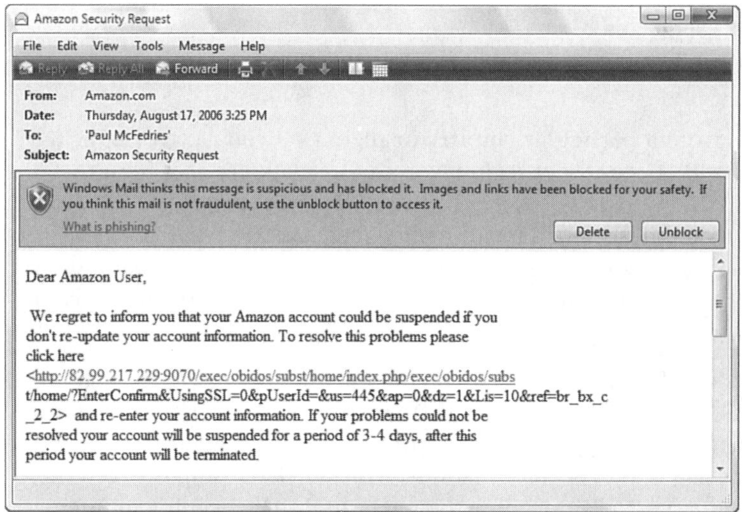

FIGURE 21.18 If Windows Mail suspects a message is a phishing attempt, it lets you know and blocks the message's links and images.

Maintaining Your Privacy While Reading Email

You wouldn't think that the simple act of reading an email message would have privacy implications, but you'd be surprised. Two scenarios can compromise your privacy: read receipts and web bugs.

Blocking Read Receipts

A **read receipt** is an email notification that tells the sender that you've opened the message sent to you. If the sender requests a read receipt and you either select the message so that the message text appears in the preview pane, or double-click the message to open it, Windows Mail displays the dialog box shown in Figure 21.19. Click Yes to send the receipt, or click No to skip it.

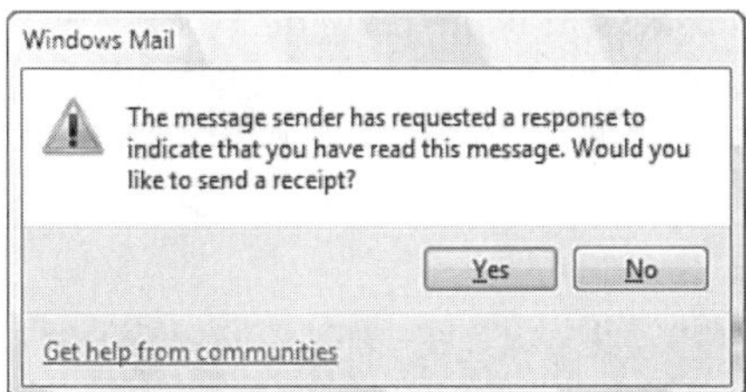

FIGURE 21.19 You see this dialog box when you open a message for which the sender has requested a read receipt.

Many people like asking for read receipts because they offer proof of delivery. It has been my experience, however, that getting a read receipt back starts a kind of internal clock that the sender uses to measure how long it takes you to respond after reading the message. Because of this annoyance, and because I feel it's nobody's business to know when I read a message, I always click No when asked to send a read receipt. (Spammers, too, sometimes request read receipts as a way of validating email addresses.) In fact, you can go one better and tell Windows Mail never to send a read receipt:

1. Select Tools, Options to display the Options dialog box.
2. Display the Receipts tab.
3. In the Returning Read Receipts group, activate the Never Send a Read Receipt option.
4. Click OK.

Squashing Web Bugs

A **web bug** is an image that resides on a remote server and is included in an HTML-formatted email message by referencing a URL on the remote server. When you open the message, Windows Mail uses the URL to download the image for display within the message. That sounds harmless enough, but if the message is junk email, it's likely that the URL will also contain either your email address or a code that points to your email address. When the remote server gets a request for this URL, it knows not only that you've opened the message, but also that your email address is legitimate.

You have three ways to combat web bugs:

- **Don't open a message that you suspect to be spam, and don't preview the message in the Windows Mail preview pane**—In fact, before you can delete the message, you have to turn off the preview pane temporarily, as described earlier in this chapter.
- **Read your messages in plain text**—In Windows Mail, select Tools, Options, choose the Read tab, and then activate the Read All Messages in Plain Text check box. This prevents Windows Mail from downloading any web bugs because it displays all messages in plain text, which means that it also thwarts other message formatting, as well.

TIP

If you get a legitimate HTML message, you can tell Windows Mail to display the formatting. Select the message and then select View, Message in HTML (or press Alt+Shift+H).

- **Block messages from displaying**—In Windows Mail, select Tools, Options, choose the Security tab, and then activate the Block Images and Other External Content in HTML E-mail check box. This prevents Windows Mail from downloading web bugs and any other items that would otherwise come from some remote server.

Sending and Receiving Secure Email

When you connect to a website, your browser sets up a direct connection—called a **channel**—between your machine and the web server. Because the channel is a direct link, it's relatively easy to implement security because all you have to do is secure the channel.

However, email security is entirely different and much more difficult to set up. The problem is that email messages don't have a direct link to a Simple Mail Transfer Protocol (SMTP) server. Instead, they must usually hop from server to server until they reach their final destination. Combine this with the open and well-documented email standards used on the Internet, and you end up with three email security issues:

- **Privacy**—Because messages often pass through other systems and can even end up on a remote system's hard disk, it isn't that hard for someone with the requisite know-how and access to the remote system to read a message.
- **Tampering**—Because a user can read a message passing through a remote server, it comes as no surprise that he can also change the message text.
- **Authenticity**—With the Internet email standards an open book, it isn't difficult for a savvy user to forge or **spoof** an email address.

To solve these issues, the Internet's gurus came up with the idea of **encryption**. When you encrypt a message, a complex mathematical formula scrambles the message content to make it unreadable. In particular, the encryption formula incorporates a **key value**. To unscramble the message, the recipient feeds the key into the decryption formula.

Such **single-key encryption** works, but its major drawback is that both the sender and the recipient must have the same key. **Public-key encryption** overcomes that limitation by using two related keys: a **public key** and a **private key**. The public key is available to everyone, either by sending it to them directly or by offering it in an online key database. The private key is secret and is stored on the user's computer. Here's how public-key cryptography solves the issues discussed earlier:

- **Privacy**—When you send a message, you obtain the recipient's public key and use it to encrypt the message. The encrypted message can now only be decrypted using the recipient's private key, thus assuring privacy.
- **Tampering**—An encrypted message can still be tampered with, but only randomly because the content of the message can't be seen. This thwarts the most important skill used by tamperers: making the tampered message look legitimate.
- **Authenticity**—When you send a message, you use your private key to digitally sign the message. The recipient can then use your public key to examine the digital signature to ensure that the message came from you.

If there's a problem with public-key encryption, it is that the recipient of a message must obtain the sender's public key from an online database. (The sender can't just send the public key because the recipient would have no way to prove that the key came from the sender.) Therefore, to make this more convenient, a **digital ID** is used. This is a digital certificate that states a trusted certifying authority authenticates the sender's public key. The sender can then include his or her public key in outgoing messages.

Setting Up an Email Account with a Digital ID

To send secure messages using Windows Mail, you first have to obtain a digital ID. Here are the steps to follow:

1. In Windows Mail, select Tools, Options and then display the Security tab.
2. Click Get Digital ID. Internet Explorer loads and takes you to the Microsoft Office Marketplace digital ID page on the Web.
3. Click a link to the certifying authority (such as VeriSign) you want to use.
4. Follow the authority's instructions for obtaining a digital ID. (Note that digital IDs are not free; they typically cost about $20 U.S. per year.)

With your digital ID installed, the next step is to assign it to an email account:

1. In Windows Mail, select Tools, Accounts to open the Internet Accounts dialog box.
2. Select the account you want to work with and then click Properties. The account's properties sheet appears.
3. Display the Security tab.
4. In the Signing Certificate group, click Select. Windows Mail displays the Select Default Account Digital ID dialog box.
5. Make sure to select the certificate that you installed and then click OK. Your name appears in the Security tab's first Certificate box.
6. Click OK to return to the Internet Accounts dialog box.
7. Click Close.

TIP

To make a backup copy of your digital ID, open Internet Explorer and select Tools, Internet Options. Display the Content tab and click Certificates to see a list of your installed certificates (be sure to use the Personal tab). Click your digital ID and then click Export.

Obtaining Another Person's Public Key

Before you can send an encrypted message to another person, you must obtain his public key. How you do this depends on whether you have a digitally signed message from that person.

If you have a digitally signed message, open the message, as described later in this chapter in the "Receiving a Secure Message" section. Windows Mail adds the digital ID to the Contacts list automatically:

- If you have one or more contacts whose email addresses match the address associated with the digital ID, Windows Mail adds the digital ID to each contact. To see it, open the `Contacts` folder—select Start, select your username, and then open `Contacts`—open the contact and display the IDs tab.
- If there are no existing matches, Windows Mail creates a new contact.

TIP

If you don't want Windows Mail to add digital IDs automatically, select Tools, Options, display the Security tab, and click Advanced. In the dialog box that appears, deactivate the Add Senders' Certificates to My Windows Contacts check box.

If you don't have a digitally signed message for the person you want to work with, you have to visit a certifying authority's website and find the person's digital ID. For example, you can go to the VeriSign site (www.verisign.com) to search for a digital ID and then download it to your computer. After that, follow these steps:

1. Open the `Contacts` folder.
2. Open the person's contact info or create a new contact.
3. Type one or more email addresses and fill in the other data as necessary.
4. Display the IDs tab.
5. In the Select an E-Mail Address list, select the address that corresponds with the digital ID you downloaded.
6. Click the Import button to display the Select Digital ID File to Import dialog box.
7. Find and select the downloaded digital ID file and then click Open.
8. Click OK.

Sending a Secure Message

After installing your digital ID, you can start sending out secure email messages. You have two options:

- **Digitally sign a message to prove that you're the sender**—Start a new message and then either select the Tools, Digitally Sign command or click the Digitally Sign Message toolbar button. A certificate icon appears to the right of the header fields.
- **Encrypt a message to avoid snooping and tampering**—In the New Message window, either activate the Tools, Encrypt command or click the Encrypt Message toolbar button. A lock icon appears to the right of the header fields.

TIP

You can tell Windows Mail to digitally sign and/or encrypt all your outgoing messages. Select Tools, Options and display the Security tab. To encrypt all your messages, activate the Encrypt Contents and Attachments for All Outgoing Messages check box. To sign all your messages, activate the Digitally Sign All Outgoing Messages check box.

Receiving a Secure Message

The technology and mathematics underlying the digital ID are complex, but there's nothing complex about dealing with incoming secure messages. Windows Mail handles everything behind the scenes, including the authentication of the sender (for a digitally signed message) and the decryption of the message (for an encrypted message). In the latter case, a dialog box tells you that Windows Mail decrypted the message with your private key.

As you can see in Figure 21.20, Windows Mail gives you a few visual indications that you're dealing with a secure message:

- The message displays with a certificate icon.
- The message text doesn't appear in the preview pane.
- The preview pane title is Security Help and the subtitle tells you the type of security used: Digitally Signed and/or Encrypted.
- The preview pane text describes the security used in the message.

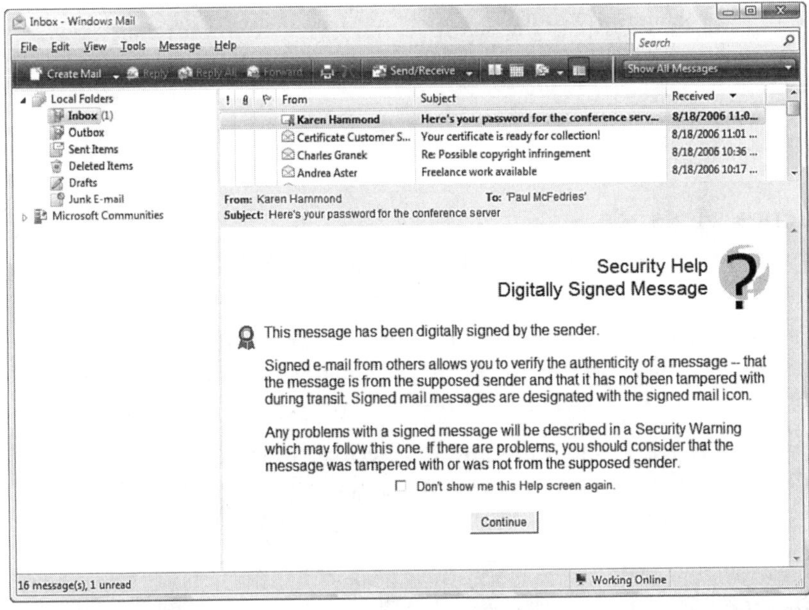

FIGURE 21.20 For a secure message, the preview pane describes the type of security used.

To read the message, click the Continue button at the bottom. If you don't want to see this security preview in the future, activate the Don't Show Me This Help Screen Again check box.

TIP

If you change your mind and decide you want to see the preview screen, you have to edit the Registry. Open the Registry Editor and head for the following key:

```
HKCU\Software\Microsoft\Windows Mail\Dont Show Dialogs
```

Open the `Digital Signature Help` setting and change its value to `0`.

Security and Privacy Options for Windows Media Player

You can set some options in Windows Media Player to ensure that media downloaded from or played on an Internet site is safe. You can also set options in Windows Media Player that enhance the privacy of the Internet media you play.

You'll find Windows Media Player's security and privacy settings in the Options dialog box, which you display by pressing Alt and then selecting Tools, Options.

TIP

You can use the Group Policy editor to hide the Security and Privacy tabs in the Options dialog box. Select User Configuration, Administrative Templates, Windows Components, Windows Media Player, User Interface, and then enable the Hide Privacy Tab and Hide Security Tab policies.

Setting Security Options

You can play Internet media either by downloading the music or video to your computer and playing it in Windows Media Player or by using a version of Windows Media Player that resides inside a web page. Either way, the person who created the media might have included extra commands in a script designed to control the playback. Unfortunately, scripts could also contain commands that can harm your computer, so preventing these scripts from running at all is the best option.

In the Security tab, there are four check boxes in the Content group that control scripting:

Run Script Commands When Present	Leave this check box deactivated to avoid running scripts in downloaded media.
Run Script Commands and Rich Media Streams When the Player Is in a Web Page	Deactivate this check box to avoid running scripts in media embedded in web pages.
Play Enhanced Content That Uses Web Pages Without Prompting	Leave this check box deactivated to have Windows Media Player ask whether you want to view a media site's **enhanced content**; that is, web pages that give you information related to the media. Because those pages could contain malicious content, it's best to have Windows Media Player ask whether you want to see the enhanced data.

Show Local Captions When Present	If the media has captions in the Synchronized Accessible Media Interchange (SAMI) format, Windows Media doesn't display them because a SAMI file might contain malicious code. If you know the media you're playing is legitimate, activate this check box to display SAMI captions.

Setting Privacy Options

When you use Windows Media Player to play content from an Internet site, the program communicates certain information to the site, including the unique ID number of your copy of Windows Media Player. This allows content providers to track the media you play, and they might share this data with other sites. So, although the Player ID does not identify you personally, it might result in sites sending you targeted ads based on your media choices. If you do not want such an invasion of privacy, you can instruct Windows Media Player not to send the Player ID:

1. In the Options dialog box, display the Privacy tab.
2. Deactivate the Send Unique Player ID to Content Providers check box.

CAUTION

Remember that some content sites *require* the Player ID before you can play any media. For example, a site might request the ID for billing purposes. In that case, you should read the site's privacy statement to see what uses it makes of the ID.

3. Deactivate the Save File and URL History in the Player check box if you don't want other people who use your computer to see the media files and sites that you play and visit.
4. Click OK.

More New Security Features

New The security features you've seen so far are certainly worth the price of admission and should be enough to make Vista the most secure version of Windows yet. But Microsoft has more security tricks up its sleeve. The next few sections take you on a quick tour of the most important or interesting of the rest of Vista's new Internet security innovations.

Preventing Rogue Services with Windows Service Hardening

If you could map out the Windows attack surface, the biggest feature in the resulting landscape would be, by far, the system and third-party services that run in the background. Services are a tempting malware target for two reasons. First, most services are "always on," in the sense that they start when Windows loads and remain running until you shut down the system. Second, most services run with a high privilege level that gives them full access to the system. Malware that manages to get into a computer can use the system services to perform almost any task, from installing a Trojan horse to formatting the hard drive.

To reduce the chance that a malware program could turn a system's services on itself, Windows Vista implements a new service security technology called *Windows Service Hardening*. This technology doesn't prevent malware from infecting a service; that's the job of Windows Firewall and Windows Defender. Instead, Windows Service Hardening limits the damage that a compromised service can wreak on a system by implementing the following security techniques:

- Runs all services in a lower privilege level.
- Strips all services of permissions they don't require.
- Assigns each service its own **security identifier** (**SID**) that uniquely identifies it. This enables a system resource to create its own **access control list** (**ACL**) that specifies exactly which SIDs can access the resource. If a service that's not on the ACL tries to access the resource, Vista blocks the service.
- Enables a system resource to restrict which services have write permission to the resource.
- Ensures that all services come with network restrictions to prevent services from accessing the network in ways not defined by the service's normal operating parameters.

Avoiding Overflows with Support for the NX Bit

One common cause of system crashes, and a common technique used by makers of malicious software, is the *buffer overflow*. A **buffer** is a memory area set aside to hold data. The buffer has a fixed size, which means it can't handle data larger than that size. A well-programmed system includes checks to ensure that the only data written to the buffer is of the correct size or smaller.

In practice, however, the desire for faster code or sheer sloppiness by the programmer can occasionally result in unprotected memory buffers. When buffer overflow occurs, either by accident or by design, the system writes the extra data to memory areas adjacent to the buffer. If these adjacent areas just hold more data, nothing terrible happens. However, if the adjacent areas contain core operating system code, the system can crash; even worse, if the adjacent areas are designed to run system control code, a clever hacker can take advantage of that to run whatever code he or she wants, usually with disastrous results.

To help prevent those nasty aspects of buffer overflow, recent CPUs have implemented the NX (No eXecute) attribute, which can brand certain memory areas as nonexecutable. As a result, even if a buffer overflows into a code area, no malicious code can run because that area is marked with the NX attribute. Windows Vista fully supports the NX bit, allowing it to brand core system areas such as the stack and the head as nonexecutable. Note that you need both components—a CPU with the NX bit and Windows Vista—to get this protection.

Thwarting Malware Randomly with ASLR

Microsoft isn't assuming that users' machines will never be subject to malware attacks. To that end, Windows Vista implements not only support for the NX bit and continued support for Data Execution Prevention (which prevents malicious code from running in protected memory locations). Vista also implements an open-source security feature called *Address Space Layout Randomization* (*ASLR*). This feature aims to thwart some common attacks that attempt to run system code. In previous versions of Windows, certain system DLLs and executables were always loaded into memory using the same addresses each time. Attackers could launch one of those processes because they knew the function's entry point. With ASLR, Vista randomly loads these system functions into one of 256 memory locations, so attackers can't be certain where a particular bit of system code resides in memory.

From Here

Here's a list of chapters where you'll find related information:

- For the details on using the Group Policy editor, refer to the "Implementing Group Policies with Windows Vista" section in Chapter 10, "Using Control Panel and Group Policies."
- To find out about scripting Windows Vista, refer to Chapter 12, "Programming the Windows Scripting Host."
- To learn how to create mail rules, refer to the "Filtering Incoming Messages" section in Chapter 19, "Communicating with Windows Mail."
- To learn how to secure your wireless network, see the "Implementing Wireless Network Security" section in Chapter 22, "Setting Up a Small Network."
- To learn how to make secure remote connections to your network over the Internet, see the "Using Virtual Private Network Connections" section in Chapter 23, "Accessing and Administering the Network."

PART V

Unleashing Windows Vista Networking

CHAPTER 22

Setting Up a Small Network

IN THIS CHAPTER

- Setting Up a Peer-to-Peer Network
- Understanding the Network Icon
- Displaying the Network and Sharing Center
- Customizing Your Network
- Turning Network Discovery On or Off
- Viewing a Network Map
- Managing Wireless Networks
- Working with Network Connections

For many years, networking was the private playground of IT panjandrums. Its obscure lingo and arcane hardware were familiar to only this small coterie of computer cognoscenti. Workers who needed access to network resources had to pay obeisance to these powers-that-be, genuflecting in just the right way, tossing in the odd salaam or two.

Lately, however, we've seen a democratization of networking. Thanks to the trend away from mainframes and toward client/server setups, thanks to the migration from dumb terminals to smarter PCs, and thanks to the advent of easy peer-to-peer setups, networking is no longer the sole province of the elite. Getting connected to an existing network, or setting up your own network in a small office or home office, has never been easier.

This chapter shows you how Windows Vista has helped take even more of the *work* out of networking. You'll learn how to set up your own simple network and how to perform some useful administrative tasks. (For the details on accessing network resources, see Chapter 23, "Accessing and Using Your Network.")

Setting Up a Peer-to-Peer Network

One of the biggest improvements in Windows Vista is in networking setup. Specifically, if you have your computers connected correctly (more on that in a second), Vista sets up the appropriate networking settings automatically. It's true plug-and-play: You plug your machine into the network and you can play with network resources within a few seconds. Note that this doesn't apply to wireless connections which, for security reasons, require a few extra steps. Although, as you'll soon see, Vista enables you to "save" a wireless connection, so the next time your computer comes within range of that network, Vista makes the connection automatically.

So what is the "correct" network configuration required for this automatic networking setup to happen? For wired networks, it requires only the following:

- Each computer must have a network connection device, such as a network interface card (NIC), a USB network adapter, a motherboard-based network chip, or a network PC Card.
- You must have an external router (or switch).
- You must active Dynamic Host Control Protocol (DHCP) on the router. DHCP automatically assigns unique IP addresses to each computer on the network.

NOTE

By default, Vista sets up each computer to use DHCP. To double-check this, select Start, Control Panel, Network and Internet, Network and Sharing Center. Click the Manage Network Connections link to see a list of your connections. Right-click the Local Area Connection or the Wireless Network Connection icon, click Properties, and enter your UAC credentials. In the connection's properties sheet, double-click Internet Protocol Version 4 and then make sure that the Obtain an IP Address Automatically option is activated. Close all open dialog boxes.

- Each computer must have a network cable running from the NIC to a port in the router (or switch).
- If you have a high-speed modem, you must run a network cable from the Internet (or WAN) port in the router to the network port in the modem. This ensures that every computer on the network can share the Internet connection.
- Each computer must have a unique name.
- Configure every computer to use the same workgroup name.

If you're not sure about the last two points, see "Changing the Computer and Workgroup Name," later in this chapter.

For wireless networks, the configuration is more or less the same (except, of course, you don't need to run a network cable from each computer to the router). Here are the differences for a wireless network:

NOTE

Networks don't have to be exclusively wired or wireless. In fact, it's quite common to have a mixture of the two connection types. Most wireless access points come with a few ports to accept wired connections.

- Each computer must have a NIC that supports wireless connections.
- You must have a wireless access point or gateway that also doubles as a router.

CAUTION

Some broadband providers are using "smart" modems that include routing and firewall features. That's fine, but these modems almost always have a static IP address, and that address is usually either http://192.168.1.1 or http://192.168.0.1, which might conflict with your wireless gateway's IP address. If you have connection problems after adding the wireless gateway, the likely culprit is an IP address conflict. Disconnect the broadband modem, access the gateway's configuration program, and change its IP address (to, say, http://192.168.1.2 or http://192.168.0.2).

- During the initial configuration, one computer must connect to the access point via a network cable. This enables you to configure the access point before the wireless connection is established.

See "Connecting to a Wireless Network," later in this chapter, to learn the extra few steps that you must run to make the wireless connection in Vista.

Changing the Computer and Workgroup Name

I mentioned earlier that to implement a flawless Vista network, each computer must have a unique name and every computer must use the same workgroup name. (I'm assuming here that you're setting up a small network in your home or small office. Larger networks are typically divided into multiple workgroups, where all the machines in each workgroup are related in some way—marketing, IT, sales, and so on.)

Here are the steps to follow to change the computer name and workgroup name in Vista:

1. Click Start, right-click Computer, and then click Properties. The System window appears.
2. In the Computer Name, Domain, and Workgroup Settings section, click Change Settings and then enter your UAC credentials. The System Properties dialog box appears with the Computer Name tab displayed.

TIP

Another way to open the System Properties dialog box with the Computer Name tab displayed is to press Windows Logo+R (or select Start, All Programs, Accessories, Run), type **`systempropertiescomputername`**, click OK, and then enter your UAC credentials.

3. Click Change. The Computer Name/Domain Changes dialog box appears, as shown in Figure 22.1.

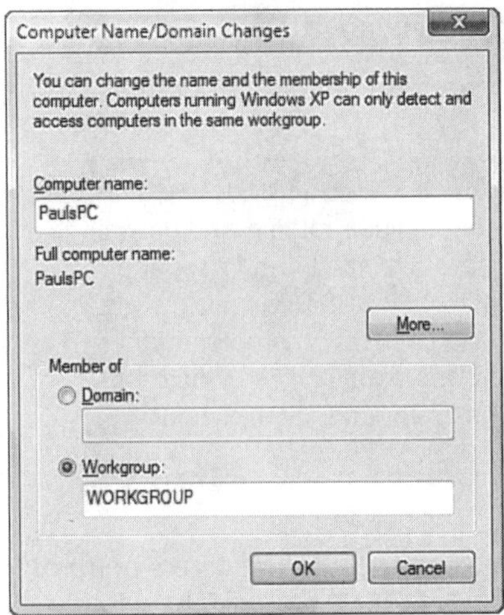

FIGURE 22.1 Use this dialog box to change your computer name and workgroup name.

4. Type the computer name.
5. Select the Workgroup option and type the common workgroup name.
6. Click OK. Vista tells you that you must restart the computer to put the changes into effect.
7. Click OK to return to the System Properties dialog box.
8. Click Close. Vista prompts you to restart your computer.
9. Click Restart Now.

Connecting to a Wireless Network

With your wireless network adapters installed and your wireless gateway or access point configured, you're ready to connect to your wireless network. This gives you access to the network's resources, as well as to the Internet, if you have a wireless gateway. Again, Vista doesn't establish the initial connection to a wireless network automatically. This is mostly a security concern because a password or security key protects most wireless networks. However, it's also usually the case (particularly in dense urban neighborhoods) that Vista might detect multiple wireless networks within range, so it's up to you to specify which network you want to connect to. Fortunately, you can configure Vista to remember a wireless network's settings and automatically connect you the next time the network is in range. So, in most cases, you need to run through the connection procedure only once.

Here are the steps to follow to connect to a wireless network:

1. Select Start, Connect To. Vista opens the Connect to a Network dialog box, which displays a list of the available wireless networks, as shown in Figure 22.2. Each network displays three pieces of information:

   ▶ The left column displays the network name (also called the **Service Set Identifier** or **SSID**).

   ▶ The middle column tells you whether the network requires a password or security key (`Security-enabled network`) or not (`Unsecured network`).

   ▶ The signal strength, as indicated by the five bars to the right (the more green bars you see, the stronger the signal). Note that the networks are in descending order of signal strength.

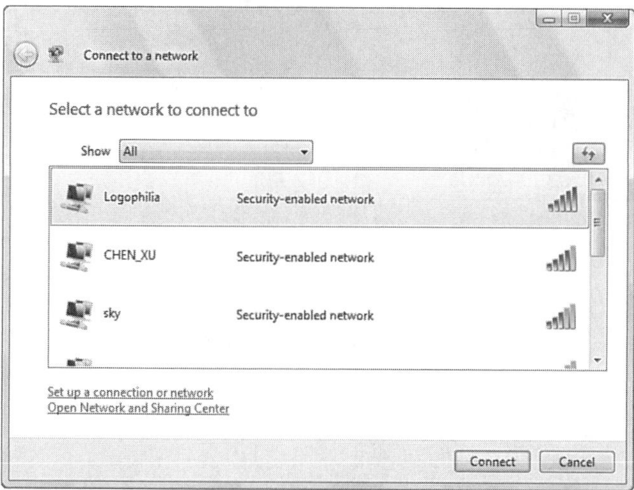

FIGURE 22.2 The Connect to a Network window displays a list of the wireless networks that are in range.

NOTE

Some of the networks might be **wireless hotspots**, which are locations that allow wireless computers to use the location's Internet connection. You can find hotspots in many airports, hotels, and even businesses such as coffee shops, restaurants, and dental offices.

2. Select the network that you want to use and then click Connect.

3. If the network that you want to use is unsecured—as are most public hotspots—Vista connects to the network immediately (so skip to step 5). However, most

private wireless networks are (or should be) secured against unauthorized access. In this case, Windows Vista prompts you to enter the required security key or password, as shown in Figure 22.3.

NOTE

Older wireless networks use a security protocol called Wired Equivalent Privacy, or WEP, that protects wireless communications with (usually) a 26-character security key. That sounds impregnable, but unfortunately there were serious weaknesses in the WEP encryption scheme, and now software exists that can crack any WEP key in minutes, if not seconds. In newer wireless networks, WEP has been superseded by Wi-Fi Protected Access, or WPA, which is vastly more secure than WEP. WPA uses most of the IEEE 802.11i wireless security standard, and WPA2 implements the full standard. WPA2 Personal requires a simple passphrase for access (so it's suitable for homes and small offices), while WPA2 Enterprise requires a dedicated authentication server.

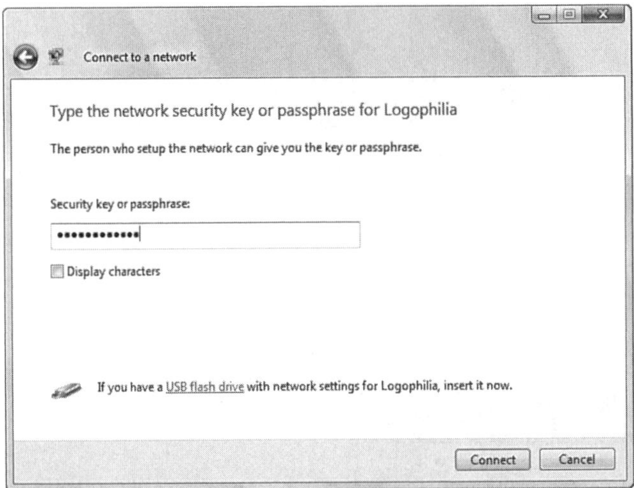

FIGURE 22.3 To access a secured wireless network, you must enter a security key or password.

4. After Vista connects to the network, you see a dialog box named Successfully Connected to *Network*, where *Network* is the name of the network. This dialog box gives you two options (both activated by default):

   Save This Network—When activated, this check box tells Vista to save the network in the Manage Wireless Networks window (see "Managing Wireless Networks," later in this chapter). You must leave this check box activated if you want to connect to the network automatically in the future.

   Start This Connection Automatically—When activated, this check box tells Vista to connect to the network automatically the next time it comes within range. If you always want to connect to the network manually, deactivate this option.

5. Click Close.
6. Click the location of your network: Home, Work, or Public Location.
7. Enter your UAC credentials and click Close.

Connecting to a Nonbroadcasting Wireless Network

You saw earlier that each wireless network has a network name: the Service Set Identifier, or SSID. The SSID identifies the network to wireless devices and computers with wireless network cards. By default, most wireless networks broadcast the network name so that you can see the network and connect to it. However, some wireless networks disable network name broadcasting as a security precaution. The idea is that if unauthorized users can't see the network, they can't attempt to connect to it.

CAUTION

You disable SSID broadcasting by accessing the wireless access point's configuration page and deactivating the broadcast setting. (Exactly how you do that varies depending on the manufacturer; see your documentation or just poke around in the settings page.) However, when previously authorized devices attempt to connect to a nonbroadcasting network, they include the network's SSID as part of the probe requests they send out to see whether the network is within range. The SSID is sent in unencrypted text, so it would be easy for a snoop with the right software (easily obtained from the Internet) to learn the SSID. If the SSID is not broadcasting to try to hide a network that is unsecure or uses an easily breakable encryption protocol, such as WEP, hiding the SSID in this way actually makes the network *less* secure.

However, you can still connect to a hidden wireless network by entering the connection settings by hand. You need to know the network name, the network's security type and encryption type, and the network's security key or passphrase. Here are the steps to follow:

1. Select Start, Connect To. Vista opens the Connect to a Network dialog box.
2. Click the Set Up a Connection or Network link. The Choose a Connection Option dialog box appears.
3. Select Manually Connect to a Wireless Network and click Next. Vista prompts you for the network connection data, as shown in Figure 22.4 (which shows a completed version of the dialog box).
4. Provide the following connection data:

   Network Name—The SSID of the wireless network.

   Security Type—The security protocol used by the wireless network. Select No Authentication (Open) if the network is unsecured.

   Encryption Type—The method of encryption used by the wireless network.

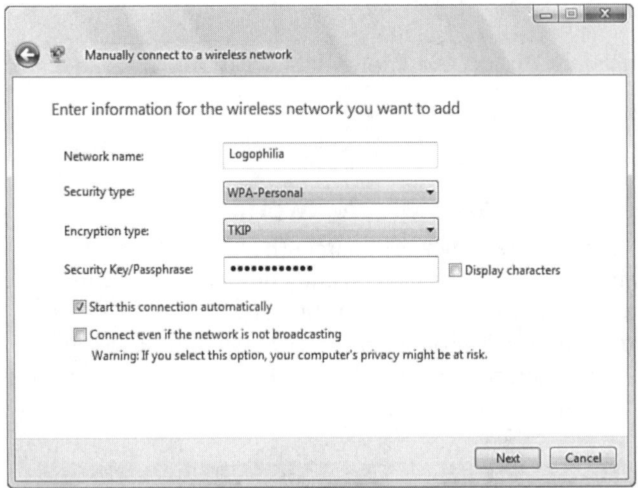

FIGURE 22.4 Use this dialog box to specify the connection settings for the hidden wireless network.

Security Key/Passphrase—The key or password required for authorized access the network.

Start This Connection Automatically—Leave this check box activated to have Vista connect to the network now (that is, when you click Next in step 5) and do so automatically the next time the network comes within range. If you always want to connect to the network manually, deactivate this option.

Connect Even If the Network Is Not Broadcasting—If you activate this check box, Vista will send probe requests to see whether the network is in range even if the network isn't broadcasting its SSID. As explained in the Caution sidebar earlier, this lessens security (because the SSID is sent in plaintext in the probe request), so you should leave this check box deactivated.

5. Click Next. Vista connects to the network and adds it to the list of wireless networks.

6. Click Close.

Setting Up a Wireless Ad-Hoc Network

New If you don't have a wireless access point, Vista enables you to set up a temporary network between two or more computers. This is an **ad hoc connection** and it's useful if you need to share folders, devices, or an Internet connection temporarily. Note that the computers must be within 30 feet of each other for this type of connection to work. Here are the steps to follow:

1. Select Start, Connect To. Vista opens the Connect to a Network dialog box.

2. Click the Set Up a Connection or Network link. The Choose a Connection Option dialog box appears.
3. Select Set Up a Wireless Ad Hoc (Computer-to-Computer) Network and click Next.
4. In the initial dialog box, click Next.
5. Provide the following data to set up the network:

   Network Name—The name of the ad hoc network.

   Security Type—The security protocol used by the wireless network. Select No Authentication (Open) if the network is unsecured.

   Save this Network—Activate this check box to save the network in the Manage Wireless Networks list.
6. Click Next. Vista sets up the ad hoc network.
7. If you want to share your computer's Internet connection, click Turn on Internet Connection Sharing.
8. Click Close.

When you finish, other people within 30 feet of your computer will see your ad hoc network in their list of available networks, as shown in Figure 22.5. (This is the view from the original machine; as you can see, it says `Waiting for users to connect` instead of a security label.) Note that the network remains available as long as at least one computer is connected to it, including the computer that created the network. The network is discarded when all computers (including the machine that created the network) have disconnected from it.

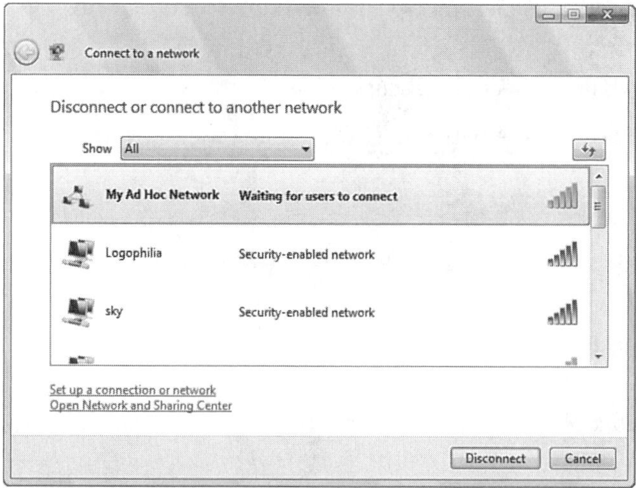

FIGURE 22.5 The ad hoc network is available to computers that are within 30 feet of the original computer.

Understanding the Network Icon

New Windows Vista always displays a Network icon in the taskbar's notification area. The version of the icon you see depends on the current network status. When Vista connects to a network with Internet access, it displays the version of the Network icon shown in Figure 22.6. For a network without Internet access, the Network icon appears without the globe, as shown in Figure 22.7. Finally, if Vista can't make a connection to any network, you see the Network icon shown in Figure 22.8.

FIGURE 22.6 The Network icon for a network with Internet access.

FIGURE 22.7 The Network icon for a network without Internet access.

FIGURE 22.8 The Network icon when there is no current network connection.

Displaying the Network and Sharing Center

New Vista's home base for networking is the new Network and Sharing Center, which enables you to do all the following network-related tasks:

- See a list of your current network connections.
- Visualize your network with a network map (see "Viewing a Network Map," later in this chapter).
- Customize the network name, type, and icon (see "Customizing Your Network," later in this chapter).
- Change your computer discovery and sharing options (see "Turning On Network Discovery," later in this chapter, and "Setting Up File and Printer Sharing," in Chapter 23).
- View the status of each network connection (discussed later in this section).
- View the computers and devices on the network (see "Browsing the Network" in Chapter 23).
- Connect to another network.
- Manage your wireless networks (see "Managing Wireless Networks," later in this chapter).
- Manage your network connections (see "Working with Network Connections," later in this chapter).
- Diagnose and repair a network connection (see "Diagnosing Network Problems," in Chapter 23).

The Network and Sharing Center is a great new networking tool that you'll probably use a great deal. That might be why Microsoft offers so many ways to open it. Here's a summary of the various methods you can use:

- Select Start, Control Panel, View Network Status and Tasks (you can also click Network and Internet and then Network and Sharing Center).
- Click the Network icon in the notification area and then click Network and Sharing Center.
- Select Start, Network, and then click Network and Sharing Center in the taskbar.
- Select Start, Connect To, Open Network and Sharing Center.
- In the Manage Wireless Networks window (see "Managing Wireless Networks," later in this chapter), click Network and Sharing Center in the taskbar.

Whichever method you use, you see a version of the Network and Sharing Center window shown in Figure 22.9.

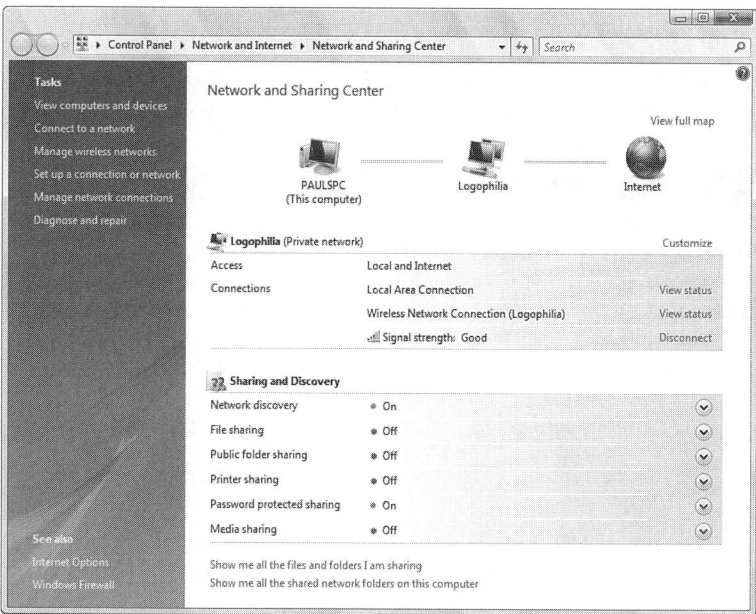

FIGURE 22.9 The Network and Sharing Center is Vista's networking hub.

The Network and Sharing Center window comprises four main areas:

- **Map**—This section gives you a miniature version of the network map: a visual display of the current connection. See the "Viewing a Network Map" section, later in this chapter.

- **Network**—This section tells you the name of the network to which you're connected, the network category (private or public), whether you have Internet access via that connection, and which of your computer connections is in use (this will usually be either Local Area Connection for a wired connection or Wireless Network Connection). If you're connected to multiple networks or have multiple connections to a single network (wired and wireless, for example), all the connections appear here.
- **Sharing and Discovery**—This area shows the current network detection and sharing settings.
- **Tasks**—This pane on the left side of the Network Center window gives you one-click access to the most common network tasks.

Customizing Your Network

New When you first open the Network Center, in most cases, you won't have a profile set up for the network, so Vista configures the network with three default settings:

- A default name, usually either *Network* or the SSID of the wireless network.
- The network type, which depends on the network location you chose when you first connected to the network. (This might have occurred when you installed Vista.)

NOTE

Windows Vista supports three types of network categories: private, public, and domain. Private networks are usually home or small office networks where you need to work with a few nearby computers. To that end, Windows Vista turns on **network discovery**—a new feature that enables you to see other computers and devices on your network—and file and printer sharing. Public networks are usually wireless hotspot connections in airports, coffee shops, hotels, and other public places. When you designate a network as public, Vista turns off Network Discovery, and file and printer sharing. The domain category applies to networks that are part of a corporate domain.

- A default network icon, which depends on the network location you chose when you first connected to the network. (In the miniature network map shown in Figure 22.9, the default Home icon is the one shown above `Logophilia`.)

To change any of these default, follow these steps:

1. Click Customize to display the Customize Network Settings dialog box shown in Figure 22.10.
2. Type a name in the Network Name text box.

3. Select either Public or Private. (You see the Domain option only if you are connected to a network with a domain.)

4. To change the icon, click Change to open the Change Network Icon dialog box, select an icon, and then click OK.

TIP

The Change Network Icon dialog box initially shows you a small collection of icons from the `%SystemRoot%\system32\pnidui.dll` file. To get a larger choice of icons, type any of the following pathnames into the Look for Icons in This File text box (press Enter after you enter the pathname):

```
%SystemRoot%\system32\shell32.dll
%SystemRoot%\system32\pifmgr.dll
%SystemRoot%\explorer.exe
```

5. Click Next and enter your UAC credentials. Vista applies the new network settings.

6. Click Close. Vista updates the Network and Sharing Center window with the new settings.

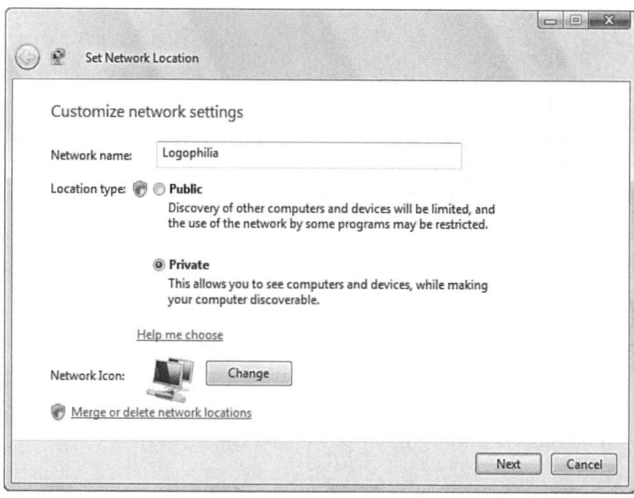

FIGURE 22.10 In the Network and Sharing Center, click Customize to display this dialog box so that you can change the network name, type, and icon.

Turning Network Discovery On or Off

New A new networking feature implemented in Vista is network discovery, an on/off setting that determines whether other computers on the network can see your computer and whether you can see them. In a public network, network discovery is turned off, which makes sense because you probably don't want other users in the coffee shop to see your computer. On the other hand, in a private network or domain, you want to see other computers (and have them see you), so network discovery is turned on.

However, there might be times when the default network discovery setting doesn't work for you. For example, there may be one computer in a private network that you don't want others to see (it might contain sensitive information). Similarly, you and a friend might want to see each other's computers in a public setting so that you can perform a quick file exchange.

If you want to change the current network discovery setting without changing the network type, follow these steps:

1. Open the Network and Sharing Center, as described earlier.
2. In the Sharing and Discovery section, click the current network discovery setting. Vista expands the Network Discovery item.
3. Click either Turn On Network Discovery (this will only work while you're connected to a network) or Turn Off Network Discovery.
4. Click Apply and then enter your UAC credentials.

Viewing a Network Map

New The new Network Map feature gives you a visual display of everything your computer is connected to: network connections (wired and wireless), ad hoc (computer-to-computer) connections, Internet connections, and the devices associated with these connections. Network Map also gives you a visual display of the connection status so that you can easily spot problems.

The Network and Sharing Center displays your local portion of the network map, and the layout depends on your current connections. You always see an icon for your computer on the left. If your computer is connected to a network (as shown earlier in Figure 22.9), a green line joins the computer icon and the network icon. If the network is connected to the Internet, another green line joins the network icon and the Internet icon on the right. If there is no connection, you see a red X through the connection line.

The Network and Sharing Center also comes with a more detailed version of Network Map. To view it, click the View Full Map link. Figure 22.11 shows an example of the full network map. If you have multiple network connections, use the Network Map Of list to select a different connection and see its map.

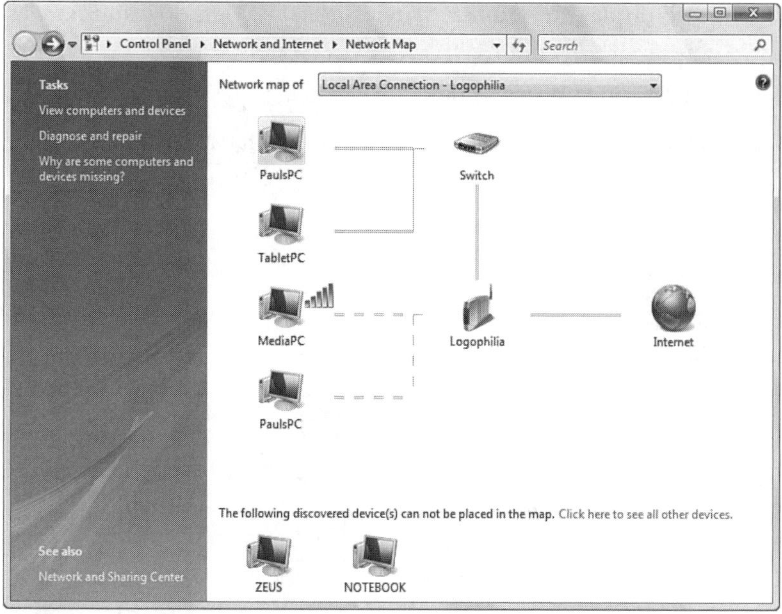

FIGURE 22.11 The full version of a network map.

Managing Wireless Networks

New It's not unusual to have multiple wireless networks configured on your computer. For example, you might have two or more wireless gateways in your home or office; you might have a wireless hotspot nearby; and as you saw in the previous section, Vista also enables you to set up computer-to-computer wireless connections to share files or an Internet connection without going through a wireless access point. Vista comes with a Manage Wireless Networks feature that lists your saved wireless networks and enables you to add new wireless connections, remove existing connections, and reorder wireless networks.

Why would you need to reorder the networks? By default, Windows Vista configures a wireless network with an automatic connection, so you get on the network as soon as Vista detects it. If you have multiple wireless networks, Windows Vista maintains a priority list, and a network higher in that list connects before a network lower in that list. If you are not connecting to the wireless network you want, it might be that the network is lower on the network priority list. To work around this problem, you can move the network higher in the list.

Here are the steps to follow to display the Manage Wireless Networks window and reorder the networks:

1. Open the Network and Sharing Center, as described earlier.
2. Click the Manage Wireless Networks link. Vista displays the Manage Wireless Networks window, shown in Figure 22.12.

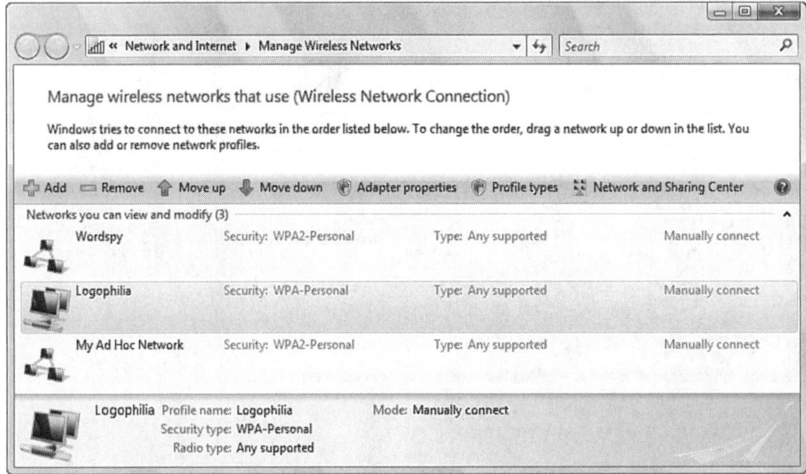

FIGURE 22.12 Use the Manage Wireless Networks feature to reorder, add, and remove wireless networks.

3. Select the network you want to move.
4. Click the Move Up and Move Down buttons to place the network in the position you prefer.

NOTE

To remove a wireless network, select it and then click Remove.

NOTE

A wireless network might change its security settings. For example, the administrator might upgrade to a more robust encryption setting or change the security key or password. To adjust the security settings for an existing network, right-click the network in the Manage Wireless Networks window, and click Properties to display the network's properties sheet. Display the Security tab and then edit the Security Type, Encryption Type, or Network Security Key.

Working with Network Connections

New Windows Vista maintains a Network Connections window that lists all your network connections, including wired, wireless, dial-up, and virtual private network (VPN) connections. Each network interface card (NIC) attached to your computer gets its own connection icon in the list, and you can use those icons to work with your network connections. Follow these steps to display the Network Connections window and work with a connection:

1. Open the Network and Sharing Center, as described earlier.
2. Click the Manage Network Connections link. Vista displays the Network Connections window, shown in Figure 22.13.

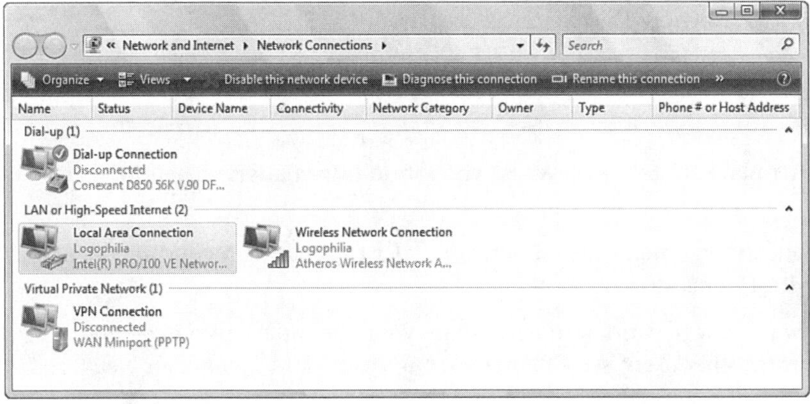

FIGURE 22.13 Use the Network Connections feature to modify your wired or wireless network connections.

3. Select the network connection you want to work with.
4. Modify your network settings using any of the following techniques (note that in some cases you need to enter your UAC credentials to complete the task):
   - **Renaming a connection**—Windows Vista supplies each connection with a generic name such as `Local Area Connection` and `Wireless Network Connection`. To assign a more descriptive name to the selected connection, press F2 (or click Rename this Connection in the taskbar), type the new name, and press Enter.
   - **Installing a networking client, service, or protocol**—You shouldn't need extra networking components in a small peer-to-peer network. Just in case you do, you can install them by right-clicking the network connection, clicking Properties (or click Change Settings of this Connection in the taskbar), and then clicking Install.

- **Checking the network status**—To see the network activity and details such as your current IP address, right-click the connection and then click Status (or click View Status of this Connection in the taskbar).
- **Diagnosing a network problem**—If you're having network problems, Vista offers a network diagnostics tool that can examine the connection and offer solutions. Right-click the connection and then click Diagnose (or click Diagnose this Connection in the taskbar). For more details, see "Diagnosing Network Problems" in Chapter 23.
- **Disabling a connection**—If you have multiple NICs and want to disable one that you don't use, right-click its connection and then click Disable (or click Disable This Network Device in the taskbar). You can enable this connection in the future by right-clicking it and then clicking Enable (or by clicking Enable This Network Device in the taskbar).

From Here

Here's a list of other places in the book where you'll find information related to networking:

- To learn about sharing media over a network, refer to "Sharing Media" in Chapter 7, "Working with Digital Media."
- To learn how to view network resources, share your computer's resources, and collaborate with other users, see Chapter 23, "Accessing and Using Your Network."
- Accessing your network from remote locations is often crucial, so I devote an entire chapter to this topic. See Chapter 24, "Making Remote Network Connections."

CHAPTER 23

Accessing and Using Your Network

IN THIS CHAPTER

- Learning Some Common Network Tasks
- Accessing Network Resources
- Sharing Resources with the Network
- Working with Offline Files and the Sync Center
- Collaborating with Windows Meeting Space

In Chapter 22, "Setting Up a Small Network," you saw that connecting to a network in Vista is either automatic (in the case of most wired connections) or requires just a few steps (in the case of most wireless networks). You also saw that the new Network and Sharing Center makes it easy to work with your network connections. So far, Vista appears to be the best Windows networking client we've seen from Microsoft to date. However, the networking proof is in the access pudding, which is to say that a networking client is only as good as its capability to access the network and use its resources. How does Vista fare in that regard? I'm afraid the results are mixed. Vista sometimes doesn't work well with remote non-Vista machines, and accessing shared folders is a bit harder because Vista no longer supports XP's **Network Places** (shortcuts to shared folders). On the plus side, Vista gives you many more options for sharing resources, it makes using network files offline a bit easier, and it comes with Windows Meeting Space—a powerful application for running networked meetings and presentation.

This chapter takes you through the good and the bad of accessing and using the resources on your network. You learn how to examine the network, map network drives, use network printers, and share your own drives, folders, and printers with your network peers.

Learning Some Common Network Tasks

Let's begin with the basic networking tasks that you'll use most often. The next few sections show you how to view network computers, add a computer or device to the network, and diagnose network problems.

View Network Computers and Devices

After you connect to the network, the first thing you'll likely want to do is see what's on the network and access the available resources. Vista gives you two ways to get started:

- Select Start, Network
- In the Network and Sharing Center, click View Network Computers and Devices

Either way, you see the Network window, which lists the main network resources, such as the computers and media devices in your workgroup. As you can see in Figure 23.1, Details view shows you the resource name, category, workgroup or domain name, and the name of the network profile.

NOTE

If you see a network resource name twice, once in the Computer category and again in the Media Devices category, it means that computer has activated Media Player's new media sharing feature (see "Sharing Media" in Chapter 7, "Working with Digital Media"). Double-click the Media Devices version of the computer name to open the computer's media library in the Media Player window.

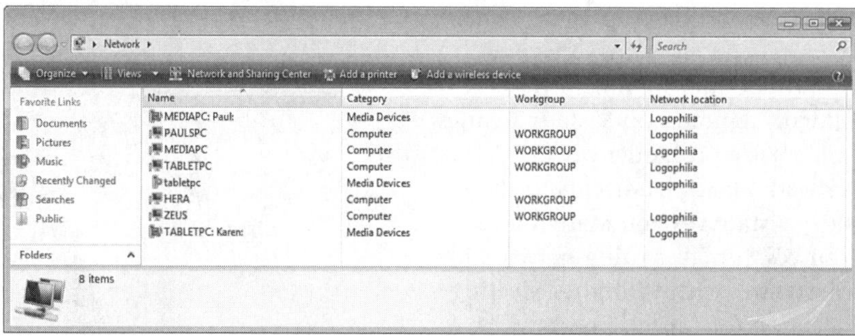

FIGURE 23.1 The Network window shows you the main resources on the network to which you're connected.

Adding a Computer or Device

Previous versions of Windows showed network resources in either Network Neighborhood or My Network Places, but those resources were mostly limited to domains, workgroups, and computers. Windows Vista is much more aware of other types of devices connected to the network, including media players, wireless access points, routers, and print servers. These devices usually appear in the network map, but some devices might not. To add those devices, open the Network and Sharing Center and click the Add a Wireless Device link in the task pane. Vista immediately begins searching for network devices. If it finds any, it displays them in a list; you can decide which ones you want to add to your network.

Diagnosing Network Problems

Windows XP came with a Repair tool that did a pretty good job of repairing connectivity problems because most networking problems can be resolved by running the Repair tool's basic tasks: disconnecting, renewing the DHCP lease, flushing various network caches, and then reconnecting. However, all too often the Repair tool would report that it couldn't fix the problem, which usually meant that the trouble existed at a level deeper in the network stack than the Repair tool could go. In an attempt to handle these more challenging connectivity issues, Vista comes with a completely redesigned Network Diagnostics tool that digs deep into all layers of the network stack to try to identify and resolve problems. Vista gives you several methods of launching the Network Diagnostic tool:

- Right-click the notification area's Network icon and then click Diagnose.
- In the Network and Sharing Center, click View Status and then click Diagnose.
- If you lose a connection to a network share, Vista displays a Network Error dialog box to let you know. Click the Diagnose button.
- In the Network Connections window (see the "Managing Network Connections" section in Chapter 22), click the broken connection and then click Repair This Connection.

When you launch the diagnostics, Vista invokes the new Network Diagnostics Framework (NDF), a collection of tools, technologies, algorithms, programming interfaces, services, and troubleshooters. The NDF passes the specifics of the problem to the Network Diagnostics Engine (NDE), which then generates a list of possible causes. For each potential cause, the NDE launches a specific troubleshooter, which determines whether the aspect of networking covered by the troubleshooter could be creating the problem. For example, there are troubleshooters related to wireless connectivity, Transport Control Protocol (TCP) connections, address acquisition, and many more. In the end, the troubleshooters end up creating a list of possible solutions to the problem. If there is just one solution that can be performed automatically, the NDE attempts the solution. If there are multiple solutions (or a single solution that requires user input), you see a Windows Network Diagnostics dialog box similar to the one shown in Figure 23.2. Click the solution or follow the instructions that appear.

Turning On Network Discovery

New You can't do much in the way of networking in Windows Vista unless you have *network discovery* turned on. Network discovery is a new setting that enables you to see other computers on your network and to work with their shared resources. Network discovery also enables other computers on the network to see your computer and access your shared resources.

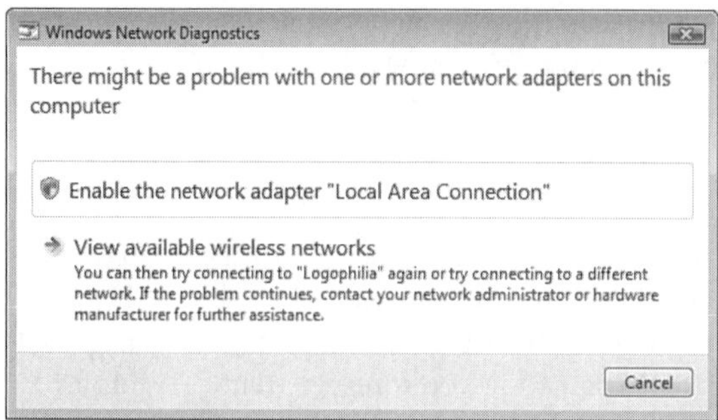

FIGURE 23.2 If Vista can't connect to a network or device, it displays this dialog box; you can click Diagnose to run the network diagnostics.

To ensure that network discovery is on, click the Network icon in the taskbar's notification area and then click Network and Sharing Center. (Alternatively, select Start, Control Panel, Network and Internet, Network and Sharing Center.) In the Sharing and Discovery section, if you see Off beside the Network Discovery setting, click Off, click the Turn On Network Discovery option, click Apply, and then enter your UAC credentials.

Accessing Network Resources

After your network has been set up, you can start using it immediately to share resources, including files, folders, programs, and peripherals. Your starting point for all of this is the Network window, which I discussed earlier.

Begin by double-clicking a resource to see what it contains. For example, if you double-click a workgroup computer, you see its shared items, as shown in Figure 23.3.

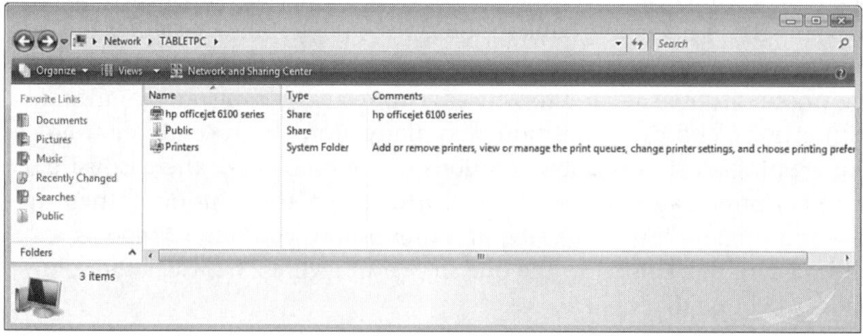

FIGURE 23.3 Double-click a workgroup computer's shared folder to see its contents.

Notice that Vista computers automatically share two folders:

- `Public`—This folder is open to everyone on the network and provides users with full read/write access.

- **`Printers`**—This folder contains the computer's installed printers. Vista usually places an icon for each shared printer in the computer's main folder, as well.

NOTE

Whether you see the `Public` and `Printers` folders depends on the remote computer's sharing settings. See "Setting Up File and Printer Sharing," later in this chapter.

Double-click a shared folder to see its contents. If you have an account on the remote computer, you should see the folder's contents right away. Otherwise, you might have to enter the username and password of an account on that computer.

Understanding the Universal Naming Convention

If you click inside the Address bar with a remote computer or share open, you see an address that uses the following format:

```
\\ComputerName\ShareName
```

Here, *`ComputerName`* is the name of the computer, and *`ShareName`* is the name given to the shared resource. This is the **universal naming convention** (**UNC**). For example, the following UNC path refers to a shared resource named `Public` on a computer named TABLETPC:

```
\\TABLETPC\Public
```

If the UNC refers to a drive or folder, you can use the regular path conventions to access subfolders on that resource. For example, if the resource `Public` on TABLETPC has a `Downloads` subfolder, you can refer to that subfolder as follows:

```
\\TABLETPC\Public\Downloads
```

TIP

The UNC offers you several alternative methods of accessing shared network resources:

- In the Network explorer, click inside the Address bar, type the UNC for a shared resource, and then press the Enter key.
- Press Windows Logo+R (or select Start, All Programs, Accessories, Run) to open the Run dialog box. Type the UNC for a shared resource and then click OK to open the resource in a folder window.
- In a 32-bit application's Open or Save As dialog box, you can use a UNC name in the File Name text box.
- At the command prompt, type **`START`** followed by the UNC path. Here's an example:

  ```
  START \\TABLETPC\Public
  ```

- At the command prompt, you can use a UNC name as part of a command. For example, to copy a file named `archive.zip` from `\\TABLETPC\Public\Downloads\` to the current folder, you'd use the following command:

```
COPY "\\TABLETPC\Public\Downloads\archive.zip"
```

Mapping a Network Folder to a Local Drive Letter

One networking conundrum that comes up repeatedly is the problem of referencing network resources (in, say, a script or command). You can reference UNC paths, but they're a bit unwieldy to use. To avoid the hassle, you can map a shared network drive or folder to your own computer. **Mapping** assigns a drive letter to the resource so that it appears to be just another disk drive on your machine.

NOTE

Another good reason to map a network folder to a local drive letter is to give certain programs access to the network folder. Some older programs aren't network-aware, so if you try to save files to a network folder, the program might display an error or tell you that the location is out of disk space. In most cases, you can solve this problem by mapping the folder to a drive letter, which fools the program into thinking it's dealing with a local folder.

To map a shared drive or folder, follow these steps:

1. Select Start, right-click Network, and then click Map Network Drive. (In any folder window, you can also press Alt to display the menu bar, and then select Tools, Map Network Drive.) Windows Vista displays the Map Network Drive dialog box, shown in Figure 23.4.
2. The Drive drop-down list displays the last available drive letter on your system, but you can pull down the list and select any available letter.

CAUTION

If you use a removable drive, such as a memory card or Flash drive, Windows Vista assigns the first available drive letter to that drive. This can cause problems if you have a mapped network drive that uses a lower drive letter. Therefore, it's good practice to use higher drive letters (such as X, Y, and Z) for your mapped resources.

3. Use the Folder text box to type the UNC path to the shared folder. (Alternatively, click Browse, select the shared folder in the Browse For Folder dialog box, and then click OK.)
4. If you want Windows Vista to map the resource each time you log on to the system, leave the Reconnect at Logon check box activated.

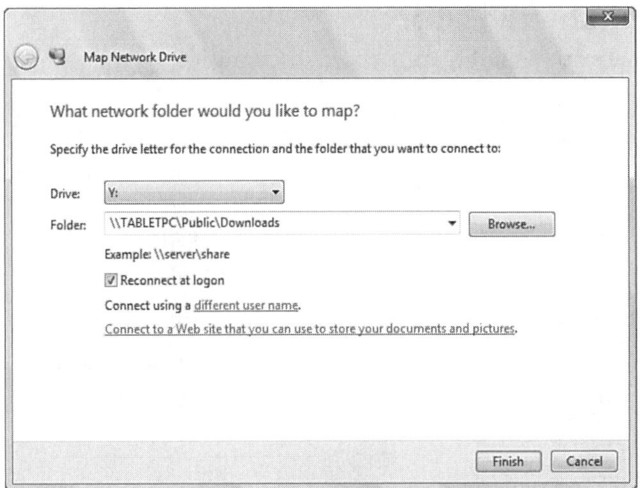

FIGURE 23.4 Use the Map Network Drive dialog box to assign a drive letter to a network resource.

5. If you prefer to log on to the resource using a different account, click the Different User Name link, type the User Name and Password, and click OK.
6. Click Finish. Windows Vista adds the new drive letter to your system and opens the shared resource in a new folder window.

To open the mapped network folder later, select Start, Computer and then double-click the drive in the Network Location group.

Mapping Folders at the Command Prompt

You can also map a shared network folder to a local drive letter by using a Command Prompt session and the `NET USE` command. Here's the basic syntax:

```
NET USE [drive] [share] [password] [/USER:user]
➥[/PERSISTENT:[YES ¦ NO]] ¦ /DELETE]
```

drive	The drive letter (following by a colon) of the local drive to which you want the shared folder mapped
share	The UNC path of the shared folder
password	The password required to connect to the shared folder (that is, the password associated with the username, specified next)
/USER:*user*	The username you want to use to connect to the shared folder
/PERSISTENT:	Add YES to reconnect the mapped network drive the next time you log on
/DELETE	Deletes the existing shared mapped to *drive*

For example, the following command maps the shared folder `\\TABLETPC\Public` to drive Z:

```
net use z: \\tabletpc\public \persistent:yes
```

Disconnecting a Mapped Network Folder

If you no longer need to map a network resource, you should disconnect it by following these steps:

1. Select Start, Computer to open the Computer window.
2. Right-click the mapped drive and then click Disconnect.
3. If there are files open from the resource, Windows Vista displays a warning to let you know that it's unsafe to disconnect the resource. You have two choices:
    - Click No, close all open files from the mapped resource, and then repeat steps 1 and 2.
    - If you're sure there are no open files, click Yes to disconnect the resource.

Creating a Network Location

New When you map a shared network folder to a drive on your computer, Vista creates an icon for the mapped drive in the Computer folder's Network Locations group. You can also add your own icons to this group. These are similar to the network places you could create in Windows XP. That is, once you create a network location, you can access that location by double-clicking the icon. This is usually a lot faster than drilling down through several layers of folders on the network client, so create network locations for those network folders you access most often.

Follow these steps to create a network location:

1. Select Start, Computer to open the Computer folder.
2. Right-click an empty section of the Computer folder and then click Add a Network Location. Vista launches the Add Network Location Wizard.
3. Click Next in the initial wizard dialog box.
4. Select Choose a Custom Network Location and then click Next.
5. Type the UNC address of the shared network folder (or click Browse to use the Browse for Folder dialog box to select it), and then click Next.
6. Type a name for the network location and click Next.
7. Click Finish.

Printing over the Network

After you connect to a network printer, you can use it just like any local printer on your system. Windows Vista offers a couple of methods for connecting to a network printer. The easiest way is to use the Network window to open the computer that has the shared printer, open its Printers folder, right-click the printer, and then select Connect. When Vista asks you to confirm the connection, click Yes. Vista installs the printer using the remote machine's printer driver files.

If you like using a wizard for these kinds of things, you can do so using the Add Printer Wizard:

1. Select Start, Control Panel and then click the Printer link under the Hardware and Sound icon.
2. Click the Add a Printer link to open the Add Printer Wizard.
3. Click Add a Network, Wireless or Bluetooth Printer. Vista searches for shared printers on the network.
4. Select the network printer you want to use. (To see a computer's shared printers, double-click the computer name.) Click Next.
5. Complete the wizard normally.

Sharing Resources with the Network

In a peer-to-peer network, each computer can act as both a client and a server. You've seen how to use a Windows Vista machine as a client, so now let's turn our attention to setting up your system as a peer server. In Windows Vista, that means sharing individual drives, folders, printers and other resources with the network.

Setting Up File and Printer Sharing

Whether it's a folder, disk drive, or printer, networking is all about sharing. Vista's sharing options have many more nuances than those of previous versions of Windows. In fact, Vista allows you to configure sharing in five different ways: general file and printer sharing, `Public` folder sharing, printer sharing, password-protected sharing, and media sharing. It all happens in the Network and Sharing Center (refer to Chapter 22), in the Sharing and Discovery section.

The File Sharing setting covers general file and printer sharing. It offers you two choices (after making your choice, click Apply and enter your UAC credentials):

- Turn On File Sharing—Activate this option to allow other people on the network to access your shared files and printer.
- Turn Off File Sharing—Activate this option to prevent other people on the network from accessing your shared files and printers. Note that turning off this setting also turns off the Public Folder Sharing and Printer Sharing settings.

The Public Folder Sharing setting covers sharing the `Public` folder, and gives you three choices (after making your choice, click Apply and enter your UAC credentials):

- Turn On Sharing So Anyone with Network Access Can Open Files—Activate this option to share the `Public` folder, but allow network users only to read files in that folder (that is, users can't create new files or change existing files).

Turn On Sharing So Anyone with Network Access Can Open, Change, and Create Files—Activate this option to share the `Public` folder, and allow network users to read, edit, and create new files in that folder.

Turn Off Sharing (People Logged On to this Computer Can Still Access This Folder)—Activate this option to prevent sharing the `Public` folder with network users (although you can still share the folder with other accounts on your computer).

The Printer Sharing setting covers sharing the `Printers` folder, and offers you two choices (after making your choice, click Apply and enter your UAC credentials):

Turn On Printer Sharing—Activate this option to allow other people on the network to access your `Printers` folder.

Turn Off Printer Sharing—Activate this option to prevent other people on the network from accessing your `Printers` folder.

The Password Protected Sharing setting covers sharing with password protection. You have two choices (after making your choice, click Apply and enter your UAC credentials):

Turn On Password Protected Sharing—Activate this option to share resources only with people who know the username and password of an account on your computer.

Turn Off Password Protected Sharing—Activate this option to allow any network user to access your shared resources.

The Media Sharing setting connects with Media Player's library sharing features. Refer to "Media Sharing" in Chapter 7, "Working with Digital Media."

Finally, you also have two links for viewing shared files and folders:

Show Me All the Files and Folders I Am Sharing—Click this link to open the `Shared By Me` search folder.

Show Me All the Shared Network Folders on This Computer—Click this link to open a folder window showing your computer's shared folders and printers.

Deactivating the Sharing Wizard

New Sharing can be a complex business when you get into file permissions and other minutiae. Windows Vista minutiae are what this book is all about, so sharing holds no terrors for the likes of you and me. However, novice users want sharing to be simple and straightforward, and to that end Vista introduces the Sharing Wizard. This wizard presents the wary with a stripped-down set of sharing options and a method for letting other people know that a shared resource is available.

The Sharing Wizard activates by default, and in a second I'll show you how to deactivate it. Just so that you know what you're giving up, Figure 23.5 shows the initial wizard dialog box. You use the list to select a user account on your computer, and then you assign that user one of three permission levels: Reader (read-only), Contributor (read and write), or Co-owner (all permissions). When you click Share (and then enter your UAC credentials), the Sharing Wizard shows the address of the share and offers a link to email the share address to other people.

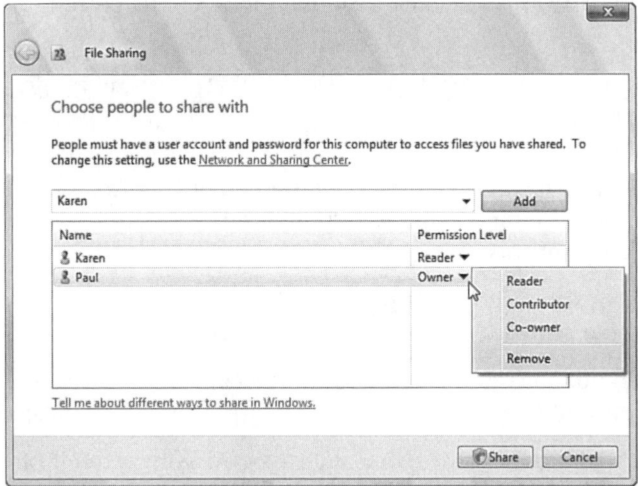

FIGURE 23.5 The Sharing Wizard offers a simple, novice-oriented interface for sharing resources.

The Sharing Wizard is actually a bit of an improvement over the brain-dead Simple File Sharing feature in Windows XP, but it's still suitable for new users. However, the rest of us want the full power of permissions and other sharing goodies. To get at them, you have to deactivate the Sharing Wizard feature by following these steps:

1. Select Start, Control Panel, Appearance and Personalization, Folder Options icon (or, in any folder window, select Organize, Folder and Search Options).
2. Display the View tab.
3. Deactivate the Use Sharing Wizard check box.
4. Click OK.

CAUTION

To use Vista's advanced sharing features, you need to supply User Account Control credentials.

Creating User Accounts for Sharing

If you activated the Password Protected Sharing option, you have to do one of the following:

- **Set up separate accounts for each user that you want to access a shared resource**—Do this if you want to assign each user a different set of permissions, or if you want the usernames and passwords to match each user's local username and password.
- **Set up a single account for all remote users to use**—Do this if you want to assign the same set of permissions for all users.

I discussed creating user accounts in Chapter 6, "Getting the Most Out of User Accounts," so I won't repeat the details here. Here are some notes to bear in mind for creating users who will access your computer over a network:

- Windows Vista does *not* allow users without passwords to access network resources. Therefore, you must set up your network user accounts with passwords.
- The usernames you create do not have to correspond with the names that users have on their local machines. You're free to set up your own usernames, if you like.
- If you create a user account that has the same name and password as an account of a user on his or her local machine, that user will be able to access your shared resources directly. Otherwise, a Connect To dialog box appears so that the user can enter the username and password that you established when setting up the account on your computer.

Sharing a Resource

Windows Vista gives you two ways to share a resource:

- If you have Public Folder Sharing turned on, make a copy of the folder or file in the `Public` folder or one of its subfolders: `Public Documents`, `Public Downloads`, `Public Music`, `Public Pictures`, `Public Videos`, or `Recorded TV`. This is the way to go if you want to share individual files, or if you worry about permissions for the `Public` folder only (the subfolders inherit the `Public` folder's permissions).

TIP

To get to the `Public` folder, open any folder window, display the Folders list, and then click Desktop. The default `Desktop` folder contains seven items: your user account folder, `Computer`, `Network`, `Internet Explorer`, `Control Panel`, `Recycle Bin`, and `Public`.

- Activate sharing and set permissions on the folder you want to share. This is the way to go if you don't want to deal with copies of your files and folders or if you want to set separate permissions for different folders.

For the latter technique (and assuming that you have the Sharing Wizard turned off), follow these steps:

1. In Windows Explorer, select the drive or folder and then click Share in the taskbar (you can also right-click the drive or folder and then click Share). Windows Vista displays the object's properties sheet with the Sharing tab selected.
2. Click Advanced Sharing and enter your UAC credentials to open the Advanced Sharing dialog box.
3. Activate the Share This Folder option.
4. In a small network, it's unlikely you'll need to restrict the number of users who can access this resource, so you're probably safe to leave the Limit the Number of Simultaneous Users To spin box value at 10.
5. Click Permissions to display the Permissions dialog box (see Figure 23.6).

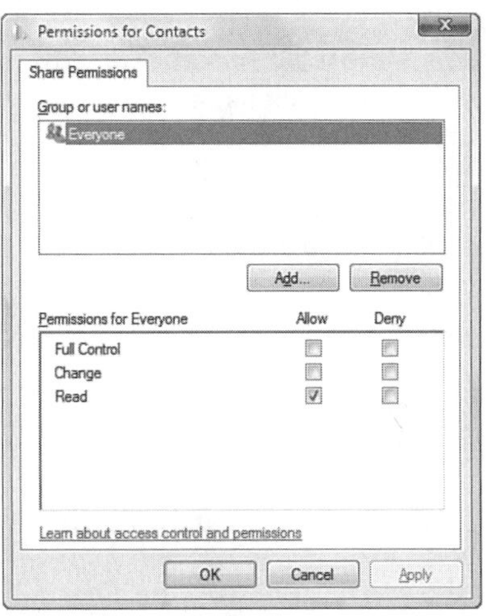

FIGURE 23.6 Use the Permissions dialog box to specify file permissions for the shared resource.

6. Select the Everyone group in the Group or User Names list and then click Remove.
7. Click Add to display the Select Users or Groups dialog box.
8. In the Enter the Object Names to Select text box, type the name of the user or users you want to give permission to access the shared resource (separate multiple usernames with semicolons). Click OK when you're done.
9. Select a user in the Group or User Names list.

10. Using the Permissions list, you can allow or deny the following permissions:

Read	Gives the group or user the ability only to read the contents of a folder or file. The user can't modify those contents in any way.
Change	Gives the group or user Read permission and allows the group or user to modify the contents of the shared resource.
Full Control	Gives the group or user Change permission and allows the group or user to take ownership of the shared resource.

11. Repeat steps 7–10 to add and configure other users.
12. Click OK to return to the Advanced Sharing dialog box.
13. Click OK to return to the Sharing tab.
14. Click Close to share the resource with the network.

NTFS SECURITY PERMISSIONS

If you want even more control over the use of your shared resources across the network, you should also set NTFS security permissions on the folder. (Ideally, you should do this before sharing the resource.) To do this, right-click the folder, click Sharing and Security, and then display the Security tab. This tab is similar to the Permissions dialog box shown in Figure 23.6, except that you get a longer list of permissions for each group or user:

Full Control—Users can perform any of the actions listed. Users can also change permissions.

Modify—Users can view the folder contents, open files, edit files, create new files and subfolders, delete files, and run programs.

Read and Execute—Users can view the folder contents, open files, and run programs.

List Folder Contents—Users can view the folder contents.

Read—Users can open files, but cannot edit them.

Write—Users can create new files and subfolders, and open and edit existing files.

Special Permissions—Advanced settings for permissions, auditing, ownership, and effective permissions.

Hiding Shared Resources

Hiding your valuables is a time-tested method of securing them from prying eyes and would-be thieves. When you share a resource on your network, however, you're displaying that resource for all to see. Sure, you can set up password-protected user accounts and set the appropriate permissions for the resource, but others will still be able to see that the resource is shared.

To prevent this situation, it's possible to share a resource *and* hide it at the same time. It's also extremely easy to do: When you set up the shared resource, add a dollar sign ($) to the end of the share name. For example, if you're setting up drive F for sharing, you could use `F$` as the share name. This prevents the resource from appearing in the list of resources when you open a remote computer from the Network window.

In Figure 23.7, for example, you see the properties sheet for drive F, which shows the drive is shared with the following path:

```
\\Paulspc\f$
```

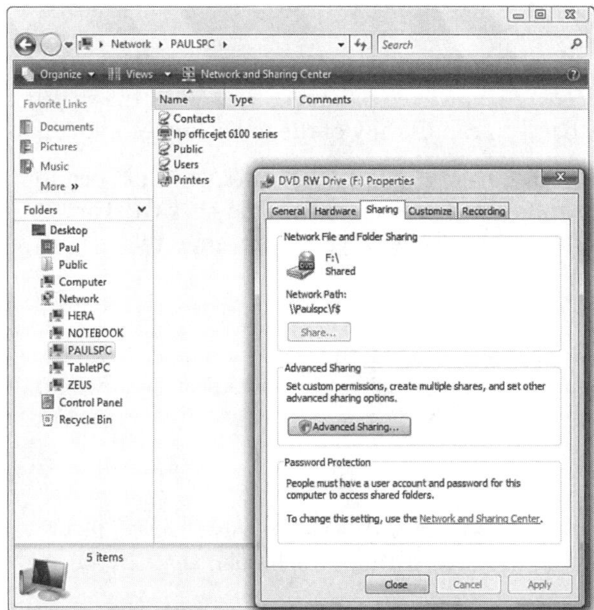

FIGURE 23.7 Hidden shared resources (such as drive F shown here) don't appear in the browse list.

That is, the drive is shared on PaulsPC with the name `F$`. However, in the folder window, you can see that drive F doesn't appear in the list of resources shared by PaulsPC.

Hidden Administration Shares

Hiding shares will work for the average user, but a savvy snoop will probably know about the $ trick. Therefore, you'll probably want to set up your hidden shares with nonobvious names. Note, however, that Windows Vista sets up certain hidden shares for administrative purposes, including one for drive C (C$) and any other hard disk partitions you have on your system. Windows Vista also sets up the following hidden shares:

Share Name	Shared Path	Purpose
ADMIN$	%SystemRoot%	Remote administration
IPC$	N/A	Remote interprocess communication
print$	%SystemRoot%\System32\spool\drivers	Access to printer drivers

You cannot delete or rename these administrative shares.

How do you connect to a hidden share? Well, you need to know the name of the shared resource, of course. When you know that, you can use any of the following techniques:

- Select Windows Logo+R (or select Start, All Programs, Accessories, Run) to open the Run dialog box, type the UNC path for the hidden resource, and click OK. For example, to display the hidden share F$ on PaulsPC, you would enter this:

  ```
  \\paulspc\f$
  ```

- In a Command Prompt session, type **start**, a space, the UNC path, and then press the Enter key. For example, to launch the hidden share F$ on PaulsPC, you would enter this:

  ```
  start \\paulspc\f$
  ```

- Use the Map Network Drive command, as described earlier in this chapter. In the Map Network Drive dialog box, type the UNC path for the hidden share in the Folder text box.

- For a hidden shared printer, follow the steps in "Printing over the Network," earlier in this chapter and, when Vista begins searching for available printers, click The Printer That I Want Isn't Listed. In the Find a Printer By Name or TCP/IP Address dialog box, type the UNC path to the hidden printer in the Select a Shared Printer By Name text box.

Working with Offline Files and the Sync Center

Vista Business | Vista Enterprise | Vista Ultimate Edition

One of the main advantages of setting up a small network in your home or office is the ease with which you can share files and folders with other users. You simply share a folder with the network, and other users can use their Network folder to open the shared folder and work with the files.

However, this benefit is lost when you disconnect from the network. For example, suppose that you use a notebook computer to connect to the network while you are at the office. When you take the notebook on the road, you must disconnect from the network. Fortunately, you can still get network access of a sort when you disconnect from the network (or are **offline**). Windows Vista (Business, Enterprise, or Ultimate) has an Offline Files feature that enables you to preserve copies of network files on your computer. You can then view and work with these files as though you were connected to the network.

Enabling Offline Files

New Vista has offline files enabled by default. Follow these steps to make sure that your system has them enabled:

1. Select Start, Control Panel, Network and Internet, Offline Files. Vista opens the Offline Files dialog box.
2. If you see the Enable Offline Files button, select it. (If you see the Disable Offline Files button instead, offline files are enabled, so skip to step 4.)
3. Enter your UAC credentials.
4. Click OK. Vista prompts you to restart your computer to put the new setting into effect.
5. Click Yes.

TIP

If you're an administrator, the Group Policy editor offers a large number of policies related to offline files. For example, you can prohibit users from configuring the Offline Files feature, set default synchronization options, prevent certain files and folders from being made available offline, and disable offline files altogether. In the Group Policy editor, open the User Configuration, Administrative Templates, Network, Offline Files branch.

CAUTION

If you want to work with sensitive data offline on a notebook computer, bear in mind that a thief could easily steal your notebooks and might be able to access the sensitive data. To guard against this scenario, you can encrypt your offline files if you have the Encrypting File System, which is available with the Vista Business, Enterprise, and Ultimate versions. Select Start, Control Panel, Network and Internet, Offline Files, display the Encryption tab, and click Encrypt.

Making Files Available Offline

New With the Offline Files feature turned on, follow these steps to make network files available offline:

1. Use Windows Explorer to open the folder that contains the shared network folder that you want to use offline.
2. Select the folders you want to use offline.
3. Right-click any selected folder, and click Always Available Offline.

Windows Vista synchronizes the folders for offline use. While the initial synchronization occurs, Vista displays the Always Available Offline dialog box. If you're using quite a few files offline, the synchronization might take a long time. If so, click Close to hide the Always Available Offline dialog box. (You can redisplay it by clicking the Sync Center icon in the taskbar's notification area.)

When the initial synchronization finishes, you can disconnect from the network and work with the files offline.

TIP

A quick way to disconnect is to open a folder set up for offline use and then click Work Offline in the task pane.

Working with Network Files Offline

New Windows XP handled offline files by creating a special Offline Files folder that contained all the shared network files that you chose to work with offline. Vista handles offline files a bit differently. Specifically, you now have two ways to work with offline files:

- **Work with the files "in place" using the remote computer's folder window**—The objects available offline display the Offline Files icon superimposed on their regular icon and, when you select an offline object, the Details pane shows `Offline (not connected)` as the Offline Status (see Figure 23.8).

TIP

You can't navigate to a remote computer's folder via Start, Network because Vista will tell you that you aren't connected to a network. Either leave the remote computer's folder window open when you disconnect or type the remote computer's UNC path into the Run dialog box or Explorer Address bar.

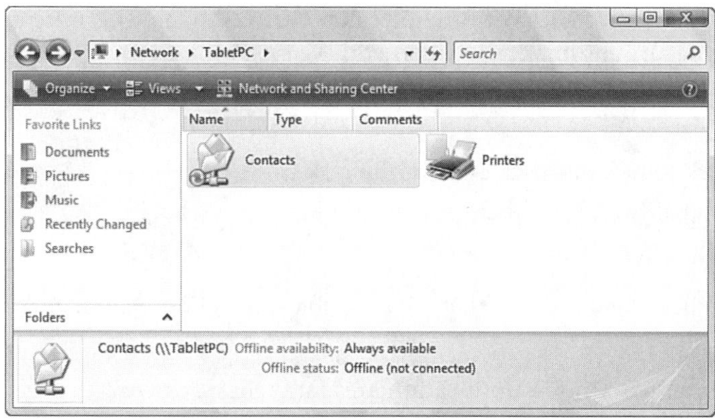

FIGURE 23.8 A shared network folder displayed offline.

- **Work with the files using Sync Center**—Select Start, Control Panel, Network and Internet, Sync Center. (Alternatively, double-click the Sync Center icon in the notification area.) Click View Sync Partnerships (although this is selected by default), and then double-click Offline Files, shown in Figure 23.9.

You can open and edit the files just as though you were connected to the network.

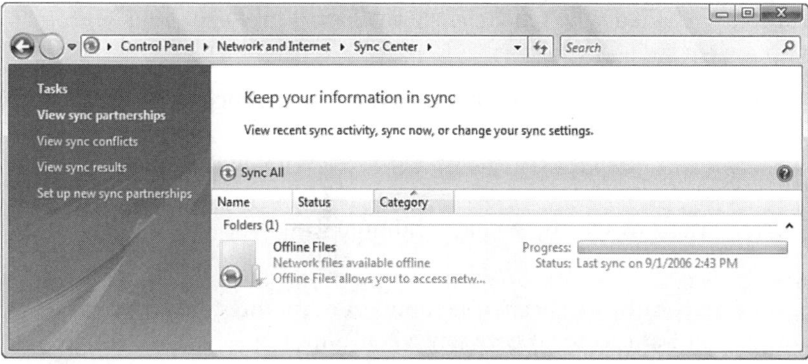

FIGURE 23.9 Use Vista's new Sync Center to keep your offline files synchronized.

Synchronizing Offline Files

When you reconnect to the network, Windows Vista automatically **synchronizes** the files. This means that Windows Vista does two things: First, it updates your local copy of an offline folder by creating copies of any new or changed files in the shared network folder.

Second, it updates the shared network folder with the files you changed while you were offline. This synchronization occurs automatically when you log on to the network and when you log off the network. You can also synchronize the offline files yourself. You have four choices:

- Open the shared network folder and click Sync in the task pane
- Open the Sync Center, click View Sync Partnerships, double-click Offline Files, select the offline folder, and click Sync
- Open the Sync Center, click View Sync Partnerships, double-click Offline Files, and click Sync All
- Right-click the Sync Center icon in the notification area, and click Sync All

You can also set up a synchronization schedule, either based on a time or on one or more events, as described in the next two sections.

Scheduling a Synchronization by Time

If you want synchronization to occur automatically, and you know when you want it to occur, follow these steps to set up a time-based sync schedule:

1. In the Sync Center, click View Sync Partnerships.
2. Click Schedule. The Offline Files Sync Schedule dialog box appears.
3. If you have already created a sync schedule, click Create a New Sync Schedule; otherwise, skip to step 4.
4. Leave the check box activated beside each folder you want to include in the synchronization, and click Next.
5. Click At a Scheduled Time.
6. Use the Start On controls to specify the date and time when you want synchronization to begin.
7. Use the Repeat Every controls to specify the numbers of minutes, hours, days, weeks, or months you want to occur between synchronizations.
8. Click More Options to see the More Scheduling Options dialog box with the following options (click OK when you're done):

   Start Sync Only If: The Computer Is Awake—Leave this check box activated to ensure that the synchronization occurs only if the computer isn't in Standby or Hibernate mode.

   Start Sync Only If: The Computer Has Been Idle for at Least *X* Minutes/Hours—Activate this check box to tell Vista to synchronize only when you're not using your computer. Use the spin box to set the amount of idle time that must occur before the sync begins.

   Start Sync Only If: The Computer Is Running on External Power—Activate this check box to avoid running the synchronization when your portable computer is running on batteries.

Stop Sync If: The Computer Wakes Up from Being Idle—Activate this check box to have Vista abandon the sync if you start using your computer.

Stop Sync If: The Computer Is No Longer Running on External Power—Activate this check box to have Vista stop the sync if you switch your portable computer to battery power.

9. Click Next.
10. Type a name for the schedule and then click Save Schedule.

Scheduling a Synchronization by Event

If you want the synchronization to occur automatically, and you know when you want the synchronization to occur, follow these steps to set up a time-based sync schedule:

1. In the Sync Center, click View Sync Partnerships.
2. Click Schedule. The Offline Files Sync Schedule dialog box appears.
3. If you have already created a sync schedule, click Create a New Sync Schedule; otherwise, skip to step 4.
4. Leave the check box activated beside each folder you want to include in the synchronization, and click Next.
5. Click On an Event or Action.
6. Specify the events or actions that trigger the sync by activating one or more of the following check boxes:

   I Log On to My Computer—Activate this check box to start the sync when you log on.

   My Computer Is Idle for *X* Minutes/Hours—Activate this check box to start the sync when your computer has been idle for the number of minutes or hours that you specify.

   I Lock Windows—Activate this check box to start the sync when you lock your computer.

NOTE

You lock your computer either by selecting Start, Lock, or by pressing Windows Logo+L.

   I Unlock Windows—Activate this check box to start the sync when you unlock your computer.

7. Click More Options to see the More Scheduling Options dialog box (described in the previous section).
8. Click Next.
9. Type a name for the schedule and then click Save Schedule.

Handling Synchronization Conflicts

When Windows Vista synchronizes your offline files, it might find that a file has changed both on the network share and on your offline computer. In that case, the Sync Center icon displays a `Sync Conflicts Have Occurred` message. Here's what you do:

1. Click the `Sync Conflicts Have Occurred` message to open the Sync Center.
2. Click View Sync Conflicts. The Sync Center displays a list of the conflicts.
3. Select the conflict you want to work with.
4. Click Resolve. Vista displays a Resolve Conflict dialog box similar to the one shown in Figure 23.10.

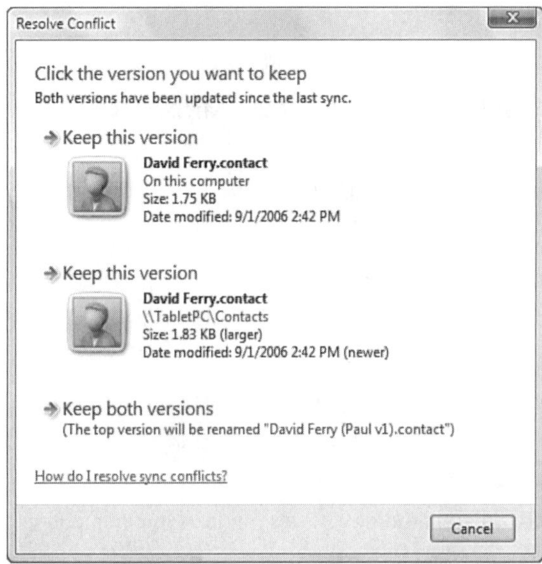

FIGURE 23.10 Use the Resolve Conflict dialog box to tell Vista how you want it to handle a file that has been changed both locally and offline.

5. Click the version you want to keep, or click Keep Both Versions to have the offline version saved under a modified filename.

Adjusting Disk Space Used for Offline Files

Vista sets aside a finite amount of disk space on your system to store both offline files and temporary offline files. (The latter are local copies of network files that you've used recently. Vista keeps these files cached automatically so that you can use them offline if you need them.) Vista assigns a limit on the amount of disk space both types of offline files can use on your system. These limits are a percentage of the size of the `%SystemDrive%`, and the larger the drive, the higher the percentage. For example, on a 15GB drive, Vista sets a limit of about 15% of total disk space (about 2GB) for both types of offline files; on a 200GB drive, Vista sets a limit of about 25% of total disk space (about 50GB) for both types of offline files. If you find these limits are too high or too low, you can adjust them by following these steps:

1. Select Start, Control Panel, Network and Internet, Offline Files. Vista opens the Offline Files dialog box.
2. Display the Disk Usage tab. As shown in Figure 23.11, this tab tells you the amount of disk space you're currently using for offline files and for the offline files cache, and it also tells you the current limits for both types.

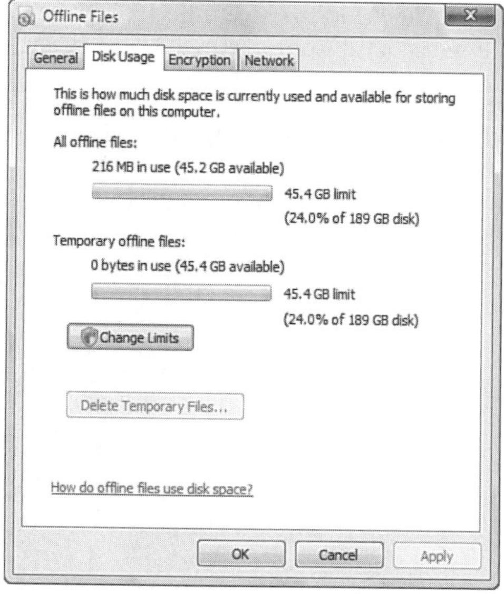

FIGURE 23.11 The Disk Usage tab shows you the disk space used by your offline files as well as the disk space limits.

3. Click Change Limits and then enter your UAC credentials. The Offline Files Disk Usage Limits dialog box appears.
4. Use the Maximum Amount of Space All Offline Files Can Use slider to set the limit for offline files.
5. Use the Maximum Amount of Space Temporary Offline Files Can Use slider to set the limit for the offline files cache.
6. Click OK to return to the Offline Files dialog box.
7. Click OK.

Collaborating with Windows Meeting Space

In previous versions of Windows, if you needed to remotely collaborate with other users by sharing a program or working together on a document, the tool of choice was Microsoft NetMeeting. Vista's replacement for NetMeeting is an entirely new program: Windows Meeting Space. As in NetMeeting, you can use Windows Meeting Space to show a local program or document to any number of remote users and you can collaborate on a document with remote users. Windows Meeting Space uses several new Vista technologies, including Peer-to-Peer Networking, Distributed File System Replicator (DFSR), and People Near Me. The next few sections show you how Windows Meeting Space works.

Signing In to People Near Me

To use Windows Meeting Space, you must first sign in to People Near Me. You do this either by starting Windows Meeting Space (see "Starting Windows Meeting Space," later in this chapter) or directly via the Control Panel: select Start, Control Panel, Network and Internet, People Near Me.

In the People Near Me dialog box that appears, display the Sign In tab and activate the Sign In to People Near Me option. Before you click OK, you might want to look at the Settings tab, which enables you to change the name and picture that other people see, and to control various other People Near Me options, as shown in Figure 23.12.

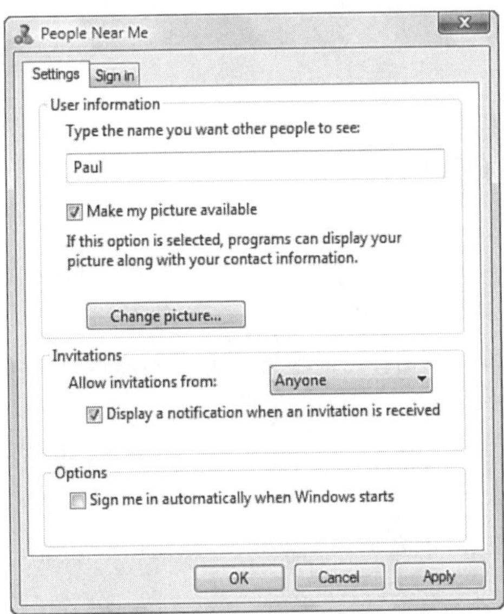

FIGURE 23.12 Use the Settings tab to configure People Near Me.

When you first sign in, Vista displays the People Near Me privacy policy, which states that the People Near Me feature discloses only your name, your computer name, and your computer's IP address. Click OK to continue.

Starting Windows Meeting Space

When you're signed in to People Near Me, you can launch Windows Meeting Space by selecting Start, All Programs, Windows Meeting Space. The first time you do this, the Windows Meeting Space Setup dialog box appears. For Windows Meeting Space to work, the data must be allowed to pass through the Windows Firewall—to do that, there must be Windows Firewall exceptions for the Meeting Space Infrastructure and the DFSR. If you click Yes, Continue Setting Up Windows Meeting Space (and enter your UAC credentials), Vista creates the exceptions for you automatically.

The Windows Meeting Space window appears, as shown in Figure 23.13. From there, you either start a new collaboration meeting or join an existing meeting, as described in the next couple of sections.

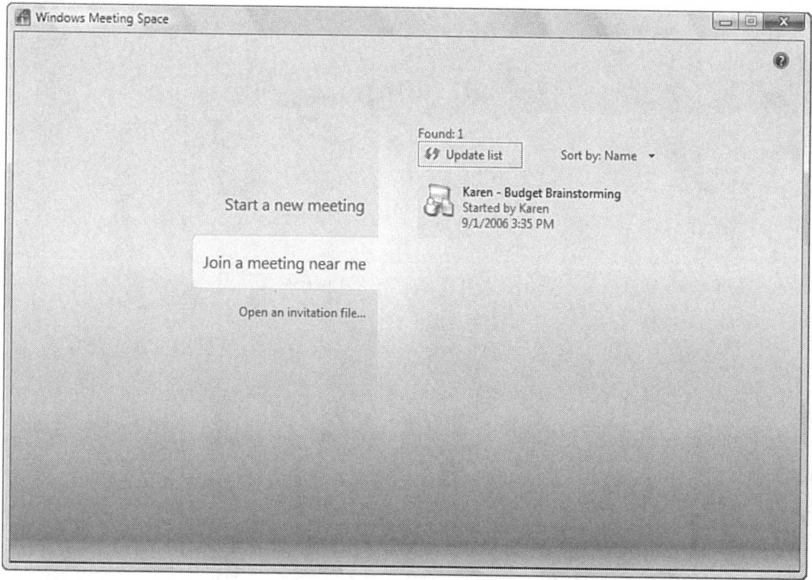

FIGURE 23.13 Use the Windows Meeting Space window to start and join collaboration meetings.

Joining a Meeting

If you know that another person has a meeting running, but you didn't receive an invitation, here are the steps to follow to join that meeting:

1. In the Windows Meeting Space window, click Join a Meeting Near Me. Windows Meeting Space displays a list of running meetings (see Figure 23.13).
2. Click the meeting you want to join. Windows Meeting Space prompts you to enter the meeting password.
3. Type the password and press Enter. Windows Meeting Space verifies your password and then joins the meeting.

Starting a Meeting

If you want to start your own collaboration meeting, follow these steps:

1. Click Start a New Meeting.
2. Enter the meeting name.
3. Enter the meeting password.
4. Press Enter. Meeting Space starts the new meeting, as shown in Figure 23.14.

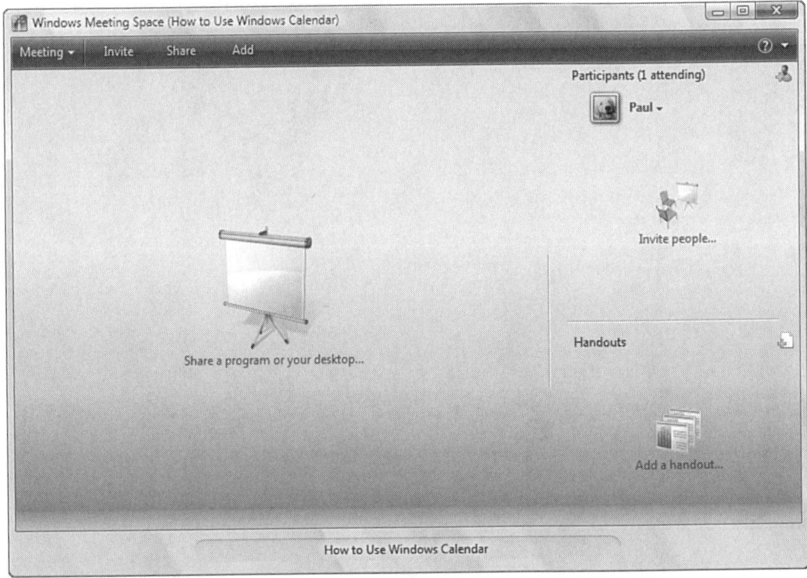

FIGURE 23.14 A new meeting, ready to begin.

Inviting People to the Meeting

You can't collaborate unless there are other people in the meeting, so your next step is to send invitations to those people you want to join the meeting. Here are the steps:

1. Click Invite in the menu bar or click the Invite People icon to display the Invite People dialog box.

2. Activate the check box beside each person you want to invite.
3. Click Send Invitations.

NOTE

The list of users you see in the Invite People dialog box consists of those people signed in to People Near Me on your network. If you want others to attend, you can send them an email message. In the Invite People dialog box, click Invite Others then click Send and Invitation in E-mail.

A user who receives your invitation first sees the notification shown in Figure 23.15. Click View (or wait a few seconds), and you see the Invitation Details dialog box shown in Figure 23.16. Click Accept to join the meeting (this also loads Windows Meeting Space on the user's machine; at this point, you enter the meeting password); click Decline to refuse the invitation or click Dismiss to do nothing.

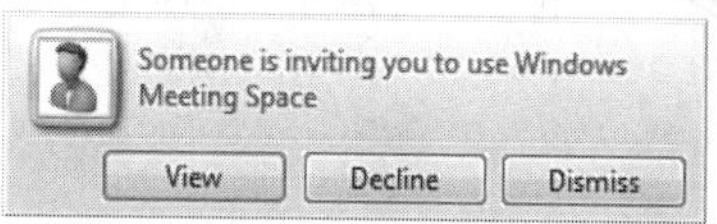

FIGURE 23.15 You see this notification when a meeting invitation first arrives.

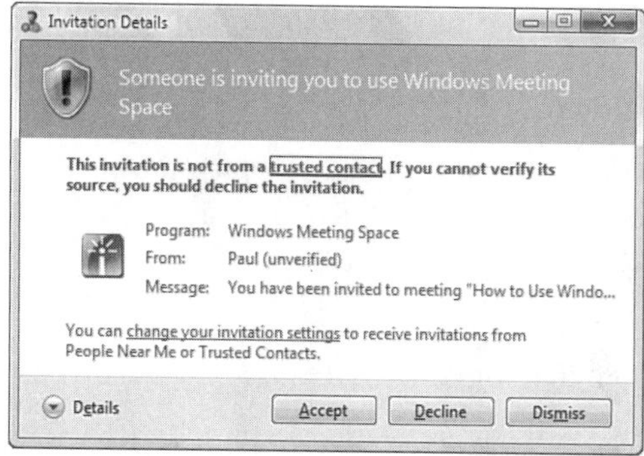

FIGURE 23.16 This dialog box appears a few seconds after the invitation arrives.

As people accept the invitations, their People Near Me name appears in the Windows Meeting Space Participants list.

Sharing a Handout

Before getting to the presentation, you might have some notes, instructions, background material, or other type of handout that you want to share with each participant. You do this by following these steps:

1. Click Add in the menu bar or by click the Add a Handout icon. Meeting Space tells you the handouts will be copied to each computer.
2. Click OK.
2. Select your file and then click Open. The file appears immediately in the Handouts area, which shows the filename and the name of the person who added it.

CAUTION

You can share any type of file you want as a handout. However, remember that the remote users will only be able to view and work with the handout file if they have an application installed that's associated with the handout's file type.

Starting a Shared Session

When all your participants have joined the meeting and you've shared your handouts, it's time to start the shared sessions. In Meeting Space, a shared session involves one of the participants performing some sort of action on his or her computer; the other participants see the results of those actions within their meeting window. You can perform three basic actions:

- **Demonstrating a specific program**—This involves running the program on your computer so that other people in the meeting can watch what you do.
- **Collaborating on a document**—This involves running a program and opening the document. The person who starts the shared sessions initially has control over the document, but control can pass to any participant.
- **Demonstrating any action**—This involves sharing your desktop, which means that the other participants see anything you do on your computer.

Follow these steps to start a shared session:

1. If you're going to demonstrate a specific program or collaborate on a document, start the program or open the document.
2. Click Share in the menu bar. Meeting Space asks whether you want the other participants to see your desktop.
3. Click OK. The Start a Shared Session dialog box appears.
4. You have three choices:
    - To share a program, select the program from the list of running applications.
    - To share a document, select Browse for a File to Open and Share.
    - To share your desktop, select Desktop.

5. Click Share.
6. If you are sharing a document, the Open dialog box appears. Select the document and then select Open.

CAUTION

Vista might automatically switch to a different color scheme if one of the participating computers can't handle your current color scheme. For example, if you're running the Aero scheme and a participating computer is running only Vista Basic, Vista switches to Basic.

TIP

To present your handout, right-click the handout and click Share to Meeting.

Controlling the Shared Session

After you begin a shared session, the Meeting Space window displays a `You are sharing X` message, where *X* is the object you're sharing. You also see two links:

Show Me How My Shared Sessions Looks on Other Computers—Click this link to see your shared session from the point of view of a remote computer.

Stop Sharing—Click this link to shut down the shared session.

Vista also displays a `You are sharing` message as well as the meeting title in a title bar across the top of the desktop, as shown in Figure 23.17. You can use the controls in this bar as follows:

- Click Pause to stop the shared session temporarily.
- Click Give Control and then click a participant's name to give that person control of the shared session.
- Click Give Control, Take Control (or press Windows Logo+Esc) to resume control of the shared session.
- Click Options, Shows Windows Meeting Space Window to switch to the Windows Meeting Space window.
- Click the Stop button to stop the shared session.

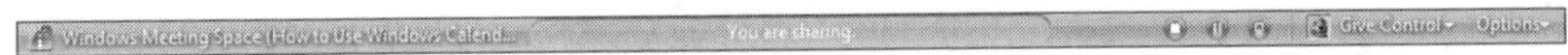

FIGURE 23.17 This bar appears at the top of your desktop after you start a shared session.

Figure 23.18 shows what the shared session looks like on a remote computer.

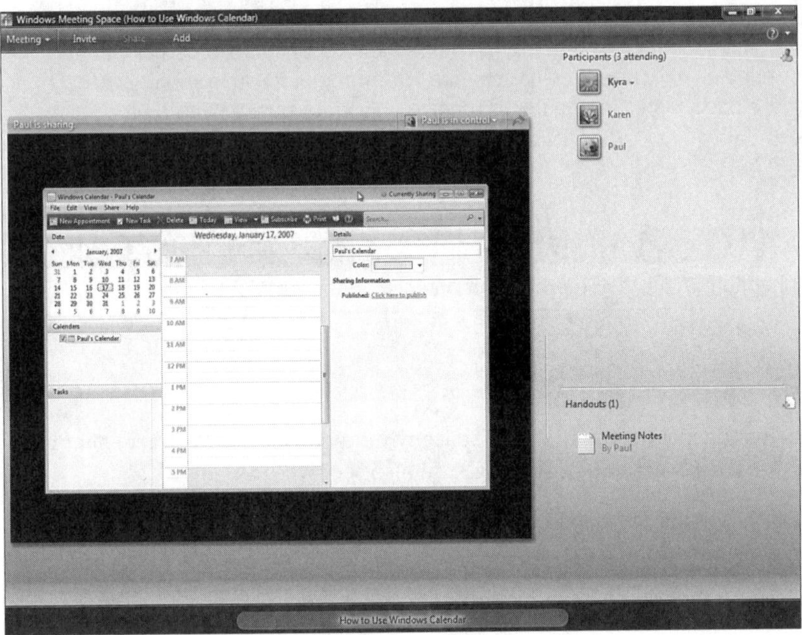

FIGURE 23.18 The presentation as seen on a remote computer.

Ending the Shared Session

When the shared session is over, click the Stop Sharing link in the Meeting Space window or click the Stop Sharing button in the session title bar. If you don't want to share anything else, select Meeting, Leave Meeting, or close the Meeting Space window.

From Here

Here are some other sections in the book where you'll find information related to the topics in this chapter:

- To learn about sharing media over a network, refer to "Sharing Media" in Chapter 7, "Working with Digital Media."
- To learn how to connect to a network and work with connections, refer to Chapter 22, "Setting Up a Small Network."
- For information on accessing your network from remote locations, refer to Chapter 24, "Making Remote Network Connections."

CHAPTER 24

Making Remote Network Connections

IN THIS CHAPTER

- Connecting to a Remote Desktop
- Using Virtual Private Network Connections

The networking techniques you've seen so far have assumed some kind of physical or local wireless connection between machines. For standard peer-to-peer and client/server networks, the computers use either a network card/cable package or a wireless NIC to connect to each other either directly or indirectly via a hub or router. What do you do, however, when a local connection just isn't possible? For example, suppose that you're on the road with your notebook computer and need to access a file on your network server. Or suppose that you're working at home and need to send a file to your office machine. Is there any way to access a network in the absence of a nearby connection? The answer is that for these remote predicaments, you *can* connect to a network and use its resources just as you can with a local connection (albeit, in most cases, more slowly).

Windows Vista offers two solutions: Remote Desktop and Virtual Private Networking. This chapter takes you through the details of understanding, configuring, and using these techniques.

Connecting to a Remote Desktop

Windows Vista's Remote Desktop feature enables you to connect to a workgroup computer's desktop and use the machine just as though you were sitting in front of it. This is handy if you can't leave your desk but need to troubleshoot a problem on the remote machine. Alternatively, if you have a network at home, you can use Remote Desktop to operate your main computer from any other computer in the house.

Getting the Remote Computer Ready to Host

Vista Business Vista Enterprise Vista Ultimate Edition

Remote Desktop is easy to configure and use, but it does require a small amount of prep work to ensure trouble-free operation. Let's begin with the remote computer, also called the **host** computer. (Note that the host software is available only with Vista Business, Enterprise, and Ultimate.)

By default, the user currently logged on to the host machine has permission to connect remotely to the host. Other users with default remote connection permissions are members of the host's Administrators and Remote Desktop Users groups. (In all cases, only users with password-protected accounts can use Remote Desktop.) If you want to connect to the host remotely, you first need to set up an account for the username with which you want to connect from the client (again, you must assign a password to this account).

You now have to follow these steps to prepare the remote computer for its Remote Desktop hosting duties:

1. Select Start, right-click Computer, and then click Properties to open the System window.
2. Click the Remote Settings link and then enter your UAC credentials. Vista opens the System Properties dialog box with the Remote tab displayed.

TIP

Another way to open the System Properties dialog box with the Remote tab displayed is to press Windows Logo+R (or select Start, All Programs, Accessories, Run), type **`systempropertiesremote`**, click OK, and enter your UAC credentials.

3. In the Remote Desktop group, you have two choices:

   Allow Connections from Computers Running Any Version of Remote Desktop—Select this option if you want people running previous versions of Remote Desktop to be able to access the host.

   Allow Connections Only from Computers Running Remote Desktop with Network Level Authentication—Select this option if you only want the most secure form of Remote Desktop access. In this case, Vista checks the client computer to see if its version of Remote Desktop supports Network Level Authentication (NLA). NLA is an authentication protocol that authenticates the user before making the Remote Desktop connection.
4. If you didn't add more users earlier, skip to step 7. Otherwise, click Select Users to display the Remote Desktop Users dialog box.

5. Click Add to display the Select Users dialog box, type the username, and click OK. (Repeat this step to add other users.)
6. Click OK to return to the System Properties dialog box.
7. Click OK.

Getting a Client Computer Ready Using Windows XP

You must install the Remote Desktop Connection software on the computer that will initiate the connection (this is the **client**). This software is already installed in all versions of Windows Vista. If you're running an earlier version of Windows on the client, you can install the Remote Desktop Connection software from the Windows XP CD (if you have one):

1. Insert the Windows XP CD and wait for the Welcome to Microsoft Windows XP screen to appear.
2. Click Perform Additional Tasks.
3. Click Set Up Remote Desktop Connection.

You can also download the latest client software from Microsoft:

www.microsoft.com/windowsxp/downloads/tools/rdclientdl.mspx

Note, too, that Microsoft also offers a client that operates under Mac OS X. Go to www.microsoft.com/downloads and search for *Remote Desktop Mac*.

Making the Connection to the Remote Desktop

On the client computer, you can now connect to the host computer's desktop. Follow these steps:

1. Select Start, All Programs, Accessories, Remote Desktop Connection. The Remote Desktop Connection dialog box appears.
2. In the Computer text box, type the name or the IP address of the remote computer.
3. If you don't want to customize Remote Desktop, skip to step 10. Otherwise, click Options to expand the dialog box to the version shown in Figure 24.1.
4. The General tab offers the following additional options:

Computer	The name or IP address of the remote computer.
Save	Click this button to have Vista remember your current settings so that you don't have to type them again the next time you connect. This is useful if you always connect to the same host.
Save As	Click this button to save your connection settings to a Remote Desktop (`.rdp`) file for later use. This is useful if you regularly connect to multiple hosts.
Open	Click this button to open a saved `.rdp` file.

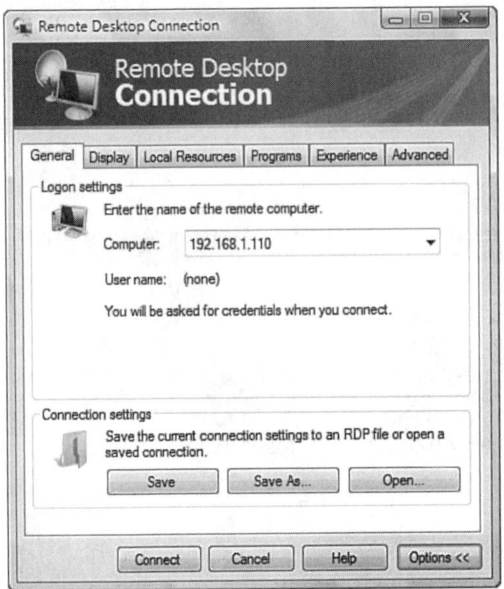

FIGURE 24.1 Clicking the Options button expands the dialog box so that you can customize Remote Desktop.

5. The Display tab, shown in Figure 24.2, offers three options for controlling the look of the Remote Desktop window:

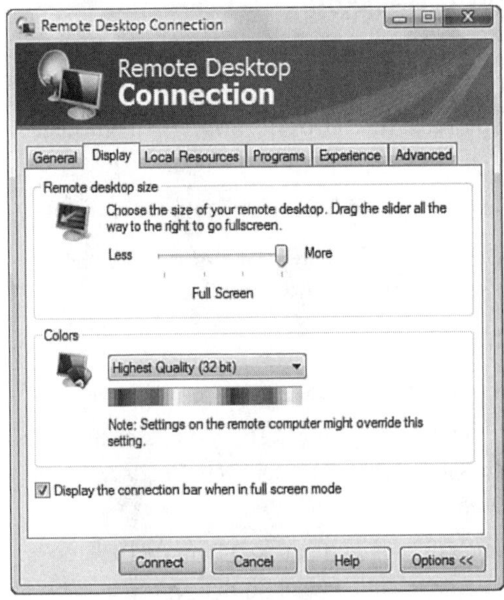

FIGURE 24.2 Use the Display tab to set the Remote Desktop size and colors.

Remote Desktop Size	Drag this slider to set the resolution of Remote Desktop. Drag the slider all the way to the left for a 640×480 screen size; drag the slider all the way to the right to have Remote Desktop take up the entire client screen, no matter what resolution the host is currently using.
Colors	Use this list to set the number of colors used for the Remote Desktop display. Note that if the number of colors on either the host or the client is fewer than the value you select in the Colors list, Windows Vista will use the lesser value.
Display the Connection Bar When in Full Screen Mode	When this check box is activated, the Remote Desktop Connection client displays a connection bar at the top of the Remote Desktop window, provided you selected Full Screen for the Remote Desktop Size setting. You use the connection bar to minimize, restore, and close the Remote Desktop window. If you find that the connection bar just gets in the way, deactivate this check box to prevent it from appearing.

6. The Local Resources tab, shown in Figure 24.3, offers three options for controlling certain interactions between the client and the host:

Remote Computer Sound	Use this list to determine where Windows Vista plays the sounds generated by the host computer. You can play them on the client (if you want to hear what's happening on the host), on the host (if you want a user sitting at the host to hear the sounds), or not at all (if you have a slow connection).
Keyboard	Use this list to determine which computer is sent special Windows key combinations—such as Alt+Tab and Ctrl+Esc—that you press on the client keyboard. You can have the key combos sent to the client, to the host, or to the host only when you're running the Remote Desktop window in full-screen mode. What happens if you're sending key combos to one computer and you need to use a particular key combo on the other computer? For such situations, Remote Desktop offers several keyboard equivalents, outlined in the following table:

Windows Key Combo	Remote Desktop Equivalent
Alt+Tab	Alt+Page Up
Alt+Shift+Tab	Alt+Page Down
Alt+Esc	Alt+Insert
Ctrl+Esc or Windows Logo	Alt+Home
Print Screen	Ctrl+Alt+– (numeric keypad)
Alt+Print Screen	Ctrl+Alt++ (numeric keypad)

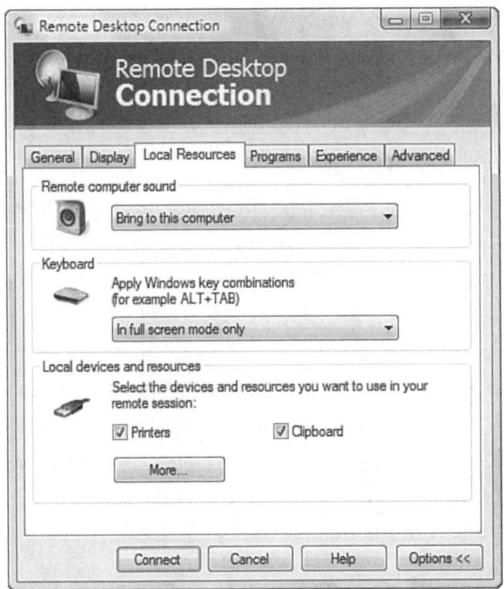

FIGURE 24.3 Use the Local Resources tab to customize how Remote Desktop handles the host's sounds, Windows key combinations, and the client's local devices.

TIP

Here are three other useful keyboard shortcuts that you can press on the client computer and have Windows Vista send them to the host computer:

Ctrl+Alt+End	Displays the Windows Task Manager (on a peer-to-peer computer) or Windows Security (on a domain computer). This is equivalent to pressing Ctrl+Alt+Delete, which Windows Vista always applies to the client computer.
Alt+Delete	Displays the active window's Control menu.
Ctrl+Alt+Break	Toggles the Remote Desktop window between full-screen mode and a regular window.

Local Devices and Resources	Leave the Printers check box activated to display the client's printers in the host's Printers and Faxes window. The client's printers appear with the syntax `Printer (from COMPUTER)`, where *`Printer`* is the printer name and *`COMPUTER`* is the network name of the client computer. Leave the Clipboard check box activated to use the client's Clipboard during the remote session.

7. Click More to see the Remote Desktop Connection dialog box shown in Figure 24.4. Use the following check boxes to configure more client devices and resources on the host (click OK when you're done):

Smart Cards	Leave this check box activated to access the client's smart cards on the host.
Serial Ports	Activate this check box to make any devices attached to the client's serial ports (such as a barcode scanner) available while you're working with the host.
Drives	Activate this check box to display the client's hard disk partitions and mapped network drives in the host's Computer window. (You can also open the branch to activate the check boxes of specific drives.) As shown in Figure 24.5, the client's drives appear in the Computer window's Other group with the syntax *`D`* `on` *`Computer`*, where *`D`* is the drive letter and *`Computer`* is the network name of the client computer (such as `PaulsPC` in Figure 24.5).

FIGURE 24.4 Use this dialog box to customize how Remote Desktop handles more of the client's local devices and resources.

Supported Plug and Play Devices	Activate this check box to make some of the client's Plug and Play devices available to the host, such as media players and digital cameras. (You can also open the branch to activate the check boxes of specific devices.)

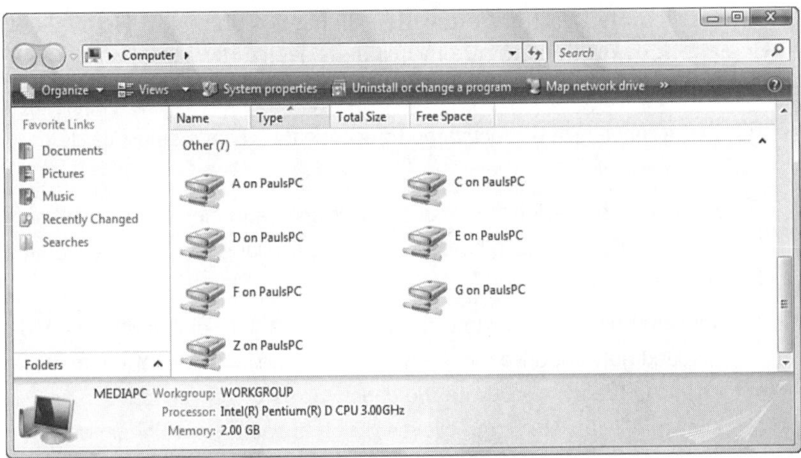

FIGURE 24.5 If you elect to display the client's disk drives on the host, they appear in the Computer window's Other group.

8. Use the Programs tab to specify a program to run on connection. Activate the Start the Following Program on Connection check box, and then use the Program Path and File Name text box to specify the program to run. After connecting, the user can work with only this program, and when he or she quits the program, the session also ends.

9. Use the Experience tab, shown in Figure 24.6, to set performance options for the connection. Use the Choose Your Connection Speed to Optimize Performance drop-down list to set the appropriate connection speed. Because you're connecting over a network, you should choose the LAN (10 Mbps or higher) option. Depending on the connection speed you choose, one or more of the following check boxes will be activated (the faster the speed, the more check boxes Windows Vista activates):

Desktop Background	Toggles the host's desktop background on and off.
Font Smoothing	Toggles the host's font smoothing on and off.
Desktop Composition	Toggles the host's desktop composition engine on and off.
Show Contents of Window While Dragging	Toggles the display of window contents when you drag a host window with your mouse.
Menu and Windows Animation	Toggles on and off the animations that Windows Vista normally uses when you pull down menus or minimize and maximize windows.
Themes	Toggles the host's current visual theme on and off.
Bitmap Caching	Activate this check box to improve performance by not storing frequently used host images on the client computer.

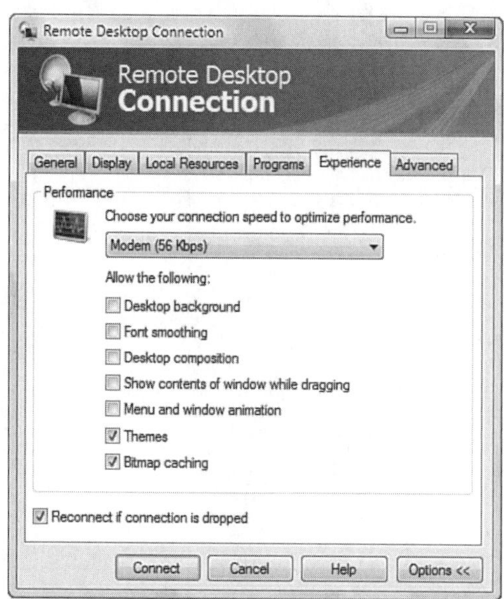

FIGURE 24.6 Use the Experience tab to set performance options for the connection.

10. Click Connect. Vista prompts you to enter your security credentials.
11. Type your User Name and Password, and then click OK.
12. If you activated the Disk Drives or Serial Ports check boxes in the Local Resources tab, a security warning dialog box appears. If you're sure that making these resources available to the remote computer is safe, activate the Don't Prompt Me Again for Connections to this Remote Computer check box. Click OK.
13. If a person with a different username is already logged on to the remote computer, Windows Vista lets you know that you'll disconnect that user, which could result in data loss. Click Yes only if you're sure that it's okay to disconnect the current user.

NOTE

The remote user has the option of cancelling your logon attempt. When you initiate the logon, the remote user sees a Remote Desktop Connection dialog box that tells the user of the remote connection attempt. He or she can then click Cancel to prevent the logon. Otherwise, the logon happens automatically after 30 seconds (or when the remote user clicks OK).

The remote desktop then appears on your computer. If you chose to work in full-screen mode, you'll also see the connection bar at the top of the screen, as shown in Figure 24.7.

24

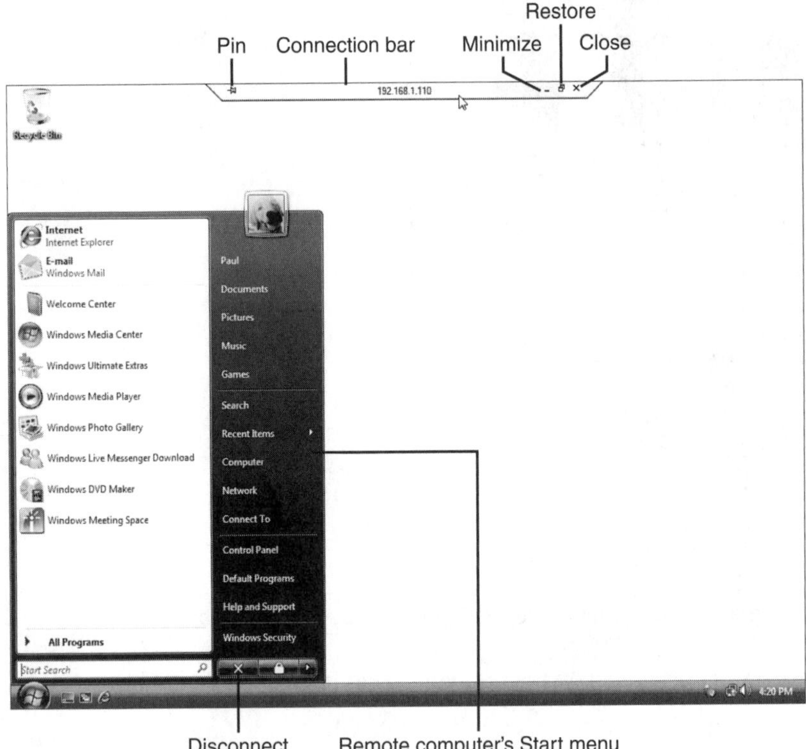

FIGURE 24.7 After you've connected, the remote computer's desktop appears on the client screen.

If you don't want the connection bar to appear all the time, click the Pin button. When you move your mouse away, the connection bar slides off the screen. To get the connection bar back, move your mouse to the top edge of the screen.

If you need to work with your own desktop, you have two choices:

- Click the connection bar's Minimize button to minimize the Remote Desktop window
- Click the connection bar's Restore button to display the Remote Desktop window

Disconnecting from the Remote Desktop

When you finish with the Remote Desktop session, you have two choices for disconnecting:

- Using the host's desktop, select Start, Disconnect (refer to Figure 24.7).
- Click the Close button in the connection bar. Windows Vista displays a dialog box to let you know that your remote session will be disconnected. Click OK.

Connecting to a Remote Desktop via the Internet

Connecting to a Remote Desktop host over your LAN is easy to set up and fast, but your LAN might not always be so local. If you're traveling, what do you do if you want to connect to your desktop or to the desktop of some computer on your network? This is possible, but it requires some care to ensure that you don't open up your computer or your network to Internet-based hackers.

CAUTION

In addition to the security precautions I present in this section, you should also set up your accounts with robust passwords, as described in the "Creating a Strong Password" section of Chapter 6, "Getting the Most Out of User Accounts." Using Remote Desktop over the Internet means that you open up a small window on your network that is at least visible to others on the Net. To ensure that other Internet users cannot exploit this hole, a strong password is a must.

Here are the steps to follow (each is explained in more detail later) to set up your system to allow Remote Desktop connections via the Internet:

1. Configure Remote Desktop to use a listening port other than the default.
2. Configure Windows Firewall to allow TCP connections through the port you specified in step 1.
3. Determine the IP address of the Remote Desktop host or your network's gateway.
4. Configure your network gateway (if you have one) to forward data sent to the port specified in step 1 to the Remote Desktop host computer.
5. Use the IP address from step 3 and the port number from step 1 to connect to the Remote Desktop host via the Internet.

Changing the Listening Port

Your first task is to modify the Remote Desktop software on the host computer to use a listening port other than 3389, which is the default port. This is a good idea because there are hackers on the Internet who use **port scanners** to examine Internet connections (particularly broadband connections) for open ports. If the hackers see that port 3389 is open, they could assume that it's for a Remote Desktop connection, so they try to make a Remote Desktop connection to the host. They still have to log on with an authorized username and password, but knowing the connection type means they've cleared a very large hurdle.

To change the Remote Desktop listening port, open the Registry Editor and navigate to the following key:

```
HKLM\System\CurrentControlSet\Control\TerminalServer\WinStations\RDP-Tcp
```

Open the `PortNumber` number setting and replace the existing value—`D3D` hexadecimal, or `3389` decimal—with some other number between 1,024 and 65,536 (decimal). Reboot your computer to put the new port setting into effect.

Configuring Windows Firewall

Now you have to configure Windows Firewall to allow data to pass through the port you specified in the previous section. Here are the steps to follow:

1. On the Remote Desktop host, select Start, Control Panel.
2. Under the Security icon, click the Allow a Program Through Windows Firewall and enter your UAC credentials. Vista displays the Windows Firewall Settings dialog box with the Exceptions tab displayed.
3. Click Add Port to display the Add a Port dialog box.
4. Use the Name text box to type a name for the unblocked port (such as *Remote Desktop Alternate*).
5. In the Port Number text box, type the port number you specified in the previous section.
6. Make sure that the TCP option is activated.
7. Click OK in all open dialog boxes.

Determining the Host IP Address

To connect to a remote desktop via the Internet, you need to specify an IP address instead of a computer name. The IP address you use depends on your Internet setup:

- If the Remote Desktop host computer connects directly to the Internet and your ISP supplied you with a static IP address, connect using that address.
- If the host computer connects directly to the Internet but your ISP supplies you with a dynamic IP address each time you connect, use the IPCONFIG utility to determine your current IP address. (That is, select Start, All Programs, Accessories, Command Prompt to get to the command line, type **`ipconfig`**, and press Enter.) Make note of the `IPv4 Address` value returned by IPCONFIG (you might need to scroll the output up to see it) and use that address to connect to the Remote Desktop host.

TIP

If you want to use Remote Desktop via the Internet regularly, constantly monitoring your dynamic IP address can be a pain, particularly if you forget to check it before heading out of the office. A useful solution is to sign up with a dynamic DNS service, which supplies you with a static domain name. The service also installs a program on your computer that monitors your IP address and updates the service's dynamic DNS servers to point your domain name to your IP address. Here are some dynamic DNS services to check out:

TZO (www.tzo.com)

No-IP.com (www.no-ip.com)

DynDNS (www.dyndns.org)

- If your network uses a gateway, determine that gateway's IP address. You usually have to log on to the gateway's setup pages and view some sort of status page. Figure 24.8 shows an example. When you set up your Remote Desktop connection, you'll connect to the gateway, which will then forward your connection (thanks to your efforts in the next section) to the Remote Desktop host.

TIP

Another way to determine your gateway's IP address is to navigate to any of the free services for determining your current IP. Here are two:

WhatISMyIP (www.whatismyip.com)

DynDNS (checkip.dyndns.org)

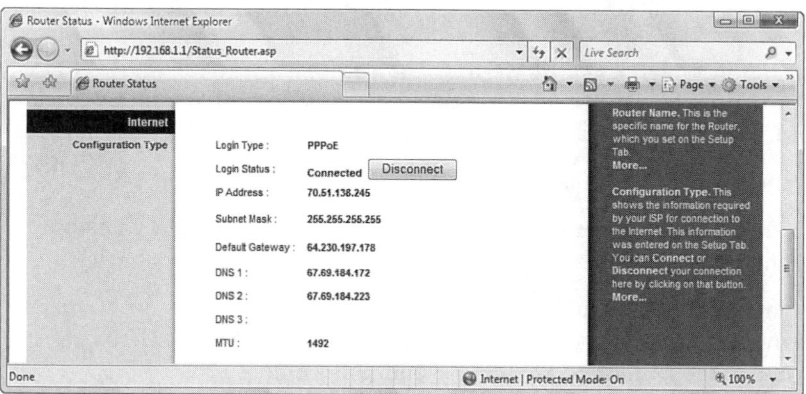

FIGURE 24.8 Log on to your gateway device to see its current IP address.

Setting Up Port Forwarding

If your network uses a router, gateway, or other hardware firewall, you need to configure it to forward data sent to the port specified in step 1 to the Remote Desktop host computer. This is **port forwarding**, and the steps you follow depend on the device. Figure 24.9 shows the Port Forwarding screen of the router on my system. In this case, the firewall forwards data that comes in to port 1234 to the computer at the address 192.168.1.110, which is the Remote Desktop host. Consult your device documentation to learn how to set up port forwarding.

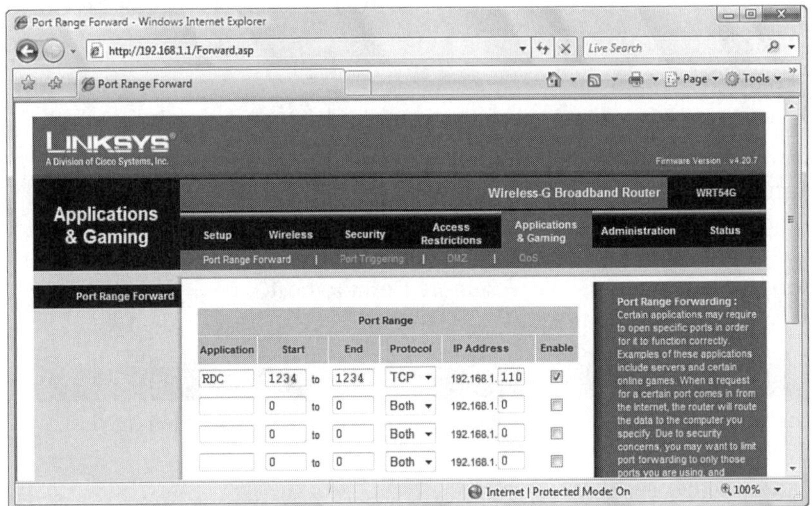

FIGURE 24.9 On a hardware firewall, forward the new port to the Remote Desktop host computer.

Connecting Using the IP Address and New Port

You're now ready to make the connection to the Remote Desktop host via the Internet. Here are the steps to follow:

1. Connect to the Internet.
2. Select Start, All Programs, Accessories, Remote Desktop Connection. The Remote Desktop Connection dialog box appears.
3. In the Computer text box, type the name or the IP address of the remote computer and the alternative port you specified in step 1, separated by a colon. Here's an example that uses the IP address 123.45.67.8 and port number 1234:

```
123.45.67.8:1234
```

4. Set up your other Remote Desktop options as needed. For example, click Options, display the Experience tab, and then select the appropriate connection speed, such as Modem (28.8 Kbps), Modem (56 Kbps), or Broadband (128 Kbps–1.5 Mbps).

5. Click Connect.

Using Virtual Private Network Connections

In the remote connections you've seen so far, the security exists mostly at the connection point. That is, you set up usernames with strong passwords, and no one can access your dial-up or Remote Desktop connection without entering the correct logon data. This works well, but it doesn't do much for the actual data that's passed between the host and client. A malicious hacker might not be able to access your system directly, but he certainly can use a packet sniffer or similar technology to access your incoming and outgoing data. Because that data isn't encrypted, the hacker can easily read the contents of the packets.

What do you do, then, if you want to transfer secure data such as financial information or personnel files, but you love the simplicity of a dial-up connection? The answer is a tried-and-true technology called **virtual private networking** (**VPN**), which offers secure access to a private network over a public connection, such as the Internet or a phone line. VPN is secure because it uses a technique called **tunneling**, which establishes a connection between two computers—a **VPN server** and a **VPN client**—using a specific port (such as port 1723). Control-connection packets are sent back and forth to maintain the connection between the two computers (to, in a sense, keep the tunnel open).

When it comes to sending the actual network data—sometimes called the **payload**—each network packet is encrypted and then encapsulated within a regular IP packet, which is then routed through the tunnel. Any hacker can see this IP packet traveling across the Internet, but even if he intercepts the packet and examines it, no harm is done because the content of the packet—the actual data—is encrypted. When the IP packet arrives on the other end of the tunnel, VPN **decapsulates** the network packet and then decrypts it to reveal the payload.

Windows Vista comes with VPN client support built in and it uses two tunneling protocols:

Point-to-Point Tunneling Protocol (**PPTP**)
This protocol is the most widely used in VPN setups. It was developed by Microsoft and is related to the **Point-to-Point Protocol** (**PPP**) that's commonly used to transport IP packets over the Internet. A separate protocol—**Microsoft Point-to-Point Encryption** (**MPPE**)—encrypts the network packets (IP, IPX, NetBEUI, or whatever). PPTP sets up the tunnel and encapsulates the encrypted network packets in an IP packet for transport across the tunnel.

IP Security (**IPSec**)	This protocol encrypts the payload (IP packets only), sets up the tunnel, and encapsulates the encrypted network packets in an IP packet for transport across the tunnel.

NOTE

A third popular VPN protocol is **Layer 2 Tunneling Protocol** (**L2TP**), which goes beyond PPTP by allowing VPN connections over networks other than just the Internet (such as networks based on X.25, ATM, or Frame Relay). L2TP uses the encryption portion of IPSec to encrypt the network packets.

There are two main ways to use VPN:

Via the Internet	In this case, you first connect to the Internet using any PPP-based dial-up or broadband connection. Then you connect to the VPN server to establish the VPN tunnel over the Internet.
Via a dial-up connection	In this case, you first connect to the host computer using a regular dial-up connection. Then you connect to the VPN server to establish the VPN tunnel over the telephone network.

Configuring a Network Gateway for VPN

The best way to use VPN is when the client has a broadband Internet connection and the server has a public IP address or domain name. This enables you to access the server directly using your fast Internet connection. What happens, however, if the Windows Vista machine you set up as the VPN server sits behind a gateway or firewall and so uses only an internal IP address (192.168.1.*)?

You can often get around this problem by setting up a network gateway to pass through VPN packets and forward them to the VPN server. (Note that some broadband routers come with VPN capabilities built in, so they can handle an incoming VPN connection automatically.)

The details depend on the device, but the usual first step is to enable the gateway's support for **VPN passthrough**, which allows network computers to communicate via one or more VPN protocols (such as PPTP and IPSec). Figure 24.10 shows a sample page in a gateway setup application that that lets you enable passthrough for the IPSec, PPTP, and L2TP protocols.

In some cases, just enabling VPN passthrough is all you need to do to get VPN up and running through your gateway. If your VPN connection doesn't work or if your gateway doesn't support VPN passthrough, you have to open a port for the VPN protocol you're using and then have data to that port forwarded to the VPN server. (This is similar to the port forwarding described earlier for Remote Desktop connections.) The forwarded ports depend on the protocol:

PPTP	Forward TCP to port 1723
IPSec	Forward UPD to port 500

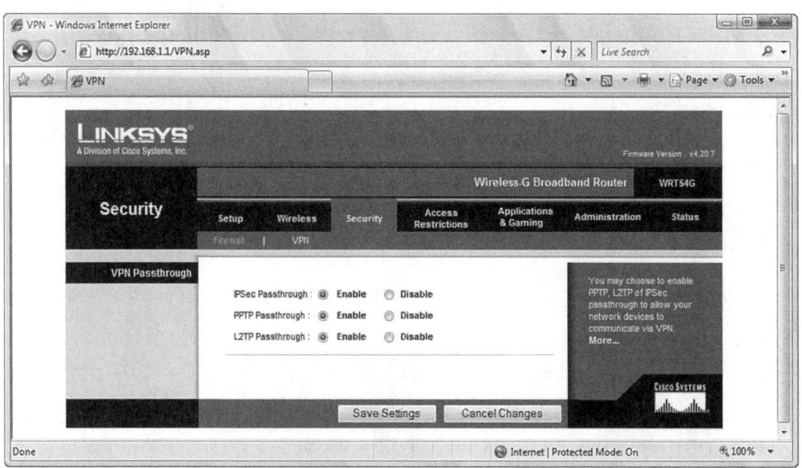

FIGURE 24.10 In your gateway setup application, enable VPN passthrough for the protocols you use.

Figure 24.11 shows an example of port forwarding.

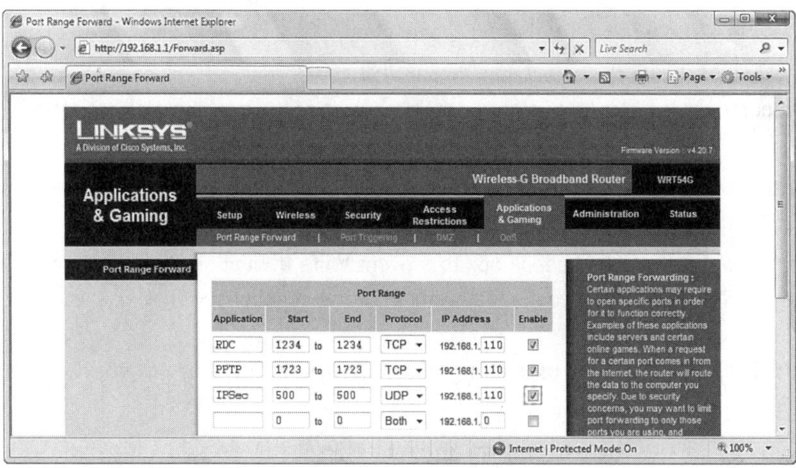

FIGURE 24.11 In your gateway setup application, forward the ports of the VPN protocols you use to the IP address of your network's VPN server.

Configuring the VPN Client

Now you have to configure the remote computer as a VPN client. Here are the steps to follow:

1. Select Start, Connect To. Vista displays the Connect to a Network dialog box.
2. Click the Set Up a Connection of Network link to open the Choose a Connection Option dialog box.
3. Click Connect to a Workplace and then click Next. The How Do You Want to Connect? dialog box appears.
4. Click one of the following two choices:

   Use My Internet Connection—Click this option if you want to make the VPN connection over the Internet.

   Dial Directly—Click this option to use a dial-up VPN connection.
5. In the next dialog box (Figure 24.12 shows the Internet connection version), configure the following controls (click Next when you're done):

   Internet Address—If you're using an Internet connection, type the domain name or IP address of the VPN server (or the network gateway that forwards your connection to the VPN server).

   Telephone Number—If you're using a dial-up connection, type the phone number used by the VPN server.

   Destination Name—Type a name for the VPN connection.

   Use a Smart Card—Activate this check box if your VPN server requires you to have a smart card security device inserted in your system as part of the server's authentication process.

   Allow Other People to Use This Connection—Activate this check box to make this connection available to other user accounts on your computer.

   Don't Connect Now—Activate this check box to prevent Vista from connecting to the VPN server right away. This is useful if you're just setting up the connection for later use.

6. Type your VPN logon data: your username, your password, and your network domain (if any).
7. Click Create. Vista creates the connection and launches it (unless you activated the Don't Connect Now check box in step 5).
8. Click Close.

Windows Vista adds a Virtual Private Network group to the Network Connections folder, and places in that group an icon with the name you specified in step 5.

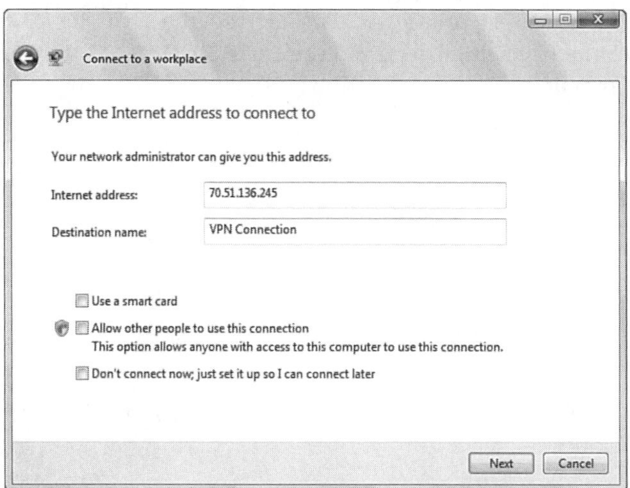

FIGURE 24.12 Use this dialog box to specify the location of your network's VPN server and other connection options.

Making the VPN Connection

With the VPN client configured, you can now use the client to make the VPN connection. Follow these steps on the VPN client computer:

1. If you need to establish a dial-up connection to the Internet before connecting to the VPN server, make that connection now.

TIP

You can configure the VPN connection to make the dial-up connection to the Internet automatically. Click Start, Connect To, and then click the Open Network and Sharing Center link. In the Network and Sharing Center window, click the Manage Network Connections link. Right-click the VPN connection icon and then click Properties to open its properties sheet. In the General tab. activate the Dial Another Connection First check box, and then use the associated list box to select the dial-up connection you want dialed. Click OK.

2. Select Start, Connect To.
3. Scroll up the Dial-up and VPN group.
4. Click the VPN connection and then click Connect. The Connect dialog box appears for the VPN connection. Type your username, password, and domain (if applicable).

6. If you want Windows Vista to remember your logon data, activate the Save This User Name and Password for the Following Users, and then activate either Me Only or Anyone Who Uses this Computer.
7. Click Connect. Windows Vista sets up the VPN connection.

From Here

Here's a list of chapters where you'll find related information:

- To learn about sharing media over a network, refer to "Sharing Media" in Chapter 7, "Working with Digital Media."
- To learn how to connect to a network and work with connections, refer to Chapter 22, "Setting Up a Small Network."
- To learn how to view network resources, share your computer's resources, and collaborate with other users, refer to Chapter 23, "Accessing and Using Your Network."

PART VI
Appendixes

APPENDIX A

Windows Vista Keyboard Shortcuts

Windows Vista was made with the mouse in mind, so most day-to-day tasks are designed to be performed using the standard mouse moves. However, this doesn't mean you should ignore your keyboard when you're not typing. Windows Vista is loaded with keyboard shortcuts and techniques that you can use as replacements or enhancements for mouse clicks and drags. These shortcuts (as shown in Tables A.1–A.13) are often a faster way to work because you don't have to move your hand from the keyboard to the mouse and back. Also, the Windows Vista keyboard techniques are useful to know just in case you have problems with your mouse and must rely on the keyboard to get your work done.

TABLE A.1 General Windows Vista Shortcut Keys

Press	To Do This
Ctrl+Esc	Open the Start menu.
Windows Logo	Open the Start menu.
Ctrl+Alt+Delete	Display the Windows Security window.
Print Screen	Copy the entire screen image to the Windows Clipboard.
Alt+Print Screen	Copy the active window's image to the Windows Clipboard.
Alt+Double-click	Display the property sheet for the selected object.
Alt+Enter	Display the property sheet for the selected object.
Shift	Prevent an inserted disc from running its AutoPlay application. (Hold down Shift while inserting the disc.)
Shift+F10	Display the shortcut menu for the selected object. (This is the same as right-clicking the object.)
Shift+Right-click	Display the shortcut menu with alternative commands for the selected object.

TABLE A.2 Shortcut Keys for Working with Program Windows

Press	To Do This
Alt	Activate or deactivate the program's menu bar.
Alt+Esc	Cycle through the open program windows.
Alt+F4	Close the active program window.
Alt+Spacebar	Display the system menu for the active program window.
Alt+Tab	Cycle through icons for each of the running programs.
Windows Logo+Tab	Launch Flip 3D to cycle through a 3D stack of running program windows.
F1	Display context-sensitive help.
F10	Activate the application's menu bar.

TABLE A.3 Shortcut Keys for Working with Documents

Press	To Do This
Alt+-(hyphen)	Display the system menu for the active document window.
Alt+Print Screen	Copy the active window's image to the Clipboard.
Ctrl+F4	Close the active document window.
Ctrl+F6	Cycle through the open documents within an application.
Ctrl+N	Create a new document.
Ctrl+O	Display the Open dialog box.
Ctrl+P	Display the Print dialog box.
Ctrl+S	Save the current file. If the file is new, display the Save As dialog box.

TABLE A.4 Shortcut Keys for Working with Data

Press	To Do This
Backspace	Delete the character to the left of the insertion point.
Ctrl+C	Copy the selected data to memory.
Ctrl+F	Display the Find dialog box.
Ctrl+H	Display the Replace dialog box.
Ctrl+X	Cut the selected data to memory.
Ctrl+V	Paste the most recently cut or copied data from memory.
Ctrl+Z	Undo the most recent action.
Delete	Delete the selected data.
F3	Repeat the most recent Find operation.

TABLE A.5 Shortcut Keys for Moving the Insertion Point

Press	To Do This
Ctrl+End	Move the insertion point to the end of the document.
Ctrl+Home	Move the insertion point to the beginning of the document.
Ctrl+Left Arrow	Move the insertion point to the next word to the left.
Ctrl+Right Arrow	Move the insertion point to the next word to the right.
Ctrl+Down Arrow	Move the insertion point to the beginning of the next paragraph.
Ctrl+Up Arrow	Move the insertion point to the beginning of the paragraph.

TABLE A.6 Shortcut Keys for Selecting Text

Press	To Do This
Ctrl+A	Select all the text in the current document.
Ctrl+Shift+End	Select from the insertion point to the end of the document.
Ctrl+Shift+Home	Select from the insertion point to the beginning of the document.
Ctrl+Shift+Left Arrow	Select the next word to the left.
Ctrl+Shift+Right Arrow	Select the next word to the right.
Ctrl+Shift+Down Arrow	Select from the insertion point to the end of the paragraph.
Ctrl+Shift+Up Arrow	Select from the insertion point to the beginning of the paragraph.
Shift+End	Select from the insertion point to the end of the line.
Shift+Home	Select from the insertion point to the beginning of the line.
Shift+Left Arrow	Select the next character to the left.
Shift+Right Arrow	Select the next character to the right.
Shift+Down Arrow	Select the next line down.
Shift+Up Arrow	Select the next line up.

TABLE A.7 Shortcut Keys for Working with Dialog Boxes

Press	To Do This
Alt+Down Arrow	Display the list in a drop-down list box.
Alt+*Underlined letter*	Select a control.
Ctrl+Shift+Tab	Move backward through the dialog box tabs.
Ctrl+Tab	Move forward through the dialog box tabs.
Enter	Select the default command button or the active command button.
Spacebar	Toggle a check box on and off; select the active option button or command button.
Esc	Close the dialog box without making any changes.
F1	Display help text for the control that has the focus.
F4	Display the list in a drop-down list box.
Backspace	In the Open and Save As dialog boxes, move up to the parent folder when the folder list has the focus.
Shift+Tab	Move backward through the dialog box controls.
Tab	Move forward through the dialog box controls.

TABLE A.8 Shortcut Keys for Drag-and-Drop Operations

Press	To Do This
Ctrl	Copy the dragged object.
Ctrl+Shift	Display a shortcut menu after dropping a left-dragged object.
Esc	Cancel the current drag.
Shift	Move the dragged object.

TABLE A.9 Shortcut Keys for Working in a Folder Window

Press	To Do This
Alt	Display Classic menus.
Alt+D	Display the pathname of the current folder in the Address bar.
Alt+Left Arrow	Navigate backward to a previously displayed folder.
Alt+Right Arrow	Navigate forward to a previously displayed folder.
Backspace	Navigate to the parent folder of the current folder.
Ctrl+A	Select all the objects in the current folder.
Ctrl+C	Copy the selected objects.
Ctrl+V	Paste the most recently cut or copied objects.
Ctrl+X	Cut the selected objects.
Ctrl+Z	Undo the most recent action.
Ctrl+E	Activate the Instant Search box.
Delete	Delete the selected objects.
F2	Rename the selected object.
F3	Display a Search window.
F5	Refresh the folder contents.

TABLE A.9 Continued

Press	To Do This
Shift+Delete	Delete the currently selected objects without sending them to the Recycle Bin.

TABLE A.10 Shortcut Keys for Working with Internet Explorer

Press	To Do This
Alt	Display Classic menus.
Alt+Home	Go to the home page.
Alt+Left Arrow	Navigate backward to a previously displayed web page.
Alt+Right Arrow	Navigate forward to a previously displayed web page.
Ctrl+A	Select the entire web page.
Alt+C	Display the Favorites Center.
Ctrl+B	Display the Organize Favorites dialog box.
Ctrl+D	Add the current page to the Favorites list.
Ctrl+E	Activate the Instant Search box.
Ctrl+F	Display the Find dialog box.
Ctrl+H	Display the History list.
Ctrl+Shift+H	Pin the History list.
Ctrl+I	Display the Favorites list.
Ctrl+Shift+I	Pin the Favorites list.
Ctrl+J	Display the Feeds list.
Ctrl+Shift+J	Pin the Feeds list.
Ctrl+N	Open a new window.
Ctrl+T	Open a new tab.
Ctrl+W	Close the current tab.
Ctrl+Q	Display the Quick Tabs.
Ctrl+O	Display the Open dialog box.
Ctrl+P	Display the Print dialog box.
Ctrl+Tab	Cycle forward through the open tabs.
Ctrl+Shift+Tab	Cycle backward through the open tabs.
Ctrl++	Zoom in on the current web page.
Ctrl+–	Zoom out of the current web page.
Esc	Stop downloading the web page.
F4	Open the Address toolbar's drop-down list.
F5	Refresh the web page.
F11	Toggle between Full Screen mode and the regular window.
Spacebar	Scroll down one screen.
Shift+Spacebar	Scroll up one screen.
Shift+Tab	Cycle backward through the Address toolbar and the web page links.
Tab	Cycle forward through the web page links and the Address toolbar.

TABLE A.11 Shortcut Keys for Working with Windows Media Player

Press	To Do This
Ctrl+O	Open a media file.
Ctrl+U	Open a media URL.
Ctrl+P	Play or pause the current media.
Ctrl+S	Stop the current media.
Ctrl+B	Go to the previous track.
Ctrl+Shift+B	Rewind to the beginning of the media.
Ctrl+F	Go to the next track.
Ctrl+Shift+F	Fast-forward to the end of the media.
Ctrl+H	Toggle Shuffle playback.
Ctrl+T	Toggle Repeat playback.
Ctrl+M	Show the menu bar.
Ctrl+Shift+M	Auto-hide the menu bar.
Ctrl+N	Create a new playlist.
Ctrl+1	Switch to Full mode.
Ctrl+2	Switch to Skin mode.
Alt+1	Display video size at 50%.
Alt+2	Display video size at 100%.
Alt+3	Display video size at 200%.
Alt+Enter	Toggle Full Screen mode.
F3	Display the Add to Library dialog box.
F7	Mute sound.
F8	Decrease volume.
F9	Increase volume.

TABLE A.12 Shortcut Keys for DOSKEY

Press	To Do This
Command Recall Keys	
Alt+F7	Delete all the commands from the recall list.
Arrow keys	Cycle through the commands in the recall list.
F7	Display the entire recall list.
F8	Recall a command that begins with the letter or letters you've typed on the command line.
F9	Display the Line number: prompt. You then enter the number of the command (as displayed by F7) that you want.
Page Down	Recall the newest command in the list.
Page Up	Recall the oldest command in the list.

TABLE A.12 Continued

Press	To Do This
Command-Line Editing Keys	
Backspace	Delete the character to the left of the cursor.
Ctrl+End	Delete from the cursor to the end of the line.
Ctrl+Home	Delete from the cursor to the beginning of the line.
Ctrl+Left arrow	Move the cursor one word to the left.
Ctrl+Right arrow	Move the cursor one word to the right.
Delete	Delete the character over the cursor.
End	Move the cursor to the end of the line.
Home	Move the cursor to the beginning of the line.
Insert	Toggle `DOSKEY` between Insert mode (your typing is inserted between existing letters on the command line) and Overstrike mode (your typing replaces existing letters on the command line).
Left arrow	Move the cursor one character to the left.
Right arrow	Move the cursor one character to the right.

TABLE A.13 Windows Logo Key Shortcut Keys

Press	To Do This
Windows Logo	Open the Start menu.
Windows Logo+D	Minimize all open windows. Press Windows Logo+D again to restore the windows.
Windows Logo+E	Open Windows Explorer (Computer folder).
Windows Logo+F	Display a Search window.
Windows Logo+Ctrl+F	Find a computer.
Windows Logo+L	Lock the computer.
Windows Logo+M	Minimize all open windows, except those with open modal windows.
Windows Logo+Shift+M	Undo minimize all.
Windows Logo+R	Display the Run dialog box.
Windows Logo+U	Display the Ease of Access Center.
Windows Logo+F1	Display Windows Help.
Windows Logo+Break	Display the System window.
Windows Logo+Spacebar	Scroll down one page (supported only in certain applications, such as Internet Explorer).
Windows Logo+Shift+Spacebar	Scroll up one page (supported only in certain applications, such as Internet Explorer).
Windows Logo+Tab	Cycle through a 3D stack of running program windows.

TIP

If your keyboard doesn't have a Windows Logo key, you can remap an existing key to act as a Windows Logo key. The trick here is to tell Vista to take the built-in scancode of an existing key and convert it to the scancode associated with the Windows Logo key. For example, when you press the right Alt key, the hexadecimal scancode E038 is generated. The scancode associated with the right Windows Logo key is E05C. Therefore, you need to tell Vista that whenever it detects the scancode E038 after a right Alt keypress, that it should send to the system the code E05C, instead. This means that pressing the right Alt key will be the same thing as pressing the Windows Logo key.

To do this, open the Registry Editor and navigate to the following key:

```
HKLM\SYSTEM\CurrentControlSet\Control\Keyboard Layout
```

Select Edit, New, Binary Value, type **Scancode Map**, and press Enter. Open the Scancode Map setting and set its value to the following:

```
00 00 00 00 00 00 00 00 01 00 00 00 5C E0 38 E0
```

Reboot your computer to put the new key mapping into effect.

APPENDIX B

Using the Windows Vista Command Prompt

IN THIS APPENDIX

- Getting to Command Prompt
- Working with Command Prompt
- Customizing the Command-Line Window

In Internet circles, a **holy war** is a never-ending debate on the merits of one thing versus another, in which people use the same arguments over and over, and nobody's opinion budges even the slightest bit one way or the other. Common holy war topics include liberalism versus conservatism, pro-choice versus pro-life, and neatness versus sloppiness.

Operating systems cause frequent holy war skirmishes, with most battles pitting either Macintosh against Windows or Linux against Windows. Years ago (I realize I'm dating myself here), the mother of all operating system holy wars was DOS versus Windows, with correspondents devoting obscene amounts of time and energy extolling the virtues of one system and detailing the shortcomings of the other. Of course, *nobody* sings the praises of DOS any more, and few mourned its demise.

So, yes, DOS is dead, but **Command Prompt** is alive and well and adjusting nicely to its current role as just another Windows Vista accessory. Yes, it's entirely possible that you might go your entire Windows career without having to fire up a Command Prompt session. But if you do need Command Prompt, you must know a few things in order to get the most out of your command-line sessions. This appendix shows you how to squeeze the best and most reliable performance out of them under Windows Vista.

Getting to Command Prompt

To take advantage of Command Prompt and all of its many useful commands, you need to start a Command Prompt session. Windows Vista (as usual) offers a number of different ways to get to Command Prompt:

- Select Start, All Programs, Accessories, Command Prompt.
- Press Windows Logo+R (or select Start, All Programs, Accessories, Run), type **`cmd`** in the Run dialog box, and click OK.
- Create a shortcut for `%SystemRoot%\system32\cmd.exe` on your desktop (or some other convenient location, such as the taskbar's Quick Launch toolbar) and then launch the shortcut.
- Reboot your computer, press F8 to display Windows Vista's Advanced Options Menu, and select the Safe Mode with Command Prompt item.

NOTE

To learn more about the Advanced Options Menu, refer to the "Custom Startups with the Advanced Options Menu" section in Chapter 2, "Customizing and Troubleshooting the Windows Vista Startup."

It's also possible to configure Windows Vista's Folder file type to open Command Prompt in Windows Explorer's current folder. To see how, refer to the "Example: Opening Command Prompt in the Current Folder" section in Chapter 4, "Mastering File Types."

Preventing Command Prompt Access

To prevent a user from accessing Command Prompt, log on as that user, press Windows Logo+R (or select Start, All Programs, Accessories, Run), type **`gpedit.msc`**, click OK, and then enter your UAC credentials to launch the Group Policy editor. Open the User Configuration, Administrative Templates, System branch and then enable the Prevent Access to the Command Prompt policy.

Using `CMD.EXE` Switches

For the methods that use the `CMD.EXE` executable, you can specify extra switches after the `CMD.EXE` filename. Most of these switches aren't particularly useful, so let's start with the simplest syntax that you'll use most often:

```
CMD [[/S] [/C ¦ /K] command]
```

`/S`	Strips out the first and last quotation marks from the *command*, provided that the first quotation mark is the first character in *command*
`/C`	Executes the *command* and then terminates
`/K`	Executes the *command* and remains running
command	The command to run

For example, if your ISP provides you with a dynamic IP address, you can often solve some connection problems by asking the IP for a fresh address. You do that by running the command `ipconfig /renew` in Command Prompt. In this case, you don't need the Command Prompt window to remain open, so you can specify the `/C` switch to shut down the Command Prompt session automatically after the `IPCONFIG` utility finishes:

```
cmd /c ipconfig /renew
```

On the other hand, you often either want to see the results of the command, or you want to leave the Command Prompt window open so that you can run other commands. In those cases, you use the `/K` switch. For example, the following command runs the `SET` utility (which displays the current values of the Windows Vista environment variables) and then leaves the Command Prompt session running:

```
cmd /k set
```

Here's the full syntax of `CMD.EXE`:

```
CMD [/A ¦ /U] [/Q] [/D] [/T:bf] [/E:ON ¦ /E:OFF] [/F:ON ¦ /F:OFF]
➥[/V:ON ¦ /V:OFF] [[/S] [/C ¦ /K] command]
```

`/Q` Turns echo off.

`/D` Disables the execution of `AutoRun` commands from the Registry. These are commands that run automatically when you start any Command Prompt session and you can find the settings here:

```
HKLM\Software\Microsoft\Command Processor\AutoRun
HKCU\Software\Microsoft\Command Processor\AutoRun
```

TIP

If you do note see an `AutoRun` setting in one or both keys, select the key, select File, New, String Value, type **`AutoRun`**, and press Enter.

TIP

The `AutoRun` Registry settings are handy if you always run a particular command at the beginning of each Command Prompt session. If you run multiple commands to launch a session, you can add those commands to either `AutoRun` setting. In that case, you must separate each command with the command separator string: &&. For example, to run the `IPCONFIG` and `SET` utilities at the start of each Command Prompt session, change the value of an `AutoRun` setting to the following:

```
ipconfig&&set
```

B

/A	Converts the output of internal commands to a pipe or file to the ANSI character set.
/U	Converts the output of internal commands to a pipe or file to the Unicode character set.
/T:*bf*	Sets the foreground and background colors of the Command Prompt window, where *f* is the foreground color and *b* is the background color. Both *f* and *b* are hexadecimal digits that specify the color as follows:

0	Black	8	Gray
1	Blue	9	Light Blue
2	Green	A	Light Green
3	Aqua	B	Light Aqua
4	Red	C	Light Red
5	Purple	D	Light Purple
6	Yellow	E	Light Yellow
7	White	F	Bright White

TIP

You can also set the foreground and background colors during a Command Prompt session by using the `COLOR` *bf* command, where *b* and *f* are hexadecimal digits specifying the colors you want. To revert to the default Command Prompt colors, run `COLOR` without the *bf* parameter. For more information, see the "Specifying the Command Prompt Colors" section later in this appendix.

/E:ON	Enables **command extensions**, which are extra features added to the following commands (in Command Prompt, type the command name followed by a space and /? to see the extensions):

ASSOC	IF
CALL	MD or MKDIR
CD or CHDIR	POPD
COLOR	PROMPT
DEL or ERASE	PUSHD
ENDLOCAL	SET
FOR	SETLOCAL
FTYPE	SHIFT
GOTO	START

/E:OFF	Disables command extensions.

`/F:ON` Turns on file and directory name completion, which enables you to press special key combinations to scroll through a list of files or subdirectories in the current directory that match the characters you've already typed. For example, suppose that the current directory contains files named `budget2005.doc`, `budget2006.doc`, and `budget2007.doc`. If you type **`start budget`** in a Command Prompt session started with `/F:ON`, pressing Ctrl+F tells Windows Vista to display the first file (or subdirectory) in the current directory with a name that starts with `budget`. Pressing Ctrl+F again displays the next file with a name that starts with `budget`, and so on. You can do the same thing with just subdirectory names by pressing Ctrl+D instead.

TIP

You don't need to start Command Prompt with the `/F:ON` switch to use file and directory name completion. Command Prompt offers a similar feature called **AutoComplete** that's turned on by default. At the prompt, type the first letter or two of a file or subfolder name and then press the Tab key to see the first object that matches your text in the current folder. Keep pressing Tab to see other matching objects. If, for some reason, you prefer to turn off AutoComplete, pull down the Command Prompt window's control menu (right-click the title bar), select Defaults, and then deactivate the AutoComplete check box in the Options tab.

`/F:OFF` Turns off file and directory name completion.

`/V:ON` Enables delayed environment variable expansion using `!` as the delimiter: `!`*`var`*`!`, where *`var`* is an environment variable. This is useful for batch files in which you want to delay the expansion of an environment variable. Normally, Windows Vista expands all environment variables to their current values when it reads the contents of a batch file. With delayed expansion enabled, Windows Vista doesn't expand a particular environment variable within a batch file until it executes the statement containing that variable.

NOTE

For an example of how delayed environment variable expansion works in a batch file, see the "Using Delayed Environment Variable Expansion" section in Appendix C, "Automating Windows Vista with Batch Files."

`/V:OFF` Disables delayed environment expansion.

`/S` Strips out the first and last quotation marks from *`command`*, provided the first quotation mark is the first character in *`command`*.

`/C` Executes the *`command`* and then terminates.

`/K` Executes the *`command`* and remains running.

`command` The command to run.

Running Commands

Although many of the Windows Vista accessories provide more powerful and easier-to-use replacements for nearly all commands, a few commands still have no Windows Vista peer. These include the REN command, as well as the many Command Prompt–specific commands, such as CLS, DOSKEY, and PROMPT.

How you run a command depends on whether it's an internal or external command, and on what you want Windows Vista to do after the command is finished. For an internal command, you have two choices: You can either enter the command in Command Prompt or include it as a parameter with CMD.EXE. As you saw earlier, you can run internal commands with CMD.EXE by specifying either the /C switch or the /K switch. If you use the /C switch, the command executes and then the Command Prompt session shuts down. This is fine if you're running a command for which you don't need to see the results. For example, if you want to redirect the contents of drive C's root folder in the text file root.txt, entering the following command in the Run dialog box (for example) will do the job:

```
cmd.exe /c dir c:\ > root.txt
```

On the other hand, you might want to examine the output of a command before the Command Prompt window closes. In that case, you need to use the /K switch. The following command runs DIR on drive C's root folder and then drops you off in Command Prompt:

```
cmd.exe /k dir c:\
```

For an external command, you have three choices: enter the command in Command Prompt, enter the command by itself from within Windows Vista, or include it as a parameter with CMD.EXE.

NOTE

When you use Command Prompt or the Run dialog box to start an external Command Prompt command, you don't need to use the command's full pathname. For example, the full pathname for mem.exe is %SystemRoot%\System32\mem.exe, but to run this command, you need only enter **mem**. The reason is that the %SystemRoot%\System32 subfolder is part of the PATH statement for each Command Prompt session.

To enter a command by itself from within Windows Vista means launching the command's file in Explorer, entering the command in the Run dialog box, or creating a shortcut for the command. For the latter two methods, you can embellish the command by adding parameters and switches. The problem with this method is that Windows Vista automatically closes the Command Prompt window when the command completes. To change this behavior, follow these steps:

1. Find the command's executable file in the `%SystemRoot%\System32` folder.
2. Right-click the executable file and then click Properties to display the command's properties sheet.
3. Display the Program tab. (Note that this tab doesn't appear for all commands.)
4. Deactivate the Close on Exit check box.
5. Click OK.

Adding Parameters and Switches to a Command Prompt Command

If you use Command Prompt or the Run dialog box to enter your Command Prompt commands, you can easily tack on any extra parameters or switches you want to use to modify the command. If, however, you start an external command from Explorer, the command runs without any options. To modify how an external command operates, you can add parameters and switches by following these steps:

CAUTION

Vista sets up the `%SystemRoot%\System32` folder as read-only for security purposes. This means that you cannot change the properties of any file in the folder, including Command Prompt stalwarts such as `MEM` and `EDIT`. To modify the properties of these programs, you must copy them to a folder within your user profile.

1. Use Windows Explorer to find the command's executable file.
2. Right-click the executable file and then click Properties to display the command's properties sheet.
3. Display the Program tab.
4. In the Cmd Line text box, add a space after the command and then add your parameters and switches. Figure B.1 shows an example.
5. Click OK.

Program Information Files

After you've modified a command's properties sheet, Windows Vista creates a **PIF**—a **program information file**—for the command. This is a separate file that has the same name as the command, but with a `.pif` extension. Unfortunately, Windows Explorer always hides the `.pif` extension. You can recognize the PIF, however, if you display Explorer in Details view: The PIF says `Shortcut to MS-DOS Program` in the Type column. If you prefer to display the `.pif` extension, head for the following Registry key:

```
HKCR\piffile
```

Rename the `NeverShowExt` setting to `AlwaysShowExt` (or something similar). When you next restart your computer, Windows Vista will show the `.pif` extensions.

B

FIGURE B.1 Use the Cmd Line text box to append extra parameters to an external command.

If you want to vary the parameters each time you run the command, add a space and a question mark (?) to the end of the command, like so:

```
%UserProfile%\mem.exe ?
```

Each time you run the command (whether from Explorer or from the Run dialog box), Windows Vista displays a dialog box similar to the one shown in Figure B.2. Use the text box to type your switches and options, and then click OK.

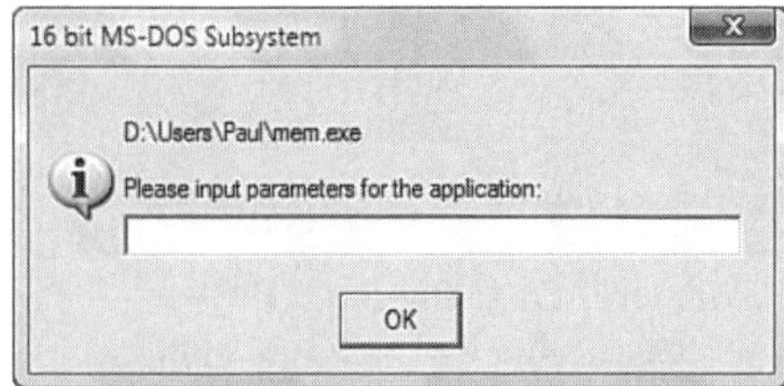

FIGURE B.2 If you add a question mark (?) to the end of the command, Windows Vista displays a dialog box similar to this one each time you run the command.

Working with Command Prompt

When you have your Command Prompt session up and running, you can run commands and programs, create and launch batch files, perform file maintenance, and so on. If you haven't used Command Prompt since the days of DOS, you'll find that the Windows Vista Command Prompt offers a few extra command-line goodies. The next few sections highlight some of the more useful ones.

CAUTION

When you're working in Command Prompt, be warned that any files you delete aren't sent to the Recycle Bin, but are purged from your system.

Working with Long Filenames

Unlike the old DOS, you can work with long filenames within a Windows Vista Command Prompt session. If you want to use long filenames in a command, however, you need to be careful. If the long filename contains a space or any other character that's illegal in an 8.3 filename, you need to surround the long name with quotation marks. For example, if you run the following command, Windows Vista will tell you that `The syntax of the command is incorrect`:

```
copy Fiscal Year 2006.doc Fiscal Year 2007.doc
```

Instead, you need to enter this command as follows:

```
copy "Fiscal Year 2006.doc" "Fiscal Year 2007.doc"
```

Long filenames are, of course, long, so they tend to be a pain to type in Command Prompt. Fortunately, Windows Vista offers a few methods for knocking long names down to size:

- In Explorer, drag a folder or file and drop it inside the Command Prompt window. Windows Vista pastes the full pathname of the folder or file to the end of the prompt.
- In Explorer, hold down Shift, right-click the folder or file, and then click Copy as Path to copy the object's full pathname to the Clipboard. Use the technique shown later in the "Pasting Text to the Command Prompt" section to paste the pathname into your Command Prompt session.
- Create application-specific and document-specific paths, as described in the "Creating Application-Specific Paths" section of Chapter 5, "Installing and Running Applications."

B

- If you're trying to run a program that resides in a folder with a long name, add the folder to the PATH. This technique enables you to run programs from the folder without having to specify the full pathname. (I talk about this in more detail in the next section.)
- Use the SUBST command to substitute a virtual drive letter for a long pathname. For example, the following command substitutes drive Z for the current user's Accessories folder:

```
subst z: "%UserProfile%\AppData\Roaming\Microsoft\Windows\Start Menu\
➥Programs\Accessories"
```

Changing Folders Faster

You probably know by now that you use the CD (change directory) command to change to a different folder on the current drive. However, Command Prompt has a few short forms you can use to save time.

You might know that both Command Prompt and Windows Vista use the dot symbol (.) to represent the current folder, and the double-dot symbol (..) to represent its parent folder. You can combine the CD command and the dot notation to jump immediately to a folder's parent folder, or even higher.

To make this more concrete, suppose that the current folder is C:\Animal\Mammal\Dolphin. Table B.1 demonstrates the techniques you can use to navigate to this folder's parent, grandparent (two levels up), and great-grandparent (three levels up) folders.

TABLE B.1 Combining the CD Command with Dot Notation

Current Folder	Command	New Folder
C:\Animal\Mammal\Dolphin	Cd..	C:\Animal\Mammal
C:\Animal\Mammal\Dolphin	Cd..\..	C:\Animal
C:\Animal\Mammal\Dolphin	Cd..\..\..	C:\
C:\Animal\Mammal\Dolphin	Cd..\Baboon	
C:\Animal\Mammal\Baboon		

TIP

If you want to return to the root folder of any drive, type **cd** and press Enter.

Taking Advantage of DOSKEY

Vista loads the DOSKEY utility by default when you start any Command Prompt session. This useful little program brings a number of advantages to your command-line work:

- You can recall previously entered commands with just a keystroke or two.
- You can enter multiple commands on a single line.
- You can edit commands instead of retyping them.
- You can create your own commands with DOSKEY macros.

In this section I'll focus on DOSKEY macros, but I'll begin with a quick introduction to the other DOSKEY features.

Recalling Command Lines

The simplest DOSKEY feature is command recall. DOSKEY maintains a **command history buffer** that keeps a list of the commands you enter. To scroll through your previously entered commands in reverse order, press the Up Arrow key; when you've done that at least once, you can change direction and run through the commands in the order you entered them by pressing the Down Arrow key. To rerun a command, use the arrow keys to find it and then press Enter.

TIP

If you don't want to enter any commands from the history buffer, press Esc to get a clean command line.

Table B.2 lists all the command-recall keys you can use.

TABLE B.2 DOSKEY Command-Recall Keys

Press	To
Up Arrow	Recall the previous command in the buffer.
Down Arrow	Recall the next command in the buffer.
Page Up	Recall the oldest command in the buffer.
Page Down	Recall the newest command in the buffer.
F7	Display the entire command buffer.
Alt+F7	Delete all commands from the buffer.
F8	Have DOSKEY recall a command that begins with the letter or letters you've typed on the command line.
F9	Have DOSKEY prompt you for a command list number (you can see the numbers with the F7 key). Type the number and press Enter to recall the command.

TIP

The command history buffer holds 50 commands, by default. If you need a larger buffer, run DOSKEY with the /LISTSIZE=*buffers* switch, where *buffers* is the number of commands you want to store. For example, to change the buffer size to 100, enter the following command:

```
doskey /listize=100 /reinstall
```

Entering Multiple Commands on a Single Line

DOSKEY enables you to run multiple commands on a single line. To do this, insert the characters && between commands. For example, a common task is to change to a different drive and then run a directory listing. Normally, you'd do this with two separate commands:

```
e:

dir
```

With DOSKEY, however, you can do it on one line, like so:

```
e:&&dir
```

TIP

You can enter as many commands as you like on a single line, but just remember that the total length of the line can't be more than 8,191 characters (which should be plenty!).

Editing Command Lines

Rather than simply rerunning a previously typed command, you might need to run the command again with slightly different switches or parameters. Rather than retyping the whole thing, DOSKEY enables you to edit any recalled command line. You use various keys to move the cursor to the offending letters and replace them. Table B.3 summarizes DOSKEY's command-line editing keys.

TABLE B.3 DOSKEY Command-Line Editing Keys

Press	To
Left Arrow	Move the cursor one character to the left.
Right Arrow	Move the cursor one character to the right.
Ctrl+Left Arrow	Move the cursor one word to the left.
Ctrl+Right Arrow	Move the cursor one word to the right.
Home	Move the cursor to the beginning of the line.
End	Move the cursor to the end of the line.
Delete	Delete the character over the cursor.

TABLE B.3 Continued

Press	To
Backspace	Delete the character to the left of the cursor.
Ctrl+Home	Delete from the cursor to the beginning of the line.
Ctrl+End	Delete from the cursor to the end of the line.
Insert	Toggle DOSKEY between Insert mode (your typing is inserted between existing letters on the command line) and Overstrike mode (your typing replaces existing letters on the command line).

Learning About DOSKEY Macros

Perhaps the most powerful feature you get with DOSKEY is the ability to combine one or more DOS commands into a single easy-to-use command called a **macro**. If this sounds like a batch file, you're close. DOSKEY macros and batch files are similar, but they differ in some important ways:

Macro Pros:

- Macros are stored in memory and batch files are stored on a disk. This means that macros execute much faster than batch files.
- Batch files must have legal filenames, but macro names can include the following symbols normally banned from regular filenames:

  ```
  * + [ ] : ; " , . ? /
  ```

- You can use macros to replace existing commands.

Macro Cons:

- Macros must be no longer than 8,191 characters, but batch files can be any length.
- There are no commands or symbols to suppress command echoing (that is, seeing each command onscreen before they execute).
- There is no macro equivalent for the GOTO and IF batch file commands.
- You have to reenter macro definitions each time you start your computer. (However, you can automate this by using a **macro library**, a batch file that stores your macro definitions. I'll explain all this later in this section.)

In general, you should use macros as substitutes for complex commands or to combine two or more commands into a single command. You should use batch files for more sophisticated tasks.

Creating DOSKEY Macros To create a DOSKEY macro, enter a command that has the following form:

DOSKEY *macroname=commands*

B

Here, *macroname* is the name of the macro and *commands* is the list of commands you want the macro to execute.

As an example, consider the following command:

```
dir /ogn /p
```

This displays a directory listing with the filenames in alphabetical order, with the subdirectories grouped first and a pause after every screen. Instead of typing this command every time, you could define a macro called SDIR instead. Here's the command that'll do it:

```
doskey sdir=dir /ogn /p
```

After you've defined a macro, you can use it like any other command. For this example, just type **sdir** and press Enter, and Command Prompt displays the sorted directory listing.

TIP

If you need to stop a running macro, press Ctrl+C.

When you're defining a macro that contains more than one command, you need to be a little careful. For example, suppose that you want to create a macro called CDD that changes to drive E and then gives you a DIR listing. Your first instinct might be to enter the command

doskey cdd=e: && dir

However, when Command Prompt sees the command separator symbol, it assumes that you're trying to run two commands: one to define the DOSKEY macro CDD and another to display a DIR listing. To avoid this confusion, use $T (or $t) instead of && inside your macro definition. Here's the revised command:

```
DOSKEY cdd=a: $t dir
```

NOTE

To make the commands easier to read, I've included spaces before and after the $T symbol. If you prefer, you can leave these spaces out when defining your own macros.

Table B.4 lists all the macro-definition symbols you can use.

TABLE B.4 DOSKEY Macro-Definition Symbols

Use	To Replace
$B or $b	Pipe symbol (|)
$G or $g	Redirect output symbol (>)
GG or gg	Append output symbol (>>)
$L or $l	Redirect input symbol (<)
$T or $t	Command separator ( )
$$	Dollar sign ($)

TIP

To delete a macro definition, use the following format:

DOSKEY *macroname*=

Using Replaceable Parameters in Macros In Appendix C's "Using Parameters for Batch File Flexibility" section, I show you how to use replaceable parameters inside batch files. Macros, too, can use replaceable parameters. Instead of the symbols %1 through %9 that are available in a batch file, use the symbols $1 through $9 for macros.

For example, the CDD macro introduced in the last section is okay, but it lacks flexibility. Instead, change the macro to the following:

```
doskey cdd=$1 $t dir
```

If you now type, say, **cdd d:**, DOSKEY replaces $1 with d: and runs the macro accordingly.

Macro Examples To get you started, this section takes you through a few of my favorite DOSKEY macros.

The first example uses the fact that, as mentioned earlier, Windows Vista represents the current directory's parent with the double dot symbol (..). One way this comes in handy is to use the following command to change quickly to the parent directory:

```
cd..
```

This is short as it is, but I prefer to use a macro called UP, which I define as follows:

```
doskey up=cd..
```

A similar macro is UP2, which I use any time I need to move up two directory levels:

```
doskey up2=cd..\cd..
```

So, for example, if you're in the Documents\Letters\Business subdirectory, entering the UP2 command takes you to the Documents directory.

Suppose that you also have a subdirectory called Documents\Letters\Personal and you want to move from the Business subdirectory over to Personal. Normally, you have to use the following command:

```
cd Documents\Letters\Personal
```

However, both Business and Personal have the same parent directory (Letters), so you can create a macro called OVER as follows:

```
doskey over=cd..\$1
```

After you've defined this macro, you can move from Business to Personal by entering the following command:

```
over personal
```

TIP

To see a list of all your currently defined macros, use the command DOSKEY /MACROS.

Have you ever lost a file on your hard drive? You know it's there somewhere, but you can't remember where it is. It's happened to me more times than I've had hot dinners, so I use a macro called ? to help out. Here's the definition:

```
doskey ?=dir \$1 /s /b
```

The /S switch causes Command Prompt to search all your subdirectories, and the /B switch displays only the filename, if one is found.

My final macro definition shows that you can use macros to replace existing commands (this is called **command aliasing**). For example, the DEL command is safer if you use it with the /P switch (Command Prompt asks you to confirm each deletion). You can actually create a macro called DEL with the following definition:

```
doskey del=del $1 /p
```

Macros take precedence over commands, so whenever you use DEL, it's the macro that executes, not the command. (If you need to run the command, you can do so by preceding it with a space.)

TIP

If you're setting up a computer for a novice user, use macros to replace dangerous commands such as FORMAT or RECOVER. Instead of running the command, just display a message telling the user the peril they're in, like so:

```
doskey format=ECHO Sorry, the FORMAT command is not available.
```

Creating a Macro Library One of the problems with macros is that your definitions are lost whenever you turn off your computer. The solution is to create a **macro library**—a batch file that contains all your macro definitions. Follow these steps to create a macro library:

1. Type the following command and press Enter (if you don't have a BATCH directory, substitute the directory where you keep your batch files):

   ```
   doskey /macros > macros.bat
   ```

2. Command Prompt redirects the output of the command into a batch file called macros.bat. Now load macros.bat into your text editor.
3. For each macro definition, add DOSKEY to the beginning of the line (be sure that you leave a space between DOSKEY and the definition).

Now, whenever you need to load your DOSKEY macros, just run the macros.bat batch file.

TIP

You'll probably need to edit your macro library quite often to remove macros you never use and add new ones. To make this chore easier, here's another macro that loads the macro library into Notepad and then runs the batch file when you're done:

```
doskey editlib=start notepad macros.bat $t macros
```

Note that you'll likely have to include the path where you've stored macros.bat to ensure that Notepad can find it. Also, be sure to run the doskey /macros > macros.bat command again right after you define the EDITLIB macro so that EdITLIB is added to the library.

Starting Applications from Command Prompt

Command Prompt isn't just for running commands. You can also use it to start applications, as described in the next two sections.

Starting 16-Bit Applications

On the odd chance that you still use 16-bit programs, you need to either change to the drive and folder where the program resides and enter the executable file's primary name from there, or enter the executable file's full pathname from the current folder. There are two situations in which you don't have to change folders or use the full pathname:

- If the program's executable file is in the current folder
- If the folder in which the program's executable file resides is part of the PATH statement

If you enter only the primary name of an executable file, Command Prompt first searches the current folder for a file that combines your primary name with an extension of .com, .exe, .bat, or .cmd. If it doesn't find such a file, it searches the folders listed in the PATH statement. Recall that the PATH statement is a series of folder names separated by semicolons (;). The default PATH for a Command Prompt session is this:

```
%SystemRoot%;%SystemRoot%\system32;%SystemRoot%\system32\Wbem
```

This is stored in an environment variable called PATH, so you can easily add new folders to the PATH right from the command prompt. For example, suppose that you have a DOS program that resides in the C:\Program Files\Dosapp folder. To start the program without having to change folders or specify the pathname, use the following command to add this folder to the PATH statement (%path% represents the PATH environment variable):

```
set path=%path%;"c:\program files\dosapp"
```

Starting Windows Applications

You can also use the Command Prompt to start Windows applications, launch documents, and even open folder windows. As with DOS programs, you start a Windows application by entering the name of its executable file.

This works fine if the executable file resides in the main Windows Vista folder because that folder is part of the PATH. But most Windows Vista applications (and even some Windows Vista accessories) store their files in a separate folder and don't modify the PATH to point to these folders. Instead, as you learned in Chapter 5, the Registry has an AppPaths key that tells Windows Vista where to find an application's files. Command Prompt can't use the Registry-based application paths directly, but there's a Windows Vista command that can. This command is START, and it uses the following syntax:

```
START ["title"] [/Dpath] [/I] [/MIN] [/MAX] [/SEPARATE ¦ /SHARED]
[/LOW ¦ /NORMAL ¦ /HIGH ¦ /REALTIME ¦ /ABOVENORMAL ¦ /BELOWNORMAL]
[AFFINITY hex value] [/WAIT] [/B] [filename] [parameters]
```

"*title*"	Specifies the title to display in Command Prompt's window title bar.
D*path*	Specifies the program's startup folder.
/B	Starts the program without creating a new window.
/I	Tells Windows Vista that the new Command Prompt environment will be the original environment passed to cmd.exe and not the current environment.
/MIN	Starts the program minimized.
/MAX	Starts the program maximized.
SEPARATE	Starts a 16-bit Windows program in a separate memory space.
SHARED	Starts a 16-bit Windows program in a shared memory space.
LOW	Starts the program using the IDLE priority class.

`NORMAL`	Starts the program using the NORMAL priority class.
`HIGH`	Starts the program using the HIGH priority class.
`REALTIME`	Starts the program using the REALTIME priority class.
`ABOVENORMAL`	Starts the program using the ABOVENORMAL priority class.
`BELOWNORMAL`	Starts the program using the BELOWNORMAL priority class.
`AFFINITY`	Starts the program with the specified processor affinity mask, expressed as a hexadecimal number. (On a multiprocessor system, the affinity mask indicates which processor you want the program to use. This prevents Vista from moving the program's execution threads from one processor to another, which can degrade performance.)
`/WAIT`	Waits until the program has finished before returning to Command Prompt.
`filename`	Specifies the name of the executable file or document. If you enter a document name, be sure to include the extension so that Windows Vista can figure out the file type.
`parameters`	Specifies options or switches that modify the operation of the program.

When you use `START` to launch a program, Windows Vista checks not only the current folder and the `PATH`, but also the Registry. For the Registry, Windows Vista looks for an `AppPaths` setting or a file type (if you entered the name of a document). For example, if you type **`wordpad`** and press Enter at the Command Prompt, you get a `Bad command or file name` error (unless you happen to be in the `%Program Files%\Windows NT\Accessories` folder). If, however, you enter **`start wordpad`**, WordPad launches successfully.

NOTE

The `START` command's `/WAIT` switch is useful in batch files. If you launch a program from within a batch file by using `START /WAIT`, the batch file pauses while the program runs. This enables you, for example, to test for some condition (such as an `ERRORLEVEL` code) after the program has completed its work.

Sharing Data Between the Command Prompt and Windows Applications

Command Prompt sessions (as well 16-bit programs) don't know about the Clipboard, so they don't support the standard cut, copy, and paste techniques. However, there are methods you can use to share data between the Command Prompt (or a 16-bit program) and Windows applications. I spell them out in the next few sections.

Copying Text from the Command Prompt

The best way to copy text from the Command Prompt or a 16-bit program is to highlight the text you want and then copy it. The following procedure takes you through the required steps:

1. If you're using a 16-bit application, place it in a window (if it isn't already) by pressing Alt+Enter.

NOTE

If you're using a 16-bit application that has a graphics mode, copying a section of the screen will copy a graphic image of the text, not the text itself. If you want text only, make sure that the program is running in Character mode before you continue.

2. Make sure that the text you want to copy is visible onscreen.
3. Pull down the window's control menu and select Edit, Mark to put the window into Select mode. (You can also right-click the title bar and then select Edit, Mark.)
4. Use the mouse or keyboard to select the data you want to copy.
5. Pull down the window's control menu and select Edit, Copy to copy the selected data to the Clipboard. (You can also either press Enter or right-click the title bar and then select Edit, Copy.)
6. Switch to the Windows application you want to use as the destination and position the insertion point where you want the copied data to appear.
7. Select Edit, Paste.

TIP

If you have a lot of text to copy, you might find it easier to activate Windows Vista's QuickEdit option. QuickEdit mode leaves the 16-bit program's window in Select mode permanently so that you can select text anytime you like. (The downside, however, is that you can no longer use the mouse to manipulate the Command Prompt program itself.) To enable QuickEdit, pull down the window's control menu and select Properties to open the properties sheet for the program. In the Options tab, activate the QuickEdit Mode check box.

Pasting Text to the Command Prompt

If you've sent some text to the Clipboard from a Windows application, it's possible to copy the text into a Command Prompt session or 16-bit program.

First, position the Command Prompt cursor at the spot where you want the pasted text to appear. Then pull down the window's control menu and select Edit, Paste (or right-click the title bar and then select Edit, Paste).

TIP

You might encounter problems pasting text from the Clipboard to your Command Prompt program. For example, you might see garbage characters or some characters might be missing. This probably means that Windows Vista is sending the characters too fast, and the Command Prompt program can't handle the onslaught. To solve this problem, find the 16-bit program's executable file, right-click the file, and then click Properties. Then display the Misc tab and deactivate the Fast Pasting check box. This tells Windows Vista to hold its horses and send the characters at a slower rate.

Sharing Graphics Between 16-Bit and Windows Programs

Unlike with Windows-to-Windows transfers, there's no clean way to transfer graphics between 16-bit and Windows programs.

If you have a 16-bit graphic you'd like to place on the Clipboard, display the program in a window, adjust the window so that the image is visible, and then press Alt+Print Screen. Windows Vista copies an image of the entire window to the Clipboard. You could then paste this image into a graphics program and remove the extraneous window elements.

Unfortunately, the Clipboard can't handle graphics transfers from a Windows application to a 16-bit program. Your only choice here is to save the image in a graphics format that the 16-bit program understands and then open this file in the 16-bit program.

Customizing the Command-Line Window

If you figure you'll be spending a reasonable amount of time using Command Prompt or 16-bit or command-line programs, you'll want to configure the windows so that you're comfortable with how they work and display. The next few sections take you through the various options available for customizing the Command Prompt window, as well as the windows used by external command-line programs and 16-bit applications.

Customizing the Command Prompt Window

Windows Vista's Command Prompt utility has its own set of customization options and settings, so I'll discuss those first. To view these options, you have three choices:

- If you want your changes to apply to all future Command Prompt sessions, open a Command Prompt window, pull down its control menu, and then select Defaults. This displays the Console Windows Properties dialog box. Note that the changes you make in this dialog box do *not* apply to the current Command Prompt session, but Windows Vista does apply them to all future sessions.
- If you want your changes to apply only to a specific Command Prompt shortcut (such as Start, All Programs, Accessories, Command Prompt), right-click the Command Prompt shortcut icon, and then click Properties.
- If you want your changes to apply to only the current Command Prompt session, pull down the control menu and select Properties.

In the properties sheet that appears are four tabs that offer options specific to Command Prompt: Options, Font, Layout, and Colors.

Setting Command Prompt Options

The Options tab, shown in Figure B.3, offers a mixed-bag of settings that control various aspects of the Command Prompt window and operation:

Cursor Size	Use these options to set the size of the cursor that Command Prompt uses to indicate where the next character that you type will appear.
Display Options (shortcut Properties dialog box only)	The Full Screen and Window options determine whether Command Prompt starts full screen or in a window.
Command History	These options control how Command Prompt stores the commands you enter: ▶ Buffer Size—Use this spin box to specify the number of commands that DOSKEY stores in its command history buffer. ▶ Number of Buffers—Use this spin box to set the maximum number of Command Prompt processes that can maintain command history buffers. ▶ Discard Old Duplicates—Activate this check box to have Command Prompt automatically discard duplicate commands from the buffer. This enables you to store more unique commands in the buffer. However, if you often rerun a series of commands, activating this option could cause problems by discarding one more commands in the series.
QuickEdit Mode	When this check box is active, you can select program text with the mouse. I explained how this works earlier in this appendix.
Insert Mode	When this check box is activated, DOSKEY starts in its Insert mode, where your typing is inserted at the cursor. If you deactivate this check box, DOSKEY switches to Overstrike mode.
AutoComplete (Console Windows Properties dialog box only)	When this check box is activated, Command Prompt enables you to complete file and folder names by pressing the Tab key.

FIGURE B.3 Use Command Prompt's Options tab to control various aspects of the program's look and feel.

Changing the Command Prompt Font

The font size Windows Vista uses to display text in a Command Prompt window isn't set in stone. You're free to make the font size larger or smaller, depending on your tastes. The Font tab, shown in Figure B.4 offers the following options:

Size	Use this list to select the font size you want to use (or Auto).
Font	Select either Raster Fonts or Lucida Console. If you select the latter, you can also activate the Bold Fonts check box to get bold text.

As you make changes to the Font, the Window Preview area shows you how the new Command Prompt window will appear, and the Selected Font preview area shows you what the font looks like.

Customizing the Command Prompt Layout

You can control the Command Prompt window's dimensions, position, and screen buffer size using the settings in the Layout tab, shown in Figure B.5:

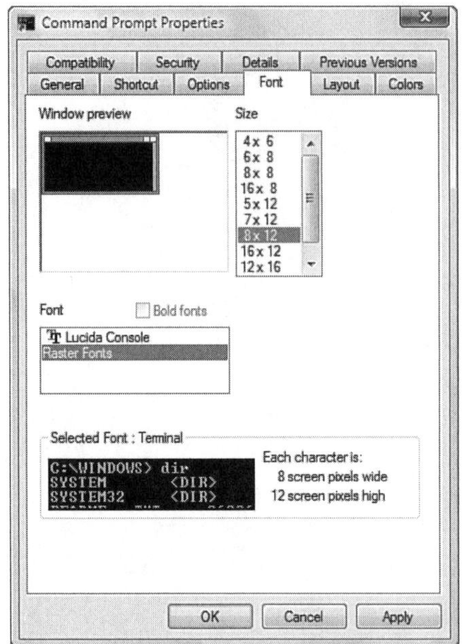

FIGURE B.4 Use the Font tab to select the font size to use in the Command Prompt window.

Screen Buffer Size
: The **screen buffer** is a memory area that stores the lines that have appeared in the Command Prompt window and since scrolled off the screen. This is useful if you run a command that displays more lines than the Command Prompt window can hold. You can use the vertical scrollbar to scroll up and see the lines you missed. You shouldn't need to change the default Width value (80 characters), but you can set the Height value up to 9,999 lines.

Window Size
: Use the Width and Height spin boxes to set the dimensions, in lines, of the window. Note, however, that Windows Vista cannot resize the window to anything larger than what your screen can hold.

Window Position
: Use the Left and Top spin boxes to set the location, in pixels, of the top-left corner of the Command Prompt window. You have to deactivate the Let System Position Window check box to enable these spin boxes.

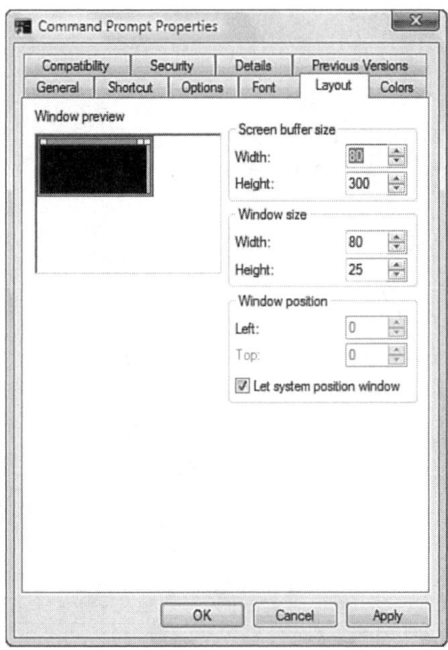

FIGURE B.5 Use the Layout tab to customize the Command Prompt window's dimensions, position, and screen buffer size.

Specifying the Command Prompt Colors

You saw earlier that you can run `cmd.exe` with the `/T:fb` switch to control the foreground (text) and background colors of the Command Prompt window. You can also use the `COLOR` utility to change the colors while you're in mid-session. An alternative to these methods is the Colors tab, shown in Figure B.6. You can set colors not only for the screen, but also for the pop-up text and background. (An example of a pop-up is the window that appears when you press F7 at the command line to see a list of the commands in the `DOSKEY` history buffer.) Activate one of the four options—Screen Text, Screen Background, Pop-up Text, or Pop-up Background—and then use either of the following techniques to set the color:

- Click one of the preset color boxes
- Use the Red, Green, and Blue spin boxes to set a custom color

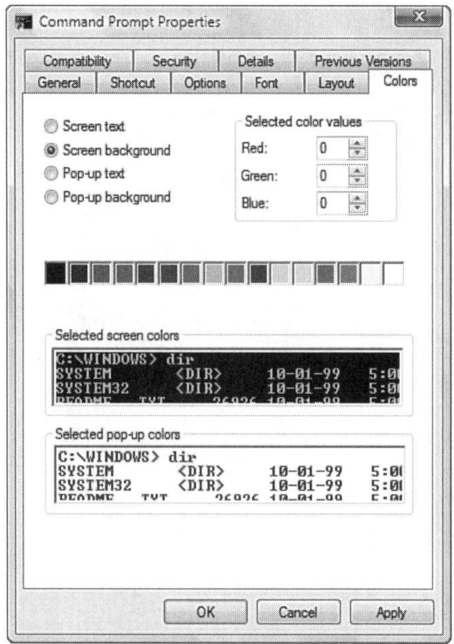

FIGURE B.6 Use the Colors tab to set the foreground and background colors of the Command Prompt screen and pop-ups.

Customizing Other Command-Line Windows

A 16-bit or command-line program, like any Windows Vista object, has various properties that you can manipulate to fine-tune how the program works. To display the properties sheet for a 16-bit or command-line program, you have three choices:

- In Explorer, select the program's executable file and select File, Properties; or right-click the file, and select Properties.
- If the program's window is open, you can get to the properties sheet from the keyboard by pressing Alt+Spacebar and selecting Properties from the control menu that appears.

NOTE

Most of the properties I discuss affect the command-line program only while it's running in a window. If your program is running full screen, press Alt+Enter to place it in a window. To change back to full-screen mode, press Alt+Enter again.

NOTE

To learn about the settings in the properties sheet's Compatibility tab, refer to the "Understanding Application Compatibility" section in Chapter 5.

Setting Program Properties

The Program tab, shown in Figure B.7, contains various settings that control the startup and shutdown of the program. The untitled text box at the top of the dialog box specifies the text that appears in the program window's title bar.

FIGURE B.7 Use the Program tab to set various properties for the command-line program's startup.

Here's a rundown of the rest of the options:

Cmd Line	This text box specifies the pathname of the program's executable file. As you saw earlier, you can use this text box to add parameters and switches to modify how the program starts.
Working	Use this text box to set the application's default folder.
Batch File	This text box specifies a batch file or command to run before starting the program. This is useful for copying files, setting environment variables, changing the PATH, or loading memory-resident programs.

Shortcut Key	Use this text box to assign a key combination to the program. For launching the program, this key combination seems to work only if you create a shortcut for the program on the desktop. When the program is running, however, you can use the key combination to switch to the program quickly. The default key combo is Ctrl+Alt+*character*, where *character* is any keyboard character that you press while this text box has the focus. If you prefer a key combination that begins with Ctrl+Shift, hold down both Ctrl and Shift and then press a character; for a Ctrl+Alt+Shift combination, hold down all three keys and press a character.
Run	This drop-down list determines how the application window appears. Select Normal Window, Minimized, or Maximized.
Close on Exit	If you activate this check box, the window closes when the program is complete. This is useful for batch files and other programs that leave the Command Prompt window onscreen when they're done.
Advanced	This button displays a dialog box that enables you to specify the locations of custom `Autoexec.bat` and `Config.sys` files for the program to use.
Change Icon	Use this command button to assign a different icon to the program's PIF. Clicking this button displays the Change Icon dialog box.

Adjusting Memory Properties

The Memory tab that enables you to manipulate various memory-related settings, as shown in Figure B.8.

Here's a rundown of the available controls:

Conventional Memory	The Total drop-down list specifies the amount of conventional memory (in kilobytes) supplied to the program's virtual machine by Windows Vista's Virtual Memory Manager (**VMM**). (**Conventional memory** is defined as the first 640KB of memory.) If you leave this value at Auto, the VMM handles the memory requirements automatically. However, it doesn't always do a good job. For example, if you run a command, the VMM carves out a full 640KB of memory for the Command Prompt virtual machine. Because most commands run happily in much less, you're either wasting precious physical memory or unnecessarily paging to the swap file. You can specify a smaller value (for example, 160KB) and save memory resources. Before changing this value, check the documentation for your program to find its minimum memory requirement.

FIGURE B.8 Use the Memory tab to customize the memory usage for a command-line program.

Initial Environment

This drop-down list specifies the size (in bytes) of the command-line environment. The environment is a small memory buffer that holds the environment variables. If you're using the Batch File text box to run SET statements or add folders to the PATH, you might want to increase the size of the environment. You shouldn't need a value any larger than 1024 bytes.

TIP

To see the contents of the environment while you're in a command-line session, run the SET command.

Protected

While your program is running, small chunks of Windows Vista come along for the ride in the system memory area. If the program is ill-behaved, it might accidentally overwrite part of the system area and cause Windows Vista to become unstable. To prevent this, activate the Protected check box to write-protect the system memory area.

Expanded (EMS) Memory	The Total drop-down list specifies the amount of expanded memory (in kilobytes) supplied to the program. If you know your program doesn't use expanded memory, you can set this value to None. If you set this value to Auto, Windows Vista supplies the program with whatever it needs. If you prefer to set a limit on the amount of expanded memory the program uses, select a specific value (1024KB should be plenty for most programs).

NOTE

To understand the difference between expanded memory and extended memory, I use the analogy of a carpenter's workshop. As a carpenter, you can increase your work space in two ways: You can *expand* the total area by erecting a separate building, or you can *extend* the existing work space itself with an addition. This is the principal difference between expanded memory and extended memory. Expanded memory usually comes in the form of a separate piece of equipment (called a *memory board*) you must install. You get extended memory, on the other hand, just by plugging memory chips directly into your computer's main circuit board. How does this extra memory help? Well, old DOS applications had to stay within the first 640 KB of memory, but small programs (called *memory managers*) shuffled bits of program code and data files between the conventional memory area and the expanded or extended memory.

For example, suppose that you're in your workshop and you need to use a lathe, but you haven't got the room. No problem. Your assistant (the memory manager) knows that the lathe is either outside in a separate building (expanded memory) or in an adjacent area (extended memory). He grabs something you don't need for now (a band saw, for instance), takes it to the expanded or extended memory area, exchanges it for the lathe, and brings the lathe to your workshop.

Extended (XMS) Memory	If your program can make use of extended memory, use the Total drop-down list to specify the amount of extended memory (in kilobytes) that the VMM allocates to the program. Again, use Auto to allow the VMM to allocate extended memory automatically. However, the VMM maps virtual memory as extended memory, so your programs might end up grabbing all the available virtual memory for themselves! Setting a limit of, for example, 1024KB prevents this from happening.
Uses HMA	This check box determines whether the program has access to the **high memory area** (**HMA**). The HMA is the first 64KB of extended memory. Programs can use it to load device drivers. By default, Windows Vista uses the HMA for MS-DOS, so it's generally unavailable to other programs.

MS-DOS Protected-Mode (DPMI) Memory This Total drop-down list specifies the amount of DOS protected-mode memory (in kilobytes) supplied to the program. Use Auto to let the VMM configure this type of memory automatically.

Setting Screen Properties

The properties sheet for a command-line program also includes a Screen tab, shown in Figure B.9, that controls various aspects of the program's display.

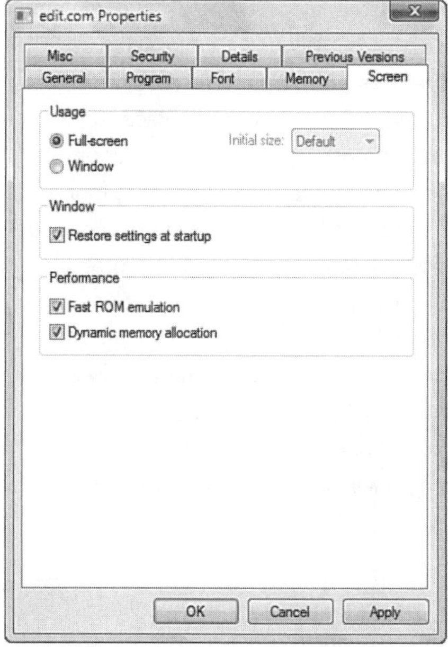

FIGURE B.9 Use the Screen tab to control the appearance of the Command Prompt program.

Here are your options:

Usage The Full-Screen and Window options determine whether the program starts full screen or in a window.

Restore Settings at Startup When this check box is activated, Windows Vista remembers the last window position and size and restores them the next time you run the program. If you deactivate this check box, Windows Vista just uses the original settings the next time you start the program; any adjustments you make in the current session are ignored.

Fast ROM Emulation	When this check box is activated, Windows Vista uses the video display VxDs to reproduce (or **emulate**) the video services (that is, writing text to the screen) that are normally the province of the ROM BIOS functions. These RAM-based VxDs are faster, so the overall performance of the program's display is improved. However, if the program expects to use nonstandard ROM calls, you might see garbage characters onscreen. If so, deactivate this check box.
Dynamic Memory Allocation	Some command-line programs can operate in both text and graphics modes, but the latter requires more memory. If this check box is activated, Windows Vista supplies memory to the program as required by the program's current mode. If you run the program in graphics mode, Windows Vista allocates more memory to the program's virtual machine; if you switch the program to text mode, Windows Vista reduces the memory allocated to the virtual machine, which makes more memory available to other applications. If you find that your program hangs when you switch to graphics mode, it could be that Windows Vista can't allocate enough memory to handle the new mode. In that case, you should deactivate the Dynamic Memory Allocation check box to force Windows Vista to always supply the program with enough memory to run in graphics mode.

Some Miscellaneous Properties

To complete our look at command-line program customization, let's turn our attention to the Misc tab of the program properties sheet, shown in Figure B.10. This tab contains a grab bag of options that cover a whole host of otherwise unrelated properties.

Here's a summary of what each control contributes to the Command Prompt program:

Allow Screen Saver	When this check box is turned on, Windows Vista allows your Windows screensaver to kick in while you're using the command-line program (that is, when the program is in the foreground). This is probably safe for most command-line programs, but if you find that the screensaver is causing your program to hang or is causing the program's graphics to go batty, you should deactivate this check box. You should definitely clear this check box if you're using a terminal emulation program or a communications program.

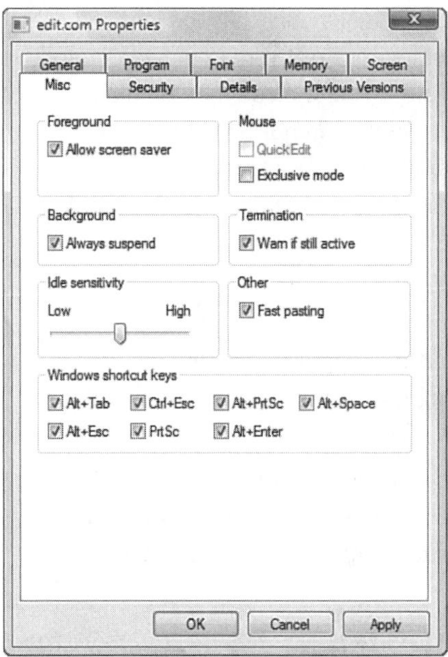

FIGURE B.10 The Misc tab contains an assortment of controls for customizing a Command Prompt program.

QuickEdit — When this check box is active, you can select program text with the mouse. (Not all command-line programs support this option, so you might find this check box disabled.) I explained how this works earlier in this appendix.

Exclusive Mode — If you check this option, Windows Vista offers the program exclusive use of the mouse. This means that the mouse will work only while you use the program; it won't be available in Windows Vista. You should activate this check box only if the mouse won't otherwise work in the program.

Always Suspend — When you activate this check box, Windows Vista doesn't supply any CPU time to a running command-line program that doesn't have the focus. (Such a program is said to be *in the background*.) If your program doesn't do any background processing when you switch to another window, you should activate this check box. Doing so improves the performance of your other applications. This is also a good idea if a background command-line program interferes with your foreground applications. (For example, some 16-bit games can mess up the sound in your foreground window.) If, however, you're using the 16-bit program to download files, print documents, or perform other background chores, you should leave Always Suspend unchecked.

Warn If Still Active	For safest operation, and to make sure that you don't lose unsaved data, you should always exit your Command Prompt program completely before trying to close the Command Prompt window. If you leave the Warn If Still Active box checked, Windows Vista displays a warning dialog box if you attempt to shut down the program prematurely. You can force Windows Vista to close the program (if it has hung, for example) by clicking End Now.
Idle Sensitivity	This slider determines how much CPU time Windows Vista devotes to the command-line program when the program is idle. See "Understanding Idle Sensitivity," later in this appendix.
Fast Pasting	This check box controls the speed at which Windows Vista pastes information from the Clipboard to the program. I discussed pasting data to Command Prompt windows earlier in this appendix.
Windows Shortcut Keys	These check boxes represent various Windows Vista shortcut keys. For example, pressing Alt+Tab while working in a Command Prompt window takes you to another open application. Your command-line program, however, might use one or more of these key combinations for its own purposes. To allow the program use of any of the shortcuts, deactivate the appropriate check boxes.

Understanding Idle Sensitivity

When it's multitasking applications, Windows Vista doles out to each running process fixed-sized chunks of processor cycles called **time slices**. Ideally, active applications get more time slices, and idle applications get fewer. How does Windows Vista know whether an application is idle? Windows applications send a message to the scheduler that specifies their current state. For example, an application might tell the scheduler that it's just waiting for user input (a keystroke or mouse click). In that case, Windows Vista reduces the number of time slices for the application and redistributes them to other processes running in the background.

Command-line programs are a different kettle of time-slice fish. In most cases, Windows Vista has no way of knowing the current state of a 16-bit program. (However, many newer command-line applications are Windows-aware and can send messages to the scheduler.) In the absence of keyboard input, Windows Vista just assumes that a program is in an idle state after a predetermined amount of inactivity, and it then redirects time slices to other processes. The amount of time that Windows Vista waits before declaring a Command Prompt program idle is the **idle sensitivity**.

You can control the idle sensitivity for a command-line program by using the Idle Sensitivity slider. The slider has a range between Low and High. Here's how to work with this slider:

Low Idle Sensitivity	Windows Vista waits longer before declaring the program idle. Use a Low setting to improve performance for 16-bit programs that perform background tasks. This ensures that, despite the lack of keyboard input, these tasks still get the time slices they need.
High Idle Sensitivity	Windows Vista takes less time to declare a 16-bit application idle. If you know your program does nothing in the background, using the High setting will improve the performance of your other running applications because the scheduler will reallocate its time slices sooner.

APPENDIX C

Automating Windows Vista with Batch Files

IN THIS APPENDIX

As you saw in Appendix B, "Using the Windows Vista Command Prompt," the command line is still an often useful and occasionally indispensable part of computing life, and most power users will find themselves doing at least a little work in the Command Prompt window. Part of that work might involve writing short batch file programs to automate routine chores, such as performing simple file backups and deleting unneeded files. And if you throw in any of the eight Windows Vista commands that enhance batch files, you can do many other interesting and useful things. That's where this appendix comes in: You'll learn what batch files are, how they work, and what commands are available.

Batch Files: Some Background

In Appendix B, I told you that the Command Prompt uses a program called `cmd.exe` to handle anything you type at the prompt. The Command Prompt has some commands—such as `COPY`, `DIR`, and `DEL`—built right in (these are called **internal** commands).

For most anything else, including your software applications and the **external** commands such as `FORMAT`, `CHKDSK`, and `FC`, Command Prompt calls a separate program. Command Prompt executes the command or program and returns to the prompt to await further orders.

If you tell Command Prompt to execute a batch file, however, things are a little different. Command Prompt goes into **Batch mode**, where it takes all its input from the individual lines of a batch file. These lines are just commands that (in most cases) you otherwise have to type in yourself. Command Prompt repeats the following four-step procedure until it has processed each line in the batch file:

1. It reads a line from the batch file.
2. It closes the batch file.
3. It executes the command.
4. It reopens the batch file and reads the next line.

The main advantage of Batch mode is that you can lump several commands together in a single batch file and tell Command Prompt to execute them all simply by typing the name of the batch file. This is great for automating routine tasks such as backing up the Registry files or deleting leftover `.tmp` files at startup.

Creating Batch Files

Before getting started with some concrete batch file examples, you need to know how to create them. Here are a few things to bear in mind:

- Batch files are simple text files, so Notepad (or some other text editor) is probably your best choice.
- If you decide to use WordPad or another word processor, make sure that the file you create is a text-only file.
- Save your batch files using the `.bat` extension.
- When naming your batch files, don't use the same name as a Command Prompt command. For example, if you create a batch file that deletes some files, don't name it `Del.bat`. If you do, the batch file will never run! Here's why: When you enter something at the prompt, `Cmd.exe` first checks to see whether the command is an internal command. If it's not, `Cmd.exe` then checks for (in order) a `.com`, `.exe`, `.bat`, or `.cmd` file with a matching name. Because all external commands use a `.com` or `.exe` extension, `Cmd.exe` never bothers to check whether your batch file even exists!

After you've created the batch file, the rest is easy. Just enter any commands exactly as you would in Command Prompt (with a couple of exceptions, as you'll see later), and include whatever batch instructions you need.

Making a Home for Your Batch Files

If you find yourself creating and using a number of batch files, things can get confusing if you have the files scattered all over your hard disk. To remedy this, it makes sense to create a new folder to hold all your batch files.

To make this strategy effective, however, you have to tell Command Prompt to look in the batch file folder to find these files. You do this with the `PATH` command, which has the following general form:

```
PATH dir1;dir2;...
```

Here, *dir1*, *dir2*, and so on are the names of folders. This command effectively tells Command Prompt, "Whenever I run a command, if you can't find the appropriate file in the current folder, look for it in any of the folders listed in this `PATH` statement." Suppose that you create a folder named `batch` in your `Documents` folder. In this case, you want to add `%USERPROFILE%\Documents\batch` to the path.

Rather than doing this each time in Command Prompt, follow these steps to change the `PATH` variable permanently:

1. Select Start, right-click Computer, and then select Properties to open the System window.
2. Click the Advanced System Settings link and then enter your UAC credentials to open the System Properties dialog box with the Advanced tab displayed.
3. Click Environment Variables to display the Environment Variables dialog box.
4. In the System Variables list, select Path.
5. Click Edit to open the Edit System Variable dialog box.
6. In the Variable Value text box, add a semicolon and the path for your batch file folder to the end of the existing value. Figure C.1 shows the Edit System Variable dialog box with `%UserProfile%\Documents\batch` added to the `PATH` value.

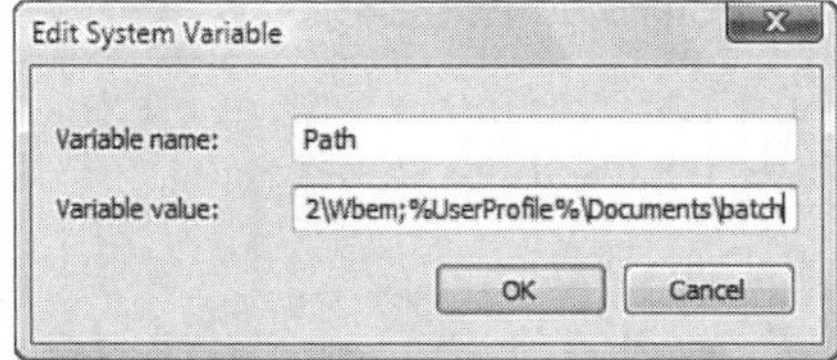

FIGURE C.1 Add the folder where you'll be storing your batch files to the `PATH` value.

7. Click OK to return to the System Properties dialog box.
8. Click OK.

Batch-File-Specific Commands

Let's begin our batch file tour with a look at a few commands that you can only use within a batch file. The next few sections introduce you to the `REM`, `ECHO`, and `PAUSE` commands.

REM: The Simplest Batch File Command

The first of the batch-file-specific commands is REM (which stands for *remark*). This simple command tells Command Prompt to ignore everything else on the current line. Batch file mavens use it almost exclusively to add short comments to their files:

```
REM This batch file changes to the Windows Vista
REM folder and starts CHKDSK in automatic mode.
CD %SystemRoot%
CHKDSK /F
```

Why would anyone want to do this? Well, it's probably not all that necessary with short, easy-to-understand batch files, but some of the more complex programs you'll be seeing later in this appendix can appear incomprehensible at first glance. A few pithy REM statements can help clear things up (not only for other people, but even for you if you haven't looked at the file in a couple of months).

CAUTION

It's best not to go overboard with REM statements. Having too many slows a batch file to a crawl. You really need only a few REM statements at the beginning to outline the purpose of the file and one or two to explain each of your more cryptic commands.

ECHO: A Voice for Your Batch Files

When it's processing a batch file, Windows Vista normally lets you know what's going on by displaying each command before executing it. That's fine, but it's often better to include more expansive descriptions, especially if other people will be using your batch files. The ECHO batch file command makes it possible for you to do just that.

For example, here's a simple batch file that deletes all the text files in the current user's Cookies and Recent folders and courteously tells the user what's about to happen:

```
ECHO This batch file will now delete all your cookie text files
DEL "%UserProfile%\Roaming\Microsoft\Windows\Cookies\*.txt"
ECHO This batch file will now delete your Recent Items list
DEL "%UserProfile%\Roaming\Microsoft\Windows\Recent\*.lnk"
```

The idea here is that when Windows Vista stumbles on the ECHO command, it simply displays the rest of the line onscreen. Sounds pretty simple, right? Well, here's what the output looks like when you run the batch file:

```
C:\>ECHO This batch file will now delete all your cookie text files
This batch file will now delete all your cookie text files
C:\>DEL "%UserProfile%\Cookies\*.txt"
C:\>ECHO This batch file will now delete your Recent Items list
This batch file will now delete your Recent Items list
C:\>DEL "%UserProfile%\Recent\*.lnk"
```

What a mess! The problem is that Windows Vista is displaying the command and ECHOing the line. Fortunately, Windows Vista provides two solutions:

- To prevent Windows Vista from displaying a command as it executes, precede the command with the @ symbol:

  ```
  @ECHO This batch file will now delete all your cookie text files
  ```

- To prevent Windows Vista from displaying any commands, place the following at the beginning of the batch file:

  ```
  @ECHO OFF
  ```

Here's what the output looks like with the commands hidden:

```
This batch file will now delete all your cookie text files
This batch file will now delete your Recent Items list
```

TIP

You might think that you can display a blank line simply by using ECHO by itself. That would be nice, but it doesn't work (Windows Vista just tells you the current state of ECHO: on or off). Instead, use ECHO. (that's ECHO followed by a dot).

The PAUSE Command

Sometimes you want to see something that a batch file displays (such as a folder listing produced by the DIR command) before continuing. Or, you might want to alert users that something important is about to happen so that they can consider the possible ramifications (and bail out if they get cold feet). In both cases, you can use the PAUSE command to halt the execution of a batch file temporarily. When Windows Vista comes across PAUSE in a batch file, it displays the following:

```
Press any key to continue . . .
```

To continue processing the rest of the batch file, press any key. If you don't want to continue, you can cancel processing by pressing Ctrl+C or Ctrl+Break. Windows Vista then asks you to confirm:

```
Terminate batch job (Y/N)?
```

Either press Y to return to the prompt or N to continue the batch file.

Using Parameters for Batch File Flexibility

Most command-line utilities require extra information such as a filename (for example, when you use COPY or DEL) or a folder path (such as when you use CD or MD). These extra pieces of information—they're called **parameters**—give you the flexibility to specify exactly how you want a command to work. You can add the same level of flexibility to your batch files. To understand how this works, first look at the following example:

```
@ECHO OFF
ECHO.
ECHO The first parameter is %1
ECHO The second parameter is %2
ECHO The third parameter is %3
```

As you can see, this batch file doesn't do much except `ECHO` four lines to the screen (the first of which is just a blank line). Curiously, however, each `ECHO` command ends with a percent sign (`%`) and a number. Type in and save this batch file as `PARAMETERS.BAT`. Then, to see what these unusual symbols mean, enter the following command at the Windows Vista prompt:

```
parameters Tinkers Evers Chance
```

This produces the following output:

```
C:\>parameters Tinkers Evers Chance

The first parameter is Tinkers
The second parameter is Evers
The third parameter is Chance
```

The following `ECHO` command in `PARAMETERS.BAT` produces the first line in the output (after the blank line):

```
ECHO The first parameter is %1
```

When Windows Vista sees the `%1` symbol in a batch file, it examines the original command and looks for the first word after the batch filename and then replaces `%1` with that word. In the example, the first word after `parameters` is `Tinkers`, so Windows Vista uses that to replace `%1`. (This is why batch file programmers often call `%1` a **replaceable parameter**.) Only when it has done this does it proceed to `ECHO` the line to the screen.

The replaceable parameter `%2` is similar, except that, in this case, Windows Vista looks for the second word after the batch filename (`Evers` in this example).

NOTE

If your batch file command has more parameters than the batch file is looking for, it ignores the extras. For example, adding a fourth parameter to the `parameters` command line has no effect on the file's operation. Note, too, that you can't use more than nine replaceable parameters in a batch file (`%1` through `%9`). However, there is a tenth replaceable parameter (`%0`). It holds the name of the batch file itself.

TIP

If the replaceable parameter is a string that includes one or more spaces, surround the parameter with quotations marks (for example, "%1").

Let's look at a real-world example. Consider the following slightly useful but highly inflexible batch file, called NEWFOLDER.BAT:

```
@ECHO OFF
CLS
MD \batch
CD \batch
```

This batch file simply creates a new folder called batch within the current folder location and then moves to it. You'll be surprised how often you need to do something like this, so it makes sense to try to automate the whole procedure.

Unfortunately, this isn't the best way to go about it. You could set up a batch file each time you need to create and move to a folder, but I assume that you want to spend your remaining years in a more fruitful enterprise. Instead, you can use replaceable parameters to add instant flexibility to NEWFOLDER.BAT:

```
@ECHO OFF
CLS
MD %1
CD %1
```

Now, if you want to create and move to a new batch folder, enter the following command:

newfolder \batch

Vista replaces each %1 in NEWFOLDER.BAT with \batch (the first word after newfolder), so the batch file works as it did before. The difference, of course, is that you can now use it for other folders as well. For example, to create a new scripts folder and move to it, use the following command:

```
newfolder \scripts
```

NOTE

If you run the NEWFOLDER.BAT batch file from the Run dialog box, Vista creates the new folder in the folder where the batch file resides.

Improving on Command-Line Utilities

Because a batch file's replaceable parameters work just like the parameters used in command-line utilities, it's not hard to create batch files that mimic—and even improve on—the standard Command Prompt fare.

Making DEL Safer

Probably 99.9% of all accidental command-line deletions occur when you use wildcard characters to delete multiple files. A question mark in the wrong place or a `*.*` in the wrong folder can lead to disaster.

NOTE

The symbols * and ? are wildcard characters. You use ? to match a single character, and you use * to match any number of characters.

It would help if you could see a list of all the files that you were about to delete and then have the option of canceling the deletion if things weren't right. The easiest way to do this, of course, is to run a `DIR` command using the same file specification you would use with `DEL`. But it's usually a pain typing two commands and making sure that you get the ?s and *s in the right place each time. This situation cries out for a batch file, and here it is (it's `SAFEDEL.BAT`):

```
@ECHO OFF
CLS
ECHO %0 %1
ECHO.
ECHO Here is a list of the files that will be deleted:
REM Display a wide DIR list in alphabetical order
DIR %1 /ON /W
ECHO.
ECHO To cancel the deletion, press Ctrl+C. Otherwise,
PAUSE
DEL %1
```

You use `SAFEDEL.BAT` just like the `DEL` command. For example, to delete all the `.bak` files in the current folder, enter the following:

```
safedel *.bak
```

The following list is a quick summary of what happens:

- The command `ECHO %0 %1` simply redisplays the batch filename (`%0`) and the file specification (`%1`) for reference.
- The `DIR %1 /ON /W` command is used to get an alphabetical listing (in wide format so that you can see more files) of everything that's about to be deleted.

- The batch file then runs PAUSE so that you can examine the files.
- If you decide to continue (by pressing any key), the DEL %1 command takes care of the job.

CAUTION

The percent sign (%) is a perfectly good character to use in a filename, but if you try to reference a file named, for example, PERCNT%.XLS, you'll run into problems. The reason is that when Command Prompt processes batch files, it mindlessly deletes any single occurrences of % as part of its parameter replacement chores. So, PERCNT%.XLS becomes PERCNT.XLS, and things go haywire. To fix this, use double percent signs when referring to the file in a batch command (for example, PERCNT%%.XLS).

Changing Folders and Drives in One Step

The CD command falls down on the job if you need to change to a folder on a different drive. You have to change to the drive first and then run CD. Use CDD.BAT to do this all in one command:

```
@ECHO OFF
%1:
CD \%2
```

For example, to change to the G drive's BACKUP folder, simply use the following command:

```
cdd g backup
```

If you hate typing backslashes, you can avoid them altogether by adding a couple of extra CD commands:

```
@ECHO OFF
%1:
CD \%2
CD %3
CD %4
```

Now, to change to the \BACKUP\123\DATA folder on drive G, enter the following:

```
cdd g backup 123 data
```

Excluding Files from a Copy Command

The wildcard characters are used to include multiple files in a single command. But what if you want to *exclude* certain files? For example, suppose that you have a WP\DOCS folder that has files with various extensions—.doc, .txt, .wp, and so on. What do you do if you want to copy all the files to drive A except those with a .txt extension? One solution is to use separate XCOPY commands for each extension you do need, but that's too much work (and besides, you might miss some). Instead, try this batch file (named DONTCOPY.BAT):

```
@ECHO OFF
CLS
ATTRIB +H %1
ECHO.
ECHO Copying all files to %2 except %1:
ECHO.
XCOPY *.* %2
ATTRIB -H %1
```

To use this batch file to copy all the files in the current folder to drive G, except, for example, those with the extension .txt, use the following command:

```
dontcopy *.txt g:
```

The secret here is that DOS won't copy hidden files. So, DONTCOPY.BAT uses the ATTRIB command to hide the files that you want to ignore. The first command, ATTRIB +H %1, does just that. Now all that's needed is an XCOPY command that copies everything that's not hidden (use *.* to do this) to the target (%2). When that's done, DONTCOPY.BAT uses another ATTRIB command to unhide the files.

CAUTION

To be safe, DONTCOPY.BAT should check to make sure that a destination parameter (%2) was entered. This can be done, but you need to use the batch file commands IF and GOTO, which are discussed later in this appendix.

NOTE

You can use the same idea to exclude files with other commands. For example, Command Prompt won't delete or rename hidden files, so it wouldn't be hard to create the appropriate DONTDEL.BAT and DONTREN.BAT batch files.

SHIFT: A Different Approach to Parameters

Although you won't be using it until later in this appendix, you should know that there's another way to handle parameters inside batch files: the SHIFT command. To see how it works, rewrite the PARAMETERS.BAT file to get PARAMETERS2.BAT:

```
@ECHO OFF
ECHO.
```

```
ECHO The first parameter is %1
SHIFT
ECHO The second parameter is %1
SHIFT
ECHO The third parameter is %1
```

If you enter the command **`parameters2 Tinkers Evers Chance`**, you get the same output as before:

```
C:\BATCH>parameters2 Tinkers Evers Chance

The first parameter is Tinkers
The second parameter is Evers
The third parameter is Chance
```

How does this work? Well, each `SHIFT` command shuffles the parameters down one position. In particular, `%2` goes to `%1`, so the following command really does display the second parameter:

```
ECHO The second parameter is %1
```

All the other parameters change as well, of course: `%3` goes to `%2`, `%1` goes to `%0`, and `%0` heads off into oblivion.

This sort of behavior is handy for two types of situations:

- **Batch files that require more than 10 parameters**—There aren't many times when you'll need this many parameters, but at least you know you can handle it when the need arises.
- **Batch files that use a varying number of parameters**—This is a much more common scenario; you'll see a couple of examples a bit later.

Note that I'm holding off on presenting `SHIFT` examples because to use it properly, you need an `IF` command to test whether there are any more parameters left to shift. I discuss the `IF` command later in this appendix (see "`IF`: Handling Batch File Conditions").

Looping with the FOR Command

Pound for pound, the `FOR` command is easily the most underutilized and misunderstood of all Command Prompt commands. That is bad news because `FOR` is an extremely powerful weapon that shouldn't be left out of any command-line guru's arsenal. The problem, I think, is that `FOR` has a somewhat bizarre syntax that makes it wildly unappealing at first glance. So, before we look at it, I'll give you some background.

Looping: The Basics

If you wanted to instruct someone on how to dress each day, you might begin with a simple step-by-step approach:

1. Put on underwear
2. Put on socks
3. Put on pants
4. Put on shirt

This is fine, but you can make things simpler by creating a list—underwear, socks, pants, shirt—and telling the person to put on everything in this list in the order in which it appears. Now, instead of a linear approach, you've got a primitive loop: The person looks at the list, puts on the first item, looks at the list again, puts on the second item, and so on.

Now you can formalize the instructions into a single, pithy statement:

```
for each item X in the set (underwear, socks, pants, shirt), put on X
```

Programmers often use loops like this to add generality to programs. Instead of writing a dozen different instructions, they can often write a single, generic instruction (something like `put on X`) and loop through it a dozen times, each time supplying it with a different input (underwear, socks, and so on).

Understanding the FOR Command Syntax

The `FOR` command is a batch file's way of looping through an instruction:

```
FOR %%parameter IN (set) DO command
```

Looks like bad news, doesn't it? Well, see how it looks if you plug in the dressing instructions:

```
FOR %%X IN (underwear, socks, pants, shirt) DO put on %%X
```

That's a little more comprehensible, so let's break down the `FOR` command for a closer look:

`%%parameter` This is the parameter that changes each time through the loop (`%%X` in the example). You can use any single character after the two `%` signs (except 0 through 9). There are two `%` signs because, as I explained earlier, DOS deletes single ones as it processes the batch file.

`IN (`*`set`*`)` This is the list (it's officially called the **set**) of choices for `%%X` (in the example, `underwear`, `socks`, and so on). You can use spaces, commas, or semicolons to separate the items in the set, and you must enclose them in parentheses.

DO *command*	For each item in the set, the batch file performs whatever instruction is given by *command* (such as put on %%X). The parameter %%X is normally found somewhere in *command*.

A Simple Batch File Example

Here's an example of the FOR command in a simple batch file that might help clear things up:

```
@ECHO OFF
FOR %%B IN (Tinkers Evers Chance) DO ECHO %%B
```

This batch file (call it PARAMETERS3.BAT) produces the following output:

```
C:\BATCH>parameters3
Tinkers
Evers
Chance
```

All this does is loop through the three items in the set (Tinkers, Evers, and Chance) and substitute each one for %%B in the command ECHO %%B. In other words, this FOR loop is equivalent to the following three ECHO commands:

```
ECHO Tinkers
ECHO Evers
ECHO Chance
```


Different Sets for Different Folks

The set in a FOR command can hold more than simple strings such as Tinkers and Evers. The real power of FOR becomes evident when you use file specifications, command names, and even replaceable parameters as part of a set.

For example, have you ever copied a bunch of files into the wrong folder? This happens occasionally, and it's usually a mess to clean up because the files get all mixed up with whatever was already in the folder. Before smashing your monitor, check out the following batch file (named CLEANUP.BAT):

```
@ECHO OFF
FOR %%F IN (*.*) DO DEL C:\WRONGDIR\%%F
```

This batch file assumes that you copied all the files from the current folder into the WRONGDIR folder. In this case, the set is given by the *.* file specification. FOR loops through every file in the current folder and, for each one, deletes it in the WRONGDIR folder.

To see how to use command names in a set, you can redo the NEWFOLDER.BAT batch file created earlier. Here's NEWFOLDER2.BAT:

```
@ECHO OFF
CLS
FOR %%C IN (MD CD) DO %%C %1
```

As you can see, the set consists of two commands: MD and CD. They substitute for %%C each time through the loop, so this single FOR command is equivalent to the two commands in NEWFOLDER.BAT:

```
MD %1
CD %1
```

The FOR command is very powerful if you use replaceable parameters inside the set. The most common use of this potent combination is to create your own versions of commands that accept multiple parameters. For example, here's a batch file (named SUPERDELETE.BAT) that deletes up to nine file specifications at once:

```
@ECHO OFF
ECHO.
ECHO About to delete the following files:
ECHO %1 %2 %3 %4 %5 %6 %7 %8 %9
ECHO.
ECHO Press Ctrl+C to cancel. Otherwise,
PAUSE
FOR %%F IN (%1 %2 %3 %4 %5 %6 %7 %8 %9) DO DEL %%F
```

To use this file to delete, for example, all files in the current folder that have the extensions .bak, .tmp, and .$$$, use the following command:

```
superdelete *.bak *.tmp *.$$$
```

Windows Vista must do two things to process the FOR command in SUPERDEL.BAT. First, it replaces the parameters inside the set so that the command looks like this:

```
FOR %%F IN (*.bak *.tmp *.$$$) DO DEL %%F
```

Then it loops through the set to delete each file specification. In the end, this is equivalent to the following three DEL commands:

```
DEL *.bak
DEL *.tmp
DEL *.$$$
```

Using Delayed Environment Variable Expansion

The FOR command is an excellent tool for understanding the delayed environment variable expansion that I discussed in Appendix B. To refresh your memory, if you start the cmd.exe with the /V:ON switch, you turn on delayed environment variable expansion, which means that Windows Vista doesn't expand a particular environment variable within a batch file until it executes the statement containing that variable.

For example, suppose that you want to use FOR to display a list of subfolder and files in the current folder. You might think that you could loop through all the items in the folder and store each one in a custom environment variable. Here's a first pass:

```
@ECHO OFF
SET FileList=
FOR %%F IN (*.*) DO SET FileList=%FileList% %%F
ECHO %FileList%
```

This code first initializes an environment variable named FileList. Then a FOR loop runs through everything in the current folder (*.*) and appends the name of each item to %FileList%. The batch file then displays the current value of %FileList%.

Unfortunately, if you run this batch file, the final value of %FileList% is just the name of the last file in the folder. The problem is that Command Prompt expands the value of %FileList% at the beginning of the batch file. Because this variable is blank to begin with, all the FOR loop is doing is adding each subfolder or filename to a blank value.

To fix this, you must start cmd.exe with delayed environment variable expansion (/V:ON) and then change %FileList% in the FOR loop to !FileList!, as shown here:

```
@ECHO OFF
SET FileList=
FOR %%F IN (*.*) DO SET FileList=!FileList! %%F
ECHO %FileList%
```

This enables Command Prompt to retain the contents of FileList with each loop, so you get a proper listing of subfolders and files.

C

GOTO: Telling Your Batch Files Where to Go

Your basic batch file lives a simple, linear existence. The first command gets processed, and then the second, the third, and so on to the end of the file. It's boring, but that's all you need most of the time.

However, there are situations in which the batch file's usual one-command-after-the-other approach breaks down. For example, depending on a parameter or the result of a previous command, you might need to skip over a line or two. How do you do this? With the GOTO batch command:

```
...
... (the opening batch commands)
...
GOTO NEXT
...
... (the batch commands that get skipped)
...
:NEXT
...
... (the rest of the batch commands)
...
```

Here, the GOTO command is telling the batch file to look for a line that begins with a colon and the word NEXT (this is called a **label**) and to ignore any commands in between.

GOTO is useful for processing different batch commands depending on a parameter. Here's a simple example:

```
@ECHO OFF
CLS
GOTO %1
:A
ECHO This part of the batch file runs if A is the parameter.
GOTO END
:B
ECHO This part of the batch file runs if B is the parameter.
:END
```

Suppose that this file is named GOTOTEST.BAT and you enter the following command:

gototest a

In the batch file, the line GOTO %1 becomes GOTO A. That makes the batch file skip down to the :A label, where it then runs the commands (in this example, just an ECHO statement), and then skips to :END to avoid the rest of the batch file commands.

One handy use of the GOTO command is for those times when you need to add copious comments to a batch file. As you know, you normally use REM to add batch file remarks. Windows Vista doesn't try to execute these lines, but it still has to read them, and this can really slow things down. Here's a way to use GOTO to get around this (literally!):

```
@ECHO OFF
GOTO START
You place your batch file comments here. Notice how
I'm not using the REM command at all. This not only
saves typing (a constant goal for some of us) but it
```

```
certainly looks a lot nicer, don't you think?
:START
...
... (Batch file commands)
...
```

As you can see, GOTO just leaps over the comments to end up at the :START label. Windows Vista doesn't even know that the comments exist.

IF: Handling Batch File Conditions

We make decisions all the time. Some are complex and require intricate levels of logic to answer (Should I get married? Should I start a chinchilla farm?). Others are simpler and depend only on existing conditions (the proverbial fork in the road):

- If it's raining, I'll stay home and work. Otherwise, I'll go to the beach.
- If this milk smells okay, I'll drink some. Otherwise, I'll throw it out.

No batch file (indeed, no software program yet developed) is sophisticated enough to tackle life's complex questions, but the simpler condition-based decisions are no problem. Here are a few examples of what a batch file might have to decide:

- If the %2 parameter equals /Q, jump to the QuickFormat section. Otherwise, do a regular format.
- If the user forgets to enter a parameter, cancel the program. Otherwise, continue processing the batch file.
- If the file that the user wants to move already exists in the new folder, display a warning. Otherwise, proceed with the move.
- If the last command failed, display an error message and cancel the program. Otherwise, continue.

For these types of decisions, you need to use the IF batch command. IF has the following general form:

IF *condition command*

condition	This is a test that evaluates to a yes or no answer ("Did the user forget a parameter?").
command	This is what is executed if the *condition* produces a positive response ("Cancel the batch file").

The next few sections discuss the various ways you can use IF in your batch files.

C

Testing Parameters with IF

One of the most common uses of the IF command is to check the parameters that the user entered and proceed accordingly. From the previous section, the simple batch file that used GOTO can be rewritten with IF as follows:

```
@ECHO OFF
CLS
IF "%1"=="A" ECHO This part of the batch file runs if A is the parameter.
IF "%1"=="B" ECHO This part of the batch file runs if B is the parameter.
```

The condition part of an IF statement is a bit tricky. Let's look at the first one: "%1"=="A". Remember that the condition is always a question with a yes or no answer. In this case, the question boils down to the following:

```
Is the first parameter (%1) equal to A?
```

The double equal sign (==) looks weird, but that's just how you compare two strings of characters in a batch file. If the answer is yes, the command executes. If the answer is no, the batch file moves on to the next IF, which checks to see whether the parameter is "B".

NOTE

Strictly speaking, you don't need to include the quotation marks ("). Using %1==A accomplishes the same thing. However, I prefer to use them for two reasons: First, it makes it clearer that the IF condition is comparing strings; second, as you'll see in the next section, the quotation marks enable you to check whether the user forgot to enter a parameter at all.

CAUTION

This batch file has a serious flaw that will prevent it from working under certain conditions. Specifically, if you use the lowercase "a" or "b" as a parameter, nothing happens because, to the IF command, "a" is different from "A". The solution is to add extra IF commands to handle this situation:

```
IF "%1"=="a" ECHO This part of the batch file runs if a is the
parameter
```

Checking for Missing Parameters

Proper batch file techniques require you to check to see not only what a parameter is, but also whether one exists at all. This can be vital because a missing parameter can cause a batch file to crash and burn. For example, earlier I showed you a batch file called DONTCOPY.BAT designed to copy all files in the current folder to a new destination (given by the second parameter) except those you specified (given by the first parameter). Here's the listing to refresh your memory:

```
@ECHO OFF
CLS
ATTRIB +H %1
ECHO.
ECHO Copying all files to %2 except %1:
ECHO.
XCOPY *.* %2
ATTRIB -H %1
```

What happens if the user forgets to add the destination parameter (%2)? Well, the XCOPY command becomes XCOPY *.*, which terminates the batch file with the following error:

```
File cannot be copied onto itself
```

The solution is to add an IF command that checks to see whether %2 exists:

```
@ECHO OFF
CLS
IF "%2"=="" GOTO ERROR
ATTRIB +H %1
ECHO.
ECHO Copying all files to %2 except %1:
ECHO.
XCOPY32 *.* %2
ATTRIB -H %1
GOTO END
:ERROR
ECHO You didn't enter a destination!
ECHO Please try again...
:END
```

The condition "%2"=="" is literally comparing %2 to nothing (""). If this proves to be true, the program jumps (using GOTO) to the :ERROR label, and a message is displayed to admonish the user. Notice, too, that if everything is okay (that is, the user entered a second parameter), the batch file executes normally and jumps to the :END label to avoid displaying the error message.

The SHIFT Command Redux

Now that you know a little about how IF works, I can show you how to use the SHIFT command introduced earlier. Recall that SHIFT operates by shuffling the batch file parameters down one position, so that %1 becomes %0, %2 becomes %1, and so on. The most common use of this apparently strange behavior is to process batch files with an unknown number of parameters. As an example, let's redo the SUPERDELETE.BAT batch file so that it can delete any number of file specifications:

```
@ECHO OFF
IF "%1"=="" GOTO NO_FILES
:START
ECHO Now deleting %1 . . .
DEL %1
SHIFT
IF "%1"=="" GOTO DONE
GOTO START
:NO_FILES
ECHO You didn't enter a file spec!
:DONE
```

The first IF is familiar—it just looks for a missing parameter and, if that proves to be the case, leaps to :NO_FILES and displays a message. Otherwise, the program deletes the first file specification and then SHIFTs everything down. What was %2 is now %1, so you need the second IF to check the new %1. If it's blank, this means that the user didn't enter any more file specs, and the program jumps to :DONE. Otherwise, you loop back to :START and do it all again.

CAUTION

As you can see from the preceding example, it's okay to use GOTO to jump backward in a file and create a loop. This is often better than a FOR loop because you can process any number of commands, instead of a single command. However, you have to be careful or you might end up in the never-never land of an endless loop. Always include an IF command that will take you out of the loop after some condition has been met (such as running out of parameters).

Using IF to Check Whether a File Exists

Another variation of IF is the IF EXIST command, which checks for the existence of a file. This is handy, for example, when you're using COPY or MOVE. First, you can check whether the file you want to copy or move exists. Second, you can check whether a file with the same name already exists in the target folder. (As you probably know, a file that has been copied over by another of the same name is downright impossible to recover.) Here's a batch file called SAFEMOVE.BAT, which uses the MOVE command to move a file but first checks the file and then the target folder:

```
@ECHO OFF
CLS
IF EXIST %1 GOTO SO_FAR_SO_GOOD
ECHO The file %1 doesn't exist!
GOTO END
:SO_FAR_SO_GOOD
```

```
IF NOT EXIST %2 GOTO MOVE_IT
ECHO The file %1 exists on the target folder!
ECHO Press Ctrl+C to bail out or, to keep going,
PAUSE
:MOVE_IT
MOVE %1 %2
:END
```

To explain what's happening, I'll use a sample command:

```
safemove moveme.txt "%userprofile%\documents\moveme.txt"
```

The first `IF` tests for the existence of `%1` (`MOVEME.TXT` in the example). If there is such a file, the program skips to the `:SO_FAR_SO_GOOD` label. Otherwise, it tells the user that the file doesn't exist, and then jumps down to `:END`.

The second `IF` is slightly different. In this case, I want to continue only if `MOVEME.TXT` doesn't exist in the current user's My Documents folder, so I add `NOT` to the condition. (You can include `NOT` in any `IF` condition.) If this proves true (that is, the file given by `%2` doesn't exist), the file skips to `:MOVE_IT` and performs the move. Otherwise, the user is warned and given an opportunity to cancel.

Checking for Command Errors

Good batch files (especially those that other people will be using) always assume that if anything bad can happen, it will. So far you've seen how `IF` can handle missing parameters and file problems, but there's much more that can go haywire. For example, what if a batch file tries to use `XCOPY`, but there's not enough memory? Or what if the user presses Ctrl+C during a format or copy? It might seem impossible to check for these kinds of errors, but it is not only possible, it's really quite easy.

When certain commands finish, they always file a report on the progress of the operation. This report, or **exit code**, is a number that tells DOS how things went. For example, Table C.1 lists the exit codes used by the `XCOPY` command.

TABLE C.1 `XCOPY` Exit Codes

Exit Code	What It Means
0	Everything's okay; the files were copied.
1	Nothing happened because no files were found to copy.
2	The user pressed Ctrl+C to abort the copy.
4	The command failed because there wasn't enough memory or disk space, or because there was something wrong with the command's syntax.
5	The command failed because of a disk error.

What does all this mean for your batch files? You can use yet another variation of the IF command—IF ERRORLEVEL—to test for these exit codes. For example, here's a batch file called CHECKCOPY.BAT, which uses some of the XCOPY exit codes to check for errors:

```
@ECHO OFF
XCOPY %1 %2
IF ERRORLEVEL 4 GOTO ERROR
IF ERRORLEVEL 2 GOTO CTRL+C
IF ERRORLEVEL 1 GOTO NO_FILES
GOTO DONE
:ERROR
ECHO Bad news! The copy failed because there wasn't
ECHO enough memory or disk space or because there was
ECHO something wrong with your file specs . . .
GOTO DONE
:CTRL+C
ECHO Hey, what gives? You pressed Ctrl+C to abort . . .
GOTO DONE
:NO_FILES
ECHO Bad news! No files were found to copy . . .
:DONE
```

As you can see, the ERRORLEVEL conditions check for the individual exit codes and then use GOTO to jump to the appropriate label.

NOTE

How does a batch file know what a command's exit code was? When Windows Vista gets an exit code from a command, it stores it in a special data area set aside for exit code information. When Windows Vista sees the IF ERRORLEVEL command in a batch file, it retrieves the exit code from the data area so that it can be compared to whatever is in the IF condition.

NOTE

Here's a list of exit codes CHKDSK might generate:

Exit Code	What It Means
0	The drive was checked and no errors were found.
1	Errors were found, and all were fixed.
2	Disk cleanup, such as garbage collection, was performed, or cleanup was not performed because the /F switch was not specified.
3	Could not check the disk, errors could not be fixed, or errors were not fixed because the /F switch was not specified.

One of the most important things to know about the `IF ERRORLEVEL` test is how Windows Vista interprets it. For example, consider the following `IF` command:

```
IF ERRORLEVEL 2 GOTO CTRL+C
```

Windows Vista interprets this command as "If the exit code from the last command is equal to or greater than 2, jump to the `:CTRL+C` label." This has two important consequences for your batch files:

- The test `IF ERRORLEVEL 0` doesn't tell you much because it's always true. If you simply want to find out whether the command failed, use the test `IF NOT ERRORLEVEL 0`.
- To get the correct results, always test the *highest* `ERRORLEVEL` first and then work your way down.

Redirecting Windows Vista

Windows Vista is always directing things here and there. This generally falls into two categories:

- Directing data into its commands from a device called **standard input**
- Directing data out of its commands to a device called **standard output**

A device called **CON** (**console**) normally handles standard input and standard output, which is your keyboard and monitor. Windows Vista assumes that all command input comes from the keyboard and that all command output (such as a `DIR` listing or a system message) goes to the screen. Redirection is just a way of specifying different input and output devices.

Redirecting Command Output

To send command output to somewhere other than the screen, you use the **output redirection operator** (>). One of the most common uses for output redirection is to capture the results of a command in a text file. For example, you might want to use the report produced by the `MEM` command as part of a word processing document. You could use the following command to first capture the report as the file `mem.txt`:

```
mem /c > mem.txt
```

When you run this command, don't be alarmed when the usual `MEM` data doesn't appear onscreen. Remember, you directed it away from the screen and into the `mem.txt` file.

You can use this technique to capture `DIR` listings, `CHKDSK` reports, and more. One caveat: If the file you specify as the output destination already exists, Windows Vista overwrites it without any warning. To be safe, you can use the **double output redirection symbol** (>>).

This tells Windows Vista to append the output to the file if it exists. For example, if you want to add the results of the `CHKDSK` command to `mem.txt`, use the following command:

```
chkdsk >> mem.txt
```

You can also redirect output to different devices. Table C.2 lists the various devices that Windows Vista installs each time you start your system.

TABLE C.2 Devices Installed by Windows Vista When You Start Your System

Device Name	Device
AUX	Auxiliary device (usually COM1)
CLOCK$	Real-time clock
COM*n*	Serial port (COM1, COM2, COM3, or COM4)
CON	Console (keyboard and screen)
LPT*n*	Parallel port (LPT1, LPT2, or LPT3)
NUL	NUL device (nothing)
PRN	Printer (usually LPT1)

For example, you can send a `DIR` listing to the printer with the following command (of course, you need to be sure that your printer is on before doing this; also note that this only works for a printer attached to a parallel port; it doesn't work for USB printers):

```
dir > prn
```

The `NUL` device usually throws people for a loop when they first see it. This device (affectionately known as the **bit bucket**) is, literally, nothing. Batch files normally use it to suppress the usual messages Windows Vista displays when it completes a command. For example, Windows Vista normally says `1 file(s) copied` when you copy a file. However, the following command sends that message to **NUL**, so you wouldn't see it onscreen:

```
copy somefile.doc a:\ > nul
```

Redirecting Input

The **input redirection operator** (<) handles getting input to a Windows Vista command from somewhere other than the keyboard. Input redirection is almost always used to send the contents of a text file to a Windows Vista command. The most common example is the `MORE` command, which displays one screen of information at a time. If you have a large text file that scrolls off the screen when you use `TYPE`, the following command, which sends the contents of `BIGFILE.TXT` to the `MORE` command, solves the problem:

```
more < bigfile.txt
```

When you run this command, the first screen of text appears, and the following line shows up at the bottom of the screen:

```
-- More --
```

Just press any key, and `MORE` displays the next screen. (Whatever you do, don't mix up < and > when using `MORE`. The command `more > bigfile.txt` erases `BIGFILE.TXT`!) `MORE` is an example of a **filter** command. Filters process whatever text is sent through them. The other Windows Vista filters are `SORT` and `FIND`, which are discussed in a moment.

Another handy use for input redirection is to send keystrokes to Windows Vista commands. For example, create a text file called `ENTER.TXT` that consists of a single press of the Enter key, and then try this command:

```
date < enter.txt
```

Windows Vista displays the current date, and instead of waiting for you to either type in a new date or press Enter, it just reads `ENTER.TXT` and uses its single carriage return as input. (For an even easier way to input the Enter key to a command, check out the next section.)

TIP

You can send keystrokes to any Windows Vista command that waits for input. You can even send multiple keystrokes. For example, a typical `FORMAT` command has three prompts: one to insert a disk, one for the volume label, and one to format another disk. If your normal responses to these prompts are Enter, Enter, N, and Enter, include these in a text file called, say, `INFORMAT.TXT`, and run `FORMAT` with the following command:

```
format a: < informat.txt
```

One common recipient of redirected input is the `SORT` command. `SORT`, as you might guess from its name, sorts the data sent to it and displays the results onscreen. So, for example, here's how you would sort a file called `JUMBLED.TXT`:

```
sort < jumbled.txt
```

Instead of merely displaying the results of the sort onscreen, you can use > to redirect them to another file.

TIP

`SORT` normally starts with the first column and works across. To start with any other column, use the `/+n` switch, where *n* is the number of the column you want to use. To sort a file in reverse order, use the `/R` switch.

Piping Commands

Piping is a technique that combines both input and output redirection. Using the pipe operator (¦), the output of one command is captured and sent as input to another command. For example, using `MEM` with the `/C` or `/D` switch usually results in more than one screen of data. `MEM` has a `/P` switch to pause the output, but you can also pipe it to the `MORE` command:

```
mem /c ¦ more
```

The pipe operator captures the `MEM` output and sends it as input to `MORE`, which then displays everything one screen at a time.

NOTE

Piping works by first redirecting the output of a command to a temporary file. It then takes this temporary file and redirects it as input to the second command. A command such as `MEM /C ¦ MORE` is approximately equivalent to the following two commands:

```
MEM /C > tempfile
tempfile < MORE
```

I showed you in the preceding section how to use input redirection to send keystrokes to a Windows Vista command. But if you have to send only a single key, piping offers a much nicer solution. The secret is to use the `ECHO` command to echo the character you need and then pipe it to the Windows Vista command.

For example, if you use the command `DEL *.*`, Vista always asks whether you're sure that you want to delete all the files in the current directory. This is a sensible precaution, but you can override it if you do things this way:

```
echo y ¦ del *.*
```

Here, the `y` that would normally be echoed to the screen is sent to `DEL` instead, which interprets it as a response to its prompt. This is a handy technique for batch files in which you want to reduce or even eliminate user interaction.

TIP

You can even use this technique to send an Enter keypress to a command. The command `ECHO.` (that's `ECHO` followed by a period) is equivalent to pressing Enter. So, for example, you could use the following command in a batch file to display the time without user input:

```
ECHO. ¦ TIME
```

A command commonly used in pipe operations is the `FIND` filter. `FIND` searches its input for a specified string and, if it finds a match, it displays the line that contains the string. For example, the last line of a `DIR` listing tells you the number of bytes free on the current drive. Rather than wade through the entire `DIR` output just to get this information, use this command instead:

```
dir | find "free"
```

You'll see something like the following:

```
2 Dir(s) 28,903,331,184 bytes free
```

`FIND` scours the `DIR` listing piped to it and looks for the word *free*. You can use this technique to display specific lines from, say, a `CHKDSK` report. For example, searching for *bad* finds the number of bad sectors on the disk.

A

B

C

D

E

F

G

H

M

N

O

P

Q

R

S

T

U

V

W

X–Z

THIS BOOK IS SAFARI ENABLED

INCLUDES FREE 45-DAY ACCESS TO THE ONLINE EDITION

The Safari® Enabled icon on the cover of your favorite technology book means the book is available through Safari Bookshelf. When you buy this book, you get free access to the online edition for 45 days.

Safari Bookshelf is an electronic reference library that lets you easily search thousands of technical books, find code samples, download chapters, and access technical information whenever and wherever you need it.

TO GAIN 45-DAY SAFARI ENABLED ACCESS TO THIS BOOK:

- Go to **http://www.samspublishing.com/safarienabled**
- Complete the brief registration form
- Enter the coupon code found in the front of this book on the "Copyright" page

If you have difficulty registering on Safari Bookshelf or accessing the online edition, please e-mail customer-service@safaribooksonline.com.